Russian Peasant
Schools

Russian Peasant Schools

OFFICIALDOM, VILLAGE CULTURE, AND POPULAR PEDAGOGY, 1861–1914

Ben Eklof

UNIVERSITY OF CALIFORNIA PRESS

BERKELEY   LOS ANGELES   LONDON

University of California Press
Berkeley and Los Angeles, California
University of California Press, Ltd.
London, England
© 1986 by
The Regents of the University of California

First Paperback Printing 1990

Library of Congress Cataloging in Publication Data

Eklof, Ben, 1946–
    Russian peasant schools

    Bibliography: p.
    Includes index.
    1. Education, Rural—Soviet Union—History.   2. Peas-
antry—Education—Soviet Union—History.   3. Soviet
Union—Rural conditions.   4. Villages—Soviet Union—
History.   I. Title.
LC5148.S65E38   1986   370.19'346'0947   84-16407
ISBN 0-520-06957-9

Printed in the United States of America

1 2 3 4 5 6 7 8 9

*To Louise,
in Memory,
and to Tamara Louise,
with Love*

Contents

List of Tables

Acknowledgments

It is a pleasure to acknowledge debts incurred over the years in the preparation of this work.

My early interest in history was kindled and nurtured by professors Kim Steele, Nicholas Clifford, and Marjorie Lamberti of Middlebury College. At Princeton University a faltering graduate student was kept on course by professors Cyril Black, Arno J. Mayer, and S. Frederick Starr. My interest in peasant studies was enthusiastically encouraged by Lucien Bianco. To all these generous individuals I can finally express gratitude deeply felt; in particular, Cyril Black's unswerving, patient, and good-humored support over a decade has been most helpful.

The research and travel undergirding this lengthy project have been funded at times by grants from the Davis Postdoctoral Fund of Princeton University, Fulbright-Hays, International Research and Exchange Board, Midwestern Universities Consortium for International Studies, International Programs, and Research and Graduate Studies of Indiana University. Grace Bareikis and John Lombardi of International Programs have been especially helpful and supportive.

At one time or another, many individuals have read and commented on parts of this manuscript. I gratefully acknowledge the assistance and criticism rendered by George Alter, Reid Gagle, John Spence, John Hartman, David Pace, Bill Reese, Harvey Graff, Scott Seregny, Joel Shapiro, Dan Orlovsky, and Neil Weissman.

I owe substantial debts to several people for unstinting personal and professional support and for considerable contributions of time and energy: to Barbara Hanawalt, for criticism and encouragement at crucial stages; to Janet Rabinowitch, for several complete readings and for unselfish advice, stern criticism, and warm support; to Alex Rabinowitch and to John Bushnell, without whose friendship, encouragement, and intervention at critical times I might well have wandered irretrievably off track or simply not have overcome many hurdles; to Charles Halperin, a fine teacher, genuine scholar, and true friend, who helped reshape the early drafts of this manuscript; and to Libby Gitlitz, for patience, support, and critical comments.

I also am pleased to acknowledge the help and friendship of some fine scholars in the Soviet Union. My visits to that country have been enlivened and enriched by the company, support, and criticism of Larissa Georgievna Zakharova of the History Department at Moscow State University and of Eduard Dmitrievich Dneprov of the Academy of Pedagogical Science. The warm personal friendship and the example of intellectual depth, curiosity, and passion of Boris Ilyich Krasnobaiev was especially inspiring; his death at an early age is a great loss to the field and a personal loss as well.

My gratitude also goes to Sheila Levine of the University of California Press for enthusiastic support and intelligent advice. Mary Renaud, my editor, helped transform a raw manuscript into a finished book, and the text is far better for her persistence and talent.

Finally, I thank Nadya Peterson for a decade of patience, support, expertise, and love. There is undoubtedly much to be said for the "strong woman" motif in Russian literature; here, if nowhere else, literature reflects reality.

A number of tables in this book, as well as sections of chapters, have previously appeared in print. My thanks for permission to use this material go to the editors of the *History of Education Quarterly* ("The Myth of the Zemstvo School: The Sources of the Expansion of Rural Education in Imperial Russia, 1864–1914," 24, no. 4 [Winter 1984]; "The Adequacy of Basic Teaching in Rural Russia: Teachers and Their Craft, 1880–1914," 26, no. 2 [Summer 1986]) and to the editors of the *Journal of Social History* ("Peasant Sloth Reconsidered: Peasant Strategies of Education and Learning in Rural Russia Before the Revolution," 14, no. 3 [Spring 1981]).

The transliteration of Russian terms in this work follows, with minor modifications, the Library of Congress system. Dates are according to the Julian calendar. Translations from Russian sources are my own unless otherwise indicated.

Regions and Provinces of European Russia

Introduction

The Russian peasant is in truth that mysterious unknown. . . .
Who can understand him? He does not understand himself!

Ivan Turgenev, *Fathers and Sons*

The Russian peasant visible in history books was a lurking, sullen presence, duplicitous and ignorant, clinging adamantly to tradition and routine, and given to sporadic outbursts of intense violence. Preliterate, prelogical, and premodern, peasants were deemed incapable not only of comprehending abstract ideas but even of perceiving their own best interests. Like children, peasants needed stern guidance; without a firm hand, they would either sink utterly into the sloth and degradation of the Russian village or release their uncontrolled emotions in *bunt*, the elemental wave of anarchic destruction that periodically swept the Russian countryside, wreaking immense damage.

The view of the peasantry as naive, impulsive, and irrational was strengthened by major intellectual currents and traditional practices. Slavophilism glorified the peasant's emotional soul, undefiled by Western rationalism, whereas Westernism blamed peasant sloth and ignorance for Russia's backwardness. A longstanding habit among the gentry, noted by Marc Raeff, of treating peasants as toys to be manipulated at will—an attitude learned in early childhood on wealthy estates—further reinforced the notion of paternalistic intervention and carried over to military affairs, bureaucratic administration, and even social reform.[1] Everyone, except a

1

few populists inspired by Bakunin, believed the peasant needed guidance. Daniel Field comments:

Standing on the other side of the cultural divide, literates supplemented whatever was oblique or obscure in peasants' utterances from their own conceptions of peasants in general. These conceptions varied in important respects, but they were uniformly patronizing. The *muzhik* was understood to be superstitious, irrational and credulous. He was less than adult, and his childishness served to justify the authority of educated adults. . . . *The peasant might be conceived as impulsive and bestial or as vulnerable and innocent. In either event, he required authoritative guidance* [emphasis added].[2]

The image of the peasant as child and of village society as characterized by a "magic mentalism" is by no means unique to Russia. Whether expressed in terms of *Gemeinschaft* and *Gesell-schaft,* primitive (folk) society and civilization, or tradition and modernity, the notion has prevailed since the Enlightenment that societies progress from simplicity to complexity and from superstition to reason and science.[3] To be sure, the polarity of folk society and civilization has been qualified by the discovery of the peasantry as a "distinct human type" emerging out of precivilized folk. Peasants constitute "part-societies with part-cultures," living in a community in which internal norms are still "personal and familial" but which also takes account of money, the division of labor, and formal and impersonal external controls. The peasant community adapts to the outside world in a narrow range of activities, while maintaining an internal equilibrium and a distinct "style of life." Anthropology has also taught that folk communities have their own "moral economy" and has even suggested that the holistic moral order of the face-to-face society is perhaps in many ways superior to modern societies, which are marked by limited, instrumental human relations and large formal institutions.[4]

Despite decades of assault by scholars unhappy with the concept of unilinear change, the notion of a continuum from tradition to modernity continues to exert considerable appeal among historians. Village cultures are viewed as essentially unchanging, though "equilibrium" is slowly replacing the word "inertia," as historians come to recognize that the transmission of culture is not a self-perpetuating process but is rather the result of a good deal of hard work by "people involved in the process of handing down traditions."[5]

The history of popular education and literacy is a good example of the way this framework has affected the treatment of social change. The history of literacy and schooling has been particularly vulnerable to what Marx called the "illusion of politics"[6]—the notion that change comes from the pens of legislators. Until recently, most histories of education described a sequence of legislative decrees passed by lawmakers and imposed by a bureaucracy. Like all change, the introduction of schooling in the village was assumed to have come from without, an exogenous process imposed by outsiders on a recalcitrant, lethargic, and ignorant community. If traditional society were a "closed, unconnected, immobile set of social worlds," how else could change be explained?[7]

This argument assumed not only that literacy and schooling were imposed on the community but also that they *necessarily* heralded major changes in rural society and in the peasant mind. Indeed, it is difficult to ignore that the three great major revolutions of modern European history—English, French, and Russian—all took place when each country was approaching a threshold of 50 percent literacy, or that a 40 percent literacy level seems to be a precondition of modern economic development.[8] But this view not only points out a correlation between literacy and revolution or economic development. It also argues that learning to read is in itself a revolutionary process, that literacy alters the mind at the same time that it changes the community and breaks down barriers between the autarkic village and society at large.

The notion is widespread that the written word has "peculiar psychological properties. Its relationship to memory and thinking is different from that of the spoken word." This theory, advanced in recent decades by P. M. Greenfield and Jerome Bruner, holds that writing promotes cognitive growth and, especially, content-independent, abstract thought. Literacy involves the mastery of "the logical functions of language apart from its interpersonal functions (of communication)" and the development of general mental capacities such as abstract thinking and the ability to perform logical operations, which "are presumed to characterize the

individual's intellectual functioning across a wide range of tasks."
Such capacities have recently been linked with Piaget's developmental stages, notably with the final stage of formal operational
thought. Thus, in acquiring literacy, children are supposedly learning a set of skills that can be transferred to other tasks. In short,
literacy has a ripple effect on traditional society.[9]

The history of literacy is an essential, perhaps causal, element
of the larger history of modernization and social mobilization. Literacy is even regarded as a convenient proxy for or indicator of
"becoming modern," implying a restructuring of world view.
Those who know how to read and write are more curious about
the outside world, optimistic about progress, and receptive to science and innovation. In the words of Daniel Lerner, "psychic mobility" accompanies geographic and social mobility; literacy is
both the index and the agent of this phase. The capacity to read
equips people to "perform the various tasks required in the modernizing society." The result is *participation* in the affairs of the
world outside the family and village.[10]

Although schooling has been seen largely as a vehicle for literacy, it has also been viewed as a melting pot facilitating national
integration, a "bridging agency" helping to replace the mores of
the traditional family with a modern world view.[11] Particularly in
the United States, schools were long viewed as instruments of democracy, promoting not only pluralism and tolerance but also
equality of opportunity. To be sure, some recent works on modernization have noted that schools can work to *preserve* "existing
distributions of power" by "indoctrinating those under their control with a subservient ethic."[12] But on the whole, the mobilizing,
liberating, and leveling potential of schooling, rather than its social
control function, has been stressed.

In the study of Russian history, several trends have reinforced
the conventional treatment of the history of education, particularly
on the issues of sponsorship and impact. First, Russian history
has often been written as the history of the Russian state. (Recall
Pushkin's famous lament that all that was missing in Karamzin's
History of the Russian State was the Russian people.) Given the
prominent role of the state, the destruction of autonomous organizations, and the tradition of state intervention in all areas, the tendency to focus primarily on legislation and policy debates has been

particularly salient in the history of Russian schools. Second, Russia has been seen as especially backward, her peasantry exceptionally ignorant and in need of guidance, and the village commune notably resistant to change. Clearly, in this view, when change came, it would strike with particular force, and it would come from the outside.

When such historical development is presented as a progression from tradition to modernity, the source of change is often identified as the state or educated elites and the object of change as village culture. Russian history of education represents an extreme statement of this approach. There have been some excellent *institutional* histories of Russian education, but the social history of literacy and schools has not found fertile soil, at least partially because traditional approaches to the history of education tuck so neatly into Russian historiography as a whole.[13]

Yet, in the West, at one time or another virtually every aspect of this traditional approach has been challenged, if not discredited. In particular, modern anthropologists and social historians have rejected the analogy between child and adult, on the one hand, and primitive and modern, on the other. They argue that traditional thought is indeed logical, a form of thought as completely and systematically socialized as our own, but applied to "different modes of experience" and pursuing different strategies. No longer "absorbed in immediate sensation, unable to concentrate or to comprehend abstract ideas, and given . . . to credulity,"[14] the peasant now strides onto the stage of history as a rational actor, even a systematic thinker.[15]

The techniques and approaches of social history have been applied to the history of literacy and popular schooling as well, and some longstanding assumptions have been discarded.[16] For example, the very notion of literacy itself is no longer clear. Elizabeth Eisenstein has cast doubt on the validity of sharp distinctions between oral and literate cultures by showing that the boundaries between the two were very porous and that what the illiterate peasant heard in oral culture had long been transformed by the advent of print.[17] Natalie Davis has shown that the first century or more of printing in France brought little change to the villages and "strengthened rather than sapped the vitality of the culture of the *menu peuple* in the cities," for they were not "passive recipients" but "active users and interpreters" of the new type of communication and "helped give . . . books form." [18]

Striking advances have been made in the study of literacy, both as a historical phenomenon and as a process linked to cultural change and cognitive modes. Harvey Graff informs us that "literacy is a process, different for different roles, and with requirements shifting as individuals and societies change." [19] Daniel and Lauren Resnick have shown how changing expectations affect estimates of the adequacy of a population's literacy, and they have traced a "sharp shift" in the meaning of literacy over time:

To illustrate, if writing one's name were what was meant by literacy, we would not be worried that illiteracy was a national problem. . . . [Yet] until well into the nineteenth century the capacity to form the letters of one's signature was not a skill shared by the majority of the population, even in the more developed nations of Europe. Even a somewhat more stringent literacy criterion would not force recognition of a major problem. If the ability to read aloud a simple and well-known passage were the measure, America would have a "few illiterates" but hardly a crisis. If we expected people to demonstrate after reading this simple passage that they had registered its contents at some low level, perhaps by saying whom a story was about or what a named character did, we would probably find a low percentage of illiterates in our adult population.

But the number would start to rise, perhaps quite sharply, if unfamiliar texts were to be read and new information gleaned from them. And, if inferential rather than directly stated information were to be drawn from the text, we would probably announce a true crisis in literacy. If we used as a literacy criterion the ability to read a complete text with literary allusions and metaphoric expression and not only to interpret this text but to relate it sensibly to other texts, many would claim that only a tiny fraction of our population is "truly literate," a charge not infrequently made in discussions about standards of literacy at the university level. [20]

Such observations have not been confined to the West or to the study of alphabetic cultures. Evelyn Rawski's pathbreaking work on popular literacy in Ch'ing China is based on an insightful distinction between levels of literacy. [21] In China, written documents were necessary for marriages, funerals, sales transactions, and clan lineage functions, as well as for dividing family property, paying and allocating taxes, coordinating the maintenance schedules of irrigation systems, and keeping registers at temples, shrines, and hostels. According to Rawski, scholars have grossly understated the degree of literacy in China by concentrating on those with full mastery of the written language (i.e., those capable of reading the classics and preparing for the examinations), while "ignoring the levels of knowledge below mastery of the elite written culture," the rudimentary levels of literacy necessary for functioning within, not moving up in, traditional rural society. Few Chinese could read the classics, but a remarkably large proportion of the rural population could handle simple figures, as well as up to one thousand characters used in everyday life.

Others tell us that mastering writing produces effects distinct from those of learning to read. Speaking of the "technology of the intellect," Jack Goody argues that the acquisition of writing produces many of the social, economic, and intellectual changes associated with modernity. Goody asserts that "setting down speech allowed men to clearly separate words, to manipulate their order and develop syllogistic forms of reasoning." In a fascinating discussion, Goody shows how oral cultures tend toward homeostasis and how writing facilitates the growth of bureaucracy, individualism, and an awareness of history.[22] François Furet and Jacques Ozouf, writing on the history of literacy in France, conclude that although restricted literacy had little effect on traditional structures, the spread of writing signaled the emergence of the individual out of the community.[23] Writing "nourished the burgeoning power of the state . . . ultimately, new communications at the personal level altered society and government and created a need for reintegration."[24] Thus, to be meaningful, the study of literacy must distinguish among stages and take into account current discussions of the differing impact of both reading and writing.

Recent work on the psychology of literacy has also focused on the environment in which literacy is achieved. Sylvia Scribner and Michael Cole, inspired by the work of Alexander R. Luria in Central Asia and informed by their own investigations of the Lai tribe in Liberia, suggest that literacy is a skill much like pottery making or basket weaving. Though highly complex, it is learned by demonstration (it is context-dependent), and it does not provide conceptual rules easily transferred to other areas of endeavor. In short, literacy may fit well into traditional ways of life.[25] If we accept the proposition that it is possible to learn how to read or to sign one's name without undergoing important psychological development, we must look more closely both at definitions of literacy and at the setting in which it is acquired.

Scribner and Cole maintain that schools (as distinct from literacy) *do* promote qualitative changes in modes of thought. Literacy is context–dependent and fits easily into a traditional matrix, but school-based learning fosters the "transfer of conceptual rules" to tasks outside the classroom. It facilitates "learning out of context," "the independent learning of techniques or instrumental skills, apart from the ends to which they will later be . . . related, . . . which do not seem to have many parallels in everyday life." In school, the child learns to separate what is taught from who is teaching and how to formulate abstract rules. Thus schooling, rather than literacy, removes learning (both skills and values) from its traditional setting, and it is here that the first steps to "becoming modern" may take place.[26] Although a worthwhile enterprise, the study of literacy should not be taken for more than it is and must not be treated as a convenient index of schooling, much less of psychological modernization or "attitudinal liberation." Schooling emerges as a distinct phenomenon, and school-based learning does have the potential to transform the way people think.

The social history of education in the West has also convincingly decoupled the *histories* of literacy and of schooling. In the words of Thomas Laqueur, "Literacy was not the inevitable product of schooling; nor was non-literacy a necessary consequence of its absence."[27] The effectiveness of compulsory education laws has been challenged—indeed, the significance of the history of all educational legislation to the history of schooling is under a shadow.[28] In general, literacy and modernization have been disassociated. It has been shown that in England the rise of mass literacy preceded industrialization, that in fact the early stages of industrialization witnessed a *decline* of literacy.[29] U.S. historians have argued that in many areas widespread literacy and schooling preceded both urbanization and industrialization and that mass education often came before government intervention and the common school.

The purpose of intervention, according to David Tyack, was to standardize and improve, to control rather than to expand, mass education.[30] Furet and Ozouf have shown that the "school system, far from being an institution imposed upon society from above, was on the contrary the product of social demand for education" and that three centuries of restricted literacy did little to modernize French society, instead leaving the French peasant a "cultural half-breed."[31] Sweden, it turns out, developed mass literacy in the seventeenth century without government intervention, well before urbanization or industrialization.[32]

Others have looked at school routines, rather than at the mastery of basic skills or the assimilation of new material, and have suggested that "it is often not what is taught, but the organization of the teaching, that matters."[33] Schools enforce values, but they also define deviance and merit, and they select and label failure and success. According to revisionists, schools "promote standardization, cultural homogenization, subordination, discipline, and hierarchy."[34] It was once argued that schools provided basic skills needed in the factories. Now, with the discovery that literacy rates have often gone down in the early stages of industrialization and the argument that capitalism "deskills" the work force, the conclusion follows that schools instill a toleration for boredom, routine, and repetition—that this is what "becoming modern" means![35] Some have argued that social control was the main goal of schooling from early times and have highlighted the darker side of Enlightenment education philosophy. Others have stressed the connection between the rise of capitalism and the emergence of the "surveillance," or "therapeutic," state, in which schools, like mental hospitals and prisons, were designed to control and shape.[36]

All of this emphasizes the need to distinguish between levels of literacy, between reading and writing as distinct skills. We must investigate literacy acquired in noninstitutional settings, as well as school-based skills and school routines. The result of recent work has been to draw a line between the overlapping but distinct phenomena of literacy and schooling.

❖

In Russian history, the investigation of peasant *mentalité* has reflected trends in Western social and cultural history. Michael Confino and Moshe Lewin have produced brilliant work demonstrating the rational component underlying dogged peasant adherence to traditional techniques of tilling the soil. Daniel Field has shown how peasant duplicity and the "myth of the Tsar"—the fabled irrational adherence to patriarchal political views—in reality represented a defensive strategy and a convenient fiction protecting the village from retribution by the state, at the same time as it deflected the blame for peasant disturbances to outsiders stirring up the "naive" peasantry. Other scholars have begun work on the peasant family, on demographics, on the "hearth" and *izba*—all in the hope of understanding the relationship between ecology and *mentalité,* in the attempt to study history "from below," and in search of ways to bypass the old problem confronting historians who try to understand how peasants think—*pas de documents, pas d' histoire.*[37]

One record of peasant activities remains largely untapped: the history of village schools in Russia. It is to that history we now turn, in an attempt to understand the peasant contribution to the rise of schools in Russia and the village response to modernity. The primary focus of this book is the expansion and the results of mass schooling. Who sponsored education, providing the funding, labor, and support? What were the essential stages in the creation and evolution of Russian village schools? How did peasants participate in this effort, and what does the nature of their participation tell us about the peasant view of the world?

Our investigation, though emphasizing popular input, will also show that there were several actors on the stage, and it will take us from the village and local government to the national level, allowing us to look at education from the top down, as well as from below, and to consider the contribution of the educated public and the state bureaucracy. We will examine how control was exerted over the schools, looking in some detail at school boards, zemstvo educational organizations, and local school inspectors. Finally, we will consider the impact of political infighting within the bureaucratic system and discuss the famous conflict between secular and religious schools, embodied at the national level in the rivalry between the Holy Synod and the Ministry of Education.

Recent work by Western scholars has provided refreshing new insights into the workings of the Russian bureaucracy and has indicated that an intense struggle over local institutions was at the heart of Russian politics at the turn of the century. The failure to create viable local government made it virtually impossible to govern Russia when the Provisional Government came to power in 1917.[38] By keeping an eye on local politics and by including institutional history, I have tried to avoid a shortcoming frequently encountered in the writing of social history: "collapsing the political into the social"—treating politics as an epiphenomenon of social forces.[39] While analyzing the strategy set by peasants, I have also tried to clarify the constraints imposed by the political structure and to incorporate the insights of recent studies on local politics and central bureaucracy into educational history. A description of the workings of local educational institutions should cast light on other aspects of local and national politics.

The second major concern of this book is the impact of schooling on village life. Some historians have argued that because schools arrived so tardily in Russia and so few children managed to enroll (with those who did staying only briefly), the prerevolutionary Russian school had no perceptible impact on the village. Others see the late upsurge in enrollments and the government campaign for universal literacy as evidence of the enormous strides made by Russia in the half century following Emancipation. They argue that given another decade or so the Russian work force would have been schooled for modernity, equipped with the proper skills and routines for the factory order, and inculcated with a world view conducive to participation in pluralistic, even democratic, political systems.[40] Of course, few would state the issue so baldly or argue that the humble rural school alone could have determined the fate of Russia. Yet familiarity with the way the European work force was domesticated in school, trade union, and army should caution us from underestimating the potential impact of even limited schooling. Most important, the question has never really been posed.[41]

How then do we go about measuring the influence of schooling? One way is to enter the school, look at textbooks, consider day-to-day routines, and, on the basis of this description, draw plausible inferences about the impact of content and routines on children. Such an approach is promising, and the material is available, but it also presents several problems. The most significant obstacle is that, despite all the recent attention given in the West to education and "reproduction" (the replication of existing social relations in the classroom), to the theory of "correspondence," and to "hegemony," there is really little agreement on just what takes place in classrooms or on how to approach the study of classroom content and "the social relations of classroom encounters."[42] The study of the Russian classroom may ultimately contribute to the debate over what happens in schools and how this affects the child's mind, as well as to an understanding of how schooling interlocks with, reinforces, or subverts processes in the outside world. At present, however, there is no consensus on how to approach the issue or even how to model the investigation.

To be meaningful, such an analysis must occur within a snug framework of quantitative dimensions—we must know how many children went to school, for how long, and with what regularity. As Karl Kaestle and Maris Vinovskis point out in their recent investigation of the expansion of American schooling, "This study is not, to any great extent, about the experiences children had within the schoolroom. We believe that a sound social history of American education . . . should begin with question of who went to school."[43] Likewise, this book will consider the timing of the expansion of schooling in Russia and the level of saturation of the countryside with schools at different times, attempting to describe how many children had access to, and actually had contact with, a school at some time in their childhood.

We will also consider the intensity of schooling. By determining the length of stay in school, the scale of absenteeism, and the rate of repetition, we can determine the scope and depth of schooling. From duration and regularity, as well as from pupil-teacher ratios and classroom size, we can establish contact time and can infer what children might plausibly have learned in the time allotted them. The difference between initial enrollment levels and length (and regularity) of stay is analogous to the contrast between signature (restricted) and comprehensive literacy. Though figures on signature literacy and enrollments are useful, only knowledge of the level of literacy and the dimensions of contact time will permit us to draw inferences about the true impact of reading skills and schooling, in terms of both instruction and socialization.

But this work will also proceed beyond the dynamics of schooling to look directly at results. Through a careful look at retention studies (reexaminations of former pupils) carried out in the villages between 1880 and 1914 and at inspectors' reports and teachers' observations of the impact of schooling, I will try to measure—admittedly in a crude fashion—the cognitive and behavioral impact of two to three years of intensive schooling on peasant children and on village culture as a whole. In particular, I look for signs that the schools were either failing entirely in their mission, as many claimed, or were successful in promoting "transfer skills." Were schools providing restricted or comprehensive literacy? Were children learning to read, or were they learning *from* reading? In addition, I will examine more fragmentary evidence of what we now call the "hidden curriculum," asking to what degree the routine and organization of schooling brought about changes in the behavior or aspirations of its wards. This same question also prompted me to include a study of the continued education of the few who proceeded beyond the basic school.

The studies cited here were usually very broad in scope, involving thousands, sometimes hundreds of thousands, and, in the case of the 1911 School Census and the 1911 Zemstvo Survey, millions of pupils at one time. Often the information was collected through visits to local school boards or zemstvo school commissions, through questionnaires sent to teachers or local correspondents, or through direct visits to the schools. In general, after poring over hundreds of such surveys and statistical yearbooks, one gains an impression of extraordinary caution and integrity in the compilation and use of data.[44]

I have also turned to another source to verify the inferences drawn from the school records: the network of zemstvo correspondents who began working in the villages in the last quarter of the nineteenth century. Made up of thousands and thousands of medical orderlies, village teachers, peasant officials, and other peasant literates, this network produced a rich storehouse of impressions gleaned from years of personal observation, conversation, and participation in village life. Used carefully in conjunction with the school records, and with due account of the gap between peasant and outsider—even resident outsider—the zemstvo correspondent records are a valuable historical source.

A sensible handling of the data on sponsorship, enrollments, denied admissions, length of stay, regularity of attendance, repetition, and frequency of dropping out will also produce a *record of peasant strategy* as well as a record of behavior. The practice of deducing world view from aggregate behavior has respectable precedents. Moreover, given the paucity of available material on peasant beliefs, school records should not be overlooked as a source.

For example, because schooling was not compulsory in Russia, peasant enrollments will tell us much about peasant estimates of the value of education. Even more significant is the incidence of denied admissions, reflecting both unmet demand and significant pressure on the state to intervene in support of education.[45] But peasants also wanted a voice in the schools once they were built and peasant children were enrolled. The dusty school records documenting length of stay, repetition, and "wastage"—carefully sifted —reflect not only the economy of the Russian countryside and the impact of poverty and child labor on the length of schooling, but also conscious efforts by peasants to intervene in a process they no longer directly controlled.

We should not expect a perfect fit between peasant goals and the way the schools actually worked. After all, the aspirations of any single class, dominant or subservient, are seldom perfectly reflected in reality, and peasants had to operate within harsh structural constraints. But we can hope to find some traces of the way villagers were thinking in the records left by their children as they passed through the rural schools. Thomas Darlington, the British inspector who traveled to Russia at the end of the century, observed:

The fact that there is nowhere in Russia proper any legal obligation to send children to school [compulsory education for children aged ten to thirteen was in place in the Baltic] gives the peasantry in practice a very real influence over the spirit of teaching and ensures its popular character. No peasant will send his child to any school, however conveniently it may be situated, if the teaching given in the school is not what pleases him.[46]

To be sure, once convinced that schooling was necessary for survival, peasants would undoubtedly enroll their children even if it meant exposing them to disruptive elements introduced by an alien curriculum or by a teacher brought in from the outside. Then, the peasants might adopt a strategy more complex than that embodied in the simple opportunity to veto a type of schooling not fitting village needs. Yet Darlington astutely saw that actual control depended not only on the determination of those who executed policy and the efficiency of the state machinery but also on the degree of compliance or resistance shown by a very willful population, even in a highly centralized state. In Russia, the peasantry, when not in open revolt, had for centuries waged a war of passive resistance against serfdom. After 1861, it used similar tactics of duplicity and feigned ignorance against tax collectors and other outside authorities. Is there any reason to believe that common villagers were incapable of pursuing their own perceived self-interests, of acting according to very practical reasoning when it came to the schoolroom as well?

A study of rural teachers will complete the description of schooling, with two issues foremost. First, it has commonly been asserted that Russian teachers were so ill-trained that they could not have taught the peasants anything of value. I will draw a demographic profile of these teachers and look carefully at their educational backgrounds (as well as self-perceptions of adequacy) to evaluate just how well prepared they were to teach the ABCs. As we shall see, notions of "adequacy" and "failure" were often applied to many education issues with little thought to clear definition or context. Applying the standards of adequacy drawn up recently by UNESCO, as well as making comparisons with teachers in other countries, will allow us to draw more balanced, impartial conclusions about the quality of these teachers.

Not only the skills of the teachers but also their place in the village will interest us. Those who argue that teachers were ill-prepared often add that they were also carriers of radical political beliefs. The more basic question is whether the teachers, virtually the only permanent outsiders in the village, were in a position to exert any influence on village culture; if so, what were their beliefs? The Russian peasant village resembled the "closed corporate" societies described by the anthropologist Eric Wolf. In such villages integration is achieved by "inhibiting direct contact" between the individual and the outside world, by "interposing between them an organized communal structure." Relations between teacher and community can reveal how intact traditional village mechanisms for dealing with the outside world were.[47]

Most peasant cultures have a highly differentiated terminology for the various categories of "outsiders" who have dealings with the rural community, from the itinerant trader to the tax collector. Teodor Shanin believes that the Russian peasant distinguished three such types of outsiders: the "plenipotentiary," the "neighbor," and the "stranger."[48] The plenipotentiary outsiders (*nachal'stva*), those with the authority to coerce and command, represented a direct threat to the village. The neighbor outsider was simply a peasant from another community who was hardly likely to serve as a vehicle of technological innovation or cultural change.

But the stranger outsider was a person who, expressing different values and acting according to different sets of rules than those governing village relations, was nevertheless distinguished from the local authorities (plenipotentiary outsiders). In Russia, the teacher was one such stranger outsider and (with the exception of those who doubled as tax collectors or police constables) was not associated in the peasant mind with the brute force and power of *nachal'stvo*. By bypassing the traditional "broker relations" maintained by the village and volost' elders between the community and the global culture,[49] this teacher could serve as a link for the transmission of techniques and skills (as well as political and cultural values). Teachers were *in* the village; were they also *of* it?[50]

Such an investigation will bring us back to the starting point of this discussion—the response of the village community to the pressures of rapid social and economic change. I have described the issues that prompted my research and have argued that the rural school offers a window on village life as a whole. The following pages represent an attempt both to come to grips with these issues and to reproduce the rich detail of village culture viewed through that window.

PART I

Institutions and Sponsors

1

Russian Schools Before the
Great Reforms

The history of Russian popular education before 1864 is one of sweeping projects occasionally passed as laws but almost never carried out in practice. From the time of Peter the Great, the government took an active interest in educating its citizenry in the pursuit of international power, military strength, and bureaucratic improvement. In J. L. Black's words, "Peter's educational system was designed primarily to train technically proficient servants of the state."[1] Peter first established navigational schools and then elementary "cypher" schools (1714), his adviser Pososhkov recommended compulsory education, and promotion in the bureaucracy was briefly attached to educational achievement. But the cypher schools, which soon merged with garrison schools, had no significance for the peasantry. In the forty-two schools opened between 1716 and 1722, half of all pupils were from the clergy, one-quarter were "soldiers' children" (*soldatskie deti*—a social category established by law in 1719) belonging to the military estate, and the remainder were the offspring of officials (*prikaznye*) and of the lower urban strata.[2] Peter also pressured the Church to educate its priests, but "no decree from Peter was going to ease the dread which most of the nation's church leaders and parish priests had of learning."[3] Although Peter saw education of his citizenry as a prerequisite of

19

national strength, the notion of citizenry did not extend to serfs and state peasants who, treated more like cattle than like human beings, constituted most of the country's population. Pososhkov's expressed opinion that the peasantry should be assisted toward literacy does little to contradict the overwhelming evidence that popular education was in no way a priority of Petrine policy.[4]

During the reign of Catherine the Great (1762–1796), the famous Legislative Comission of 1767 recommended obligatory education for the entire male population; and when Boards of Public Welfare—the forerunners of local school boards—were established in 1775, they were instructed, among other things, to look after primary education, both rural and urban. In 1783, Catherine invited the Austro-Serbian educator Iankovich de Mirievo to Russia and appointed a Commission for the Establishment of Schools to design a school system. The result was a statute (1786) that set up *Trivialschulen* ("Minor Schools") and *Hauptschulen* ("Major Schools") on the Austrian model and established the rudiments of a national school administration.[5]

Catherine is known to have felt that too much education for the *chern'* (plebes) was dangerous to the social order. Yet a prominent prerevolutionary historian of education, S. V. Rozhdestvenskii, suggested that the elimination of the class element from education and the introduction of obligatory attendance for all male pupils were two salient principles of the educational projects undertaken in the first years of Catherine's reign.[6] Indeed, as Paul Dukes has shown, a specific concern for peasant education was evident among some of the local committees of the 1767 Legislative Commission; some believed that educated serfs would be more productive, whereas others hoped that schooling would tame the wild beasts. Describing the murder of a noble family by its serfs, Count Stroganov speculated that "if this kind of people were enlightened, then, of course, we would not be witnesses to such bestiality."[7] Thus, although hostility to primary education, based on the apprehension that educated peasants would be unsatisfied with their place in society, was undoubtedly present, such an attitude was not universal among the elite. Even in the eighteenth century, the Enlightenment view of education was that it not only could liberate minds from tradition and superstition but also could encourage economic productivity and order, particularly if properly supervised from above and if the common man was "educated in the virtues appropriate to his calling and station in life."[8]

The 1786 Statute detailed the subjects to be taught at each level and described the methods to be used. It provided for high schools and primary schools in the provincial capitals, and primary schools in the district towns. The primary schools consisted of two classes, each of one year, and were to teach the three Rs as well as grammar and moral education; the high school had four classes (five years, the final class lasting two years) and boasted an ambitious curriculum including architecture, physics, history, and languages. Schools were free and coeducational for all but serfs.[9]

These reforms, though in theory representing a major breakthrough by spreading at least limited education to the provinces and opening the door to basic education even to free peasants, in practice remained a dead letter. As Black has noted, this situation resulted from Catherine's failure to open her purse "for public schools as she did for elitist institutions." The sums spent on education never even approached those spent "on the trappings of imperial glory and on gifts, even palaces, for her favorites."[10] It has been calculated that by 1801 there were twenty-two thousand pupils in all public schools—both Major and Minor—in all of Russia. The fact that peasants composed a large proportion (36 percent) of children in public schools should not obscure the truth that the total number enrolled was minute and that, in a population of perhaps forty million, the life chances of an individual peasant receiving any formal schooling were insignificant. Interestingly, as Catherine pointed out in 1761, the only place where a peasant's son might have had the opportunity to receive some schooling was the army; and apparently this remained true throughout the century. In the unofficial peasant schools scattered throughout the villages, retired soldiers were prominent as teachers, indicating that some at least were literate; nevertheless we should keep in mind that soldiers were conscripted for twenty-five years, and relatively few survived to return to the village. Thus, for all practical purposes, educating peasant soldiers did not have a significant impact on the peasant community as a whole.

Finances were not the only consideration preventing the realization of the pious hopes expressed in the Legislative Commission and in Catherine's earlier education projects drawn up in collaboration with Ivan Betskoi. This failure, as explained by Nicholas Hans, stemmed from two other causes:

Firstly, the establishment of schools among peasants involved many practical difficulties. The majority of peasants were the private property of the landowners, and the government did not wish to open state schools among serfs without the consent of their owners. Secondly, the peasant revolutionary movement under Pugachev frightened Catherine and the nobility, and she decided not to proceed [with the establishment of rural schools]. The absence of rural schools in the Statute of 1786 was a serious drawback, and the system, instead of being nationwide, became a school system for the town population only.[11]

Catherine is known for her promotion of female education; she is also justly praised for the restoration of an "ideal of education as a harmonious development of the intellectual and bodily powers"—at least for the "public," if not for the *chern'*, whose education was to be vocational and narrowly practical—for restoring, that is, a moral and aesthetic component to the narrowly utilitarian view of education prevailing under Peter.[12] But most of all Catherine is known as the founder of the Russian school *system*. To be sure, only a small segment of the system was actually built in her lifetime; nevertheless, she left an indelible stamp on the structure of Russian education. From this period on, the system was built primarily from the top down, with emphasis on secondary and university education. Even as late as 1900, traces of Catherine's legislation were still visible in the cumbersome edifice of Russian education—this multi-tiered structure, which developed over two centuries, was endlessly redesigned and modified by rulers and reformers, but almost always by accretion and elaboration, by modification, rather than by removal of any of its parts. For this reason one could count as many as sixty-seven different types of primary schools in existence by 1914, as well as a bewildering profusion of advanced elementary and secondary schools.[13]

Alexander I, while building on the Catherinian legislation, introduced fundamental structural changes of great significance. The reforms began with the establishment of the Ministry of Education in 1802; in 1803 the Main Administration of Schools (Glavnoe upravlenie uchilishch) came into being, and on 24 January 1803, Preliminary Rules followed, converting Catherine's three-tiered system into a four-tiered one. The rules also divided Russia into six (subsequently twelve) education circuits, each encompassing several provinces, and made the university an administrative link by requiring that these higher institutions be responsible for supervising the lower levels of education within each education circuit. Although the university was subordinated to the curator of each circuit (who was a member of the Main Administration), it nominated the director of schools for each province and directly appointed the local inspector (*smotritel'*) of district schools, who was also responsible for supervising primary education. (The university was divested of its supervisory function in 1834.)[14]

Many historians regard the 1803 Rules and their codification and further elaboration in the 1804 Statute to be major landmarks in Russian history. They represented a turn from German to French models; the 1804 Statute was modeled, at least partially, after Condorcet's *Sur l'instruction publique,* submitted to the French National Assembly in 1792.[15] Alexander's Unofficial Committee, which helped shape the reform, borrowed two related principles from the French Revolution: the notion of the "unified school"—an all-embracing system, cross-connected for ease of transfer; and the "ladder," or arrangement of all levels of instruction to allow advancement from lower to secondary and higher schools, along with coordinating curriculum to facilitate such advancement. The first rung in the ladder was the parish school, offering one year of instruction, which was to be built in every urban and rural settlement. Supervised by the inspector of the district school, sponsored by priests in state peasant villages and by gentry in serf villages, the parish school was to provide instruction in the three Rs, the Bible, civics (*nravouchenie*), and guided reading from an official sourcebook on health, nature, and agriculture. The mission of the parish school was to "provide children from families of agriculturalists and other occupation groups relevant information [*im prilichnye svedeniia*], to make them better from a physical and moral point of view, to provide them with precise information about natural phenomena, to eradicate superstitions and prejudices, so injurious to their well-being."[16]

District schools, which the statute required each district town to open with its own resources, were the second rung in the educational ladder. Open to all children of all classes who had completed the parish school, they in turn provided direct access to the gymnasiums.

N. Karamzin was among the first to point to the potential significance of the statute for rural education. According to him, "the main legacy of the statute will always be the establishment of rural schools . . . [which] will prove far more useful than all the lycées. . . . Between people who can only read and write and the completely illiterate, the gap is wider than between the layman [*neuchënyi*] and the world's leading metaphysician. Reading and writing open up a new world to the individual, especially in our time, with the rapid advances of the mind."[17]

Admirable as this scheme was, it had one fatal flaw: it left the establishment of parish schools to the initiative of municipalities, the clergy, and landowners. As a result, only about six hundred such schools were established by 1825, half of them in towns. Even the district schools languished; in 1825, there were no schools at all in at least 131 district towns in European Russia.[18] According to the official historian of the St. Petersburg school circuit, "In general all official village schools lacked roots, and the majority closed their doors for good soon after they first opened."[19] Alexander's entire grandiose project remained largely on paper, though worked out in fine detail and embracing generous principles. Nicholas Hans's judgment seems correct: because there was no provision for funding of peasant schools, "the basis of the whole scheme was lacking."[20]

The main result of the Alexandrine legislation was to continue the sponsorship of secondary and higher education begun under Peter, while leaving popular education to the distant future. This may or may not have been a wise strategy; some argue that allocating scarce resources to specialized training yields greater economic dividends than a policy of promoting universal primary education. In this case, however, without the first rung of the ladder the principles of universal access and free promotion throughout the system remained pious wishes.

The first quarter of the nineteenth century brought great educational ferment to Russia, marked by discussion of and experiments with the Lancaster method of instruction (later repressed by the government in Alexander's waning years) and the translation and circulation of the works of advanced thinkers such as the prominent Swiss educator Heinrich Pestalozzi, who left a permanent imprint on Russian pedagogy. Despite this activity, however, the government failed to become involved in funding primary education, thereby condemning the goals of the 1804 Statute to failure. To be sure, few other countries in Western Europe had traditions of active government intervention in primary education at this time, either. Nevertheless, Russia entered the nineteenth century with fewer than one in two hundred of its school-age population under instruction, and the situation can hardly have improved in the period following the promulgation of the 1804 Statute.[21]

Soon after Nicholas I (1825–1855) came to the throne, he instructed his Committee for the Establishment of Schools to modify the entire system in the interest of uniformity throughout the Empire. Nicholas, whose guiding principle has been summarized as "a place for everyone and everyone in his place," was concerned not so much to integrate as to dismantle the ladder; yet it is one of the minor ironies of history that this paternalistic autocrat, who had little use for the Enlightenment principles toyed with by his elder brother and who worked hard to dismantle the ladder system, did far more than Alexander to promote primary education.[22]

In 1827, a rescript was issued requiring that "instruction be appropriate to the likely future destination of the pupil" and recommending that individuals be discouraged from "striving to excessively improve upon the situation in which fate had placed them." As an example, the rescript pointed to serfs who had advanced to the gymnasium and even to the university. This mobility was deemed especially harmful because

on the one hand, these youth often bring baneful habits along with them to the school; on the other hand, those who excel in application and are successful become accustomed to a way of life, to notions and to a style of thought not appropriate to their situation; the inevitable burdens of their life now become intolerable and they fall into despondency, succumbing to baneful dreams and base passions.[23]

The rescript forbade universities and gymnasiums to admit serfs, and a ministerial circular explained that the three-year district schools were to serve the "children of merchants, officers and clergy."

Throughout his life, and notably in comments on official documents (1837, 1843, and 1847), Nicholas reaffirmed his belief that education should fit one's station in life. In his famous secret speech of 1842, referring to the evils of serfdom but also to the impossibility of changing the system at the time, Nicholas criticized the carelessness of certain gentry who had provided their household serfs with an education inappropriate to their standing, thereby rubbing salt in wounds.[24]

The Statute of 8 December 1828, which superseded the 1804 Statute, embodied and codified these sentiments and brought the school system back in line with the old Prussian system established under Frederick the Great (which by 1828 had been replaced in Prussia by a school structure modeled and promoted by Wilhelm Humboldt). According to the 1828 Statute, district schools were in principle open to all classes, but the curriculum at the successive rungs of the ladder was no longer coordinated to facilitate transfer from lower to higher schools. Henceforth, the goal of the parish school would be to spread "rudimentary information"—the three Rs and the Bible—and instruction in health and natural science was to be dropped. Schools could be opened "wherever the resources could be found," but, as in 1804, it was left to the discretion and initiative of the gentry whether or not to educate their serfs. For the first time, the law tightly regulated the sequence, content, and hourly course work of the parish school, permitting only books approved by the Ministry of Education to be employed. Corporal punishment, eliminated (at least on paper) in 1794, reentered the school with the blessings of the government in the 1828 Statute. Of course, for rules, regulations, and specifications to have more than symbolic significance, there had to be schools in which they could be applied.[25]

As William Mathes has justly observed, Nicholas's aim was not to eliminate education but rather to control and channel it. A fear of excess permeated his approach to governing and caused him to restructure the system. A. S. Shishkov, briefly Nicholas's Minister of Education, made explicit the notion that education, like salt, should be taken in good measure; or, as Karamzin had declared earlier, "to seek the superfluous is as bad as to reject the necessary."[26] This sentiment, perhaps the first utterance of a position later embodied in the notorious "Cooks' Children" circular of 1887, was perhaps reprehensible and at times was a mere fig leaf for utter lack of concern for peasant well-being. But a concern for social stability was not identical to indifference to popular education; it is a fundamental misreading of Russian educational history to assume that because rulers wished to restrict social mobility through the schools, they also sought to prevent even basic education. It was perfectly possible for a ruler and for officials to recognize that basic education was useful to the state, while at the same time resisting the ladder principle or the "unified school." Undoubtedly, basic education was not a high priority of the government in the first half of the nineteenth century; but there were also few people *outside* government circles who paid more than lip service to the cause of peasant schooling.

Unless we keep in mind the difference between hostility to education per se and opposition to "excess," it is difficult to understand why primary education made considerably more progress under Nicholas I than it had under Alexander I. During the latter's reign, grand principles were proclaimed, but virtually no one attempted to enact these principles. Under Nicholas, even though the government imposed strict limits on the scope and content of education, it encouraged rural primary education across a rather broad front. Although all schools except those under the Holy Synod had to conform to the 1828 Statute and were thus ultimately under the Ministry of Education (MNP), this was in reality a period of ministerial pluralism and (admittedly small-scale) efforts by a number of authorities to build schools. In the decades following the 1828 Statute, a bewildering variety of state-sponsored primary schools emerged in the countryside, each under the jurisdiction of a different ministry, or department within a ministry. Few records were kept on these schools, and there is good reason to suspect that many existed only on paper. Historians differ in their estimates of the total number of primary schools in the countryside during this period, though few would argue that they were widespread.[27]

Volost' schools, established under the supervision of several ministries, were the first permanent rural schools, appearing in Russia for the first time in the 1830s. (The volost' was a unit of peasant administration including several communes.) These schools concentrated on training petty functionaries such as clerks, assistant *fel'dshery* (medical orderlies), land surveyors, and others. Because the Ministry of Education was not directly linked to these schools and because they were listed as providing a vocational, not a general, education, the MNP kept no records of them. Thus these schools, for the most part, remained unregistered, unstudied, and ephemeral; very little is known about them. According to the Soviet historian N. A. Konstantinov, however, they were the only rural primary schools in Russia in the second quarter of the nineteenth century with a planned organizational structure.[28]

The Ministry of Appanages (Ministerstvo udelov) was also concerned with rural schools. When first established in 1797, it called for establishing parish schools for children six to ten years old who "while yet unable to withstand hard physical labor should not be left idle," and it sought to maintain a flow of literate clerks for the appanage offices. In 1804, however, the ministry abandoned the effort to build schools and instructed each local office (*prikaz*) to choose three boys to send to district schools at the expense of the peasant commune. In 1827, when the MNP inquired about the conditions of schools under the Ministry of Appanages, the former could locate only five rural schools in the entire Empire.[29]

On 25 October 1828, the Ministry of Appanages was instructed by Imperial decree to establish rural schools under each *prikaz* to provide peasants with rudimentary literacy and, again, to train minor peasant officials. According to the Instruction, priests were to serve as teachers and the Lancaster method of using monitors was to be employed, but no set program or length of stay was established. In 1865, the Ministry of Appanages turned over 1,376 such crown schools with 11,394 pupils to the Ministry of Education; some progress in school construction had clearly been made.[30] In theory, the *prikaz* elders were responsible for selecting pupils from village families; in practice, rich peasants often bought their children *out* of these schools—schooling, like military service, when linked with later employment for the state, was avoided whenever possible. By the 1840s, the Ministry of Appanages was providing subsidies of 5 to 30 rubles to parents of children in such schools and guaranteeing exemption from military conscription for other family members. Yet an investigation in Samara province showed that the enrollments recorded on paper grossly inflated the true number of pupils in schools. By inflating official enrollment figures local officials could reap double benefits: they levied a tax on the entire community to provide for the schooling of pupils theoretically enrolled, while pocketing the state subsidies sent to parents of these "dead souls" (and perhaps extorting yet more money from families to allow their children *not* to enroll!).[31]

The Church also became involved in rural education under Nicholas I. Earlier in the century (notably in 1804 and in 1818), the Holy Synod had expressed an interest in peasant schooling, but it was only in 1836, with the issuance of Rules of Village Education, that the Church central bureaucracy sent out orders to local clergy to organize schools in their parishes. Between 1837 and 1853, the recorded number of Church-sponsored schools increased rapidly, followed by a sharp decline until 1857 when Alexander II expressed an interest in Church schools and the Holy Synod again sent out instructions to the local dioceses to sponsor schools and to send in monthly reports on them. According to official reports, the number of Church schools was 1,500 in 1838, 4,820 in 1853, and 2,270 in 1857; increasing to 9,283 (with 159,000 pupils) in 1861, and to 21,420 (with 413,524 pupils) in 1865; but dropping precipitously after that, until only 4,000 schools survived in 1881.[32]

Few historians accept these figures uncritically. N. N. Mosolov noted, for example, that in some provinces the numbers provided by the local ecclesiastical offices exceeded the total number of schools of all types known to be in operation in those provinces. The local clergy were under considerable pressure from their superiors to open schools; schools that closed down when the pressure eased were often kept on the books and entered as new schools when they were once again "opened" as pressure was renewed (for example, in 1857). A. N. Kulomzin noted that where these schools existed they rarely enjoyed the support of the local population. Instead of teaching, the local clergy often forced the children to "cut wood, carry water and feed the livestock," and parents soon withdrew their children, justly feeling that they could be put to equally good use at home.[33] Count P. D. Kiselëv, who became famous for his reforms of the administration of state peasantry and for building schools in the villages of the state peasants (bound peasants,

who rendered obligations to the state, rather than the landlord),
noted in 1837 that "the clergy doesn't pay the slightest attention to
the matter of educating our village youth." In 1850, Kiselëv drew
up a plan by which the Ministry of State Domains would build
schools, with the clergy maintaining them and supervising curriculum; when he submitted this plan to the Synod, he received no
response.[34]

Speaking of the period immediately following Alexander II's
expression of interest in religious schools for the peasants, N. V.
Chekhov noted:

At first glance one is struck by the surprisingly rapid increase in the number of such schools. The local priests, the psalmist, the deacon—all
opened schools, whether at home or using Church facilities, and they
opened these schools when it was least convenient for peasant children,
namely, in May or June. If one looks closer, yet another peculiarity becomes evident: sometimes in the same small hamlet two or three schools
were opened simultaneously, or in short order one after another, and in
one school the priest would teach five, the deacon three, and the psalmist
one pupil. Generally, the average number of pupils in such schools was
fewer than ten, and sometimes, dozens of schools in populous villages
had from three to five pupils each. . . . Among the surviving population
from that era, the memory lingers of these schools run by priests; if you
ask an elderly literate how he learned how to read, he'll answer you: "Ah,
that was when the priests were still the teachers."[35]

Chekhov concluded that Alexander's 1857 decree had had some
effect: it *was* put into force, though often perfunctorily, for the
size and haphazard nature of these schools show that they were
hastily organized, transient, and scarcely deserving the appella-
tion of "school." Yet, as Laqueur notes, widespread literacy preceded the industrial revolution in England; indeed, "most children
learned to read and perhaps to write from their parents or neighbors, unlicensed and untrained, in settings which we today and indeed nineteenth-century observers would have hesitated to call
schools."[36] By restricting the history of education to the search for
certified, formal, permanent schools, historians have long ignored
the popular origins of literacy and schools. Chekhov's observations
simply suggest that priests were working on that frontier of popu-

lar literacy before the formalization of schooling. He implies that priests and Synod *conspired* to inflate the number of working schools in the countryside; in fact, the passage suggests that priests who had been occasional literacy teachers were now pressured by central authorities to officially register these small groups of children as "schools." If someone in the diocesan offices forgot to take this "school" off the books when it disbanded, no harm was done.

Chekhov, however, not only misses the informal nature of early peasant schools and the significant role played by priests, but he also fails to mention that the attitudes of the Church bureaucracy, on the one hand, and the local parish priest, on the other, toward popular literacy could be radically different. The important role played by individual priests in promoting literacy can be seen in the memoirs of a worker who was taught to read and write during the 1860s by a priest who patiently helped him proceed through the several stages of literacy and who intervened at different points in the worker's childhood to help and to persist. At times, this worker met with the priest individually and, at others, with a small group of fellow village children, sometimes after Church services. How would such interaction and sponsorship be entered in record books in terms of schools and enrollments?[37]

The accusations that few schools listed on the books functioned on a long-term basis or were even working in any given year and that many were "multiple listings" are accurate. Nevertheless, the contempt that Church education efforts have encountered among historians is unjustified and one-sided. Many Udel schools also were thriving enterprises only on paper and only for those "running".these fictional entities. The same practices were observed in the villages of the state peasants, where most historians consider the school effort to be the one bright light in a dismal period; one historian noted that it was a common practice here as well for peasants to "buy out" (*otkupit'*) their children from the schools. An investigation conducted in 1849 revealed that many state peasant schools existed only on paper. In 1850, an on-the-spot investigation of Olonets province (considered to be "doing well") discovered that the number of pupils enrolled on paper exceeded the number in the schools by a factor of 1.5. A year later, similar discrepancies between reports and reality were observed in nearby Viatka province. In 1855, the Minister of State Domains ordered the "conscription" of orphans of both sexes to fill up the empty seats in the schools for state peasants.[38]

The comic unreality of statistics-gathering at the local level in Russia in the first half of the nineteenth century is well known to historians; thus it is unfair to single out the Church, and the local clergy in particular, to be criticized for doctoring records. Moreover, many of the clergy indicted for indifference to education were in fact willing to teach, but only for the highest bidder; Count Kiselëv found that many priests were uninterested in teaching the state peasants because the Udel paid more.[39] The Church itself paid its priests nothing, expecting the impoverished local clergy to collect fees from the parishioners, as it did for all services. The clergy did this; all sources testify that where unofficial schools existed in the countryside the local priest was often the tutor, collecting fees individually from peasant families. But if he was to maintain an official school, why not collect a salary as well as fees? Thus it was common to find that although Church schools existed only on paper, the local priest was active in education, busy teaching for another department of the state. As we shall see, the very same phenomenon appeared at the close of the nineteenth century, when local clergy neglected the parish schools to teach Bible in the zemstvo schools, where they were remunerated for their efforts.

Other state agencies sponsored rural schools, among them the Mining Department and the Ministry of the Interior, which had four thousand rural schools in 1855. Unfortunately, no information about these schools has been unearthed.[40] But the schools established for the Ministry of State Domains (itself first organized in 1837) were unquestionably the most widespread and best organized and made the most lasting impact in the villages. Numbering 2,795, with 153,000 pupils in 1853 (the number declined slightly in the following decade), the schools formed an integral part of Count Kiselëv's economic, administrative and cultural reforms, which, some historians argue, did much to improve the lot of the state peasants.[41]

Before 1837, state peasants had been entrusted (if that is the word to describe the inhumane, even bestial treatment they received from local officials) to the Ministry of State Finances, which ran a total of sixty volost' schools with only 1,880 pupils. In 1838, an Instruction [Nakaz] directed the Ministry of State Domains to provide for "the character education and spread of useful information commensurate with one's station in life, to which end [it should] establish parish schools in the village."[42] Initially, the ministry moved cautiously, testing demand and slowly preparing the peasants for the establishment of a network of permanent schools, for "it wished to avoid spurious rumors" generated by too hasty activity in this area.[43] (This was not as absurd as it seems. According to N. M. Druzhinin, the memory of the hated military colonies, which had regimented peasant life and had been disbanded as recently as 1831, was still very fresh in the villages.)[44]

However, when inspectors claimed to have discovered a demand for education among the peasants and added that "without guidance and direction from above, without confirmation of the rules of faith and morality" this desire could lead the peasants along a "false path," particularly in those many villages with large numbers of seasonal city workers,[45] the ministry stepped up its activity and in 1842 produced a general school code that remained in force until 1866 when the state peasant schools were turned over to the zemstvos. Kiselëv placed great hopes in this code and actively campaigned to win the support of the clergy, gentry, and even peasants in implementing it. The schools, which, according to the able Soviet historian Druzhinin, were set up "not only to spread knowledge . . . but mainly to impart to the peasants the rules of the faith and the duties of a subject, as the foundation of morality and order," provided a three-year program, free instruction to individual peasants (a levy was imposed on the entire community), a curriculum offering the three Rs and a heavy dose of religious instruction, and instruction by priests who were to receive 85 to 115 rubles a year.[46]

Although the number of such schools increased rapidly until 1853—when inspections curbed the enthusiasm of some overzealous keepers of ledgers—the figures for 1866 probably reflect rather accurately the maximum level of expansion achieved by schools under the Ministry of State Domains. In that year, the ministry had 2,754 schools and 132,582 pupils, 16,579 of whom were girls. In addition, beginning in 1860, the ministry started to sponsor more modest literacy schools, of which, by 1866, there were 3,842, with 83,182 pupils.[47]

The state peasant schools had enthusiastic sponsorship, firm guidance, an elaborate school code, and financial support; but there is every reason to believe that in many areas their existence was as precarious or ephemeral as the "paper schools" flourishing under other authorities. Internal investigations between 1845 and 1849 revealed that in many areas, despite instructions, no schools had been opened and no funds set aside. In 1852, so many schools were nearly empty that it was necessary to reduce the number of schools to one for each volost' the following year. Again in 1855, after reports that many schools were virtually empty, the ministry decided to fill them with orphans of both sexes, for whom daily attendance became compulsory. Resistance to such schools was often very high in areas with non-Russian minorities, especially among the Tatars. But resistance was also strong among the Old Believers, who had no intention of letting their children be instructed by *nikoniane,* or Orthodox priests. (Nikon was the Patriarch under Alexis the Quiet in 1667 when the schism in the Orthodox Church occurred; those who broke with Nikon came to be known as Old Believers for their adherence to the Old Rituals.) Nor was resistance limited to ethnic and religious minorities for, as we shall see, observers of the countryside shortly after the Emancipation noted that peasants often regarded enrollment in the state schools as a form of conscription.[48]

How many schools were there before 1864? Reports seeped out into Western Europe that the Russian schools had turned into havens for innumerable "dead souls," and in 1834, stung by ridicule in the foreign press, Minister of Education Count S. S. Uvarov solicited information from all departments and ministries on the number of enrolled pupils at all levels in the school system. The results were published in French in 1837. The *Précis,* as it was titled, solemnly proclaimed that one of every fifteen peasants and one of every forty-eight subjects in the entire Empire was enrolled in school. It concluded that Russia was making remarkable progress and soon would be in the forefront of the civilized world. Despite the sparsely settled expanses and nomadic ways of the minority tribes in many areas, Russia already occupied "by no means the last place" among European nations.[49]

The results of a survey published in Russian by the MNP in 1838 revealed a much less cheerful situation. According to this study, only one pupil was enrolled per 208 population in fifty provinces of European Russia and, significantly, 58 percent of all students could be found in only sixteen provinces.[50] If these figures bear any relationship to reality, some progress was achieved in the next three decades: Darlington estimated that the ratio of enrollees to population rose from 1:200 in 1834 to 1:170 in 1854 and to 1:117 in 1864. Using data collected by the Central Statistical Committee in 1856, G. A. Fal'bork and V. I. Charnoluskii showed that there were 450,000 pupils in *lower schools,* in a population of almost 64 million—a ratio of 1:143.[51]

These figures both understate and overstate—radically—the number of enrolled pupils in the countryside. Not only do we know that many of the enrolled pupils were "dead souls," but it is also clear that the official figures grossly overstate the ratio of enrolled to population for rural areas. Though the bulk of the population of the Empire resided in villages in 1856, fewer than a quarter of all schools were located in the countryside. Thus, if one of every seventeen urban inhabitants was in school, the ratio for rural dwellers was certainly lower than 1:143, though by how much is anyone's guess. Moreover, since the enrollment level was far higher in the Baltic provinces (2.7 percent in Kurland, 4.6 percent in Lifland, but only .56 percent in Estland), in other provinces it was that much worse.

Estimates of the number of official schools in the Empire from 1801 to 1856 do show a pattern of substantial growth: from 62,000 pupils in 1800 to 245,500 pupils in 1834, to 432,889 in 1856, and to 1,155,800 in 1863. That the 1863 data are entirely unreliable is indicated by the fact that only six years later, in 1869, the number of pupils in the Empire was set at 675,000. Still, excluding the 1863 figures, the number of schools increased more than tenfold in almost seventy years, while the population increased by a factor of 1.59, from 37.2 million in 1795 to 59.2 million in 1857.[52] Thus in 1795 a child had one chance in 600 of receiving some public education; in 1857 a child's chances were one in 138.

The figures on schooling are inexact for yet another reason: they ignore the universally acknowledged but never counted domestic (*domashnye*) or "free" (*vol'nye* or *samovol'nye*) schools, which were peasant-sponsored and peasant-run (see Chapter 3). Because of state distrust of private initiative, such schools had long been frowned on and even actively suppressed. A statute in 1834, addressed against *pensions* and other private schools in the cities but applied to primary schools in the countryside as well, limited the pool of teachers to free subjects, graduates of official schools of Christian faith, "of certifiably high moral caliber."[53] Although teachers who limited their instruction to primary education did not require certification, they were not to be free of government supervision, either. Indeed, one salient aspect of continuity in the Russian tradition of education since the time of Peter the Great has been only limited tolerance for, and even suppression of, private education.[54]

In the countryside, where control by the central government was haphazard and where the majority of peasants were in any case under the tutelage of the *pomeshchiki* (serfowners), the laws against private instruction had little meaning except perhaps to keep most peasant-sponsored schools off the books. Who would take notice of an informal arrangement by which a retired soldier, clerk, or other literate villager agreed, for a fee, to teach a few local children to read—or who, for a slightly larger sum, taught them to read with comprehension, and for a few more kopecks, to write as well? This was true in Europe as well: schooling and informal education of this sort preceded organized, institutionalized schooling by generations, if not centuries. Darlington is almost certainly correct in saying of these literacy schools that "their existence as a class was no secret to anybody; but individually they managed to evade official control and enumeration."[55]

Since at least the eighteenth century in the Ukraine, "wandering teachers" had done much to spread basic education. M. I. Demkov has provided a description of these itinerants:

The wandering teacher who arrived in the village always stayed in the school, which at that time served also as an overnight lodging for travelers. The school was also the permanent residence of the deacon. Sometimes the wandering teacher entered into an agreement, that is, hired himself out to the local *pomeshchik* to teach his children, and on occasion, when there was no school in the village, went from house to house teaching the children. There can be little doubt that such wandering teachers made a major contribution to basic schooling and that some of them helped promote a love of learning. An outstanding example of the wandering teacher of the eighteenth century was Grigorii Skovoroda.[56]

Peasants, though often resisting government measures to herd them into schools, had shown at least some interest in basic education. As for private serfs, it is Demkov's judgment, unsubstantiated to be sure, that in the first half of the nineteenth century peasants clearly understood the utility of literacy, but that the *pomeshchiki* remained indifferent. In many areas, the priests tried valiantly to establish and maintain schools but, without material help from the gentry, such schools soon folded, though the priest may have continued to teach, moving from home to home. According to the inventories of private estates drawn up in Tula in 1858 in preparation for the Emancipation Statute, more than half the local *pomeshchiki* declared that there were no literate peasants on their property. Where there was literacy, it was spread through the efforts of parents or the parish priest. If the landlord played any role, it was usually in the selection and sponsorship of youths for future employment as land surveyors or employees in the manorial offices. The *pomeshchiki* also referred frequently to instances where peasants taught themselves and each other.[57]

HOW THEY WERE TAUGHT

Where schools existed, what was instruction like? Anticipating the famous comment by Napoleon III's minister of education that at any time on any day he could look at his watch and tell just what all the schoolchildren throughout the country were doing, an entry in the journal of Alexander's Commission for the Establishment of Schools boasted on 14 April 1800:

All schools are in complete uniformity: no matter what school the child may enter, he will read the same textbooks, the teacher will employ the same methods of instruction and follow the same schedule . . . since in the most distant corners of the Empire learning is organized in the same manner and according to the same timetable as it is in the capital itself.[58]

Of course, this description was mere wishful thinking. According to reports from local officials, instruction in the Udel schools was entirely haphazard and unplanned; reading was taught without any explanatory discussions or attempts to improve comprehension, rote memorization was the rule, and harsh discipline prevailed.

Perhaps the most influential description of schools in the pre-reform era was given by S. I. Miropol'skii in his widely read work, *School and State: Compulsory Education in Russia*. The description, cited in part or in full in nearly every Russian-language history of Russian education, made as indelible an impression on the minds of the educated public as did the famous paintings of Bogdanov-Belskii in the last quarter of the nineteenth century—particularly the sad portrait of the wretched village urchin standing wistfully at the entrance to the school, watching the uniformed teacher instructing better-dressed and well-groomed children in the secrets of the printed page. Accurate or not, the Miropol'skii description has become a historical document in its own right. Miropol'skii commented that the old folksaying "When there are seven nurses, the children remain unsupervised" applied to the Russian school system—virtually every department in the Russian bureaucracy was a "nurse," a governess of the school, but the child ran around unfed, half-dressed, and untutored. Official descriptions of the schools were virtually worthless, for the venerable Russian tradition of *pokazukha* ("window-dressing") was firmly entrenched, and the bureaucratic-administrative method of supervision resulted only in occasional forays into the lower school, preceded by prior warnings allowing the teacher to prepare the buildings and children for inspection.[59]

Pokazukha surely prevented reliable descriptions of the schools from making their way into the official records. Moreover, there is every reason to believe that where peasant schools existed, discipline was harsh and conditions very primitive. Nothing in the relationship between state peasants and serfs, on the one hand, and gentry and local officials, on the other, suggests that peasant children would have been treated with kindness and consideration in the schools. Russian pedagogy in the eighteenth century was a peculiar blend of the writings of Comenius, Locke, Fenelon, the harsh strictures of the *Domostroi* (the sixteenth-century "family management" book), and the work of Pososhkov, Peter the Great's peasant adviser whose "rules of life" in his *Paternal Testament* enjoined parents and teachers to "diligently [*neploshno*] teach the faith, and to keep children in dread."[60] Although the first half of the nineteenth century saw considerable interest in Pestalozzi, the Lancaster system, and child-centered pedagogy, it is hard to believe such concerns seeped out beyond urban areas and educated circles to the primitive schools in the countryside.[61] Most likely, where rural schools existed, discipline was harsh and learning took place by the old alphabet method, with an emphasis on rote memorization. Marc Raeff has pointed out that in many seminaries for the clergy, rote learning was so pervasive that the students often learned how to recite the contents of an entire book by heart but could not read another line independently. If this was the case, and if clergymen were often the teachers of peasants, one can only imagine what the quality of instruction may have been.[62]

Fortunately, some first-hand descriptions survive from the 1860s. The chairman of the Berdiansk district zemstvo board in Tavrida reported to an early session of that zemstvo assembly:

There is no set program, there are no textbooks, and the pupils have to make do with whatever comes their way. There is no set time to begin or to finish learning how to read, there is absolutely no supervision over the schools; discipline is applied by the teacher as each sees fit, and in many schools is very severe.[63]

In Moscow, detailed reports presented to the zemstvo assemblies described the condition of rural schools. By 1867, there were an estimated 268 registered schools, with an enrollment of 9,411 pupils, taught almost exclusively by rural priests and deacons. Assistants to these teachers were also from the clergy (deacons, sextons, and so forth), and none had any pedagogical training. Indeed, the various journals and reports of the district zemstvos in Moscow province are full of dismal surveys indicating the lack of materials, poor results, and incompetence of the teachers in the school system—if such it can be called—inherited from the pre-Emancipation period. One report by the Volokolamsk district zemstvo board stated that all earlier schools were located in the homes of priests or unordained clerics who taught during their free time for a negligible sum. These schools were most ephemeral. They would open, shut down, then open again. There were no textbooks and often no furniture. For the most part, instead of desks and chairs, there would be plain boards placed across stumps. What books there were were ill-suited for instruction.[64]

In Kolomna district, a report to the zemstvo executive board in 1869 lamented that

in almost every school without exception the teaching methods are highly unsatisfactory. Youths who have spent nearly two years in school are barely able to read, and their rote recital is limited almost exclusively to the psalter, to reading without the slightest comprehension of the material at hand. Instruction is limited to the rudiments of literacy; little or no attention is paid to developing the pupil's mental faculties. Hence school attendance, even over the course of several years, brings with it little essential benefit.[65]

Perhaps the most graphic descriptions of schooling on the eve of and shortly after the Emancipation come from Tula.[66] A teacher from Orel volost' (Bogoroditsk district) with long experience in the countryside described the old schools:

The teachers had no pedagogical training: they included semi-literate peasants, a deacon, a psalmist, and even the wife of the local priest, who could scarcely make out a word. Literacy consisted of the ability to read Old Church Slavonic and a smattering of writing.* For textbooks, there were the Church Slavonic *azbuka* and the psalter. In our Kibensk school, the teacher was a local peasant named Boris, who was sixty years old. His literacy consisted of being able to read the psalter for the deceased; I think he knew virtually the entire book by heart. School was held in his house, a wooden building six *arshins* [in length?], with only one window, and of the black *izba* type.† The teacher received payment individually from

---

*Here the Russian is ambiguous: *otchasti* could mean "a smattering," or it could mean "sometimes." Thus, the writer could have meant that some pupils learned how to write or that all or most learned a little writing.

† *Topilas' po kurnomu.* Until the twentieth century, many peasant huts had no chimneys. In the winter, the smoke from the stove simply accumulated indoors, and the huts, because of the accumulated soot, were known as "black." Here, the phrase is "heated in the smoky way."

the pupils—50 kopecks each for the winter, along with an apartment. The school year lasted from the first snow 'til the snow disappeared from the ground.

We learned by the alphabet method. The teacher would choose the lesson by pointing with his finger [in the book] "from here to there" and would begin, as they used to say, by "leading" [*provodit'*] the pupils—he would say along with them: "*Az! Az! Buki! Buki!*" and so forth [the *names* of the letters A and B; the names did not correspond to the sounds of these first two letters in the alphabet]. So, several voices would sing out together, the teacher loudest of all, so that the pupils could hear him; this is how he "led" the pupils through each new lesson in sequence. Sometimes he would lie on the stove while running the lesson and shout out as loud as he could. From the school issued forth an unremitting clamor from morning to dinner.* After dinner, the noise began again, for reading in unison was the only skill our "pedagogue" had.

He taught writing by requiring memorization of the alphabet book, and sometimes the poor pupils studied for two winters and still didn't know how to write the letters of the alphabet. . . . A pupil with a good memory began to write no earlier than Lent. For them to retain what they had learned by rote, each morning upon arriving in class the pupils had to repeat what they had just learned; during this time one could also hear a concert of voices of children aged ten to seventeen. . . . If, God forbid, one of the pupils had failed to memorize his homework, then fists, shoves, and hairpulling were brought into use, while for a weak performance a flogging was administered. . . . As far as scientific information and intellectual development are concerned, these teachers suppressed rather than encouraged them.

When he was absent for several days in a row, the teacher turned over the class to his son Daniel. Daniel was entirely illiterate; he could not even name a single letter. So in his father's absence, Daniel would take a switch, or even a stick, and walk around the classroom striking each pupil in sequence, saying: "Read! Read!" The pupils could not complain to their parents, because the mother or father would simply add some punishment, saying, "You idiots won't learn anything without the rod"— of course, parents had learned this cruelty in their own treatment by their masters. And all of the teachers named above—the deacon, the psalmist,

---

*Baron Korf observed in his handbook that peasants frequently asked, "I wonder why I can't *hear the school?*" ("*Chto-to ot shkoly nichego ne shlyshno?*")

and the old widow of the priest—applied the same method and the same discipline as did Old Boris. The only variation was in the way fees were levied. Boris took money, the deacon and psalmist were paid in kind— someone brought flour, or grain, another brought a hen or a piglet, yet another, a wagonful of straw, and so forth.

Another teacher from Tula explained how pupils learned by the old alphabet method, first putting together the names of letters, pronouncing and combining the sounds (*buki-az-ba*)—a method known in Russia as *po skladam*. Then, working backwards, the teacher pronounced a syllable—*de*—and required the pupils to identify and pronounce the letters in the ABC book (*de: dobro-est'-de-de*)—known as working *po tolkam*. Then the memorization proceeded in sequence (*po riadam*), as the pupil moved from the chapter heading to the words under the subheading to the prayers, fables, Bible history, multiplication tables, and to the psalter. After the psalter, writing began,

but not writing as we know it: to be able to compose words and speech from letters. In their understanding, writing means to be able to copy down elegant cursive script in letter combinations entirely incomprehensible to them, to take down from a copy-book.

The teacher added that sometimes the memorization of numbers from one to one thousand was included, but as purely mechanical memorization without any understanding of the principle of numeration. This work exhausted the full course of study—the "program,"

which around here ordinarily costs 7 rubles and 50 kopecks for the works [*gurtom*] with promised results [*za vyuchku*], or from 1 to 2 paper rubles for each month of instruction. For a long time I couldn't figure out how, despite such instruction, some pupils were learning to read, and finally figured it out with a simple mathematical calculation. In the ABC book on the average there are fifty pages, with twenty-five lines on each page. If initially the pupil is given two lines of verse a day, and toward the end eight a day, then the average for the year is around five lines. In three hundred days, according to this calculation, the pupil will have learned by heart the entire *azbuka;* that is, in just about a year, which is what happens with a diligent and strict teacher. Another year is spent on the psalter, and another on the copy-book—so we have three years, which coincides with the time it ordinarily takes the diligent teacher to bring the good pupil to a state of readiness [*v polnuiu vyuchku*].

Finally, this description from Tula:

In Podosinkovsk school I spent a long time, in the absence of the teacher, trying to get something out of the pupils. As soon as I turned to one of them, he would stick his nose in a book and begin repeating to himself a verse, completely ignoring me. I would look around, searching for signs of vitality, and once in a while would catch someone whose eyes had left the book and gazed intelligently and attentively at me; I would approach him and inquire—but at that moment a film would come over his eyes, and once again he would begin to repeat his verses. I tried to ask questions from history: the elder psalter-boy began with the chapter entitled "A Short Bible History" and recited for me some twenty verses, but stumbled when it came to the creation of Woman. To prod his memory, I asked him: "Did Adam have a wife?" He broke out crying.

Finally, announced by some obedient boy, the teacher appeared. He was crippled, used crutches, had a week's growth on his chin, and a puffed-up, grim, and vindictive face. . . . I asked him to demonstrate his methods, and he began to step up to each of the pupils; as he did, I noticed how each boy grimaced and hunched his shoulders, seeming to sense the teacher's approach without looking up. During the lesson and the recess he conducted himself just as the old field elder did in former times, carrying a stick as he followed the women to work on the master's fields, and at the approach of the *barin* shouting: "Get on, wenches; get working, *babas*," regardless of the fact that these "*babas*" ["wenches"] already knew how to pretend to be working, without his encouragement. "Hey you, quiet now, in turn," he shouted at the children, as they crawled out from behind the desk, nudging them in the back, and with a rapid, imperceptible motion of his wrist plucking at whatever he came across. Before leaving the desk, each pupil would cross himself . . . kiss his . . . book and recite the verse he had memorized for that day. . . . Everyone also prayed before the icon. The teacher explained that he hadn't yet but intended soon to teach them to recite the prayers before and after their lessons. . . . The pupils left the school dull and in a stupor, walked a few yards as if stepping out of the grave, and only then, when they had gained some distance from the school . . . began to liven up.

Druzhinin has produced archival evidence that the schools run by the Ministry of State Domains for state peasants were also harsh and primitive. Even according to inspectors of these schools, buildings were crowded and filthy, textbooks and school supplies inadequate. In one school in Kiev province, pupils slept on the bare floor and ate only what their parents, living ten to fifteen versts away, brought them once or twice a week.[67] (One verst was two-thirds of a mile.) Reports from Astrakhan', Kursk, Riazan', Voronezh, and elsewhere complained that the local priests were extremely negligent in their teaching responsibilities and were interested only in emoluments. Pupils were often left alone for entire days without instruction or supervision. In many schools, the results of one or two years of instruction seemed to be meager indeed. Druzhinin drew the following comments from inspections carried out in Viatka between 1842 and 1856:

Except for awful Church Slavonic textbooks, there are almost no books in the schools, and the children are more likely to end up sextons than literate peasants. . . . So little attention is devoted to lessons that for half the year they never go to school. . . . After attending school for more than a year, the boys can barely read, and at that only slowly and hesitatingly; they can't write even two words correctly, even when they are regarded as having completed the program.[68]

At the Belilovskoe school in the region of the right-bank Ukraine (west of the Dniepr River), there were two classes, the first with thirty boys and eight girls, and the second with thirty-one boys and two girls. According to the inspector, the local priest (Alexander Matskevich, a graduate of the academy in Kiev) taught by rote memorization:

In the upper class, when I asked what the pupils were studying, they quickly answered, "The catechism and history," then fell silent and looked at the teacher questioningly. When questioned by their teacher in the two subjects, each pupil replied rapidly from memory, but when I asked them to explain how they understood what they were saying, not one could answer; it was even rare that any one could understand the questions given in the textbook.[69]

In many schools, pupils almost never finished the program in three years; the entire first half of the school year was often spent repeating the material the pupils had forgotten during the previous summer. From Novgorod it was reported that pupils in Valdaisk region who had been in school for five years could barely carry out simple addition problems, whereas others could read only in a stumbling manner. Reporting on some schools in Perm', an inspector declared that in fifteen years he had "yet to find a [male] graduate of the schools whom he could call fully literate." From Vil'no and Grodno, it was observed that graduates were unfit to serve as village clerks. In Perm' in 1846, the peasants complained that their children were left without supervision in school, went over the same ABC book year after year, and achieved little despite a lengthy stay in school.[70]

Commenting on the quality of rural schools before the 1860s, the historian-activist E. A. Zviagintsev concluded:

[The reports] all demonstrate the extremely impoverished conditions of the school, the abysmal level of instruction, the transience of individual schools, and popular indifference—in fact, some parents and children in state peasant villages regarded school attendance as a means of fulfilling their state-imposed obligation.[71]

At least some authorities who examined the records believed that, of the twenty thousand rural schools on record on the eve of the Great Reforms in the 1860s, many more than half were no longer or had never been in operation,[72] and at least some observers believed that graduates of the rural schools were incapable of coping even with the work of a village clerk. (It was said of graduates of appanage schools that they made trustworthy clerks: you could give them the most confidential documents to copy without fearing that they would understand or remember a word.) All in all, the situation was not very promising. Note in particular that several of the comments above distinguished between mere literacy and moral or character education, concluding that, without a moral component, schools were not doing anything useful except turning out a handful of clerks and literate elders to help the nobility run their estates and to provide staff in the lowest government offices.

Yet Druzhinin also notes that in several areas inspectors turned in satisfactory reports on the results of schooling. In state peasant villages, to be sure, *pokazukha* may have been at work, but then why were the reports dismal in other areas? Interestingly, Druzhinin points out that the program of study had been organized and the basic readers drawn up by V. F. Odoevskii and A. P. Zablotskii–Desiatovskii, both working in the Academic Committee under the Ministry of State Domains. The books contained stories and fables by well-known writers, as well as maps and a profusion of illustrations, and included in popular form basic information on natural science, agriculture, and the geography and history of Russia. Noting sententiously that the readers "still bore the stamp of officious-conservative ideology," Druzhinin concedes that "they nevertheless broadened the peasants' world view and represented, for the time, a major advance in methodology."[73]

There is good reason to put the harsh, and undoubtedly true, accounts in comparative perspective. Throughout Europe at the time, where rural schools existed, discipline was severe and teachers were semi-literate; learning was by rote memorization, school facilities were extremely primitive, and an inspector's visit was cause for great anxiety and "dressing up," both literally and figuratively.

In France, according to Eugen Weber, the teacher

in the first half of the nineteenth century . . . could well have been a retired soldier, a rural constable, the local barber, innkeeper. . . . [In Rennes] seven of the fifteen teachers were ex-convicts. . . . Such schoolbooks as could be found were ancient. Authorities denounced them as Gothic, anachronistic, and absurd. They seem to have been all of these things. We hear of an alphabet book in Latin, of a work called *Christian Civility* printed in Gothic characters; of a life of Christ dating back to the fifteenth century, "full of miracles, superstitions, and fear of devils," of a text telling how the Virgin Mary spent her youth in the temple learning the psalter and the prayer book, as a good saint should. . . . One hears of village schools that imparted a good fund of knowledge, and of countrymen who knew how to read and actually did read. But these were the exceptions. Most country schools must have been more like the one at Selins in the 1840's which was conducted by Sister Gandilhon, who could teach only prayers, the catechism, and the first two rules of arithmetic ("she had heard of a third, but never learned it"). In consequence, if poor men read, it was because they had taught themselves. . . . It takes real effort today to conceive of such an educational system, one in which both teacher and taught were ignorant of the material they were dealing with, and in which the capacity to draw letters or pronounce them completely outweighed any capacity to comprehend. Letters, words and sentences were formulas and spells . . . writing was a stage of learning to which few aspired, the few because it called for higher fees.[74]

Even in Prussia, which in the early nineteenth century developed the most comprehensive elementary school system in Europe, conditions were often harsh and results paltry. Recent research has shown that "at the not very subtle urging of ignorant, often brutal schoolmasters, pupils learned to read by rote memorization and by monotonous repetition of psalms, verses of hymns, verses from the Bible, and biblical stories." From these schools the German peasant emerged with a reading ability "not much greater than his or her understanding of the spiritual meaning of Scripture." According to this research, "the teaching methods in German primary schools constituted nothing less than an anticipation of the drill that the boys would later encounter on the military parade ground," and virtually no schools taught geography, history, or the natural sciences.[75]

As we shall see again and again, public criticism of state-run or peasant-organized schools in Russia was often overstated and began with the assumption that any operation organized and controlled by the central government had to be a failure because it functioned through command and coercion and because it stifled local initiative; it also assumed that peasants were too ignorant to know what they wanted. Such criticism was often just, but at other times it obscured the uncomfortable facts that the notions of education and child development entertained by society were not always shared by the peasant community and that the results the educated public sought in the schools were sometimes different from those pursued by peasants. Preconceptions particularly affected the descriptions of the Church schools at the end of the century and the evaluation of the success of rural schools as a whole. But they also colored the criticisms, leveled largely by historians and educators writing after the Great Reforms, of the schools operating in the period that has been labeled the era of state pedagogy (from Peter the Great until 1861). My own familiarity with documents from a later period suggests that nearly all historians who discussed schools of the first half of the nineteenth century approached the limited material available with strong prejudices and a predisposition to criticize.

✤

On the eve of the Crimean War and the Great Reforms, the state, though spinning out grandiose educational projects, creating an elaborate administrative scaffolding, and suppressing private initiative—at least in the cities, where state control was effective—had made only fitful, woefully limited attempts to educate the peasantry. Because of the nature of the historical sources and because of the haphazard, generally unorganized way "schools" were organized and run, it is unlikely that historians will ever gain any precision of detail. Yet the general contours of the situation are clear, drawn by Gerold T. Robinson a half century ago:

In the decades that intervened [between the 1804 Statute and the Emancipation] some progress was made in establishing official primary schools among the peasants . . . and an indeterminable number of unregistered primary schools, maintained sometimes by the peasants themselves and sometimes by the landlord. A beginning had thus been made, but the great mass of the serfs on the private estates and of the peasants on the State domain had hardly been touched by the cultural changes which since Peter's time had so deeply affected the nobles and the bourgeoisie.[76]

Despite the paltry results of state-sponsored popular education in the almost 150 years following the Petrine reforms, certain principles became firmly entrenched during this period and were carried over into the era subsequent to the Emancipation. Among these principles were the suspicion of private or local initiative, "the reluctance characteristic of the historic bureaucratic polity to long endure initiatives from below";[77] a concentration on advanced rather than basic education; the imposition of a uniform system of education; and a belief that the schools should be "nondisruptive of Empire, state and society . . . [and in fact should] strengthen all

three, [built on] the premises of authority, status, hierarchy and social stability." Along with this went the notion of streaming and
selection—the belief that everyone had a place in the social order
and occupational structure and that the scope of education should
be tailored accordingly.[78]

This principle, and the corollary of reserving the upper schools
almost exclusively for the gentry, was not restricted to the time of
Catherine, nor was it, according to Mathes, "the aberration of a
handful of reactionary ministers since 1800. Rather it was almost
an *idée fixe,* venerable in Russian history, and consistent with the
rulers' visions and goals and with the political balance they sought
to maintain."[79]

Yet it should be added that another *idée fixe* from the time of
Peter the Great was the recognition that if Russia were to compete
internationally, her people needed skills that could be provided
only by schools. Until the late nineteenth century, the state was
concerned mostly with borrowing specialized information and
training bureaucrats and officers, and thus it focused largely on the
promotion of advanced schools. Nevertheless, the efforts launched
in the second half of the nineteenth century, particularly after 1890,
were entirely consistent with a long tradition; the only difference
was that the focus turned to popular education as the source of national strength as well as of social order. As for the serfowners,
there was little evidence in the half century preceding the Emancipation that they saw any virtue in popular education; it must be
said, too, that the state posed no obstacles to local education under
the guidance of the serfowner. The first half of the nineteenth century gave little cause to believe that when the local gentry came
together in the zemstvo assemblies created after the Emancipation
to administer local affairs, they would be active supporters of peasant education. To the contrary, whereas earlier the landowner had
needed a few literate serfs to run his manorial offices, or in extreme
cases, to play in his serf orchestras or to act in serf theaters, after
Emancipation the peasants were no longer the landowner's personal property or playthings. Thus why bother to teach them to
read? Perhaps so they could make sense of their new legal rights
vis-à-vis the landlord?

2

The Great Reforms and the Zemstvos

As Alexander II's official biographer wrote, "The issue of spreading primary education among the people, of teaching the peasants literacy, flowed directly from the changes taking place in their daily lives with the onset of the emancipation from serfdom."[1] Unquestionably, the liberation of the serfs in 1861 removed one of the obstacles to support for primary education: the fear that to educate an unfree man was to make him aware of his chains. The reforms of primary education embodied in the statutes of 1864 and 1874 and in accompanying decrees, rescripts, and instructions were but one component of a general restructuring of the entire educational system from top to bottom, including a substantial overhaul of secondary and higher schools. In turn, all the educational reforms brought about in the 1860s were but one part of a larger series of reforms affecting the judiciary, the military, finances, municipal and rural local self-government, and, most important for this study, the establishment of zemstvo institutions at the provincial and district level. It is unfortunate that of all the Great Reforms, only the 1864 Education Statute, which represented the culmination of long debate, even struggle, among several departments of government and which developed with considerable public input, has not yet received the attention it deserves from Western historians. The following chapter will provide background needed to understand the relationships between the main actors in the educational world—the Ministry of Education, the zemstvo, and the peasant community—and will mention briefly both the issues that concerned legislators and the solutions embodied in legislation.

One major change wrought in the 1860s was the introduction of zemstvos. Essentially the vehicles of gentry organization at the local level, they represented, with some important qualifications, the viewpoint of the educated elite concerning peasant schooling. The mission and activities of the zemstvos are of great importance to our story, and they deserve considerable attention.

Among the other issues singled out for mention here are curriculum legislation, the administration and financing of schools, control over teacher appointments (and removal), and the functions of local school boards. Three major pieces of legislation implemented after 1878—the 1884 Regulations for Church Parish Schools, the 1897 Model Programs for Schools, and the 1908 School Bill—receive attention in other chapters. The specialist in Russian institutional history may find little new in this chapter; my intent is to clarify the institutional background—in a very cluttered landscape—for the social historian of education.

THE 1864 EDUCATION STATUTE

Two events ushered in a new era in educational policy and set in motion the forces that eventually led to zemstvo involvement in primary education. The first was the publication (in *Morskoi sbornik,* July 1856) of an article entitled "Questions of Life" by the famed surgeon-turned-educator, N. I. Pirogov. His attack on early specialization for practical vocations and his call for a general humanitarian education touched off a debate on educational methods and goals that provided the framework for Russian pedagogical thought during the following half century.[2]

The second—and not unrelated—event was the resurrection of the Academic Committee in 1856 under the Ministry of Education. The committee had been established in 1817 by Alexander I but disbanded under his successor. Under E. P. Kovalevskii, who was Minister of Education at the time, the Academic Committee in 1858 began to consider proposals for a new school statute. The evolution of these proposals, from the first published version in 1860 to the final edition, provides fascinating insight into the interplay of bureaucratic intrigue, societal pressure, political needs, and economic realities in this era of reform but is well beyond the scope of this work.[3] It should be noted in passing, however, that a number of points included in the 1860 draft reflected a new awareness of the need for major restructuring and expansion of the primary school network.

The draft called for eliminating class distinctions in access to the various rungs of the "ladder," for maximum accessibility of primary education, for compulsory measures to ensure enrollment, for freedom of initiative by societal and private associations, and for eliminating excessive bureaucratic control in the administration of schools. According to the draft, primary education would be provided by three types of institutions: literacy schools, and both lower and higher elementary schools. The two lowest rungs would be opened at the initiative of and financed by private individuals and communities, whereas the government would underwrite the costs of the higher elementary schools. The former would offer a one-year program and the latter a four-year course with instruction in geography, natural science, and history. Reflecting the views of Pirogov, elementary schools were to provide a complete primary education while preparing the more gifted for a secondary education, either classical or vocational.[4]

As the Soviet historian V. Z. Smirnov sententiously remarks in his study of the debates over the 1864 Education Statute, it was one thing to proclaim principles and quite another to realize these principles in specific measures. Between the two intervened the intractable realities of poverty, class privilege, obdurate tradition, and political struggle.[5] Kovalevskii's project, the establishment of a new education code, "began its passage through the long process of emendation that threatened to emasculate every Russian legislative act."[6] After consideration by the State Council, the revised third draft of the statute was finally signed into law by Alexander II on 14 July 1864.

Rozhdestvenskii, the official historian of the Ministry of Education, argued that the 1864 Education Statute "set primary education on a broad and firm foundation," but, at the time, liberal reformers severely criticized it. Ironically, after the later 1874 School Statute was promulgated, liberal historians came to assess the early law more positively. In the words of a prerevolutionary specialist (and no friend of the government), "The 1864 Statute opened a new era in public education since, together with the promulgation of the Zemstvo Statute in the same year, it gave the population of the zemstvo provinces the opportunity to take public education into their own hands."[7]

The goal of primary education, according to the first article of the statute, was "to impart religious and moral notions among the population and to spread useful, basic knowledge."[8] Only the lowest rung of schools proposed in the earlier drafts was preserved, although a bewildering variety of departments were allowed to maintain such schools. The ministries of Interior, State Domains, Appanages, and Mining, as well as the Holy Synod and the Ministry of Education, were confirmed in their role as sponsors of primary schools. Elementary schools "established and maintained" by private individuals or "financed by society" (i.e., the peasant community) were also given the nod, but such schools needed the preliminary approval of the newly established school boards (*uchilishchnye sovety*) (Article 10). Now, however, curriculum and choice of textbooks were to be controlled by the Ministry of Education; only the Holy Synod remained independent of this control (Article 5). Instruction was to be exclusively in Russian, and the question of fees was left to the discretion of each school's sponsor; no measures for compulsory enrollment were provided by the statute.

The program of the primary school was to include religion, "reading in secular and religious books," penmanship, the first four functions of arithmetic, and (optionally) singing (Article 3). Although it was assumed that the elementary schools would offer only a one-year course of instruction, the length of the program remain undefined, as did the number of hours to be devoted to each subject. This omission was surprising, for the various drafts of the statute had devoted considerable attention to this question, and it provided an obvious loophole for school sponsors to or-

ganize curriculum as they saw fit. Nor was a proper school age
defined.

The statute did, however, pay great attention (16 of 33 articles)
to the question of administration and supervision of the school
system, creating special district school boards to oversee the primary schools. Each district school board was composed of two
delegates from the zemstvo assembly and one member each from
the ministries of Education and Interior, the Orthodox Church,
and other departments. Because the chairmen of these boards were
elected by the members, and all issues were decided by majority
vote (Articles 19 and 30), the struggle between the Holy Synod
and the Ministry of Education that helped shape these school
boards resulted in a significant, if temporary, devolution of authority—into the hands of local government.[9]

The local boards were to supervise instruction, open and close
schools, certify teaching, and distribute approved texts and teaching aids. More specifically, any nongovernmental organization
wishing to establish a school had to obtain the prior consent of the
local school board. With the exception of clergy appointed by the
Holy Synod to teach religion in all schools, teachers had to be confirmed in their posts by the board after it had received testimony
from "known persons" verifying their "moral character and reliability" (*blagonadëzhnost'*) (Article 16). Assigned responsibility
for finding funds to maintain schools, the boards were also granted
the freedom to select textbooks from among those approved by
the Academic Committee under the Ministry of Education.

The provincial board, whose membership included the bishop,
the governor, the director of schools, and two zemstvo deputies,
reviewed the district boards' reports and proposals, distributed
funds allocated by the Ministry of Education, and removed unsuitable teachers. Although the zemstvos were given only two
votes on each provincial board, no ministry was given a controlling hand, either. Complaints against the provincial boards were
arbitrated neither by higher officials in the education district (under
the MNP) nor by officials of the ministry but were decided by the
Senate, on a national level. The composition of the school boards
reflected the rivalry between the Holy Synod and the Ministry of
Education for control of school affairs; the situation was further
complicated by the presence of the governor (under the Ministry

of the Interior), whose power over education was enhanced by later legislation.[10] During the decade following 1864, this rivalry between departments worked to the benefit of the zemstvo, as no one institution was able to exert control over the boards.

Obvious parallels exist between the 1864 legislation and the 1804 Statute of Alexander I. Particularly noteworthy was the state's decision in each case to wash its hands of the problem of funding education, while carefully maintaining a measure of control over the direction of schooling throughout the Empire. In 1804, the state had left the initiative to local *pomeshchiki;* now, in 1864, the government, "reflecting the spirit of the time" and with the overwhelming support of the educated public, also decided to leave the question of *providing* education to "local initiative." It adopted the "English," rather than the "Prussian" or the "French," model; that is, individual compulsory education (Prussia) was rejected, as was legislation requiring the community to provide schools (France), in favor of private initiative with state support, and state supervision where state support was requested.[11] (Ironically, the "English system," which had no precedent in Russia, was itself on the verge of radical transformation in the direction of state intrusion, with the Foster Act of 1870.) But there was a difference between the measures of 1804 and 1864, contained in the phrase "local initiative."

Given the administrative vacuum created by the dissolution of the juridical bonds of serfdom and the absence of any tradition of local self-government, corporate organization, or even local initiative in Russia, what did the framers of the Education Statute have in mind? It is significant that at this point the newly created zemstvo institutions entered the fray. They were unmentioned in earlier drafts of the Education Statute and initially given no representation on local school boards; it was only in the State Council's discussion of the education legislation in 1863 that a role for the future zemstvos in sponsoring schools came under consideration. Because I have used the zemstvo in this book as a proxy for the educated public as a whole and because the assessment of the zemstvos' place in late Imperial history is a matter of considerable dispute,[12] we must digress here from the basic narrative in the area of education legislation to consider the organization, structure, functions, and powers of the local zemstvos. To some, they were the seedbed of democracy in Russia; to others, they were the "fifth wheel" of the Russian autocracy. What were the zemstvos? Who ran them? How much freedom did they have in the area of education? Whom did they represent?

ZEMSTVOS

The zemstvos were formally brought into existence by the Statute of 1 January 1864,[13] but the first organs of local self-government did not begin to function until as much as a year later; some provinces had to wait as long as a decade. (Twenty-seven provinces received zemstvos between 1865 and 1866, another six between 1867 and 1876.) It cannot be emphasized too strongly that these institutions were established during the era of post-Crimean reforms, in line with the reorganization of local administration and the abolition of the judicial and administrative powers of the nobility. Much ink has been spilled in arguments over the origins and functions of the zemstvos, but we should not lose sight of the fact that they were created to fill an administrative vacuum in the countryside. What then is the disagreement among historians?[14]

To liberal reformers of that day, their successors a generation later, and some modern Western historians, the zemstvos represented the crowning edifice of an era of humanitarian aspirations— the creation of a body of representative institutions defending the interests of local society as a whole rather than of a particular class or corporate estate. According to this "societal" theory of local self-government, the interests of local society were distinct from the needs of central government, and the zemstvos were representatives of the "creative forces" of Russia, struggling to liberate society from the oppressive weight of bureaucracy. In short, the zemstvos were the embryo of democratic government.[15]

Soviet historians have remained content with Lenin's dictum that the zemstvos were the "fifth wheel of the Russian state administration." To the Soviets, the establishment of the zemstvos marked the turning point in the transition from feudal to bourgeois legal norms—a generality so vapid and elusive as to be meaningless.[16] In contrast, the works of George Yaney, S. Frederick

Starr, and Alexander Vucinich have provided a more realistic, if still incomplete, appraisal of the workings of the zemstvo. According to Vucinich, the zemstvos were the "most tangible and original contribution of the reform–oriented government [of Alexander II] . . . the zemstvos were among the principal forces which transformed Russia's social life along completely new lines of citizenship." Yet, at the time, "in practice the autocratic government did not surrender any of its functions." The work of the zemstvo simply consisted of fulfilling obligations to the state and completing tasks "with which the state was not traditionally concerned."[17] Yaney is more deprecating: "In theory the zemstvos represented all classes, but in fact they consistently adopted policies and programs that suited gentry interests. . . . Until about 1890 they generally had little contact with the peasants, exerted little influence over them, and took little interest in them."[18] To Starr, the zemstvos "inherited many attitudes from the old gentry assemblies," particularly concerning relations with the peasantry, but after 1864 the "center of gravity in zemstvo life [was transferred] from the political to the administrative level," and the zemstvos did much to correct the "underinstitutionalization" of Russian provincial life.[19] Thus there is some authority for viewing the zemstvos as semi-autonomous local agencies concerned with the administration of services in the countryside.

The viewpoint expressed by Starr, Vucinich, and others, including some Soviet historians, resembles the state theory of self-government that gained currency in Russia at the end of the century. According to this theory, local society assumed certain tasks assigned to it by the central government and so was responsible for policy implementation rather than formulation. Indeed, this theory was close to the designs of those who formulated the Education Statute, and particularly close to the views of Alexander II: as Kermit McKenzie has recently noted, the original 1864 legislation included no mention of *samoupravlenie,* or self-government.[20] For the purpose of studying peasant education and elite participation, it is useful to keep in mind a recent comment by Thomas Fallows:

Underlying these two theories on the nature of self-government lie two basic tendencies in the way historians study the zemstvo. One approach is to define the zemstvo *politically,* as a forum for Russian liberals. The other is to define this institution *administratively,* essentially as a welfare agency serving the educational health and economic needs of the population.[21]

This distinction is useful, for, as we shall see, the zemstvos took advantage of control over the *administration* of education to give shape and emphasis to *policy.* Below we shall consider elite control over peasant education and the nature of the fabled conflict between the democratic (elective) and bureaucratic principles.

Whom did the zemstvos represent, and who determined the direction and set the pace of zemstvo activities? Zemstvos were established at two levels of administration, the province (*guberniia*) and the district (*uezd*). (As McKenzie has noted, the zemstvo did not *displace* the existing bureaucratic offices at the provincial level, though it did assume some functions previously in the hands of the bureaucracy.) At both levels, the zemstvo consisted of two bodies: an assembly of delegates, which met only briefly once a year and was elected for three years, and a permanent, salaried executive board (*uprava*—sometimes translated as "directory"), whose members were elected by the zemstvo assemblies. The chairman of the assembly was *ex officio* the local marshall of the nobility, whereas the chairman of the executive board, though elected, had to be confirmed in office by the Minister of the Interior. The government, fearful of the emergence of a regional or even national elective body, energetically suppressed all attempts at communication or joint projects among zemstvos at the provincial level. Thus, the provincial assembly remained the highest forum for zemstvo activity. If the zemstvo lacked a "roof" to crown the edifice of local self-government, it was just as much in need of a "foundation" (in the parlance of the time). The district zemstvo assembly, made up of thirty to fifty delegates, represented rather extensive territorial units (in Moscow province, for example, the units ranged from 1,621 to 3,069 square versts) and a large population (again in Moscow, a range of 55,000 to 222,000 in 1897). All attempts to establish a smaller basic unit of self-government (*mel'kaia zemskaia edinitsa*), to bring zemstvo services closer to the population, were firmly resisted by the government.[22]

Delegates (*glasnye*) to the district assembly were elected on the basis of a "curial" system. According to the 1864 Zemstvo

Statute, no class distinctions were observed; instead, a property qualification formed the basis for participation. The first curia consisted of rural landowners meeting a rather sizable property qualification, the second consisted of those owning property in the city, and the third was made up of delegates elected directly from the peasant volosts. Delegates to the provincial assembly were elected by the district assemblies from among their own members, regardless of class. Although the zemstvos were in theory all-class and, until 1890, peasant representation at the district level (38.5 percent) nearly equaled that of the nobility (42.4 percent), from the outset the provincial zemstvos were firmly controlled by the gentry (81.6 percent) with only a sprinkling of peasant representatives.[23]

Except for the four so-called peasant zemstvos (Olonets, Perm', Viatka, Vologda), the zemstvos were hardly representative of local society, for the peasants had but a minority of the delegates. Even worse, after 1890, peasants were no longer directly elected by their own community (although even before that date, their election had to be confirmed) but instead were *selected* by the governor from among candidates chosen at volost'-level assemblies. (These assemblies included all village elders, who were themselves confirmed in office by the local authorities, and who seldom were genuine leaders in the peasant community.)[24]

Who were the peasants chosen by the governor to represent their peers in the zemstvos? No information is available for the period preceding the 1890 legislation, but in 1900 more than half the peasant delegates in Moscow province were selected from the local administrative apparatus, and of this figure, 75 percent were serving as volost' elders. In one district, Serpukov, all ten delegates were from the local administration, and eight of these ten were elders. Of the remaining peasant delegates in the districts, 20 percent were employed in factories or trade, 12 percent were Church elders or zemstvo functionaries of peasant origin, and only 12 percent were engaged exclusively in agriculture. According to an inspection (*reviziia*) of Moscow province conducted by the Ministry of the Interior in 1903, the government preferred to select delegates either from the local administration or from among those engaged in agriculture rather than industry; the local lists of candidates included a much higher percentage of peasant factory workers than did the final list of delegates. Although there were 166 volosts in Moscow province, there were only 108 peasant delegates; that is, more than one-third of all volosts, each including several villages, were disenfranchised. Expressed in terms of landholdings, each delegate from the nobility represented 4,815 desiatinas, whereas each delegate from the peasantry represented 16,189 desiatinas.[25] (One desiatina was the equivalent of 2.7 acres.) Not surprisingly, most accounts agree that peasant interest in zemstvo elections was low.

From the start, the peasants played a largely passive role in the assemblies. Intimidated by their former lords, after 1889 they often voted according to the instructions of the local land captains. (These officials, who first appeared in 1889, were selected from among the nobility to watch over the peasantry and were granted many of the prerogatives earlier held by serfowners, notably the right to impose corporal punishment.) B. B. Veselovskii was present at a session of the Moscow district assembly in which the gentry representatives were seated around a table in the center of the hall, while the peasants were allotted wooden benches in the corners; many other observers also noted the persistence of the "spirit of serfdom" in zemstvo procedures and relations. Even George Fischer, a staunch defender of the zemstvos, conceded that "above all, education, self-confidence and social status gave the nobility a preeminence that neither the peasantry nor the small town bourgeoisie ever sought to challenge."[26] Significantly, peasants themselves often confused the zemstvo with the hated land captains—in Russian, the words are close.[27] Although we frequently encounter the assertions that, in nineteenth-century Russia, society was lined up against the government and that the zemstvo *represented* society, in truth the zemstvo represented only the elite and not the people. To the village peasant, there was little distinction between the zemstvo and the government; both represented brute authority. In the words of an experienced zemstvo activist writing in 1911:

The zemstvo was and remains an organization that is foreign to [the peasant]: a name for some kind of undefined administration [*nachal'stvo*], whether identical with the district office, the marshall of nobility, the policeman, the land captain, or distinct from them—it is not clear.[28]

Before 1890, the gentry claimed 89 percent of membership on district boards and 61 percent on provincial boards. After 1890, the proportion was 94 percent and 75 percent, respectively.[29]

In addition to the elected delegates, however, there were the "Third Element" employees, hired to implement the growing number of services administered by the zemstvo. As zemstvo activity changed from political to administrative, and effective power moved from the assemblies to the staffs of the executive boards, these Third Element functionaries and specialists came to play an important role in policy making. By the 1890s, they exercised control—though not unchallenged—over most of the committees spawned by the executive board to draw up position papers, reports, and proposals. Then, as now, expertise was a source of power, for the zemstvo delegates met but once a year and had little opportunity or inclination to review the complexities of educational issues or agricultural measures. Instead they normally accepted the budget and policy recommendations of the executive boards. According to Veselovskii, by 1912 there were eighty-five thousand Third Element professionals working for the zemstvos— over fifty employees for each elected delegate.[30] Many of these professionals were motivated by the "small deeds" mentality that marked the transformation of much of the intelligentsia from radical populism to collaboration with the liberal gentry in extending services to the population; these Third Element employees were at least partially responsible for the upsurge of zemstvo activity observed throughout the country in the 1890s. In turn, they suffered disproportionately in the right-wing reaction that swept the country after 1905, when the political and economic demands voiced by the zemstvo collided with each other and many gentry assemblies turned against their own staffs.[31]

These professionals were anything but a homogeneous stratum in terms of their training, their backgrounds, and their standard of living. Fully 70 percent of the zemstvo employees were teachers, *fel'dshery* (medical orderlies), and midwives (60 percent of whom were women). The training of these low-grade specialists was often inadequate, their salaries minimal, and their morale often even lower. Conflict with the upper echelon of employees (doctors, hospital and school administrators, and statisticians, who enjoyed comfortable salaries and considerable status) was endemic.

The contrast in living standards between the upper and lower levels of employees prompted some to label the latter the "Fourth Element," or plebeians (*chernaia kost'*), in the zemstvos.[32] (The zemstvo doctor received 1,200 rubles per annum, the *feld'sher* or midwife, 300 rubles. By 1912, the zemstvo agronomist in Moscow was receiving 3,000 rubles, the statistician 3,600, the superintendent of education 3,600, and the teacher 300–350.)

Still, salaries and backgrounds aside, there can be no question that the zemstvo employees as a group were largely responsible for establishing whatever rapport existed between the zemstvo and the local population. Although the peasants had little concern for the representative aspects of the zemstvo, they did sometimes view these institutions as "slightly improved versions of the local government apparatus," and when positive contact between zemstvo and peasant did take place, it was through services to the population—through the work of the doctor, the teacher, or the agronomist. Thus, "the Third Element, to some degree, formed the connecting link between zemstvo and population."[33] All talk of local self-government, however, was rightly seen by the peasants as nonsense, unless .39 percent of the population (the nobility in rural Moscow) could have voted on behalf of 91.3 percent (the peasantry) and the situation been labeled self-government.

Mention must also be made of the functions of the zemstvos, the powers granted them by the central government, and the freedom allowed in the disposition of revenues.[34] A vacuum had been created by the dissolution of the ties of serfdom, and the zemstvos were established largely to carry out the local services that had been at least theoretically administered by the nobility in the pre-Emancipation period. These services included promoting agriculture, commerce, and industry; administering public health, charity, and relief; preventing fires and providing fire insurance; constructing and maintaining roads; providing veterinary services; and advancing education. Initially, activity in these spheres was restricted by government regulations that distinguished between obligatory and nonobligatory activities and forced the zemstvos to contribute a large share of their revenues to the upkeep of the local volost' administrative apparatus, the court system, the jails, and the salaries of police and other low-level functionaries.

Zemstvo revenues came from a combination of duties from trade documents, patents, property taxes on residences, and levies imposed on lands, factories, taverns, and commercial enterprises. The specific mix of revenues and the opportunities to fund welfare measures with these revenues varied from province to province, depending on the economic profile of the given region. (In the peasant zemstvos in the north, revenues were generated by high levies imposed on *state*-owned land!) Budgets were subject to government approval, and the 1864 Zemstvo Statute, though empowering the zemstvo to raise revenues through taxation, failed to establish tax agents responsible to the zemstvo or to provide zemstvos with enforcement power. Instead, the zemstvo had to rely on the local police for tax collections, and the latter often gave zemstvo taxes low priorities among their other tasks (which included tax collection for the central government). As a consequence, arrears in tax collection long remained a serious problem for zemstvo finances; often the only result of tax increases was a corresponding rise in the arrears registered in the zemstvo tax rolls.[35]

What, specifically, was the role of the zemstvo in local education? Initial consideration of the Zemstvo Statute defining zemstvo powers made no allowance for participation in education, but during debate over the final shape of the statute in the State Council, former Minister of Education Kovalevskii won insertion of a clause including under local services "participation, primarily through material aid [*v khoziastvennykh otnosheniiakh*], and with boundaries provided by law, in the sponsorship of education."[36] This clause, whose deliberate ambiguity resulted from a prolonged struggle between proponents and antagonists of local self-government, gave the zemstvo a foot in the door; yet, although it allowed the zemstvos to help provide schools, it seemed to give them no voice in how such schools would be run.[37] Indeed, this was the thrust of the much-misunderstood Great Reforms as a whole: to mobilize local energy to participate in the enactment of centrally defined goals—not to promote local democracy.[38]

The compromise embodied in the Zemstvo Statute did not complete the story, for zemstvo participation in local education was also alluded to in the 1864 Education Statute. During the discussion over the third draft of the Education Statute, drawn up by the MNP in 1863, Baron N. A. Korf, director of the Fourth Chancery, argued that the proposed local school board would simply be another bloodless interministerial government institution, staffed by functionaries whose responsibilities in other areas left them no time and provided them with no expertise to deal with rural education. Instead, Korf suggested that all the functions of the proposed boards be turned over to the soon-to-be-created zemstvos. The Minister of Education, A. V. Golovnin, agreed that the zemstvos should be allowed to organize schools, but he argued that control should be vested in the Ministry of Education. Discussion of the issue in the State Council led, again under Kovalevskii, to a surprising compromise: as noted above, the zemstvos were given two representatives on local school boards, whose mixed composition and elected chairman now virtually assured that no central ministry would control the schools. In effect, whereas the Zemstvo Statute had offered the zemstvo the right to *provide,* the Education Statute now offered the zemstvo the right to *participate* through local school boards whose organization—the result of a factional struggle among branches of government trying to prevent the hegemony of any one branch, as well as between proponents of local self-government and centralization—now assured a large dose of decentralization.[39]

EDUCATION MEASURES, 1864–1874

It was only a short time before the central government began to retract those aspects of the 1864 Education Statute granting a measure of decentralization and pluralism in school administration. On 13 May 1866, a month after the failed attempt by the deranged Karakozov on the life of the Tsar (which many historians see as a dividing line between the liberal and conservative periods of Alexander's reign), Alexander II issued a rescript to the Committee of Ministers emphasizing that henceforth the goal of the MNP in primary education would be to strengthen religion—notably Orthodoxy—among the people and to help preserve the existing political system. In the same year, the government introduced the censorship of textbooks under the supervision of the Academic Committee in the MNP. In fact, censorship was embodied in Article 5 of the Education Statute, which permitted the use of only those textbooks approved by the MNP. In 1865, the liberal Golovnin strengthened the Academic Committee's control by prohibiting the use of any textbook not sanctioned by that committee; two months later, the MNP began to publish cumulative annual catalogs of books permitted in the classroom. Finally, on 19 May 1869, a special textbook section for elementary schools was established under the Academic Committee and was instructed to "evaluate the political, moral, and pedagogical qualities" of all prospective primary school texts. Thus at the same time that overall concern for censorship of the press and secular literature was being removed from the MNP to the Ministry of the Interior (MVD), notably in the 1865 Temporary Regulations establishing the Main Committee for Censorship, the MNP gained full control over schoolbooks—completing a process that had begun before the attempt on the life of the Tsar.[40]

In 1866, curators of education circuits received instructions that tightened supervision over private schools, domestic instruction, and private tutors, and on 19 February 1868, an important law began to require that those wishing to establish private schools must receive a clean bill of moral and political health from the local school authorities and to mandate that teachers in such schools be certified. Since this was a year prior to the establishment of inspectors, it is unclear who the authorities were; but the effect of this ruling (and subsequent elaboration) was to drive unofficial peasant schools in the countryside underground, to open up such schools to harassment from local authorities, and to make the numbers of such schools very hard to estimate. Even after domestic schools were legalized in 1882, a legacy of mistrust accompanied a tradition of arbitrary interference, which meant that peasants were understandably less than forthcoming to the authorities about such schools.[41]

Yet another important indicator of this period was the decision in 1867 to turn over all elementary schools except those under the Church to the Ministry of Education. Thus, responsibility for funding Udel and state peasant schools in the thirty-four zemstvo provinces was shifted over to the zemstvos; elsewhere, these schools were assigned to peasant land societies. Everywhere these schools came under the direct supervision of the MNP.

A far more important measure of centralization was the establishment on 26 May 1869 of the post of inspector of primary schools in each province.[42] These inspectors were empowered to take over the supervision of primary education from the directors of secondary schools who had been responsible since 1804 for the supervision of *all* schools in their respective provinces. The slow rate at which the inspectorate grew in the quarter century following the 1874 School Statute, and the quickened pace after 1900, offer a significant clue to the nature of educational politics in the Russian countryside and support the argument made below that until 1905 zemstvo-government relations were generally harmonious as the zemstvos slowly took over a peasant-sponsored school system; after the turn of the century, the provincial zemstvos saw "their" system slowly taken from them as the MNP began to tighten a very tenuous grip over the countryside.

The 1869 legislation establishing the post of inspector was concerned less with political control than with the sponsorship of education, largely through establishment of model schools in the villages. Instructions issued in 1871, however, considerably expanded the powers and responsibilities of the inspectors and substantially increased the authority of inspectors over curriculum, the hiring and firing of teachers, and the course of primary education in general. These regulations, though often attacked as outmoded, remained in force until 1917 and constitute one of the most significant elements of the legal edifice of tsarist education in late Imperial Russia. (See Chapter 5.)

During this period, the central government also moved to gain control over teacher training institutions. Initially the government hesitated and considered allowing the zemstvos to take charge of this essential area of schooling. In 1869, the Novgorod zemstvo, followed by the Moscow, Riazan', Chernigov, Tver', Viatka, Kostroma, Kursk, Samara, Petersburg, and Olonets zemstvos, established teachers' seminaries, acting on the basis of 1868 legislation tolerating (as well as limiting) private schools. (Restrictive legislation often helped promote the activity being regulated by making explicit the terms and conditions of its existence.)

But the Ministry of Education soon began to encircle these efforts with red tape and then to establish state-run closed seminaries on the Prussian model. In 1871 five such seminaries were established, in 1872 six more, and between 1873 and 1875 another eleven. After 1875, the ministry's efforts in this direction flagged, yet the restrictions on zemstvo efforts were never lifted, and the shortage of qualified teachers remained a persistent, even crippling, problem until 1914. Ironically, because of persistent shortages, the expanding school system was consistently forced to turn to applicants who had received an incomplete secondary, or even an informal, education, and the degree of control exerted over teacher preparation was consequently much vitiated.[43]

Apprehensive that the radical populist ideas spreading among university youth on the eve of the great "going to the people" movement would infect future rural teachers and then be passed on, like bacilli, to the rural population through the schools, the government made a concerted effort to locate teachers' seminaries in sleepy provincial or district towns and to provide stipends allowing rural youth to enroll and become teachers. At the same time, it limited the curriculum of the teachers' seminaries and training schools to what was essentially a repetition, at a slower pace, of the advanced primary school program. Daily life in these closed institutions was closely regulated by Instructions issued on 4 July 1875, which remained in force until the 1917 Revolution.[44]

The drive for centralization, political security, and protection from radical infiltration of the schools led the Tsar to issue yet another rescript, this one on 25 December 1873, summoning the nobility to "stand guard over the schools to protect them from pernicious and baneful influences." Soviet historians rank this statement, together with I. Delianov's notorious "Cooks' Children" circular of 1887—arguing that poor children shouldn't be educated beyond their rank in society—as examples of two of the most important and *representative* features of tsarist education policy: a desire to restrict social mobility and a concern to ensure political loyalty. There is considerable truth in this point of view; nevertheless, it oversimplifies a more complicated reality. In fact, competing pressures for modernization and for political stability resulted in a search for "controlled participation." Political support for an endangered estate—the nobility—was combined with dynamic promotion of economic growth, which in turn entailed at least a limited recognition that considerable social mobility from the lower orders would inevitably result. Moreover, although the prevailing

Soviet interpretation treats the tsarist bureaucracy as a monolithic entity, recent research by both Western and outstanding Soviet historians reveals a far more complex reality, a network of feuding patronage systems, each with its own agenda.[45]

Qualifications aside, it was unquestionably fear of political radicalism, as well as a desire to centralize control over local school boards and restrict the powers of the zemstvos, that helped shape the revised School Statute of 1874. Even after the political fears of the moment had passed, this statute remained in force until 1917. Thus, the Instructions of 1871 and the 1874 School Statute remained the cornerstones of tsarist policy in the following decades of expansion and elaboration of a system that had hardly existed in organized form when the measures were first implemented.

The revised School Statute, issued on 31 May 1874, introduced virtually nothing new in terms of goals, curriculum, language of instruction, choice of textbooks, or the question of funding, but it did bring about changes in the composition and competence of the local school boards.[46] The right to shut down schools because of "disorders" or "harmful instruction," formerly entrusted to the boards, was now granted to inspectors under the Ministry of Education. Trustees were to be confirmed in office by the provincial, rather than the district, board. The statute placed the inspectors on the district board and directors (also functionaries of the Ministry of Education) on the provincial boards; moreover, the statute required the presence of the inspector or a representative of the Ministry of Education at all school board meetings. Inspectors received the all-important power of confirming teachers in their posts and, jointly with the local school board, of removing these teachers at their discretion. The new statute removed school trustees from the boards and substantially narrowed the functions of the school boards themselves.

Overall responsibility for ensuring the "proper moral direction" of the schools was assigned to the local and provincial marshalls of the nobility, who were also made *ex officio* chairmen of the district and provincial school boards (Article 32), but administration of the schools and responsibility for curriculum were placed in the hands of the inspectors.

The effect of the 1874 School Statute—which followed on the heels of the "going to the people" movement and reflected government concern for greater control over primary education—was twofold. On the one hand, the independence of school boards in educational affairs was greatly reduced, whereas on the other hand these organs were brought firmly under the control of the Ministry of Education. Concerning 1874, Allen Sinel writes: "The Ministry of Education had finally become an omnipresent force in elementary education." [47] This description is an overstatement, for the statute left several loopholes by which other institutions could affect the course of primary education. Supervision of Bible courses and "the religious-moral direction of instruction in the elementary schools" remained the prerogative of the Holy Synod (Article 17). The marshalls of the nobility, as Sinel himself points out, were given a good measure of power and were not answerable to any ministry. Finally, the governor, who was subordinate to the Ministry of the Interior, was entrusted with "overall supervision over the state direction of primary education in the provinces" (Article 34). Despite this, the school boards in practice now became organs of the Ministry of Education, subordinate to the local inspectors.

The Senate was still to arbitrate complaints against the provincial school boards, but ultimate control over decisions of curriculum (*po uchebnoi chasti*) remained in the hands of the Ministry of Education (Article 37). To be sure, a later Senate ruling (1893) facilitated zemstvo participation in school affairs by legalizing zemstvo school commissions and rejecting a narrow interpretation of the 1874 Statute limiting the zemstvo to the provision of schools (*khoziaistvennaia storona*). [48] The Senate ruled that the zemstvos had the right to be active in setting curriculum as well as in funding schools. Nevertheless, the 1874 School Statute remained on the books with few modifications until 1917 as the basic law dealing with the administration of primary school affairs, and—with the reservations noted above—the Ministry of Education became the ultimate authority over the schools.

3

Who Built the Schools?

Zemstvo and Peasant Community

The decade of the 1860s was a period of considerable, though short-lived, ferment in Russian educational thought. Violating all precedent, the Ministry of Education had circulated early drafts of the 1864 Education Statute to leading educators in Russia and the West. Pedagogical journals and societies sprang up, and the ideas of Korf, Ushinskii, and Pirogov were widely discussed in the flush of excitement following the Emancipation. How was the peasant to be educated? How much education was appropriate, and what skills and values should be imparted? Who should pay for the schools? Where were teachers to be found? This decade was also a period, as we have observed, of diminished bureaucratic control over schooling: no one official had been given a dominant position on the local school boards, and zemstvos had been allowed two representatives on these boards.[1]

Yet this decade of ferment did not see a substantial expansion of basic education. In fact, one prominent educator, V. P. Vakhterov, later pointed to the first decade of zemstvo activity as a step *backward* in educational history. In the words of S. F. Starr:

Throughout Russia before 1870 the zemstvos commonly sought to pass responsibility for education either to the local arbiters of the peace, to church institutions and parish priests, or to the very peasant communes which presumably were the object of the campaign for enlightenment.[2]

In contrast, the activities of the zemstvos during the 1870s and 1880s—ironically, *after* government inspectors had been given broad powers over local school boards and *after* the revised 1874 School Statute had considerably restricted zemstvo initiative in education—have won applause from both contemporaries and historians, Soviet as well as Western. The British school inspector Darlington commented that "the educational work of the zemstvo marks an epoch in the history of Russia." A recent Soviet text on the subject conceded:

Despite all obstacles created by the government, zemstvo institutions played an important role in improving the local economy and promoting culture. Their efforts to spread primary education were particularly successful. The zemstvo was the first to lay a firm foundation for the rural public school in Russia.[3]

Admittedly, the pace of zemstvo activity slowed during the eighties, but—so the argument goes—this was the consequence of bureaucratic repression and the harsh suppression of zemstvo initiative rather than of the withering of zemstvo initiative or idealism.

This interpretation does not hold up under close investigation. To be sure, a handful of district and provincial zemstvos, prodded by the efforts of educators such as Korf, N. Blinov, D. Shakhovskii, and others, made a substantial contribution to peasant education. More than that, it was in the sixties and seventies that the distinctively zemstvo school emerged, with one teacher and a three-year program. But on the whole, zemstvo education endeavors languished. This chapter traces the early efforts of the Moscow zemstvo and the emergence of a school policy in zemstvo Russia, as well as discussing the issue of initiative, or sponsorship of the remarkable expansion of schooling that did occur in these three decades. We will discover both that there was a substantial escalation of schooling in Russia and that the zemstvo contribution to this development was meager.

A ZEMSTVO SCHOOL POLICY

By law, the zemstvos were allowed, but not required, to allocate funds for education; they could also establish schools with the permission of the proper authorities, present candidates for teaching posts, and elect two members to the local school boards. First, however, the zemstvos had to confront a number of issues. Information had to be collected on the existing network of schools in the province, and a professional staff assembled to administer education as well as road building, livestock insurance, health care, and agricultural services. Priorities had to be determined and funds allocated accordingly. The zemstvos had to decide what type of school best fit local needs and where to find competent teachers. Ushinskii had written in 1861:

We don't have a single public school in the entire boundless expanse of Russia. . . . The very notion of a Russian public school has only superficially been touched upon in our literature. . . . There are no questions more timely and urgent than the following: What exactly should our Russian public school be? How and where should schools be built? What should be taught and how? Where will we find teachers? Who should these teachers be? What should the relationship be between school, society, and the educational bureaucracy?[4]

In Moscow, the provincial zemstvo sessions of 1865, 1866, and 1867 discussed a number of theoretical and practical issues pertaining to primary education. Teaching methods and curriculum were hotly debated, the merits of a professional versus a general education were contrasted, the virtues of Sunday school classes for adults were pointed out, and the importance of instruction in geography, Russian history, drawing, and choir was emphasized. In 1866, the provincial zemstvo Commission on Needs and Uses recommended the adoption of the Lancaster system of instruction, and the assembly voted to accept this recommendation.[5] Some delegates spoke in favor of entrusting instruction exclusively to the clergy as guardians of peasant morality, although others noted that clergymen were too busy with other responsibilities to serve simultaneously as teachers and that in parish schools absenteeism by teachers rivaled that of pupils. One delegate proposed the introduction of instruction in crafts and agriculture. In his words: "It will be quite an achievement if by disseminating certain basic agricultural concepts we succeed in dispelling those superstitions prevailing over how the peasant works his land."[6] This proposal was contested by the majority of delegates. D. I. Shipov believed that the amount of practical information that could be conveyed in the elementary schools would be virtually worthless, and he spoke in favor of a curriculum that would focus on the ABCs.

This debate in turn led to a discussion of how many years pupils would be expected to remain in school. Although the commission proposed that instruction should be continued to the age of fourteen, Shipov noted that most families could not spare their children from work, either at home or in the local cottage industries, for such a protracted period. Another delegate replied that "the longer children, under the prevailing way of life, are separated from the domestic hearth, the better for both children and parents."[7] The journals of the Viatka, Iaroslavl', Tver', and other zemstvos indicate that similar issues occupied the delegates in other provinces during the late sixties.

No stone was left unturned during these debates, and much of the detail makes fascinating, if rather quaint, reading. (For example, when the burning issue of coeducation was brought up, Count Uvarov pointed to the examples of "highly developed" Germany and Belgium, where pupils were not segregated by sex until the age of fourteen, and he added, "As far as Russia is concerned, the people are so sober and pure in their healthy notion of life [*zdravoe poniatie*] that we have nothing to fear from coeducation.")[8] But it is difficult not to be struck by the comic unreality of arguments over curriculum, teaching staff, and coeducation, when the basic issue of who would pay for the construction and maintenance of schools had yet to be confronted.

This issue soon came to the forefront in the zemstvo debates, and not only in Moscow. Prince A. I. Vasil'chikov, delegate to the Novgorod zemstvo and author of a controversial book, *On Self-Government,* argued that education should be free and that schools should be constructed at the initiative and expense of the local community. Vasil'chikov was supported in the press by the renowned educator Baron N. A. Korf, who added that in those villages desiring to build schools, the zemstvo and government should also step in to help. But A. I. Koshelev from Riazan' demurred, arguing that as long as the sponsorship of schools was left to the rural community, there would be no schools. Thus two positions were articulated, one arguing that initiative should rest with the rural community (with the zemstvo merely establishing a system of supports, or *pooshchreniia*), and the other calling for active zemstvo sponsorship and commitment of funds.[9]

To many zemstvo representatives, it was not at all clear what priority education should receive among all the other concerns of the zemstvo. But the debate over education went even further, questioning principles as well as priorities. Because only peasant children were likely to study in rural schools, and the zemstvo was charged with the well-being of all residents of an area, some felt it improper to channel money in that direction. It is difficult to determine how much genuine conviction was behind this argument; certainly today it sounds a bit forced and self-serving. Even a sympathetic historian conceded that the early policies adopted by the zemstvos were but an attempt to shrug off the burden of education. Acknowledging that initially the zemstvo had only limited funds at its disposal, P. F. Kapterev added:

The zemstvo showed little enthusiasm for public schooling. Indeed, many believed that the rural school was not a proper area of activity for the zemstvos; after all, such schools taught peasants only and should be run by peasants. Landowners and people of other estates did not enroll their children in village schools, and the zemstvo was obliged to serve all rural inhabitants, not just one estate. Thus, at first the zemstvo was not entirely reluctant to rid itself of rural schools, leaving their fate largely, if not entirely, to the village community.[10]

Perhaps because of the multitude and complexity of the questions thrust before them, the zemstvos throughout Russia at first attempted only to gather information from local school committees on the state of education in the localities. In the first four years after the zemstvos were established, 109 districts, almost one-third of the total, allocated no funds to public education. Another forty allocated paltry sums, others used available funds for secondary education, and still others neglected to spend allotted sums.[11]

In provinces later known as leaders in primary education, such as Iaroslavl', Vladimir, and even Viatka, the historian B. B. Veselovskii detected almost no interest in peasant education at early zemstvo meetings. In his recollection of the zemstvo in Nizhnii Novgorod province, the moderate educator N. N. Iordanskii noted that despite revenue surpluses on hand, a number of district assemblies, pleading poverty, declined peasant requests for help and voted down allocations for schools.[12]

But where was money for the schools to be found? According to the Zemstvo Statute, the chief source of revenue was to be a tax on agricultural and forest land; in fact, this levy yielded 75 percent of zemstvo income in the 1860s. The balance came from taxes on other immovable property and from a number of minor levies on capital gains, turnpike traffic, and so forth. But the gentry and peasantry were united in their opposition to increases in land taxes, whereas the ministers of Finance and the Interior were adamantly opposed to the "excessive" taxation of trade and industry. Yet existing revenues fell far short of meeting immediate needs in nearly every province. It is no wonder that confusion and hesitation reigned among zemstvo leaders in this early period.[13]

During the 1860s, the government did indeed hobble the activities of the newly established zemstvos by severely restricting sources of revenue and by mandating that a large proportion of zemstvo funds be spent on maintaining local administrative offices and jails. It is also undeniable, however, that by following the "English model" (private funding and state supervision) the 1864 Education Statute allowed local bodies considerable freedom to promote primary education. The truth is that, by and large, many zemstvos simply evaded their responsibilities during this first decade. Most zemstvos either refused to shoulder educational costs or allotted only insignificant sums.

In early 1867, the question of funding became urgent throughout the zemstvo provinces when the State Council announced the termination in the following year of the special education tax collected from state peasants for the maintenance of their schools— schools that had recently been turned over to the zemstvos. In Moscow, a crisis was temporarily averted when the provincial zemstvo, after initial resistance, backed down and allocated 30,288 rubles for the schools, to be distributed according to the number of revision souls (tax units) in each district. Up to this point, the zemstvos had generally been unwilling to discuss funding, arguing that they had no right to allocate money to schools that provided an education to specific estates—here, the state peasants—and refused access to others.[14]

Thus, the government decision to terminate the education tax forced the hand of the Moscow zemstvo, and in January 1868 the executive board presented another report, which drew up guidelines for future involvement in elementary education. After a brief statement acknowledging "the vital importance of the urgent tasks" confronting the zemstvo, the executive board made a proposal that subsequently became the cornerstone of zemstvo educational policy throughout Russia until the 1890s:

Having recognized the total impossibility of carrying out those tasks that would confront the zemstvo if it decided to promote public education in Moscow province at zemstvo expense, . . . the board suggests that the sole possible, and therefore useful and well-founded, service that the zemstvo can provide [to the cause of] education is in the extension of subsidies and other forms of support to existing and newly organized schools, in appeals to private individuals and societies to open new schools, . . . in the prompt rendering of material aid to these schools, . . . in the purchase of textbooks and school equipment where necessary, and in incentives, both moral and material, to the best teachers.[15]

Because the district zemstvos would have the closest ties with the local population, the board proposed that subsidies be provided to the community by district zemstvos. The provincial zemstvo would assume responsibility for teacher training. Even though the Moscow provincial zemstvo soon began to devise measures to supersede its self-defined limits by intervening directly to prod the district assemblies into action, and the actual division of functions was never as clear in practice as in theory, at least now the would-be zemstvo educators were armed with guidelines for action. These guidelines were, in brief, the "incentive" (*pooshchrenia*) system. In its most benevolent form, this system was a version of "helping those who help themselves"; in most zemstvos, it was a convenient rationalization for inaction.[16]

Nevertheless, this early period witnessed the emergence of a distinctively "zemstvo" school. A number of outstanding educators, among them Korf, Blinov, I. Derkachev, I. Paul'son, V.

Vodovozov, and N. Bunakov, devoted their efforts to developing teaching methods; determining the most appropriate scheduling, length of program, age of pupils, and class divisions; and compiling a number of popular ABC books and readers. By far the most influential educator during these decades was Baron Korf, a graduate of the Aleksandrov Lycée, who retired from the Ministry of Justice to first become a delegate to the Ekaterinoslav provincial zemstvo assembly and then to serve on the school board in the Aleksandrov district. In the following five years (1867–1872), Korf helped establish over one hundred village schools funded by communal taxes in his district, and his success in mobilizing peasants in this effort won him considerable prominence.

The Korf schools had one teacher who presided over three one-year divisions. The school day included two three-hour periods, separated by a two-hour lunch and recess. The course of instruction included not only reading, writing, and arithmetic, but also history, geography, natural science, and Russian grammar. The basic textbook used was Ushinskii's *Rodnoe slovo* (*Native Word*), supplemented by the reader *Nash drug* (*Our Friend*), written by Korf himself, which focused on subjects from rural life familiar to the pupil. Although Korf never gained a reputation as an innovative thinker, his handbook *Russkaia nachal'naia shkola* (*The Russian Primary School*), rich in practical advice, won immense popularity among zemstvo teachers, and the Korf three-year school soon became indistinguishable from the zemstvo school.[17]

But by the 1880s it had become clear to many observers that the incentive system was making only limited headway. Most blamed peasant sloth, ignorance, hostility to schooling; peasants, they said, would not contribute to the expense of building and maintaining schools. Everyone agreed that zemstvo efforts were little more than a drop in the proverbial sea of rural illiteracy. Why, then, given such limited progress, did the zemstvos cling to a program based on peasant initiative, even as they often argued that peasant *indifference* was the main obstacle to the expansion of schooling?

It is true that the incentive system paralleled the strong currents of localism (*uezdnichestvo*) running through zemstvo politics in the late seventies and eighties. The *uezdniki*—those who favored concentrating zemstvo activities and powers at the district rather than the provincial level—argued that the only proper functions of the provincial zemstvos were to supplement and coordinate, when requested, the activities of the district zemstvos. Although the powers vested in the provincial zemstvos by the 1864 Zemstvo Statute (Article 62) and retained in the 1890 Statute were considerable, district "independence" and *uezdnik* views held sway until the mid-1890s. Rumblings were even heard during the eighties advocating the abolition of the provincial zemstvos on the grounds that they had no "local roots"; if these rumblings turned into a groundswell only in the nineties, it was because until that decade the provincial zemstvos exerted little effort to challenge *uezdnik* dominance. The only exceptions to the *uezdnik* program of decentralization were the Kherson medical program, the Riazan' and Kazan' road-building programs, and the Moscow educational program.[18]

But the sway of the *uezdniki* over zemstvo politics was not the only explanation for the appeal of the incentive system. Other reasons were the timidity of the zemstvos in the face of the tasks confronting them and the low priority given peasant education, evident in early discussions about universal education. This latter subject had been broached on a number of occasions before 1890. For example, the *principle* of universal education had been heatedly discussed during the debate over the conflicting drafts of the 1864 Education Statute. (In theory, the statute supported universal education, but the adoption of the "English system" of private support for primary education in reality relegated universal education to the distant future.) As the Education Statute was being revised in 1874, A. S. Voronov, a member of the Council of the MNP, had submitted drafts favoring the introduction of universal compulsory education.[19] Then, in 1876, the Ministry of Education had sent out an elaborate questionnaire to all inspectors and directors of education to determine the feasibility of universal education.

Outside government circles, too, voices in favor of universal education were not difficult to find. In the 1840s, S. A. Maslov presented a report to the Moscow Agricultural Society calling for universal education. The St. Petersburg Literacy Committee heard a similar paper in 1861, and in 1866, the Moscow Literacy Committee sponsored a debate on universal literacy. The topic was extensively discussed at the Second Agricultural Congress in Moscow in 1870 and at the First Congress of Technical Education in 1889. In the zemstvo assemblies, a handful of districts and provinces in the 1870s addressed petitions to the government calling for universal education, but many of the most prominent zemstvo educators, including Korf and Koshelev, spoke against the idea as premature.[20]

What prevented even the most ardent supporters of education from working for universal primary education? Part of the answer lay in the widespread recognition that there simply weren't enough teachers for the enormous task at hand and that the effort would swallow up all the country's intellectual forces. There was also the mutual distrust of government and society, the one fearing the concentration of control and the other dreading the release of initiative on such a large scale. Yet, as a later chapter will show, such friction was limited and does not adequately explain the lack of activity.

Another important reason for the withering of initiative seems to have been the genuine conviction, widespread among educators within and outside government, that the costs of such a project were enormous, indeed prohibitive, that "because we are poor, we cannot afford education." A number of attempts had been made to calculate the costs of introducing universal education, and all had been sobering. Voronov's proposal estimated that to have one teacher for every forty school-age children (one school for every two hundred fifty inhabitants), the number of primary schools in Russia would have to be increased from twenty-three thousand to three hundred thousand—or more than thirteen times. Concluding that in the foreseeable future there would be far too few teachers to staff that many schools, Voronov suggested proceeding slowly in response to petitions from individual zemstvos. A. V. Dubrovskii, analyzing the results of the school census of 1880, concluded that the implementation of universal elementary education in European Russia would require an increase in outlays from the existing 6 million to 82 million rubles, or from 9 kopecks per person to 1.24 rubles.[21] As late as January 1893, the mathematician and prominent educator A. N. Strannoliubskii presented a paper to the St. Petersburg Literacy Committee arguing that "the attainment of universal, correctly organized, primary education, given the present conditions and outlays on education, is impossible even in the distant future." He stated that Russia needed two hundred fifty thousand new schools and yearly outlays of 125 million rubles to make universal education a reality. This report was published in a St. Petersburg journal and received considerable attention.[22]

Some Soviet historians have argued that the Ministry of Education deliberately used these "frightful" calculations to "intimidate the common taxpayers."[23] But a truer summation of the dominant position in the Ministry of Education was the response to zemstvo petitions for universal obligatory education: "No matter how desirable the introduction of compulsory education, it is simply impossible at the present time."[24] The belief that Russia lacked the resources to carry out such a massive project was not limited to the government; it was genuine, widespread, and shared by most leading educators. We should also recall that zemstvo finances before 1890 were pinched, that sources of revenue were very limited, and that the zemstvos had no means of enforcing tax collection, having to rely instead on the local police, who collected zemstvo taxes last, after other levies had been gathered. As arrears on peasant taxes mounted in the 1880s, it seemed senseless to increase zemstvo land taxes; the ultimate result might even have been a net loss in zemstvo revenues.

Nevertheless, the belief that "because we are poor, we cannot afford education" also reflected the low priority given schooling before the 1890s, the conviction that popular schooling was a frill, a luxury that could be dispensed with since it had value only to the individual and not to the nation. Only in the nineties, when universal literacy was seen virtually as the condition of national salvation, did the costs suddenly seem manageable.

Zemstvo inertia was also perpetuated by the reluctance of gentry zemstvo delegates to allow tax reassessments that would have distributed the burden of zemstvo taxes more equitably between lord and peasant. Incredible as it may seem, gentry land taxes before the 1890s were derived from estimates of size and quality of holding provided to the assessor by the individual owner himself. For this reason, large tracts of gentry land went entirely untaxed; between 1871 and 1900, zealous zemstvo statisticians discovered over 30 million desiatinas of previously untaxed gentry land—and many lost their jobs as a reward. In Moscow province, a thorough land survey conducted in the nineties resulted in a call for a 55 percent increase in gentry land taxes; despite government prodding, however, the provincial zemstvo rejected the findings. Moreover, land under plow was more heavily taxed than forest or pasture; because gentry holdings were less intensively cultivated than were peasant lands, the rate on gentry lands (at least those under taxation) was lower than that imposed on peasant holdings.[25]

Granted, in Russia the central bureaucracy cornered 85 percent of all government revenues.[26] Moreover, until the 1890s the central government directed a large proportion of zemstvo revenues to the upkeep of local administration, leaving little for human services and rural needs. Arrears on peasant land taxes also mounted in the 1880s, squeezing available zemstvo revenues even more tightly. But it must also be acknowledged that the zemstvo coffers were often empty because the gentry themselves had rigged local taxes so that they were contributing almost nothing—even though many of the services provided by the zemstvos benefited the gentry more than the peasantry.

The low priority given peasant education is also evident in the successive waves of enthusiasm demonstrated by zemstvo assemblies in the 1880s for alternatives to the Korf-type school. Though Korf himself regarded a three-year program as inadequate and had developed his handbook in full recognition of the poverty of the villages and of the limits this poverty imposed on the rural school program, many treated the Korf school as a luxury. In the words of Kapterev:

Baron Korf . . . taught the zemstvo that the primary school must develop the person, not the professional; that it must provide not literacy but education, however limited; and that it must be staffed by trained and [at least] minimally educated teachers; and so forth. He was not the only one to point this out. But the zemstvo, guided primarily by economic rather than pedagogical considerations, persistently tried, when it couldn't hand over responsibility entirely to the rural community, to build schools even more simply and cheaply and spent a good deal of time looking for an inexpensive version of the public school. Whenever something appeared on the pedagogical market, the zemstvo rushed in headlong, jumping at whatever cost less. During the seventies, someone thought up mobile, or "ambulatory," schools, temporary schools in the districts run by traveling teachers . . . and the zemstvo eagerly turned in this direction [but was soon stopped by the government, fearful of wandering political agitators]. Some zemstvos dreamed of turning the primary schools into literacy schools because of the latter's simplicity and low overhead, others of giving the primary schools a narrowly vocational nature. . . . [In the eighties] many zemstvos ecstatically seized upon the idea of Church parish schools when they appeared, thinking that they could now say, "God's will be done," . . . and the zemstvos began to subsidize parish schools. . . . Certain zemstvos went even further and turned over existing schools to the clergy, regarding their zemstvo obligations to the cause of public education as fulfilled.[27]

Here Kapterev succinctly recapitulated the history of zemstvo education endeavors between 1864 and 1890. From the beginning, the search was for a "cheap way out," and the essential stages proceeded from support for the mobile (or filial) school[28] to the literacy school and the Church parish school. As we have seen, the search for an inexpensive means of spreading literacy was somewhat justified, for estimates of the cost of realizing universal literacy were truly intimidating. But the simultaneous effort to divest the zemstvo of *all* responsibility for peasant education, the reluctance to invest funds in other areas of the rural infrastructure that would have largely benefited the peasantry, and gentry reluctance to tax themselves to promote general (that is, peasant) education all suggest the low priority the gentry accorded peasant literacy.

Thus the debates in zemstvo circles over how to educate peasants, where to find money, who was to build schools, and who was to take initiative were characterized by a blend of inertia, expediency, and disagreement over principles; the debates lasted from the 1860s until the 1890s. Historians have often argued that the 1874 School Statute, which considerably curtailed zemstvo freedom in school affairs, dampened enthusiasm for education and led to efforts to turn schools over to other institutions in the eighties. But in reality, there was no fundamental discontinuity in 1874. Instead, the reality was one of slow, fumbling steps, backtracking, and the gradual dawning of an awareness of the many dimensions involved in introducing formal education to the countryside. During this period, government measures were of only secondary importance in determining the level of zemstvo energy in school affairs. The fundamental decision made by the zemstvos was to encourage existing peasant education activity by applying limited grants according to the Moscow-inspired incentive system and by contributing expertise to improve school organization.

There was a certain irony to the initiative taken by the Moscow provincial zemstvo, for although this zemstvo was the first in the country to adopt the incentive system that subsequently spread throughout the country, it was the gradual *abandonment* of this system that placed Moscow in the forefront of school affairs. Before the 1890s, Moscow was the only provincial zemstvo to launch an active program of school construction, teacher training and salary subsidies, and library promotion, all funded by matching grants to the district zemstvo from the provincial level. The irony was that no sooner had Moscow devised the incentive system than the zemstvo moved away from it and became a model of direct educational sponsorship.[29]

PEASANT INITIATIVE

Before 1890, it seems, the Russian gentry active in the zemstvos paid lip service to popular education but managed to avoid the uncomfortable problem of how to fund a large-scale school construction effort. They argued, first, that Russia was simply too poor, and, second, that initiative should come from below, that the only function of the zemstvo should be to encourage such initiative by timely but limited grants. In some areas, zemstvos sought, particularly in the eighties, to escape all responsibility for schooling by turning over supervision and budget allocations to the Holy Synod or to the local school board. The zemstvos have usually been forgiven for this retreat because of the widespread belief that the imposing weight of the Imperial bureaucracy had smothered zemstvo initiative and engendered widespread demoralization and apathy by this time.

We have, however, an uncomfortable set of facts to confront. Despite the evidence of a slowdown in zemstvo activity, some historians have detected a steady expansion of schooling beginning in the 1870s and lasting throughout the last quarter of the nineteenth century (see Chapter 10). Even more striking, as military observers discovered after 1874 when they began to keep records on the literacy of recruits, peasant literacy began a slow but inexorable climb in this period. Who was building the schools, and what was the source of peasant literacy?

It is highly likely that between 1864 and 1890 peasants themselves were the driving force behind the progress in literacy registered in official statistics. As late as the end of the century, noninstitutional sources accounted for a remarkably high proportion of the literates in the countryside. Historians often refer to data showing that 36 percent of the literate factory population had learned how to read or write outside the schools—that is, in "unregistered" schools, from literates (*gramotei*) hired individually by parents or collectively by villages to teach their children. In Saratov, between one-half and three-fourths of all literates had received no formal education; in Iaroslavl', the figures were 48 percent for men and 38 percent for women.[30]

Undoubtedly, the vast majority of "unschooled" literates learned their ABCs in the so-called free, or "wild," schools (*vol'nye shkoly*) that proliferated in the Russian countryside despite regulations established in 1869 to restrict private education. Until they were legalized in 1882, these schools functioned furtively; even later, they frequently escaped documentation. Yet sources demonstrate their presence and testify to their considerable vitality and popular support.[31] N. V. Chekhov, an enthusiast of the zemstvo school, commented in 1923:

Much more important [than the gentry-promoted schools organized by Korf, Tolstoy, and others] was the independent initiative of the peasant population, expressed by the opening in the sixties of thousands of literacy schools. Despite the extremely impoverished circumstances of these schools, the barely literate teachers, . . . and despite the complete absence of textbooks and amenities, or even of permanent quarters [the teacher lived and worked by moving from house to house—a type of payment in kind by the parents], these schools turned out to have the greatest vitality and formed the cornerstone for the zemstvo schools, into which they were gradually transformed in the seventies and eighties.[32]

In Kashirsk district of Tula province in 1873, investigators discovered that in addition to seven registered schools, forty-five "small schools" (*mel'kie shkoly*) were in operation—thirty-two taught by priests and ten by peasants (the other three unspecified).

In Vladimir twenty years later, when 426 teachers were asked to comment on if and where (and by whom) peasants had been educated before the establishment of official schools, 21 percent cited other villages; 29.5 percent, local *gramotei* and retired soldiers; 43.5 percent, the local clergy; and only 5 percent observed that there had been no schooling. Detailed research carried out in Voronezh at the turn of the century showed that in forty small villages located far from population centers and having no official schools, 16 percent of the population was nevertheless literate. According to this study, 39.2 percent of the literates had learned to read from the military, 33.8 percent from fellow villagers, 21.2 percent were self-taught, and 5.8 percent had learned in school. In Tavrida in 1900, after a large-scale school drive and the establishment of a network of rural schools, 7 percent of those who came to school were already literate; two-thirds of this number had learned to read or write at home or in a free peasant school.[33]

Detailed studies in the 1880s by Bunakov, A. Prugavin, N. Rubakin, and V. I. Farmakovskii showed that in Tver' and other provinces literacy was quite widespread, even in districts with no official schools. Prugavin, for example, discovered that in one district in Vladimir 83 percent of all literates had learned to read and write in *vol'nye* schools; in Iukhovskii district, Smolensk province, 175 of 704 villages had functioning free peasant schools in the 1880s. In Dorogobuzhsk district, also in Smolensk, there were 154 villages with access to twenty-five official schools in 1885; of the remaining 479 villages, 108 hired their own teachers and maintained unsupervised schools. In yet another district (Gzhatsk), of 551 villages with no access to official schools, 230 hired their own teachers. *Vol'nye* schools were particularly popular among religious sectarians, but they enjoyed widespread support anywhere the population had no direct access to official schools.[34]

It is most important to recognize that the free peasant school in most cases served as the foundation for the zemstvo *and* Church parish schools that emerged in the Russian countryside in the last quarter of the nineteenth century. The official school system was deliberately and explicitly built by incorporating, formalizing, "improving" schools that had originally been organized and funded by the peasant community. For this reason, we should not assume that the increase in the number of schools in *official statistics,* before 1890 in particular, always represented a net increase in the number of schools actually in the villages. In large measure, the increase merely represented the formalization (registration) of existing peasant-sponsored schools, their incorporation within the official network. As Veselovskii noted, before the 1880s,

the zemstvo school led an ephemeral existence; it opened and closed its doors with great ease. This was because such schools had no buildings of their own, but were located in Church facilities, the local bath house, and so forth. But it was also *because the general zemstvo attitude was one of providing subsidies to existing schools* [*rather than opening new ones*] [emphasis added].[35]

This attitude was indeed a deliberate policy pursued by most zemstvos (and later by the Church), following the incentive system. To paraphrase an expression used by Karl Kaestle to point out that in the United States widespread informal schooling preceded the government intervention of the 1840s, one could say that in Russia the "sleepy period" of zemstvo inactivity (1864–1890) was also a "sneaky period" of active, but often furtive and undetected, peasant sponsorship of basic education.

Even once schools were officially registered, the peasant contribution remained substantial; until the close of the century, peasants continued to pay a considerable proportion of the direct expenditures on education in the official schools (both Church and zemstvo). The formula worked out by many zemstvos—that the community would pay for the purchase or rental and the upkeep of a school building, while the zemstvos would provide textbooks and pay teachers—was only partially implemented before 1900. As late as the end of the 1880s, local communities were still funding 30 percent of teachers' salaries and outlays on books, as well as meeting all expenses for facilities (except in Moscow and a few other provinces). In 1893, only one in ten zemstvo schools was funded exclusively by zemstvo monies. In 1903, the government set conditions under which zemstvos would be eligible for direct subsidies, including requirements that zemstvo teachers receive an annual salary of at least 300 rubles from the zemstvo and that village communities be freed from all direct expenditures on schools. But many district zemstvos still found these stipulations too burdensome and declined government offers to help pay for the schools.[36]

When measuring the relative contributions of the elite and the peasantry to total school costs, some additional facts must be kept in mind. First, most estimates did not include outlays on facilities, which the peasants bore solely, ordinarily as a form of labor due. A. N. Kulomzin estimated that the peasant contribution in 1898 accounted for 17.9 percent of education costs, but that if such labor and material obligations were included, the figure was actually 43 percent. Recall, too, that until the 1890s most zemstvo revenues were collected through land taxes based on arbitrary assessments by which the gentry consistently forced a grossly disproportionate share of the tax burden onto the peasantry.[37]

Thus, except in those zemstvo provinces fortunate enough to supplement their revenues with taxes on industrial and urban property, the lion's share of money came from peasant lands—and in many cases, the zemstvo assemblies fought stubbornly against government efforts to prod the zemstvos into reassessments. Moreover, the taxes collected from the peasantry and earmarked for education often went into secondary rather than primary schools. In 1877, the thirty-four provincial zemstvos spent more than three-quarters of all sums earmarked for education on secondary schools and scholarships to secondary schools. Information on district zemstvos is harder to obtain, but of forty-six districts in 1877–1879, ten districts allocated over 50 percent of their total outlay on education to secondary schools; thirteen districts allocated 40–49 percent, twelve districts 30–39 percent, eleven districts 20–29 percent, and no district allocated less than 20 percent.[38]

There were individual zemstvos whose efforts were wholly and consistently dedicated to primary education; among them were Perm' and Viatka—where there were no gentry. Moreover, many zemstvos defended spending peasant money on secondary schools with the argument that before you could have schools you had to have teachers and that to provide teachers you needed secondary schools.[39] (In the early 1870s, the government had blocked zemstvo efforts to establish independent seminaries for teachers.) Still, the gentry did not attend the village schools; they *did* enroll in the secondary schools, and thus the net effect of the policy was to subsidize the education of the gentry. It would in fact be more accurate to say that peasants were sponsoring not only their own but also the gentry's education.

Before the 1880s, zemstvo schools had been established and organized by the peasant community; by the 1880s, the zemstvos had begun to provide salary supplements for local teachers and to poke here and there into other aspects of schooling. During that decade, much of the zemstvo effort went into supporting the less expensive and less ambitious literacy schools (which generally offered only two years of instruction rather than the minimum of three required by the Education Statute), into subsidizing Church schools, or even into turning over all of the existing schools to the Church. As late as the turn of the century, peasants were paying as much as 43 percent of the direct costs of schooling. The zemstvo school was in all but name a peasant school.

INTERVENTION AFTER 1890

What happened after the 1880s? The following pages complete the description of school finances by carrying the story up to 1911, even though in so doing we intrude into a new era of zemstvo history. A revolution in school finances occurred in the 1890s, the result of a joint government-zemstvo endeavor—both had given low priority to popular education until 1890, but both moved rapidly after that date to bring about universal education. (The reasons for this change in attitude are the subject of the next chapter.)

Table 1 indicates that between 1879 and 1911 the burden of direct financing of public education gradually shifted away from the village commune. Even allowing for the distortions caused by omitting the costs of fuel deliveries, janitorial services, and other labor dues provided by the peasantry, the proportional monetary contribution of the village community as a share of all outlays on schools declined significantly—this during a time when the general quality of the school buildings, furniture, textbooks, and equipment seems to have been steadily improving. Moreover, in absolute terms, the peasant contribution rose only threefold between 1879 and 1911 whereas that of the zemstvo increased nearly

Table 1
Sources of Funding for Rural Schools,
1879 and 1911

	PERCENTAGE OF FUNDS SUPPLIED	
	1879[a]	*1911*
Central government	11.3%	45.0%
Zemstvo	43.4	29.6
Village commune	32.3	14.8
Church and philanthropic organizations[b]	1.3	1.3
Private	6.4	6.0
Fees	3.0	1.6
Other	0.7	1.6

SOURCES: Compiled from MNP, *Odnodnevnaia perepis'* 16:51, 117; Fal'bork, *Vseobshchee obrazovaniie v Rossii,* 208–209; Johnson, *Russia's Educational Heritage,* 292; Hans, *History of Russian Educational Policy,* 229–232; Fal'bork and Charnoluskii, *Narodnoe obrazovanie,* 194–198; Veselovskii, *Istoriia zemstva* 1:568–570; *Svodka svedenii,* sec. 11, 15.

NOTE: The 1879 study included the fifty European provinces, whereas the 1911 School Census covered the entire Empire. However, because schooling was so infrequent outside European Russia, the data remain roughly comparable.

[a] The figures in the original data add up to only 98.4 percent.

[b] Includes local parishes and monasteries. The budget of the Holy Synod came from the central government.

seven times, and the central government's share increased forty-one times.[40]

Granted that by 1910 the financial contribution of the peasant had declined and others had picked up the bill for the direct cost of schooling; for our purposes it is more important to determine precisely when this change occurred and gained momentum. In terms of the zemstvos' outlays on education, the period from 1869 to 1895 was one of slow but steady increase, both in the absolute sums spent on education and the proportion of the total zemstvo budgets spent on schools (schooling at all levels). A radical break occurred after 1895 and particularly after 1900, when zemstvo ex-

Table 2
Zemstvo Outlays on
Education, 1871–1910

	AMOUNT (IN RUBLES)
1871	1,600,000
1876	4,091,000
1880	5,200,000
1890	7,225,800
1895	9,128,600
1900	16,924,300
1906	25,314,000
1910	42,882,000

SOURCES: *Svodka svedenii,* sec. 11, 15; Veselovskii, *Istoriia zemstva* 1:567–580.

penditures on education increased from 17 million to 43 million rubles in the ten years between 1900 and 1910. (See Table 2.) (Between 1871 and 1898, the total increase had been only 8.1 million.) The average annual increase in the education allotments in zemstvo budgets was 12,400 rubles in the seventies, 5,900 rubles in the eighties, 11,800 between 1890 and 1895, 38,200 between 1895 and 1900, and 86,000 each year during the decade from 1901 to 1910 (with considerable variation from province to province). Similarly, as a proportion of growing overall zemstvo budgets, education outlays rose from 5 percent in 1868 to 14 percent in 1895, then increased to 31.1 percent by 1914.[41]

Expenditures by the central government on primary education increased at a snail's pace between 1862 and 1895, then rose from 2 million to 5 million rubles in one year, doubled between 1896 and 1900, doubled once more by 1907 (despite the severe financial strains created by the war and revolution), and then soared from slightly over 19 million in 1907 to 82.2 million in 1914— more than fourfold in seven years. As a proportion of the regular state budget, all government outlays on education at all levels stood at 2.69 percent in 1881, declined to 2.44 percent in 1895, rose again to 3.22 percent in 1900 and then to 7.21 percent in 1914.[42]

It took nearly forty years for expenditures on *primary* education to rise from .3 percent to .6 percent of the state budget. This percentage actually declined between 1897 and 1908, but then increased nearly fourfold, to 2.25 percent in 1913. Considering primary education outlays as a percentage of the total budget of the MNP alone shows a much more dramatic increase: from 18 percent in 1900 to 44 percent in 1914. (Although it was lower than the 20.8 percent of 1868, the 1900 figure was an increase from the low point of 14 percent recorded in 1884.) [43] Thus, the turn of the century was a watershed for the government as well.

Is it valid to distinguish between the contribution made by *officialdom* to primary education and that made by the *public* (the zemstvos)? This distinction has often proven to be false and misleading; even when appropriate, it works to the disadvantage of the zemstvo. Arguments frequently cited in support of the distinction stem from data comparing zemstvo and nonzemstvo provinces, zemstvo and government (Church) schools, and public and government outlays on education, as well as from the contention that the two elites were locked in struggle, were at loggerheads, and that for the first thirty years after 1864, the government's main objective was to stifle zemstvo efforts or, failing that, to promote its own schools. We need to examine more closely, then, the information on sources of funding—public and official—and comparisons of regions of zemstvo activity with those administered solely by officialdom.

Consider the problem of investments in education. As a proportion of total budget, zemstvo expenditures on education far exceeded those of the central government; champions of the zemstvo have often pointed to this as a sign of the zemstvo commitment. But a moment's reflection shows that such a comparison is fatuous; after all, zemstvos did not have to raise armies, conduct foreign policy, and so forth. It is worth pausing to ask, however, how zemstvo budgets managed a radical increase in outlays on education around the turn of the century—an increase not only in absolute outlays but also as a proportion of total budget. At least part of the explanation lies in decisions made by the central government that relieved the zemstvos of other responsibilities and allowed them to redirect the flow of finances.

During this period, the government gradually released the

Table 3
Zemstvo Outlays on Local Government
Institutions, 1890–1913

	AMOUNT (IN RUBLES)	AS PERCENTAGE OF TOTAL ZEMSTVO BUDGET
1890	12,227,000	25.9%
1900	6,840,000	7.7
1910	8,313,000	4.9
1913	10,234,700	4.0

SOURCE: B. B. Veselovskii, "Zemskie finansy," in Veselovskii and Frenkel', *Iubileinyi zemskii sbornik,* 170.

zemstvos from financial responsibility for local administration, courts, jails, and police, which initially had consumed a large part of the zemstvo budget. These so-called mandatory expenditures—which had effectively turned the zemstvo into an arm of the local bureaucracy—declined slowly but steadily from 63 percent of all zemstvo expenditures in 1868 to 39.6 percent in 1890 (25.9 percent allocated directly to local offices). During the 1890s, however, the central government moved to assume most of the remaining mandatory expenditures, and by 1913 the zemstvos were paying only 4 percent of their budgets for the upkeep of local institutions, as shown in Table 3.

The reduction of mandatory expenditures was in effect a release of large sums to be spent at the discretion of the zemstvo on medicine and education. Thus, in this area at least, it is unfair to draw a sharp line between official and zemstvo monies, for the central government could just as easily have spent the money itself, while continuing to require that the zemstvo pay for the upkeep of local offices. Instead, by freeing funds for local use, the government was providing the zemstvos the opportunity to build more schools.

At the same time, subsidies *to* the zemstvos from the central government were increasing; subsidies rose from 9.5 million rubles in 1900 to 67.6 million rubles in 1913—or from 10.7 percent to

26.6 percent of the zemstvo budgets. Perhaps more to the point, 22.5 percent of the combined provincial and district zemstvo educational budgets in 1910 came from government subsidies.[44] Earlier we saw that the slow pace of increases in zemstvo educational budgets *before* 1890 could be largely explained by the recognition among the gentry leaders that any increase in zemstvo revenues would have had to come from land reassessments, bringing into line the taxes paid by gentry and peasantry on land of similar quality—something the zemstvos everywhere resisted, even when prodded by the government. *After* 1890, much of the zemstvo energy in school construction can be explained not by measures that involved any financial sacrifice by the gentry (such as tax redistribution), but rather by the initiative of the central government, which both provided direct subsidies and released monies from other uses.

Historians have often contrasted zemstvo and official efforts by comparing progress in the zemstvo and nonzemstvo provinces. Although educational gains were far more rapid and extensive in the provinces with zemstvos, and average outlays per school, per pupil, and per capita were far higher in the zemstvo provinces by 1911 (see Table 4), such comparisons have several glaring shortcomings.[45]

First, the thirteen European nonzemstvo provinces had a far higher concentration of non-Russian, particularly non-Orthodox, minorities. (This, of course, was even more the case for the Baltic and Asian regions.) Because Russification and religious conversion were pursued by the state through the schools, particularly after 1881, the population in these areas often had good reason to resist the spread of official schooling. In the Baltic and Polish provinces, where schooling had been quite advanced by 1864, enrollments actually declined in the last quarter of the century. This undoubtedly reflects poorly on the policies of the Russian government, but it tells us little about the level of zemstvo energy in neighboring provinces.

Second, as late as 1911, zemstvo schools were a minority of all primary schools in twenty-four of the thirty-four zemstvo provinces; zemstvo teachers were a minority of all teachers in nineteen provinces, and only a minority of all enrolled pupils were in zemstvo schools in fifteen zemstvo provinces. In no province did the

Table 4

Average Outlays on Education in Zemstvo and Nonzemstvo Provinces,
1879 and 1911 (in rubles)

| | 1879 | | | 1911 | | |
EXPENDITURE	34 Zemstvo Provinces	13 Nonzemstvo Provinces	50 European Provinces	34 Zemstvo Provinces	13 Nonzemstvo Provinces	50 European Provinces
Per school	374.80	194.00	305.00	850.00	573.00	753.00
Per pupil	6.70	5.20	6.00	13.50	9.60	11.90
Per capita	.098	.06	.09	.62	.38	.51

SOURCES: MNP, Odnodnevnaia perepis' 16:51, 117, 194; Charnoluskii, Zemstvo i narodnoe obrazovanie 1:68; Veselovskii, Istoriia zemstva 1:471–472, 581.

NOTE: Statistics presented here for European Russia, excluding ten Polish provinces.

number of zemstvo schools exceed 62 percent of total schools, the number of zemstvo teachers exceed 85 percent, or the number of pupils in zemstvo schools exceed 72 percent. In a few zemstvo provinces, only three out of ten schools were zemstvo schools, and in one province, Bessarabia, the figure was only one in ten. Thus, even in the most basic measure of educational expansion—the number of schools, teachers, and pupils—progress in the zemstvo provinces was a joint government-zemstvo venture. Moreover, as we have already seen, individual zemstvo schools after 1900 were jointly financed by state and zemstvo.[46]

We should also measure the gains in education in each province relative to conditions prevailing there before the establishment of zemstvo institutions (a task which should be combined with studies of the politics of individual zemstvos, but which is beyond the scope of this work). In addition, we should note that when the government committed itself to a campaign to implement universal schooling after 1907, it began by granting subsidies to the zemstvo provinces, on the assumption that it was best to complete the school network in those areas where it was already most developed and then to proceed to other areas of the country. Thus, government policy after 1907 provided additional advantages to provinces that had already taken the greatest strides in primary education.

For all these reasons, it makes little sense to distinguish between a "public" (nongovernment elite) and an official effort in primary education. This is not to say that the zemstvos contributed nothing to the cause, either before or after 1890, but rather that the scope of their contribution has been grossly overstated—and the scope of the government contribution understated. In particular, given the decision by the government to release funds for the zemstvos to spend at their own discretion, the distinction between sources says little about relative commitment. Thus, we may speak only of elite indifference before 1890 and of joint elite intervention after that date, not of a tug-of-war between a benevolent zemstvo and an obscurantist government.

What then can be said about elite funding of primary education on the eve of World War I? Before 1890, elite intervention took place on a small scale only. The occasional and short-lived efforts by the zemstvo to promote education were local rather than national in scope and ordinarily consisted of subsidies and aid extended to existing peasant schools. After 1890, the government and zemstvo rapidly—and jointly—took over the funding of primary education. By World War I, Russia had reached the stage considered by Carlo Cipolla to be a precondition of the rapid expansion of basic education: the direct costs of schooling had been assumed by the state, leaving only the indirect, opportunity costs to the parent.[47] But why, exactly, did the 1890s witness this sharp departure from the tradition of elite indifference to one of massive intervention?

4

Intervention:

The Transformation of Elite Attitudes

The 1890s marked a major turning point in zemstvo efforts to promote primary education in the countryside. The new surge of energy in school affairs can be explained not only by the shock waves generated by the major famine that hit large sections of Russia in 1891–1892 and by the changing of the guard after the death of Alexander III in 1894, but also as a specific political conjuncture, when "for the first time, the old socialist dreams of 'going to the people' coalesced in practice with the ideals of small deeds liberalism."[1] Press accounts—perhaps unjust—of government ineptitude and callousness during famine relief efforts in the Volga region in the spring of 1892 began a decade of widespread agitation for the extension of political freedoms. This agitation merged with the growing labor movement in the cities after 1896; with student disorders, which assumed threatening dimensions by 1898; with growing unrest among minorities in the Russian Empire; and finally in 1902 with peasant disorders, which were occurring on a scale unseen in the nineteenth century. The wave of political energy crested in the 1905 Revolution and then subsided, leaving a shaken but intact political structure. The movement of "society" against "government" was clearly a number of movements—and although they were not entirely synchronic and certainly not harmonious in their goals and demands, such differences were often overlooked during the 1890s in the rush for change.

One demand on which all forces seemed to agree was the need for universal primary education as a precondition of progress. A delegate to the Khar'kov zemstvo said in 1897:

Poverty and ignorance—here are the main reasons for all our ills. Which of these two sores is worse is difficult to say. We are only sure that they are tightly and inseparably connected and causally interdependent: we are poor because we are ignorant, and ignorant because we are poor—how can we escape this vicious circle, which ill should we cure first?[2]

The concern for public education became so widespread in Russia in the nineties that enrollment rates and per capita expenditures on schooling came to be regarded by the educated public as the best measurements of a country's strength and level of civilization. Relentlessly the message was driven home: if too much education was dangerous for the unsophisticated, too little education was dangerous for the nation's health. As in the West, the assumption that literacy and progress were identical became part of progressive dogma, even reaching deeply into governmental circles.

By this time, the question posed in Khar'kov had been resolved in the minds of many, and the solution differed radically from that offered a decade earlier. Darlington summarized this change in attitudes: "Whereas in the early eighties the prevalent note of the discussion had been, 'we are poor, and therefore we cannot have schools,' the general drift of the discussion ten years later might with equal aptness be summarized in the words, 'we are poor, and therefore we must have schools.'"[3]

This change in elite attitude justifies calling the 1890s the beginning of a new period in the history of Russian education. Insofar as we can speak of the central government as a single actor rather than as a conglomeration of forces often tugging in opposite directions, the decision to actively promote the cause of mass education came a decade later and gained full force in the last years of the Empire.[4]

It has been customary to see the humanitarian impulse as a constant among zemstvo leaders and to attribute the slow pace of zemstvo educational activity before 1890 not to indifference but to the weight of government restrictions.[5] In fact, as N. V. Chekhov—

a party to this myth—pointed out, the first decade of heightened zemstvo activity coincided with a plethora of new government regulations intended to harness zemstvo energies. I shall argue that the nineties witnessed, if not a change in attitudes, then certainly a shift in priorities, with primary education emerging at the top of the list.

Certainly school reform was an ideal focal point for the combined efforts of the new professional intelligentsia, zemstvo liberals, and reform-minded industrialists. The St. Petersburg and Moscow Literacy Committees (under the Imperial Free Economic Society and the Moscow Agricultural Society, respectively) became the headquarters of progressive zemstvo notables and Third Element workers until these committees were closed down in all but name by the government in 1895 and 1896. Membership in the school board under the Society for the Dissemination of Technical Knowledge, founded in 1871, jumped from 150 in 1880 to 397 in 1897. Three congresses organized by the Permanent Pedagogical Commission of this society (the first in 1888–1889 in St. Petersburg, the second in 1894–1895 in Moscow, and the third in St. Petersburg in 1903–1904) brought together thousands of industrialists and education specialists to discuss a wide range of problems and elucidate the links between education and productivity in industry and agriculture. In 1898, the Moscow Pedagogical Society of the Imperial University was founded and became the meeting place for professors, secondary school teachers, school physicians, and educational writers.[6]

Although most activists deserted the literacy committees in the two capitals after the Ministry of Education took control of them in 1895, the slack was soon taken up by other organizations. One was the Khar'kov Literacy Society, which, despite its membership of over seven hundred in 1900, its sponsorship by such figures as A. Rubinstein and F. Chaliapin, and its energetic efforts, has received little attention from Western historians. Other literacy societies mushroomed after 1900 in provinces such as Poltava, Nizhnii Novgorod, Ekaterinoslav, Tambov, Kursk, Orenburg, and even Irkutsk. In 1898, 135 of these societies existed; by 1917, the number had risen to 270.[7]

Perhaps the most important and prominent forum for educators after 1905 was the League of Education, established in 1906 by former members of the Moscow Literacy Committee. The league created a network of local organizations that brought together progressive educators, but its most notable activity was drafting a proposal to implement universal education, a proposal that it submitted to the Second Duma and circulated throughout Russia for discussion. This proposal formed the core of the platform for school reform advocated by progressive educators after 1905.[8]

Another sign of the growing interest in primary education was the emergence of a specialized pedagogical press. Most of the Russian journals concerned exclusively with education and pedagogy date from the early 1890s. Indeed, two of the most prominent Russian educational journals, *Russian School* (*Russkaia shkola*) and *Messenger of Education* (*Vestnik vospitaniia*), were founded in 1890. By 1899, interest was so great that one indexer listed over eleven thousand separate articles and books published on education in Russia. After 1905, pedagogical activity, measured in terms of the output of specialized journals, increased even more: of the 157 pedagogical journals published between 1860 and 1917, roughly 100 first appeared after 1905.

This interest spilled over into the so-called thick journals such as *Russian Opinion* (*Russkaia mysl'*), Russian Wealth (*Russkoe bogatstvo*), and *Russian Messenger* (*Russkii vestnik*). It is difficult to find an issue of these journals from the 1890s without at least one lengthy article devoted to the question of universal literacy, to the strenuous efforts to educate the *muzhik* in this or that province, to peasant reading habits, to the miserable living conditions endured by the valiant rural teacher, or to the current congress of education in one of the capital cities.[9]

Promoters of education took every opportunity to present their needs and goals to the educated public. In the words of one contemporary:

After the terrible famine of 1891–1892, the question of education became urgent. One of the striking features of the nineties was that at even the most specialized congresses and during discussions of the most varied problems imaginable, it was unanimously concluded that the promotion of education was indispensable.[10]

The Second Congress on Technical and Professional Education was really the first *general* convention on education—its Ninth
Section (General Affairs) was devoted exclusively to education and
was by far the most widely attended session.[11] Although the Ministry of Education had published regulations in 1881 and 1885
making the convening of teachers' congresses virtually impossible,
teachers met at the Nizhnii Novgorod Exhibition of 1896, calling
openly for an all-Russian teachers' union. After the Ministry of
Education liberalized the rules governing congresses, three hundred delegates representing twenty-five thousand teachers met in
Moscow over the winter vacation in 1902–1903. At yet another
gathering, the Fourth All-Russian Agricultural Exhibit held in
Moscow in December 1895, the Moscow Literacy Committee organized a large display. The famous Zemstvo Congress of 6–7
November 1904, held in St. Petersburg, included a number of
points concerning education in its political demands to the government. (Conversely, gatherings ostensibly organized to discuss education were sometimes used as a cover for more narrowly political
activities—the Kursk Education Exhibition of 22–30 June 1902 is
one outstanding example.)[12] Even the local committees of Sergei
Witte's Special Commission on the Needs of Local Industry, convened in 1902, produced a chorus of pleas for the spread of general
education as the first step in improving conditions in the countryside. Likewise, a survey of zemstvo assemblies found a virtually
universal belief that a solution to the agrarian crisis could only be
found through literacy.[13]

After a brief spell of inactivity following the turmoil of 1905–
1907, the level of public activities connected with primary education rose again. Although the press devoted the most attention to
the All-Zemstvo Congress on Education held in Moscow in 1911,
the years immediately preceding World War I were also host to an
All-Russian Congress on Public Education (22 December 1913–
3 January 1914), an All-Russian Library Congress (1–7 June 1911),
a Congress on Extramural Education, and a Congress on Educational Statistics in Khar'kov in 1913. All congresses were well attended and were the focus of considerable public attention.

Many of the activists in the various committees and organizations and on the editorial boards of journals were in fact employed

by the zemstvos, and it was the zemstvos who mounted the most sustained drive to promote education. The turning point was clearly in the period from 1894 to 1897, when, after three decades of indifference to primary school concerns in the districts, the provincial zemstvos throughout the country actively took up the cause. In this three-year interval, twenty-four provincial assemblies addressed the question of universal education; seventeen of these actually undertook systematic statistical work to determine the state of education in the province, and twenty set up special loan and grant funds to help construct schools. An even more serious signal of intent was the establishment of permanent school commissions in twenty-three provinces, and school bureaus—nineteen by 1908—in nearly all the remainder of the thirty-four zemstvo provinces. By the end of the century, many provincial zemstvos had accepted the responsibility of offering loans and subsidies for the construction and maintenance of schools, for supplements to teachers' salaries, for school libraries, and, in some cases, for school breakfasts and night lodgings for pupils who otherwise could not attend school. In turn, the principle of free education, initially accepted only by Moscow and a few other provinces, was now nearly universally recognized.[14]

Finally, zemstvo petitions to the government, a venerated if useless tradition (since the government seldom bothered to reply), increased sharply in number in the 1890s. These petitions called for increased aid to the schools and, somewhat incongruously, for total decentralization of the school system. According to Veselovskii, no one really expected these efforts to be successful; instead, the petitions served to propagandize zemstvo goals and provide a platform around which progressive forces could be rallied.[15]

EDUCATION AS THE CURE

What prompted this fundamental change in attitudes throughout elite society? What moved a society fond of debate and idle projects to immediate action? Many historians allude to the 1891–1892 famine as the explanation for the step-up in activity in the 1890s. The "democratic movement," so the argument goes, needed to recruit peasants into the struggle against the Tsar—and the only way peasants could participate intelligently in politics was if they were educated.

Certainly many who were politically active in Russia had learned from John Stuart Mill that basic education is a prerequisite of democracy, and even more had drawn the same lesson from the writings of Jules Simon, a popular, if sententious, contemporary French educator. There is an element of truth to the argument that the zemstvos "approached the problem of elementary education in the spirit of nineteenth-century European liberalism."[16] Still, it is hard to read the journals and conference papers of the time without coming away with the impression that other, more powerful forces were at work.

What was emerging, in fact, was a confluence of forces promoting general education as a solution to the core problems often associated with the transitional phases of modernization. Some saw the problem as one of labor productivity and labor discipline. To others, it was one of agricultural output and techniques; to still others, one of military strength. Finally, some saw the schools as a means of ensuring social control. And certainly the efforts of Western European countries in promoting primary education were a stimulus, for any major development in Europe was likely to have an impact in a country that was acutely aware of its relative backwardness and eager to emulate the West.

Soviet historians, who noted some thirty years ago that "the very fact of the rapid development of industry and agriculture placed on the agenda the question of manpower resources, of literate, educated, capable workers," have focused—albeit fuzzily—on one of the key elements of the picture.[17] The concern with labor resources was indeed widespread at the time. One of the most widely cited publications was a collection of articles entitled *The Economic Significance of Education,* composed of several reports to the Second Conference on Technical and Professional Education. The publicity given to the volume and the broad credence given to the authors' arguments make this source an excellent barometer of public opinion and indicate a high level of concern for the relationship between literacy and labor productivity.[18]

The editor of the volume, the renowned economist I. I. Ianzhul, provided a general framework for understanding the relationship between education and work with the observation that "work with machines calls for order, precision, accuracy, the ability to conceptualize; that is, all those qualities which can only rarely be found in the completely uneducated person."[19] More specialized papers by A. Gorbunov, L. Gavrishev, and P. Shestakov presented detailed studies of workers in individual factories. Summarizing the conclusions, one Professor Dukhovskoi was quoted in *Russian Opinion:*

All the answers received [in the surveys] lead to the recognition that literacy unquestionably makes the worker more productive; that the worker who has made it through the public school is more resourceful, better understands the nature of the work given him, and is more skillful at preserving and economizing material . . . that he requires less supervision [*kontrol'*]; and finally, that such a worker can learn how to handle machines and tools more rapidly.[20]

We are not concerned with testing the validity of these studies, but simply record the broad acceptance of these conclusions. The methods used by these investigators—studying wages as a firm index of labor productivity—would raise some eyebrows today; recent studies of the relationship between education and industrialization in the West question the simple cause-and-effect description so evident in these reports. Few today would accept the argument presented in the *Popular Encyclopedia* volume on education, which matched two columns, one showing the rise in education expenditures in England in the second half of the nineteenth century, the other demonstrating a corresponding increase in national income. The conclusion? Education was the direct cause of England's rising prosperity! Only the fact that the link between education and productivity had become an integral part of the liberal canon could have allowed such fatuity to pass without question.[21]

One more element of the labor productivity question must be mentioned. Would the costs of education balance the gains in the factory? The answer was provided by a contribution to *The Economic Significance of Education:*

The higher the level of culture, the more productive is labor—whether factory or cottage industry. . . . The cost of school education for the future worker is inconsequential compared to the profit to be derived from the acquisition during his studies of the habit of thinking through [problems] and successfully using the knowledge he has gained.[22]

A similar logic was evident among specialists in agriculture. Learned treatises, popular brochures, and resolutions voted by congresses proclaimed that the mounting agricultural crisis required improvements in rotation systems and cropping methods as well as land redistribution, that knowledge of improved methods could best be spread through the written word, and that the peasant with a general education would be far more receptive to innovation. A contributor to *The Economic Significance of Education* asked rhetorically: "How can improved methods be conveyed to the agriculturalist when he doesn't even have access to the most basic tool for the dissemination of ideas—literacy?" Some also pointed out that a general basic education would ease the transition from agricultural to industrial labor.[23]

Not only industry and agriculture but also the health of the population was perceived to be at stake. In 1896, a congress of Russian specialists on syphilis complained that "the ignorance of the population and the low level of culture is hindering the success of the struggle with syphilis in the rural localities of Russia."[24] Concerning child care, Nancy Frieden has recently written of the medical profession in Russia: "Having diagnosed the basic ailment as cultural backwardness, physicians recommended education as the cure."[25]

The perceived utility of education spurred Russia to build schools for one other reason—the belief that literate conscripts were necessary to handle modern weapons and fight wars. An article on elementary education in the prestigious Brokgaus-Efron Encyclopedia claimed that Prussia's devastating victories over Austria in 1866 and France in 1870, along with the widespread belief that "the Prussian schoolteacher was responsible for the victory at Sedan," helped push through the English school reforms of 1870 and contributed to the passage of the 1874 Military Statute in Russia.[26] This thought remained in the minds of educators in the early twentieth century. The *Popular Encyclopedia* published by I. D. Sytin for the new mass reader stated in the introduction to the volume on education that Japan in 1904 had five times as many teachers relative to its population as did Russia and concluded, "From these figures it is clear why the Asiatics defeated us: they are better educated than we!"[27]

Thus the notion of the utility of education found wide recognition among the educated public. Today, the socialization functions of the school environment gain just as much attention from specialists. To cite one authority: "Punctuality, quiet, order, work in large groups, response to orders, to bells, to timetables, respect for authority, even tolerance of monotony, boredom, punishment, lack of reward and regular attendance at place of work are habits to be learned in school."[28]

Although the strong note of cynicism would have been out of place in Russian writings of the time, in 1893 the prominent journal *Russian School* carried an article by the educator A. N. Strannoliubskii, extolling precisely these same classroom qualities:

The school is valuable not only in that it develops and enlightens the mind, providing ennobling and useful knowledge . . . but also because it fosters character and disciplines the personality. The regularity and sequential order of course work, which do not allow for deviations because of arbitrary whim, encourage the habit of correct daily labor, order, and symmetry, and teach the pupil to value time. . . . The authority of the teacher, who is independent in his actions not only of the will of the student but also of [the] parents, fosters trust in the authority of rational power, the ability to consciously and willingly submit to this power, and the habit of respect for the law and sows the conviction, based on personal experience, that law-abiding behavior leads to well-being, while violations of the law can only bring harm.[29]

Readers might feel that we are descending a great slope of perceptions, from a roseate view of human nature and the liberating functions of education, the ideal of "preparing the child for life and democracy" that governed progressive pedagogy, to a more calculating notion of the school's "utility" and the need for basic skills to ensure national strength, and finally, to a chillier proto-Foucault vision of schools as institutions of social control, where teachers resemble wardens. We reach the sunless bottom as we encounter those proponents of education whose only use for the school was as a means to replace the discipline and hierarchy of the old serf order, as a dam to hold back the waves of *buntarstvo,* the rebellious outbursts that seemed to sweep over the lower orders with increasing frequency as accelerated social change swept away old restraints. This fear was a strand in the thought of even the most distinguished zemstvo educators. It certainly loomed large in Konstantin Pobedonostsev's ruminations on education, and it also contributed to the government decision in the early twentieth century to actively promote education. Essentially, this decision represented a shift from the belief that teaching peasants to read and write would introduce them to harmful concepts and foster dissatisfaction with their station in life, or even foster "chaos and sedition," to a new fear of the looming and imminent dangers of uncontrolled literacy or, even worse, a total release of social control accompanying the breakdown of traditional institutions. As Shipman has observed: "In societies which are starting to modernize, with new working conditions, mobility, and the decline of traditional institutions, a void appears which is filled by the schools."[30] The essential shift, then, was from resisting change to attempting to direct change through control over the schools.

The attempt to restore control and consensus in a society undergoing the strains of rapid modernization provided the impulse to educate the people and explains the transformation in elite attitudes. Addressing a similar situation in the West, Harvey Graff writes:

With the breakdown of traditional patterns of deference, in the face of capitalism's social transformations, the inculcation of morality and its behavioral attributes without literacy was increasingly seen as impossible. Education now substituted for paternalism as a source of order, cohesion, and hegemony in a society stratified by social class rather than by rank.[31]

The notion of using education to combat the deleterious effects of social change was not entirely new in Russia. At the annual meeting of the Imperial Moscow Agricultural Society in 1844, S. A. Maslov, speaking in favor of schools for peasants, declared that "the morals of the Russian people are visibly declining with the influx of new notions, with the gradual move of the folk from a simple rural and agricultural life to one of the factory and manufacturing." He suggested that Russia borrow a measure proposed by Lord Russell, "who introduced a bill in the English

House on the necessity of spreading the foundations of a religious and moral education among the people."[32]

Zemstvo leaders also saw that the dangers of illiteracy exceeded those of literacy. Baron Korf, the leading light in zemstvo education during the sixties and seventies, wrote:

The education of the masses is an essential need of state and society, who must therefore act upon this need; for the more educated and developed the masses, the better for the rights of property and civil order, on which the state rests. . . . How deeply Russia has already suffered from the ignorance of the masses! How much the Pugachev revolt [*Pugachevshchina*], cholera riots, and hopes for a second liberation have cost Russia![33]

This fear of *buntarstvo* expressed by the founder of the zemstvo school can also be detected in the most prominent and ingenuous proponent of education in the nineties, V. P. Vakhterov. Expressing the old Lavrov-populist notion that the Russian intellectual had been given the leisure time to pursue self-development by education only through the sweat and toil of the less privileged masses, Vakhterov added a certain urgency to the conclusion that only service to the people could repay this accumulated debt.

The people need knowledge and futilely search for it under every stone; from sorcerers, magicians, wanderers, religious dissenters; in broadsides, oracles, dreambooks; in pagan beliefs and traditions. And . . . certainly the members of the intelligentsia can and must share their knowledge with the people who feed them. Today it is particularly important to underscore this fact. Innumerable signs indicate that the moment we are living through is both serious and critical. If we let the moment pass, if the broadest measures to promote public education are not undertaken by the government, and equally by public institutions and private individuals, if right now a universal crusade against ignorance is not declared, then it will be too late. The tavern, the village kulak, the factory, the inn, and other products of contemporary economic relations will gain the upper hand against the healthier sides of the life of the people and will produce such public morals that schools and libraries will then be powerless to halt the degeneration and decay.[34]

A similar sentiment was prominently expressed in the pages of the *Journal of the Ministry of Education* (*ZhMNP*) in 1906. The author, V. V. Akimov, described the events caused by the circulation of a pamphlet in the countryside in 1899. Written by one Professor Fal'b and entitled "Doomsday, 13 November 1899," the pamphlet included passages such as this: "The earth was plunged into the pitch dark of night, heavy stifling air made breathing difficult, people and animals suffocated; the inhabitants of the area hid in their cellars. And then at noon a comet appeared and with stunning speed hurtled toward the earth, leaving a fiery red glow. Suddenly a frightening thud was felt. . . . If the world ends on 13 November 1899, I advise you to be ready." As that day approached, peasants refused to sign labor contracts effective after 10 November, the local taverns filled up, and crowds became increasingly unruly; in Khar'kov, peasants slaughtered and consumed their stock and even left the crops to rot in the fields. Others dressed in their finest, lit "*strastnye*" candles in front of icons, and caroused all night long, "waiting for the last trumpets of the Archangel." Akimov, obviously alluding to the ongoing disorders in Russia as well as to this minor event, wrote:

It is only against a background of endemic ignorance that popular disturbances, now relentlessly increasing and threatening to reach ominous dimensions, could have erupted. After all, even the most absurd notion, the most fantastic rumor, finds in the country today fertile soil for dissemination, and when we realize that we are talking about tens of millions of people mired in ignorance, the full import of this dire situation stands out in sharp relief.[35]

The growing fear of disorders stemming from popular ignorance and superstition was linked to the sudden collapse of faith in the rural commune as a bulwark of stability, traditional values, hierarchy, and loyalty to the throne, a change of attitude among the elite that led directly to the Stolypin reforms and the effort to dismantle the rural commune in the countryside.

But along with this fear of "darkness," as the Russian phrase had it, went a growing fear of the wrong kind of light penetrating the village. The elite feared the growing phenomenon of "wild" or extra-school literacy (*dikaia gramotnost'*); it was in the 1890s, as we have seen, that numerous books and articles produced evidence of the existence of peasant-sponsored schools in the countryside, showing that the urge to read and write was outpacing the abilities of the formal school network. In his influential proposal to implement universal education, A. N. Kulomzin of the Ministry of Finance asked rhetorically whether public literacy or ignorance was more dangerous politically and asserted that the fact that literacy was growing more rapidly than the school system represented a "major political danger."[36]

"WE MUST, WE CAN HAVE SCHOOLS . . ."

All of these considerations, arguments, fears, and points of view came together in the discussion over universal education. This discussion had long roots in Russian history, but it now gained a strong sense of urgency. Public opinion took a sharp turn in the 1890s after a speech by V. P. Vakhterov.

The public was electrified when Vakhterov, who was then inspector of schools for the city of Moscow and a member of the Moscow Zemstvo Commission on Education, gave a speech to the Moscow Literacy Committee in January 1894 favoring the immediate implementation of universal education. The committee responded by forming a special Commission on Universal Education and producing thousands of copies of the speech for distribution throughout the country. When the speech was printed later that year in *Russian Opinion,* it caused an enormous outpouring of comment in response.[37]

Vakhterov began his address with a brief summary of the history of debates on universal education in Russia. Russia, he said, in deliberating over the drafts for the 1864 Education Statute, had chosen the worst aspects of various foreign educational systems: tight control over curriculum by the central government, combined with funding of schools strictly on the basis of local, private initiative. As a result, the number of primary schools in the country had dropped substantially in the decade following 1864.

Vakhterov then turned from the familiar litany of government sins to point the finger at his listeners. The government, he declared, had rejected universal education in the sixties and seventies, "as a result of a misunderstanding . . . shared for decades by all educated persons in Russia." All estimates of the funds needed to implement universal primary education had been based on the European method of including in the school-age population all children from the ages of seven through fourteen. Confusion stemmed from the fact that most schools in Russia accepted children of these ages, *but only for a three-year stay*. In Western Europe, however, the program was far more extensive, and children were supposedly expected to complete seven full years in the schools.

Estimates of the number of schools required to meet the demands of universal education in Russia had been based on Academic Buniakovskii's calculation that in 1872 the school-age cohort (ages seven through fourteen) made up 15 percent of the total population. Instead, Vakhterov noted, the proper length of school attendance in Russia was three years, preferably beginning at the age of eight and concluding by the time the child was eleven years old. Relying on more contemporary calculations of age cohorts (i.e., Dubrovskii's), Vakhterov argued that in reality the eligible school-age cohort made up between 6.5 percent and 6.7 percent of the entire population.

Vakhterov then tried to arrive at a figure for the number of schools needed to implement universal education. But first he introduced an important caveat. "In principle," he argued, "we stand for universal, free, and also compulsory primary education." But compulsory education could succeed only if supported by the vast majority of the population—and this majority supported such education only for boys. "We fully support the widely held opinion that to teach a girl, the future mother of a family, is to ensure the literacy of her offspring." But Vakhterov predicted that, except in the case of the urban population, the compulsory education of girls would cause "rumblings" among the population. He concluded that the projected school system should include the entire school-age male population and all girls in urban areas, but only that percentage of village girls who were already enrolled (with a small allowance for annual increments). This, in substance, was Vakhterov's redefinition of universal primary education.

Strannoliubskii had claimed that Russia needed two hundred fifty thousand new schools, but Vakhterov now explained that Russia really needed only twenty-five thousand schools in the countryside and six thousand more in the cities, at an annual cost not of 125 million rubles, but rather a mere 11 million. If Vakhterov's figures were correct, universal education, the cure for all Russia's woes, was within reach! Vakhterov managed to cut these figures even more by explaining that because only a small proportion of urban budgets (7.7 percent) was being spent on education, cities could easily find the money to build and maintain six thousand schools. This left only a sum of 8.4 million rubles to be raised.

At this point, Vakhterov clarified his strategy of untangling and dealing separately with the issues surrounding universal education. On the question of where to find 8.4 million rubles, he noted:

It is possible to find numerous weighty arguments supporting the idea that the Treasury assume the major burden of education costs; but it is far more practical to separate the issue of universal education from all others. . . . For universal education to have the largest possible number of active supporters, we must not connect the issue with that of reforming sources of distribution, or with the transformation of the type of primary school which has emerged out of practice, or even with reforms in the system of control over schools. . . . For these reasons, in our calculations [of costs] we have used only the norms worked out by life itself.

Using the existing distribution of costs between government, zemstvo, and commune (roughly 10 percent, 60 percent, and 30 percent, respectively), Vakhterov concluded that in the zemstvo provinces the annual expense of new schools would cost the state 1.3 kopecks per citizen, the zemstvo less than 5 kopecks per citizen, and each commune 3 kopecks per desiatina. These figures were based on an average cost of 332 rubles for running each school—an estimate Vakhterov calculated by taking the 1880 school census figure of 271 rubles and making allowances for increased costs since that time. More important than the precise figure, however, was the fact that Vakhterov was effectively endorsing the existing school system and the low wages paid to teachers.

In the conclusion of his speech, Vakhterov proposed the establishment of "filial" schools with reduced courses taught by apprentice teachers, or boarding schools in sparsely populated areas. He waved aside the problem of opportunity costs by noting that, although the population often thought of children in terms of "labor power," the school year did not actually conflict with summer agricultural work. The cost of winter clothing and shoes was more important, but only as long as schools were few and far between and the distance covered every day by the schoolchild considerable. Finally, in the last moments of his speech, Vakhterov swept aside all objections to compulsory education and argued simply that the time was ripe.

In sum, Vakhterov made his case by discussing separately three issues that had been commonly lumped together under the phrase "universal education": the question of the accessibility of schools, the issue of compulsory education, and the problem of who was to pay. Most important, Vakhterov argued that regardless of who paid, estimates of the amount of money needed had been grossly exaggerated and based on a faulty notion, borrowed from the West, of the proper school age for children. Finally, Vakhterov made the argument for universal primary education more plausible by changing the very definition of the term to exclude most girls.

The response to the speech was truly remarkable. Vakhterov's main conclusions were endorsed by such prominent figures in the world of education and zemstvo affairs as V. I. Farmakovskii, F. Ol'denburg, I. Belokonskii, and N. Bunakov.[38] Within the government, a number of directors and inspectors of local school systems came forward with practical suggestions on how to begin the process locally.

To be sure, there were critics of the speech. In particular, many criticized his exclusion of girls from universal education plans. The harshest criticism, however, was printed in *Education* (*Obrazovanie*) and focused on Vakhterov's estimated cost of 322 rubles for each school. In the eyes of his critics, this sum was wrong for two reasons. First, it seemed to endorse the existing two- and three-year schools (Church and zemstvo, respectively) just at a time when educators were mounting a campaign for an expanded program. Second, it condemned the rural teacher to a life of continuing poverty. "Wouldn't it be better," one article asked, "to dream about improving the existing schools than to double the number of schools from which impoverished teachers are sending forth youths [who have achieved] a very dubious level of literacy?"[39] Finally, most educators, even those most sympathetic to Vakhterov's report, rejected the notion of compulsory education.[40]

But it was not such specifics that gave the report its significance. Paul Miliukov, the historian and future leader of the Kadet Party and a member of the Commission on Universal Education under the Moscow Literacy Committee, noted that although Vakhterov's cost estimates were too modest, they "had a psychological impact. Compulsory education in Russia no longer seemed utopian, and the question of universal education was again given priority." Another prominent figure, A. I. Chuprov, wrote that Vakhterov had managed to foster in the zemstvos and society a "belief in the attainability of universal education in Russia and to infuse its advocates with burning energy."[41] In short, this speech, and the response to Vakhterov's critics at the Second Congress on Technical and Professional Education in 1895–1896, caught and held public attention because for the first time a prominent educator was arguing that universal education was not only desirable and necessary but also feasible.

Thus the change in attitudes that took place in the 1890s was indeed a shift from the belief that "because we are poor, we cannot afford education" to the conviction that "because we are poor, we *must* have education." Once it was decided that a basic education was necessary for the nation's health and for social tranquillity, earlier qualms about excessive government control, sources of funding, and a curriculum that concentrated on the basics rather than on broader aspects of child development were simply swept aside. In many ways, the Vakhterov speech was a sleight of hand: by redefining the very notion of universal education and cutting school budgets to the bone, he gave the country's educators a concrete and realizable goal. The tenuousness of his calculations and the fact that the schools he proposed violated many of the precepts of progressive pedagogy suggest that the speech was but a spark, that contemporary developments had already convinced his listeners to place basic education on the nation's agenda, and that the other concerns of curriculum, decentralization, child development, and the "ladder" system were now secondary to this urgent need.

THE GOVERNMENT STEPS IN

The growing sense of urgency affected the government as well. Nicholas II's marginal notations on numerous reports reveal mounting concern for the basic education of the population, both boys and girls.[42] Within the ranks of the central bureaucracy, there was growing acceptance of the need, even urgency, of educating the multitudes. By the turn of the century, the Ministry of Education (which the great populist N. Mikhailovskii had sneeringly called the "Ministry of Obscurantism"),[43] was quite willing to print in its official journal an article that stated dramatically:

[Anyone with] the slightest bit of humanity will find it impossible to accept the fact that millions of people who produce the wealth of modern society are wallowing in a mental world lower than that of the primitive. Without education, there can be no true religious sense, no public order, no public health, and no firmness or intelligibility of moral habits and convictions.

All these truths have already become truisms; we all more or less recognize their irreducible veracity. Still, the darkness of ignorance, like some kind of fantastic being, continues to hold the village in its clutches.[44]

To emphasize the point, Minister of Education P. M. von Kaufman, speaking to the Duma on 4 May 1907 in favor of the recently introduced government bill on universal education, declared:

Schools that are universally accessible and healthy [the codeword for a curriculum and teaching profession free of revolutionary ideas] are the cornerstone of national well-being. . . . It is obvious that it is no longer possible to put off universally available, if not obligatory, education; we must give our people the opportunity to see, we must lift them out of darkness. . . . No matter how great the sacrifice from the state and the people needed to provide public schools, the ministry has not hesitated before these difficulties and has accelerated its efforts to bring its proposals before the legislative bodies for confirmation, in the profound conviction that such an investment of public funds is the *most profitable* outlay of capital ever made in Russia [emphasis added].[45]

This interest was not limited to pious—or fearful—expressions of support. In 1902, the Ministry of Education established a special commission to draw up a new report on education needs. In 1903, V. I. Farmakovskii, a high official in the ministry and a well-known educator, published his plan for universal education.[46] At virtually the same time, an alternative proposal sponsored by A. N. Kulomzin in the Ministry of Finance was being circulated to the local committees of the Special Commission on the Needs of Local Industry. This proposal was picked up by the Ministry of Education and sent for comment to the curators and school directors in the bureaucratic hierarchy. The Kulomzin report, modified in its wanderings through numerous committees between 1904 and 1905, formed the core of the bill on universal education presented to the Duma in 1907.[47]

On 20 February 1907, the day the Second Duma convened, von Kaufman submitted a bill providing for the implementation of universal education. The short-lived Second Duma sent the bill to a newly formed, fifty-five-member Education Commission but had little time to act before the Duma itself was dismissed. When the Third Duma convened, von Kaufman introduced three separate bills on universal primary education, the first providing guidelines for introducing universal education throughout Russia, the other two authorizing the allocation of credits of 5.5 million and 1.4 million rubles for this purpose. In subsequent years, a number of other measures were proposed or introduced, including a bill creating a special school construction fund (22 June 1909) and a bill entirely rewriting the 1874 School Statute (23 March 1909).[48]

Because the Duma simultaneously considered a plethora of measures, some historians have confused the various bills and erroneously reported that the legislation signed into law on 3 May 1908 was a complete bill providing for the implementation of universal education.[49] In reality, the law only authorized the issue of credits and set terms similar to those presented in the 1907 Duma bill. Aside from these credits and the 1909 establishment of the school construction fund, no other law made its way through both chambers of the bicameral legislature.[50] Both the bill on universal education and the new School Statute foundered when sharp disagreement arose between the Duma and the State Council over including Church parish schools in the proposed school "network," granting state subsidies to Church schools, and transferring supervision of Church schools from ecclesiastic school boards (established in

1884) back to the secular school boards dominated by the Ministry of Education.[51] When the war broke out in 1914, both the bill on universal education and the new School Statute were held up in committee with no realistic expectation of passage. Nevertheless, it is worth noting that the terms established by the 3 May 1908 law for receiving credit and subsidies from the state treasury closely matched the specific terms of the general bill on universal education—an indication that in 1908 the Russian government began de facto, if not de jure, to move in the direction of universal education, leaving the controversial questions of jurisdiction, curriculum, and language of instruction for future resolution.

The terms governing credit and subsidies in the 3 May 1908 law bore the clear imprint of the zemstvo programs of the 1890s. In the nonzemstvo areas, the existing policy of granting subsidies of up to 700 rubles for each one-class school was simply continued. In the zemstvo provinces, however, zemstvo and municipal schools were granted subsidies of 390 rubles for every fifty students between the ages of eight and eleven, inclusive. To be eligible, the district zemstvos had to submit a plan for realizing universal education within ten years; the zemstvos were also required to maintain existing outlays on education and to relieve the peasant communities of all fees or obligations for maintaining school facilities. In addition, all schools had to have fully certified teachers and offer a four-year course of instruction (although this rule often seems to have been waived). The school network had to be based on the three-verst radial plan first proposed by Moscow province in 1896, and buildings had to meet approved hygienic standards.[52]

The 22 June 1909 law provided a further stimulus by establishing direct grants for school construction. Up to 1,500 rubles were allowed for wood-frame buildings and 2,000 for those built of stone; in no case was the grant to exceed half the actual construction costs. In addition, however, loans were made available at 3 percent, payable in twenty years. (In 1912, an amendment extended the time to forty years.)[53] By 1914, 398 district zemstvos (91 percent) and 281 municipalities (35 percent) had concluded agreements with the MNP making them eligible for grants and loans. Between 1909 and 1915, some 61.46 million rubles were spent on school construction alone. (By contrast, the entire budget of the MNP for all levels of education and for maintaining the educational bureaucracy in 1900 was only a little over 33 million rubles.)[54] There can be no question that within the zemstvo provinces the goal of universal enrollment through the combined efforts of government and zemstvo had been placed on the agenda.

But the sudden infusion of massive government subsidies also disrupted the fragile balance between provincial and district zemstvos throughout Russia, a balance that had already been disturbed by the chaotic events and tensions of 1905–1907. The government monies provided by the 1908 law were primarily in the form of subsidies to teachers' salaries, raising the question of who really employed the teachers. Because money went directly to the district zemstvos, the provincial organizations, which had recently been at the forefront of zemstvo educational efforts, were now faced with the possibility of losing all control over the school system and over the district zemstvos as well. In addition, because the zemstvo schools were under the control of the Ministry of Education, and government grants and loans were to cover up to four-fifths of all construction costs, who actually owned the buildings?[55]

In one sense, the 1908 law was a logical outgrowth of the ferment in the educational world. After all, the provisions governing grants were very close to those that had been worked out by Vakhterov and the Moscow zemstvo in the 1890s and adopted since then by a number of provincial zemstvos. The logic is the more convincing if we cast aside the old stereotypes of this period as one in which government and "society" were locked in deadly combat and realize that the interchange between society's elite and the middle levels of the bureaucratic hierarchy was considerable. In particular, it was not uncommon for members of the elite to move between government and zemstvo, and a cross-fertilization of educational ideas and plans was inevitable.

But in another sense, the 1908 law did represent a major landmark in Russian history, a break with tradition as radical as the contemporaneous Stolypin reforms, which in 1906 began a wholesale assault on the Russian peasant commune in favor of individual farms. Until 1901, the MNP had exerted direct administrative control over the school system, but only in that year had it begun direct subsidies to zemstvo schools, and only in 1908 did the subsidies become massive in scale. In effect, the ministry was borrowing a leaf from the provincial zemstvos' book: by granting huge

subsidies, the MNP became indispensable to the school system,
and by attaching strings to these subsidies, it began to assume indirect control.

$$\clubsuit$$

It is possible, then, to see that Russian education after 1864
developed in three stages. In the first, peasant-sponsored *vol'nye*
schools spread rapidly; during the second, the zemstvo "organized"
the schools and then began slowly and only partially to assume the
burden of maintenance costs. In the third, beginning after 1900 but
gaining momentum after 1908, the Ministry of Education gradually took over the zemstvo schools, first increasing control by doubling the number of inspectors in the countryside and then, in
1908, by assuming most of the costs of school construction and
maintenance—using grants to set the rules on how schools should
be built and run and who should teach. The zemstvos had done
precisely the same thing to the peasant community a generation
before.

5

Control of the Schools:

Zemstvo, Inspector, and Local School Board

A prominent theme of most histories of education is the struggle between locality and center for control of education—between self-government and bureaucratic administration, between private (or, in Russian parlance, public [*obshchestvennoe*]) and government supervision. Yet such an approach is seriously inadequate for Russian history. Linked with a polemical defense of the "forces of democracy" (the zemstvos) against the stifling weight of the bureaucratic leviathan (the autocracy), the description turns from history to morality play. As Allen Sinel astutely points out, a locally elected, representative assembly offers no automatic guarantee of a successful school program, nor does state control inevitably harm education.[1]

Recent American and Soviet scholarship contends that the degree of conflict between zemstvo and central government has been considerably overstated. As Daniel Orlovsky notes, "Preferring to concentrate on conflicts between government and zemstvos, historians have downplayed the considerable harmony and cooperation that existed between them."[2] An opposition movement did develop in the zemstvos during periods of intense crisis (though it never won a majority of delegates), and it has been common to infer from this liberal political movement, which sought political representation at the national level and protection of gentry prerogatives at the local level against the "impersonal" and alien bureaucracy, that the zemstvo also promoted welfare, education, and health care in the provinces. As Veselovskii convincingly demonstrated three-quarters of a century ago, however, the delivery of social services to the population by the zemstvo was lackluster— except when such services immediately and tangibly benefitted the gentry as well as (or instead of) the peasants. (The example of zemstvo enthusiasm for the telephone comes to mind.) Sinel makes this point forcefully:

Fundamentally opposed to autocratic government, . . . scholars believed that liberal institutions like the zemstvos could only benefit Russia and that attempts to curtail their powers were by definition retrogressive. Judging developments in elementary education in this light, they credited all successes to local societies, particularly the zemstvos. . . . For these critics the zemstvos were the major fount of pedagogical wisdom, the inspectors merely ministry policemen who had usurped functions rightfully belonging to private initiative.[3]

The pages that follow continue the discussion of the issue of control over the schools begun in Chapter 2, turning first to the Ministry of Education's struggle for a monopoly over the administration of schooling, then moving to the local level and looking more carefully at the person and functions of the local inspector, the activities of the local school board, and the effective influence of the zemstvo on teacher appointments, school supervision, and decisions of both school board and inspector. I argue that only after 1908 did the MNP gain something approximating hegemony over school affairs; that there was an enormous gap between passage of a law and its implementation at the local level; that at the local level relationships between zemstvo and Ministry of Education were generally amicable and mutually supportive; and that, although historians have given considerable weight to the inquisitorial function of the local inspectors, their role as benefactors of education has been unjustly overlooked.

THE MINISTRY OF EDUCATION AND THE
LINES OF CONTROL

At first glance, it seems easy to establish who controlled local education. Although the 1874 School Statute allowed local zemstvos to provide for schools, it was the Ministry of Education, through the network of inspectors, directors, curators, and commissions or councils at the center, that had the last word on all important issues: when and if a school could be opened; who was competent to teach, and who should be dismissed or transferred; what the content and schedule should be; what textbooks and instructional aids were permitted in the classroom.[4]

Concerning private and locally sponsored education, Darlington observed:

Some of the higher technical colleges, real-schools, and primary schools are maintained partly by state subventions and partly by funds locally contributed; others again, including nearly half the primary schools and some of the most important places of technical and commercial instruction, depend almost wholly on local funds, with little or no aid from the Imperial Treasury; and finally many are private venture schools, pure and simple. These distinctions, however, make practically no difference to the kind and degree of control exercised by the State. The State in Russia assumes control of all educational institutions, however provided and maintained, dictates their curricula, and assures itself by exactly the same means in private as in State-provided schools that its requirements have been complied with. Private schools are officially recognized as existing in order to cooperate with the views of government, and the English ideal of the School as having rights in the shape of freedom from Government inspection and the like which it can barter away to the State in exchange for Treasury grants or other privileges is one which is entirely foreign to Russian habits of thought.[5]

Yet, as should be apparent from the plethora of government departments and ministries involved in primary education, the MNP never gained a complete monopoly over primary education in the Russian Empire. During Count Dmitri Tolstoy's term as head of the MNP (1861–1880), the ministry worked hard to reverse "the legacy of Alexander I"—the failure to have precisely defined the jurisdiction of the MNP at its establishment in 1802. Miropol'skii noted that the salient feature of the school system under Nicholas was its fragmented nature; in Tolstoy's first years in office, schools in the Polish provinces, the Baltic Area, Eastern Siberia, Turkestan, and the Caucasus, as well as Arkhangel'sk and Orenburg provinces, remained outside his authority. (The 1864 Education Statute applied only to the thirty-four zemstvo provinces and the Don region, which temporarily had zemstvo institutions.) In the last quarter of the nineteenth century, at great political cost, schools in the Baltic and Polish areas were brought under MNP control: local school boards were stripped of authority, the Lutheran and Catholic churches were forced out, and the local Polish and German gentries were unceremoniously divested of all say in school matters. As a result, primary education in these areas, which since the 1840s had been far in advance of European Russia, declined precipitously. In addition, as late as the turn of the century, large areas of the country, including the Amur region, Eastern Siberia, and Turkestan, had still not been organized into educational districts, and primary education remained under the immediate control of the Governor-General of each area.[6]

But the larger failure of the MNP, if the goal was hegemony within the bureaucracy, lay in the attempt to "usurp the educational prerogatives of other bureaus." Tolstoy "acquired only those schools that his competitors wanted to get rid of." When he came to office, his major competitors in the field of education were the Holy Synod (which, of course, he also headed), the Fourth Section of the Imperial Chancery, and the War Ministry, which was headed by the progressive reformer Dmitri Miliutin. According to Tolstoy's biographer, "at the end of his term, Russia maintained her pluralistic approach to education. Even under the greatest centralizer in its history, the education department itself probably controlled less than half of Russia's schools."[7]

The fortunes of the Church parish schools are traced in another chapter. But who were the other rivals? The Fourth Section was not in reality a major rival in the field of primary education; its efforts were concentrated on secondary and higher schooling for girls. Yet to the extent that the structure of secondary education affected streaming policies, it is important to recognize that beyond the primary-school level the Fourth Section, as well as the

Ministry of Finance, had an independent say in the management and direction of education in the country. With its own Educational Committee (*Uchebnyi Komitet*), body of government inspectors, and local councils of curators, the Ministry of Finance maintained a large, popular, and growing network of "commercial schools" after 1888 under the Department of Trade and Manufactures. The commercial schools (despite their name) offered a general secondary, rather than a narrowly vocational, education and provided an important springboard of social mobility for the lower middle classes, undermining the MNP's interminable efforts to regulate advancement in society by controlling the curricula and the entrance requirements for the pro-gymnasiums and gymnasiums. Thus, if the goal of the Ministry of Education was to sponsor widespread basic education without promoting (indeed, while restricting) social mobility, it was never able to successfully limit such mobility, if only because of the simple fact of ministerial plurality. No sooner had the Minister of Education in 1887 uttered his notorious phrase about "cooks' children" and their proper place in life than the Ministry of Finance began to promote social mobility through the expansion of commercial schools.[8] (See Chapter 15.)

The efforts of the War Ministry in the sphere of primary education remain obscure. Under Miliutin, the dynamic reformer and Tolstoy's rival, the War Ministry spent 4 to 5 million rubles annually on educational institutions. With the introduction of universal conscription in 1874, all regiments were instructed to establish reading and writing schools for illiterates, and the bibliographies of readers and textbooks issued in the last quarter of the nineteenth century and the first decade of the twentieth list a number of basic readers drawn up specifically for the recruit.

There is indirect testimony that the army played a major role in spreading literacy. Before Emancipation, conscription had been, in effect, a life sentence, and thus the army could have had little impact on village life, except to deplete it of manpower. However, since conscripts now spent six years, instead of twenty-five, in the service, there was a chance that literate, army-trained peasants would return to their villages. According to Patrick Alston, the army introduced more than 1.5 million peasants to reading and writing between 1874 and 1891. John Bushnell argues that "the Tsarist army became the single most important source of literacy for Russian peasants," with 25–30 percent of all males of draft age entering the army in the final quarter of the century. Darlington's writings concur; he repeated an assertion he heard in Russia: "It is stated to be a rare thing for a soldier to leave the army at the end of his term of obligatory service without being able to read and write." Darlington estimated the number of military detachments in which there were soldiers' schools in 1898 at about 7,500.[9]

These estimates must be accepted with caution, however. Bushnell also notes that the War Ministry was most active in pursuing literacy in the 1870s; required instruction was dropped in the mid-1880s and then "even when literacy instruction was required . . . it frequently, perhaps ordinarily, remained a dead letter." He cites several officers' memoirs to substantiate the suspicion that many of the army schools, particularly after the time of Dmitri Miliutin, were fictitious operations. Moreover, Bushnell concludes from War Ministry data that the army was *not* providing literacy instruction during the period between the Russo-Japanese War and World War I: the literacy rate among conscripts was virtually identical to the literacy rate reported for the army as a whole. According to this evidence, not more than 2 to 3 percent of the soldiers, or 6 to 9 percent of all illiterate conscripts, could have been acquiring even semi-literacy (the ability to read, but not to write) in the army. That figure may even be too high—all re-enlistees would have been literate (a requirement for NCOs), a fact exerting a slight upward bias. The army's main contribution may, in fact, have been its encouragement of schooling in the countryside, of literacy gained *before* induction; until 1906, the recruit's term of service was reduced if he could produce a certificate of graduation from a primary school or could pass a test demonstrating competence in the three Rs.[10] These privileges not only spurred interest in education; they also had a tremendous impact on curriculum. According to a survey of teachers in Moscow province in the 1890s, the 1885 Regulation, which stipulated exactly what the recruit had to know, dictated how much time teachers spent on each subject and how they approached teaching. Thus, until the 1897 Model Program was issued, army regulations often set course content in the schools.

Education was of central importance to anyone concerned with national integration, social mobility and elite formation, cconomic development, or political control, and the Russian autocracy tolerated or even encouraged a great measure of overlapping authority, pluralism, multiple hierarchies of control, and diversity of sponsorship. To be sure, with the implementation of the 1908 School Bill the MNP finally undercut, perhaps irreparably, the position of the Holy Synod, as well as of the provincial zemstvo, and for the first time acquired a virtual monopoly over primary education. But a great diversity of schools—as many as sixty-two different types, by one Soviet historian's count—were still left, along with a vast no-man's-land in the all-important sector of secondary education. Most attempts at streaming—controlling the flow of pupils from one level to the next—were thus vitiated, almost nullified, and the Ministry of Education lost the power to stand guard over the gateways of social mobility.

Darlington was basically correct in his observation that underneath the bewildering profusion of types of schools there existed a basic uniformity of control, supervision, and even curriculum in Russian schooling. But as late as 1914, lines of conflicting authority, multiple jurisdiction, and competing interests still survived. The commonplace conception that power in Russia was centralized in the hands of a few administrators in the major cities, who executed their decisions through local functionaries, who in turn brooked no opposition, is simply not true. Moreover, the crazy-quilt distribution of power and authority in education operated to ensure a high degree of autonomy at the local level for anyone who was smart enough to take advantage of the loopholes and opportunities provided by fragmentation and interministerial rivalry.

THE INSPECTORATE

The issue of bureaucratic plurality, important as it is to an understanding of Russian history, must be subsumed under a more general problem: the degree of *effective* control exerted over schooling. Starr has written of the early nineteenth century: "Policies could be announced with pious resolution at the parade grounds in Petersburg, but they became concrete facts in the lives of most Russians only when applied at the provincial level." [11] To what de-

gree and with what effectiveness did the authority of the central
government reach into the village, and in particular into the village
schools?

The instrument of state control over the primary school was
the school inspector, to whom, along with the local marshall
of the nobility, the 1874 School Statute gave the power to influence
the entire direction of primary education in the countryside. The
Ministry of Education, because it could not find the funds to move
more rapidly, was very slow in establishing new inspectors' positions; indeed, the changes in the size of the inspectorate between
1874 and 1914 provide an excellent yardstick of the degree of involvement by the MNP in local education. Numbering only 34 in
1871, the cadre of inspectors increased to 102 in 1874 (three in each
province, with one becoming the director to whom the other inspectors were subordinate); in the next two years, another 76 new
posts were added. During the period from 1869 to 1874, most inspectors received their assignments in zemstvo provinces; between
1876 and 1900, however, when only 150 new positions were added,
the great majority set up shop in the nonzemstvo provinces. In this
latter period, then, when the zemstvo school system came into
being and grew substantially, the size of the official inspectorate in
those areas serviced by zemstvos remained virtually the same. Beginning at the turn of the century, the Ministry of Education received funding for many new posts, and by 1907 there were 489
inspectors, in addition to a director in each province. Between
1907 and 1912, another 215 positions were added, and by 1914
there were 784 inspectors, 60 percent of whom (421) worked in the
original thirty-four zemstvo provinces. (In 1911, new zemstvos
were established in seven provinces.) If the 78 directors of schools
are included, the official inspectorate numbered 862 in 1914. Thus,
during the last quarter of the nineteenth century, the number of
inspectors increased by only 150 (from 178 to 328), although in the
following fourteen years it increased by 456.[12]

A look at the Temporary Instructions of 1871 and the 1874
School Statute reveals not only that the inspector's powers were
broad but also that his responsibilities were so sweeping that he
could not have fulfilled them all conscientiously. The inspector,
who generally lived in the provincial capital, had to rely heavily on
others for information and help in carrying out his decisions; real-

istically, he had to set priorities, selectively fulfilling only the most important or most urgent of his duties.[13]

As the educator Miropol'skii stressed at the time, the legislation defining the functions of the inspector envisioned him as both benefactor and inquisitor, as facilitating the expansion and improving the quality of primary education, as well as controlling its direction. Miropol'skii was on firm ground when he argued, in response to an outcry in the press against the 1871 Instructions, that the inspector's mission outlined in these regulations was to help promote local education and to provide guidance to teachers. Yet Zviagintsev, a prerevolutionary authority on the inspectors, observed that what soon developed was the "diminishing of the creative, positive mission in favor of the formal, police tasks," the emergence of petty bureaucrats exclusively concerned with the observance of rules, filing of reports, and maintenance of order. That inspectors sometimes harassed and even persecuted defenseless teachers is abundantly clear from the periodical press and teachers' memoirs. After a MNP circular in 1879 instructing school officials to verify the "moral qualities and political reliability of all teaching candidates" before admitting them to their posts, the police functions became even more salient.[14]

Nevertheless, the powers and responsibilities of the inspectors were broad enough to allow enormous leeway for individual interpretation. Alone, the inspector could not possibly hope to fulfill more than a fraction of his responsibilities, which could, in any case, be interpreted in different ways. Thus the personality and training of the individual inspector were very important.

Who were these inspectors? Charnoluskii, like Zviagintsev a socialist and opponent of the government, argued that inspectors were a heterogeneous lot: there were passive bureaucrats, confining their activities to paper-pushing; others who were energetic administrators; some who empathized with zemstvo efforts and offered help when they could; and enthusiastic sponsors of education who worked closely with the zemstvos. Even Soviet historians admit that not all inspectors were bad. To be sure, E. N. Medynskii complained fifty years ago of the low quality and poor qualifications of inspectors, but a recent authoritative survey by F. G. Panachin concludes that they were a "mixed lot." In the West, Sinel argues that many inspectors and directors were well-educated and "did not limit their activities to invigilation alone." In his study of rural teachers, Scott Seregny notes that inspectors often had to intercede between teachers and local authorities and that "the MNP did contain many enlightened officials, experts who understood the importance of a general, largely secular education."[15]

As examples, we have, on the one hand, the extraordinary father of Lenin: I. N. Ul'ianov, inspector, and later director of Simbirsk province and Kazan' education district. Even allowing for the virtual deification of all Lenin's relatives in Soviet hagiography, the briefest acquaintance with this man's biography convincingly demonstrates that he was indeed a dedicated, tireless, inspiring inspector with an almost missionary zeal and faith in the civilizing powers of the school. Other progressive and well-known educators who also served as inspectors or directors included Flerov, Krasev, Iordanskii, Lubenets, Ovchinnikov, Belliustin, Geertz, Vakhterov, Demkov, and D. P. Martynov, who literally worked himself to death.[16]

On the other hand, we have the monstrous example of M. T. Iablochkov ("Mr. Apple") from Tula province, whose work *Russian School: A Director's Instructions* made him the laughingstock of the pedagogical profession, but who terrorized the defenseless teachers in his province with an unending stream of ridiculous regulations governing virtually every aspect of their public and private behavior (see Chapter 8). His book, justly infamous before the revolution, is still cited by Soviet historians as typical of pre-revolutionary "officious [*ofitsioznaia*] pedagogy," and Iablochkov is described as the typical school inspector.[17] Zviagintsev collected a long list of outrageous instructions, threats, and deeds committed by inspectors, all drawn from the periodical press in the forty years after 1874. Names such as Garusov and Iankovskii became almost household words, and incidents such as the "Berdiansk episode" in the 1870s, when a local director ran amok, virtually destroying the new school system before finally being removed, caused loud protests in the press. Many a teacher's life was made miserable, if not ruined, by such bureaucratic arbitrariness.[18]

Though most inspectors were not this controversial, some were undoubtedly ill-suited for their tasks, as evidenced by numerous heartfelt laments from educators. Even the Ministry of Education publicly admitted that its school inspectors were sometimes not up to the demands of the job. In 1909, the official journal of the MNP published an unsigned article in which the author conceded that "not all inspectors [were] adequately trained" or understood the "complexity of school affairs" and that few had "a firm grasp of methodology"; too few "adequately understood the burdens and hardships imposed upon the teacher."[19]

Unfortunately, very little is known about the inspectors as a professional group. One contemporary source asserted that a significant minority of directors and inspectors had a higher education and prior teaching experience in specialized pedagogical institutions; it is noteworthy that outstanding educators such as Vakhterov and Flerov did hold such posts. A larger number were graduates of ecclesiastical academies: in this contingent, some had first gained considerable experience in pedagogical institutions, whereas others had stepped directly into the position of inspector of primary schools from lower ecclesiastic schools or seminaries. Versed largely or even exclusively in the catechism, Church law, the liturgy, homiletics, and ancient languages, many such inspectors demonstrated "bookishness," "pedantry," and ignorance of new teaching methods, as well as *pokaznaia ispravnost'*—a tendency to formalism. Finally, many other inspectors had received their education at teachers' institutes, or sometimes seminaries, and had worked as inspectors or teachers at district or municipal schools.[20] (N. N. Iordanskii, the prominent inspector and progressive educator, was a product of the seminary.)

In a circular dated 11 October 1911, the Ministry of Education admitted that individuals without sufficient education, pedagogical experience, or adequate character had sometimes been appointed as inspectors or directors, and it called for additional effort in the search for talent. This problem is surely the reason that the Education Commission of the Third Duma pressed to increase inspectors' annual salaries, finding the 2,000 rubles then current insufficient to attract competent educators. Thus, the MNP did have recruiting problems, but it was aware of shortcomings and acting to remedy them. (Ironically, the very awareness of deficiencies tends to generate documents that the historian may later seize upon to bolster an assumption that the deficiencies were typical, even pervasive.)[21]

The image we have of the school inspectors comes almost entirely from Zviagintsev's compilation of newspaper reports, but even he cautioned that "by no means all inspectors conducted themselves as did the inspector-monsters exposed in the press." A single volume of reported "incidents" (and a slim volume, at that) covering forty years, or a listing of a dozen or so incidents in one year (1913) is not convincing evidence that all or even the majority of inspectors were incompetent or abusive. The periodical press reported sensational episodes, crimes, and conflicts; then, as today, it would not have found newsworthy an item proclaiming that, say, in Tambov province, relations between inspectors and teachers were normal or even friendly.[22]

Two complaints were addressed most frequently to the inspectors: they allowed their police, or inquisitorial, function to supersede all else; and they often became little more than paper-pushers, concerned exclusively with observing regulations, filing reports, and collecting information (with little concern for accuracy). That the inspectors were often swamped with paperwork is no surprise considering the multitude of tasks entrusted to them; this fact was amply documented and acknowledged by the MNP to be a serious problem. In some areas, given the quality of the inspectors, it was perhaps best that they occupied themselves with paperwork in their offices and seldom ventured out from the provincial capital.

Yet whatever the personal inclinations and training of the inspectors—and certainly not all of them were bad—they were in fact not physically in a position to regulate the day-to-day affairs of schools in any but the most perfunctory way. For the most part, this was still an age when communication was linked to transportation; to receive or gather information, one had to travel from one location to the next. Understaffed, overwhelmed by a multitude of duties, and responsible for a territory as large as Ireland (and often, an "Ireland" with no paved roads), the inspector could at best maintain a semblance of order and try to avoid egregious violations of the law pertaining to the classroom routine, health conditions in the school, or the personal lives of the teachers. What is more, there is some reason to argue that the tenuous hold exerted over the schools by the inspectors in 1874 was relaxed, rather than tightened, in the zemstvo provinces during the next quarter century. If this is true, it becomes very hard to accept the frequently encountered argument that government harassment was the main obstacle interfering with zemstvo efforts to promote schools in the Russian countryside in the decades following the establishment of the zemstvos.

Sinel correctly points out just how inadequate was the surveillance of schools under Dmitri Tolstoy. According to the ministry, each elementary school inspector should have had no more than fifty schools under his supervision; but in 1874, the ratio of inspectors to schools was 1 to 71 in Moscow, 1 to 163 in Khar'kov, and 1 to 114 in Kiev (though somewhat lower in Vil'no and Odessa). Because the official school system was in its infancy, the distance between schools was enormous, and the territory each inspector had to cover was formidable:

The staff in St. Petersburg, for example, faced an expanse considerably larger than Texas; that in Moscow, a region almost equal to France. The comparatively smaller Khar'kov district still exceeded California in area, and had a single inspector. Poor transportation facilities magnified these already immense distances. The first autumnal rains, first wet snows, and vernal thaws made Russian roads virtually impassable in late fall and early spring, precisely when most schools were in session.[23]

Despite a doubling of the number of inspectors in the last quarter of the century, the perfunctory supervision that existed in 1874 in the zemstvo provinces actually slackened in these subsequent years. Indeed, N. V. Chekhov, working in the 1890s as a zemstvo-appointed school supervisor in Tula province, recalled in his memoirs that many schools under his surveillance had not been visited by an official inspector in more than five years. When the inspector did visit, what took place could hardly have been called an inspection: "The inspector would arrive, step down from his sleigh, exchange greetings with the teacher, and announce: 'Well, fine, now I have visited your school this year,' get back in the sleigh and depart."[24]

Two reasons seem to account for the attenuation of what was already inadequate supervision. First, the increase in primary schools during this quarter century occurred particularly in the nonzemstvo provinces, thereby increasing the need for at least minimal supervision in these areas. Second, the increase in the number of schools, both zemstvo and nonzemstvo, in all areas easily outstripped the increase in the number of inspectors. Although there were approximately 350 inspectors in the Empire by 1900, the number of schools under ministry supervision was 32,980 by that time[25]—94 schools for each inspector. In the zemstvo provinces, the number of zemstvo schools alone rose from 10,000 in 1877 to 16,400 in 1898 and to 45,000 in 1914.[26] Although this was not remarkable progress, it meant an increase between 1877 and 1898 of 6,400 schools with virtually no change in the number of zemstvo inspectors in the zemstvo provinces. This situation could only have produced an attenuation of control. Admittedly, financial stringencies were very important in keeping down the number of inspectors' posts established. But the priority given to non-zemstvo provinces during the quarter century following 1874 indicates that the Ministry of Education did not feel that tightening control over zemstvo schools was a matter of urgent concern.[27]

The Duma school commission mandated to draw up plans for universal education established the ratio of one inspector for every seventy-five schools as a target; by 1911, this goal had been reached in a few zemstvo provinces, and several other provinces were within striking distance. Only a few provinces had an inspector-school ratio of over one to one hundred (see Table 5). This increased capacity to exert guidance or control over the school fits with the general observation that 1908—not 1864, 1874, or any other date—was the major turning point after which the MNP significantly increased its leverage over the school system. It now provided the money to build and maintain schools, and it underwrote salaries and determined the standards of eligibility for grants, thereby undercutting not only the Church schools but also the hitherto dominant provincial zemstvos, which had once employed the same tactic to spur into action and to control the district zemstvos. The ratio of inspectors to schools was finally beginning to decline. Perhaps more important, as the number of inspectors increased, the area for which each was responsible shrank; accordingly, the amount of time the inspector had to spend on the road traveling between schools also declined. For example, in Moscow province, although the ratio of inspectors to schools remained virtually the same between 1874 and 1911 (approximately one to seventy), the

Table 5
MNP School Inspectorate, 1911

PROVINCE	AREA (IN SQUARE MILES)	MNP SCHOOLS	INSPEC- TORS	AREA PER INSPECTOR	SCHOOLS PER INSPECTOR
Bessarabia	17,135	993	11	1,558	90
Vladimir	18,824	1,081	14	1,345	77
Vologda	155,305	863	11	14,119	78
Voronezh	25,461	1,083	13	1,959	83
Viatka	59,334	1,668	17	3,490	98
Ekaterinoslav	24,483	1,303	11	2,226	73
Kazan'	24,586	963	13	1,891	74
Kaluga	11,953	744	10	1,195	64
Kostroma	32,449	1,005	12	2,704	84
Kursk	17,936	1,331	16	1,121	75
Moscow	12,853	1,584	18	714	88
Nizhegorod	19,793	1,118	14	1,414	80
Novgorod	45,775	1,355	15	3,052	90
Olonets	49,360	459	7	7,051	66
Orel	18,061	911	11	1,642	83
Penza	14,995	548	8	1,874	69
Perm'	127,563	1,745	16	7,973	109
Poltava	19,274	1,340	16	1,204	84
Pskov	16,680	604	7	1,043	86
Riazan'	16,187	898	12	1,349	75
Samara	58,337	1,038	10	5,834	104
Petersburg	17,233	1,428	14	1,231	102
Saratov	32,641	968	13	2,511	74
Simbirsk	19,109	655	8	2,389	82
Smolensk	21,625	861	13	1,663	66
Tavrida	23,314	1,173	11	2,119	77
Tambov	25,722	1,092	13	1,979	84
Tver'	24,983	1,485	16	1,561	93

SOURCES: Compiled from Zviagintsev, *Inspektsiia narodnykh uchilishch,* 10; Trutovskii, *Sovremennoe zemstvo,* 229; Malinovskii, "Nekotorye vyvody," 74–75.

Continued on next page

Table 5—*continued*

PROVINCE	AREA (IN SQUARE MILES)	MNP SCHOOLS	INSPEC-TORS	AREA PER INSPECTOR	SCHOOLS PER INSPECTOR
Tula	11,953	929	13	919	71
Ufa	47,118	1,055	11	4,283	96
Khar'kov	21,024	1,187	14	1,502	85
Kherson	27,341	1,388	13	2,103	107
Chernigov	20,281	981	13	1,560	75
Iaroslavl'	13,725	574	7	1,961	82

area covered by each inspector declined sharply; instead of two inspectors to travel the 12,853 square miles (6,427 miles each), there were eighteen officials (each covering 714 square miles). Still, there were areas where the sheer physical demands on the inspector remained staggering. In Samara province in 1911, each inspector was responsible for 104 schools and 5,834 square miles of territory; in Perm', each one covered 109 schools and 7,973 square miles; and in Vologda, inspectors averaged 78 schools and a territory encompassing 14,119 square miles (Table 5). (Given this variety of conditions and demands, it is particularly interesting that there is no correlation between the number of inspectors for each school and the political leanings of an individual zemstvo. If the only function of the inspector had been inquisitorial, we would expect that the highest number would have been in provinces with the highest concentration of zemstvo liberals in the assemblies and the most active professional staffs. But this does not seem to have been the case.)

The frequency and length of visits paid by inspectors to individual schools tell us more about the degree of effective control exerted by the MNP. According to annual reports preserved in the MNP archives, inspectors made a point of visiting each school at least once a year. In Kazan' educational district in 1880, inspectors visited 428 of 465 schools in Viatka province, all 413 schools in Simbirsk, and 314 of 444 schools in Saratov. In Penza in 1897, two inspectors claimed to have visited 241 schools; in Khar'kov, scven inspectors visited 549 schools; and in Tambov, ten inspectors visited 708 schools (all but 5 of the total). Later, in 1911, the Mirgorod district zemstvo reported that the local inspector had visited all but 4 of its 84 schools. In Rostov district, where a "first-rate" inspector looked over the schools, of 114 zemstvo institutions, 1 was visited twice, 73 once, and 40 not at all. Still, the press reported that it was not unusual, even in European Russia, to find schools that had not been visited in two, three, or more years—this on the eve of World War I. Moreover, in truly remote areas, such as the Trans-Baikal region, where the inspector of schools visited the Shilkin village school three times in twenty-one years, government supervision remained a pious wish.[28]

The reader will recall Chekhov's description of a school inspector in the 1890s—an exchange of greetings with the teacher and a hurried departure. Judging by the figures just cited, many inspectors' visits must have been just as perfunctory two decades later. If the school year lasted one hundred fifty days, and each inspector visited each of seventy-five schools (in fact, as noted above, they claimed to have visited far more), he would have had two days for each school. But even in 1914, it often took an entire day to travel from one school to the next, even without taking into account inclement weather, impassable roads, or the enormous amount of time the school inspector had to spend at school board meetings or in his office filing reports. Annual reports had to be in by June 1; thus his most intensive work period in the office coincided with the last month of the school term and the time when the annual certifying examinations were under way. (When Lenin's father, Ilya Ul'ianov, began his career as inspector, paperwork kept even this dedicated educator from visiting the villages until four months on the job had elapsed.)[29]

The most systematic description of inspectors' visits comes from a questionnaire published in the journal *Public Teacher* (*Narodnyi uchitel'*) at the close of the 1912–1913 school year. The questionnaire asked the teachers to describe who had visited the school, what occasioned the visit, when it took place, who visited the class in session, and what commands, requests, or advice ensued. The journal received 243 responses from fifty-six provinces, scattered throughout the Russian countryside.[30]

These 243 responses recorded a total of 435 visits to 205 schools. School authorities made up approximately half the total number of visitors. But in terms of *schools* visited (rather than number of visits), inspectors entirely missed 90 of the 243 schools in 1912–1913 (or 70 of 229—31 percent—if Church schools are excluded). Of 133 zemstvo schools, inspectors visited 85 (64 percent); in other words, these schools do not appear to have been the object of special attention (or harassment, as the case may be).

Individual comments by schoolteachers who had seen the elusive inspectors make it clear how superficial the supervision of the schools was. From Samara:

The inspector visited, but his stay was so brief—an hour and a half for all three sections—that he limited his inquiry to requiring one or two pupils to read a line each.

In Vladimir, the inspector made, to put it mildly, a cursory survey of school conditions:

In my fourth grade, the inspector recommended that we move the desks away from the window where there was a draft. He asked if we had gotten to fractions. He never talked to the pupils; this was the entire inspection. He said he was in a rush, but promised to return.

Haste seemed to be the rule in Novgorod as well:

How do the pupils behave? . . . Looking at the written work, he paid attention only to penmanship and neatness. He required the pupils to read in turn, cutting them off in the middle of sentences and words, as if he were hurrying to a fire—faster, faster, faster!

One inspector limited his comments to a recommendation that curtains be hung on the windows, and another told the teacher to make sure pupils washed their hair more often; still another asked the pupils what a "country" was and what kind of government existed in France, but left without waiting for the answer and without offering advice or direction. When advice was given, it usually concerned superficial matters of discipline or warnings to concentrate on grammar, penmanship, or Bible instruction, and brief comments on the textbooks in use.

The teachers seemed divided: some who had been visited

found the inspection a nuisance; some who hadn't been visited and many who had only seen the inspector "on the run" rued the lack of guidance or positive reinforcement. A certain number of the teachers were generally content with the advice and support provided, as well as with the thoroughness of the visit, but they were apparently a small minority. Some teachers felt that the inspectors were incompetent bureaucrats concerned only with formal requirements and external appearances, but an equal number of teachers were disappointed with the *lack* of contact, the superficiality of the visits, and the seeming inability or unwillingness of the inspectors to act as benefactors of the schools. Many teachers wanted *more,* not less attention.

If the inspector hoped to keep an eye on the schools, either politically or pedagogically, he had to rely heavily on the help of others, primarily the school boards and the local zemstvos. He could also tap an extensive network of informers, from the village priest to the local landlord or even the volost' peasant authorities, who sometimes seemed to delight in making life miserable for the vulnerable teacher. Nevertheless, if we accept the argument that not all inspectors were by nature tormentors of the poor teacher and that many, lacking the time to provide personal guidance, were concerned that minimally satisfactory conditions be maintained and acceptable instruction provided, it was inevitable that they would come to rely heavily on the existing infrastructure in the countryside—namely, the zemstvos.

LOCAL CONTROL OF EDUCATION

And so they did, as N. V. Chekhov observed in his landmark history of nineteenth-century Russian education. Because the inspectors were saddled with an enormous territory and multiple responsibilities, yet had virtually no staff and preferred to live in provincial towns, they "naturally could not become the true masters [*khoziaeva*] of the situation."[31]

In Chekhov's opinion (and note that he himself on a number of occasions suffered political persecution from the Russian bureaucracy and had no reason to understate its degree of control), the true master of the school was the zemstvo, acting through its executive board and its representatives on the local school boards. Although the right to directly supervise the schools, which had been provided to the zemstvo representatives by the 1864 Education Statute, had been formally rescinded a decade later, in reality, it remained in place.

> The zemstvo appointed and, in substance, fired teachers; it supplied the schools, visited them far more frequently than did the inspectors . . . and conducted the [graduating] examination in most districts.[32]

What were the relationships between the local zemstvo and the school board and between the zemstvo and the inspectorate? A brief look at scattered reports from the localities suggests that Chekhov's judgment was indeed valid. In most areas, the school boards tended to be inactive; when they were active, they were dominated by zemstvo personnel and, until the turn of the century at least, the inspector often had to prod or plead with the zemstvo to aid him in his efforts to promote education.

Before 1908, when the massive intrusion of government funds and significant expansion of the inspectorate began to alter the relationship of central government and local institutions concerned with primary education, the control of schooling in the zemstvo provinces evolved in three basic directions. One was the growing dependence of the local inspector on the local zemstvo for financial, organizational, and secretarial help in managing school affairs. A second was the establishment of zemstvo hegemony over the school boards through the widespread use of hired zemstvo personnel to carry out board functions. The last was the gradual emergence of permanent zemstvo organizations to deal with curriculum, organization, and economic and information-gathering functions pertaining to the schools. Where local school boards were active, they often came to be dominated by these organizations and, in the more extreme cases, school board functions were sometimes usurped.

Although there were districts where the zemstvo remained inactive and the school boards moribund, and others where the school boards seemed to act without the help of an indifferent zemstvo, and still others where the inspector had to operate on his own without assistance from either school board or zemstvo, the general pattern seems to have involved features of all three developments noted above. The interlocking of local organizations, both official and semi-official, through the flow of trained personnel from the zemstvo and (especially in the 1890s) the establishment of permanent zemstvo organizations to handle school affairs represented the dominant trends.

Zemstvos and Inspectors

From the start, in many areas of the country, the zemstvos responded favorably to the establishment of the post of inspector and worked very closely with these officials. As the zemstvo financial contribution to primary education increased and the zemstvos began to hire educational personnel, inspectors in some provinces came to rely heavily on zemstvo personnel and resources. "Under such conditions, the role of the inspector was often muted"—that is, he had to bow to the wishes of those providing the much-needed help.[33]

In the 1870s, a number of zemstvos began to offer free secretarial and clerical help to the overburdened inspectors, to provide subsidies for their travel expenses, and to offer the use of post horses for travel. Finally, when it became clear that the government was not going to provide money to hire more inspectors, and when zemstvo petitions to set up the post of zemstvo school inspector were turned down, the zemstvos themselves in sixty districts between 1874 and 1900 provided money for the salaries of *government-appointed* inspectors in order to ensure that the schools received more adequate supervision.[34] Surely the fact that zemstvos were willing, even eager, to help find money to establish more government (not zemstvo) inspectors—a practice that lasted until 1904—is an important indication that in many areas the relationship between the local MNP officials and the zemstvo was not marked by conflict or antagonism. Most zemstvos were happy to work closely with the MNP authorities.

Within the zemstvo milieu the awareness was very dim of the urgent need for local independent organizations to run school affairs, and trust was high in bureaucratic means of running the schools from above, in official inspectors, and in "paper control" [*bumazhnyi kontrol'*].[35]

This attitude continued into the 1890s, for as plans for major school expansion took shape in the zemstvos, petitions to increase the number of government inspectors also began to proliferate. In many areas, the inspector acted almost as an employee of the zemstvo executive board. Financial subsidies and other forms of support

sometimes forestalled the occurrence of recriminations or of resistance by inspectors to zemstvo activities; in other cases, the inspectors, brought closer to the zemstvos by one or another measure [of zemstvo support], even carried out zemstvo requests or directives and acted as liaisons for the zemstvo with the circuit [*okruzhnye*] educational authorities or with local peasant land societies.[36]

Contemporary observers noted that in cases of friction between inspector and zemstvo, the former often lost out because he was of inferior social status and lacked the connections with higher circles on which the marshall of the nobility (chairman of the zemstvo assembly) or the chairman of the zemstvo executive board could draw in case of need.[37] Quite simply, the *formal* powers of the inspector were inferior to the *informal* ties linking the liberal gentry to the upper levels of the bureaucracy. In many cases, the zemstvos simply ignored the instructions of the local inspector.

Did the amicable relationship between inspector and zemstvo change after 1905? Zviagintsev argued that it was possible to produce a long list of testimonies to conflictual relationships between official inspectors and the zemstvos, all dating from 1908 to 1913. Because the inspectors now resided in the districts, attended school board meetings, and received more money from the government for secretarial help, they became both free for more fieldwork and more independent of the zemstvo. More important was the power of the purse; inspectors were required by the 1908 School Bill to supervise those schools receiving government grants to ensure that the stipulations attached to these funds were met. Inspectors were to make sure that peasants had been released from all school expenses, that school buildings met official standards, and that teachers were qualified. According to Zviagintsev, attempts to enforce these regulations and the vagueness of the law caused increasing friction between zemstvo and inspector in the countryside, where a universal enrollment campaign was underway.[38]

Given the purge of the zemstvo activists following the 1905 Revolution and the predominantly right-wing, antidemocratic, or apolitical orientation of the zemstvos in the following decade, it would be misplaced, however, to treat friction between inspectors and zemstvos as evidence of a conflict between local self-government or democracy and the bureaucracy. Moreover, after 1908, despite the right-wing orientation of the zemstvos, most showed a renewed interest in primary education and justified this interest in much the same terms as did the government, making it unlikely that much tension was generated over conflicting visions of the goals and purposes of education.[39] Finally, though Zviagintsev was generally an objective observer and though a struggle for control was inherent in the extension of representatives of the central government to the countryside, even he concedes that in 1914 the conflict was still largely potential rather than actual.[40]

Western and Soviet historians have recently documented the powerful resurgence of the provincial nobility after 1905 and the nobility's attempt to consolidate control over the district zemstvos for use as fortresses against the intrusion of a hostile, alien central bureaucracy. With this return to the countryside of the old service nobility, efforts to reform local government in directions that implied democratization or the attenuation of estate (*soslovie*) distinctions met growing resistance. Viewed from this angle, rather than from the perspective of a struggle between bureaucratic and elective institutions, suspicion of the growing power of the inspector may sometimes have reflected this resistance to government intrusion in local affairs and a defense of privilege *against* reform. (This conflict was interwoven with another one—the joint zemstvo-government effort to persecute Third Element radical zemstvo activists, particularly after the All-Russian Teachers' Congress in 1913–1914; thus, zemstvo assemblies could often support purges of teachers while pressing for "local autonomy" in their affairs within the sphere of education).

Zemstvos and School Boards

The second trend in local school politics was the interchange of personnel between zemstvo and school board and the establishment of a zemstvo voice in, or even hegemony over, school board operations. In the decade following the 1864 Education Statute, the boards "often constituted no check upon zemstvo activities. . . . Given [their] heterogeneous membership, any group that could form a bloc would wield considerable influence."[41] Interministerial rivalry and reluctance to give the MNP monolithic control opened this loophole for zemstvo activity (although in reality, only a few zemstvos took advantage of the opportunity at the time; not until the close of the decade did most zemstvos turn to education as an area of possible endeavor). During this decade, most local school boards failed to file annual reports as required, and we can infer that they were not very active, if they met at all.

As for the provincial school boards, they seem to have been stillborn. At no time did they play a significant role in either promoting or limiting primary education. Chekhov noted sardonically that the activities of the provincial boards, which often did not convene for long years at a stretch, were soon reduced to two functions: the purely formal confirmation of local trustees, and the rejection of (or failure to act on) complaints against local school boards.[42]

The revised School Statute of 1874 secured the domination of the school boards by MNP officials and shifted several functions from these boards to the local inspector, but it did not grant Minister of Education Tolstoy's request to seat the inspector as the chairman of the board. Instead, as a compromise, the local marshall of the nobility assumed this post. The appointment of the marshall reflected the growing fear of the revolutionary movement, as well as the spirit expressed in a newly issued rescript admonishing the local nobility to be vigilant in the fight against sedition.

In practice, however, this move unlocked a back door through which, under proper circumstances, the zemstvo could easily dominate the local school boards. The local marshall of the nobility was *ex officio* chairman of the zemstvo assembly and frequently also held the position of director of the zemstvo executive board. In such cases, zemstvo influence was often very strong. According to Article 41 of the School Statute, the local marshall of the nobility could select (with approval of the provincial school board, which routinely approved all local school board activities) "trusted local residents" to assist him in school affairs and to visit schools, reporting to him on these visits. In 1876, the MNP issued an explanatory note specifying that the number of such "assistants to the chairman" could be determined by the local school board.[43] These local residents were predominantly zemstvo deputies, especially Third Element zemstvo employees working in education, and as the school system began to grow, the number of these assistants rapidly increased.

Often the zemstvos made a concerted effort to strengthen their voice through such participation. In Kostroma, for example, the zemstvo executive board established an education section nominally concerned with school economic management but in fact dealing largely with curriculum matters, and the zemstvo worked hard to see that representatives of the section were always voting members or invited consultants on the school boards (Article 41). Regulations passed by the Moscow provincial zemstvo in 1900 governing subsidies to district schools stipulated that the receiving district had to include its school business manager as a consultant to the school board if it wished to receive such grants.[44]

Because the majority of board members were officials with a multitude of other concerns in many provinces and districts, the consultants soon performed the lion's share of the board's tasks. Although they had no vote at board meetings, votes were uncommon; the most important business was carried out between meetings. These assistants were very active in inspections and other visits to the schools and were often in charge of the certifying examinations, which were perhaps the single most important factor in determining the direction and tone of classroom instruction. The addition in 1887 of the local zemstvo doctor as a voting member of the local school board increased the preponderance of zemstvo-affiliated representatives. In Moscow, where the beady eye of the *revizor* (senate inspector) N. A. Zinov'ev scrutinized the cozy relationship between school board and zemstvo, it was discovered in 1903 that of fifty-five assistants helping the local school boards, forty-six were from the Moscow zemstvo; of this number, the majority were Third Element employees rather than zemstvo delegates.[45]

How active were the school boards after 1874? The School Statute did not specify how often the boards should convene, but stipulated that the presence of the inspector or other MNP official was necessary and that a quorum of three (in addition to the chairman) was required to act on any pending concern (Articles 30–35). Reports presented to a 1901 conference on public education in Moscow, however, indicate that the boards often met without the inspector. A local marshall of the nobility in Smolensk reported that he knew of only one instance in his district in ten years where an inspector had attended a school board meeting. In another district in the same province, *no* inspector had attended a meeting in the two decades before 1900. The *reviziia* of Moscow province in 1903, however, reported that the local inspectors, together with the zemstvo delegates, were the most active and faithful in attending meetings. In many cases, a quorum in Moscow province was reached by the attendance of only the inspector and the zemstvo delegates, whereas the majority of representatives of other institutions seldom attended the sessions and almost never visited the schools. According to *revizii* of Kursk and Viatka provinces, the local school boards at the turn of the century were virtually inactive and exerted no independent influence over the direction of education.[46]

The records of school board meetings from three different areas (St. Petersburg and Kazan' education circuits and Moscow province) between 1885 and 1909 show that in most local districts the school boards met about six times a year, or every other month. Although the average changed little over time, the range of frequency was considerable from district to district: in Viatka province, although one district board met only twice in 1909, another met fourteen times; in Simbirsk, the range was from four to thirteen times; in St. Petersburg province (1885), from two to twelve; and in Vologda, from four to thirteen times. If the frequency of meeting is an indication of the vitality of these institutions, it changed little in the more than two decades following 1885. In each province, some district boards were reasonably active and others could hardly muster the energy to gather once every six months.[47]

Zinov'ev, the cantankerous Ministry of the Interior inspector, pointed out that the district boards were "not distinguished by exceptional vitality." After perusing several years of journals from local school board meetings, he could find only a few ripples of discussions of substance; for example, a debate on moral education had engaged the attention of the Moscow district board on 10 March 1903 but was then dropped after one session. For the most part, the laconic entries concerned only formalities such as confirming newly appointed teachers, accepting annual school reports, allocating schools to examination boards, and considering nominations for awards. Zinov'ev could find very few examples of a zemstvo petition or motion that had been denied by a local school board in Moscow. (Most concerned transfer or appointments.) The most significant disagreement among board members took place at a meeting of the Moscow board on 23 March 1903 when a local Bible teacher filed a complaint alleging that an unnamed teacher at the Bitsevsk school was a pernicious influence on her charges. The zemstvo delegate present objected to investigating this allegation, and he was supported by three nonvoting consultants. By a vote of three to two, the board decided to drop the matter.[48]

If there was widespread evidence of friction between the zemstvos and school boards following 1874, Veselovskii claims that his search failed to find it; indeed, he denies that the 1874 School Statute had any impact whatsoever on these relations, which were, and remained, predominantly "amicable." In fact, during the 1870s and 1880s, a large number of district zemstvos turned over their allocations for primary education to the local school boards, to be distributed as the boards saw fit. (Veselovskii explicitly rejects Fal'bork and Charnoluskii's contention that the practice was limited to a few zemstvos.)[49] Because no strings were attached to these funds, it is unlikely that this was an attempt to influence decision making by selective subsidies, a practice that did emerge later when the provincial zemstvos became active in primary education. Instead, it represented part of a widespread movement among the zemstvos during this period to relinquish all responsibility for primary education, a movement that also led to frequent attempts to turn over the maintenance and control of all zemstvo schools to the Holy Synod or to restrict zemstvo educational activities to subsidies to Church schools. Indeed, where conflict did erupt between the two institutions, it was commonly over the zemstvos' attempt to *avoid* financial commitments to the schools rather than over board attempts to stifle zemstvo initiative.

Tension between school boards and zemstvos did surface in the 1890s. A regulation of 1894 required local authorities to approve all consultants appointed under Article 41, and a ruling of 1895 placed the new land captain on the school boards with a vote on all issues of concern to him.[50] Moreover, in the debates over a new Education Statute that took place at conferences on education and on the floor of the Duma (and in its special Education Commission), the role of the school boards was considered at length. The Fifth Section of the 1911 Zemstvo Congress recommended eliminating the school boards, and the general session approved this motion by a vote of eighty-seven to twenty. This vote is significant, for those attending the session had been carefully screened by the government to exclude radical democrats or socialists such as Charnoluskii; the vote, therefore, represented the voice of a very moderate sector of the world of education. Being pragmatic men, these educators recognized that school boards would *not,* in fact, be eliminated and added (by a vote of seventy-four to eleven) that teachers, elected by their own profession, should be included as voting members and that the post of inspector should be eliminated or stripped of all police powers.[51]

Moreover, the Duma proposal for a revised Education Statute removed supervision from the directors and inspectors and placed it entirely under the school boards, whose composition was modified and which would be chaired not by the marshall of the nobility but by a person elected by the local zemstvo assembly.[52] In contrast, a Ministry of Education proposal in 1900 attempted to significantly reduce the jurisdiction of the school boards and strengthen the powers of the inspectorate. Although the proposal soon disappeared, it is indicative of sentiment within the MNP about the school boards.[53] It appears that these boards had few friends: they were assailed by the MNP, the Duma, progressive educators, and the zemstvos.

Zemstvo Commissions

The final way in which the zemstvo established its role in rural education was to hire professional staff or set up permanent organizations that gradually usurped the functions of the school boards, turning the boards into rubber-stamp institutions—precisely what Zinov'ev felt they had become in Moscow province. Perhaps because the pace of zemstvo education activity was muted throughout the seventies and eighties, the independent establishment of zemstvo posts or organizations proceeded quite slowly. When embryonic organizations did appear, they clustered around the new statistical bureaus (*kantselarii*), as "education desks," first at the provincial and later at the district level, but there is no evidence that any were sizable, particularly active, or long-lived. Indeed, zemstvo organizations emerged more rapidly in other areas such as medicine and agronomy.[54]

In the 1890s, permanent school organizations spread throughout zemstvo Russia in response to the growing public clamor for universal education. Two types of organizations emerged: school bureaus and permanent school commissions. School bureaus, established to gather information and do routine paperwork, existed at the provincial level in all zemstvo provinces by 1910 except Orel, Novgorod, Smolensk, and Ufa. They had from two to eight permanent employees and small budgets of from 2,000 to 5,000 rubles. Permanent school commissions, the first of which was established in Moscow in 1891, were more broadly conceived: their tasks were to coordinate all school activities, plan the implementation of universal education, set education policy, and supervise the school bureaus, over which they had executive powers. Veselovskii counted twenty-three such school commissions founded between 1891 and 1905.[55] Although widespread purges, including dismissals of personnel and dismantling of economic, education, and health organizations, followed the 1906 "righting" of the zemstvos, twenty-five provincial and sixty-five district-level education boards were still in operation in 1908.[56]

Whatever the politics of the local zemstvos, most agreed that universal literacy was an urgent goal for the nation's survival. In order to qualify for government funds to build schools after 1908, the zemstvos had to present a complete plan based on detailed statistics, which in turn required personnel and organization. Since financial contracts and plans were now drawn up, submitted, and negotiated at the district level, it is likely that the center of gravity of zemstvo educational organization shifted at this time from the provincial to the district level, which before 1905 had shown few signs of activity and had relied largely on provincial personnel and funding to draw up plans for universal education.

There were still other ways in which the zemstvo could directly influence education. After 1900, several zemstvos also resurrected the post of business director, first in Moscow, after a very narrow vote of twenty-one to twenty in the zemstvo assembly, and then in Kursk and Tavrida, as well as in a handful of district zemstvos. In addition, at least in Moscow at the turn of the century, school boards were being bypassed at the district level by informal meetings between representatives of teachers from each volost' and the local zemstvo executive board. Such monthly meetings were the source of exchanges and even litigation between the zemstvos and local authorities. At first, school inspectors labeled the meetings illegal, but by the turn of the century these officials were joining in the meetings as a chance to meet with teachers living and working in distant villages. Although the local school boards registered perfunctory objections and the governors began to make inquiries, these meetings apparently continued.[57]

Far more widespread was the rapid establishment after 1907 of so-called collective guardianship over the schools. Guardians, or trustees, of the schools had been established in the 1874 School Statute; selected by the school sponsor—whether peasant community or zemstvo—they were confirmed in office by the local school board, in which they were then allowed to participate with a vote. Their responsibilities included the "closest supervision over the school" and the maintenance of order. These guardians apparently played only a minor role. On occasion a local philanthropist or benefactor of the school assumed the voluntary, unremunerated post; elsewhere, a local peasant, perhaps attracted by the guardians' access to the same privileges given local peasant functionaries, became the school guardian. An 1898 zemstvo study of Vladimir province concluded that the guardians fulfilled their obligations perfunctorily at best. In most cases, peasants avoided the position of trustee, because, like other peasant posts in the countryside, it made them responsible to the authorities for whatever might go wrong. Only the legal privileges accompanying the position or the opportunity to rake off a small profit could tempt peasants into the role of negotiating between village and government and answering to the government for the actions of the village.[58]

The Statute on Guardians (26 March 1907), a response to petitions from the zemstvos dating from 1900,[59] changed this situation drastically by permitting the guardian to be not an individual but a collective body, by allowing this new organization to watch over several schools, and by allowing teachers as well as zemstvo representatives and elected community representatives to serve. Although this new statute empowered the new organization only to look after the economic needs of the school, to provide textbooks and other equipment, and to sponsor teaching candidates, the provision of the 1874 School Statute specifically entrusting guardians with management ("*zavedovanie*") of the school also remained in effect. This word, an 1891 circular noted, implied "a direct influence upon the course of instruction of youth."[60] According to information collected for the 1911 Zemstvo Congress, collegial trustee boards had been established within three years (1907–1910) in fifty-seven districts in twenty-one of thirty-four zemstvo provinces; that is, in about 20 percent of all district zemstvos, most commonly in Voronezh, Samara, Perm', and Iaroslavl'.[61]

The lifespan of the collegial trustee boards was too brief to allow them to leave a mark on Russian educational history. Still, these boards did spread rapidly, and their legally defined functions were broad enough to allow them to act as local organizations overseeing all aspects of rural education. One study concluded that their activities spanned philanthropic, organizational, and academic concerns.[62] Serving even as shadow school boards, they offered yet another opportunity for the zemstvo to influence the course of education in the countryside and to avoid government restrictions.

These organizations existed in great profusion, and they often included representatives of officialdom as voting or consulting members. Although the Ministry of the Interior, through the governor, often sought to circumscribe the activities of these organizations and to restrict participation by Third Element personnel, the participation of inspectors and the very spread of these organizations despite pressure to confine them suggest a good deal of vitality. In areas where zemstvo organization was not particularly vital, local school boards may have been successfully coping with the demands of education, obviating the need for independent zemstvo organization. What is clear from the survey of these organizations is that, combined with influence over the local inspector and prominent representation on the school boards, independent zemstvo education organs provided substantial input into peasant education.

CONCLUSIONS: ZEMSTVO DOMINANCE OF LOCAL SCHOOLS

Zemstvo opportunities to shape local education were by law confined to the provision of schools. Yet it is abundantly clear from the observations of those directly connected with these organizations that the independent zemstvo boards and commissions, like the collective guardian boards, influenced, indeed sometimes dominated, all aspects of rural education. For example, N. V. Chekhov served as supervisor of the economic affairs of schools in Tula province in the 1890s, but in reality he ran the schools and worked closely with the teachers on a daily basis. He wrote in his memoirs:

I should note that legally I had no right to supervise instruction or to inspect the quality of teaching, since this was the role of the school inspector; but since by instruction of the board the selection of teachers, material provision for the school, and supervision of exams was in my hands, I had far greater claim to be the master of the schools than did their occasional visitor—the MNP inspector.[63]

To be sure, Chekhov was dismissed from this post in 1897. However, the initiative to fire him came not from the local inspector or from the Ministry of the Interior, but from the new zemstvo executive board chairman, one Count Bobrinskii, who had begun a campaign to support parish schools and found Chekhov's secular zeal and moderate populism incompatible with this aim.[64] The *government* apparently had no objection to Chekhov, as the school manager employed by the zemstvo, carrying out educative functions legally belonging to the inspector.

The leading role of the provincial zemstvo school commissions was emphasized by the *revizor* who surveyed all zemstvo institutions in Kursk:

The leading force in education in Kursk, at both the provincial and district levels, is the Commission on Education . . . to which most of the credit for the step-up in activity that took place in the nineties belongs. The commission in many instances is the initiator and supervisor of major measures taken at both provincial and district levels. The commission discussed all of the most important concerns of education, whether economic or curricular. . . . Its conclusions carried great weight in the zemstvo assembly and, with few exceptions, were adopted as policy.[65]

Admittedly, the *revizor* had an axe to grind: he wished to show that institutions dominated by the Third Element were usurping the functions of the zemstvo assembly and that in many areas the zemstvos were overstepping the legal boundaries circumscribing their field of activity. Nevertheless, a Novgorod zemstvo survey of twenty-one provinces, carried out by zemstvo employees, came to the same conclusion. The survey found that within the zemstvo assemblies, the commissions framed the basic issues for discussion, carried out the preliminary work before consideration by the assembly, and then developed the general guidelines to carry out policy approved by the assembly. Moreover, whatever the letter of the law, the commissions paid little attention to the distinction between the provision of education and curriculum concerns and busied themselves equally with both. We can see why even stalwart antigovernment, zemstvo-affiliated educators conceded that "the zemstvo executive boards, in appointing teachers, selecting textbooks, and in the entire organization of school affairs, had a greater impact than the remote inspector."[66]

Approximately ten years after the Novgorod study, a zemstvo congress survey polled district and provincial zemstvos for information on the administration of education and came to virtually the same conclusions.

Although the curricular and moral aspects of education are not directly within the purview of the zemstvo, nevertheless, through a series of auxiliary measures such as textbook selection, the establishment of school museums and book depositories, the organization of external education, and the promotion of consultative sessions with teachers, as well as the direct elaboration of educational issues as a whole—the latter commonly undertaken at the provincial level—the zemstvos in practice succeed in exerting their influence on all aspects of education.[67]

The survey stressed that zemstvo participation in managing the schools was particularly prominent in the selection of teachers and the choice of textbooks. Joint decisions and activity involving both inspector and zemstvo executive board (or commission) were most common. The zemstvo board generally recommended, and the school board and inspector confirmed, the selection of teachers. But in some instances, admittedly infrequent, the executive board usurped all stages, including the right to transfer or dismiss.

As for textbooks, before the school year began, the inspector would usually send out a list of textbooks, from which the executive board would choose. Visual aids and library books were selected directly by the zemstvo, but usually from the official *Katalog* or from lists provided by the inspector. In a few provinces such as Nizhnii Novgorod or Vladimir, the local school board rather than the zemstvo board did the selecting. Often, according to the survey, the teacher had the final voice or at least participated in the selection through the zemstvo school commission. The striking variety of textbooks and readers in use and the prominence of primers written by Tolstoy, Vakhterov, Bunakov, and many other liberal and progressive educators confirms the suspicion that a considerable measure of de facto local control existed in textbook selection.[68]

Much depended on the personal relations between the inspector and the zemstvo. Although the potential for abuse was obvious, the available evidence and the zemstvo studies of the actual relationships between the zemstvos and the inspectors, as well as official investigations of links between zemstvos and school boards, demonstrate that conflict was the exception rather than the rule. Admittedly, the same zemstvo survey cited above complained that zemstvo influence was greatest on the boundaries between school funding and curriculum affairs—that is, in the provision of schools, books, and teachers—and that in the final result, the curriculum was only indirectly affected by zemstvo measures. Still, if one had to select pressure points where influence in schooling could be most forcefully exerted, it is hard to imagine more important spots than the selection of teachers and textbooks. This is all the more true in a country where outside inspection of schools took place once or twice a year at most.

If we consider the evidence concerning the role of the inspector in the countryside, the relationship between zemstvo and local school boards, the use of zemstvo resources and personnel to administer and supervise schools and to staff school boards, and the power of the zemstvos to participate in the essential decisions concerning personnel and instructional materials, *it is hard to avoid the conclusion that there was a high degree of local (elite) control of the rural schools.* The government did impose limits on this freedom, and with the increase in the number of inspectors after 1908, the potential for central control definitely increased. But the degree of standardization and centralization taking place in Russia was not notably greater (and may even have been less) than that in Western Europe and the United States. The level of activity manifested by the zemstvos, then, was a measure of their commitment to the cause of public education, not of the scope of freedom allowed them by the government.

6

Wretched Imitations?

The Church Parish School

Zemstvo control of local school boards and autonomy in managing secular schools did not necessarily provide the local elite with a monopoly over peasant schooling. Beginning in 1884, the Holy Synod, with the encouragement of first Alexander III and then Nicholas II, launched a campaign to combat the spread of secular values and to promote basic literacy, patriotism, and the Orthodox faith through the establishment of Church parish schools. This campaign, which lasted until 1906, was portrayed by liberal educators as a struggle between officialdom and local self-government, between official and zemstvo (*kazënnye* and *zemskie*) schools—words suffused with an emotional message—as well as a struggle between secular and religious education.

This chapter describes the emergence, spread, and decline of the Church parish schools, their complicated relationship with the zemstvo world, and their internal structure and organization. (Chapter 1 discusses Synod educational activities before the Emancipation.) There is no question that between 1884 and 1906, the parish schools were essential components of the school system, sometimes as friends of the Ministry of Education and the local zemstvo schools, at other times as rivals. Contrary to the claims of many historians and partisans of zemstvo schools, the internal or-

155

ganization of these parish schools was generally very similar to that of the zemstvo schools.[1] The Church school was often a poor relative, but a relative just the same, of the zemstvo school, and both were offspring of the same parent, the peasant school. In studying the results and impact of rural education on peasants and the village community, I have turned largely to zemstvo sources. But to judge by the organization of the parish schools, as well as by the surviving evidence discussed below, the conclusions derived from a study of zemstvo schools may also be applied, with caution, to the village parish schools—and thus to nearly all village schools.

A BRIEF HISTORY

During the eighteenth century, schools for the clergy may well have been the only institutions in the countryside—in district towns, that is—where peasants could receive an officially sanctioned education. But by the first half of the nineteenth century, the Holy Synod was only one of many government organs sponsoring rural schools (see Chapter 1). In the fifteen or so years following the 1836 Rules of Village Education, which encouraged village priests to establish and run schools in their settlements, the number of such schools increased rapidly, but then declined after 1853. Shortly after Alexander II came to the throne, the number of Church parish schools (under the supervision of the *shtatnyi smotritel'* of the district schools, an MNP official) again increased rapidly, particularly after 1858.

All sources agree, however, that these marked fluctuations reflected signals sent from the central government rather than actual circumstances in the villages. The 1858 increase came soon after Alexander II read a governor's annual report noting that here and there in the countryside local priests were teaching peasants how to read and write. Alexander expressed his approval and called for monthly reports from the dioceses; the Holy Synod in turn sent down instructions to the local priests to set up schools and produce monthly reports. Monthly reports were indeed produced, but how many schools were actually in operation is anyone's guess.[2] Since no funding was forthcoming from the central Treasury or the

Holy Synod, and all parish schools were to be funded out of local parish money—thereby competing with other Church needs, including the salary of the priest—we have good reason to be skeptical about results. Not until 1893 did the Holy Synod establish paid school inspectors, until then relying instead on the unremunerated services of the clergy to check on conditions in Church schools. Moreover, until at least the 1880s, "schools" in the countryside, whether secular or religious, seldom had permanent quarters. It is therefore difficult to give much credence to the numbers offered by the Synod. It was perhaps at this time, roughly between 1836 and 1864 when pressure was occasionally exerted from above on the local priest but no money provided or inspections carried out, that the Synod became infamous as the sponsor of thousands of fictional "paper schools" in the Russian countryside.[3]

For a brief time under Alexander II, during deliberations over the forthcoming Education Statute (specifically, during E. V. Putiatin's term as Minister of Education), an effort was launched to place the Holy Synod in control of all rural primary education. In reality, this effort was probably a bargaining strategy, a defensive move by the Synod to prevent the MNP from gaining uncontested control of basic schooling, as had indeed been projected in the early drafts of the education bill sponsored by the MNP's Academic Committee and the Editing Commissions. Political negotiations at higher levels resulted in a session of the Committee of Ministers on 18 January 1862 where Alexander II expressly stated his wish that the Holy Synod retain control over existing Church schools as well as those to be opened in the future.[4] The final version of the statute, however, subordinated Church schools in the villages to the local school boards, bringing the schools under the control of *secular* officials and local representatives. To be sure, the Synod actually gained some influence over secular schools at the same time, for the local priest was now obligated to teach Bible in the secular school and to keep a watchful eye over the moral quality of education and the conduct of the local teacher (Articles 16–17).[5] To judge from the accounts of teachers, many priests took this obligation very seriously and sometimes ruthlessly harassed teachers on issues of dress and overall appearance, friendships and recreation, as well as political beliefs or classroom conduct.

Briefly in 1865, when the Ministry of Education and the Holy

Synod locked horns over control of education in the western borderlands, and in 1866, soon after the attempt on the life of the Tsar, the government again considered turning over all primary education to the clergy, but even the Church recognized that it lacked the funds, administrative apparatus, and trained personnel to shoulder such a burden.[6]

Whereas priests were allowed to spy on secular schools, the local school boards were to report on conditions in Church-sponsored schools, and it may well have been these reports seeping into the press, often via the zemstvo assemblies, that convinced most people that the Church was in no position to assume the burden of popular education. In the words of O. Blagovidov, a historian sympathetic to the Church:

The vast majority of school boards drew from their first-hand contact with Church parish schools the conviction that the clergy, burdened with their obligations to the Church and with work at home [priests were allotted land by the commune and often engaged in agriculture], have no opportunity to carry out with any success the demanding tasks connected with teaching; as a result, the conditions in such schools are highly unsatisfactory.[7]

According to Blagovidov, these sentiments were shared by many local priests and Church officials at the diocesan level. Beginning in the late 1860s, as the zemstvos started to express at least nominal interest in local education, many priests shut down their schools or turned over teaching functions to literate peasants or retired soldiers, entrusting supervision to the zemstvos. Of twenty thousand schools existing under the Synod in the 1860s, only four thousand survived into the next decade.[8]

Yet the decline in numbers may have been as little reflective of reality as the increase recorded in previous decades. As the result of on-the-spot verification by the zemstvos, many paper schools that had appeared in response to Alexander II's note of interest were now "closed down"—that is, discovered not to exist. (It bears repeating that Church schools, though most roundly condemned, were not the only fictional entities; when Baron Korf began his school promotion campaign in Ekaterinoslav province in 1867, he discovered that only a small fraction of the schools registered in the province were actually in operation.)[9]

In some areas, the clergy actively promoted local education; often, the decline in numbers of Church parish schools did not signify a reduction in the clergy's activities, but rather a migration to the newly emerging secular schools. Throughout the sixties and seventies, the concept of the zemstvo school was ill-defined; most rural schools were peasant-sponsored, as well as peasant-maintained, receiving only salary subsidies from the local zemstvo. Thus, it was clearly in the best interest of the local clergy running schools for the peasants to establish an affiliation with the zemstvo—they could then be relieved of their unpaid teaching obligations or could receive a salary supplement not offered by the diocesan authorities. *In other words, the 1870s may have seen the Holy Synod withdraw from primary education at the top level, but at the local level, what took place was more a transfer of energy from Church to zemstvo.* Even the militantly anti-Church activist Charnoluskii conceded that the hostility of Synod officials to secular education did not accurately reflect the attitudes of the local clergy, who

as the more educated segment [of the rural population] contributed their share to the spread of public education, beginning in the epoch of the Great Reforms. From their milieu emerged more than a few dedicated teachers of both sexes, as well as zemstvo delegates, and many of the Church schools served as the cornerstones of properly organized ministerial and zemstvo schools.[10]

It is one thing to give the local priest his due as an active sponsor of peasant schooling; it is quite another matter to claim that priests could have served as the backbone of the teaching profession or that the Holy Synod could have energetically promoted primary education. Although the rural priest sometimes played a significant role in rural disturbances, siding with the peasant community in disorders before and after the Emancipation and identifying with the lower classes rather than with the elite monastic ("black") clergy or the privileged estates in the countryside, in other areas peasants clearly saw the priest as a parasite and outsider to the *mir* (commune). Some records document the contribution to education made by priests, but other records show that in places they were lazy, indifferent, and incompetent; testimony to this effect was sometimes produced by Synod officials.[11]

Whatever the balance sheet may ultimately be, one irrefutable fact is that there simply were not enough members of the clergy to meet the demands of the growing school system. (There were far fewer parishes than villages.) Several high officials, searching for a solution to the teaching shortage, expressed the hope at one time or another that the clergy could run the schools. This would have been an inexpensive solution because the clergy required no salary and because there would have been no need to invest in teacher training schools; in addition, clergymen would have been politically reliable. Ultimately, however, most realized that to rely on priests alone to educate the peasants was futile.[12]

Although the Holy Synod did operate a school council in St. Petersburg, it had no administrative apparatus in the provinces or countryside to deal with primary education and thus no large-scale bureaucracy engaged in promotional activities favoring the Synod's services and the expansion of its own budget. Some historians, such as E. G. West, have applied the "economics of bureaucracy" to the study of school system expansion and the history of government intervention in schooling. According to this notion, an internal dynamic in bureaucracies draws its energy from the link between internal promotion, on the one hand, and the growth of bureaus under senior officials in a bureaucratic system, on the other. Expansion fueled by the needs of the bureaucracy (rather than the needs of the country) in turn "leads to calls for mergers, coordination, centralization, and eventually, one exclusive monolithic body."[13] The lack of such an apparatus, the circumstance that Tolstoy served as both head of the Ministry of Education and head of the Synod, and the high Church hierarchy's general indifference to popular welfare may explain the Synod's lack of internal pressure to expand its domain in the sphere of education. Ideologically, the Church did press for control over the content of local school curriculum, for the restriction of learning to the ABCs and a heavy dose of religion, but it did so with little effort to alter the administrative apparatus of school control and with no internal pressure from the Synod bureaucracy to counteract the growth of the Ministry of Education, to increase personnel, or to gain larger grants from the Treasury.

The situation began to change in 1879, however. This year witnessed both an attempt on the life of the Tsar by a schoolteacher named Solov'ev and a discussion in the Committee of

Ministers of the relationship between Church and schooling. On 12 June 1879, the Committee of Ministers resolved that "the spiritual development of the people, which is the cornerstone of the entire state edifice, cannot be achieved without providing the clergy with the dominant role in management of the schools."[14]

Yet at the time, the Committee of Ministers declined to take concrete steps to act on this pious resolution. Only in 1882, in the atmosphere of retrenchment and counterreform following the assassination of Alexander II, were the first moves made to create a rival system of primary schools and then, later in the decade, an independent supervisory apparatus under the Synod. (By this time, Tolstoy had long been out of office, succeeded in the Holy Synod by the powerful figure of Konstantin Pobedonostsev.[15] Tolstoy's successor as Minister of Education [after the brief term of liberal Baron Nikolai] was the incompetent and universally ridiculed I. Delianov, whom one of his colleagues called the stupidest man in the Empire.) On 26 January 1882, the Committee of Ministers again issued a resolution in favor of promoting Church schools, but this time it established a commission (including the distinguished Miropol'skii and the "Christian populist" S. Rachinskii) to draw up a statute for Church schools.[16] Two years later, the Holy Synod published Regulations for Church Parish Schools (13 June 1884), and in 1886, an official program to govern school curriculum appeared. These legislative measures, together with a statute in 1896 consolidating the administrative structure of the new Church educational bureaucracy, served as the cornerstone of the Church parish school system and, like the 1874 School Statute for MNP schools, remained in place until 1917 with only slight alteration.

The 1884 Regulations provided for parish schools to be opened by the clergy with the object of "strengthening the Orthodox faith and Christian morality among the people and imparting useful elementary knowledge." Two types of schools were established: one-class schools with a two-year course, and two-class schools with a four-year course. Later, a revised statute in 1902 lengthened the program of the one-class school to three years and that of the two-class school to four or five years. It was apparent from the beginning that two years were inadequate to fulfill the program demands, and a circular issued in 1898 allowing Church parish schools to provide a three-year program merely legitimized wide-spread practice. As we shall see, even when the two-year program remained in place, the average length of stay of the pupil was hardly affected and closely approximated the intensity of school-ing in secular schools that had a longer official program.[17]

In one-class schools, the curriculum consisted of Bible, Church choir, reading and writing in Church Slavonic and Rus-sian, and the rudiments of arithmetic. In two-class schools, the only addition was some basic instruction in Church and Russian history. (In 1902, geography, a smattering of science, and drawing were added.) The 1884 Regulations enjoined the parish school to impart a love for the Church and the liturgy and to help promote the habit of regular Church attendance. Although the assumption was clear that the parish priest or deacon would be the teacher (Ar-ticles 10–12), Article 13 also permitted laypersons with proper certification to teach. This concession proved to be significant: de-spite regulations issued in 1885 and 1892 requiring the deacon to teach in the Church schools or forfeit part of his salary, and despite other measures stipulating that before a member of the clergy could take a post as parish priest he had to serve at least two to three years as a parish school teacher, by the turn of the century most teachers in the greatly expanded parish school system were unordained. Sometimes such teachers were impoverished members of clerical families who could find no other employment, but often they were from other estates and had received a secular education. The revised statute of 1902 stipulated only that the teacher should have at least a secondary education or formal certification.[18]

The 1884 Regulations established the important provision that graduates of Church schools were entitled to the same military ex-emptions provided by the certifying examinations in the secular schools.[19] More important in establishing the groundwork of an independent system rival to the MNP, however, was the setting up of a rudimentary administrative structure, which in subsequent years became far more highly articulated and was codified in the 1896 Church School Administrative Statute. Articles 21 and 22 of the 1884 Regulations placed general supervision of the schools in each diocese (generally coterminous with the province) under the bishop, who was to be assisted by a school council made up largely of Church officials, but including the MNP director of schools as well. Although even apologists for the Synod concede that these diocesan-level boards, like their counterparts under the MNP, remained dead letters,[20] Articles 21 and 22 did remove supervision of Church parish schools from the Ministry of Education and created the rudiments of a parallel system of school administration.[21]

That high Church officials were in earnest about promoting rural education became clear when in 1888 district sections (*otdeleniia*) of the diocesan school boards were established; by 1891, some 496 were in operation. Even more important, beginning in 1893, the Church established the salaried post of local inspector (*nabliudatel'*) in thirteen dioceses in European Russia. In 1895, another sixty-three positions were funded, and beginning in 1900, local inspectors were also established at the parish level with yearly salaries of 1,200 rubles. Before the establishment of the inspectors' posts, the same priests who were charged with setting up and running schools were responsible for inspection. Although the Synod had begun requiring annual reports based on standardized forms in 1887, these reports remained largely ritualistic, almost incantational, until the mid-1890s. At roughly the same time that a salaried inspectorate was established, the annual reports lost their ritualistic flavor and often became candid appraisals of the local Church schools—appraisals that are now of great value to the historian.[22]

In its zeal to demonstrate peasant preference for religious over secular education, the Church did itself more harm than good. By falsifying records in at least one case, it incurred the ridicule of the press and reinforced the inaccurate belief that Church schools were largely fictional entities. In this instance, the Synod presented information at its stall at the Nizhnii Novgorod Exhibition in 1896 alleging that in 1882, before peasant literacy schools were Church-affiliated, only three hundred had existed in Russia and that by 1893, two years after all literacy schools had been turned over to the Holy Synod, the number had risen to more than eighteen thousand. A quick search of directors' reports to the Ministry of Education showed, however, that in 1883 there were more than three hundred literacy schools in Moscow province alone, another four hundred in Vladimir, and so forth. Moreover, the diagrams displayed by the Holy Synod at the exhibit grossly understated the number of zemstvo schools in operation at the time of the fair. This fact was soon noticed by a representative of the Kursk zemstvo, who produced documents forcing the Church representatives to erase their figures for each province and insert a number nearly double the original for zemstvo schools in Kursk, Tula, Penza, Smolensk and Khar'kov. In the following months, the periodical press picked up the story and produced evidence that the Synod figures for *Church* schools were often falsified as well. In the Don region, Church authorities had "borrowed" pupils from secular schools to produce photographs for the exhibit; in Novouzensk district, a zemstvo teacher had been ordered to "share" his pupils with the local parish school. Here and there, spot checks showed that Church schools shown on the exhibit map could not be located in the villages.[23]

The Synod's crude propaganda reinforced the strong impression derived from an earlier period that the Church schools in the countryside were largely fictitious entities, the products of the fantasies of local priests or Church officials anxious to prove to their superiors in "Piter" (St. Petersburg) that all was well in the countryside. Times were changing, however, and for the first time local parish schools were in fact developing a permanent and independent identity. One reason for this was the establishment of a separate educational hierarchy responsible for the promotion and supervision of rural education.

Perhaps even more important than the articulation of bureaucratic structure was the fact that in the 1880s the Synod began to receive large subsidies for primary education from the central government. Until 1882, such subsidies from the Treasury amounted to only 55,000 rubles a year; even worse, this money came via the MNP, which could decide how to spend the funds. In 1882, the Holy Synod began to receive its allocations directly, and in 1887, the annual sum was increased by 120,000 rubles. In 1893, another 350,000 rubles were added, and in the following year, yet another 350,000. But the real increases were still to come: from 875,500 rubles in 1895 to 3,454,645 rubles in 1896; another 1 million added the following year; an increase to almost 7 million in 1900, and to 10.3 million in 1902. (In contrast, the MNP allotted 1.6 million rubles to its primary schools in 1896 and 5 million in 1902.)[24]

As a result, the number of Church schools in the Empire rose rapidly, from 5,517 in 1884 to 44,421 in 1903, until they actually outnumbered zemstvo schools, though the number of teachers employed and pupils enrolled in the latter always exceeded those in Church schools. According to those who have studied the Church records closely, the increase in Church parish schools in the decade following 1884 preceded the opening of the government coffers; in Vladimir, for example, as late as 1896 the lion's share of funding for local schools came from local sources. After 1896, however, Church parish schools became in effect official (*kazënnye*) state schools funded by the central government. But even with this funding, the Church could never match the money available to the zemstvo after 1890 and was forced to charge fees or require pupils to purchase their own textbooks and writing paraphernalia.[25]

The rapid rise in the number of Church parish schools can also be explained by the subsidies some zemstvos provided and by the occasional transfer of control from zemstvo to Church (a reversal of the process observed in the 1870s). But the most significant reason was a 4 May 1891 ruling placing all literacy schools under the supervision of the diocesan school boards and the Holy Synod.[26] These *shkoly gramoty,* or reading-and-writing schools, had emerged into the sunlight of official recognition after 1882 when the central government had removed the 1868 ban on private instruction in village schools and had legalized peasant-sponsored one- and two-year informal schools in the countryside. *Shkoly gramoty* had been the pet projects of many zemstvos in the 1880s, as the zemstvos were anxious to find a cheaper, more expedient way of spreading rudimentary literacy and were intimidated by an official survey that had produced staggering estimates of the costs necessary to educate the entire population. Now, after 1891, such schools were only legal if supervised by the clergy; and with one swoop of the bureaucratic pen, the Synod gained thousands of schools. Even allowing for the addition of *shkoly gramoty,* however, the increase in Church parish schools was rapid in this period. Moreover, during the two decades following 1891, the local Church school authorities succeeded in converting the vast majority of these one- and two-year institutions into full-fledged parish schools—which in most cases involved providing new school buildings, hiring qualified teachers, and supplying school equipment.[27]

During this period—specifically, between 1887 and 1897—the government seriously considered turning over all primary schools under the MNP to the Holy Synod. On 12 May 1887, the State Council instructed the Minister of Education and the Chief Procurator of the Synod to "prepare a joint report on the advisability of concentrating the whole control of primary education within a single state department." When by 1893 no progress had been made on such a report, similar instructions were repeated, this time urging haste. But in 1897, the commission was disbanded and the question, for all practical purposes, was buried for the last time.[28]

Not exactly buried, however. After 1896, proponents of secular education began to wage a bitter campaign—initially defensive, but later offensive—against the Church schools, which for the first time seemed to be in a position not merely to compete with but possibly even to drive out the new zemstvo schools. Articles appeared in prominent journals arguing that a dual administrative structure for primary education was a costly luxury Russia could ill afford and that because Church schools were clearly inferior in quality to the zemstvo schools, the former should be scrapped or at least excluded from all projected universal education networks.[29] The critics showed that teachers in the Church parish schools were untrained and incompetent, school buildings and equipment were in terrible condition, essential supplies were lacking, local priests generally ignored their supervisory functions, and, most important, the peasantry clearly preferred to send their children to zemstvo schools when the choice was available and (by implication) liked the secular instruction offered there more than the heavily religious and catechismic character education served up in the parish schools.

Ironically, many of the most vitriolic attacks on the Church schools were based on information drawn from the reports of the local diocesan inspectors; yet at the same time zemstvo supporters often complained that Church school inspectors were bumbling fools concerned only to impose harsh discipline and to propagate a rosy image of the Church school at work.[30] Of course, mud was slung in the other direction as well, with Church authorities blaming the politically suspect zemstvo teachers and the secular curriculum for the upsurge in social discontent and crime in the countryside at the turn of the century.[31] But by 1900, the Church parish school was clearly on the defensive.

It should be stressed that much of the conflict between Church and zemstvo school took place at the national level. B. B. Chicherin even argued that this famous conflict was not visible at the local level, that there was no friction between Church and zemstvo schools in the village, and that they continued to coexist amicably.[32] This assessment was probably an overstatement, for in some areas the local Church authorities did resent—even resist—the spread of zemstvo schools. Nevertheless, the point is valid; for example, in many areas zemstvo subsidies to Church schools continued into the twentieth century. But friction was clearly present after 1900 in the *high levels* of the central bureaucracy, between Holy Synod and Ministry of Education officials, and even pleas from the Tsar for cooperation seemed to fall on deaf ears.[33] It was at approximately this same time that the progressive educational press began to urge the zemstvos to stop subsidizing the inferior Church schools.

After 1906, the axe fell on the parish school, and it was the MNP who dealt the blow. The decline began with the Duma debates and subsequent passage of legislation providing yearly funding for the implementation of universal education. The district zemstvos were called on to draw up plans for universal education and to administer the grants provided by the central government, and the Holy Synod was effectively squeezed out of the massive expansion program launched in 1908. To be sure, defenders of the Church role in education were powerful enough in the Duma (especially in the upper chamber, the State Council) to block and permanently table new legislation that would have replaced the outdated 1874 School Statute—mainly because the Duma sponsors of the new bill wished to include a clause subordinating all local schools to a unified school board under the Ministry of Education.[34] The *expansion* of education did not, however, require a new statute, and the funds now pouring into the countryside were directed to the district zemstvo and zemstvo school. Moreover, the terms of these grants specifically excluded *shkoly gramoty* because they offered only two years of instruction and almost never had buildings that met eligibility requirements for inclusion in the official networks. Even the parish schools offering a full three-year program were often excluded because they were unable to attract properly certified teachers.

In short, because the Church schools lacked the funds to attract and keep certified teachers and to build proper school buildings, they were ineligible to receive MNP subsidies. This lack of funds only exacerbated conditions by increasing the flight of qualified teachers from these schools. It also placed the Synod in a disadvantageous position in the competition for peasant enrollment because it was forced to charge fees and require pupils to purchase textbooks and writing materials. A vicious circle was created: the Church school was criticized for being poor, and, because conditions were often inadequate, it was excluded from receiving grants, which only worsened these conditions.[35]

The irony of this major coup in school politics, the triumph of the zemstvo school and the decline of the Church school after 1906, was that it took place when the zemstvo school was for the first time becoming tightly attached to the MNP hierarchy through the greatly enlarged inspectorate and the strings attached to grants available to the district zemstvos for universal education. The schools first built and run by the peasantry, often with the help of local priests, had been slowly brought under the control of the provincial zemstvos in the last half of the nineteenth century through subsidies and zemstvo educational organizations and through zemstvo participation in, even dominance of, local school boards. These same schools were now being incorporated, by a similar process of grants and subsidies with strings and the tightening of an organizational framework, into the network of the Ministry of Education. The provincial zemstvos, which since the 1890s had been most actively engaged in the spread of education and which had generally succeeded in subordinating district-level educational efforts to their control, were now hoist on their own petard. In a very important sense, the decline of the Church parish school was another, though contemporaneous, stage in this process. The very argument used by progressive educators to destroy the Church schools—the need for unified control of the schools—was used against zemstvo schools when progressives argued against the central bureaucracy for the virtues of local self-government and administration of the schools.[36]

SIBLING RIVALRY

Even though the Church parish school began a precipitous decline after 1906, it undeniably played a major role in the history of Russian primary education in the countryside. In the following chapters, I focus largely on the dynamics of enrollment and the results of instruction in the zemstvo schools; is it possible to assume that the Church parish schools functioned in essentially the same way? To judge from the contemporary press, this assumption would be rash indeed. For example, an article in *Vestnik Evropy (European Herald)* in 1901 concluded a long diatribe against the quality of instruction and results produced by the Church parish school with the following lament:

The spread of inadequate schools can only be considered a net loss for the cause of public education. The children filling these schools are, in substance, receiving no education, no solid knowledge, and thousands of these spurious disseminators of enlightenment exist without bringing any good, but only interfering with the establishment of genuinely useful schools in those locations where they have been set up. Therefore, we look with anxious alarm at the fate of public education as the Church school system grows with every passing year.[37]

This attitude is very similar to that of the Soviet historian of rural libraries, K. I. Abramov, who excludes the thousands of Church libraries from his count of libraries in Russia before 1914 simply because the Church's facilities were stocked primarily with religious tracts and lives of the saints.[38] N. Bratchikov, the former teacher with so many clear insights into the dynamics of Russian schooling, commented in 1909:

Public opinion about the school is formed largely by political viewpoints rather than by a genuine study of the facts of the matter. The progressive press and public [have approached the question with the a priori opinion] that the zemstvo school, created by public efforts, is the best type of school, that it answers the demands of the public, and that it fully meets public needs.[39]

It is true that the Korf school differed in inspiration from the Rachinskii school; that the zemstvo school theorists prided themselves on a progressive, up-to-date methodology closely tuned to developments in the international educational community; and that Church school educators explicitly shunned all links with German, French, and then American educators, citing instead the Russian, and particularly Orthodox, tradition for guidance. Moreover, Church pedagogy was closer to talk-and-chalk approaches than to the child-centered routines advocated by progressives. The contrast, however, has often been overdrawn.

Although progressives attacked Church educators for being almost exclusively concerned with the promotion of religion and religious practices at the expense of instruction, progressive educators themselves seemed blissfully unaware of the deep-seated intellectual paternalism involved in their own concepts of childhood and their strong belief that peasant children had to be civilized, wooed away from the traditions and superstitions of their families and community. Indeed, these educators stated over and over again that education would be meaningless and would bring no changes to the village if it were confined to rote learning and basic skills; in their concern for the development of the "whole child" and the promotion of modern values and their despair at the apparent failure of school graduates to rise above the village milieu, they practiced a pedagogy no less intrusive than that advocated by the Church. That one was religious and the other secular is of little matter; each valued character education over instruction.

Moreover, whatever the arguments in the pedagogical press between proponents of religious or zemstvo approaches, at the local level the schools seemed to function in essentially the same manner. The official programs of the Church schools (1886) and zemstvo schools (1897) were virtually identical; again and again, studies of time allocation showed that Church and zemstvo schools spent almost the same proportion of the day devoted to each subject; at most, the Church schools gave more attention to Church Slavonic. As Darlington noted long ago, "Such differences as do exist are differences of proportion and emphasis."[40] My own perusal of lists of textbooks and readers used in the two types of schools shows that although the zemstvo had a greater variety, the books were chosen from essentially the same lists and most readers contained essentially the same mix of fables, natural science, edification, and travel stories.

Most important, until 1906 the requirements of the military qualifying examination really determined the approaches adopted by teachers and the time allotted to each subject. In zemstvo and Church schools alike, the teacher, whose competence was judged by the proportion of candidates who passed these examinations, adopted the rote methods and drill tactics most likely to bring success in this area and paid little attention to the great debates at the national level. F. D. Samarin, in an address to the Moscow zemstvo in 1892, was entirely correct in arguing that "instruction in the two types of schools is carried out in virtually the same spirit and, from the point of view of curriculum and upbringing, there are no grounds for juxtaposing . . . or drawing a firm line between secular and Church schools."[41]

One of the most striking ironies of this situation was that, by all accounts, the quality of Bible instruction was much higher in the zemstvo schools. The priest often neglected the parish school in his own village, traveling to the zemstvo school to teach Bible, where he received a salary based on lessons taught; as a result, Bible instruction in the parish school was often left to the secular teacher who had been trained (at best) in a gymnasium or other secondary school and often knew no Church Slavonic and only a smattering of the Bible. The compiler of the reports to Witte's famous Commission on the Needs of Local Industry in 1902 summarized local elite complaints: "Although the local priest is entrusted with supervision of the school, because of multiple obligations both to his flock and often as a relatively well-paid zemstvo Bible teacher he generally has no time to supervise the parish school or even to teach Bible in it—which instead is often left to a secular teacher."[42]

The reports of the Church archives are full of complaints that the parish school teachers were entirely incapable of teaching choir and could not themselves read old Church Slavonic, whereas the results of the 1911 Zemstvo Survey showed that in many areas former pupils of zemstvo schools did very well when tested in Bible. (This result might have also reflected the frequent references to the Bible and the fondness for lives of the saints observed by those who recorded peasant reading habits.) Thus, apparently, the Church school concentrated on basic skills, while the zemstvo school enjoyed the services of the priest!

It was often argued that the heavy hand of the Church bureaucracy stifled all initiative and creativity in the local schools and that the Church school inspectors were reactionary incompetents. Witte's commission recorded the following consensus among local people about the Church school bureaucracy:

Literacy and Church parish schools, by the general testimony of the local committees, are in unsatisfactory shape. An explanation for this can be found in the incorrect organization of school affairs, which are impeded by superfluous paperwork and formalities. The entire direction of these schools, in reality, is in the hands of the provincial diocesan board, which lags far behind the school; the condition of each individual school depends on the energy and views of the chairman of this board. The activities of the district sections of the board are paralyzed by the provincial board, since every improvement, every urgent need of the school must be considered and resolved at the provincial level. The chairman of the district section is entirely dependent, in service terms, on the Church authorities, and he involuntarily tries to conform to the views and demands—often quite impossible to fulfill on location—of the chairman of the provincial board.

Local people [*mestnye liudi*—a code word for the progressive educated public] included in the district sections of the diocesan board, who become convinced that their sincere desires to make a contribution are often fruitless, lose energy and cease to vitally participate in the operations of the bureau which, in effect, turns out to consist solely of the chairman. The provincial Church inspector is merely a pen-pushing bureaucrat engulfed by a mass of incoming and outgoing paperwork, and who accordingly has no time to visit all of the Church schools in the province. Since he has no opportunity to become personally acquainted with each school, what he does know about any given school is by happenstance or by denunciation; his annual reports are compiled from the reports of the district inspectors, who have received prior instructions from above. The district inspector, who actually does have first-hand knowledge of the schools, cannot always speak or write impartially about them in his report. First, he has the claims of the Church authorities; second, of the provincial inspector; and third, of the zemstvo. Under such circumstances, the position of the local inspector is very difficult and tenuous. His activities provoke constant complaints, resolutions from the zemstvo, and petitions to the diocesan authorities, and the result is high turnover of personnel, which also has a detrimental effect.[43]

I have argued above that the same complaints were leveled against officials of the MNP, but that the evidence supporting the argument that the typical inspector was abusive, pedantic, and incompetent is overdrawn. With some caution, I feel that the same may be said about the Church school inspectors. My own, admittedly incomplete, study of a sampling of Church parish archives from the 1890s and the five-year interval just before World War I produced a strong impression that at least some of these inspectors were genuinely devoted to the spread of education, aware of modern approaches and debates, and very candid in their appraisals of the shortcomings of the Church parish schools, both material and instructional. Time and again in the reports, inspectors are appalled by the difficult physical conditions confronted by pupils and teachers. On many occasions, there are references to overzealous teachers being reprimanded for resorting to harsh disciplinary methods (this, in particular, after a Synod decree in 1892 called for an end to corporal punishment in the schools). Most striking, I found that in their evaluations of the results of instruction in the Church schools, many of these inspectors seemed very concerned that the schools promote comprehensive learning rather than rote memorization and recitation. Although the Church school lagged far behind the Korf zemstvo school in switching over to the phonic methods of teaching reading, the old alphabet method had virtually disappeared from the parish schools by the end of the nineteenth century. (It is a further irony that in the early twentieth century the zemstvo schools began to change over to the "American" whole word method—a method that, Soviet educators soon discovered, is inappropriate for teaching reading in Russian, which is a more phonetic script than English. The parish schools remained with the phonics approach, which, although not as "advanced," was more suited to Russian needs.)

Understandably, both Church and zemstvo educators claimed that peasants preferred *their* type of school over the other. Chekhov was probably accurate when he commented that until the 1890s the peasants showed little preference (further evidence that the two types of schools differed little), but that at the end of the century and in the following decade peasant communities began to express a clear preference for the zemstvo schools. Indeed, the Church archives, particularly after 1905, are full of complaints about a massive flight of peasant children from the Church schools. Some communities even wrote petitions asking the Church to transfer the parish school in their village to the zemstvo network. The average zemstvo school enrolled seventy-one children at the turn of the century, whereas the Church school had only half that number. In addition, the results of a number of questionnaires sent to the villages demonstrated a clear peasant vote for the zemstvo school: a 1903 Perm' study showed that in 180 of 375 cases (48 percent), correspondents noted that peasants chose the zemstvo over the parish school; in 29 (8 percent), they preferred the Church school; in 85 (23 percent), peasants expressed no preference; and in 81 (22 percent), they said they would send their children to the closest school.[44]

This argument is not completely convincing; what it *does* suggest is that peasants would send their children to the school best equipped to provide a basic education at the least expense and inconvenience, and no more. As the Church parish system proved incapable of funding schools as well as the zemstvo did, particularly after 1900, and placed a larger share of expenses on the village community (even imposing fees and requiring pupils to purchase textbooks), peasants naturally chose the best available bargain. The progressive press pointed out that Church parish reports frequently referred to peasants' unwillingness to meet their share of expenditures on Church schools and that peasant resolutions in favor of Church schools were often forcibly extracted from the community by the local authorities.[45]

Indeed, such reports were true, but they missed a few points. By the turn of the century, peasants were paying a general land tax (*zemskii sbor*), part of which went to the zemstvo schools throughout the district. If an individual village had a parish, rather than a zemstvo, school, it had to pay an additional school levy to the diocesan authorities. Thus, peasants perceived that they were paying a school tax to the zemstvo and receiving nothing in return, while paying an additional fee for their children's education. It was understandable that peasants resented the second levy and only logical to seek to convert the local parish school into a zemstvo school in such cases.

Moreover, the records of the Moscow zemstvo show that when the 1896 plan to expand rural education was presented to peasants in that province, most districts had great difficulty convincing them to contribute to building upkeep or to take out loans for school construction. Undoubtedly, one reason for this reluctance was that the official chosen to explain the financial terms to the communities was the land captain, whom the villagers often feared and distrusted—after all, here was yet another *barin* come to the village to trick them out of their meager earnings! Elsewhere, it was reported, villages were asked to take out loans jointly with other communities against whom they often harbored historical grudges. Because schools had to serve more than one village, these longstanding feuds often presented major obstacles.

Thus the peasant reluctance to provide money was not confined to Church schools. The Perm' study did note that among the 48 percent of respondents who cited a preference for zemstvo schools, many claimed that the teachers were better and that the zemstvos were more amply provided with textbooks and other necessities (including night lodgings)—but this takes us back into the circular argument about the relationship between funding and quality of instruction. Moreover, it is worth noting that, despite the multiple advantages accruing to zemstvo schools by the turn of the century, more than 52 percent of the Perm' respondents reported that peasants either chose the parish schools or made no distinction between the two types.

Finally, we should keep in mind that the earlier zemstvo strategy of beginning to first establish schools in the bigger villages and more populous areas meant that when the Church entered the field, it was often left with districts where population was scattered and schools were consequently smaller. Again, financial exigencies intruded; because Church facilities were smaller and less capacious, it is logical that enrollments were lower. The literacy schools included in the calculations of average size only further reduced the average Church school enrollment.[46]

In brief, when a peasant preference between the two types of schools could be detected, it was based on utilitarian concerns; the stronger position of the zemstvo schools after 1900 reflected only the shifting financial fortunes of the two types of schools. Instruction in all rural schools was shaped largely by the overriding concern for maximizing the success rate on the certifying examination. Differences in pedagogical approaches between the two traditions tended to disappear in the classroom. Though instruction was undoubtedly better in the zemstvo schools, this difference was largely a matter of degree and stemmed from the school's endowment rather than from instructional approaches or philosophies. There is reason to believe that many officials in the Church school bureaucracy were genuinely concerned with education and sensitive to alternative approaches.

Although by 1900 the Church school was clearly a poor cousin of the zemstvo school (and the gap only widened in the next fifteen years), one can reasonably argue that the descriptions of the dynamics of the zemstvo school system, the peasant strategies for schooling, and the results of instruction found in the following chapters, though drawn largely from zemstvo school records, apply to Church schools as well. In fact, many of the studies contributing to this narrative of school history, although zemstvo-sponsored, look at both zemstvo and Church schools and show the same processes at work in each type of school. It is fair to argue, and I believe further research will demonstrate, that the Church parish schools have been unjustly ridiculed by historians, who have drawn too uncritically from militantly anticlerical sources and who have indiscriminately lumped together the views of Pobedonostsev and the high Church bureaucracy with the activities and beliefs of the local parish priests.[47]

PART II

The Outsider in the Village: Russian Teachers

7

Mere Craftsmen:
Teachers and Professional Adequacy

Writing after the 1917 Revolution, former Minister of Education Pavel Ignatiev commented:

Many schoolteachers, to whom life in the country was a novel experience, looked upon their present occupation as having a casual and temporary nature. Devoid of adequate training, unfamiliar with his surroundings, and inclined to look upon his work as a stepping-stone to something better, the village schoolmaster was not merely incapable of educating the younger generation, but was also incapable of satisfying the countryside's demands for enlightenment, and so failed to become an influential social worker in the district that fate had assigned to him.[1]

The rural teacher is a familiar and sad character in Russian literature. But little hard information has been forthcoming to verify the impressions gleaned from fiction. Western and Soviet historians have been content to point out that teachers eked out a miserable existence, that they were usually dropouts from advanced schools, and that they were often of a radical cast of mind—stemming either from their student days or from the experience of life among the peasants.[2]

Recently, however, the long-neglected Russian teacher has received attention from historians interested both in the part teachers played in political events on the national level and in the emergence of the professions in Russia—the corporate organization and autonomy of groups engaged in various specialized activities and the ability of these groups to free themselves from state tutelage. In these terms, the professionalization of teachers in Russia before 1914 was a failure—Russian primary school teachers failed to gain the right to organize, to set and police their own standards of competence, even failed to win the respect of the more prestigious professions requiring a higher education for entry.

Yet the status and power of the teaching profession, defined as autonomous activity and corporate organization, should not be confused with an assessment of the effectiveness and influence of teachers in the village community. If the measure of professionalization is in some way related to the ability to deliver services to a population, then, in the case of Russia or other developing countries, corporate organization and autonomy may be irrelevant criteria, no matter how important they are to the teacher's self-esteem and standard of living. In Russia, many of the external features associated with professionalization, such as claiming privileges based on possession of esoteric knowledge and (for teachers) donning a uniform, obstructed close contact with the village. It might even be argued, as the teacher P. Salomatin did, that the less professional teachers were, and the more closely they resembled the old *gramotei* who had taught in the villages before zemstvo-appointed teachers arrived, the better they fit in the village and the more effective they were at instructing the peasants.

If we accept delivery of services to the population (and to the country) as the proper criterion of effective performance, then we must ask what these services are and how we measure them. Ignatiev complained that the village teacher provided neither education nor enlightenment to the rural population. This chapter assesses this claim and argues that, although Ignatiev was correct in distinguishing between education (instruction) and enlightenment (socialization), his estimation of the performance of rural teachers was unduly bleak.

The next two chapters draw a collective profile of the village teacher that specifically addresses the questions of the teacher's ability to provide the rudimentary instruction demanded by the villagers and the teacher's impact as a role model and agent of external values. The personality, intellectual resources, and integrity of the individual teacher—qualities not easily quantified—were clearly important, but there are also a number of measurable features that help us estimate the place of teachers in the community: *gender*—male teachers had a far easier time gaining respect than did female teachers; *age*—the peasant community closely linked age with position in the village hierarchy; *origins*—the village was more receptive to change suggested by one of their own; *family status*—it was important to have a "hearth" (*osedlost'*) in the village; *length of stay*—it took time to win respect and trust; and *material and legal status*—a teacher in rags, dependent on village support, scorned and mistreated by the authorities and educated society, was in a very vulnerable position and unlikely to gain a voice in the village. Finally, the question of *competence* can be addressed directly. A careful look at the educational background of teachers reveals that most had the skills necessary to teach what the village community wanted.

In the discussion below, I have included descriptive passages and commentaries by teachers, but I have relied most heavily on quantitative indicators for a profile of the teacher. This approach reflects my general suspicion of the tone of most descriptive renditions of what was "typical" or "representative" in the countryside. Conditions were indeed harsh; but the tone of these descriptions often reflected not an objective assessment of the schools but rather the disillusionment that set in with the realization that literacy did not necessarily civilize the masses. Quantitative analysis such as that presented here involves crude assumptions and allows no place for considering the individual gifts of a teacher, but it does highlight the demographic dynamics at work in the profession and provide a backdrop against which individual comments and descriptions may be evaluated.

THE SUPPLY OF TEACHERS

As early as 1868, the Moscow zemstvo board turned its attention to the question of finding qualified teachers and noted that "the level of teaching in rural schools will be fully satisfactory only when the post is not a secondary obligation or a temporary and purely chance means of earning a bit to eat, but the concern of people devoted to and specially trained for the task."[3]

The few schools existing in the countryside at the time were taught by "the dregs of society [*vsiakoe otreb'e*], bureaucrats driven from the service, dropouts from various schools, retired soldiers, . . . all those who had nowhere else to turn." Where schools existed, local clergy had often been forced against their will to act as teachers and, instead of teaching, forced the children to perform chores. Numerous studies conducted by local zemstvos in the late 1860s produced evidence of the dire shortage of teachers and the lamentable quality of those who were available. Indeed, in one early effort to improve the quality of teachers, the Kashirsk district zemstvo in Tula province sponsored a contest in 1872 with prizes of up to 100 rubles for the teacher who could best demonstrate mastery of the phonetic method of teaching reading—but the contest was canceled when nobody showed up to compete.[4]

Until nearly the end of the century, however, the only major qualification that concerned authorities was political and moral reliability. Perhaps because it was widely believed in Russia, as elsewhere, that anyone could teach what everyone knew and that working with children required no special training, the first priority became simply finding enough teachers to fill the existing schools and to expand the system without excessive cost to the government. At various times it was suggested that the government recruit retired noncommissioned officers and solicit help from among the clergy, who would take up the work of teaching as an additional pastoral duty. Finally, in an attempt to avoid spreading the contamination of urban life to the rural commune, the government under Tolstoy launched a halting effort to build teachers' seminaries in the countryside to train literate peasants as teachers at government expense and then send them back to the villages. At least until the end of the century, however, particularly in Church parish schools, a substantial proportion of teachers continued to work in the schools as a supplementary occupation or as work to tide them over after retirement.[5]

Between 1880 and 1914, the profession of teaching at the elementary level emerged, and its ranks grew so rapidly that teachers outnumbered any other free profession by 1914, including the only other group with its face to the countryside: doctors and medical orderlies (*fel'dshery*). In 1880, the census showed that in the sixty European provinces of Russia there were 24,400 teachers, of whom 19,500 were male. By 1911, the number of rural teachers in the Empire had increased to 126,501 (of whom 61,400 were male), and the number of all primary school teachers, including those working in the cities, had risen to 153,360. Approximately 46,000 of the primary school teachers were employed in zemstvo schools, and 42,000 in Church parish schools. (In addition, there were 9,000 teachers in Jewish *khedery,* and 12,600 in Muslim *mektebe* and *medresse.*)[6]

This substantial increase signaled the establishment of a major profession. By comparison, a Soviet historian estimates that the total number of professionals engaged in industry in 1897 was only 61,027. In 1913, approximately 24,000 doctors and 30,000 orderlies were at work in the Russian Empire. The number of primary school teachers in the Empire in 1913 roughly equaled the combined numbers of ranked officials (60,000) and unranked employees (90,000) serving in the civil government bureaucracy in 1897. Thus, although they were deprived of essential elements of professionalization (corporate organization and corporate autonomy) and although they stood at the lowest rung of prestige, primary school teachers by 1914 represented a formidable army of workers with *potentially* great influence over the life of the country. No other profession had comparable contact with the village: whereas 46,000 zemstvo teachers were employed in the thirty-four zemstvo provinces, there were only 2,335 doctors in the villages; in addition, there were only between 3,000 and 5,000 veterinarians in the entire Empire, and only 9,000 trained agricultural personnel (of whom 4,300 were employed by the zemstvos). The only group comparable to rural teachers in both professional standing and place in the countryside was the *fel'dsher*—and there were five times as many teachers as orderlies. Moreover, none of these other groups actually lived in the villages where they worked.[7]

How many teachers did the country need to provide for universal literacy? Estimates and projections varied enormously; the disparities stemmed from disagreements over the proper size of the school-age cohort, over population growth estimates, over the acceptable size of schools (pupil-teacher ratios), and over the maximum radial distance to be serviced by each school. Differences over any of these factors implied adjustments in the number of teachers needed.

An influential position paper drawn up by the League of Education in 1908 and later submitted to the Duma estimated that by 1914 Russia would need 370,464 teachers, 200,000 more than were available in 1908. The most widely accepted projections placed Russia's annual need at 15,000 teachers to fill new positions and 8,000 more men and women to offset normal attrition—23,000 new teachers each year for a decade, or 230,000 in all.[8]

How close was Russia to meeting the demand for teachers?[9] In 1914, specialized pedagogical institutions were probably producing no more than 5,000 teachers each year for the rural school system.[10] Despite the rapid growth of pedagogical institutions in Russia, particularly teachers' seminaries (whose numbers more than doubled between 1905 and 1915), it would have been unrealistic to have expected the Treasury to find the 170 million rubles one specialist estimated were needed. Russia, like other developing countries (and indeed like many Western nations at the end of the nineteenth century), had to find other institutions to provide recruits, and did so.

For this reason, estimates of supply and demand that demonstrate an enormous shortfall of graduates from specialized pedagogical institutions (no more than 5,000, whereas 23,000 were needed) are misleading; they overlook the substantial pool of graduates from general secondary schools (233,000 male students and 324,000 female students in general secondary secular schools in 1914), as well as from advanced primary schools and from secondary schools under the Holy Synod. Although the MNP had little hope of attracting all these students to primary school teaching, the belief was that if it could tap but a small proportion and provide them with some pedagogical education, the gap between need and availability could be substantially narrowed. As early as 1896, the yearly pool of graduates from general secondary schools providing some pedagogical training *exceeded by ten times* the number graduating from specialized pedagogical institutions. More than 16,000 girls were enrolled in the pedagogical classes of the gymnasiums alone in 1911.[11]

Thus, to determine the true size of the gap between the demand for teachers and the supply of recruits, we must look beyond the teachers' seminaries and consider the process of certification in Russia.[12] The legal right to teach was automatically conferred on all graduates of secondary schools who had at least one year of pedagogical training. This category included most graduates of the ecclesiastical seminaries (boys) and diocesan schools (girls) under the Holy Synod, as well as most women's gymnasiums and pro-gymnasiums (schools offering the first four years of the gymnasium program, for children nine to thirteen).[13] Because the number of students enrolled in these schools far exceeded the demand for primary school teachers, the issue of supply must be rephrased: how many of these graduates were attracted to the rural schools, and how well qualified were they to teach the peasants? To policy makers of the time, the question was somewhat different: how much money should be put into teacher training, and how much into improving salaries of those already working in the system in order to retain them?

Answering such questions poses formidable problems (including determining the alternative employment opportunities for secondary school graduates) that would take us far afield. The main point here is that although the institutions created to produce teachers for the villages were not graduating enough recruits to keep up with attrition, let alone to fill new positions, a pool of educated graduates of other institutions was sufficient to make up the difference. Who were these teachers, how well trained were they, and how well did they fit in the village?

To further complicate the picture, because of the school system's rapid rate of expansion and because of attrition from the teaching profession, the government and the zemstvo had to set their sights even lower than the general secondary school graduates. They were forced to recruit graduates of advanced elementary schools, using certifying examinations to provide some assurance that these recruits were adequately educated to teach the rudiments. The tsarist government clearly had to resort to stopgap measures to provide teachers for its universal literacy campaign; did this mean, however, that teachers with such a variety of backgrounds could not be effective, or that the campaign was bound to fail?

A DEMOGRAPHIC PROFILE

As noted above, the potential influence of the individual village teachers often hinged on personal qualifications not subject to detection in the dry school records. Nevertheless, gender, social background, marital status, age, and length of stay in the village all helped measure the reservoir of good will on which teachers could draw or the depth of the suspicion and contempt they had to overcome.

The most salient change in the teaching profession in rural Russia between 1880 and 1914 was the *feminization* of the profession. In this respect, Russia was following the same pattern as England, where in 1914 about three-quarters of all elementary school teachers were women, but not the pattern of Germany, where in 1911 only 21 percent of teachers were female, working almost exclusively in the cities.[14] Table 6 indicates how the change proceeded in Russia.

Table 6
Feminization of Teaching Profession in Rural
Schools, 1880–1911

PROVINCES	WOMEN TEACHERS AS PERCENTAGE OF ALL RURAL TEACHERS		
	1880	*1894*	*1911*
34 zemstvo	27.5%	41.4%	62.2%
13 nonzemstvo	10.8	23.9	35.8
3 Baltic	1.9	1.6	9.8
50 European	20.6	38.6	54.9
10 Polish	14.0	10.8	24.0
60 European (total)	20.0	36.4	53.8

SOURCE: MNP, *Odnodnevnaia perepis'* 16:89, tables 32–33.
NOTE: Data included 26,000 teachers in 1880, 69,098 in 1894, and 126,501 in 1911. For provincial tabulations, see MNP, *Odnodnevnaia perepis'* 16:88, table 31.

According to Chekhov, women teachers had first appeared in the countryside in the 1870s, but as late as 1880 they accounted for only one in five teachers in rural Russia (exclusive of Poland). By 1894, however, this number had increased to nearly four in ten, and by 1911 women constituted an absolute majority (54.9 percent) of rural teachers. Moreover, although women made up only a narrow majority of teachers in Church parish schools (52.2 percent), they accounted for 71 percent of all teachers in zemstvo schools in Russia and for as many as four in five teachers in Iaroslavl', Viatka, Tver', and Kaluga zemstvo schools. In only six provinces did male teachers predominate in zemstvo schools. Interestingly, the proportion of female teachers was highest in the industrial provinces and lowest in the northern forest provinces, prompting investigators to suggest that greater employment opportunities for males caused them to spurn primary education in the Central Industrial region, whereas a lack of employment opportunities in the north led to stiff competition for teachers' places. Much of the imbalance, however, was also caused by the highly irregular distribution of male and female teachers' seminaries and other secondary schools.[15]

The tsarist government on numerous occasions expressed its preference for women teachers, whom it considered more politically reliable and pliant. The Marxist educational historian Samuel Bowles suggests that the replacement of male by female teachers in the West represented a move to promote the *internalization* of discipline over harsh coercive measures and "reflected a view that schools increasingly become an extension of the family, or when necessary, its substitute." In other words, the feminization of the profession was but one aspect of a general hidden agenda: to use the schools to inculcate the values and behavior desired by the dominant class and to ease the transition to modernization by promoting a docile work force. Yet another view, that of Lawrence Stone, associates the feminization of the teaching profession—indeed, the very emergence of a profession as such—with demographic factors such as a plentiful supply of unmarried women caused by an unbalanced sex ratio, a pattern of low marriage rates, or a very late marriage age.[16]

Whether the explanation was demographic, political, or occupational, the feminization of the profession, particularly in the zemstvo schools, meant that the teacher who was to bring knowledge and enlightenment to the village was now a woman. Although it would be incorrect to overstate the importance of this change, there can be no doubt that the female teacher enjoyed less prestige than her male counterpart in the village. In the words of S. T. Semënov, the writer who left a detailed description of rural life in the Moscow countryside:

[The peasants] expected no serious advice from the woman teacher because she was a *baba* and her hair was long [*volos dolog,* an allusion to the peasant proverb *"volos dolog—a um korotok"* ("the hair is long but the mind short")]. I had the occasion to observe this attitude toward not only our local teacher but many others as well. [17]

Other authorities such as Chekhov also noted that these *chernichki,* as they were sometimes called (from *chernichestvo* [nuns], because many women teachers were from families of the clergy), met with obdurate suspicion and even hostility from the local population; such feelings were not easily dispelled. The disillusioned teacher Salomatin, writing late in the period under study, argued that although some peasants would turn to the male teacher for advice, they would seldom approach the woman, whom they considered a *baryshnia.* This term meant that she was from another milieu; she was a "lady" who was concerned with her "toilet" and knew or cared little about the peasants' problems. According to Salomatin, peasants believed that a woman teacher was incapable of disciplining their children; they didn't trust her knowledge; and they believed she should be paid less than a man who taught. Even when they felt she was a good person, they would not seek her advice. "They will treat her gingerly, show her respect, when providing transportation help her as they would a child. A little lady, in short. But when looking after their affairs, they will never turn to the school." [18]

In some instances, peasants showed outright hostility and sought to drive women teachers out of the village, petitioning the zemstvo or local school board for a male replacement, holding back salaries, and generally making life miserable for the vulnerable city women. [19] Sexual assault was not infrequent. There is scattered evidence that when the 1917 Revolution swept the villages of Russia, unleashing a torrent of violence, the female teachers often suffered most from the outburst of hostility toward the outside world.

Yet, who can measure the impact that such "ladies" had on young village girls growing up in the twentieth century and exposed for the first time to contact with women who espoused values, conduct, and aspirations generally inimical to the usual role of beast of burden assigned to women in the Russian countryside? Although the village structure was generally intact in the early twentieth century, there were also abundant signs that in some areas young women resented their treatment and eagerly sought opportunities to escape. The new woman teacher may have played a significant part in encouraging such aspirations.

Describing the social origins of rural teachers is complicated by the heterogeneity and changing sex ratio of the teaching profession. However, one can make some general observations. Between 1880 and 1911, the proportion of teachers who were peasants rose from 30 percent to 40.8 percent. The proportion of clergy in the profession declined from 37.8 percent to 22 percent, and the proportion of nobility from 10.9 percent to 6.7 percent. Together, by 1911, peasants and *meshchane* (the social estate usually translated as "petty bourgeoisie") were an absolute majority of all teachers in rural Russia.[20]

Among male teachers, the most marked change was the sharp increase in the proportion of peasants (from 36.1 percent to 61.9 percent) and the decline of clergy (from 36.3 percent to 10.4 percent). Among female teachers, daughters of the clergy were still a substantial part of the work force, although their numbers had declined from 43.6 percent to 32.6 percent. The proportion of women teachers from the nobility declined by two-thirds, however, from nearly 30 percent to only 10.2 percent. The proportion of peasants among women teachers increased threefold (from 6.5 percent to 21.6 percent) and the proportion of *meshchanki* doubled (from 11.3 percent to 20.7 percent). The striking feature about the social origins of women teachers as late as 1911 was their heterogeneity; no single category accounted for more than a third of the whole group. Soviet historians are correct in noting that women rural teachers were increasingly of humble origins, for four out of ten were either peasant or petty bourgeois, and if children of the rural clergy are included, more than seven out of ten were from the lower strata. Nevertheless, the continuing diversity of origins precludes any general statement except that by 1911 the "lady" had by and large left the rural school, replaced by a woman of humbler origin (although to a large extent this interpretation depends on where one placed children of the rural clergy on the social ladder).[21]

The question of the geographic origins of rural teachers was never brought up in any of the major educational surveys, and we must be content with scattered information from an earlier period. For example, Orlov's study of Moscow in the eighties shows that 30.5 percent of male teachers were of urban origin and 69.5 percent were from rural areas; for women, the corresponding figures were 55 percent and 45 percent, respectively. A zemstvo survey of Novgorod province conducted in 1885 shows that although only 25 percent of all teachers were at work in their native villages, fully 65 percent were teaching in their home districts, and 92 percent were working in their native provinces. The social composition of teachers as a group changed significantly in subsequent decades, and these early studies of place of origin must therefore be used with caution. Yet a study of Iaroslavl' teachers at the turn of the century, when the school system was already largely in place, produced similar results. Of 943 teachers polled, the overwhelming majority of both sexes were working in their province of origin; only 5.5 percent were from a town or village in another province. Four out of ten teachers were of "urban" origin, but many were from the local district town rather than a large urban center.[22]

Did the teacher have a "hearth" in the countryside? In the most literal sense, yes. During the last half of the nineteenth century, the teacher commonly lived with the peasants, moving from house to house like a common day-laborer, or rented a vacant peasant hut. By 1911, however, the vast majority of teachers had been given rent-free quarters by the local zemstvo or lived in apartments adjacent to the school. Teachers' comments make it abundantly clear that the provision of housing was an improvement not only in their material status but also in their standing in the eyes of the villagers. Whereas before teachers had been little more than itinerant *gramotei,* now they no longer depended on the whim of the villages for a place to sleep.[23]

But in most cases, by "hearth" (*osedlost'*), peasants meant family, and it was the marital status of teachers, as much as origin or domicile, that gave them a place in the village. Circumstances, however, conspired to place overwhelming obstacles in the way of marriage and family life for teachers. As budget studies showed, a village teacher's salary made it extremely difficult to bring up children; with more than two mouths to feed, virtually all a teacher's wages would have been spent on food. Moreover, as Vladimir surveys showed in both 1898 and 1910, very few teachers could have hoped to educate their children above the elementary level; 56 percent of teachers said that they had not been able to provide their children with an appropriate education.[24]

Economic circumstances were not the only forces pulling against marriage and the family. In some provinces, including St. Petersburg, as well as Arkhangel'sk, Tobolsk, and other outlying regions, marriage meant automatic dismissal for women teachers. In Olonets, a woman teacher who married could remain employed only as an assistant to her husband. In Moscow circuit and elsewhere, women could remain at work only as long as they could "fulfill their teaching responsibilities" (were not pregnant); in still others, the power to retain or dismiss a woman teacher after marriage was left to the local inspector. (In a few provinces, marriage had no effect on the teachers' status.) Reports to the 1902 Teachers' Mutual Aid Congress are full of complaints and graphic descriptions of inspectors and other local authorities persecuting teachers who aspired to marry. One report cited a survey sent to seven hundred teachers (although only seventy replied): when asked why teachers remained unmarried, 88 percent cited external causes, including 43 percent who listed the "school administration" and 52 percent who pointed to "material conditions." (There were some double listings.) Interestingly, many women referred to *rumors* that teachers could not marry or to "fear of losing their jobs," rather than to actual instances or specific information. Nevertheless, in many areas, and as late as 1911, inspectors clearly preferred that teachers remain single in the belief that they would be more devoted to schooling, could be transferred more easily, and were cheaper to maintain.[25]

As a result, most women teachers were unmarried; in 1911, as in 1880, more than four in five women teachers were single

Table 7
Marital Status of Rural Teachers in Sixty
European Provinces, 1880 and 1911

	MALE TEACHERS		FEMALE TEACHERS	
	1880	*1911*[a]	*1880*	*1911*
Single	50.6%	53.7%	85.2%	80.6%
Married	47.8	44.2	10.4	15.7
Widowed/divorced	1.6	1.4	4.4	3.7

SOURCE: MNP, *Odnodnevnaia perepis'* 16:86, table 28.
NOTE: The 1880 data included 26,000 teachers; the 1911 School Census surveyed 126,501 teachers.
[a] Figures in the original data total slightly less than 100 percent.

(Table 7). (The number married rose slowly, from one in ten to about one in six.) In zemstvo schools, 50 percent of male teachers were married, a considerably higher proportion than in Church schools (40 percent). These figures strongly suggest that the male teacher was much more likely to put down roots in the village. Chekhov argued that this was because teaching was a supplementary income for many male teachers of peasant origin; like a cottage industry, it was used to fill the long hours between the harvest and the sowing season. Moreover, if we look at the number of teachers who remained in the village during vacations, the importance of marital ties in establishing permanent status becomes obvious. In Moscow in 1891, only 23 percent of single male and 22 percent of single female teachers remained in the village in the summer, while 80 percent of married men and 75 percent of married women stayed at home.[26]

Male peasants who had graduated from primary school and received a teaching certificate often took up farming after receiving work in a village near home; these teachers married and maintained homes in the community. As for graduates of clerical seminaries, few of them stayed in a village long enough to put down roots. Very few women married; when they did, they soon left. If marriage and a hearth improved the teacher's rapport with the peasants, the feminization of the profession, and especially of the zemstvo school, meant that the profession was losing a vital link with the villages. In 1911, only 38,000 of 126,500 rural teachers, or 30 percent, were married, and of all zemstvo teachers, only one in four (26 percent) had established a home.[27]

Another indirect indication of the authority enjoyed by the teacher was age, for peasant culture venerates age and links it with wisdom and authority. It is impossible to pinpoint a time at which villagers gained, by virtue of age, a voice in village affairs—was it when they took up the plow, gained independent incomes, married, or became a *bol'shak* (head of household)? It is worth noting, nevertheless, that in 1911, as in 1880, the overwhelming majority of teachers were young, under thirty years of age (Table 8).

Among men teachers, the most remarkable fact was that in 1911, as in 1880, roughly seven of ten were under thirty years of age. Among women, change over time was more apparent. In 1880, 90 percent of women teachers had been under thirty; by 1911, the proportion in this age group had dropped to 80 percent, despite the large influx of women recruits. Moreover, the proportion of women teachers who were under twenty years old dropped from 38 percent to 27 percent. (These figures suggest that the ex-

Table 8
Age of Rural Teachers in Sixty European
Provinces, 1880 and 1911

	MALE TEACHERS		FEMALE TEACHERS	
	1880	*1911*	*1880*	*1911*
20 years or younger	9.4%	11.6%	37.9%	26.6%
21–25 years	34.9	37.8	37.9	37.2
26–30 years	24.7	21.1	13.1	14.8
31–40 years	18.4	16.1	7.6	12.9
41 years and older	12.6	13.4	3.5	8.5

SOURCE: MNP, *Odnodnevnaia perepis'* 16:91, table 35.
NOTE: The 1880 data included 26,000 teachers; the 1911 School Census surveyed 126,501 teachers.

pansion of schools and the influx of new recruits to fill openings
was offset by the aging of those who remained at their posts and
made teaching a career; that is, several mutually canceling forces
were at work.) Still, as late as 1911, more than one in four female
teachers were under twenty years old, and only one in five was over
thirty. Thus, their youth, like their social background, gender, and
marital status, inevitably put these teachers at a tremendous disadvantage when it came to winning respect and authority among the
villagers.

In zemstvo schools, a higher proportion of men teachers were
over thirty years of age (35 percent) than was the case in Church
schools; fewer women (23 percent) were under twenty in zemstvo
schools, as compared to Church schools, where 32.6 percent had
not yet reached that age. Although two in three zemstvo teachers
were thirty or under, in Church schools four in five (82 percent)
were that young. (This concentration was true for men as well as
women.) Since the Church school system was expanding much
more slowly than the zemstvo network and therefore should have
been recruiting new, younger teachers more slowly, these statistics
on age offer confirmation of the frequent observations that parish
school teachers were more transient than zemstvo teachers, that
they moved to zemstvo schools when the opportunity arose, and
that they left the profession earlier than did the zemstvo teachers.[28]

TEACHER TRAINING AND CERTIFICATION

By comparing the 1880 and 1911 census data, one can assess
the degree of change and continuity in the level of teachers' educational qualification. Ignoring for the moment the feminization of
the profession, we see, overall, remarkable continuity in the level
of training. The proportion of teachers in all rural schools with
a general secular secondary education increased, but only from
9.7 percent to 14.1 percent; the proportion with a secondary religious education declined slightly, from 19.9 percent to 17.1 percent; and those with a secondary pedagogical education declined
from 21.5 percent to 16.0 percent. In 1911, as in 1880, the main
contingent of teachers had an elementary education and teaching
certification, which meant that they had passed a special qualifying

examination testing their knowledge at the six-year municipal school level and had served a probationary period as an assistant under a fully qualified teacher. Note that the baseline of competence was the equivalent of a six-year education (and most pupils entered the municipal school with prior formal education) and an apprenticeship under an experienced teacher.[29]

Because the zemstvo school and the woman teacher were, after 1900, the cornerstones of rural education, it is worth looking closely at the level of training of the female teacher and the zemstvo teacher, respectively. In 1880, of the 4,878 women teaching in rural schools, slightly more than a third came from gymnasiums and pro-gymnasiums, 28 percent came from diocesan schools, 14 percent from municipal schools, and 15.5 percent had no formal education. In 1911, of 64,851 women rural teachers, 26.7 percent had a secular (general) secondary education, 28.9 percent had a religious secondary education, 3.5 percent had a pedagogical secondary education, and 40.9 percent had an elementary or informal education (compared to 57.5 percent in 1880). Although the number of women teaching in the countryside had increased by nearly 60,000, the proportion with only an elementary education had declined 17 percent. In short, close to six in ten women rural teachers had a general secondary education (and one or two years of pedagogical education or training while in school), and the remaining four in ten had the equivalent of six years of general education. Not surprisingly, the women teachers with a secular secondary education gravitated to the zemstvo schools (where they accounted for more than one-third of zemstvo women teachers), and those with a religious secondary education were drawn to the Church parish school (43.9 percent of all parish school teachers).[30]

In 1910, the largest contingent of zemstvo teachers of both sexes came from the clerical seminaries (19.8 percent) and from specialized pedagogical institutions (18.8 percent), followed by those from three- and four-class pro-gymnasiums (16.7 percent), elementary schools (that is, through qualifying examinations—12.3 percent), women's gymnasiums (11.1 percent), municipal schools (10.3 percent), five- and six-class pro-gymnasiums (5.2 percent), and secular secondary schools without pedagogical instruction (4.5 percent).[31] This variety of sources complicates any assessment of the adequacy of teacher training in Russia. But let us consider the quality of general education and pedagogical training offered by the schools that produced the largest overall contingent of teachers: teachers' and clerical seminaries, gymnasiums, and diocesan women's schools. Some idea of the course offerings is essential to an understanding of the teachers' world view and their capacity to act as agents of change in the village or, conversely, to fit well into village culture. The picture is complicated by the special schools and requirements for teachers in areas with ethnic minorities and by the privately sponsored (duma or zemstvo) teacher training schools that were allowed to draw up their own programs and curricula; we shall thus concern ourselves only with broad strokes and a few generalizations on which most observers agreed at the time.[32]

Teachers' seminaries (first established in 1870 and governed until 1917 by regulations issued in 1875) were deliberately located in rural areas or district towns to ensure that the pupils' intellectual and political views would not be tainted by the influence of big-city life. These schools accepted adolescents and young adults aged sixteen to twenty-two who had certificates from two-class elementary schools (five to six years), and they allowed graduates of the basic primary school to enter a remedial (preparatory) two-year course prior to the three- or four-year program. Because the seminaries offered modest stipends, they were heavily attended by peasants, who in 1900 made up 64 percent of the students.[33]

The intellectual content of the courses seldom exceeded that of the two-class rural school program, and progressive educators at the time lamented that these seminaries were turning out "teacher-taskmasters" or drillmasters, not the committed idealists that were called for. Even Farmakovskii, a defender of the system, conceded that with the exception of Bible studies, all other courses were taught at a level of comprehensiveness and complexity much lower than that found in the institutes that trained teachers for the municipal schools. For example, Russian language instruction in the seminaries excluded all references to the history of literature; in mathematics, no algebra was taught; general history and geography were provided only as supplements to Russian history and geography; natural science was reduced to "explanations of natural phenomena"; and so forth. In short, a graduate of a teachers' seminary would have only rudimentary general knowledge.[34]

Yet criticism of the curriculum of teachers' seminaries, fair as it is, should be separated from the more general indictment that the seminaries were "inadequate to their mission." Even a harsh critic of these seminaries conceded that by the time the future teachers graduated, they had a reasonable knowledge of the basic subjects, a grounding in methodology, and a familiarity with the variety of textbooks available for use in the primary schools. Recent historians agree that the seminaries exerted a positive role in the expansion of the Russian school system for the simple reason that, although discipline was severe in these institutions and the program of general education little more than a repetition of the elementary school program, considerable emphasis was placed on practice teaching and observation, as well as on methodology.[35]

Formal training in didactics and methodology began in the second half of the second year, as did observation of classes in session in rural elementary schools. During the third year, apprentice teachers spent at least five hours a week visiting classes and had to plan and teach lessons in each subject area, first presenting them to a review board, which carefully scrutinized the content, level, and organization of the material, and then presenting them in the classroom. During the first half of the school year, apprentices worked with only one section (class); but during the final half of the year, they worked simultaneously with three sections. Thus they were gradually introduced to the environment they would confront in the village school. In the final stage of training, they conducted a full week of unassisted lessons in language, arithmetic, explanatory reading, and penmanship. These lessons were observed by the director, the teacher of the affiliated primary school, and teachers at the seminary and were then evaluated at a special meeting, where the apprentices were first asked to explain their approaches and evaluate their success. Other student apprentices were given the opportunity to comment, and the director and seminary faculty then gave a final opinion.[36]

The Soviet historian Panachin concludes his evaluation of teachers' seminaries with a revealing comment:

They carried out significant work in the preparation of a cadre of teachers, in working up a methodology of primary school instruction, and in spreading education in Russia. Their contribution in this area was utilized by the education organs of state in the early years of Soviet power. First pedagogical courses, and then *tekhnikumi* and schools—which played an enormous role in preparing Soviet teachers—were based on these teachers' seminaries and zemstvo teachers' schools.[37]

Allen Sinel's estimation of the role of teachers' seminaries is no less positive, though for somewhat different reasons. He concedes that the seminary had "humble academic goals" and an extremely limited program stressing syntax and composition, penmanship, and drawing, and that "teachers at the seminary were instructed to tell their students what they should know, but not to encourage questions or discussion." Sinel continues:

While rarely stimulating the future instructor's intellect, the seminary curriculum did prepare him in a practical way for his chosen career. In addition to his considerable time as observer and student teacher at the special primary schools set up under the seminary, he gained valuable help in readying himself for life outside the classroom. The pedagogy course, if superficial, did cover the typical problems he would face in Russia's backward villages. . . . The ministry gave the prospective instructor's practical training higher priority than his overall mental development.[38]

Sinel defends this MNP policy because of the poor quality of many applicants to the seminaries, because of the enormous shortage of teachers, and because of the rudimentary nature of the courses the graduate would have to teach, all of which made a more prolonged course "impractical, if not unnecessary." This observation is very important; as we shall see, the experience of the developing world today is that beyond a certain point, further increments of teacher training are not only superfluous but also actually counterproductive.

It seems fair to conclude that as craftsmen trained to instruct villagers in the rudiments of reading and writing, graduates of the teachers' seminaries (who composed nearly 40 percent of the male teaching staff of the zemstvo schools in 1911) were adequately prepared for their craft. Could the same be said for graduates of general secondary schools, whether secular or religious?

A main source of teachers for the primary schools was the religious seminary, offering a curriculum roughly equivalent to the gymnasium and accepting mainly, but not exclusively, children of the clergy.[39] Thousands of graduates of these schools became primary school teachers, but they were nearly always only "temporary guests," biding time until they received a place in a parish from the Holy Synod. Because their stay was so brief, it is unlikely that these teachers had a major impact on the school system or on the village, despite their numbers, and they need not concern us here.

The diocesan women's schools accepted children from the age of eleven and offered a six-year program. (After 1900, a seventh year, devoted to pedagogy, was introduced.) During the first three years, the bulk of classroom time was spent on Russian and Church Slavonic (four hours weekly), religion (Old and New Testament, the Gospels, Acts of the Apostles, translations from Church Slavonic into Russian), and arithmetic (four hours a week, including complex numbers, addition and subtraction of fractions, and itemized bills). In the second three years, the amount of time allotted to religion, Russian, and arithmetic was reduced to three hours each weekly, while instruction in Russian literary models, Russian and world history and geography, and basic geometry and physics was added. During the sixth year, the student received two hours a week of pedagogical instruction.[40]

The women's gymnasiums under the Fourth Section of the Chancery provided a seven-year course (beginning at age eleven) with thirty hours of instruction weekly, emphasizing modern languages, math, geography, and history, with less time devoted to religion or penmanship. In the last year, the *gimnazistka* received two hours of weekly instruction in pedagogy, which focused largely on the general principles of child psychology rather than on methodology or practice teaching. Other gymnasiums under the Ministry of Education offered an eighth year with additional pedagogical instruction, including practice teaching in the junior grades of the gymnasium itself rather than in an affiliated school with pupils in lower classes.[41]

Graduates of the standard program of the general secondary schools, both secular and religious, accounted for over half of all women rural schoolteachers and for six in ten women zemstvo teachers. These women had a secondary education that today would be considered quite rigorous and thorough. The general secondary schools provided a broad range of course offerings and wide intellectual horizons, but graduates received only limited pedagogical instruction, entirely inadequate practice in the classroom, and almost no exposure to village life or to conditions in the rural school. In contrast, the specialized pedagogical institutions provided a very limited general education, but a surprisingly rigorous, thoughtful, and adequate grounding in pedagogy, both in coursework and in practice teaching.

But studies of individual provinces carried out between 1894 and 1906 (Kursk, Kostroma, Poltava, Tula, Novgorod) showed that as the school system expanded, and even as wages crept upward, the formal qualifications of teachers as a group were declining.[42] Because there were not enough qualified teachers to fill the number of places created each year or to make up for the large numbers lost to attrition, new recruits were picked up from the pool of graduates of municipal schools or other advanced elementary schools (with courses of five to six years) and from young men and women with an incomplete secondary education. To qualify to teach in an elementary school, an applicant with an incomplete secondary or complete elementary education had to pass a set of written and oral certifying examinations—testing municipal school–level knowledge—and had to demonstrate teaching competence by conducting sample lessons. The certifying examinations, codified in 1896, differed in thoroughness according to the level of education completed. The basic principle was that the lower the level of formal education, the more thoroughly the applicant had to be tested.[43]

How seriously were these examinations treated? Since by 1896 one of every five teachers under the MNP and, by 1911, one of every two male and one of every three female teachers had qualified by certification, this question takes on a great deal of importance. There is some reason for skepticism about the rigorousness of the tests, for even in the 1890s there were severe shortages of qualified teachers in many provinces, particularly where universal literacy programs had been launched, and in 1896 one in every twenty teachers was serving without any formal qualification to work. It was not uncommon to appoint uncertified teachers on condition that they soon receive certification, but when no one qualified to replace them, it is unlikely that such conditions were strictly enforced.[44] These uncertified teachers were employed mainly in the borderlands, but, given the shortage of eligible candidates in many areas, inspectors and examination boards were probably willing to stretch the regulations and be lenient in conducting the examinations.

Nevertheless, there is also evidence that the examinations were taken seriously. For example, the MNP official Farmakovskii insisted that the regulations were applied literally, the examinations conducted rigorously, and the decisions, protocols, and written answers filed and saved for review by the inspector's superiors. Moreover, the former teacher Salomatin, in his general indictment of the school system, refers to items from the contemporary periodical press documenting instances in which the local inspector gave all teachers one year to pass the qualifying examinations or face dismissal, for "there [were] many qualified graduates looking for work, while uncertified teachers remain[ed] on the job." Salomatin cites these episodes as further examples of the legal vulnerability of the teacher and the arbitrary nature of inspectors' decisions, and he complains that preparing for the certifying examinations was no easy task.[45] So it appears that uncertified teachers felt some pressure and that the qualifying examinations *were* more than formalities.

What then did these examinations test? According to the regulations, successful candidates knew the prayers included in the school Horologium, New and Old Testament history, the brief catechism, liturgy, and sacred history, all at the level of the district and municipal school textbooks. They could read and pronounce Church Slavonic and fluently translate from the Gospels, and they showed familiarity with basic etymology and syntax. In Russian, they of course read and wrote fluently and correctly, and they also knew the contents of at least one reader approved for the primary school and could recite poems and fables from this reader. They knew the content of a basic course in grammar, at the level of the senior class of the municipal school or the third class of the gymnasium. They were familiar with basic methods of teaching reading and felt at home with one of the primers approved for MNP schools. In arithmetic, the examinees had to know flawlessly a textbook used at the municipal school level and had to be competent at written and oral problem solving at the same level; they had to know basic geometry and be at ease discussing the basic approaches to teaching arithmetic applied in any elementary school arithmetic book. They had to know world geography at the level provided in the widely used text by Putsykovich, and Russian geography from a municipal school textbook (Baranov).[46]

The requirements of the examination were fairly modest, but when enforced they provided an adequate grounding for competent instruction in the rudiments of reading and writing. As a stopgap measure, employing certified teachers who had the equivalent of six years of formal education (as well as those with an incomplete secondary education) was a rational policy for a developing country with limited reserves of human capital and an urgent timetable for achieving universal literacy.

Consider, by comparison, the qualifications of teachers in Great Britain in 1900. There, of twenty-five thousand certified male teachers, 28 percent had no formal training; of thirty-nine thousand certified female teachers, 51 percent had no pedagogical training. In addition, a substantial and growing proportion of teachers had no certification whatsoever, and these "supplementaries" had no training for their positions. Indeed, many rural areas preferred the untrained assistant, who had only to be eighteen years of age and vaccinated against smallpox to receive permission to teach. According to a report in 1900, there were 17,513 such supplementaries. Pamela Horn, combining the various categories of teachers, calculates that the proportion of trained and certified teachers dropped in the quarter century following 1875 from 70 percent to 66 percent of male teachers and from 57 percent to 32 percent of females. The proportion of women teachers who were both untrained and uncertified rose from 13 percent in 1875 to 41 percent in 1914. In America, David Tyack writes, "teachers in rural schools could hardly be considered members of a profession . . . they were young, poorly paid and rarely educated beyond the elementary subjects."[47]

Can we equate the level of education of primary school teachers with their actual state of preparation for the tasks facing them and the difficulties of rural life? Statements by individual teachers indicate that no such equation can be made. The data collected for the 1911 All-Zemstvo Congress on Education reveal that of 13,812 teachers only 10.3 percent felt their preparation had been adequate for the job of primary school teaching. Nearly three-fourths of all

Table 9

Teachers' Educational Backgrounds and Perceived Adequacy of Preparation for Teaching
(based on teachers' comments)

TEACHERS' EDUCATION	RECEIVED SUFFICIENT PREPARATION OVERALL	HAD INSUFFICIENT PEDAGOGICAL KNOWLEDGE	HAD INSUFFICIENT PEDAGOGICAL EXPERIENCE	HAD INSUFFICIENT GENERAL KNOWLEDGE	RECEIVED INSUFFICIENT PREPARATION FOR LIVING CONDITIONS
Teachers' seminaries	14.2%	21.8%	54.9%	18.0%	31.8%
Women's gymnasiums	8.2	35.7	67.6	6.6	45.8
Clerical seminaries	10.2	41.4	68.1	10.6	27.7
Urban schools (male teachers)	7.1	51.3	68.0	13.6	24.8
Women's pro-gymnasiums	9.9	44.4	58.3	14.4	30.2
Teacher certification examinations	10.1	51.0	66.8	15.7	22.6
Secondary and specialized education	11.3	32.7	62.9	12.6	33.0
Primary and incomplete secondary education	9.0	48.8	64.2	14.6	25.9
All respondents	10.3		72.3	13.3	30.2

SOURCE: *Anketa*, 21–42, tables 11–14.

NOTE: There were 13,812 respondents. The survey considered only teachers who had been working for at least three years. It should be noted that the lead question in the survey was weighted to emphasize shortcomings: "At the initial stages of your teaching career, in which of the following areas and subjects did you experience the most severe shortcomings in background, training, and experience?"

answers (72 percent) pointed to the inadequacy of training in pedagogical skills, 13 percent referred to insufficient general knowledge, and fully 30 percent reported a "lack of awareness of the conditions in which the teacher would be required to work and live."[48] (See Table 9.)

The last two categories in Table 9 register the perceptions of insufficient general knowledge and of inadequate preparation for living conditions in the countryside. Some 30.2 percent of all teachers complained they had not been prepared for the conditions in the village or for the sharp contrast between the urban life to which they had been accustomed and the hardships of the rural environment in which they were forced to teach. Dissatisfaction with their surroundings was most evident among graduates of the women's gymnasiums (45.8 percent), whereas the graduates of the teachers' seminaries and diocesan and urban schools were most comfortable in their surroundings. To judge by the reports to the Zemstvo Congress, the greatest difficulties faced by rural teachers stemmed from the lack of preparation for the "culture shock" encountered in moving from the city to the countryside and from their inability to provide useful answers to practical questions broached by the adult population. It would seem that peasants expected the teacher to be lawyer, agronomist, doctor, and social commentator, as well as educator.

It bears repeating that graduates of teachers' seminaries and clerical schools were the most comfortable in the rural environment. The state, for security reasons, preferred employing graduates of precisely these schools because such an arrangement supposedly preserved the peasants from direct contact with the cities.[49] Such a policy may well have been justified, for the dissatisfaction expressed in changing from an urban to a rural environment by graduates of urban-based schools was easily channeled into political discontent. The distress of the teacher whose only experience in education had been instructing a small group of children of the intelligentsia and who now had to cope with three large classes of illiterate and unruly peasants can well be imagined. (See teachers' comments in Chapter 8.)

Yet is it fair to conclude from this general dissatisfaction that the teacher was unprepared to provide instruction in the basics? Of the nearly 14,000 zemstvo teachers who commented on their level of preparation for teaching in rural schools, 9,990 (or nearly three in four) complained that their general level of *pedagogical* training was inadequate. Interestingly, only 1,813, or 13.3 percent, explicitly noted inadequate *knowledge* of subject matter. More specifically, teachers felt they lacked knowledge in natural science (4.4 percent), Russian literature (1.8 percent), local languages (2.2 percent), and child psychology (1.5 percent), with psychology, math, history, Church Slavonic, hygiene, discipline, and school accounting each cited by less than 1 percent. In no area did a sizable proportion of teachers feel that their level of general knowledge was not adequate to allow them to teach, at least at the level of the official elementary school program. In provinces with non-Russian groups, a larger minority of teachers complained of inadequate knowledge of the local language, but even there the proportion was small: 16 percent in Bessarabia, 12.2 percent in Kazan', 5.3 percent in Viatka, 5.2 percent in Olonets, and between 2.3 percent and 4.6 percent in Penza, Simbirsk, Samara, Ekaterinoslav, Tavrida, St. Petersburg, Ufa, and Kherson. Whereas seven in ten (72 percent) complained that their pedagogical preparation (meaning both experience and knowledge) was inadequate, only four in ten (41 percent) noted that their *knowledge,* or background, in pedagogy was insufficient. Of the 8,898 who complained of lacking pedagogical experience, few were specific; but of those who were, the most frequent complaints were about language arts training in Russian grammar and phonetics (811 respondents) and about lack of practice in teaching three sections simultaneously (808). Only 347 noted shortcomings in the methodology of teaching arithmetic and 105 in working with new (younger) pupils.[50]

It is particularly interesting to compare the evaluations of teacher training expressed by those with only a primary or incomplete secondary education (and certification) to the responses of those with a secondary (general and pedagogical) education (Table 9). A far greater proportion of the former felt at home in the countryside, although nearly half again as many felt that their pedagogical education had been inadequate. Because their self-evaluation in those areas corresponds with what we know of their background and education, it is striking that only 14.6 percent (compared with 12.6 percent of teachers with a secondary education) judged their level of general knowledge insufficient. In other words, although they felt the lack of pedagogical knowledge, they believed their limited general education was sufficient to teach rural children.

If we can extrapolate from this fragmentary, tantalizing evidence, we can draw what are perhaps the most important conclusions from this study: that only a small proportion of teachers felt their general education was deficient; and that although a large minority believed their level of *pedagogical* knowledge was inadequate, in pedagogical preparation it was *experience* rather than *knowledge* that was most wanting when teachers first began their careers. These are striking findings, for if we may believe the teachers' self-assessments, the widespread belief that the Russian rural teacher was inadequate to teach even the ABCs must be revised, or perhaps discarded. Most teachers felt their level of general and pedagogical knowledge was adequate; experience could be, and surely was, gained after taking up the job (painful though the process might have been).

LENGTH OF STAY

Common sense tells us that a reasonable length of stay, or tenure, in the village was a prerequisite, a necessary though not always a sufficient condition, for village teachers to win the trust and respect of the community. As one veteran of the countryside noted:

The longer a teacher works in his profession, the more professional experience he gains. The longer he works in a village and comes to know at first hand peasant *byt* [way of life], the better and closer he will forge links with the local population. . . . This requires not one, or two, but many more years of contact and experience.[51]

Peasants also felt that tenure was important. As an Iaroslavl' teacher commented, they insisted that to be successful a teacher had to spend a lifetime, "or at least ten to fifteen years," in the same school and village.

We should keep in mind the distinction between time spent in the teaching profession and time spent teaching in the same village, for the two were quite different in the Russian experience. Although the length of one's teaching career was undoubtedly an important index of overall pedagogical effectiveness and experience, the contact and interaction that allowed a teacher to win a place in the community were developed only through spending a substantial period of time in a particular village.

It is useful to compare data collected on thirty-three provinces by the Moscow Literacy Committee in 1894 to the results of the 1911 School Census.[52] If we take into account the ongoing expansion of the school system and the consequent yearly influx of new teachers, the figures reveal that by 1911 those already working in the schools were beginning to stay on the job longer. In 1894, 43.1 percent of teachers had been working fewer than five years; in 1911, the proportion was 48.1 percent—68,300 teachers, of whom 60,000 taught in the villages. But from 1906 through 1910, 20,245 schools had opened their doors for the first time, and these new openings thus accounted for more than one-third of the teachers who had worked for fewer than five years in 1911. The remaining two-thirds—some 40,000 teachers with little experience—represented about one-third of the total number of rural teachers in 1911 (126,000). Thus, if the effects of expanding the school system are removed from the picture, we find that a lower percentage of teachers (30 to 35 percent) fell into the less-experienced category in 1911 than the 43.1 percent who fit this description in 1894—in other words, a general lengthening of service can be seen. Moreover, by 1911, 31 percent of male rural teachers and 24 percent of female rural teachers had been working for ten years or more in the countryside.[53]

Separate zemstvo studies record that in those areas where the school system had been intact for some time, the amount of time each teacher spent in the schools had increased. In Vladimir province, for example, progress had been slow but measurable: the proportion of male teachers who had been working for five years or more increased from 52 percent to 60 percent between 1898 and 1911; among women, the increase was from 39 percent to 45 percent.[54] In Moscow in 1891, only 28 percent of male teachers had worked more than ten years; by 1910, that proportion had increased to 54.7 percent. In 1891, only 19 percent of women teachers had served more than ten years; by 1910, this figure had increased to 42 percent. The proportion who had served five years or less had declined from approximately 40 percent to 25 percent of

men and from 45 percent to 35 percent of women.[55] The importance of the Moscow data is that there, by the turn of the century,
the school network was nearly complete and the system stable;
thus, the official measurement of teachers' length of employment
in 1910 more closely reflected the actual professional life spans of
the teachers. These data suggest that the frequent observation that
the school was a way station and that rural teachers were transients
in their profession must be modified to account for the distortion
created in census statistics measuring length of stay without adjusting for the influx of new teaching recruits who filled positions in
recently opened schools.

Zemstvo studies of length of service uncovered a very disturbing negative correlation between educational qualifications and the
length of teaching careers. Studies of Iaroslavl', Moscow, Tula, and
Vladimir in the 1890s all produced the same results: "The lower the
education, the more tenaciously rural teachers clung to their posts,
and vice versa." These studies also showed that among teachers
with secondary education, most were actually dropouts. For example, in Iaroslavl', men with a degree from a clerical seminary
stayed in teaching eight years on the average; dropouts from clerical seminaries stayed more than fourteen years. In Moscow, the
same relationship prevailed—those with a degree stayed seven
years, those without a degree twelve years.[56] Studies of the relationship between length of stay and education add force to the argument that it did not make much sense to try to radically upgrade
teachers' qualifications: additional increments of education simply
prompted the teacher to seek more highly paid work elsewhere in
the economy, creating a new loss for the school system.

A growing average length of stay in the profession did not
necessarily entail increasing contact between individual peasant
community and teacher. In fact, the teacher-pioneer, as Chekhov
put it, was also a teacher-itinerant. As one study noted:

All the advantages accruing to a school from lengthy service by one
teacher disappear without a trace when he is transferred to another school.
The teacher's knowledge of local conditions, of the people, and of the *byt*
of the inhabitants . . . all the experience of adapting a pedagogy to local
needs, as well as the personal ties and influence of the teacher in his locale,
even the simple familiarity with one's surroundings and population so es-

Table 10
Turnover: Number of Schools at Which
Teachers Had Been Employed

PROVINCE	ONE SCHOOL	TWO SCHOOLS	THREE SCHOOLS	FOUR OR MORE SCHOOLS	UNKNOWN
			Male Teachers		
Moscow	48%	26%	15%	9%	2%
Iaroslavl'	36	29	13	9	13
Pskov	29	42	17	12	0
Vladimir	37	26	15	21	1
			Female Teachers		
Moscow	49%	34%	11%	6%	0%
Iaroslavl'	43	34	9	6	8
Pskov	54	34	10	2	0
Vladimir	47	30	16	7	0

SOURCES: Vladimirskaia gubernskaia zemskaia uprava (Vladimir), *Sbornik statisticheskikh* 3:141; Statisticheskoe biuro Tavricheskogo gubernskogo zemstva (Tavrida), *Sbornik po shkol'noi statistike* 2:41; Sheremet'ev (Tula), *Narodnye uchitelia*, 31; Moskovskaia gubernskaia zemskaia uprava, Otdel khoziaistvennoi statistiki (Moscow), "Svedeniia ob uchashchikh," 98; Evteev, *Trudy pervogo vserossiiskogo s"ezda* 1:257.

NOTE: The studies from which the data are drawn were all conducted in the 1890s.

sential to a sense of well-being—all of this is destroyed with one stroke of the pen, and lost to the schools.[57]

In Iaroslavl', for example, only 42 percent of male and 46 percent of female zemstvo teachers had spent their entire teaching career in the same school.[58] The pervasiveness of this internal turnover is illustrated by material from several studies carried out in the 1890s, summarized in Table 10.

Only in Moscow were nearly half of all male teachers still serving in their first school; elsewhere, the proportion was closer to one-third. More women than men were still working in their first school; whether this can be explained by greater stability of tenure or by the more recent influx of women into the profession is not clear. In most areas, more than 25 percent of the teachers were serving in at least their third school since entering the profession. Although this turnover may not seem remarkable, we should keep in mind that in almost all provinces the average stay in the profession was under ten years—and in some it was closer to five. Thus, in most provinces the teacher seldom spent more than two or three years in the same school.

In Vladimir, it was calculated in 1900 that in any given year one in three male teachers and four in ten female teachers were new to the schools in which they were working. In Tavrida, the average professional tenure of the zemstvo teacher was 11 years, the average number of transfers in that time 2.5, and the average length of stay in the same school 4.5 years. In Iaroslavl', the average accumulated teaching time was 5.8 years (for both sexes) but the average stay in one school was only 3.8 years for men and 3.2 years for women. In Tula, men had stayed in the profession 7.5 years and in the same school 3.4 years; comparable statistics for women were 6.2 and 3.5 years, respectively. In Moscow, men stayed in the profession 9 years, but only 5.2 years in the same school; women stayed 8.1 and 5.2 years, respectively.[59]

To be sure, if Vladimir province was representative, the situation was slowly improving. There, even as the proportion of teachers who were new but had prior teaching experience elsewhere increased between 1898 and 1910 (from 54 percent to 65 percent of male teachers, from 45 to 46 percent of female teachers), so did the average length of stay in the same school. In Vladimir, the proportion of teachers, both male and female, who were dealing with a new community in 1910 had dropped sharply—from about 40 percent to roughly 25 percent. Still, the percentage of teachers with more than five years in the same school had increased only very slightly. As late as 1910, only one in three teachers had been working with the same community for five years or more.[60]

The high incidence of turnover within the system was the source of frequent comment by teachers and by the periodical press. In many cases, turnover was the result of political persecution or harassment by local authorities; in others, it was an attempt to protect the teacher from irate local inhabitants—the village *starosta,* the priest, or the community itself. Inspectors generally preferred to transfer teachers rather than dismiss them; in dismissal cases, approval of the local school board and considerable paper-work were required, whereas in the case of transfers the inspector's command sufficed and could not be questioned. In some cases, the transfer was specifically a demotion and involved two moves: one teacher was sent to a school out in the wilderness, and another (completing probation) was returned to what was deemed—rela-tively speaking—civilization.[61]

Information on two provinces sheds light on the reasons for the high incidence of turnover. In Vladimir in 1910, vacancies cropped up in 16 percent of all schools (and in 10 percent of these schools, vacancies occurred at least twice during the year). In Moscow in 1914, excluding the sixty-three males who were mo-bilized and the four females who became nurses, 13 percent of all teachers left their posts. Between two-thirds and three-fourths of vacancies were caused by internal turnover (moving from one school to another) and, in Vladimir at least, nearly 87 percent of such moves were involuntary—that is, initiated at the order of the local inspector. Just how disruptive these transfers were to the school routine is suggested by statistics showing that 59 percent of transfers occurred in the middle of the school year and that with 13 percent of these vacancies (that is, excluding those occurring over the summer) schools were closed for more than a month.[62]

CONCLUSIONS

Rural teachers came from a variety of educational back-grounds. Those with the best general education seemed to ex-perience the greatest discomfort in the countryside (they were generally from cities); those with the limited education provided at teachers' seminaries seemed best prepared for life in the village and teaching in a rural school. Although all complained of shortcom-ings in pedagogical preparation, in most cases lack of experience was felt more sharply—experience that was soon, if painfully, gained. Because of the rapid expansion of schooling, a slim major-ity of teachers had only an advanced elementary school background, at the level of the 1872 municipal (six-year) schools. The general education of these teachers was limited but was probably adequate for the mechanics of basic instruction; the certifying exams did require a basic familiarity with the readers used in the primary schools and with the most common approaches to teaching reading and math.

A study of the educational background of rural teachers suggests strongly that those teachers with the broadest intellectual backgrounds and with urban experience—carriers of new values—were the least prepared to establish close ties with the village. Those whose education and (perhaps) intellectual horizons were limited to the rudiments of reading, writing, and arithmetic and a smattering of geography and history, as well as more detailed vocational skills, were the most likely to feel at home, establish roots, and make their presence felt. Of peasant background, these teachers were at home in the village. But their experience and education were very limited—although they may well have been quite effective in teaching the basics, it is unlikely that they were carriers of new values to the villages. The tenure of teachers, measured by length of stay in the profession, slowly increased after the 1890s, and by 1911, 37.5 percent of male teachers and 28.4 percent of female teachers in zemstvo schools had been working in their profession for more than ten years. Although a considerable number had been working for under five years, this figure was artificially inflated by the continuing expansion of the school system, which tended to increase the proportion of new recruits. The data also indicate that the lower the educational qualification of teachers, the longer they stayed in the villages. The better educated they were, the more likely they were to leave the system entirely in search of better work.

Any discussion of the adequacy of teacher training must come to grips with the subjective judgments involved in determining competence. In particular, we should keep in mind that the standards current at the time were deeply colored by the widespread belief in the civilizing mission of education and the insistence that the teacher had to be the spearhead of a general drive for enlightenment, which in turn would transform all Russia. This missionary faith spurned mere instruction in the basics and emphasized the role of teacher as *vospitatel'* ("upbringer"—someone concerned with the whole child), as role model for the children.

Our faith in the civilizing mission of schooling has declined in the intervening years, and "mere" instruction is not as universally scorned. More important, we may introduce entirely different criteria of adequacy, based on the experience of the developing world today. One can distinguish between *humanitarian* (child-centered) and *developmental* (national laborpower needs) standards; for example, a UNESCO expert has recently argued that there are six essential components to teacher training for developing nations, three of which are "pedagogical" (instructional) and three "general." The three pedagogical components are these: 1) teachers should be familiar with curriculum content and ways of presenting it; 2) they should know how to encourage learning aptitudes and how to create productive teaching-learning situations; and 3) they should have a knowledge of the various textbooks and teachers' aids in use. As to the "general" components: 1) teachers should have a sense of their social role in the community; 2) they should learn how to encourage children to participate with and learn from one another and to learn as individuals; and 3) their minds should be open to innovations and reforms. Most teachers in Russia qualified in the first and third of the pedagogical categories; admittedly, few were well trained in child development or motivational theory. Concerning the three general components, it is arguable how far such qualities have been encouraged even in modern school systems in the more advanced countries.[63]

From the standpoint of UNESCO-based criteria, it is quite reasonable to argue that a minimally adequate teacher training program in Russia, a developing nation, was also an optimal program. UNESCO studies have shown that increments in training beyond the basic level are counterproductive and that the better-trained teacher is ultimately lost to the primary school system:

A general scarcity of trained teachers results in a tendency for those qualified for primary teaching to teach in lower secondary schools and for those qualified to teach in lower secondary schools to move to upper secondary education, the result being a general lowering of teaching standards. Even worse, it is common for teacher training colleges to be used to attain a diploma, which in turn helps the graduate gain employment in the economy or civil service—in any case outside the education profession and generally away from the villages.[64]

In Russia, upgrading training would have diverted funds that could otherwise have been spent on salaries or school expansion, while providing no guarantee that these improved skills would have been employed in the rural school system. Whatever one may think of the tsarist government's priorities or political views, from a developmental perspective it made good sense to maintain the intellectual horizons and training of the prospective rural teacher at a low level. It was the best way to ensure that these skills were used in the village, rather than used for individual career advancement by the teacher.

Although the training of rural teachers was adequate to the tasks they faced, the evidence presented above indicates that in many cases their origins, background, age, and family status meant that they had a hard time earning a voice in the village. Few remained long enough to establish a hearth; it was the exceptional village where the teacher resided long enough to set down firm roots in the community and to win the trust and respect coming from lengthy service with more than one generation of children. In truth, contact with the same village seldom lasted more than three years. Of course, just as it would be frivolous to argue that a long stay in the village guaranteed the teacher a voice in the community, so it would be inane to argue that *no* teacher could have won the hearts of the villagers in short order; in individual cases, the teacher's personality was dominant. Yet as a rule, a reasonable tenure in the village was a necessary, if not sufficient, condition for exerting an impact. Moreover, teachers from the lower classes and the rural clergy were the ones who stayed longest—those who already "fit" best and who were less likely to be agents of change. Thus, although teachers had the necessary skills to teach reading and writing, the quantitative evidence suggests that they remained outsiders, to be exploited and utilized, but not to be trusted.

8

Teachers in Village Society

Writing to the bureau that carried out the 1911 Zemstvo Survey, one teacher remarked, "These days, because of his poverty and subjugation to a crowd of authorities, the teacher enjoys no respect or authority among the peasants."[1] This chapter continues our investigation of teachers by considering their political values, intellectual activities, and participation in teachers' organizations. My concern is not so much to draw an exhaustive profile of their spiritual world or political and corporate activities as to assess their standing in the community and overall impact on village life.

STANDARD OF LIVING

Perhaps because of the low esteem in which the craft of primary school teaching has traditionally been held, few countries have paid their teachers well. In Russia, too, the material status of the teacher left much to be desired. According to Chekhov, the yearly wage paid a teacher in the 1860s fluctuated from 12 to 150 rubles; even as late as 1891 in Moscow province, which pioneered the practice of salary supplements, 78 percent of all teachers were making under 250 rubles a year.[2] What such a salary meant was spelled out in reports to the Moscow Literacy Committee, where many teachers complained of the material hardships and sacrifice accompanying the job. One teacher wrote:

The situation of the teacher . . . is most unenviable. He is often forced to do without even the essentials; meat and even the necessary clothing often have to be foregone. There is no money left to order books which would give him the opportunity to supplement his knowledge and keep up with the latest methods and discussions; newspapers and journals are financially out of reach. . . . For a family man, there can be no talk of saving any money or sending his children to a school with tuition, for he can't even afford shoes for his offspring.[3]

The Moscow Literacy Committee data from thirty-three provinces show an average salary of 270 rubles for male zemstvo teachers in 1894; for women, salaries averaged 252 rubles. In only six provinces were the salaries of male teachers over 300 rubles; in only four could female teachers hope to achieve that level. (See Table 11 for additional information on salary ranges.) In Church schools, the pay scales were considerably lower. In Iaroslavl', for example, yearly wages ranged from 0 to 500 rubles, but averaged 134.[4] (Priests sometimes taught without remuneration.) Extreme

Table 11
Yearly Salaries of Zemstvo Teachers, 1894

	UNDER 120 RUBLES	120–180 RUBLES	180–240 RUBLES	240–360 RUBLES	OVER 360 RUBLES
Male teachers	6.9%	8.6%	25.9%	41.9%	14.7%
Female teachers	6.4	14.4	36.4	36.2	6.6
Male assistants	57.1	35.7	3.9	3.6	0
Female assistants	6.9	37.2	33.9	22.0	0

SOURCE: L. Blinov, "Narodnyi uchitel' v Rossii," in Shakhovskii, *Vseobshchee obrazovanie,* 75–76.

NOTE: Data compiled from 2,314 zemstvo teachers in thirty-three provinces. Figures for male teachers and male assistants add up to slightly less and slightly more than 100 percent, respectively, in the original data.

disparities in salaries in different areas and in different kinds of schools caused a good deal of turnover, as teachers fled the villages in the spring looking for greener pastures—within the profession, but in a different district, province, or type of school. In Moscow at the turn of the century, more than one in five teachers in factory schools, where the average yearly pay exceeded 400 rubles, had previously taught in a zemstvo school, whereas only two factory school teachers had foregone a higher salary to work in zemstvo schools.[5]

Attempts to boost teachers' salaries were an essential part of zemstvo and government programs for achieving universal education. Beginning in the 1890s, provincial zemstvos offered salary supplements to districts that provided a stipulated minimum—commonly bringing the salary to 300 or 360 rubles—and also offered graded increments according to length of stay. In addition, several provinces launched pension programs in an attempt to provide teachers with some security in their old age.[6]

The government was also aware of the teachers' plight and of the need for improvements, and in 1900 it set up a pension plan for teachers, allowing rural zemstvo teachers to participate voluntarily. The pension plan (revised in 1906 and again in 1910) did not substantially improve the teachers' standard of living—indeed, the operating funds were drawn primarily from their salaries—but it did offer some basic security during illness or old age.[7] With the 1908 School Bill, which set terms for the Treasury's distribution of huge sums of money to the growing school system, the Ministry of Education took over the payment of subsidies and loans directly to the district zemstvos in an attempt to bring salaries throughout Russia to a minimum of 360 rubles, a figure that had gained widespread recognition as the lowest possible amount on which a single rural teacher could survive.[8]

Another bill was introduced in the Duma to provide regular salary increments and to increase to 600 rubles the salary of those teachers who had already worked more than five years, but the amount of money needed to implement such measures staggered even liberal educators sympathetic to the teachers, and the proposal was voted down in the Duma. The issue of the teacher's material status was seldom framed in terms of whether the teacher deserved or needed a better salary—few denied the need—instead, it was seen as a question of priorities. The commitment to universal literacy involved enormous outlays on school construction and new personnel; such expenses meant that improvements in existing schools (and thereby salaries) had to be postponed. The question became whether a child was to be deprived of education or a teacher was to be denied the amenities of life, a debate that did not place liberals or conservatives unambiguously in either camp. The zemstvos had faced the same dilemma in the 1890s and had generally chosen new schools over higher salaries.[9]

As a result of zemstvo efforts and government intervention, however, salaries improved considerably in the decade after 1905, doubling and even tripling in some areas. In Vladimir, for example, the average salary rose from 260 rubles to 382 rubles between 1898 and 1910.[10] The 1911 School Census placed the average salary of rural teachers at 343 rubles for males and 340 rubles for females.[11] The average salary in zemstvo schools in 1911 was 403 rubles for men and 365 for women;[12] in Church schools, salaries averaged 284 and 269 rubles, respectively. (It was no wonder that Church school inspectors complained of a drain of talent to the secular schools; zemstvo teachers, too, kept their eyes open for vacancies in factory or municipal schools, where the annual salary was between 560 and 642 rubles for men and 488 and 497 rubles for women.) The figures collected by the Moscow Literacy Committee show that salaries between 1894 and 1911 improved by 49 percent for men and 45 percent for women. To the increase in salary should be added, of course, the free housing (or rental money) that 96 percent of zemstvo teachers now received.[13]

Where did this place teachers on the country's scale of incomes? During roughly this same period, the average salary for chairmen of zemstvo provincial executive boards was 5,000 rubles; zemstvo statisticians received 3,600; most lawyers received between 2,000 and 10,000 rubles; agronomists, 3,000; zemstvo doctors, 1,200. Hardly recognized as professionals, rural teachers were removed entirely from that social world by their income. In fact, their salaries were close to those of factory workers; in all industries, the average yearly wage was 264 rubles, ranging from 192 rubles in textiles to 396 in the metal industries. Primary school teachers were paid the same as *fel'dshers,* those medical orderlies who stood on the same low rung on the status ladder, although they too provided vital services to the population. Indeed, a close analogy can be drawn between the relative status and material security of *fel'dshers* and doctors, on the one hand, and primary school teachers and professors, on the other.[14]

How adequate was this income for the teachers' needs?[15] Abundant direct testimony documents that extreme hardship, sacrifice, and deprivation resulted from such an income and that marriage and raising a family were very difficult. Studies of teachers' budgets conducted in Tver', Iaroslavl', Pskov, and Moscow in the 1890s graphically illustrate this point.[16]

When salaries were below the 600-ruble level, or even the 360-ruble entry norm adopted by the majority of the zemstvos, teachers had two choices: they could supplement their salaries, or they could cut back on expenditures. In the 1890s, individual zemstvo studies, as well as the Moscow Literacy Committee survey, revealed that moonlighting was widespread where work was available, but that such work was often very hard to find.[17] The teachers' other choice was to make do with what was available. Numerous budget studies conducted between the 1890s and World War I observed that the lower the salary or the larger the family, the less money was allotted to books, travel, and other cultural expenditures. In most cases, however, basic demands so far exceeded income that married teachers had to cut back on food and clothing and even then would still go into debt. A study of 127 teachers in Moscow district soon after 1900 reported that of this number only 19 were free of debt and that among the remainder the average indebtedness was 77 rubles.[18]

Thus, teachers' complaints that they were underpaid were fully justified. It is true that a single teacher could get by on 350 rubles (or even less, as other budgets showed); it is also true that some married teachers had two incomes, with both spouses working in the rural school system. Yet both as an investment in human capital and as a matter of simple justice and compassion, salaries were certainly too low and failed to keep teachers in the field whenever their training and circumstances allowed them to find work elsewhere. If the goal was to make the teacher a permanent part of the community, low salaries accomplished just the opposite by encouraging high turnover, particularly of married teachers. At the prevailing wages, one teacher wrote to the 1911 Zemstvo Con-

gress, "only martyrs, accepting the burden of poverty and deprivation, or those unable to hold a job anywhere else" would remain
in the profession. As a consequence of the low salaries, another
teacher from Ekaterinoslav wrote, "The best talent leaves this profession, seeking service offering better material remuneration. . . .
Many take up the career of teaching simply as a temporary expedient, pursuing one or more of the following goals: to take advantage of the military deferments or to wait for the opportunity to
meet the right man and get married."[19]

Government intervention after 1908 helped boost and standardize salaries. Moreover, a pension plan implemented in 1900,
although not generous, at least reduced the prevalent fear of a
"hungry old age." Nevertheless, salaries still differed greatly from
region to region; in some areas, salaries remained so low that
teachers took supplementary work whenever it could be found,
despite heavy workloads, and continued to leave the profession for
more lucrative work.[20]

LEGAL AND SOCIAL STATUS

The legal position of the teacher was unenviable, even intolerable. As one teacher wrote in reply to a Moscow Literacy Committee questionnaire:

Even cultured people almost always treat the teacher as a common laborer, as an instrument for bringing to the people a wide variety of moral
and cultural benefits, as a jack-of-all trades in the area of enlightenment;
and in so doing, they often forget that he is a human being. . . . In what
way is he independent? What is he able to do? Who will protect him, defend his rights, who will even recognize that he has rights, who will
defend his interests? Who, indeed! But who, on the other hand, does not
make demands of him? Tell me who does not claim to have a precise
understanding of his obligations! It would also be a terrible mistake to
think that even the local populace respects the teacher; people respect
strength and believe rights accompany it; but who respects weakness?[21]

Another letter to the same committee complained that "the
unenviable position of the teacher is exacerbated by his dependent

relationship not only with his direct superiors but in general with everyone. He is under the supervision not only of those individuals and institutions specified by the law but also of everyone who considers himself a rural official, big or small."[22]

As Scott Seregny observes, teachers, "lacking an esoteric knowledge base," were at best "semi-professionals."[23] In Russia, the low social status of teachers was compounded by the progressive feminization of the field and by the increasing tendency for teachers to be drawn from the lower social orders. Teachers as a group were situated somewhere between the world of the intelligentsia and the *pomeshchik* estate, on the one hand, and the peasant milieu, on the other. Their position was perhaps analogous to that of the lumpenproletariat in the economic world. Teachers complained that the "village intelligentsia" looked down on them, and evidence shows that even the Third Element zemstvo doctors and statisticians often regarded the rural teacher as a social inferior, like the *fel'dsher,* whose wages were comparable. In Ivan Bunin's depressing tale "Teacher," the village teacher, Nikolai Ilyich Turbin, the son of a village deacon and graduate of a seminary, is ecstatic to learn he has been invited to a gathering at the home of a local *pomeshchik,* who is an intellectual light in the area. But once at the gathering, Turbin senses that he is a fish out of water. Out of self-consciousness, he begins to act foolishly and ends up drinking himself into oblivion to drown his awareness of inferiority and boorishness.[24] Precisely this sentiment is repeated in a report to the 1902 Teachers' Congress:

Our peasants are not yet sufficiently developed so one could discuss with them things that one has read. Neighbors with whom one could bare one's soul, as you know, hardly exist. And really, to visit neighbors like the local gentry, both time and proper clothing are required, to say nothing of the burden on the soul the teacher must endure in visits to people who look down on him.[25]

The social backgrounds of teachers, the "generic traits" (as Seregny calls them) of the teaching profession at the elementary level, and the wall of condescension separating polite society and the unwashed plebeians were all structural impediments preventing teachers from acting as conduits of outside values or links between the two worlds. In effect, teachers were forced to choose, or else they were placed, in one or the other society. They could, to be sure, become part of the semi-intelligentsia, part of semi-officialdom, but by placing themselves in that sphere, they remained outside or removed themselves from the moral world of the peasant village. The "hinge men," or brokers, who fit in the interstices between the peasant community and the "global culture" and negotiate between the two worlds seldom enjoy genuine authority or prestige in village affairs (see n. 49, p. 496). At best, teachers joined the fringes of the peasant community, hobnobbing with those who brought the wares of the outside world—whether material (the trader) or spiritual (the priest)—and being simultaneously contaminated by that contact.

But it was their legal position, more than the social origins or the insecure professional status of rural teachers, that often made their lives miserable. As one teacher noted, everyone seemed to be aware of the teachers' obligations, while no one recognized their rights. It was frequently observed that teachers were beholden to some eighteen different officials or authorities, including the inspector, the marshall of the nobility, the chairman of the local zemstvo board, the local land captain, the village priest, all members of the local school board, the diocesan Church hierarchy, and the peasant volost' office, including the clerk, the elder (both volost' and village), and the constable, along with the school trustee.

This control extended far beyond the confines of the school day, reaching deeply into the teacher's personal life. The government was extremely apprehensive about political contamination of the village community by radical teachers, and because it could not supervise classroom routine on a day-to-day basis, it tended to overreact to claims that teachers were spreading sedition or corrupting youth. In turn, anyone familiar with the ways of the political system could threaten to complain that the teacher was politically suspect in order to extort, blackmail, or terrorize the teacher on virtually any issue. Richard Pipes observes, concerning serfs and serfowners, that it was the arbitrary nature, the ill-defined juridical status of the relationship, rather than the actual incidence of abuse, that corrupted such relationships and demoralized all those involved. The same could be said of the juridical position of the rural teacher.[26]

Teachers' vulnerability began with the legislation concerning hiring, confirmation, and dismissal. An unending stream of litigation began in the 1860s soon after the zemstvo won the right to participate in the selection of teachers, and it continued until 1914, for all sides recognized that teacher selection was undoubtedly the single most important means of exerting effective control over schooling.[27]

But the power to appoint, promote, transfer, and dismiss was only one side of official control; another was the right, appropriated by the inspector and embodied in many circulars, to intervene in every aspect of the teacher's personal life. In the words of Stepan Anikin, a well-known activist, "Clothes, food, leisure time, acquaintances, all sides of a teacher's private life are subject to control."[28] The absurd lengths to which this control sometimes went can be seen in the infamous instructions given to teachers by Inspector Iablochkov from Tula. In addition to forbidding criticism of the authorities, calling for strict morality, barring teachers from marrying without the permission of the school director, and pronouncing long hair on male teachers "disgusting," Iablochkov intoned:

The teacher can wear a beard and have a moustache, but he is not to wear brightly colored jackets or ties or to smoke tobacco, which is not in accord with human nature; animals do not know tobacco and get along without it, and humans, too, for a long time after the creation of the world were ignorant of it, yet were healthier and lived longer than today. Women teachers must also dress modestly and must avoid contemporary fashions and must not put flowers, birds, or feathers in their hats; they must keep a simple hairdo, avoiding curls [*zavivat'*] or styles with hair falling over the forehead.[29]

The inspector often appropriated the right to "safeguard" the teacher's internal passport and to decide when and if the teacher could leave the village, even during vacations. Perhaps the most extreme case of supervision on record was that of the local school board in Chistopol'sk, which in 1912 required prospective women teachers to submit not only a certificate of political reliability but also medical certification of their virginity. Almost as humiliating was the stipulation that although teachers of peasant origin had been released from vulnerability to corporal punishment by Senate decision in 1867, their children remained subject to beatings inflicted by volost' courts and, later, by the land captains. All these types of interference and abuse were the subject of numerous petitions, and protests against them were included in every list of demands put forth at every teachers' gathering between 1890 and 1914.[30]

Yet the typical inspector was not abusive and arbitrary; many were dedicated and supportive. Moreover, inspectors tightly controlled the personal and moral lives of teachers in Europe and America as well at the turn of the century. Although one would have to be morally blind to ignore the potential for abuse and the vulnerability of teachers (Anikin wrote, "Just read the pedagogical chronicle in the education periodicals, and your hair will stand on end"),[31] it is likely that extreme instances have been treated as representative and that, in fact, teachers were treated comparably in Russia and the West.

Among the authorities who exercised some control over the teacher's life, particular mention should be made of the local priest who, according to Article 17 of the Education Statute, was responsible for the moral and religious tone of the school. According to Salomatin, conflict between teacher and priest was usually ignited by pupils performing poorly at their Bible lessons or on certifying examinations in this subject. He recorded instances when teachers ran into trouble for refusing to teach Bible classes for the priest, who was himself too busy (but wished to keep the fees).[32] The priest sometimes took offense if the teacher or the pupils failed to attend Church regularly or to help out with the services and work with the choir. Teachers were sometimes dismissed after being denounced by the local priest for attending a gathering at which there was vodka and dancing. In contrast, at least one teacher felt that he had first run into trouble because he did *not* like to drink or play cards or dance and had, for that reason, been suspected of political unreliability—after all, how *else* could he have been spending his time? Indeed, Salomatin claims that in most cases the teacher and priest lived together "like cat and dog."[33]

Another figure who sometimes made life miserable for the teacher was the local trustee (*popechitel'*). Assumption of this position offered the trustee the opportunity to make money through small-time embezzlement and profiteering, but it also made him legally liable for the "moral health" of the school. He often arrogated the right to meddle in the private life of the teacher, as well as to interfere with classroom routine.[34] The trustee, as noted earlier, was sometimes the local *pomeshchik* but more often was a local peasant representative of the "village intelligentsia" who could harass the teacher in many different ways if he or she didn't "fit" into their way of life.

THE TEACHER AND THE VILLAGE
COMMUNITY

The local trustee was only one in a swarm of local peasant officials who could torment the teacher. To be sure, one teacher and writer, who had his ear to the ground and generally maintained a refreshingly objective viewpoint on many education issues, argued that teachers often gravitated to the milieu of the "peasant bourgeoisie" and the clergy.[35] But teachers were a heterogeneous lot. According to Chekhov, some remained "lords and ladies," successfully hobnobbed with the local elite, and had no ties with the local population. Others merged with the local "middle class," including the village priest, storekeeper, clerk, elder, and constable. These teachers were primarily from the seminaries; they looked down their noses at the common *muzhik* and, as *arrivistes* on a small scale, had little positive moral impact on the villagers. There were also peasant teachers who fit snugly into the village culture, but only by spurning the ways they had learned outside the village. As Chekhov noted, the committed teacher—the untarnished bearer of new values and higher culture—was an isolated individual indeed.[36]

A 1903 instruction from the Chernigov governor tells us a good deal about the teacher's relationship with local village authorities:

The Gelendzhiski village elder and clerk have conducted themselves disrespectfully and coarsely with the local teacher. . . . These officials, taking advantage of each opportunity when the teacher had to contact them on school matters, not only rendered no assistance but also interfered peremptorily with her teaching, asked impertinent questions, and even pried into her personal life. Although the main villains were the assistant elder and clerk, who have been dismissed, still I recommend a strict reprimand for the elder as well, for allowing this to happen. . . .

Having every reason to believe that insufficient respect is shown the rural teacher by local authorities elsewhere as well, I find it necessary to include in this instruction a proposal to all local authorities to persuade peasant officials under their jurisdiction to show the necessary respect to teachers of both sexes . . . and to point out that simply because a village society contributes to the upkeep of a school, this does not give rural authorities the right to interfere in school affairs.[37]

The instruction confirms the suspicion that because peasants continued to contribute to a teacher's salary and to school upkeep, they felt they had a perfect right to intervene in the running of the school. Other sources show that peasants often tormented unpopular teachers by being slow to provide firewood or other supplies and by holding back salaries.[38] Popular or unpopular, as the Chernigov example shows, the teacher was often at the mercy of the loutish peasant official. But the instruction also shows that in some instances the provincial authorities or the Ministry of Education intervened to *protect* the teacher against abuse by rural peasant officials (or by the *pomeshchik* or rural priest).

One reason for peasant officials' hostility toward teachers is that the wares introduced by the teacher spelled an end to the privileges held by those who had previously monopolized communication beyond the boundaries of the oral culture. An end to socially restricted literacy jeopardized the officials' traditional functions of interpreting the law, mediating with the outside world, and interpreting the sacred texts. On a simpler level, expanded literacy meant that anyone could verify the accounts of the village and volost' offices. Given the notorious peculation of these officeholders, the clerk and elder may well have looked askance at the arrival of a teacher or the spread of literacy. At the very least, these local powerbrokers and taskmasters must have sought to put one of "their own" in the school, and as Chekhov noted, many peasant graduates of the seminaries *did* return to happily take their places among this small-time village elite—an understandable occurrence, given the psychological dynamics of small-scale social mobility.

According to some reports, it was often the village clerk, the local elder, or the *kulak*—and not the entire community—who held the teacher hostage. Suspicious of literacy, fearing it would give the villagers independence and an opportunity to keep track of operations in the volost' offices, these rich peasants often made life miserable for the eager new teachers, particularly those who didn't fit into the village milieu. According to Miropol'skii, "because of this antagonism to literacy, without help from above, the teacher [was] often in a dismal situation." Reports from Kursk, Voronezh, and Poltava showed that the village elite used the purse strings to control teachers. In Tula district, when a teacher was fired by the village community at the insistence of the volost' elder, an investigation by the local school board revealed that the elder had been embezzling funds and was afraid the teacher was on his track.[39]

The local elite often resisted the spread of schooling, but given the village's weak social differentiation—characterized more by cyclical mobility than by class division, and attenuated by cultural and kinship solidarity—one should not see the teacher as invariably victimized by grasping *kulaks* intent on preserving their exploitative ways. Everyone saw that literacy was useful, even necessary. But most villagers, especially the older generation, were concerned about the impact of education, and thus all were vitally interested in the choice of teacher. As Furet and Ozouf note, with the coming of the school, "the secret of good conduct passed out of the hands of the old—who had been its trustees because they had lived through so much—and into those of the schoolmaster because [he had] read so much. . . . General literacy claimed two victims, the parish priest and old people, by robbing the former of the secret of his prestige and the latter of the utility of [their] memory."[40]

As long as schools were peasant-sponsored and taught by retired soldiers, local priests, and sextons, there was little cause for conflict. But once the zemstvo appropriated the right to select teachers and the government began to control curriculum, peasant participation in schooling was reduced to the exercise of a veto—peasants could refuse to enroll their children, take them out early, or resist the appointment of undesired teachers. The elite, as well as popular, village response to schooling *in general* must be distinguished from the response to *particular* teachers. In many cases, villagers actively supported schools but resisted the arrival of certain teachers. At the very least, the evidence presented throughout this book suggests that it was the attempt to introduce literacy while preserving village ways—not a struggle between village poor and rich—that explains community relations with teachers and village insistence on exercising some choice in teacher selection. If there was conflict in the village, it was probably between generations as much as it was between classes, at least in this area of community life.

The comments of teachers themselves suggest that the entire village community, or at least all adults, often kept the teachers at arm's length and, when dissatisfied, could turn on them with great cruelty. Among the first to observe these relationships were V. I. Orlov and I. P. Bogolepov in their study of Moscow province in the 1882–1883 school year. Summarizing teachers' observations, Orlov noted that peasants were generally respectful of teachers, asked them for advice about children's illnesses, and even asked teachers to be godparents. Yet,

there is no close tie to be observed between the population and the teacher. Their contacts, though amicable, are of a superficial nature. In the eyes of the peasants, the male teacher is a figure alien to their world, quite remote from their vital interests. They regard him as a "little impoverished gentleman" and the schoolma'am as a "nice, poor lady." Teachers are learned, "lettered," the peasants' betters, but nevertheless alien to the village world. . . . Indeed, teachers keep a distance from the peasants, maintaining relations only through the children. This is only logical, for as of yet teacher and peasant have nothing in common. The teacher is a newcomer, lacking a hearth in the community and having no personal interest in communal affairs other than that of the school. He is a transient, knowing little and understanding less of the life of the peasantry.[41]

More than a decade later, V. V. Petrov found peasant attitudes toward teachers identical to those expressed in 1882–1883. Reports even specified that when a teacher remained in the same locale for several years, relations with the population did not substantially improve. Some teachers complained of the widespread lack of respect for their profession, attributing this phenomenon to the humiliating legal status of teachers, who were subject to the arbitrary whim of even the lowest authorities. Others pointed to material deprivation as the source of their low status.[42]

Even when teachers were of peasant origin, they were not always recognized as members of the commune (*mir*)—and justly so, because they were no longer subject to corporal punishment or to the onerous labor and tax dues imposed on the peasants, and they had no vote at the village gathering. Because teachers no longer bore the yoke, or *tiaglo* (a measure of both the taxes due from a peasant household and the laborpower of that household), they were no longer eligible for the modicum of welfare and security the commune afforded its aged and ill. As I. M. Shigin pointed out to the 1902 Teachers' Congress, an incapacitated teacher was in a terrible position—usually ineligible for state benefits but not a part of the commune:

The village society will not take him in because he, a *former* peasant, no longer fits [*im ne podstat'*]; he is learned, a *barin,* no longer a peasant. Commonly they look upon such a peasant as one of the intellectual proletariat. . . . And, in fact, so it is. The teacher has broken the ties with his society; unlike a genuine peasant, he has departed far in his views and habits, he no longer plows the land together with them, nor participates in the gatherings, nor serves in elective posts. . . . One could say that he left one shore without reaching the other.[43]

Shigin claimed that teachers were seldom nominated to electoral lists for volost' and village gatherings, the volost' courts, or the zemstvo. Perhaps this is overstated; we know that some peasant teachers *did* continue to plow the land and that some *did* exert an influence at village gatherings. Nevertheless, the point is suggestive—the peasant teacher was neither "one of us" (*nash*) nor "one of them" (*prishlyi*—literally, "newcomer"). These teachers were outsiders or fringe figures in their own villages. And if this was true for some teachers of peasant origins, it becomes that much more difficult to believe that the *barin* or the *baryshnia* had found a place in the community.

Consider once again the reports by teachers to the 1911 Zemstvo Congress on their level of preparedness for work and life in the villages (Chapter 7, pp. 202–206, and Table 9). Thirty percent of all teachers complained that they had not been prepared for living conditions in the villages or for the sharp contrast between the urban life to which they had been accustomed and the hardships of the rural environment. Lack of familiarity with village life merged with a feeling of inadequacy concerning "general topics" of interest to the peasant:

After living your entire life in the city, without any acquaintance with the countryside except from a train window, you find yourself unfamiliar with the most ordinary and essential aspects of life in the village, such as the *plug* or *sokha* [types of plows]. Peasants sometimes even make fun of teachers. The majority of us teachers from the gymnasium can't tell one grain from another, and the pupils are always correcting us. In these conditions, how can there be talk of explanatory readings, not to mention field excursions? We are the ones who need explanatory readings and excursions with a guide! We know a lot about pedagogical methods, about the different systems of teaching, but our experience is limited and at first, it is as if you conduct your classes blindfolded.[44]

Graduates of the women's gymnasiums expressed the most dissatisfaction with their surroundings (45.8 percent), whereas graduates of the teachers' seminaries and the diocesan and municipal schools were most comfortable in their surroundings.

Perhaps the most graphic depiction of teacher-peasant relations came from Tver' district, where a teacher named Andrei Arkadov wrote in a report to the 1902 Teachers' Congress of his relations with the village community:

In truth, there is no sympathy for you where you thought you would find it. Those people, women and elders, whom you began to serve, for whom you were willing to sacrifice your life's labors, your health, are so benighted that their own children, having caught even a sliver of light and some notion of the terrible ugliness of village life, find it intolerable living any longer with their elders and run off to the city . . . and our brother the teacher finds it that much harder to cope with the countryside, to come to terms with its inhabitants . . . with their mundane, practical views . . . which often differ little from immorality, and with their religious views bordering on extreme superstition.

The *stariki* [elders] won't understand him, though they may all speak in the same dialect; they'll ridicule him for his opinions and actions, they'll take advantage of him if he is kindhearted; finally they'll avoid him, [regarding him] as an *odd* one [*chudak*], as someone who voices all kinds of nonsense about some kind of morality, about superstitions, and complains about their familial scandals. Yes, some will fail to understand, others will intentionally fail to understand, and still others will treat him like a *chudak,* will give him no respect, and most likely will hold him in utter distrust.[45]

Arkadov related an incident in which a family tried to get even with a teacher for failing their "lazy lout" of a son. They bribed the volost' clerk, who then complained to the zemstvo, accusing the teacher of driving the boy to his sickbed, of beating pupils, of incompetent teaching, of holding peasants in contempt, and of failing to keep accurate financial records for the school. The zemstvo executive board sent a representative to investigate, then completely exonerated the teacher.[46]

Arkadov concluded:

I can say that some teachers have experienced no ill from the peasants, but neither have they felt any good will or respect, not to mention trust. Such teachers live in the school and are happy within these confines and have no contact with the population, don't know these people, nor do the people know them. . . . In such cases, there can be no pretense of exerting influence over the population. It is only very seldom that the population respects and trusts a teacher, for it is extremely difficult to win their trust, to convince them of the desire to help, to make them regard the teacher as one of their own, to whom they can open up their hearts.[47]

THE TEACHER–BEGGAR

The material and the social status of teachers were intertwined, as the difficulty teachers had in collecting their pay (*poluchka*) demonstrates. The way in which teachers had to virtually beg for their salaries shows just how compromised they were by their location between two cultures.

In the words of Ignatiev, the former Minister of Education, "The lack of financial security weighed upon and oppressed the local schoolteacher and prevented him from getting thoroughly acquainted with the local population and school and from furthering his knowledge." [48] The low salaries of teachers—until at least 1900 smaller than that paid the local liquor manager—compromised them in the eyes of the local population. But even more degrading than the size of the salary were the "fractional salaries" many teachers received at least until the turn of the century, with part coming from a sponsoring institution such as the zemstvo and part from the village community. Because of this dependence on the community, teachers could not count on prompt payment, and wages frequently arrived several months late, particularly in the springtime when the village coffers as well as the cooking pots were often empty. But scarcity did not always cause the delay; when a teacher was not in good standing with the local peasant officials, they could pull the pursestrings as a method of humiliation and harassment. One vicious peasant clerk and his drunken friends entertained themselves by forcing the village teacher to dance for them every time he came for his salary. [49]

This clerk was an extreme example, but complaints of late payments were very frequent. The salary payment, like the provision of fuel and maintenance of the rural school, offered one way in which the village as a whole could exercise a veto or at least show its displeasure with the teacher selections made by outsiders. Although problems with salary payment sometimes stemmed from sheer poverty, ignorance, and indifference, they also often reflected dissatisfaction with particular teachers rather than proverbial peasant sloth.

A local history of Belevskii district, Tula province, records a number of conflicts between the zemstvo and the village community over teacher selection, during which the villagers expressed a clear preference for their own "semi-literate" instructors. In such instances, the villagers malingered in the collection of the school tax, once forcing a new teacher to wait over a year for his first payment. In the village of Budugovische, the peasants refused to send their children to school when the school board appointed a priest as teacher; they felt attendance would have been a total waste of time. In 1873, villagers from Aransk requested that the teacher sent by the local school board be replaced by a fellow villager, a retired soldier, who "could be much more useful teaching our children." Studies of individual districts in Tula province, all from the 1860s and early 1870s, make it abundantly clear that villagers could support schooling with great persistence while opposing particular teachers sent from the outside. Often when peasants refused to allocate tax money, in effect closing a school, it was because they felt their children were not learning to read and write, not because they were indifferent to schooling as such. In Tula district, an inspector named Krachkovskii investigated a number of such closings and learned that in one instance the local priest had skipped so many lessons that the peasants had decided there was no point in paying him. In another village, the peasants complained that the children weren't learning anything and that the teacher was lazy and frequently drunk. When he conducted exams to verify the claim, Krachkovskii discovered that of sixty-two former pupils, not one could read a passage and retell it in his or her own words. The inspector concluded that the peasants, far from being indifferent to schooling, had justly decided that it made no sense to throw good money after bad.[50]

Even when relations between the village officials and the teacher were reasonably good, payments were not always forthcoming. According to numerous sources, peasants commonly felt that the teacher had a soft job. Reports to the Moscow Literacy Committee in 1894 showed that many villagers thought teachers were "well off" and "highly paid" and that they "did nothing." How could one avoid physical labor and yet complain of poverty?[51] Peasants could not understand why teachers should be allowed to spend the summer "idly" while all others had to work.

This sentiment was not necessarily an expression of ill will. Instead, peasants' ideas about teachers' work routines and salaries stemmed from the old *vol'nye* schools, where the teacher had received payment per lesson (*pourochno*) or per head (*na dushu*). Teachers were viewed by the peasants as day laborers in the village school: like the old literacy teacher (*master gramotei*), teachers should be paid for the hours or days they worked—what they did with their idle time, well, that was their own affair, but peasants shouldn't be asked to pay them! Thus, a conflict arose between the teachers' perceptions of themselves as state employees and professionals and the village belief that they were day laborers to be rewarded only for time on the job. For this reason, teachers writing to the 1911 Zemstvo Congress observed that wherever teachers were dependent on the village for a part of their salaries, their positions were most severely compromised.[52]

Such difficulties were most frequently reported when the school serviced several village societies and payment had to be collected separately from each. Boundary conflicts ("neighbor-outsider" disputes), stemming from the entangled land relations and intermingled strips surviving from the times when several villages belonged to one serfowner, exacerbated the intervillage strife endemic to peasant societies in general. Moreover, the volost' and village community collected the school tax per person, whether or not each household had a child enrolled, although most peasants adhered to the traditional belief that teachers should be paid only for the pupils actually enrolled in school. It was asking a lot to demand that the entire community pay for schooling; but when the tax was collected from several village societies, peasant resentment at subsidizing the education of children from still other communities was often considerable. In some cases, peasants had to pay tuition fees for their own children who were enrolled in the local Church parish school, while paying a school tax for the free zemstvo school in another village. Anyone who has difficulty suppressing a chortle at peasant localism and reluctance to subsidize the education of other children should consider contemporary debates in our own society about property taxes and schooling, vouchers, and tax credits for private education. In any case, although teachers were not always the objects of hostility, they were often the victims of the conflict between peasant notions of just taxation and the collection of school land taxes.[53]

The teacher indeed had difficulty receiving a regular salary from the peasant community; but the zemstvo assumption of responsibility for teachers' salaries in the 1890s did not always provide relief. In many districts, payment from the zemstvo was highly irregular and was accompanied by coarse and indifferent treatment of the teacher. This poor employee sometimes had to travel long distances over poor country roads to appear as a supplicant before the district board, spending not only an entire day or more on the road every month but also paying at least 2 rubles (out of a monthly salary of 20 to 30 rubles) to hire a horse, wagon, and driver for the ride to town. Such a trip is the subject of Anton

Chekhov's short story "The Schoolmistress," which describes how the zemstvo teacher Marya Vasilyevna traveled all day only to find the zemstvo offices inexplicably closed. Chekhov vividly conveys the sense of isolation and helplessness of the rural teacher:

She felt annoyed with the Zemstvo board at which she had found no one the day before. How unbusiness-like! Here she had been asking them for two years to dismiss the watchman, who did nothing, was rude to her, and hit the schoolboys; but no one paid any attention. It was hard to find the chairman at the office, and when one did find him he would say with tears in his eyes that he hadn't a moment to spare; the inspector visited the school once in three years, and knew nothing whatever about his work, as he had once been in the Excise Duties Department, and had received the post of school inspector through his influence. The school Council [board] met very rarely, and there was no knowing where it met . . . and goodness knows to whom she could appeal with complaints or inquiries.[54]

How often did the zemstvo mistreat the teacher? A few studies conducted by zemstvo specialists in the 1890s inquired just how widespread these difficulties with payment were. In Iaroslavl', where 90 percent of zemstvo teachers and 30 percent of Church parish teachers were paid monthly, about one in five teachers (19 percent of zemstvo and 20 percent of church teachers) complained of difficulties in receiving their salaries. In this province, teachers traveled up to forty versts to and from Church or zemstvo offices and in the summer could often find no transport. In Tula, more than one in four teachers (28 percent) complained, and only 32 percent declared that they had no problems (the remainder had no comment). Complaints came from nearly every district in Tula that payments were tardy and that securing payment involved much expenditure and loss of time. Tula teachers were particularly unhappy with their treatment by the zemstvo and complained that the "fractional" salary, with partial payment coming from volost' authorities and the rest from the zemstvo, did not improve their situation but instead simply doubled the humiliation, delays, and expenditures. When queried as to why they didn't simply ask a local peasant who was traveling to town to pick up their money, teachers replied that at best peasants always kept a percentage and at worst drank up the entire salary on the way home.[55]

Episodes reflecting such difficulties are also scattered throughout the reports to the 1902 Teachers' Congress. In Tver', for example, six teachers had to travel sixty kilometers on foot to petition the zemstvo to pay them. Their petition was ignored, and the teachers finally had to take the zemstvo to court. In another zemstvo, it was customary to be six months late in paying teachers. In 1894, the Minister of the Interior felt compelled to send a circular to local governors requiring verification that zemstvo executive boards were not falling behind in paying teachers. Yet over a decade later, complaints were still surfacing in the papers. Salomatin cites prolonged delays in payment from city dumas, rural zemstvos, and the Holy Synod. According to the compilers of the survey of teachers for the 1911 Zemstvo Congress, some zemstvos had begun to offer travel money to teachers who were summoned to the district board for business purposes, but there was no mention of the monthly trips for salary. Some zemstvos had begun to send salaries through the mail, but this practice only helped the occasional teacher living near a postal station. As for the rest, other zemstvos had begun to pay teachers through the volost' offices—which of course can hardly have been a significant improvement, and simply takes us back to the beginning of this sad story.[56]

The fact that teachers had to grub for their salaries before the local zemstvos speaks eloquently of their low standing among the nobility running these institutions. Even more important, such humiliation had to tarnish the image of teachers in the eyes of the village community: although not "one of us," they were also not people of importance in the world outside—otherwise why were doors slammed in their faces and why were they treated as inferiors? In the worst cases, this perception made the teacher doubly vulnerable; peasants saw that the teacher would seldom find protection or support from the zemstvo or school board and so could be abused at will. (Of course, we must keep in mind that teachers were not a homogeneous lot. The teacher of peasant origins might have been scorned as "neither a beauty nor a crow" but was not likely to have encountered the resentment and abuse heaped on teachers from the privileged classes once they were seen as fair targets for the expression of longstanding resentments.)

At the very least, the difficulties with payment were demoralizing and certainly lowered teachers' standings in the community, whatever their origins. The lament of one teacher (serving in a Church parish school, but encountering a problem widespread throughout the school system) illustrates this well:

We receive our salary three times a year: at Christmas, Easter, and at the end of the school year. The greatest inconvenience here is the receipt of salary on the eve of a holiday. The teacher, a person of limited means, is often required to acquire new clothing and footwear for the holidays. Because of extremely late and delayed payments the teacher is often left empty-handed and forced to greet the holidays in threadbare clothing and worn-out shoes. The infrequency of payment also sometimes forces the teacher to do without the necessary sustenance or to beg it as a loan from the children's parents. All of this, in my opinion, humiliates the teacher in the eyes of the people and even interferes with successful instruction.[57]

This comment illustrates the teachers' sense of wounded pride and their feeling that although they were pursuing a noble profession—even a mission—their salaries prevented them from living in a way befitting that mission. This hurt pride was particularly evident when teachers were denied servants by the local community and were "even forced to carry their own firewood and water." As one teacher noted, "I consider [these tasks] incompatible with the lofty title of teacher."[58]

The teacher was often called a "cultural pioneer," but this description has limits, for the exploration of the cultural frontier in Russia was not accompanied by a respect for manual labor and a leveling of class barriers. Instead, rank-and-file teachers, while trying honestly to bring enlightenment to the villages, were often equally conscious of their ambiguous status as "semiprofessionals." Although wishing to be recognized as members of the intelligentsia—or even as officials of the school system—they were in truth neither fish nor fowl, for they did not have the recognition of the elite. Even worse, they were neither integrated into the village community nor respected for their station. The mundane complaints about the difficulties with salary payment bring out remarkably well the link between material and status deprivation and the uncomfortable location of the rural teacher between the community and the outside world.

SINKING TO THE LEVEL OF THE
COUNTRYSIDE

At best balanced precariously between peasant and nonpeasant worlds, teachers lacked the corporate organizations and professional activities that might have sustained them psychologically and intellectually. Teachers' mutual aid societies, which proliferated in the 1890s, claimed a membership of forty-five thousand (one in four teachers) in 1914, but evidence shows that many of these organizations eked out a meager existence, maintained only minimal contact with local teachers, and required only payment of annual dues for continued membership. Even less impressive as a corporate organization was the All-Russian Teachers' Union, which— whatever its national political role—existed only from 1905 to 1908 and had a peak membership in 1907 of 13,400.[59]

The most likely source of corporate solidarity for teachers would have been their participation in teachers' congresses and summer courses. In the late 1860s, the zemstvos had begun to organize short-term courses during the summer months to upgrade the skills and general knowledge of rural teachers, as well as organizing congresses where more advanced teachers and educators could meet with the zemstvo and various officials to talk over issues, conflicts, and plans. For a brief time, these courses and congresses were extremely popular, with such famous educators as Korf, Bunakov, Vakhterov, V. I. Vodovozov, and D. I. Tikhomirov participating. In 1871, congresses were held at forty-eight district and provincial centers, while courses were sponsored at fourteen; in 1872, fifty-three such centers held congresses, with courses at ten. At this time, the courses focused on upgrading the general education rather than the pedagogical skills of the teacher. According to oft-cited testimony by Bunakov and the recollections of other teachers, these gatherings were of enormous psychological, as well as pedagogical, significance for teachers, making them feel they were part of a common enterprise, encouraging them to continue to grow intellectually, and reducing the cultural deprivation and isolation of the countryside.[60]

On the heels of the great populist campaign in the countryside, however, the government concluded, not entirely without foundation, that many radicals had taken teaching posts in order to establish contact with the population and that teachers' gatherings could have baneful political consequences. The government imposed increasingly strict control over the courses in 1875, limiting them to narrowly vocational subjects (pedagogy, agriculture, local crafts), and in 1885 banned courses and zemstvo-sponsored teachers' congresses altogether. According to a deputy from the Ministry of the Interior, Lt. General Orzhevskii, the police had detected "the infiltration of the teaching profession by politically unreliable elements with the goal of disseminating pernicious ideas among the rural population" and believed that teachers wished to use these congresses as organizational forums to draw up a plan of action. Summer courses were later resumed in 1896, and in 1899, new regulations once more broadened the scope and content to include general education subjects; teachers' congresses were legalized as well. Finally in 1907, the new law on public assembly (4 March 1906) was extended to include courses and congresses.[61]

Nevertheless, even these liberalized regulations gave dictatorial powers to the local inspector and narrowly circumscribed the rights of participants. A survey conducted by the Ufa zemstvo in 1903 showed that two-thirds of the seventeen provincial and twenty-one district zemstvos replying had experienced significant resistance from the authorities in attempts to organize courses. Repeated in 1910, the study then showed that between 1903 and 1910 two-thirds of all provincial zemstvos had again met obstacles (several, such as Vladimir, Novgorod, and Ufa, had been refused several times); but only one-quarter of all district zemstvos had experienced difficulty. In most cases, the provincial zemstvos had tried to organize general education courses, whereas the district zemstvos, generally more conservative, had endeavored only to upgrade the pedagogical skills of their rural "craftsmen" and had received government approval in doing so.[62]

But government suspicion of the teachers' courses and congresses was only a part of the problem. As Seregny points out, lack of sponsorship by the zemstvo impeded the spread of these congresses and courses as much as did government repression. Annually between 1901 and 1905, not more than five (of more than three hundred fifty) district zemstvos sponsored congresses. The reason, quite simply, was that "in the district zemstvos, where more conservative gentry opinion predominated, the notion that the lowly teacher could have no advice to offer his superiors was quite prevalent." The average zemstvo representative, influenced by "the deeply conservative attitudes and jealously guarded prerogatives of traditional institutions in the Russian countryside," was not prepared to accept the teacher as an expert.[63]

Congresses, meant to improve relations among teachers, zemstvos, and officials, never received meaningful support, and general education courses sponsored by the provincial zemstvos were successfully blocked by officialdom. But the narrowly pedagogical courses sponsored by the district zemstvos and encouraged by the government continued to thrive after 1905. According to N. V. Chekhov, interest in courses remained quite high, and applications always exceeded places by a considerable number.[64] These courses represented one more link in the Ministry of Education's strategy to wrest control of rural schools not only from the Church but especially from the provincial zemstvos, which had dominated rural education since the 1890s. By providing direct grants to the districts for school construction and by assuming the burden of teacher salary supplements, the MNP effectively cut the financial strings that had given the liberal provincial zemstvos enormous power. By allying with the conservative district zemstvos in promoting courses that would upgrade narrowly pedagogical skills, the MNP was successfully excluding the provincial zemstvo from having any voice in teacher training.

Whatever its cause, teachers' lack of corporate organization prevented the type of interaction that might have overcome their sense of isolation. Certainly government restrictions on teachers' conventions and refresher courses reinforced the intellectual stagnation of life in the countryside.

Living in the back-of-beyond, experiencing cultural isolation as well as occasional hostility from the local inhabitants, lacking any means to supplement one's education—these are the conditions in which the soldier in the "army of national salvation," that is, the teacher, is forced to work and live. It is a difficult and depressing life. Is it surprising that many of them leave the field of battle and that those who remain, for the most part, lose their weapon—knowledge—in the struggle with ignorance, become dull, morally degraded, and turn into mere craftsmen, Chekhov's men in footlockers, living corpses?[65]

One teacher in Shuiskii district so described his plight to the Vladimir provincial zemstvo board in 1904. Recent research confirms the argument that teachers living in the villages soon found their "weapon" blunted in the struggle against ignorance. Seregny's impressive chronicle of the teachers' movement in Russia documents the emergence of a powerful national organization but concedes that the Teachers' Union represented "the cream of politically conscious and militant teachers"; as for the rank and file, "many merely vegetated in the countryside, barely equipped to combat illiteracy in the classroom, let alone act as viable cultural agents within the community at large."[66]

Perhaps the most convincing evidence of the teachers' low intellectual horizons and lack of interest in the outside world can be found in the many studies of teachers' reading habits carried out near the turn of the century. Teachers were potential conduits of modern culture, but if they read little, they were not likely to be sources of information on the outside world for schoolchildren or neighbors.[67]

Petrov's study of Moscow province showed distressing results concerning teachers' reading habits and access to books. Teachers' responses to one questionnaire disclosed that more than 58 percent had fewer than fifty books in their possession and only 20 percent had more than one hundred. The growth in the number of libraries in Moscow province had not brought culture to the teachers, for in Vereia only 17 percent, in Dmitrov 29 percent, and in Volokolamsk 30 percent of teachers used these collections. To be sure, in districts where communications were better established (Kolomna, Moscow, Bronitsy), the figure was as high as 80 percent. Yet in the four-year interval between 1894 and 1898, the professional libraries housed in the facilities of the district executive boards (normally in the district town) were used by *only eighty-one teachers out of a body of roughly eight hundred.* Five of these teachers visited the libraries only once; thirteen visited twice; twenty-four made six to ten visits; and thirty-nine teachers used the libraries more than ten times. Library sign-out lists showed that professional interest in pedagogical literature was low: of 4,241 sign-outs, 88 percent (3,740) were for literature, whereas only 138 were for pedagogical works and 236 were for scientific and agricultural books. The content of teachers' personal libraries corresponded to the preferences expressed in the library sign-out lists: 50 percent of all personal books were belles-lettres, 13 percent were scientific, 11 percent agricultural, and 7 percent religious (18 percent unknown).[68] Even worse, in Moscow, 150 of 478 teachers did not own any personal books or subscribe to periodicals; of these 150, 38 specifically noted that they never read anything at all except for the books they used in the classroom.[69]

Studies in other provinces pointed to even more serious situations. In response to a questionnaire in Iaroslavl', only 52 percent of zemstvo teachers and 19 percent of Church parish school teachers affirmed that they could obtain either books or periodicals or both. Only one in four zemstvo teachers and one in five Church school teachers subscribed to a periodical of any sort. (A few more noted that they did not subscribe but had access to periodicals from the local gentry or priest.) In Kostroma district in 1904, 44 percent of zemstvo schools and in Mar'evskii district (also in Kostroma province) 62 percent received no periodicals. In Kursk in 1904, 430 of 810 teachers received no periodicals—though 170 did receive an occasional paper or journal from the local priest. Similar or worse situations were found in Novgorod, Pskov, Tula, Tambov, and Simbirsk, where one teacher added: "In the last six years I have read nothing but the official textbooks and Eruslan Lazarevich over and over."[70]

Was the lack of reading material caused by censorship or by internal stagnation? An eloquent speech by E. Vakhterova to the 1902 Teachers' Congress made it clear that government censorship of libraries played a major role. But whatever the cause, the result was generally the same. As one teacher wrote from Kazan':

I am supposed to spread enlightenment and truth, but I myself have no sources of replenishment. I live in a village where there is no one to share thoughts with, where I am surrounded by brawling, rank ignorance, miserable poverty. . . . It is terrible. I give my whole soul to the school, but on returning home become aware of my spiritual isolation. Some might say read, but what is there available to read? I could be happy, yes, delighted, to read something, but find me a book! I would buy a book or subscribe to a journal, but my salary suffices only to ward off starvation and keep me out of rags![71]

The sense of intellectual stagnation was profound; "the light . . . is feeble, flickering," wrote one teacher, while another felt himself "growing dull in the boondocks, never hearing a live human voice." A teacher from Moscow wrote:

Looking at the overall situation, . . . one comes to the sad conclusion that the village teacher is almost completely deprived of spiritual nourishment. Spending the entire year far from books and periodicals, removed from the educated world, he is not able to continue his education and consequently it is inevitable that regression takes place. He begins to feel this and, if fate allows, he leaves the village to find employment in the city. Every year our educational institutions turn out a large number of teachers of both sexes; still, a severe shortage is evident to this day. Where are they going? It is very simple: after serving for the required number of years [stipulated in the zemstvo stipends for students], they then leave the schools. Those who remain, by force of circumstance, *gradually sink to the level of the countryside* [emphasis added].[72]

THE TEACHER AS POLITICAL CONDUIT

What were the political leanings of rural teachers? How much political influence did they wield in the village? Most accounts agree that populism was very strong among teachers, and Soviet historians concede that the Socialist Revolutionaries (populists), rather than the Marxists, had the allegiance of most teachers. Many prominent educators of the time promoted the idea that progress in education and social change were mutually interdependent because direct links had been established between poverty and poor performance in schools. Moreover, the relentless government harassment of teachers' attempts to organize, attend refresher courses, or simply improve their own lot through mutual aid societies did little to convince teachers that help was forthcoming from that direction.

The evidence seems compelling that economic deprivation, popular contact, and political and professional persecution politicized teachers. Resolutions by teachers' congresses, reports by local police and land captains that teachers were active participants in village meetings and agitators for radical causes, the enormous number of teachers driven from their jobs in the repression following the 1905 Revolution—all add credence to this view. It only remains, it would seem, to determine to which political party the vast majority of the 150,000 or so teachers really belonged or with whose radical aims they sympathized.

Yet the evidence on political activism is not so unambiguous. If teachers learned anything from their ambivalent and isolated positions in the villages and their inability to develop corporate organizations, it was that they were politically vulnerable, could be harmed by either community or government, and should keep a low profile. Teachers may often have been populist in sympathy (if by this term we understand the core of beliefs stemming from Lavrov's notion of *service* to the people—small-deeds *abramovshchina*), but, as Seregny astutely notes, being pioneers on the cultural frontier of society, teachers were also abundantly aware of the enormous potential violence, explosive resentment, and destructive capacity of the village community. Teachers received a taste of anti-intelligentsia violence in early 1905, when a tide of xenophobia (urged on by the Church) swept several areas of the country. They were to receive even larger doses of violence in 1917, during the civil war, and, finally, during collectivization. Because teachers worked at unsheltered outposts, it is doubtful that they shared the Bakuninist faith in a *Pugachevshchina,* or elemental peasant uprising, to sweep away the old order, for "there was no way of predicting in which direction popular fury might turn."[73] Teachers recognized that they, too, might well be caught up in such fury, and they were aware of the specific forms peasant violence could take.

True, the 1902 Teachers' Congress was dominated by an oppositionist spirit and the later Teachers' Union was controlled by the Socialist Revolutionaries. But it is questionable how representative these organizations were of rank-and-file sentiment—in fact, fewer than half the delegates to the 1902 Congress were teachers, and the Juridical Commission, which passed thirty-two resolutions on the legal status of teachers, was dominated by educators already under police supervision. In Russia, pedagogical activism and political liberalism were strongly correlated, and we should thus be very hesitant to regard the political views of delegates to national congresses as representative of sentiment in the country-side. The Teachers' Union itself had only 5,000 members in 1905 and never grew to more than 13,400 members. The concerns of the rank and file may have been quite different from those articulated at the various congresses, even if for every member there were two or three sympathizers. Seregny has produced a remarkable statement from a participant in the teachers' movement, which illustrates superbly the personality of the so-called "zemstvo rabbit," the frightened, apprehensive, rural teacher:

These were the characteristic traits of the teacher: timidity, shyness, dis-comfiture, unsociability, a tendency to lose his identity in the rural morass, a lack of experience in gatherings, and an inability to clearly and con-cisely formulate his thoughts—all of this constituted a considerable ob-stacle to his corporate activity and unification.[74]

Among the thousands of teachers in the Russian villages, many had willingly accepted material hardship and cultural isola-tion, believing they had a debt to the people and convinced that service to the cause of enlightenment was socially meaningful. Some activists believed excessive concern with the material well-being of teachers was wrong at a time when the population chroni-cally lived on the verge of starvation. Many even boycotted salary discussions at the 1902 Congress. Yet at the same congress, I. M. Shigin suggested that teachers be formally incorporated into the state service and given rank, and a common complaint in many of the reports to the congress was that the committed activist of the seventies had been replaced by the talk-and-chalk disciplinarian from the seminary, concerned only with rote learning, examina-tions, and the opportunity to put on the official state uniform.[75] Social mobility was undeniably the primary goal of large numbers of teachers of humble origins, as demonstrated by the turnover in personnel and by the persistent requests for free tuition and espe-cially for free boarding facilities (like those given the nobility) for their children in urban schools.

Unquestionably, teachers were dissatisfied with their work and their status, both material and juridical. But it is not clear that this dissatisfaction stemmed exclusively from the high-minded, populist-derived ideals of radical culture. It is even less clear that the resolutions of the several national teachers' congresses reflected the sentiments of rank-and-file teachers. Additionally, it does not seem to follow from the documentary evidence or from what we know of the background, aspirations, or position of teachers that unhappiness with their lot put them in the forefront of the wave of both organized and spontaneous discontent that swept Russia between 1904 and 1906. Acute dissatisfaction with the lowly status of the teaching profession was accompanied in many cases by the hope that the government would improve the teachers' lot. This is precisely what happened in 1908 with the implementation of the bill requiring zemstvos to pay teachers a minimum of 360 rubles. For zemstvo teachers, the government drive to remove rural schools from zemstvo control and incorporate them directly into the Ministry of Education hierarchy was not a challenge to battle but rather was a hopeful sign. The zemstvo had long treated teachers as hirelings; perhaps, they thought, the government might at least put uniforms on them and give them rank.

We must also disentangle two separate threads in the discussion of political activism: agitation for professional status and material improvements; and political influence on the village, the capacity to sway the rural masses. Seregny's recent work, based heavily on archival as well as published contemporary accounts, notes that teachers did enter the political arena in large numbers in 1904 but that the role of political agitator was thrust on them "from below" by the peasants, whose interests had shifted from local, parochial concerns to the national arena. The population needed "decoders" of the political terminology and concepts in the newspapers now flooding the villages. Thus, peasants sometimes forced teachers to take part in events; teachers were also urged on by the liberal and radical zemstvo activists who were temporarily ascendant in the zemstvos. These activists were men who, though a minority in the zemstvos, had won the trust of teachers in the previous decade by sponsoring their interests and participating in the day-to-day concerns of education. But when the revolution receded and the zemstvo reaction swept the countryside in the following year, teachers were left sitting high and dry and suffered accordingly. In short, the archives show that teachers were thrust into political participation by a political conjuncture. The position of reader, interpreter, or decoder in the village did not necessarily imply trust, for the peasants also recruited rural priests and other local literates for the task. Moreover, Seregny's study of some of the sixty thousand peasant resolutions sent to the Tsar in 1905, often drawn up with the help of teachers, convinced him that in most cases the teacher did not necessarily play a significant role in shaping the content of these resolutions.[76]

Of course, the more than thirteen thousand members of the Teachers' Union who were active in 1907 were a formidable political force at the national level; but if we turn our face to the village, the evidence suggests that the vulnerable, isolated, anxious, and neglected teacher was likely to remain inconspicuous. When teachers did look for help, they turned as often to the state as to the zemstvo or to corporate organizations.

CONCLUSIONS

Teachers were isolated; they were not members of a recognized profession or a professional organization nor were they formally members of the village society, for they had no voting rights at the village gatherings, nor could they hold office. They were not members of the bureaucracy, for officially the government regarded them as "public" (*obshchestvennyi*) rather than state (*gosudarstvennyi*) employees. Though employees of the zemstvo, they had no voice in that institution and were generally treated as mere unskilled laborers with no contribution to make to policy. Society regarded the mission of civilizing the peasant as an important, even elevated, task, but this view did not imply that lowly teachers should be elevated into the ranks of the elite. To the villagers, teachers were "outsiders," newcomers, not to be trusted but also not to be feared, for teachers had no way to impose their will—on the contrary, they could be abused at will. To educated society, teachers were social inferiors teaching a craft that required no esoteric skills, something that "everybody knew," and they were seen as contaminated by contact with both children and peasants. Even when the belief that educating peasants was the way to national salvation (*kul'turnichestvo*) swept the zemstvo and educated society in the 1890s, the teacher remained a subordinate partner in the great civilizing endeavors launched by the zemstvo.

Teachers were largely passive, apolitical, and "uncultured," pushed by events into political activity. Their participation was limited and short-lived, and their influence on peasant actions is unproven. In the political arena, as in the school, teachers were used by peasants (as well as by others) for their own ends. Considering the position and backgrounds of rural teachers, their precarious positions in the village community, their isolation from fellow teachers, their vulnerability to political or personal vendettas—and their own often inferior education—it should come as no surprise that narrative accounts of the events of 1905 concede that the activist in the political arena, like the committed teacher in the school, was the exception rather than the rule.

Despite the great importance of the teachers' movement to the liberation movement in Russia, it is unlikely that teachers' organizations, or congresses, ever fostered a true corporate spirit among the rank-and-file village teachers, managed to destroy teachers' continued dependence on the government, or helped overcome the stupefying isolation experienced in the countryside. Those organizations that did thrive, surviving the rapid eclipse of the Teachers' Union, were narrowly concerned with providing aid in times of personal distress. They required a very limited allegiance and participation or, like the League of Education, were dominated by educators (not teachers) in the capital cities as well as by secondary-school and university professionals. Despite the liberalized regulations of 1899, teachers' congresses never achieved the scope or frequency that might have significantly changed the ethos of the teaching profession. This failure was partly the result of government repression, but it was also the outcome of traditional zemstvo indifference to the opinions and contributions of rural teachers.

PART III

Peasant Pedagogy and the Emergence of a School System

9

Peasant Pedagogy

Let us introduce the peasant as educator. To those who argue that preliterates are illogical, impulsive, and unsystematic in their thinking, the very notion of a peasant pedagogy is fatuous. Of course peasants could build schools; but did peasant sponsorship indicate a coherent strategy? Or was it an elemental force, an inchoate wave arising in response to the intrusion of the market, the spreading use of written documents in daily life, the growing contact with the city, the breakdown of the folk community's moral order? If peasant striving for literacy was simply an unthinking response to changing conditions, then we need not consider the question of participation in school affairs. Moreover, regardless of who built the school system, once it was intact and the state in control of curriculum, teacher training, and textbook selection, the issue of popular pedagogy becomes moot.

Such arguments find little support among historians of education or peasant specialists today. Because it is now widely recognized that preliterate peoples are fully capable both of setting life strategies and of practical reasoning, we may well speak of a popular pedagogy—notions of how children should and should not be educated. Because historians of education now argue that legislation is of limited importance in promoting or restricting popular schooling, we must consider the goals set by peasants before judging the success or failure of the school system in Imperial Russia. Success in whose terms? Failure by what standards?

We must keep in mind that peasants not only could sponsor education but also could decide whether and how to participate in a system organized by others—deciding if, when, and for how long to enroll their children. By maintaining a veto power once the school system had been built, peasants could choose whether to use the schools in the ways envisioned by those who "controlled" them or to use them for purposes entirely incompatible with the objectives of the state or the educated public. The very content and structure of basic education could be deeply affected by peasant choice. John E. Craig observes that "the ambition, effort and other attributes of individual students and their families . . . set the parameters within which instructional activity is organized." Attempts to remove the constraints set by the population, in Craig's opinion, have seldom been effective in the West.[1]

A rural teacher from Viatka province described precisely how peasants could shape the content of education and resist outside efforts to impose unwanted routines or curriculum:

For the secondary school pupil, the diploma has great significance, for it is linked with privileges in the civil service and one's social position in general. For the pupil in the primary school, the graduation certificate has no such significance. [These lines were written soon after the military exemptions were abrogated.] The parents of secondary school pupils will make every effort to ensure that their children make it all the way through to the end, for without the diploma the door to civil and public jobs will be slammed in their faces; for this reason, the parents and pupils will submit to the rules of the secondary school, no matter how distasteful they might be. In contrast, if the son of a peasant leaves school during his first year of study, this will have no effect on his standing in society. In the hands of the teacher in the secondary school is a powerful weapon to influence the pupils: marks and expulsion. He doesn't have to worry about weak pupils or teaching methods; he knows that the parents have to obtain an education for their children and will find tutors for their slow children. The secondary school teacher can limit his activities to covering the required lessons, listening to his pupils' [responses], and giving them grades. The primary school teacher is in another world. In response to repressive methods such as forcing a student to repeat a year or applying strict punishments and to poor teaching, the pupil can reply by refusing to study. While a member of the urban intelligentsia will tell his son, "Study, or if you don't, you won't find decent work," the peasant can respond to his son's wish to study by saying that the boy won't be a clerk, he's studied a bit, and that'll do! In a word, the primary school teacher can attract and retain pupils in the school only by competent teaching and by meeting the demands of parents and pupils.[2]

Although we know that peasants had leverage in the school system even after it had been incorporated into the state bureaucracy, how do we know what they wanted? As M. J. Maynes notes of French peasants, "Unfortunately for the historian, . . . average families rarely left records of their perceptions of schooling and its value; . . . their hopes must be inferred from their behavior" and from a knowledge of the "structural constraints" within which choices were made.[3] In short, the proof of the pudding is in the eating—that is, in peasant actions. The following chapters examine the educational activities of peasants, as reflected in the cycle of enrollment and dropping out, and consider the "structural constraints" imposed on these activities: the economy and the availability of schooling. I argue that peasant actions strongly hint at a strategy of support for basic schooling but resistance to outside intervention, a classic peasant *adaptive* strategy for changing conditions. This strategy, elicited in later chapters from the musty school records, found its first direct expression in the attitudes recorded—often in troubled voices—by zemstvo correspondents and educators in the village.

We must keep in mind the difficulty of demonstrating peasant intent, for peasants seldom left any explicit record of their opinions. As Daniel Field reminds us, "What we learn about the *narod* . . . is what individual members of educated society tell us. Our defining concepts and most of our raw material consist of perceptions and imputations made across a cultural gulf."[4] If peasants were inveterate dissimulators when forced to interact directly with those regarded as outsiders (*ne nashi*), how can we use statements made to "them" and recorded by "them"? Such statements are intrinsically suspect.

Yet, by the last quarter of the century, changes had taken place in the composition of local literate society, those recording peasant opinions. Although Field argues that "literates" and elite society (*obshchestvo*) were virtually the same, by 1900 the networks of local correspondents reporting annually to zemstvo boards were often dominated by people of peasant origin—including teachers, agricultural specialists, farmers themselves, rural priests, and others; the line was beginning to blur. One might plausibly counter that literate peasants were no longer peasants because new patterns had been introduced into their minds; yet the documents written by these correspondents have a ring of authenticity and often record sentiments and observations that must have been painful to the observer. Used with care, such documents deserve credence, or at least careful consideration.

EARLY STUDIES

During the first two decades following the emancipation of the serfs, the zemstvos had only occasional contact with peasant society and had at best only fragmentary information with which to formulate policy. Because the networks of local correspondents had not yet been established and very few professionals were at work in the countryside, statements concerning peasant attitudes toward education were generally based on preconceptions and unfounded assumptions rather than on empirical observation. Yet a few keen observers did record their experiences. The most thorough and insightful of these observers were Baron Korf, who labored for years in Ekaterinoslav province; M. Sukhomlinov, whose careful comparison of archives, official records, and actual practice in the schools of Iaroslavl' and Chernigov provinces in the 1860s give his comments unusual force; and N. Zolotov, whose travels to promote the phonic reading method provided an opportunity to gauge public attitudes. These men, whose observations of peasant life date from the 1860s, detected contradictory and confusing attitudes among the peasantry toward literacy and schooling.[5]

In most areas visited by Sukhomlinov, Korf, and Zolotov, peasants seemed enthusiastic about learning to read and write.

Moreover, Korf was perhaps the first in a long line of educators to contrast peasant children's enthusiasm for education to the indifference, hostility, and unruliness of urban schoolchildren.

In many areas, the level of literacy far outstripped the figures on school enrollment; reading and writing were often taught by siblings, parents, or private tutors (most often retired soldiers). Sukhomlinov calculated that in Chernigov literates who had been taught outside the schools outnumbered those who had learned their ABCs through the schools by a ratio of three or four to one.[6] N. Bunakov, at that time a gymnasium teacher in the north, noted that in the town of Vologda in the early 1860s 744 men and 54 women had a primary education, whereas 3,327 men and 2,520 women were literate.[7] In Iaroslavl', where the enrollment rate ranged between fifteen and sixty per thousand inhabitants, the level of literacy was as high as five hundred per thousand in some districts.[8] Iaroslavl' was, of course, an area where commerce and migratory labor (*otkhozhie*) were exceptionally developed; Sukhomlinov did observe village gatherings in Chernigov where the ratio of literates to illiterates was very low indeed (in one village, 9 out of 185; in a second, 9 out of 284; and in a third, only 1 person out of 217). He noted:

The number of literates is so low that no one could be found to administer vaccines against disease, since one has to know his letters to do this, so they were forced to choose one of the estate *fel'dshery*. The village elders are all illiterate. When a corpse is found in the vicinity, everyone summoned as a witness is illiterate, so the necessary documents [*protokoly*] remain unsigned.[9]

Nevertheless, whatever the literacy rate, it clearly exceeded the capacity of the school system. Moreover, whenever schools opened their doors, they soon were filled to overflowing. The peace arbitrators placed in the countryside to negotiate the terms of the land settlements between peasants and nobles after Emancipation often recorded a high degree of enthusiasm for learning, a willingness to make material sacrifices, and even a "universal surge" of pro-literacy sentiment. In Anan'evski district, the local zemstvo noted that "the willingness with which most peasant societies move to open schools, and to make what are often significant allocations to maintain these schools, clearly shows that the peasant population of the district is sufficiently aware of the need for schools."[10]

European Russia had scarcely begun to move in the direction of industrialization in the 1860s, and for most peasants contact with the monetary economy was secondary to their involvement in the subsistence economy of the peasant farm. Nevertheless, peasant understanding of the value of literacy, at least for boys, was very widespread. Literacy was valued not only for its utility but also for the social prestige accruing to one who possessed an item of relative scarcity and for the sheer pleasure of being able to read either to oneself or out loud.

Summarizing a survey of peasant opinions on the need for schooling conducted in the early sixties, N. P. Malinovskii wrote:

"You don't have to feed it, or treat it to drink, or carry it on your back; instead of being harmful, it is useful," say the peasants, who see a vital need for literacy for the following reasons: a) It enables one to fulfill official positions better. This explains why the majority of volost' and village elders favor literacy. Their experience has taught them how difficult it is to get by without it, what a yoke is often imposed by the volost' scribes, "who often lord it over these ignorant people." The sons, daughters, nieces, and nephews of these elders are always the first to knock on the door of the school the minute it opens. b) Literacy is necessary to be able to read statutes and other decrees concerning peasants, and especially concerning taxes. "Today the agencies collect taxes, and who knows that they're not taking too much?" say the peasants. "Well, if we were literate, we'd find out and know for ourselves." . . . c) Boys need to be literate in case they're conscripted; the literate soldier has a better chance of becoming a noncommissioned officer, and he'll have a better time of it. The more developed peasants also spoke of literacy being necessary to understand the Scripture—to know and understand the prayers.[11]

In Chernigov, a study conducted by the Office of State Domains through village elders also concluded that the main motivations for literacy were the popular perception that education would help in the army and the social prestige resulting from possession of a rare skill. It was said that in the peasant household, next to the father, a literate family member carried the greatest weight (*pochët*). Reading was also widely treasured for the enjoyment of having at least one literate family member or co-worker who could read aloud during long winter nights or in dreary, repetitive cottage industries. Zolotov found "well-worn" copies of books in nearly every home in Tver'. Sukhomlinov observed that

peasants, even the illiterate, love to hear oral readings; neighbors gathering during the winter after dinner demand [from the literate] a reading of a good book. In their understanding, the best books are those dealing with God and the saints; fairy tales and other entertaining works are also acceptable.[12]

One peasant proudly displayed his collection of books, noting that it was actually much larger than met the eye, for he had lent a number of books to the local shepherds who also gathered at night to hear books read out loud. Reports also noted that there were "great enthusiasts of reading" among women in the area.

Thus even before the onset of rapid industrialization in Russia, considerable, if scattered, recognition of the value of literacy existed among the peasant population. Still, "to value something highly is not the same as being able or willing to attain it."[13] Indeed, all our informants recorded instances that pointed to indifference or sometimes even hostility toward official schools, instances of peasant reluctance to allocate funds for school construction or to pay taxes levied for such a purpose, and frequent closings of schools once they had opened. Zolotov, who noted that in Tver' there was "some support for schooling" but that Moscow province remained virtually an educational wasteland, observed that peasants regarded all attempts to impose communal school taxes as a form of quitrent and were extremely devious in trying to avoid payment. Sukhomlinov wrote that "the peasants produce money for schools just as reluctantly as for other public institutions."[14]

It was also obvious that the cause of educating girls enjoyed virtually no support among the peasantry at that time; although Sukhomlinov, Korf, and Zolotov sometimes saw things differently, on this one matter they were unanimous. Korf lamented that his persistent efforts to encourage parents to send their little girls to school were a total failure. In his rendition of peasant opinion,

"It's a woman's business to look after the pots, not to read books." . . . In order to get married [Korf continued], a woman needs a dowry, which she must begin preparing [literally, weaving] at an early age. It takes a long time for a girl to weave it, to put it together thread by thread; . . . a peasant girl has to begin at about age ten. In the summer, she's in the fields, but in the winter, while her brother, without whom the family can get by, is learning how to read, she is learning how to weave. . . . Such is the situation of the majority . . . but even those families prosperous enough to allow at least one daughter to go to school [sometimes refuse, arguing that] literacy is not for the women.[15]

Korf, Sukhomlinov, Zolotov, and others were puzzled by these seemingly inconsistent attitudes. Most observers blamed the indifference or hostility on peasant passivity, the "heritage of serf-dom," and a sharp distrust of anything that smacked of official-dom. Peasants simply couldn't believe that anything sponsored or supported by "them" could operate to the benefit of the peasant community. In one instance, a peasant *mir* refused to put up money to build a school because its members were convinced that the local *pomeshchik* would simply appropriate the building for his own purposes as soon as it was completed.[16]

In a number of cases, peasants were convinced that official attempts to enroll their children were a ruse to steal their offspring; in Tver', Zolotov noted a widespread fear that children, once in school, would be shipped out to work in factories "in the Caucasus or Siberia." In Chernigov, when a local official tried to persuade peasants to send their little girls to school, the parents refused, convinced that the girls were to be married off to soldiers or "sent off into the steppes" (for what reason remains unclear). In Iaroslavl', peasants refused to send their boys to school in state peasant villages because they were sure that the boys would be dragged away into the army.[17]

This distrust was sometimes deep enough to negatively affect peasant attitudes toward even basic literacy: "Lord save us from literacy; as soon as you can read, you'll be whisked away as a recruit or the *pan* [lord] will take you away to be a clerk or a domestic!"[18] Popular dread of all official or gentry attempts to persuade or cajole peasants to do anything was certainly not confined to the sphere of education: thirty years earlier, well-meaning attempts to quarantine the sick during a cholera epidemic had led to furious riots in Russia, and there are countless other examples of violent peasant resistance to gentry tinkering with their way of life. Certainly the instances in which peasants refused to carry out labor obligations for the lord, arguing that by sending their children to school they were fulfilling their *barshchina* obligations, fit this pattern.[19]

In the villages, opponents of literacy argued that it was simply a useless frill, of no value to the peasant way of life—that it wouldn't change the amount of bread on the table or help reduce the burden of work. Other peasants heatedly presented this syllogism: the volost' clerks are all literate; the volost' clerks are almost all drunkards as well—therefore, literacy ruins the individual. In Chernigov, some spoke out against literacy, saying, "You can't eat it [*Khlebom ne godue*]." At the exhortation of some soldier that knowledge pleased God, peasants replied, "We're not likely to be chosen as saints, so God will take us as we are." Malinovskii argued that the provincial and official diocesan journals of the time were full of such testimony. At the same time, he added, the schools were full to overflowing![20]

Observers were quick to note that a variety of local factors were often decisive in determining popular response to efforts to promote education. Bunakov, for example, noted that in Vologda the crown peasants were far better educated than the state peasants simply because separate schools for girls were available to crown peasants—many peasant families strongly opposed coeducation and would not have otherwise sent their daughters to school. Among former serfs, the level of literacy fluctuated wildly according to who had previously owned them. Malinovskii noted that the make-up of the local zemstvo was often decisive in the 1870s, for considerable red tape had to be cut before official schools could be established. Another important factor was the settlement size; a larger community could more easily find the funds to maintain a building and pay a teacher. Finally, the level of interest in literacy was generally far higher in villages with a high rate of employment in trade or outside factory work than it was in purely agricultural settlements.[21]

The director of schools for the Simbirsk educational district in 1872 observed that enthusiasm for schools increased markedly when peasants felt the teacher was competent. In contrast, when the peasants saw no visible results, they were justifiably disillusioned. Miropol'skii tells of one school that had graduated twenty-five boys every year for ten years—yet after ten years, only five literates could be found in the entire village.[22]

In Poltava, the school inspector noted:

The reason for popular indifference to the schools can be found in the schools themselves, since certain of the teachers are obviously unprepared and make no attempt to improve; hence the quality of teaching suffers. Others, even when they know their work well, do little better. In certain schools, almost nothing is taught to pupils in two or three years: little attention is devoted to clear and precise [*razdel'noe*] intelligent reading, penmanship, or practical problem solving in math; in others, they don't teach Church singing to the children. In still others, no effort is made to do things that would serve to recommend the school to society, for example, by preparing readers [*chetsov*] and singers for the Church, which the population greatly treasures. For these reasons, the population cannot understand the school or appreciate it enough to spend their last kopecks on it; for these reasons, we find dissatisfaction and abuse heaped on the schools.[23]

Miropol'skii notes that many schools made little effort to prepare children to play a role in Church services. But in those areas where schools enjoyed popular support, singing was often a prominent part of the school day; as we shall see, singing lessons and preparation for participation in Church services (particularly by lessons in Church Slavonic) continued to be a major reason for peasant support of the school system and mandatory curriculum into the twentieth century.

Above all, observers noted that previous experience with schooling was often critical in shaping peasant attitudes toward official education. Korf pointed to an instance in which a village of state peasants had maintained a school for thirteen years at the cost of 4,400 silver rubles, but only four literates could be found in the village. A teacher told Korf that when he arrived in the village, a parent offered him a sack of potatoes in exchange for releasing his child from school. An accusing finger was pointed, probably unjustly, at the Church schools for ruining the good name of education by antiquated teaching methods, harsh discipline, and even exploitation of children. But even in schools adopting a more modern approach (phonics), undue haste or the hiring of an in-experienced teacher could result in disaster.[24] Korf and others argued: first *better,* and *then* more schools! Peasants agreed that there was no sense in packing their children off to study if the children didn't learn or else soon forgot how to make sense of the printed page. Although in some cases what we now call crude literacy was all that parents demanded, in others parents were outraged that they had paid "good silver rubles" for such meager results: "They read and read, but don't understand a damn thing."[25]

Peasant preference for *vol'nye* schools over official schools was widespread. One obvious reason was that the former cost the village much less: teachers were paid a pittance, sometimes in grain rather than cash; "school" could meet in a peasant home, obviating the need for major outlays on construction and maintenance of a school building; and the teacher could be put up in outbuildings, moving from one peasant household to the next.

In one village not far from Khar'kov, where the land-poor peasants engage in petty trade and other industries that require literacy, they opened up their own school. They hired a teacher, a bright young fellow, and sent him about twenty-five boys, even over the holidays. The costs were very low: for a building, the peasants rented a room with heat for 1 ruble a month; they paid the teacher 40 rubles [a winter?], and then added 20 for his efforts; and the parents themselves bought the books.

The peasants from two villages in Shenkurskii district, not having the opportunity to build a permanent school, set up their own mobile school, which had no permanent residence but met by turn in the homes of the villages. In each house the school and teacher [who was put up by the occupants] remained about a week.[26]

Direct expense was not the only consideration, however. Even in this early period, the conviction was widespread among peasants that too much schooling ruined a child, that allowing a child to "finish up" (*douchivat'*) was far worse than illiteracy. Korf reported that in a village school taught by a priest, the peasants specifically asked that their children be taught . . . but not too much (*chtoby detei ikh uchili, no ne douchivali*). Such a request came as no surprise, as Korf indignantly pointed out, because this was an old (Church) school which did virtually nothing for the vast majority of pupils, but tore a few away from their native hearth, from their normal employment as tillers of the soil, made them clerks and planted them like vampires on the head of the village community; is it any wonder that the peasants ask us not to overeducate their young?[27]

But the "old" Church schools were not the only offenders, according to Malinovskii's transcriptions of peasant opinion. Speaking of secular schools, peasants complained:

In general, they teach pretty badly; the child only wastes his time and as a result of his schooling loses his taste for working around the home. But if you improve the teaching, that's even worse: the child gets hooked on learning and won't go back to the plow at all![28]

Indeed, parents seemed to prefer the subject matter taught in the Church schools. "When they send their children to school, parents want their children to return knowing their prayers, when the holidays fall, able to read the saints' lives."[29] From Tver', it was reported that "all the peasants insist that first of all their children learn Church Slavonic, and then modern Russian, because in their understanding the whole purpose of literacy is to be able to read the psalter; thus, when they send their children off to be taught, they pay 1 ruble for [learning] the *azbuka* [ABC book], 1 for writing, and 2, 3, or more for reading the psalter." (Zolotov noted that by learning Church Slavonic one could turn a tidy profit as well: "The psalter, *batiushka* [Little Father], makes money; they'll pay you well to read it at a wake.") Moreover, Zolotov insisted that the peasants had as of yet absolutely no recognition of the "edificational" side of literacy or of its potential for improving the material well-being of the family.[30] In Iaroslavl',

the least demanding peasants, when they turn their children over to the school, say, "Teach 'em to read, and a bit of writing. Don't bother with the Bible; what use is it to them? They won't be sextons. It's up to you, the priests, to read books. You don't have to pay dues, so you've got time for books, but we don't have time for both!" The majority, however, want their children to have Bible instruction, and especially to learn the psalter, so they'll be able to say mass for the parents [when the parents die], and arithmetic, which the peasants say is necessary.[31]

Although the attitude toward literacy undoubtedly varied considerably from region to region, it also seems likely that the apparent contradictions in attitude perceived by educators resulted from their own misperceptions. Peasants knew what they wanted—but their desires differed greatly from the educators' goals. (Zolotov was then convinced that the school's main goal should be to exert moral influence over the whole family through the children.) In many ways, peasant desires dovetailed nicely with the content of the Church parish schools, though perhaps not with their methods of teaching. Parents wanted their young to learn to read with comprehension and were unsatisfied when the children came home able to make out a letter but unable to make sense of a paragraph. Nor did parents want the school to provoke too much curiosity about the outside world or to change the children's habits—to spoil them for the plow. This interpretation is the only plausible explanation that brings together the often jumbled and contradictory reports from the countryside. Add to this the strong desire to keep expenses to a minimum and the hardly muted hostility to anything sponsored by "them"—whether *pomeshchik* or government official—and the preference for *vol'nye* schools becomes clear.

PEASANT ATTITUDES, 1890–1914

In the mid-1880s, the annual rate of industrial growth in Russia leaped from 4 percent to 8 percent. One might plausibly expect a corresponding leap in peasant interest in schooling, for much recent scholarship presumes a connection between industrialization, literacy, and the spread of schooling.[32]

Peasant attitudes toward literacy and education again came under close scrutiny in the 1880s, this time through the zemstvo networks. The networks soon discovered that the desire for literacy had become virtually universal—and now included girls. Even the pockets of indifference were being wiped out. Yet, despite the clear intensification of peasant strivings for literacy, the same reservations about formal schooling remained. Although investigators did not always make a clear distinction between literacy and schooling, peasants had no trouble doing so. Despite an outpouring of edificational literature, self-help manuals, and how-to books, and despite the rapid industrialization process, which was fully launched by the 1890s, peasants retained their belief that too large a dose— or the wrong type—of education would ruin their offspring. Perhaps it was *because* of the pressure for change, both economic and social, that peasants held firm to this belief; indeed, a note of stubbornness could easily be detected by this time, a stubbornness in some cases intensified by what might have been a growing generational struggle in the villages over family authority, independent outside earnings, and the spread of urban clothes and habits among the young.[33] The following pages survey peasant attitudes recorded in the years between 1890 and 1914.

As early as the 1890s, 90 percent of the respondents to a Moscow Literacy Committee survey claimed that the need for education was universally recognized, that the only pockets of opposition were among the Muslim populations of Simbirsk, Kazan', Samara, and Viatka provinces. Moreover, nearly an identical percentage noted that enthusiasm for education had become more pronounced in recent years. Examples abounded of peasant initiative in school construction, despite foot-dragging and indifference by local zemstvos and webs of red tape spun by local officials. Every fall when school doors opened, the premises were soon overflowing with pupils, and parents would not allow teachers to deny their children admission. A rural teacher from Murom district, Vladimir province, described such a scene:

Well before the school opens, on holidays and Sundays, peasant children begin to gather in crowds in front of the school. . . . Each of them tries to register early to be guaranteed a place in school. The parents often don't learn whether or not their son or daughter has been accepted until they find out from the children themselves that they've managed to register. Each year we have to turn away large numbers, despite the fact that we take far more than we are supposed to.[34]

In Tambov, parents simply wouldn't take no for an answer and insisted that their children could stand during classes if there were not enough seats available. Nor were such instances exceptional. In the words of the compiler of the survey, "You can't escape

the facts; the evidence is so overwhelming that instances of nega-
tivity are simply engulfed in the floodtide of a universal search for
education."[35]

In Russia, as in France, "when going to school was the thing
to do, all would do it."[36] Attendance could not be obstructed by
poverty, inclement weather, or distance. A former justice of the
peace from an unidentified region wrote:

There is a stunning desire to learn among peasant children. I don't have
the faintest idea how to explain it, for it would seem that every imaginable obstacle has been put in the way of the peasant child: the daily trek
over snow-covered roads for long distances in the winter frost and in
flimsy clothing; lessons the entire day, and then [spending] their evenings
crowded together, under low ceilings in rooms short of oxygen, with a
meager diet largely composed of bread and water. A few of them manage
to bring along potatoes or cabbage to supplement their dinner . . . but
none of these discomforts dampens their enthusiasm for study.[37]

Other investigations carried out at the time produced similar
comments. A survey of Perm' province concluded that more than
four out of five parents willingly sent their children to school.[38] At
times, village enthusiasm clearly surpassed that demonstrated by
the zemstvo; in Kostroma province, when a local school burned
down, the district zemstvo refused to help rebuild or even to pay
the teacher's salary, but the village commune went ahead on its own.

Perhaps most striking are the comments left behind by village
teachers, who often touchingly observed the eagerness and joy of
peasant children coming to school. The experience of teachers in
other countries, the grim physical conditions of schools in the
countryside, and the frequent complaints by teachers that the
MNP and the Holy Synod mandatory syllabuses imposed rote
learning and mechanical drills on the school system would all suggest just the opposite—that peasant children should have avoided
the schools like the plague. Yet the impression of enthusiasm was
virtually universal and peppers the recollections of teachers of
diverse ideological persuasions: S. Rachinskii, P. Mironositskii,
Bunakov, and Demkov, along with Tolstoy the religious anarchist,
and countless anonymous teachers.

In his famous work on village schools, Rachinskii noted:

Our children enter school with a firm intention to become literate; for the most part, they come at their own insistent request, fully ready to study without respite from morning to evening. The parents are fully behind them. . . . [The children's] regular attendance, their genuinely insatiable appetite for learning leaves the attentive teacher no choice but to increase the number of classroom hours, especially during the first half of winter. . . . Such intensive study is not coercion of the children, but a concession to their demands; they came to study, and besides the school, they have nothing else to do. To get them to leave, you literally have to drive them away. Directly connected with this serious attitude manifested by our schoolchildren, we note their excellent, energetic, and happy, but modest and calm, behavior in school. They don't have time for mischievous pranks or fighting. They don't have a trace of that repulsive vulgarity of thought and language which has so infected our urban schools.[39]

We might be inclined to believe that such gushing stemmed from a bad case of excessive populism and antiurbanism, yet report after report by teachers stressed the honesty, discipline, seriousness, and sense of responsibility of the peasant schoolchild. Bunakov noted that "the impressions made by the school on the peasant children and their responsiveness to learning are deeper, stronger, and more lasting; their attitude toward school and toward their studies is more serious, businesslike, focused, and concentrated."[40]

Teachers saw no mystery in these attitudes. Baron Korf had noted a generation earlier in his handbook for teachers that "the home life of a peasant boy is so wretched that you don't need to do much to make him feel good about school."[41] Rachinskii argued that the peasant child differed radically from children of the privileged estates: "Though he has not yet seen an ABC book, he knows well the ABCs of life." The hardships of rural life made children extraordinarily receptive to schooling:

[The family has no time] to hide from him the filth and darker sides of life. He knows everything, not from amusing tales, but from immediate, bitter experience. He has seen death and all its terrifying details, with all its solemn grandeur, and has learned to regard it simply and soberly, with humility and hope. Though uneducated by comparison with the five-year-old child from the educated classes, he is immeasurably more mature than the twenty-year-old youth brought up in a wealthy and enlightened family. He comes to school gladly. A life awaits him here which is relatively unencumbered and free, without backbreaking work . . . here awaits a luxury which is really a necessity of childhood, a luxury for which there is no time in his own family life: constant attention and concern for him by his elders.[42]

In short, by the 1890s, evidence was overwhelming that peasant children were enthusiastic about learning; they flocked to schools in such numbers that overcrowding was becoming a serious problem in many areas (see Chapter 10). Given earlier observations, one might well ask whether these attitudes represented a change in the countryside or whether the blinders had simply fallen off the eyes of urban intellectuals—indeed, the observations of Korf, Rachinskii, and Bunakov extend from the 1860s through the 1880s. That the latter may well have been the case is suggested by the concluding comments to the Moscow Literacy Committee survey:

Earlier I felt, as does everyone who lives in the city, that the popular striving for education was more or less limited to major industrial centers, that village Russia was an area still largely untouched by schools and with a population 70 percent illiterate. *It seemed to me that it was the mission of the government and of educated society to introduce to the benighted masses the very idea of the necessity of enlightenment, and I thought that it would take several more decades before the people felt the need for schools.* Now, after becoming acquainted with these live voices not only from zemstvo Russia but also from the borderlands, I see . . . that the people already fully recognize the need for education and recognize it with equal force throughout the country [emphasis added].[43]

It seems clear why peasant children might have welcomed the opportunity to learn, but what value did adult peasants place on their children's schooling? The author of the above survey notes that "the facts led me inexorably to yet one other conclusion, namely, that the population regards the school primarily as a source of material well-being. 'In the school,' writes one teacher, 'the population sees a powerful means of support in the struggle for survival.'"[44]

For many, "well-being" meant survival, not mobility. V. V. Petrov, in his influential study of popular education, cited a Mos-

cow correspondent who claimed, "Without doubt, the peasant today must deal with various 'papers' much more frequently than in
the past, both as a soldier and as an apprentice—everywhere literacy is demanded."[45] As the byways between city and countryside
widened with industrialization, increasing the population pressure
on the land and forcing more and more peasants to flock to work
in the cities or in other provinces, the importance of reading for
sheer survival became painfully obvious. This need was expressed
in a number of pithy proverbs: "The illiterate person can't find his
way farther than his own hut"; "He who can read does well at the
marketplace." Perhaps most important, though harder to measure,
was the growing conviction that literate people were less easily
cheated by their "betters": "It's much easier to cheat the illiterate
person, while he who can read doesn't get caught so easily." Trying
to explain his thoughts, one peasant said that sending an illiterate
out into the world was like sending an untrained civilian into battle
(*s nego seichas bashku doloi*). Another declared, "Times have changed,
people have learned how to read and have become slyer. You sell
some oxen, and you can't even tell what kind of paper [money] you
get in return!" Yet another explained, "Without letters, you're lost;
you put some money down and you don't know if it was entered in
the book. It happens that they give back the book saying they
wrote it down, and then later they take your money again." These
are statements of fear and distrust; literacy was a defensive weapon,
not a tool for social mobility or a source of cultural enrichment.
Bunakov also noticed the same desire to avoid being hoodwinked
among peasants anxious to teach their children the ABCs.[46]

HOW MUCH SCHOOLING?

The growing enthusiasm for schooling did not necessarily
translate into a desire for an expanded curriculum or even an urge
to take full advantage of the existing, minimal three-year program.
As had been the case thirty years earlier, peasants—or at least parents—seemed to set their sights lower or in a different direction
than that pursued by educators. From Moscow:

Even the poor peasant makes sure that his sons are literate, for today an illiterate wouldn't even be given a job as a doorman. But many children don't wait until the final exams [to leave school]. . . . The parents take them out, saying, "We have no need of an examination; our children won't be clerks!"

The peasants in our regions are engaged in a brisk trade and acutely feel the need for literacy. Every family keeps up a cottage industry, and the account books must be maintained. . . . The demand made of the school, incidentally, is minimal: that the boy can "read a bit," "make out a letter," "write a note." This explains why few pupils reach the senior division and why, as soon as they can read and write freely, they leave the schools.

The peasants take their children out of school if they see that, once able to read well, the children run into difficulty with arithmetic or grammar exercises. They say that such exercises are unnecessary and that it is foolish to overburden the children with trivia.[47]

Such beliefs were not limited to Moscow. The 1911 Zemstvo Survey, studying the reasons for early departure from the schools, found that "family attitudes" contributed to 70 percent of all such cases—and that in nearly all instances such attitudes signified a lack of awareness of any need for or advantage in completing the full three-year program. From Iaroslavl': "We've studied our fill, so let's be done with it—after all, we're not going to the royal court!" From Kostroma: "They can read and draw up a short letter. What else do you want? They won't be priests, after all!" From Kherson it was reported that "many take the trouble to educate their children because they'll be taken into the army, and not because a son will better understand his work but because he'll be beaten less there."[48] (See also the discussion in Chapter 11.)

Other instances demonstrated peasant resentment of the schools: "Certain of the parents look on the school as encroaching on the mores and customs of the peasant and blame it for the changes taking place in peasant life."

The path taken by the contemporary school is not fully comprehended by the locals. Although they recognize the usefulness [of schools], a lot of what is taught is considered a necessary evil to be suffered through in order to gain the ability to read and comprehend what is written and to count.

Finally, others argued that "school destroyed all interest in work and made the child effete."[49]

Numerous studies reported that the peasant definition of literacy and adequate schooling was very practical and narrowly circumscribed. A questionnaire sent out in 1900 to graduates of primary schools in Kursk province asked what benefits peasants saw in schooling. The vast majority of responses pointed to the practical daily advantages of being literate: the ability to avoid being cheated, to find one's way in the city, to keep records at home, to get through one's term in the military more easily or even to make it to NCO rank, to read letters from relatives, to make sense of notices from the volost' officials.[50]

In his account of a decade spent teaching children in a small village in Voronezh province, Bunakov speaks of the peasant understanding of literacy:

I have often heard from peasants the opinion that the pinnacle of literacy and learning in the peasant milieu is the ability to read and compose a letter; whoever cannot *compose* . . .—yes, even if he can write, but keeps asking "What should I write?"—if he cannot compose, he hasn't yet made it all the way to real literacy [*eschchë ne doshel do dela, do nastoiashchei, zapravskoi gramotnosti*].[51]

Interestingly, Yuri Samarin, a delegate to the 1868 Moscow zemstvo assembly, noted that many village schools imposed one fee for teaching reading and writing and a second fee for teaching reading with comprehension, indicating that peasants distinguished between decoding and content assimilation.[52]

A study of Nizhnii Novgorod province on the eve of World War I confirmed the impression that peasants were still concerned with limiting the length and scope of study. A teacher commented:

The main reason children attend school poorly is simple negligence. In this, they enjoy parental connivance, which stems from the latter's backwardness and lack of understanding of the usefulness of any instruction that does more than teach the peasant more or less to read and write;

many boys, and especially girls, leave after studying for one-and-a-half to two years.[53]

We can gain insight into peasant strategies through studies of the level of satisfaction with the minimal program offered by the zemstvo and Church schools. Was there any indication that the peasants wanted more than this meager diet—the pauper's fare of intellectual sustenance? Were there signs of interest in either an expanded curriculum or a more extensive program that might last from five to six years? In truth, despite complaints by zemstvo educators that the scanty fare provided during the school day, the concentration on Church Slavonic and Bible study, and the unadventurous, often turgid readers promoted by higher authorities were all poisoning the schools and destroying peasant enthusiasm, the evidence seems clear that what was offered was precisely what the parents demanded.

In the 1860s, Sukhomlinov and others had discovered that a basic program of reading, writing, arithmetic, and a smattering of Bible studies coincided with peasant aspirations.[54] Thirty years later, after the secular zemstvo schools had gained a foothold in the countryside, teachers were asked whether the program taught at the schools met peasant needs. In a revealing survey of their responses, Vakhterov noted that *teachers* almost unanimously believed that reading and writing alone were not sufficient: "Teaching reading alone gives nothing but mechanical ability; it is not capable of instilling in a child an urge for reading. But without this urge the ability itself disappears!" Teachers called for the promotion of "conscious literacy" and for a reduction in the emphasis on grammar, an end to the "cult of the *jet*" ("semi-consonant," which caused innumerable difficulties for children—and foreigners—trying to master Russian spelling). Specifically, teachers suggested that the curriculum should promote curiosity, an urge for self-development, basic knowledge in history, geography, and civics, and, especially, moral development.[55]

Yet Vakhterov conceded that the demands of the population fit poorly with those articulated by teachers, many of whom admitted that the peasants had little use for "progressive" pedagogy. "The peasants," wrote one teacher from Iaroslavl', "are happy if the boy can write sensibly, read tolerably [*skladno*], and make out a

business letter. I think otherwise." From an unidentified agricultural province, another teacher noted that "the peasant demands
are meager: the ability to read Russian and Church Slavonic, *with
or without the observation of spelling rules,* but neatly, precisely, and
with meaning. The peasants think two years are fully sufficient for
this [emphasis added]."[56]

The indifference to correct spelling is a significant observation,
which we shall consider later. Here the most important points are
the continuity in popular demands on the schools and the clear recognition that teachers and parents could differ in setting goals. To
be sure, Vakhterov, a highly influential proponent of "general education" and mainstream progressive pedagogy, argued that peasants demanded the ability to *read with comprehension.* This skill
could not be achieved solely through rote recitation and memorization, but only through the promotion of overall intellectual facility; thus, he argued, the implicit demand of peasant parents was
for an extended program and self-development. But this argument
should be seen for what it was—a sleight of hand designed to conceal the embarrassing gap between parental demands and progressive pedagogy.

A major point of controversy between educators and the official bureaucracy at the turn of the century was the 1897 Model
Program adopted by the Ministry of Education, which limited the
curriculum of the elementary school to reading, writing, arithmetic, Church Slavonic, and Bible lessons (see Appendix). Although progressive educators wanted to include geography, history, and natural science as formal courses and to rid the schools of
what they saw as the barren, scholastic textbooks recommended
by the Ministry of Education (such as Baranov's *Nashe rodnoe*), parents seemed to be indifferent or even seemed to prefer the official
curriculum. In Perm', when local zemstvo correspondents were
asked if the peasants were happy with the "existing organization of
the schools," they reported overwhelmingly in the affirmative
(78.6 percent); another 7.1 percent reported indifference; and only
14.3 percent noted dissatisfaction. Dissatisfaction was often linked
with regressive illiteracy, in which children soon lost the meager
skills they had once acquired and were unable to compose a letter,
understand written documents, or read out loud to the family.
Peasants, however, did not blame the official curriculum for this

slippage; instead, they complained that their children forgot the basics because the schools "spent time on trifles [*izlishye*], on stories about pigs or dogs" and taught "songs and fairy tales."[57] (Peasants often referred to the poetry learned by their children as songs.) Similarly, a study of attendance patterns in Nizhnii Novgorod concluded that only 1.3 percent of the nonattendance recorded in the province could be blamed on dissatisfaction with the existing school program.[58]

If anything, it was the tolerance of the authorities in permitting progressive readers into the schools that annoyed and aggravated parents. Because these readers often used the phonics method, peasants thus sometimes rejected both the methodology and the content of the progressive tradition.[59] The director of schools for the St. Petersburg educational district pointed out in 1870 that Ushinskii's *Rodnoe slovo*, though praiseworthy for its methods of promoting both mechanical and comprehensive literacy, was unsatisfactory in content. The peasants were accustomed to linking literacy with "something sacred"; they "saw in it the key to understanding the word of God [*slovo bozhiia*]." Ushinskii mixed together pictures from Bible history, fables, and fairy tales, and "this extremely irritated the peasants," both Orthodox and Old Believers, so much so that sometimes they took their children out of school. The same inspector noted that peasants also disliked a reading exercise book compiled by Glavinskii because it contained stories from "peasant life," which they "had no use for."[60]

In Moscow, local zemstvo correspondents reported considerable sentiment that schools were wasting the child's time:

The peasants looked with suspicion on the methods of instruction; they thought it a waste of time to conduct preliminary discussions with the children on a wide range of themes merely to establish a measure of rapport with the pupils and to groom them to answer properly. They looked with mistrust on the early exercises given to children, asking them to break up words into sounds and groups of sounds, for they could not see the connection between this [the phonic method] and literacy. They were quite unhappy that the children's readings began not with the works of the Church, but rather with secular literature. They regarded with scorn the idea that their children would read numerous tales about chickens and roosters rather than the holy books.[61]

The writer of this passage did observe that when parents saw their children's success in learning to read and write, their attitudes toward the teaching methods employed in the zemstvo schools changed. But the dislike of the material included in progressive textbooks remained.

This irritation at mixing the sacred and the profane is easily understandable if we recognize that religious books "played a significant physical role in a world in which demons and other supernatural beings had a place."[62] The sacred books themselves were seen as being imbued with magical qualities. As a famous study of Moscow province in 1883 observed, "There are certain superstitions surrounding the psalter, namely that he who reads it from cover to cover forty times is absolved of certain sins, and that it serves as a means of divining [*gadanie*], particularly in those cases where the perpetrator of a theft of property is to be found."[63]

Elaborate rituals surrounded the use of the psalter, and the study reported that readings were often given without any thought to meaning, often as an accompaniment to local folk traditions having nothing to do with the Church. Indeed, the psalter, like the icon, had to be placed in the proper corner of the *izba*. Possession of the book did not necessarily mean the owner was literate. Because the psalter was believed to have magical properties, we can understand why peasants would have been dismayed to open their children's schoolbooks and find selections from it indiscriminately mixed with illustrations from the best-known folk and fairy tales.

But there was an even more prosaic objection to the use of progressive readers. Many peasants frowned on the fables used in these primers, calling them "entertainment, a waste of time, and frivolous." The emphasis was on utility: time is money, the peasant seemed to say. "You can learn tales [*skazki*] without knowing how to read—better to spend your time learning something useful." Ushinskii's tales of animals so irritated many parents that they refused to let their children do the assigned homework.[64] Educators must have scratched their heads in bewilderment. At a time when the countryside was flooded with cheap editions of *skazki,* when edifying books on hygiene and morality collected dust in the city bookstalls, peasant objections to "frivolous tales" seemed to apply only to schools.

Peasants had a narrow definition of what was useful, and this definition did not seem to include instruction in skills beyond basic literacy and numeracy, particularly if those skills ran counter to instruction commonly provided by the family itself or posed an implicit threat to the division of labor and family hierarchy of authority. In the early 1880s, Orlov asked teachers if horticulture was taught in Moscow schools; many answered that the population was unsympathetic to such efforts. One teacher in Bogorodskii district, for example, wrote that he had rented land from the local priest, set up a garden, and sown clover, as well as purchased books on agriculture. But the peasants objected strongly to such "trivia" (*pustiaki*) and said that with time their children "would learn these skills at home . . . that [the teacher's] job was to teach them to read and write!"[65]

Thus, religious and practical considerations combined to line up peasant sentiment against progressive methodology (phonics) and, more important, against the drive to secularize the curriculum and introduce character education. Two of the reports cited above pertained to the earlier period of zemstvo education activity, but even in the 1890s, much evidence supported the claims of the Church that "peasants are happy with the results achieved [in Church schools], especially with reading and singing. They prefer the Church over the zemstvo schools and are specifically attracted by the religious side."[66]

Certainly the claims of a school bureaucrat within the Holy Synod may be suspect; perhaps the unwitting comment of a Church school authority from Kazan' in the 1890s is closer to the mark in discussing peasant motivations: "The local population is very happy with the Church schools; they particularly like the religious emphasis, the pupil participation in Church services and choir, and the opportunity to receive military deferments."[67]

When considering the overwhelming evidence that the peasants highly valued the schools for teaching the ability to read in Church Slavonic and to participate in choir and Church services, we should not leap to the conclusion that the Russian peasant was deeply pious, if by pious we understand a knowledge and acceptance of the tenets of faith as well as of ritual. Bunakov, who spent a decade teaching in one village in Voronezh province, graphically described the persistence of "dual faith" (*dvoeverie*) in the area and observed that the impulse to send children to Bible lessons was a major source of enthusiasm for schooling: "The good school, in peasant opinion, provides knowledge of the Bible [*Zakon Bozhiia*] and leads not only to an understanding of Church services but also to children's participation in them, participation which parents deeply value." [68]

At the same time, Bunakov devoted an entire chapter in his account of life in this village to the persistence of animism and to the interweaving of Christian and pagan holidays in the peasant milieu. He stressed that the Bible program adopted for schools by the Church Synod in 1880 stressed the catechism and rote learning of the articles of faith for participation in services, rather than study of the moral code of Christianity. Lamentably, Bunakov noted, teaching from the Gospels, where the students might have learned directly from the life of Christ, was relegated largely to Church Slavonic lessons; in Bible classes, the much more difficult psalter and Horologium dominated. Even singing, which Bunakov and many others valued highly for its uplifting impact on peasant life—and which peasants also seemed to genuinely treasure—was ordinarily given short shrift in rural schools. Priests who were well prepared to teach singing had no time or inclination, and secular teachers usually lacked the training. [69]

The course content of the *vol'nye* schools offers indirect confirmation of this argument. [70] Because parents paid individually to keep their children in these schools, which generally remained free of outside supervision, they had a direct say in the books used and subjects taught. In the words of Prince D. Shakhovskii, "The distinguishing feature of literacy schools is that they are much more directly under the control of the population than are the zemstvo schools; the parents, paying the teacher directly for their children, believe that they have the right to demand that the teacher put the most effort in what they see as important for the child, and they supervise closely what happens in these schools." [71] An extensive study of *vol'nye* schools in Tver' province in 1888 showed that 87 percent (388 of 446) taught both Church Slavonic and modern Russian. The limited nature of instruction is illustrated by the facts that nearly three out of four teachers (72.6 percent) were peasants; that 39.5 percent had no formal education; and that 35.4 percent had been trained in zemstvo or parish schools. Thus, for the majority of teachers, their knowledge was probably limited to the official program set down by the MNP. A study of another district in the same province shows that textbooks were limited to ABC books, breviaries, psalters, and, in a few cases, Paul'son's well-known reader *Pervaia uchebnaia knizhka*. (Surprisingly, only one out of three schools had abacuses.)[72]

It would be wrong to simply infer that parents chose religious over secular books, for the Holy Synod worked actively to spread religious works to the countryside (and often subsidized their cost); thus, the findings above probably reflect what was most available. The point is that parents were concerned with the skill of reading, did not object to religious books, and may even have found them more acceptable than the progressive readers. For parents, the value of education was found in the mechanics, not the content, of reading. Yet when the parents were offered a choice, they voted for religious readings. Such a choice did not stop peasants from delighting in *skazki* outside the school, but it did indicate that peasants did not share the views of progressive educators.

To this point, I have been referring to parental demands. But we must keep in mind the important possibility that a conflict was developing between what parents wanted for their children and the aspirations and inclinations of the children themselves. Allusions to such a conflict can be found in frequent peasant complaints that their children were being ruined by the schools, in the oft-observed enthusiasm with which rural children took part in school activities, even in instances of children—particularly girls—trudging off to school in the face of parental resistance. Surely such differences between parent and child existed; just as surely they depended as much on the personality and approach of the teacher as on the school program. But whatever the degree of generational strife, it seems obvious from the pervasive high dropout rate that the parents ordinarily had the last word.

LITERACY FOR GIRLS?

By the turn of the century, nearly forty years had passed since Sukhomlinov and Zolotov had investigated rural schools, and Russia was undergoing a rapid industrial revolution, as well as a rural population explosion, both of which exerted tremendous pressure on the peasant way of life. Certainly these economic changes were related to the growing intensity of interest in schooling perceived by the Moscow Literacy Committee and others. These changes also had an impact on peasant notions of the value of educating girls; yet it is striking how persistent old beliefs were.

The 1894 Moscow Literacy Committee (MKG) study detected a very strong disparity between town and country in attitudes about educating girls. Although three of every four urban respondents noted that parents gave equal weight to the education of boys and girls, in the countryside only one of nine came to the same conclusion.[73] To be sure, since 1856 the ratio of girls to boys in the rural schools had nearly trebled and would increase even more sharply in the next decade. Moreover, the same study noted a growing interest in educating girls throughout the country. In Vladimir province in 1911, 55 percent of rural teachers reported that the population looked favorably on the education of girls.[74] Moscow studies showed that only 3 percent of all cases of absenteeism among girls could be traced to "parental foot-dragging" (*neradenie*) and that only 4 percent of girls who dropped out did so because of "parental negligence."[75]

Despite these signs of growing support for educating girls, abundant evidence of persistent hostility or indifference remained among some segments of the population, pointedly expressed by one peasant: "Why literacy? You don't need it to make cabbage soup!"[76]

A careful look at the statements of individual teachers and other rural reporters suggests that although actual hostility to educating girls was dissipating by the end of the century, female literacy was given low priority and was not considered worthy of much sacrifice. In addition, girls were far more useful at home as babysitters, whereas boys only got underfoot during the idle winter months, making the opportunity costs of educating girls higher. Economic pressures were intertwined with the low priority accorded education.

"Why should we teach our girls?" ask the peasants. "They won't be taken as soldiers, or as clerks in the stores. They're too busy to read books. On weekdays they work at heavy labor side by side with their men, either in the fields, the woods, or in the garden. They have an equal amount of work waiting for them at home, preparing meals for the family, tending the cattle, taking care of the children, and sewing the clothing. On holidays they are busier than ever!"

Another teacher added, "The local peasants believe it unnecessary to teach girls the ABCs, since girls won't go anywhere [*nikuda ni postupaiut*]; instead, they will stay at home.[77]

Data gathered by Bogolepov in 1893 point to the same popular attitudes. Women didn't need literacy because "they won't be behind the counter in a store," or because "just the same, they'll have to get behind the plow." One peasant expressed this reasoning very concisely: "If you send her to school, she costs money; if you keep her home, she makes money."[78]

Others reported that when the peasant girl was sent to school, it was because her future husband would most likely be away six months a year, making reading and writing essential not only to conduct the affairs of the household but also to communicate with her spouse. The more prosperous families who were engaged in commerce and cottage industries often sent the daughters to school to prepare them to handle accounts and other records.[79]

Bogolepov's study indicated that families or villages engaged exclusively in agriculture objected most strongly to the education of girls. The utility of education was seen in terms of the ability to keep accounts, read letters, and recite from the prayer book; thus when the *bol'shak,* or head of the family, was home throughout the year, there was no need or reason for the peasant woman to read. But frequent references to prevailing mores were also heard. Such curt answers as *"ne priniato," "ne zavedeno,"* or even *"mody net"* (all meaning roughly "that isn't the way it's done") reflected the belief that literacy was not an end in itself. The family was concerned with marrying the daughter off, and, as one peasant remarked sardonically, literacy was not considered a notable addition to the dowry. There were even reports that if a girl was sent to school, the neighbors and even the elders might accuse the parents of shirking the communal tax burden and the result might well be a *nakidka,* or supplementary tax.[80]

A turn-of-the-century Vladimir survey provided one of the most detailed studies of parental attitudes and female enrollment. The zemstvo statisticians in that province observed that in cases of overcrowding, girls were always the first to be denied admission. Direct testimony from teachers documented this situation, as did the observation that factory schools, which generally had more ample space, had more balanced sex ratios in the classroom than either zemstvo or parish schools. Church schools, in contrast, tended to be housed in more crowded facilities and had relatively fewer girls than did either zemstvo or factory schools.[81] As the school network spread and the problem of overcrowding eased, then, a marked growth in the proportional enrollment of girls was to be expected, which indeed seems to have been the case throughout the Russian Empire in the early twentieth century (see Chapter 10).

When Vladimir teachers responded to the question of why girls enrolled less frequently and dropped out more rapidly, "attitude" and "work at home" together account for more than 80 percent of all responses.[82] The problem with such studies is that many of the teachers' responses listed *both* parental attitude *and* the need to help at home. This same combination of reasons can be seen in studies of Moscow province, suggesting that such investigations should have considered not what value parents gave education, but instead what *priority* they gave it. Weber noted a very similar situation in France; until literacy had some tangible use, parents often claimed that their children were needed at home or that they were too poor to send their children to school. Once literacy was perceived as useful, indeed necessary, however, previously insurmountable economic obstacles suddenly vanished or at least no longer seemed quite so insurmountable.[83]

This point becomes clear in a Moscow report when the education of the sexes is compared:

Although in Volokolamsk, Dmitrov, and Klin districts, the value of education is recognized equally for boys and girls, nevertheless wherever there are mills employing female labor, the proportion of girls registered in school dips. It is clear that when the mother and older sisters leave for the mills, it is mainly girls of school age who are left to watch over the home and little children. *The majority of the same parents send their boys to school, however, even when good wages are offered at the mills!* [emphasis added][84]

Thus, when the economy impinged on female enrollment, it usually did so indirectly. Parents left to work in the factories, and older girls had to stay home to watch over the younger siblings. Yet, as Lawrence Stone noted concerning England, this situation could have an opposite effect. In England, parents were often willing to pay to get children off their hands so that they, the parents, could leave for work. The schools therefore could also serve a crèche function.[85]

The contradictory reports on peasant attitudes toward educating girls actually reflected a failure to consider the *priority* given to education. If no obvious benefit, even in survival terms, came from female literacy, it was easy enough to keep girls busy at home—indeed, the home was a school of its own, teaching domestic crafts to young girls. For boys, in contrast, simple literacy and arithmetic were minimal tools of survival; thus even when good wages were offered at the mills, parents sent their boys to school and kept them there long enough to learn to read and write. For girls, reading and writing might have been useful, particularly when the men were away at work, but these skills were expendable.

CONCLUSION

We can see, through the often unwitting comments of teachers and other observers, how peasants viewed basic education, how they understood literacy, and what they demanded of the schools. Although the need to read and write became more urgent as the century progressed, the basic demands made of the school system by peasants remained remarkably constant: teach the children their ABCs. If peasants had been aware of the struggle between progressive educators and the Church—and they may well not have been, for we have seen that the curriculum in the zemstvo schools and that found in the Church schools were virtually identical—they certainly would have favored the latter. It also seems clear that peasants—or, at least, parents—did not agree with the basic tenet of Russian progressive education. This tenet, stated first by Pirogov in the 1860s and reaffirmed in an influential article by Bunakov in the 1890s, held that the purpose of education was to prepare the student for "life" rather than for a trade.[86] Peasants wanted their children to acquire useful tools in the schools and felt that they could prepare their own children for "life," thank you! Parents saw very little practical use for educating girls and often found work for them to do at home instead, even if such work was not a vital economic necessity for the family. Often, however, when space was available and direct costs removed, hostility evaporated.

It bears repeating that this survey of peasant attitudes finds a basic consistency over time in attitudes toward literacy and schooling. Recall the confession by one author, noted above, that he traveled to the villages expecting to spread the word among the ignorant and found instead that peasants were eager and anxious to take advantage of the schools. Such accounts, further supported by data on peasant-sponsored (*vol'nye*) schools and by the sea change occurring in elite attitudes in the 1890s, only reinforce the suspicion that *it was the discovery of the peasant—and not the peasant discovery of education—that spurred the growth of the school system at the turn of the century.* If there was a change in popular attitudes between 1864 and 1914, it was that by 1914 *everyone* in the villages recognized the utility of basic education for survival; the press of written communications, travel to remote regions, work in factories, and the need to find one's way in the cities made the acquisition of literacy an urgent task. In 1864, although its usefulness had been widely recognized, acquiring a basic education had not carried such a sense of urgency. Perhaps more important, primary education had by 1914 simply become more available—the provision of schooling had improved.

10

The Expansion of Schooling

As Carlo Cipolla has succinctly observed, "It is one thing to have schools and teachers available, and quite another to convince parents to send their children to school."[1] To determine how many school-age children ever saw the inside of a school, we must next consider the dynamics of the school system, particularly the "escalation of schooling" and the "saturation" of the countryside.[2] Additionally in this chapter, I trace a crude demographic profile of the pupils and examine the issues of denied admission, pupil–teacher ratios, and the enrollment of girls. Our focus is on the relationship between opportunity and enrollment: how available were schools, and how widespread was schooling before the revolution?

THE RESULTS OF INTERVENTION

After nearly two decades of elite intervention, how close was the Russian Empire to establishing universally accessible primary education? By 1911, 398 district zemstvos (90 percent of the total) and 218 towns (35 percent) had concluded agreements with the MNP making them eligible for grants and loans to implement universal education in accordance with the terms of the 1908 School

Bill. There can be little question that within the zemstvo provinces the goal of universal enrollment had been placed on the agenda. Of 441 district zemstvos, 15 (more than 3 percent) had already built a school within three versts of every village in the district and had provided certified teachers, as well as schools that met the building code standards. Among the other zemstvos that had signed agreements with the MNP, 62 percent were within five years of achieving that goal, 30 percent were within five to ten years, and only 8 percent were more than ten years away.[3]

Of course, these figures dealt only with the zemstvo provinces, and even there they projected an overly optimistic picture, for they seldom took into account population growth between the time a plan was introduced and its completion. Even the estimates of the eligible school-age population at the outset of a plan may have been far from the mark; although most estimates began with the 1897 Census and assumed an annual growth rate of 1.49 percent, local studies found increases as high as 2.35 percent. In addition, the general assumption that the four-year age cohort (ages eight through eleven) made up between 9 and 10 percent of the entire population was subject to extraordinary local variation.[4] According to Kapterev, one could argue that there were either 12 million or 18 million school-age children in the Russian Empire in 1911. This may have been an extreme statement, but if Kapterev was correct, the margin of error was the size of the entire enrolled school population in Russia.[5] (More recent studies accept a figure closer to the 12 million estimate.)[6] Moreover, there is reason to believe that in some provinces many villages remained "*za bortom*" (literally, "overboard"), or outside the plan. Before 1908, when Chernigov province drew up a plan for universal education, it announced that 1,565 schools were needed to supplement the existing 569 units; but Kulomzin discovered that this plan left 1,347 villages (of 5,619) outside the network.[7] Data presented in Tables 12 and 15 make it readily apparent that the zemstvo provinces, and European Russia in general, were far ahead of the rest of the Empire in establishing schools. Universal education may have been on the agenda, but this was the case only in European Russia (where, to be sure, the bulk of the population lived).

Table 12
Percentage of School-Age Children Enrolled
in Primary Schools, 1911

PROVINCE	ENROLLMENT AS A PERCENTAGE OF CHILDREN 8–11 YEARS OLD
Tambov	48.2%
Moscow	84.2
Viatka	46.2
Arkhangel'sk	54.0
Smolensk	58.4
Bessarabia	40.3
Lifland	79.9
Saratov	61.3
Kovno	21.6
Vologda	45.8
Irkutsk	49.3
Stavropol	41.1
Orenburg	30.4
Fergana	1.6
Samarkand	2.4
Semirech'e	9.4
Thirty-four zemstvo provinces	53.5
Russian Empire	44.2

SOURCE: Compiled from Malinovskii, "Nekotorye vyvody," 74–75.

NOTE: The figures include students and schools under the jurisdiction of the Ministry of Education and the Holy Synod. If the scattered schools under other ministries are included, the number of schools would increase from 93,407 to 100,295, and the number of pupils from 5,862,409 to 6,180,514, thereby increasing enrollment figures as a percentage of those eligible from 44 percent to 46 percent. For a criticism of the method used in arriving at these figures, see Ia. Ia. Gurevich, "O chisle detei shkol'nogo vozrasta, ostaiushchikhsia vne shkoly," *Russkaia shkola* 22, no. 5–6 (1911): 93–95.

The prediction that universal education could be achieved by 1922 was clearly unrealistic. Even Kulomzin, who claimed that such an achievement would take ten years in the towns, fifteen in the villages of European Russia, twenty in Siberia and the Caucasus, and twenty-five in Central Asia, was probably unduly optimistic. Yet the Soviet assertion that the tsarist system would not have achieved universal primary education for another two hundred years (that is, in the year 2100) is also erroneous—and is based on estimates published in 1906, before the 1908 School Bill.[8] Setting a precise date for when universal education might have been achieved is perhaps not so important; after all, the Empire did collapse in 1917 and just how close Russia was to achieving its goal in this area made little difference in the final outcome. What is important is that the educational efforts of the tsarist Empire were gaining ground—despite the unprecedented population growth at the beginning of the twentieth century.

It would be unjust to ignore the significant expansion of schooling after 1890. Although the timetables were overly optimistic, the tsarist government and the zemstvos, building on a base provided by the peasantry, had established the foundation of the school system upon which the Soviet authorities would later build in their great push toward universal literacy, launched in 1929. Granted, many of the gains were dissipated in the destruction of World War I; and the decade following 1914 may even have seen a radical decline in literacy—there certainly was a decline in schooling. Granted, too, teachers as a profession suffered enormously in World War I and the civil war, and many who survived were so hostile to the Soviet authorities that they were of little use to the new educational system. But although the edifice was severely damaged—even razed—after 1914, the records show that by that year, the tsarist Empire was well on its way to achieving full universal primary education. Of course, simply because Russia was building a school system, we should not infer that social stability was increasing or social differences declining—a tenet of the "optimist" school regarding the general condition of Russia on the eve of World War I. But the inaccuracy of such a conclusion does not taint the fact that educational progress was indeed being made.

AVAILABILITY AND BASIC ENROLLMENTS

The number of primary schools in the Empire is a useful measure for analyzing the changing level of elite commitment to primary education. According to the annual reports of the Ministry of Education and the Holy Synod, the number of primary schools, rural and urban, increased from approximately 8,000 in 1856 to nearly 25,000 in 1878, to 87,000 in 1896, and to over 100,000 in 1911 (Table 13).[9] The number of pupils rose from 450,000 to nearly 1.1 million, to 3.8 million, and to 6.6 million in the same years. These figures seem to indicate that the greatest expansion of the school system took place between 1878 and 1896—but there are serious problems with the data. First, the 1878 figures do not include literacy schools (then illegal), of which there were at least

Table 13
Development of Primary Education, 1856–1911:
Growth Indicators

	1856	1878	1896	1911
Number of pupils	450,002	1,065,889	3,804,262	6,629,978
Number of primary schools	8,227	24,853	87,080	100,749
Girls as a percentage of all pupils	8.2%	17.7%	21.3%	32.2%
Ratio of pupils to population	1:143	1:77	1:33	1:24
Ratio of primary schools to population	1:7,762	1:3,299	1:1,443	1:1,499
Pupils as a percentage of population	0.70%	1.20%	3.02%	4.04%[a]

SOURCE: Piskunov, *Ocherki istorii shkoly,* 518; Chekini, "Nachal'noe narodnoe obrazovanie," i–iv.

NOTE: Data for both rural and urban schools throughout the Russian Empire.

[a]This figure was 5.48 percent for boys and 2.6 percent for girls. If only European Russia is included, the figure is 4.43 percent for sixty provinces (6.06 percent for boys and 2.83 percent for girls). At the time, the most common estimate of the figure necessary for full enrollment was 9 percent.

25,000 in 1895. Second, although the number of enrolled pupils almost doubled between 1896 and 1911 (increasing by 2.8 million, nearly the same increase as between 1878 and 1896), the number of *schools* rose by only about 13,000.

Even more puzzling, the increase in schools between 1878 and 1896 recorded by the MNP and the Holy Synod bears no relationship to more reliable data collected during the school census of 18 January 1911. This census recorded the year of founding for all schools in the Empire and came up with a very different periodization of school expansion, shown in Table 14. These figures show

Table 14
School Openings: Year of Founding for
Schools Existing in 1911

	AVERAGE ANNUAL NUMBER OF OPENINGS		
	MNP Schools	Synod Schools	All Schools
1851–1860	99.6	34.4	142.8
1861–1863	375.0	248.0	649.3
1864–1868	652.6	92.0	766.0
1869–1873	809.0	72.8	943.8
1874–1878	857.6	66.6	970.8
1879–1883	735.6	179.2	952.0
1884–1888	587.0	1,183.2	1,877.6
1889–1893	475.0	1,280.8	1,885.0
1894–1898	1,051.6	1,545.6	2,838.2
1899–1903	1,493.4	1,054.6	2,764.6
1904–1908	2,234.0	500.0	2,961.6
1909	4,009.0	714.0	5,036.0
1910	4,660.0	609.0	5,620.0

SOURCE: MNP, *Odnodnevnaia perepis'* 16:65.

NOTE: Of 100,749 schools registered in the 1911 School Census, the date of founding was unknown for 3,812. Of this number, 1,546 were MNP schools, 1,592 were Church parish schools, and 484 were literacy schools (also under the Holy Synod). The total number of openings is greater than the sum of openings by the MNP and Holy Synod not only because other ministries were peripherally involved but also because I have not listed literacy schools separately.

two major turning points: the first in 1884 when the state began to promote Church parish schools, and the second after 1894 when zemstvo schools began to increase rapidly. Between 1896 and 1900, the increase in Church parish schools kept pace with the growth of zemstvo schools; but in 1900 this pattern changed, and by 1903 more than twice as many zemstvo as Church schools were opened.

The large discrepancy between the official reports compiled between 1878 and 1896 and the 1911 School Census may partially reflect the fact that some of the schools opened between 1878 and 1896 subsequently closed their doors; but this explanation is hardly likely to account for such a large gap. Instead, the difference is probably a good indication of the unreliability of both Ministry of Education and Holy Synod records, a situation of which specialists in educational history have long been aware. *Whichever set of figures we accept, however, it is possible to argue that the expansion of the official (that is, registered) school system began in the 1880s and continued steadily until 1914, but that elite input into this system, measured in terms of financial contribution, began on a large scale only after 1895.*

This argument reinforces the notion that much of the school system's expansion was in reality a process of formalization, of registering and incorporating previously functioning peasant schools into the official network. Although after 1890 the expansion of rural schooling was genuine and large-scale, before that date much of the expansion was in reality a conversion of informal literacy schools into zemstvo-supervised and partially subsidized schools. In other words, the growth of the school system prior to the outpouring of funds substantiates the argument that the formalization of schooling preceded the increased funding of the 1890s and that the money to build schools came first from the peasant community and at its own initiative.

How available were official schools to the population by 1911? To establish accessibility, the growth of the school system must be compared with the growth of the population. Table 15 shows that throughout European Russia the level of geographic saturation of the countryside with schools increased markedly from 1880 to 1894, increasing once again between 1894 and 1911. Surprisingly, the degree of progress was just as substantial in the nonzemstvo as in the zemstvo provinces; the only exception was the Baltic area, where the provision of schooling had actually worsened between

Table 15
Availability of Schools, 1880–1911

	1880	1894	1911
	Square Versts per School		
34 zemstvo provinces	233	71	43
13 nonzemstvo provinces (European)	1,077	287	162
3 Baltic provinces	33	28	27
50 European provinces (total)	207	126	60
Russian Empire (including Central Asia and Siberia)	—	311	187
	Population per School		
34 zemstvo provinces	3,823	1,698	1,409
13 nonzemstvo provinces (European)	4,160	1,498	1,521
3 Baltic provinces	740	793	889
50 European provinces (total)	3,251	1,650	1,461
Russian Empire (including Central Asia and Siberia)	—	1,943	1,627

SOURCES: MNP, *Odnodnevnaia perepis'* 16:50–57, 66–68, 138–140; Fal'bork and Charnoluskii, *Nachal'noe narodnoe obrazovanie v Rossii* 1:x, 2:vii–xxi; Kovalevskii, *Proizvoditel'nye sily Rossii*, sec. ix, 73–81.

1864 and 1911. It is true that in 1911 the area served by each school in Vologda was still twenty times as great as in Moscow, but overall, progress recorded since 1880 was impressive.

In most provinces, substantial gains were registered in the first decade after 1880, but the availability of schools, as measured by the ratio of population to schools, advanced much more slowly than the raw increase in numbers of schools would suggest—and in some provinces actually declined—between 1894 and 1911. In this latter period, even in the provinces with the most ambitious school construction projects, population growth came close to outstripping the expansion of the school system. This trend is confirmed by the persistently high incidence of denied admissions based on lack of space (to be discussed shortly). For the school system to have merely kept pace with the enormous rural population explosion in the Russian countryside in the early twentieth century meant that it was in fact making giant strides. Still, even when measured by the area each school served, the biggest strides were clearly made in the 1880s, before the zemstvo became actively involved (financially) in building schools.

The most commonly used index of enrollment, in the West as well as in Russia, was based on population, rather than on an age group.[10] The level of saturation in European Russia, measured in enrollments as a percentage of population, was 1.5 percent in 1880, rising to 2.9 percent in 1894, and then to 4.5 percent in 1911. Measured as a percentage of the total population, Russian school enrollment lagged far behind that of other countries. Enrollment figures (1900–1910) stood at 15.7 percent in the Austro-Hungarian Empire, 17.4 percent in Great Britain, 17 percent in Germany, 14.2 percent in both France and Sweden, 19.4 percent in the United States, and 11 percent in Japan.[11]

These figures were often used by prerevolutionary educators to show just how backward Russia was, and Soviet historians have continued to use them uncritically with the same purpose in mind. Russia did lag; yet we should note that, with the huge rural population growth in European Russia during the turn of the century, the increase in enrollment figures from 1.5 percent to 4.5 percent between 1880 and 1911 signified an increase of 379 percent in actual primary enrollments in the fifty European provinces, despite the net decline in the Baltic area. Most important, pertinent as the population-based figure may be to human capital theorists, it is deceptive as a measure of *basic* schooling. Unless allowance is made for national differences in the ages of school entry and school leaving, it is unfair to make retrospective judgments about whether or not there was an "educational failure" in Russia based on such comparative—but not comparable—data.[12]

The proper way to determine the number of children who saw the inside of a school in rural Russia is to begin with the school-age cohort. Even here, however, the conventional presentation of data is seriously flawed. Until the 1890s, most educators, looking only at the West, used the eight-year span between the ages of seven and fourteen as the proper school-age base, despite the fact that rural and town elementary schools were designed to offer only three and (less often) four years of basic schooling. According to estimates based on these assumptions, rural enrollment in Russia increased only from 8.7 percent in 1880 to 15.6 percent in 1894, and to 23.8 percent in 1911. It is often thus hastily concluded that fewer than one in four children (24 percent) in rural Russia had any schooling whatsoever.[13]

This type of approach to school attendance records has been criticized by specialists. In England, the Kerry report of 1833 showed that only 24 percent of school-age children were in school. But as E. G. West has demonstrated, not one in four but as many as nine in ten children actually received some schooling at the time. The discrepancy stemmed from the application of an improper yardstick: although the Kerry Commission believed the proper school age was between six and fourteen, in fact the average length of stay in school was only two to three years, and the usual age at leaving was ten. (As late as 1870, the average stay was only two-and-a-half years.) Thus, on a single day, most of the children in the "school-age cohort" who were not in school had either *not yet enrolled* or had *already completed* their two- to three-year stay. It could not be otherwise.[14]

The same considerations applied to Russia, once educators finally began to regard the age-span between eight and eleven as the proper school-age base and began to stop making comparisons with an ideal situation in the West (a situation that didn't, in fact, exist). Most population experts in Russia placed the proportion of the population aged eight to eleven at 9 percent (sometimes 9.5 percent) of the total.[15] Calculations based on the enrolled and eligible populations in each province turned up a great variety in levels of enrollment; in Table 16, however, it can readily be seen that in Russia half or more of all boys of school age were *present* in school on 18 January 1911. (Vil'no educational district, where Russification policies had severely damaged the effort to expand education, was the most notable exception.) A provincial breakdown of the 1911 data would show that attendance figures among girls were much lower, ranging from as low as one in six of those eligible to one in

Table 16

Crude Enrollments: Percentage of School-Age
Children Attending School on 18 January 1911
(ages eight through eleven)

	PERCENTAGE OF BOYS ATTENDING SCHOOL	PERCENTAGE OF GIRLS ATTENDING SCHOOL	TOTAL PERCENTAGE ATTENDING SCHOOL
Village youth	58%	24%	42.0%
Urban youth	75	59	66.5
All youth	60	29	44.8
Including enrollment in confessional schools[a]	65	30	48.0

SOURCE: MNP, *Odnodnevnaia perepis'* 16:2–3, 104.
NOTE: Survey included 6,062,967 pupils. The 1911 School Census used the figure 14,799,916 as an estimate of all children aged eight through eleven in the Empire.
[a] The census did not include schools designated for a particular faith or nationality.

three. Still, by 1914, attendance figures had climbed to 51 percent of the entire school-age population in the Russian Empire.

Duly corrected, the initial enrollment figures for 1911 and 1915 provide the best overall indicators of how widely basic schooling had penetrated the countryside by World War I or, more precisely, of the percentage of children who had made contact with a school. In 1915, in all but six of the provinces of European Russia, more than half of all school-age children were registered on the school rolls. In many provinces, this figure was as high as two-thirds, and in two provinces, it was four-fifths or greater. In other areas of the country, the spread of schooling was much less extensive; in a few regions, as well as among many minority nationalities, the rate of enrollment was abysmally low. But the European provinces encompassed well over half the population, and it is thus reasonable to speak of *pockets* of backwardness, of deprived areas where education had not yet reached by 1914, whereas it is manifestly unjust to speak, as Soviet historians frequently do, of a heritage of "ubiquitous" (*pogolovnaia*) ignorance and educational deprivation in late Imperial Russia. In 1914, Russia was clearly on the way to becoming a schooled society, in the countryside as well as in the cities. What remained was a "mopping-up" operation—a phrase employed by Richard Altick to describe the situation in England before the passage of the Foster Act in 1872.[16]

The enrollment statistics still do not tell the whole story. Enrollment figures calculated as a percentage of eligible children aged eight to eleven, though far higher than those derived from using the age cohort of seven- to fourteen-year-olds, were themselves significantly understated. Specifically, the 1911 School Census included only those children enrolled *and* attending school on 18 January; approximately 7 percent of the enrolled schoolchildren were probably absent. Moreover, and perhaps most significant, in 75 percent of all rural schools the course of instruction lasted three years, although the most commonly used school-age base included four years (ages eight through eleven). As we shall learn in Chapter 11, detailed studies of the countryside showed that the average stay in school, once a child was enrolled, was approximately two-and-a-half years. Recalling West's comments on the Kerry report—that a head count of schoolchildren attending school on any one day will greatly underestimate the true extent of schooling—we can see that Russia, with a four-year school-age base and an average stay of two to two-and-a-half years, would be subject to similar miscalculations. Unfortunately, it is one thing to point out that the estimates are understated and quite another to say with confidence by just how much. Suffice it to say here that as many as two in three boys and four in ten girls may have been enrolled sometime during their school-age years.[17]

A household survey of education in Moscow province (1891–1892), which became famous for its conclusions about the impact of the economy on schooling, also produced unique information that allows us to apply E. G. West's arguments to Russia and to see by just how much the proportion of children who had had some schooling exceeded the proportion enrolled at any given time. The surveyors, who visited every home in two districts, asked parents which of their school-age children were currently in school, which had already been "schooled," and which had had no schooling.

Table 17
School Enrollment in Moscow Province,
1891–1892

	PERCENTAGE OF SCHOOL-AGE BOYS	PERCENTAGE OF SCHOOL-AGE GIRLS	PERCENTAGE OF SCHOOL-AGE CHILDREN
	Moscow District		
Currently enrolled	39%	18%	29%
Previously enrolled (and subsequently left)	26	18	22
Never (not yet) enrolled	35	65	49
	Mozhaisk District		
Currently enrolled	38%	11%	24%
Previously enrolled (and subsequently left)	20	7	13
Never (not yet) enrolled	42	84	64

SOURCE: Bogolepov (Moscow), *Gramotnost' sredi detei*, 24.
NOTE: Percentages are rounded off to the nearest whole number. Total N in this survey was 14,352 boys and 14,350 girls. "School age" refers to ages eight through eleven.

Table 17 shows that in 1891–1892 nearly 30 percent of school-age children in Moscow district and nearly 25 percent in Mozhaisk district were currently enrolled in school. Twenty-two percent of the children in Moscow and 13 percent in Mozhaisk had already had some education and had left school. Thus, more than one-half of all school-age children in Moscow and one-third in Mozhaisk were either currently or had once been enrolled in a school; the percentage "currently enrolled" would have to be increased by as much as one-half to two-thirds to accurately represent the degree of contact between school and population.

Moreover, there is powerful evidence, first, that even these figures underrepresent total enrollment and, second, that at a later date the gap between currently enrolled and all children who had some schooling would have been even greater. The Bogolepov Moscow survey (cited in Table 17) showed that pressure for admission far exceeded the capacity of the schools; in Mozhaisk, girls had been virtually excluded from schools because of lack of places. In that district, three in ten children with some schooling had received it in *vol'nye* schools outside the formal network. This survey was conducted on the eve of the great school drive, and it is thus fair to assume that one or two decades later, with the expansion of the school network and the increase in opportunities to study, the proportion of children not currently in school but having once been enrolled would have been even greater.

Yet another factor artificially depressed the enrollment statistics. With the press of applications and the high level of denied admissions, children aged eight and nine commonly had to wait a year or two before finding places in the schools—thus, illiteracy and nonenrollment were virtually universal at these ages. However, children aged twelve, thirteen, and fourteen who had never received any schooling were far fewer than we might assume simply by looking at current enrollment figures. Even in Mozhaisk, where the provision of schooling was so inadequate that 80 percent of eight-year-old boys were unschooled, only 15 percent of fourteen-year-olds were unschooled (though only 38 percent were currently enrolled). Because of the shortage of places, the gap was only 11 percent for girls, with 94 percent of eight-year-olds and 83 percent of fourteen-year-olds unschooled. In Moscow district, which had a more advanced school system, the pattern was much clearer for both sexes. There, only 18 percent of eight-year-olds were currently enrolled or "schooled," but 91 percent of boys ten, eleven, and twelve years old had received some schooling. Only 13 percent of eight-year-old girls had some schooling, but the figure rose to 45 percent for girls eleven and older.[18]

Now we can evaluate the full significance of the gap between current enrollments and the actual percentages of eligible children who had received some school education. *As early as 1891, in Moscow district, only four in ten boys and fewer than two in ten girls were enrolled in the schools, while more than nine in ten boys and four in ten girls aged eleven to fourteen had received some schooling (or were currently enrolled) at the time of the survey*. A large proportion of those remaining outside the school doors did so because they could not find places. Thus, with the increased provision of schooling in the following two decades, the same gap found in Moscow province between figures for those currently enrolled and figures for both currently and previously enrolled would have been present—perhaps to an even greater extent—in other provinces. This projection signals that the number of children who had some schooling may have been at least twice, and perhaps three times, as great as the number enrolled at any given date.

Distance between home and schoolroom was instrumental in raising the age of initial school enrollment. Many educators regarded the vast expanses of the country rather than the poverty of its inhabitants as the chief barrier to education, and the completion of a network placing schools within a three-verst distance of the overwhelming majority of the population was regarded as a precondition for universally accessible education. Darlington, the British school inspector whose nuts-and-bolts observations of the Russian school system still make highly informative reading, noted that the Russian winter made basic education far more expensive for parents by requiring the purchase of warm clothing and boots, while distance caused complications not faced in the West:

The sparseness of the population . . . greatly complicates the question of providing an efficient school within reasonable distance of each child's home. This circumstance has to be borne in mind in accounting for some characteristic phenomena of the recent history of Russian education, such as the attempts to develop and organize the literacy school. The same cause, coupled with the severity of the climate and other physical conditions, has had another important consequence. The short days, the extreme cold, the deep snow in winter, the terrible state of the roads in early spring and late autumn make it impossible for children who reside at a considerable distance from the school to return home daily; and it therefore becomes necessary in many cases to provide some sort of overnight lodgings for them in connection with the school.[19]

In 1911, few areas in Russia were close to achieving the degree of saturation of the countryside necessary to bring schools within the projected three-verst distance of all school-age children. It is revealing that of the children attending classes on 18 January 1911, the vast majority lived at most two versts away. Two out of three children in the village classrooms (64.5 percent) lived within one verst, another 30 percent resided between one and three versts away, and only 5.3 percent were more than three versts distant. Even in Petrograd circuit, which encompassed such enormous, sparsely populated provinces as Vologda and Arkhangel'sk (where each school served 214 and 1,337 square versts, respectively), only 10 percent of the pupils lived more than three versts from their school. The conclusion seems inescapable that despite remarkable progress in school construction, the problem of distance had not yet been fully confronted. As enrollments crept upward, the task of bringing in more children would likely have become progressively more difficult, for the average distance of residence from school increased as the school network reached out to the more remote areas. (Provincial studies showed that in many areas a substantial number of children spent the entire week in school without returning home. Paradoxically, as schools came to more and more villages, reducing travel and hence the need for overnight lodgings, the impact of schooling on the enrolled population, which would then have been spending evenings at home instead of in the school, may have declined overall.)[20]

The importance of settlement patterns for the success of education can hardly be exaggerated, for the way population was distributed directly affected enrollment (the further a family lived from the school, the less likely was the child to enroll). But these patterns also had an indirect impact by making the provision of education far more expensive in sparsely settled regions with dispersed households. Despite this effect, however, clustered villages with at least one hundred households (yielding, it was calculated, thirty-four school-age children), were in fact the rule in much of Russia. Thus in theory, despite the vast expanses of land, the provision of education should have been relatively cheaper in Russia than in, say, rural America—at least in that part of Russia dominated by the repartitional commune and clustered village.[21]

Just how important was the rational location, as well as the sheer number, of schools? Iaroslavl' statisticians carried out some complex calculations to show that when schools were distributed more closely to all settlements, the proportion of enrolled pupils increased, regardless of local economic conditions. Thus, both settlement patterns and population density were important considerations in the availability and unit cost of schooling.

Two additional points merit attention here. First, the majority of pupils of both sexes in most schools lived in the same village as their schoolmates. Intervillage mixing of peer groups, though sometimes occurring in the classroom, was not a widespread phenomenon. In this sense, the schools did not seem to be breaking down barriers between isolated villages. Second, although the 1911 data and many other surveys of individual provinces showed that the percentage of eligible children enrolled in school declined sharply when households or villages were located more than two or three versts from a school, it is not always clear whether this decline occurred because the travel distance was too great and the expenses of overnight lodging prohibitive or because schools supported by one community would enroll local children in preference to admitting outsiders—in short, it is not clear whether supply or demand is being measured.

One thing was clear, however: increasing unit costs caused by the sparseness of population as schools spread from more populous to more remote villages would have made further progress both more difficult and more expensive. Studies of literacy and schooling in developing countries strongly suggest that a midway point, when approximately half of all children are enrolled in school, usually marks a significant divide. From this point on, in the experience of these countries, a "mopping-up operation" involves reaching out to isolated villages and farmsteads, requiring small schools, a lower pupil-teacher ratio, and much higher unit costs. A UNESCO survey of recent worldwide efforts to eradicate illiteracy stresses precisely this difficulty.[22] If the experience of the developing world today offers a pertinent comparison, Russia, after several decades of rapid progress, faced a situation in 1914 in which further increments in increased enrollment would have been much more painfully achieved. Thus, although appreciating the advances that had been made before 1914, we should not understate the obstacles that remained before the school edifice could have been completed.

DENIED ADMISSIONS

The number of denied admissions provides significant insights into the dynamics of rural schools in Russia. Many reports by teachers (cited in Chapter 9) indicate that peasant families were virtually breaking down the school doors to gain spaces for their children, even insisting that teachers allow the children to stand at the back of the room if no seats were available. In many areas, schools introduced a policy of opening their doors to new pupils only in alternate years to reduce the crush of applicants.[23] Elsewhere, parents who despaired of enrolling their offspring finally gave up and hired private tutors.

Just how severe was the crunch? An estimate is important because, when compared with figures on the expansion of the school system and the school–population ratio, the number of those denied admission is a reasonably accurate yardstick for measuring the unmet demand for basic schooling. Like unemployment figures, the number of rejections most likely understates the amount of unsatisfied demand, for once word got around that a school was full, many parents must certainly have given up without trying. Obviously, though, if schools were being imposed on a reluctant and resistant population, there would have been few or no rejections for lack of space. Thus, the incidence of denied admissions may well understate the strength of popular demand for education, but it is unlikely to overstate it.[24]

Before the 1911 School Census, information on denied admissions was only occasionally solicited, and then seldom for more than one district or province at a time. According to statisticians in Vladimir and Iaroslavl', nearly all schools in the 1890s were overcrowded, which "is one of the best proofs of peasant attitudes [toward schooling]." Farmakovskii reported that "denied admissions for lack of space occur everywhere throughout the Empire, from Bessarabia to the far reaches of remote Siberia." Fal'bork wrote that the "popular striving for education is growing faster than the schools are expanding; as a result a veritable struggle is taking place for the few openings in the schools." Both he and Bogolepov argued that one of the best indicators of overcrowding was the composition of the student body: when schools were overcrowded and denied admissions high, girls and the youngest applicants were first turned down.[25] The slowly increasing initial enroll-ment age was a sign of demand outstripping supply. But most important, the low percentage of eligible children enrolled and the disproportionate representation of boys in the schoolroom re-flected not only traditional attitudes toward the education of girls but also the decision to admit boys first when there was not space for children of both sexes.

In Vladimir province in 1900, over 2,000 children were re-jected for lack of space—1,423 boys and 610 girls. This figure amounted to roughly ten pupils per school and equaled nearly 10 percent of the enrolled school population; the statisticians who collected this information warned that it was very incomplete, however, and that they suspected the number of rejections was much higher. Similarly, reports from Moscow put the number of rejections at zemstvo schools at 1,350 in 1886 and 2,000 in 1888 (with a school enrollment of slightly over 30,000). (In 1889, how-ever, when 486 zemstvo schools were functioning in Moscow, at least 32 of them never opened their doors to new applicants at all—thus, on paper, there were *no* rejections.)[26]

In Tavrida, too, at the turn of the century admissions were de-nied in 378 of 779 schools (49 percent) and "no room was left" in 94 percent. MNP model schools were the most likely to turn away applicants (100 percent), followed by zemstvo (62 percent), Church parish (56 percent), and literacy schools (54 percent). Where appli-cants were rejected, the average number—twenty-two—was quite high. Note that both Moscow and Tavrida zemstvos were consid-ered pioneers in education.[27]

The 1911 School Census yields eloquent testimony to the as-pirations and blocked hopes of an anonymous, silent population. In 1910, some 999,852 children—very nearly a million—were for-mally denied admission to the elementary schools, out of an es-timated school-age population of 12 million (with 6.6 million children enrolled).[28] Reasons for refusing admission included late registration and improper age. But overcrowding was responsible for between one-half (in Moscow and Petrograd) and three-fourths (in Warsaw) of all rejections.[29] Also, many of those rejected for late registration were actually turned away for lack of space, for in areas with adequate space in the schools, children were commonly ad-mitted well after the harvest was in.[30]

Both the Holy Synod and representatives of the zemstvos expended a good deal of paper and energy trying to demonstrate irrefutably that their type of school and style of instruction were best suited to peasant needs and aspirations. Since in numerous instances Church and zemstvo schools were located in the same village, competing for the same constituency, one might expect the peasants' true preferences to emerge in the respective numbers of denied admissions. Surprisingly, in 1911 the number of rejections as a percentage of all applicants (in all grades) was higher in the Church schools (16 percent for boys and 17 percent for girls) than in the zemstvo schools (11.2 percent and 13 percent). Of course, such a small difference could reflect relative availability as much as preference. Yet one might expect that the allegedly overwhelming peasant preference for the progressive zemstvo schools over the musty parish schools would have been mirrored in greater overcrowding of the former—but if anything, the opposite was true.[31]

The scale of repressed demand may be assessed in different ways. Thus, we may say that every year one out of twelve school-age children was denied admission (for whatever reason) *or that for every six children in school, at least one wanted entry but could not be accommodated.* Juxtaposing the number of denied admissions to the total enrollment in the first grade may be the most accurate reflection of unmet demand. As Table 18 shows, in the towns, for every

Table 18

Number of Children Denied Admission to First
Grade, 1911 (for every one hundred admitted)

	BOYS	GIRLS
Russian Empire		
Urban schools	30.0	28.7
Village schools	30.5	33.6
All schools	30.4	32.6
Zemstvo schools	25.4	24.8
Church parish schools	34.9	31.4

SOURCE: MNP, *Odnodnevnaia perepis'* 16:58–59, table 11.

100 boys admitted, 30 were turned away; for every 100 girls admitted, 29 were rejected. In the villages, the corresponding numbers rejected were 31 boys and 34 girls for every 100 pupils of each sex admitted. The pressure being applied by the population for expansion of formal schooling was massive, though it fluctuated in intensity from region to region.

We will consider below the extraordinary dropout rate prevailing in the school system; fewer than one in ten children managed to complete even the three-year course offered by the primary school. It seems incomprehensible, then, that at the same time children, or their parents for them, were trying to beat down the doors of the schoolhouses to gain admission. Parents must have known that even when they did secure a place their child would only stay for two years or so. Unless we assume that peasants were lemmings, blindly rushing to the schools and just as blindly leaving at the beck and call of forces beyond their control, some strategy must have been in operation. But the question of what strategy they followed must be answered in another context; here, it is important to underline the irrefutable fact that if one million children applied for admission and were turned down, there clearly was a degree of enthusiasm for schooling that the existing network was unable to satisfy. This inability reflected the failure of funding to keep up with popular demand, a problem that might well have increased in severity as time passed and could be added to the debit side in the ongoing debate over the progress of education in tsarist Russia. But this is mere quibbling. What is important here is the expression of demand, of a call by the peasants for schooling for their children.

CLASSROOM SIZE AND PUPIL–TEACHER RATIOS

The pupil–teacher ratio is one of the best indicators of the *quality* of schooling. Once we establish how long children stayed in the schools, this ratio provides one of the most reliable sources of material evidence for assessing what, in the best circumstances, pupils could have been learning. Unfortunately, in the case of Russia, there seems to have been no representative ratio, for classroom size varied greatly from area to area and among types of schools. Ol'denburg, certainly one of the most knowledgeable and cautious specialists in school statistics, estimated that in the 1890s the typical zemstvo school had between fifty and seventy students, the Church parish school had twenty-five to fifty, and the literacy school fifteen to twenty-five. Even at this time, however, a small but growing number of zemstvo schools had two teachers, and the pupil-school ratio was not an exact measure of classroom size. In Iaroslavl', slightly more than a third of one-class (three-year) schools (36 percent) had more than one teacher. In Tavrida's zemstvo schools, more than seven out of ten teachers were responsible for only one or two groups—meaning that more than one teacher taught in such schools. But in most other provinces, the three-grade, one-teacher school continued to prevail.[32]

Another factor complicating the use of pupil-teacher ratios as an index of educational quality is that the number of *grades* for which each teacher was responsible greatly affected the number of pupils the teacher could effectively instruct. For example, most educators at the turn of the century considered a ratio of 40:1 the optimum and 60:1 the maximum for effective teaching; but it obviously made a difference if the pupils were all in one grade or were divided into two grades of thirty each or three grades of twenty each, since the teacher had to keep each grade busy at separate tasks.

In the twentieth century, with encouragement from the Ministry of Education, the proportion of four-year schools with two teachers began to rise—although the chronic shortage of qualified teachers worked to counteract this progress. This development was seen as a choice of quality over quantity: rather than having more schools distributed throughout the provinces, providing at least a minimal education in admittedly bleak surroundings, it seemed better to have educators work to build better schools at a slower pace, offering a more thorough education with teachers working together (and providing each with support in the wilderness). By 1911, 28 percent of all rural schools offered four or more years of instruction; among zemstvo schools, roughly 30 percent offered such programs, with 17 percent of parish schools and only 5 percent of literacy schools (also under the Synod) doing the same. Generally, but not always, schools offering more than three years of instruction had two teachers. Thus, of ten thousand zemstvo schools offering a three-year program in 1910, 63.7 percent had only one teacher, 16.5 percent had two teachers, and 7.8 percent had three. Of 2,846 four-year schools, 78 percent had two teachers, 10.3 percent had four, and 4 percent had only one. In brief, two out of three three-year schools had one teacher, and three out of four four-year schools had two teachers.[33]

With these considerations in mind, it is useful to look at the crude figures for pupil-teacher ratios from 1880 to 1911. In 1880, there were 46 rural pupils for every teacher (excluding ordained Bible teachers) in the fifty European provinces; in the zemstvo provinces (including nonzemstvo schools), the ratio was 50:1. In 1894, the ratios were 47:1 and 48:1, respectively. Literacy schools, which received their first official recognition in the census data of the 1890s, had a pupil-teacher ratio of 28:1.[34]

Data from individual provinces in the 1890s indicate that, although the pupil-teacher ratio nationally may not have been unreasonably high, schools existed where the teachers were responsible for so many pupils that they must have spent all or most of their time simply trying to maintain order. For example, in Iaroslavl' in 1900, a single teacher taught over 60 pupils in 43 out of 246 zemstvo schools. (There were, however, 62 zemstvo schools where the teacher had fewer than 40 pupils.) In Tavrida at the turn of the century, the pupil-teacher ratio was between 61:1 and 80:1 in 35 percent of all zemstvo schools, and in 8 percent each teacher had more than 80 pupils. In Mogilev, it was said, one teacher often taught as many as 120 pupils.[35]

For 1911, it is possible to disaggregate these figures and determine the true size of the classroom in the different types of schools. Although the overall ratio of pupils to teachers for the Empire was 41:1 (villages only), ratios varied considerably by type of school, as indicated in Table 19. With the exception of literacy schools, most teachers in the Russian Empire, regardless of type of school, were dealing with between forty and fifty pupils each; remarkably, this situation had changed little since 1880. What had changed, however, was that a fairly large percentage of schools (29 percent) employed more than one teacher, so that at any given time each individual teacher was responsible for one or two, instead of three, sections. Thus, the share of each day pupils spent interacting with

Table 19

Classroom Size, 1911

	TWO-CLASS SCHOOLS (FIVE- TO SIX-YEAR PROGRAMS)	ONE-CLASS SCHOOLS (THREE- TO FOUR-YEAR PROGRAMS)
	Pupils per School	
Zemstvo schools	145	69
Church parish schools	119	52
All elementary schools		
Urban	97	
Rural	62	
	Pupils per Teacher	
Zemstvo schools	41	43
Church parish schools	40	44
All elementary schools		
Urban	40	
Rural	44	

SOURCE: MNP, *Odnodnevnaia perepis'* 16:60, table 15.

their teacher, rather than doing unsupervised exercises while the teacher dealt with more advanced or younger pupils, was increasing (though the size of each contingent of pupils was also larger).

Comparing pupil-teacher ratios in other countries is instructive. West indicates a ratio of 27:1 in six towns in England at common day schools in the 1830s (and ratios of 30:1 in English primary schools as recently as 1967); yet it is common to find references to ratios as high as 70:1 for London in the nineteenth century. Figures offered by Middleton and Weitzman indicate that the ratio of pupils to teachers in England in 1870 was 160:1, dropping only to 130:1 in the following decade. To be sure, there were also several thousand teachers' assistants "of dubious quality," but even if they are included in the count, the ratio scarcely drops below 100:1. Russian rural schools were undoubtedly overcrowded at the turn of the century, but English primary schools were doubly so. Canadian instructors in Kingston, Ontario, "each day . . . faced classes averaging seventy pupils, classified or unclassified by age or attainment, with a potential numbering twice that if all those enrolled were to attend simultaneously." Enrollment ratios exceeding 100 : 1 (with daily attendance of about 70 : 1) apparently remained common at least throughout the 1870s in other cities of Ontario as well. Similarly, Russian classroom size compared favorably with ratios prevailing in the German countryside, where there were on the average 117 children per school, 65 pupils per teacher, and 53 children per class.[36]

Thus, although Russian teachers were struggling with a difficult situation, the pupil-teacher ratio they confronted was by no means unheard of in North America and in the rest of Europe. In terms of *teacher-population* ratio, Russia lagged far behind most of Europe and had not reached the threshold at which, according to Carlo Cipolla, universal literacy is within reach. Yet because initial enrollments were lower than in much of Europe, the classroom size need not have been any bigger than in those countries with a better teacher-population ratio. For this reason, we must heed Cipolla's warning that data on the supply of teachers and the ratio of teachers to inhabitants must be "supplemented with detailed qualitative information," particularly when we wish to discover what those pupils who entered school were learning and do not want to simply assume a correlation between supply of teachers and national progress.[37]

AGE DISTRIBUTION OF PUPILS

Both the 1880 and 1911 censuses studied the age of the student population in rural schools (Table 20). In 1880, between five and six of every ten enrolled children were aged eight to eleven (inclusive); by 1911, roughly seven out of ten boys and eight of ten girls were in this age group. Comparing the sets of data for the two years shows a decline in the numbers of enrolled children *both* under the age of eight and over the age of twelve. In 1880, only 6 percent of schoolchildren had been under the age of eight, and

Table 20
Age Distribution of Rural Pupils, 1880 and 1911

AGE	BOYS		GIRLS		ALL CHILDREN	
	1880	*1911*	*1880*	*1911*	*1880*	*1911*
7 years	5.5%	1.8%	7.4%	2.4%	5.9%	2.0%
8 years	10.4	9.6	12.0	12.9	10.8	10.5
9 years	14.2	17.0	14.4	21.6	14.2	18.3
10 years	17.0	23.1	16.3	26.3	16.8	24.0
11 years	15.3	19.7	14.4	18.6	15.2	19.3
12 years	14.8	16.1	12.8	11.5	14.4	14.7
13 years	10.3	7.8	9.8	4.4	10.2	6.8
14 years	6.6	3.4	6.6	1.7	6.6	2.9
15 years or older	5.9	1.7	6.3	0.6	5.9	1.4
7–14 years	94.1	98.5	93.7	99.4	94.1	98.5
8–11 years	56.9	69.4	57.1	79.4	57.0	72.1

SOURCES: Fal'bork and Charnoluskii, *Narodnoe obrazovanie,* 171; MNP, *Odnodnev-naia perepis'* 16:50, table 3a, 104, table 46.

NOTE: The 1880 figures are drawn from rural schools in fifty provinces (1,140,915 children); the 1911 data apply to the Russian Empire (5,564,666 children). The 1911 figures are rounded off to the nearest tenth of one percent. If urban pupils are included, 98.6 percent of schoolchildren were 7 to 14 years old and 72.5 percent were 8 to 11 years old.

this proportion declined to 2 percent by 1911. But the greatest decline took place in the proportion of pupils over twelve years old—although even in 1911 nearly 16 percent of schoolchildren were twelve years old, a figure higher than the percentage of eight-year-olds in the system.

The popular view—one shared by most Russian educators since Ushinskii—held that until the age of eight a child was too young to learn how to read, to withstand the rigors of the classroom, or to travel to and from the school.[38] Thus, most children began school in Russia one, two, or even three years later than in the West. By the time they entered the gates of the school, they had seen a good deal of life and had already received a family education in the ways of the village community. More than one in four schoolchildren (27 percent) were over eleven years old, but of these, almost two out of three were twelve, and fully 98.6 percent were under the age of fifteen. As will become evident, this simple fact indicates that for the overwhelming majority of families, the school and the economy were not in competition. But with one in four schoolchildren over eleven years old, estimates of the percentage enrolled using the age span of eight to eleven as the school-age base must be corrected to account for these "stragglers"; that is, the number of enrolled as a percentage of all those eligible must be adjusted downward (although it is difficult to estimate by how much).[39]

ENROLLMENT OF GIRLS

The education of girls became a distinct priority for the Russian elite by the turn of the century. By then, the belief was widespread that teaching girls to read and write was an efficient way of spending scarce resources on basic education, for such education had a multiplier effect: the literate mother was likely to teach her children to read and write or to send her children to school. Yet educators had long observed a substantial measure of peasant resistance to sending girls to school. Darlington wrote that "it is not too much to say that the slow progress which primary education in Russia has made even among the male population is largely due to the backward state of public opinion among the peasantry with regard to the education of girls." This resistance unquestionably reflected the general indifference and brutality with which women were treated by male peasants.[40]

Peasant parents generally recognized that boys who could not read or write were at a tremendous disadvantage in the outside world, but such skills were considered a luxury for girls, who, it was believed, could better spend their time learning traditional skills such as weaving, knitting, plaiting, ceramics, and so forth. Because demand was weak, the literacy and enrollment levels of girls lagged far behind those of boys throughout the second half of the nineteenth century. Those who were directly involved in rural education often took Baron Korf's advice to heart: trying to recruit and keep girls in school was futile. Korf had tried and failed miserably, and his handbook, undoubtedly the single most influential work on primary education in nineteenth-century Russia, counseled teachers to bow to the inevitable and concentrate on teaching boys.[41] Apparently, some teachers went even further, for scattered reports indicated that when schools were overcrowded teachers denied admission to girls until all boys had been enrolled.

But we have shifted the issue. Because the supply of schooling was inadequate to meet demand, gender ratios may have often reflected competition for scarce resources and not necessarily peasant antipathy to education. Peasant resistance to the principle of educating girls is also easily confused with reluctance to send girls to mixed schools where they would spend their entire day with adolescents of the opposite sex (although legislation placed a maximum age of eleven on school attendance, one of four children in school was over eleven years old), supervised only by a teacher who was often an outsider to the village and whose morals were sometimes suspect. These parental anxieties must have been heightened by the necessity of traveling long distances to the school, perhaps after nightfall, or by the need to keep the child in overnight lodgings, either at the school or in the village.[42] It is no wonder that statisticians concerned with the impact of distance on school enrollments showed that the farther the school was located from a family's home, the more likely all children, but especially girls, were to remain unschooled.

The parallel growth of schools and female enrollment in Moscow suggests that female enrollment was closely related to local opportunities for schooling; quite simply, as schools became more available, more girls entered the doors.[43] Peasant attitudes, difficult to ascertain, were not the determining consideration. One of the most outstanding achievements of the schools in late Imperial Russia was the steady increase over time in the distribution percentage of girls enrolled in the primary schools (that is, girls as a percentage of all enrolled), *even as the absolute number of both boys and girls receiving instruction was also rapidly rising.*

Just how significant was this increase? Scattered data indicate that the number of girls as a percentage of all pupils in pre-Emancipation Russia was small, but that it differed by type of school and region. In Church parish schools, girls accounted for

10 percent of the enrollment; in schools for the state peasants, about 13 percent of the students were girls. In Moscow educational circuit in 1850, girls were only 7 percent of all primary school pupils; in Dorpat (later Riga) district they were 30 percent.[44]

From one in every ten pupils in 1850, the proportion of girls in the classroom rose to two in ten in 1880, and then to one in three by 1911. In this progression, the 1890s did not mark a radical turning point; instead, that decade stood at the midpoint of a gradual gradient. Because the total number of pupils in urban schools was only slightly over a million, compared to 5.6 million in rural schools, combined statistics obscure the noteworthy fact that in the lower elementary schools in towns girls were almost equally represented (44.6 percent of the students). One of every eleven girls of school age in the Empire lived in a town; one of every four girls enrolled went to an urban school.[45]

Not only was the composition of the classroom changing, but the proportion of all school-age girls who had gained some schooling (access percentage) was also increasing overall. Unfortunately, as noted above, Russian statisticians had for decades stubbornly considered ages seven to fourteen to be the proper school age and thus persistently understated the true level of enrollments. But even using their yardstick, we can see that the increase in access percentage was considerable: from 3.2 percent in 1880, to 6.1 percent in 1894, and to 15.2 percent in 1911. In other words, the chances of a girl between the ages of seven and fourteen receiving some education in European Russia increased fivefold between 1880 and 1911. In fact, this estimate is certainly a gross understatement, for the proportion of girls of these ages who had at one time been in school but were no longer enrolled on the day of the 1911 School Census (or indeed, who had not yet but would later enroll) was much higher in 1911 than in 1880.[46]

Although we can only roughly approximate the change over time in differences in access percentage by sex, we can use the 1911 one-day survey to find out roughly what percentage of school-age girls were actually enrolled on that one date. In almost half the European provinces, less than 21 percent of school-age girls attended school on 18 January 1911. In seven out of ten European provinces, between 11 percent and 30 percent attended; in only three (Moscow, St. Petersburg, and Iaroslavl') did the figure exceed 40 percent.

These results are dismal, but they must be tempered by two major qualifications, which significantly boost the estimate of how many Russian children ever attended school. First, the incidence of absenteeism for rural schoolgirls on that day was 7.3 percent. Adjusting for those enrolled but not in attendance on the day of the survey, we learn that in rural European Russia *roughly 25 to 35 percent of all school-age girls were enrolled in primary school on 18 January 1911.* If we allow for that contingent of school-age girls who had already passed through the schools (see the discussion of West's estimates, above), the proportion of girls with some contact with schools *could have been as high as 40 percent of Russian peasant girls.*[47] Most important, even this base figure, giving the number of school-age girls attending school on one day in 1911 as a percentage of all girls aged eight to eleven, is higher by a factor of three or four than the figures derived from using a school-age base of seven to fourteen years—figures commonly used by historians to illustrate backwardness.

In short, we know that during the decades under study the proportion of girls in the classroom (distribution percentage) rose considerably and showed no sign of abating. We know, too, that the chances of any girl going to school were higher in urban areas than in the villages; as late as 1911, fewer than one of four school-age girls in the villages were in school on the day of the census, though the proportion of girls who had been to school by age twelve was likely to have been as much as twice that number. Throughout the Russian Empire, despite the steep fluctuation in male enrollments from district to district and the variety of economic conditions encompassed, girls enrolled in schools roughly one-third to one-half as frequently as boys. The gap between the sexes was always far smaller in urban areas and, as overall enrollment crept upward, this gap tended to narrow.[48]

In some areas, female enrollment was high, but in others—and not only in the Central Asian regions—the figures were lower. Quite a few reasons could have accounted for the disparities in enrollment patterns: population density and the saturation of a given area with schools, the nature of the local economy, and popular attitudes toward education and coeducation—particularly attitudes toward the education of girls and toward instruction of any kind in the Russian language—all might have contributed. Although the most consistent correlate of female enrollment was urban residence, it should be emphasized that zemstvos in the agricultural provinces generally had access to less outside money for school construction and that the availability of schools in these provinces was therefore often sharply less than in the industrial provinces. The entire question of schooling and literacy of girls merits much closer study. Only meticulous local investigation will uncover and clarify the particular mix of factors hindering or promoting the education of peasant girls.

Can it be argued that regardless of locality, occupation, or composition of the population, female enrollment increased as schools became available for girls in 1911? If, after more detailed investigation, this argument turns out to be true, then the question again shifts from one of demand to one of supply. We could then say that as schools became less crowded, peasants would send their girls and that until that point the low enrollment level simply reflected the *relatively low priority* accorded female literacy, rather than outright opposition to female education. There is a subtle but important difference between outright opposition by peasants to the education of girls and a decision to send a boy to school when space was available only for one of the two. One position reflects absolute values, while the other is a decision made in a context of scarcity, where a choice must be made between two outcomes, each of which may be seen as a good in itself.

Moreover, as schooling became more available, it seems logical that female enrollment would have increased with particular rapidity. The harmful impact of distance and overcrowding on enrollments would have been reduced accordingly; because distance most severely affected enrollment levels for girls, the extension of the school network especially benefitted female enrollment. Finally, as women teachers came to dominate the profession, much residual peasant hesitation about sending girls to school may have evaporated.

❖

In this discussion of the growth, or "escalation," of schooling in Imperial Russia, we have once again seen peasant policy reflected in statistics, in choices made in a context of scarcity, and in massive pressures for the rapid construction of a school network capable of serving the entire population. We have seen, too, that the reach of schooling in late Imperial Russia was far more extensive than a cursory look at school censuses would suggest. The study of enrollments, distance from school, denied admissions, and enrollment by gender all suggest that the single most important determinant of peasant enrollments was the availability of schooling. There was no need to lead this horse to water; it was already thirsty and looking for a drink.

11

The School Calendar:

Rhythm and Intensity

A new tempo and discipline accompany the transition from farm to factory, from the harvest cycle and village routines to the machine speeds and close-ordered sequence of the urban day. In this transition, the school plays a major role; the sequence of lessons, the school bell, and the daily routines help provide new concepts of time and space. One reason absenteeism was endemic and schooling short-winded in early village schools in the West was the collision of school and farm, modern clock time and harvest cycle. The adjustment was difficult and protracted, reflecting the slow evolution from traditional to modern ways.[1]

Can we apply this stereotype to the Russian experience? Schooling was widespread in Russia, but how long did children remain in school? For peasants to be taught to read and write with any degree of sophistication, they had to be kept in school for two or three years; for this time span to be sufficient, attendance had to be regular and the school year of adequate length. If instruction was erratic because of repeated school closings or individual truancy or so brief that the children returned to the community only to forget the little they had learned, how could the school leave a lasting imprint or achieve even the limited goals the peasant community set for it?

It is a longstanding belief that school attendance in rural areas has always been erratic and short-lived. Theodore Schultz argued in 1963:

The average daily school attendance of children from farm homes tends to be lower than that of children from non-farm homes. There is much work on farms that children can do and many farm families are relatively poor, which makes the value of the work that children can do for them by missing a few days of school now and then comparatively high.[2]

Similarly, E. G. West commented that "it is now a recognized world-wide phenomenon that absenteeism from schools is more common in agricultural areas, whether their education is compulsory or not." Of course, most discussion has concerned countries where the school age ranged from six or seven years of age to fourteen or fifteen years and has made no distinction between attendance in the early and late years. Yet I suspect that Schultz, West, and many others have exaggerated the degree of conflict. West himself notes the economic pull in the other direction: the crèche function of the school, which often served as a babysitter for working parents and "provided a substantial external economy."[3] (Chapter 12 considers evidence that the extent of child labor in rural Russia may have been substantially overstated by historians.) Moreover, David Tyack argues that rural schools (rather than individual farm children) could adjust their schedule to farm needs by opening later and closing earlier:

Schools in farm areas could adjust the academic calendar to match the need for child labor in agriculture, thus eliminating the need to forego the earnings of children. In cities, by contrast, work opportunities were generally not seasonal.[4]

Tyack's argument finds substantiation below. Individual attendance at school and the length of the school year are related phenomena. The school's ability to adjust to the community calendar often determines the regularity of attendance and establishes a "symbiosis" of school and village culture. Because Russian schools accepted the seasonality of village life and accommodated their schedules to this seasonality (rather than seeking to impose a new order), they were able to exact a remarkable attendance level from the village youth. Much as the book was to find its way into the Russian village by dressing in village garb and speaking a village dialect, so the school had to shed its urban sense of time to function successfully. What made the school so integral a part of the village was that it did adjust and accommodate.

THE SCHOOL YEAR

According to Chekhov, the year in early village schools lasted only from 1 November (the day of the prophet Naum) until Easter (that is, until the spring flooding) or, at best, until the first of April. Excluding the frequent holidays that disrupted the calendar, the school year lasted only 60 to 75 days.[5] If Chekhov's calculations were accurate, the length of the school year had doubled to 152 days by 1911, signifying that there had been a sharp escalation, as well as an expansion, of schooling. Thorough research from the 1890s, however, suggests that even then the school year was substantially longer than Chekhov claimed. Information from several provinces shows that, although there was considerable local variety, the school year often lasted 150 days or more.

In Moscow province in 1896, 75 percent of the schools opened their doors in the first half of September, 17 percent in the second half of that month, 5 percent in October, and only 1 percent in November. Eighty-five percent closed their doors in May, 13 percent in June. From 1889 to 1894, the length of the average school year ranged from 159 days in Moscow district to 176 days in Mozhaisk. The labor demands of Moscow's widespread truck gardening partially explain the abbreviated school year there; in other areas where schools were new, the year tended to be shorter. (This tendency somewhat artificially reduced the length of the year reflected in school statistics as the school system rapidly expanded.) Petrov's Moscow studies also showed that the school year lengthened between 1886 and 1896, by as much as a half month at each end in many schools. Thus, Chekhov may have been right, and the lengthening may have begun in the 1880s. In Iaroslavl', Vladimir, and Viatka, the school calendar closely resembled that of Moscow.[6]

Data compiled by zemstvo statisticians who, unlike teachers

and inspectors, had no vested interest in papering over the defects of the rural schools show clearly that schooling lasted a little less than half the calendar year. Again, there were exceptions—perhaps one in ten schools—where an abbreviated school year fell under 125 or even 100 days, but the statisticians noted that in any given year most delayed openings and early closings were caused not by seasonal labor demands but rather by "organizational" defects. Ordinarily, this explanation meant that a teacher had been transferred or become physically incapacitated or that building repairs had not been completed on time.[7]

Information collected for both the official MNP census and the 1911 Zemstvo Congress brings us to the immediate prewar period. According to the Model Program, the school year was to last at least 163 days; in reality, it lasted 178 days in the towns and 151 in the villages. Throughout the Empire, the school year in the countryside varied from 128 days in Vil'no province to 179 days in Batum, although in European Russia almost all provinces had school years lasting from 145 to 160 days.[8] In the northern provinces, the school year began in the first half of September and ended in the beginning of May. In the agricultural heartland, schools opened as much as a month earlier and often ended in April.

One local cynic in Poltava province noted, however, that opening and closing dates had little meaning:

You might say that there are three different schedules: officially, the school year extends from 15 September to 1 May; in reality, it runs from 25 September until the end of April; but serious work proceeds from 25 October until the first of April.

Elsewhere, it was observed,

the school year begins on 15 September, but all the pupils begin to show up around 1 October, since until then the majority are busy with work around the farm: carrying firewood, driving stock out to night pasture. In the spring the children leave en masse—except those preparing for the examinations.[9]

Thus, the date of school opening and the time at which all pupils were first in their seats to greet the teacher were not the same. This difference did not mean that schools were not "really opening," but rather that pupils arrived in shifts, the youngest first and the oldest last. Indeed, after the 1917 Revolution, Chekhov suggested that the authorities heed this pattern and arrange the curriculum accordingly. He noted that the peak labor demand in the countryside was between April and September, but that this hardly affected children under the age of twelve, especially not the seven- to eight-year-old age group.[10] (Teachers' memoirs suggest that such curricular arrangements existed before the revolution.)

Of thirty-two provincial committees commenting on the length of the school year for the 1911 Zemstvo Survey, thirty-one observed that agricultural work, particularly tending livestock, cut into the schedule; ten noted that both migratory labor and cottage industries affected the school year; fifteen mentioned children's lack of warm clothing during inclement weather. Recurrent epidemics, particularly of smallpox, forced school closings in twenty-five provinces; periodic markets cleared out the schools for as much as a week at a time in twenty provinces; and local holidays, lasting several days, caused problems in twenty-three others. Inclement weather—the fall *rasputitsa* (the infamous "roadlessness"), the spring floods, the winter frosts—caused schools to close for lengthy periods in only nine provinces.[11]

At first glance, it does not seem that Russian schools adjusted well to village needs—in fact, the school appears to have been on the losing end of a persistent conflict between agriculture and education. But these reports often failed to distinguish between the length of the school year and the incidence of closings once school had begun. More important, these comments were responses to the general questions of whether schools closed, opened late, or shut early, and why. We have seen from the data collected in the 1890s that a minority *did* have to roll back the school year. But the pertinent questions are how many, and with what frequency.

Information from Moscow province in 1913–1914 makes it clear that schools had in fact adjusted successfully to the seasonal labor demand by allowing staggered entries, which also suited well the needs of a teacher trying to work simultaneously with three grades. More than four-fifths of the schools opened their doors between the first and the fifteenth of September, while two-thirds began their summer vacation between the first and the fifteenth of

May; most of the remainder had closing dates during the second half of May. In Moscow, opening and closing dates were listed separately for each class (section) of each school; the staggered dates suggest that during the first month or so the teachers concentrated on teaching beginning reading to the first grade, which commenced earlier, and began serious work with the intermediate and advanced divisions sometime in October.[12]

Thus, staggered entries, late beginnings, and early closings were characteristic of the school system but were not necessarily disruptive. Potentially far more damaging were school closings in the middle of the year, which would have destroyed any semblance of routine and continuity even the most gifted teacher could have imposed on three grades simultaneously. Yet in Moscow, in the four-year period from 1889 to 1893, only 12 percent of the zemstvo schools were forced to close for three days or more at a stretch. The greatest villain was contagious disease, which accounted for 116 out of 283 such incidents, 1,713 out of 4,298 days (40 percent). A similar number of closings were occasioned by the absence of the teacher, not only for reasons of illness or death but also because of transfers (103 instances, 1,830 days). Flooding and inclement weather explained only 32 instances and 298 days (although it should be kept in mind that closings of fewer than three days were not included in this study). These statistics present an enviable record: only one school in thirty in any given year was forced to close down for three or more consecutive days.[13]

A similar study was conducted after the 1913–1914 school year. In a school year averaging 165 days for 1,282 zemstvo schools, a total of 2,737 school days were lost because of epidemics (30 percent of lost days), teachers' illness (22 percent), teachers' absence (26 percent), building repairs (13 percent), spring flooding (2 percent), and various other reasons (7 percent). Village holidays accounted for another 2,326 days. Thus, *only about 2 percent of the school calendar year was lost because of closings, including local holidays* (1 percent if holidays are not included). In a school year lasting 165 days, then, roughly 3.3 days were lost.[14]

Village holidays affected virtually all schools equally, and only slightly.[15] School closings for other reasons affected fewer schools (199 of 1,282) but were more disruptive than the average would suggest (Table 21). Nevertheless, not only were school closings a

Table 21

School Closings, Moscow Province, 1913–1914

CAUSE OF CLOSING	NUMBER OF SCHOOLS AFFECTED	AVERAGE LENGTH OF CLOSING (IN DAYS)
Epidemics	47	18
Illness of teacher	45	14
Absence of teacher	45	15
Repairs	24	19
Spring flooding	4	11
Various other	34	6
Overall	199	14

SOURCE: "Obzor narodnogo obrazovaniia," in *Statisticheskii ezhegodnik Moskovskoi gubernii za 1913* (Moscow, 1914), 232–236.
NOTE: This study included 1,282 zemstvo schools.

relatively minor problem for the educational system but also *two-thirds (64 percent) of all days missed* (excluding holidays; one-third, or 35 percent, if holidays are included) *were caused by conditions internal to the school, which could not be blamed on the local economy.* Once the school year began, weather, the local economy, and popular attitudes had little effect on its smooth functioning (with the minor exception of brief local holidays that took away only one to two days a year for each school). Nearly all the blame for disruptive closings could be placed on epidemics, as well as on the unavoidable fact that in a one-room schoolhouse, everything depended on the health and presence of the only teacher in the village. (And in fact, illness, and even mortality, was high among teachers.) Yet, despite these factors, school closings were not a large-scale problem.[16]

In summary, the length of the school year in the Russian village was shorter than in the city, was on the average slightly more than ten days shorter than the year called for by the Model Program, and fluctuated considerably from province to province. The school year was adjusted to accommodate the local economy, but these adjustments seemed to most affect school openings and closings, rather than the continuity of lessons once classes began. It is worth noting that a school year of 150 days was comparable with school terms elsewhere. Consider the United States, the favorite model of Russian educators. Tyack put the school year at 134 days in 1890; the U.S. Bureau of Education claimed schools were open 153 days in 1908, and another source suggests considerable regional variety.[17] Yet Bowles and Gintis argue that

as recently as 1870, less than half of the children age five to seventeen attended school; among those enrolled, the school year averaged seventy-eight days, or less than a quarter of the year. Today, virtually all children . . . attend school for an average of half of the days in the year.[18]

I suspect that international comparisons, largely to the detriment of the Russian school system, miss the point here. As Craig points out in the case of compulsory education, legislation forcing enrollment has historically been effective only once most children were already in attendance; until that time, such legislation has largely been symbolic. A similar situation existed with regard to imposing a school calendar from above; if the school year was too long for local needs, absenteeism, late enrollments, and early withdrawals soared. When the calendar fit local needs, attendance increased. This pattern is precisely what Iaroslavl' zemstvo statisticians saw; the local economy did impose certain limits on the length of the school year, but because the school bowed to these demands and stayed within these limits, it could exact a high level of attendance from the local children.[19] This situation may also explain the enormous discrepancy in daily attendance figures between Russia and the West, an issue to which we now turn.

DAILY ATTENDANCE

Daily attendance figures can be very revealing. Spotty attendance could mean that parents recognized the value of schooling but also needed the children at home (or in the shop), or perhaps that nature and health conditions conspired to keep children out, despite the best intentions. Irregular attendance could also signal popular indifference to schooling, resistance to the best efforts of the elite to instruct and uplift. In contrast, regular attendance without compulsory measures could only mean a firm commitment to basic schooling, the absence of conditions preventing the child from spending each day in the classroom, or both. To be sure, regular attendance *figures* could mean that the records were being doctored; this was often the case in England where, after 1862, teachers' fees were adjusted according to the number of pupils being taught.

In Russia, because most teachers worked simultaneously with three grades, a high incidence of absenteeism could wreak havoc with learning and teaching plans. Petrov noted in the 1890s:

No matter how many school days are eliminated by breaks [caused by holidays, epidemics of contagious diseases, etc.], the cumulative effect of individual absenteeism is much more harmful. . . . One of the most difficult goals to attain, in a school with one teacher and three sections, is the maintenance of a uniform level of knowledge and skills among all pupils in a grade. This uniformity [*odnosostavnost'*] must be acknowledged to be one of the supremely important conditions permitting the teacher, according to Ushinskii's phrase, "to work with his class, as one works with a responsive and well-tuned instrument." Interruptions of the school year . . . do not upset this homogeneity and equality, and this is why, given their comparative infrequency, they are not nearly as disruptive as individual days missed. The latter often results in the student who missed a few days holding back the entire class and disrupting the order and sequence of instruction. This is why the question of absenteeism is of the utmost importance in school affairs.[20]

Much information can be squeezed out of the most prosaic of records, the attendance statistics. The entire course of instruction and socialization depended on regular attendance; regardless of the reading method employed in the schools, there could be little hope for substantial achievement unless the pupil came to school daily. In Russia, because the teacher's task was made infinitely more difficult by the need to keep three discrete groups working simultaneously, the stakes were particularly high. In short, good attendance was a necessary, though perhaps not a sufficient, condition for successful schooling.

In the West, poor attendance plagued most schools and persisted into the twentieth century. In the United States, the percentage of those enrolled who attended classes daily was as low as

64 percent between 1840 and 1890. In England, according to Pamela Horn, teachers were often driven to despair by erratic attendance; they needed their pupils in class regularly, but they were also anxious not to offend school board members (often major land-owners in a parish) who might be using child labor. Though child labor laws were passed and prizes offered for good school atten-dance, the problem persisted (according to Horn, it lasted until the full mechanization of agriculture), and as late as the 1890s it was not uncommon for schools to achieve only three-quarters of poten-tial attendance. In Kingston, Ontario, daily attendance was 50 per-cent or less of those enrolled, and fewer than 20 percent of five- to sixteen-year-olds attended regularly.[21]

Most records produced by the Russian school system show that daily attendance was remarkably high. The material is so sharply at odds with the image of the rural school repeatedly pre-sented in the literature that it is worth pausing to examine it in detail.

Although no systematic studies of attendance were compiled before the 1890s, as early as 1870 Baron Korf lamented that atten-dance was very irregular in Ekaterinoslav. If there was a wedding in the village, the schools would empty out. If there was frost on the ground, many children were too poorly clothed to venture out—or if they did, would catch cold. Others had to stay home to help with chores or had to accompany their parents to work. Nevertheless, Korf added that statistical data gathered for various teachers' congresses clearly showed that "the better organized the school, the better the attendance." This observation is important: when parents could see visible results, they left their children in school and made do. "In those schools that have earned the favor of children and parents, you will see that the overwhelming majority of children attend very regularly, and only a few miss now and then." To support his argument, Korf pointed to one school with thirty-four pupils, in which over a period of three months only ninety school days were missed and sixteen pupils had perfect at-tendance records. (The other eighteen pupils missed an average of five days each.) Moreover, most of the ninety days were missed when an epidemic swept the area. Because school generally met six days a week in Russia, we can figure a total of 2,618 school days (for thirty-four pupils, assuming seventy-seven school days in three months) and can thus calculate an attendance rate of 96.6 percent.[22]

Korf undoubtedly overstated the faithfulness with which children attended school. Perhaps he selected an atypical school; certainly there were a number of holidays and school closings during this period. Korf was considering a three-month winter interval, and later studies by Orlov in the 1880s showed the highest incidence of absenteeism in September and October during the harvest and laying in of supplies of wood. Absenteeism was next highest in May, when agricultural work began in earnest and some children were sent out to watch the herds at night.[23]

Yet systematic studies conducted in the 1890s confirmed that Korf's estimates of attendance were in line with other areas of Russia. Petrov, who studied the records of the Moscow district zemstvo executive board, arrived at the figures shown in Table 22 for a five-year interval (1891–1895).[24]

From such records, it is possible to calculate that in a school year lasting 160 days, the typical schoolboy missed 11.9 class days (7.4 percent) and the typical girl 10.7 (6.7 percent). More than one out of five children missed more than 15 days, but very few missed more than 35 (22 percent of school time).

Information from schools in three other districts of Moscow province for the school year 1893–1894 produced similar results.

Table 22
Annual School Attendance, Moscow District,
1891–1895

	BOYS	GIRLS [a]
Perfect attendance	10.6%	13.6%
Missed 1–15 days	64.5	63.3
Missed 16–35 days	18.4	18.0
Missed 36–80 days	6.1	4.5
Missed 81 or more days	0.4	0.1

SOURCE: Petrov (Moscow), *Voprosy narodnogo obrazovaniia* 1:144–145.
NOTE: This survey included 17,506 pupils.
[a] In the original data, as here, these figures total 99.5 percent.

In Dmitrov (forty-three schools), Serpukhov (forty-two schools), and Zvenigorod (fifteen schools), on any given day, between 3.1 and 3.2 children in each school failed to show up. Each pupil missed a yearly average of 11.4 days in Dmitrov, 9.8 days in Zvenigorod, and 8.7 days in Serpukhov—in each case, significantly less than 10 percent of the school year calendar.[25] Districts with different economic and occupational profiles produced nearly identical attendance patterns, strongly suggesting that the economy, and particularly child labor, did not bite deeply into attendance.

More than a decade later, the 18 January 1911 School Census of the entire Empire compared the number of children attending school that day with those actually registered. The results were remarkably similar to those of school board studies and district zemstvo records. In the villages of the Russian Empire, 6.7 percent of registered pupils (6.4 percent of boys and 7.3 percent of girls) were absent from school on 18 January; figures ranged from 12.3 percent in Warsaw educational circuit to 3.3 percent in St. Petersburg circuit.[26]

What kept children home? Petrov's study of almost 350,000 instances of absenteeism provided the breakdown shown in Table 23.[27] We must not misread this table. Poverty, disease, the economy, and the weather explained most absenteeism; parental negligence was blamed for less than 4 percent of all missed days. But it is important to distinguish between the *causes* and the *actual incidence* of absenteeism. Although zemstvo statisticians complained bitterly about the disastrous effect of poverty on the schools, absenteeism was not unduly high. The bleary-eyed Moscow statisticians, studying 344,507 cases of absenteeism, lost sight of the fact that these took place over six years and that for every day lost the average student appeared faithfully for fourteen or fifteen days. Anguish or compassion for peasants living in dire poverty filled these reports and fostered the impression that schools were laboring under extraordinarily difficult conditions. But the numbers show that *most* registered children attended school most of the time. Even a low rate of absenteeism disrupted teachers' schedules and made it difficult to keep three groups of pupils marching together. But this problem was inherent in a system that required a teacher to instruct three groups of children simultaneously. *No*

Table 23
Causes of Absenteeism, Moscow District,
1891–1895

	BOYS' ABSENTEEISM	GIRLS' ABSENTEEISM
Conditions at home[a]	43.5%	40.1%
Disease	34.8	36.1
Weather, distance, age	13.2	17.2
Parental indifference	2.9	2.4
Malingering	1.7	1.3
Church holiday	1.7	1.6
Other	2.1	1.6

SOURCE: Petrov (Moscow), *Voprosy narodnogo obrazovaniia* 1:146–147.

NOTE: This survey recorded absenteeism for 17,506 pupils. Figures in this table are rounded off to the nearest tenth of one percent.

[a] Work at home accounted for 37.6 and 37.7 percent of all absenteeism for boys and girls, respectively; poverty (i.e., lack of warm clothing) caused 5 percent and 2.6 percent. The remaining absenteeism in this category was caused by illness of relatives, relocation, or signing up for work in factories—all of these in very small numbers.

matter how miserable life in the countryside was at the turn of the century, the problems of the school system were not caused by poverty alone. The absence of poverty would not have substantially increased attendance.

Yet Petrov's work, which concluded that poverty severely disrupted the schools, was cited by others investigating conditions in the countryside, and his conclusions, rather than his evidence, became the accepted wisdom. The same misconception developed with studies of dropouts. For example, a study of Moscow by Bogolepov showed that poverty underlay the failure to enroll; but in a review of this study, Strannoliubskii observed that most school-age children did in fact attend school.[28] The surveys showing the impact of poverty dealt with only a minority of children, as did many studies of attendance and school closing figures.

From the time of Korf until World War I, attendance throughout European Russia remained close to 90 percent. This figure suggests that, although the school year in Russia was briefer, it was more productive and less disturbed by individual absenteeism than school years in the West. Once again we see that, by adjusting to the village cycle, Russian schools assured that nearly all children, once enrolled, would come regularly. Attendance figures also suggest that children and their parents saw a positive value in schooling. If parents had been using schools only for occasional babysitting, attendance would not have been as consistent.[29] The problems encountered in interpreting attendance figures make it clear that, first, those closest to the facts sometimes lost perspective on the dimensions of the phenomena they were observing and that, second, discussions of the relationship between poverty and school enrollments must be approached with extreme caution.

INTENSITY: THE DISTRIBUTION PATTERN

Once pupils enrolled and actually came to school, how long did they stay? This section considers the apparent paradox that although attendance was faithful, the duration of a student's stay in the schools was limited. Determining duration (or intensity) will allow us to see how much education children received and will help to gauge the impact of schooling, in terms of instruction and socialization. The pattern of high enrollment, regular attendance, and pervasive early departure can illuminate a later discussion of peasant motivation and the relationship between economy and schooling.

The duration of schooling was investigated by plotting the distribution of pupils by grade or by comparing the number of graduates and dropouts to the total number of students enrolled. If we assume that mortality was not a significant factor (accounting for only 1 percent of depletion) and that incoming classes were of uniform size, it follows that in a three-year program each grade should have included 33 percent of all pupils (25 percent in a four-year school). Each graduating class should have equaled one-third of the total enrollment. The number of third graders and the number of graduating pupils (not the same thing) should have been approximately equal to the number of incoming students each year.

Contemporary UNESCO studies discuss repetition and dropping out—deviations from this abstract model of an ideally functioning system—as "wastage." Although "wastage" is not cost-efficient, it may in fact reflect an adjustment to the "natural cycle" of the village, not a "malfunction" of the system.[30]

We can compare scattered grade distribution surveys made at the turn of the century with more systematic information collected on nearly seven hundred thousand pupils for the 1911 Zemstvo Congress and on nearly seven million children for the 1911 School Census. By comparing these surveys, looking separately at the records for zemstvo and Church schools, and examining carefully the year-by-year fluctuations in one province, we may draw some firm conclusions. (See Table 24.)

First, although a few provinces displayed significant anomalies, the general pattern of steady attrition in enrollment from first to third grade was pervasive and ubiquitous. In both zemstvo and Church schools, about 40 percent of the boys and 50 percent of the girls were enrolled in the first grade, roughly one-third of both boys and girls were enrolled in the second, and nearly 20 percent of boys as well as between 13 and 15 percent of girls in the third. Once he enrolled, a boy's chance of reaching (though not of completing) the third grade was less than one in two; a girl's chance was one in four or five. Because attrition from first to third grade was considerably higher for girls than for boys, classes were increasingly dominated by males.

Second, the studies conducted over a two-decade period of intensive investment in education and expansion of initial enrollments show no measurable changes in the distribution pattern. In Moscow province, after initial adjustments with the expansion of the school system, the distribution of pupils by grade remained remarkably constant after 1900, seemingly impervious to outside forces. There was no marked distinction in distribution by grade between zemstvo and Church schools.

Between one- and two-thirds of those who enrolled reached the third grade, but attrition was high at that level. Studies suggest that close to 40 percent of the pupils who reached third grade left before completing it. The 1911 Zemstvo Survey shows that 59 percent of third graders and 72.7 percent of fourth graders finished. Zemstvo studies conducted a decade earlier show a higher propor-

Table 24
Percentage Distribution of Pupils by Grade

	FIRST GRADE	SECOND GRADE	THIRD GRADE	FOURTH GRADE
Zemstvo Schools, 1910–1911				
Three-Year Schools				
Boys	44.1%	36.1%	19.8%	—
Girls	53.9	33.0	13.0	—
Four-Year Schools				
Boys	36.4	30.0	21.4	12.2
Girls	49.1	29.7	14.8	6.3
All Rural Elementary Schools, 1911 Census				
Ministry of Education Schools				
Boys	44.3%	31.2%	18.1%	4.8%
Girls	53.4	29.2	13.2	3.2
Church Schools				
Boys	46.5	32.5	18.4	2.2
Girls	55.5	30.2	12.9	1.2

SOURCES: Bratchikov, "Uchebno-vospitatel'naia," no. 1, 102; Vikhliaev (Moscow), *Ekonomicheskie usloviia,* 22–23; "Obzor narodnogo obrazovaniia," in *Statisticheskii ezhegodnik Moskovskoi gubernii za 1910* (Moscow, 1911), 29; MNP, *Odnodnevnaia perepis'* 16:114, table 16; *Svodka svedenii,* sec. 1, 19–20, tables 8 and 9.

NOTE: Figures in this table are rounded off to the nearest tenth of one percent. The 1911 data for zemstvo schools were from 7,987 three-year schools in 149 districts and twenty provinces, with a total of nearly 500,000 pupils, almost 70 percent of them boys. For four-year schools, information arrived from 80 districts in nineteen provinces, with a total of 2,038 schools and 189,000 pupils (with approximately the same proportion of boys).

Continued on next page

Table 24—*continued*

	FIRST GRADE	SECOND GRADE	THIRD GRADE	FOURTH GRADE
		Schools in Moscow Province		
		1896–1897		
Boys	48.0%	35.0%	17.0%	—
Girls	55.9	33.2	10.8	—
		1903–1904		
Boys	43.0	37.0	20.0	—
Girls	53.0	34.0	13.0	—
		1910–1911		
Boys	43.0	37.0	20.0	—
Girls	51.0	35.0	14.0	—

tion of completions: 67 percent of the boys and 69 percent of the girls. One investigator calculated from zemstvo figures that 31 percent of boys and 18 percent of girls entering school completed the full three-year program.[31]

In Iaroslavl' province, where 14 percent of all enrolled pupils graduated each year (i.e., 44 percent of "normal" flow), statisticians collected data in several stages throughout the year. Of every one hundred pupils of each sex enrolled in the third grade, eighty-eight boys and eighty-seven girls were preparing to take the certifying exams, seventy-five boys and seventy-six girls took the exams, and virtually all (seventy-four boys and seventy-five girls) passed the exams. According to these figures, more than 10 percent of the third graders in both Church and zemstvo schools were not preparing for examinations.[32]

COMPLETERS

In theory, a perfect school cycle would produce graduates at the rate of one-third or one-fourth of all pupils each year in three-

and four-year schools, respectively. Early Ministry of Education school records, not entirely reliable, indicate that the percentage of all enrolled pupils graduating in the 1870s and 1880s fluctuated from 5 to 10 percent (one-sixth to one-third the "normal" flow). More rigorous investigations of Moscow in the 1880s put the figure at 10 percent.[33]

Other studies in the 1890s produced similar results. An MNP-directed inquiry in 1896 discovered a successful completion rate of 9.9 percent for the thirty-four zemstvo provinces (zemstvo and Church schools) and for the sixty provinces of European Russia, although the rate was as high as 18.6 percent in the Baltic and as low as 3.5 percent in tsarist Poland. Most investigations of individual provinces in European Russia, as well as estimates for the entire country, were close to 10 percent.[34]

Table 25 provides a rough comparison of the "effectiveness"[35] of the school system at two points: in 1894, at the outset of the major school expansion campaign; and in 1911, after nearly two decades of effort. Comparing the percentage of pupils graduating in 1894 and in 1911 reveals a high degree of consistency, despite the radically increased availability of education. The most noteworthy changes were the 2 percent decline in the proportion of girls finishing zemstvo schools and the slight increase in the proportion of boys graduating from Church schools. A number of qualifications must be mentioned, however; for example, the 1894 study measured data from the sixty European provinces, whereas the 1911 study was concerned with the entire Empire. More important, the number of zemstvo schools with four-year programs jumped from virtually zero in 1894 to one in four in 1911 (with a four-year program, a perfectly functioning school—no repeaters, no dropouts—would produce a graduating class that equaled 25 percent of total enrollment). Moreover, the literacy schools under the Synod, which generally offered a two-year program, had virtually disappeared by 1911, and many Church parish schools had also converted from a three-year to a four-year program. Thus, it is likely that small but significant changes in the percentage of pupils graduating might not be apparent in these statistics.

Fortunately, as shown in Table 26, we can precisely compare the percentages of enrolled pupils who completed three-year zemstvo schools in several provinces in the years 1903 and 1911. In

Table 25
Effectiveness of Schooling, 1894 and 1911

	GRADUATES AS A PERCENTAGE OF ENROLLED	GRADUATES AS A PERCENTAGE OF "NORMAL" FLOW
	Zemstvo Schools	
Boys		
1894	10.5%	31.5%
1911	10.8	32.4
Girls		
1894	9.2	27.6
1911	7.0	21.0
	Church Schools	
Boys		
1894	9.4%	28.2%
1911	10.7	32.1
Girls		
1894	8.1	24.3
1911	8.2	24.6

SOURCES: Bratchikov, "Uchebno-vospitatel'naia," no. 1, 103–104; MNP, *Odnodnevnaia perepis'* 16:56, 59.

NOTE: The figures for 1894 and 1911 are not precisely comparable. The 1894 study measured the sixty European provinces (2,131,164 boys and 648,849 girls), and the 1911 study dealt with the entire Empire (4,499,845 boys and 2,130,133 girls). In addition, the Synod figures for 1911 do not include literacy schools, which generally had two-year programs. Literacy schools can be included for 1911, but as a percentage of all Synod schools (which were then beginning to convert to four-year programs), they were far fewer in 1894 than in 1911. Also, according to the 1911 Zemstvo Survey, 24 percent of all zemstvo schools were then offering four-year, rather than three-year, programs.

Table 26
Percentage of Pupils Completing Three-Year
Zemstvo Schools, 1903 and 1911

PROVINCE	1903	1911
Voronezh	11.3%	9.3%
Kazan'	12.5	12.8
Moscow	14.7	12.3
Nizhegorod	12.8	11.9
Olonets	14.3	14.0
Orel	8.2	8.1
Penza	17.7[a]	10.5
Smolensk	10.0	9.3
Tambov	11.0	10.4
Tula	10.2	7.7
Ufa	12.7	10.9
Kherson	8.1	7.9
Chernigov	9.8	10.3

SOURCES: Compiled from Shkol'naia komissiia Iaroslavskogo gubernskogo zemstva (Iaroslavl'), *Kratkii obzor zemsko-shkol'nogo,* 9 (for 1903 data); and *Svodka svedenii,* sec. 1, 23, table 10.
[a] I have no explanation for the peculiarly high completion rate in Penza.

virtually every province, the percentage of pupils finishing the full program declined slightly—though this decline may have partly reflected the imbalance caused by attrition, as well as the rapid pace of school expansion, which put larger numbers in the first grade than in the graduating class. Nevertheless, neither a decade of fast-paced school construction nor the 1906 repeal of military benefits for graduates with certificates made a significant impact on the proportion of children who remained in school to complete the program.[36]

How long did it take graduates of the primary schools to complete the three- and four-year programs? Surveys conducted at the turn of the century addressing this question are summarized in Table 27. In zemstvo and Church country schools, between 50 and 60 percent of boys who graduated did so on schedule, but between one-third and one-fourth required a fourth year. Only a tiny proportion completed the program in less time, and virtually all who finished in one year (100 percent) or two years (94.8 percent) had entered in the second or third grades. (These figures were for zemstvo schools; in the Church schools, 10 percent of boys who finished in two years had enrolled in the third grade.) Among girls who completed the program, the length of stay seemed to be considerably abbreviated (exam commissions were often much less

Table 27

Length of Stay in School for Graduates of Three-Year Schools, Iaroslavl' (1899) and Vladimir (1900)

	BOYS		GIRLS	
	Vladimir	*Iaroslavl'*	*Vladimir*	*Iaroslavl'*
	Zemstvo Schools			
One to two years	5.3%	4.7%	6.0%	8.1%
Three years	50.2	62.8	63.4	81.8
Four years	37.0	29.8	28.8	8.9
Five to six years	7.6	2.7	1.8	1.2
Average stay (in years)	3.46	3.29	3.25	3.00
	Church Schools			
One to two years	8.6%	9.7%	10.2%	14.5%
Three years	60.2	64.5	70.2	76.2
Four years	28.3	24.4	17.7	8.9
Five to six years	2.9	1.4	0.0	0.4
Average stay (in years)	3.23	3.16	3.04	2.93

SOURCES: Iaroslavskoe gubernskoe zemstvo (Iaroslavl'), *Svedeniia*, 30–31; Vladimirskaia gubernskaia zemskaia uprava (Vladimir), *Sbornik statisticheskikh* 3:117. NOTE: N = 2,633 boys and 737 girls in Iaroslavl'; N = 3,814 boys and 2,166 girls in Vladimir.

stringent with girls). Only in the zemstvo schools of Vladimir province did a similar proportion (28 percent) remain for an extra year; everywhere else, the percentage of girls who finished on schedule, as well as those who finished in fewer than three years, was higher than among boys. Moreover, in Iaroslavl' a very substantial percentage of the few girls who finished in two years— 26.5 percent in the zemstvo schools and a remarkable 63.1 percent in the Church schools—had enrolled in the beginning class, thus completing a three-year program in two years. Interestingly, this pattern did not hold true for town schools.[37]

Perhaps most striking is that the length of stay for graduates of Church parish schools, which overwhelmingly consisted of a two-grade program at the turn of the century, was very close to the length of stay in zemstvo schools in both provinces. Apparently, there was a common core of materials and skills to master, and the official length of the program mattered less than the actual time required for assimilation. Moreover, this finding offers further evidence that the programs of Church schools and zemstvo schools were comparable.

The 1911 Zemstvo Survey confirmed that the patterns exhibited earlier in Vladimir and Iaroslavl' were not atypical and that they had not changed in a decade of rapid school expansion. In twenty-one provinces and 6,579 three-year schools graduating 45,531 pupils, 65 percent of the students completed their work in three years, 29.7 percent in four, and 5.3 percent in five or more. In 1,913 four-year schools graduating 12,971 pupils, 75 percent finished in four years.[38]

DROPOUTS

How long did dropouts spend in school? Were dropouts also failures? Learning how long it took the minority of students to complete the full course is important for gauging the "fit" between the official program, the exam requirements, and actual classroom performance; but in doing so we learn little about what educators now call "wastage," about the amount of time the majority of students actually spent in the classroom and at what precise point in their studies they left.

Before the turn of the century, few zemstvos tried to move beyond investigating the distribution of pupils by grade to a more precise determination of length of stay in school. Contemporary comments on the school system placed the average time spent in school at "one or two winters"—a logical estimate, considering that 80 percent of pupils were concentrated in the first two grades. The detailed 1896 Iaroslavl' study was perhaps the first to provide specific information, and the results were somewhat surprising. The average length of stay of all pupils—both those finishing and those dropping out midway—was 3 years for boys and 2.4 years for girls in MNP schools, 2.8 years for boys and 2.3 years for girls in Church parish schools. When children left school in Iaroslavl', *whether as dropouts or graduates,* and whether from zemstvo or Church parish schools, half (48 percent) of all boys and seven in twenty girls (36 percent) had been studying for three years; between 25 and 29 percent of boys and 42 to 44 percent of girls had been enrolled two years. Notably, between 15 and 25 percent of boys had studied four or more years, and a mere 1 to 6 percent had attended only one year. With girls, the extremes were reversed: although 14.4 percent left after one year, only 6 to 7 percent stayed four years or more.[39]

The situation in Iaroslavl' may well have been somewhat anomalous, for the percentage of pupils graduating annually was higher than the overall percentage in Russia at the time. Nevertheless, the Iaroslavl' study made it clear that the grade distribution tables frequently cited by educators understated the true length of stay. The grade reached or completed did not always reflect the number of years spent in school.

Another investigation conducted in Vladimir at the time measured the length of stay for dropouts only. Of 51,742 primary school pupils enrolled in Vladimir schools in 1900, 11,524 pupils, or 22.2 percent (19.5 percent of boys and 31.7 percent of girls) dropped out during the course of the school year, while 11 percent of boys and 7 percent of girls successfully completed the program. For boys who dropped out, the average length of stay was 2.2 years in zemstvo schools and 1.9 years in Church schools. For girls, the figures were 1.8 and 1.7 years, respectively.[40]

At what stage in their studies did the one in five students who left every year depart? (The distribution of dropouts by grade is

Table 28
Points of Departure from the School System,
Vladimir, 1900

POINT OF DEPARTURE	PERCENTAGE OF ALL MALE DROPOUTS	PERCENTAGE OF ALL FEMALE DROPOUTS
	Zemstvo Schools	
First grade	35.0%	45.1%
Second grade	49.4	48.2
Third grade	15.6	6.7
	Church Schools	
First grade	41.5%	40.5%
Second grade	43.0	54.5
Third grade	15.5	5.0

SOURCE: Vladimirskaia gubernskaia zemskaia uprava (Vladimir), *Sbornik statisti-cheskikh* 3:110.

NOTE: Data for this table are based on pupils who dropped out of a grade before completing it, not those who completed a grade and simply never returned to school.

shown in Table 28.) Fifteen percent of all male students and 30 percent of female students left school in Vladimir during their first year of studies. During the second year, the attrition rates increased to 21 percent and 44 percent, respectively. If one hundred boys entered school in a given year, eighty-five remained after one year; after two years, sixty-seven; after three, fifty-one. Of every one hundred girls entering, seventy remained after the first year, thirty-nine after the second, and twenty-four after the third. Severe as this attrition rate was, it meant that as a rule, although nearly 80 percent of all children left school before reaching the third grade, more than 50 percent had remained in school for at least three years. Put in other terms, an average boy in a Vladimir zemstvo school who dropped out of the first grade had been in school for 1.43 years; a girl, for 1.28. A boy who dropped out of the second grade had ordinarily studied for 2.4 years; a girl, for 2.2.[41]

Surveys conducted at the turn of the century in Viatka and Kherson—provinces economically very different from Vladimir and even more so from each other—produced virtually the same results. *Two-thirds of those dropping out had studied two years or more, and one-third of all boys and one-fourth of all girls who dropped out had completed three or more years in the school system.*[42]

The only study to fully integrate the question of length of stay with point of departure was the 1911 Zemstvo Survey, which investigated 41,872 pupils in 2,737 schools. According to this study, 42 percent of all dropouts left from the first grade, 38 percent from the second, and 20 percent from the third. For four-year schools, dropouts were similarly clustered: 36 percent from the first grade, 30 percent from the second, 23 percent from the third, and 11 percent from the fourth.[43] The distribution of time spent in school by dropouts by grade is shown in Table 29.

This study, which collected material from ninety-six districts in seventeen provinces, suggests that the patterns discovered at the turn of the century continued a decade later, even after the schools had made enormous strides in bringing education closer to the population. As earlier, only one-third of the pupils who left school

Table 29
Years Spent in School by Dropouts, 1911
(three-year schools)

POINT OF DEPARTURE	ONE YEAR	TWO YEARS	THREE YEARS	FOUR YEARS	FIVE YEARS
First grade	72%	19%	2%	0%	7%
Second grade	13	60	20	3	4
Third grade	5	10	58	18	9
All dropouts	35	33	20	5	7

SOURCE: Modified from *Svodka svedenii,* sec. 1, 28–29, table 14.

NOTE: Total N = 29,222. Figures in this table include pupils who completed first or second grade but did not return for the next year, as well as pupils who dropped out before completing a grade.

in a given year were departing with only one year or less of schooling; but fully one-quarter of those who quit school in or after the first grade had been in school longer than one year. Thus, if 40 percent of dropouts left from the first grade, and if 72 percent of this number had studied one year or less, then the proportion of all dropouts who left within or at the end of their first year of study was 28.8 percent.[44]

The 1911 Zemstvo Survey also investigated 25,172 pupils in 1,078 four-year schools. In these schools, 31 percent of dropouts left during the first year (27.2 percent if first-year dropouts from upper grades are excluded), 28 percent during the second year, 23 percent during the third, 12 percent in the fourth, and 6 percent in the fifth year of study. Notably, in the four-year schools there was a closer fit between years of study and the point of dropping out; that is, 81 percent of dropouts from the first grade had studied only one year; 69 percent from the second grade had studied two years; 67 percent from the third grade three years; and 67 percent of those who left from the fourth grade had been in school for four years.[45] These figures do not mean that pupils dropped out earlier—indeed, roughly the same proportion dropped out after only one year of study—but rather that when pupils dropped out at a certain grade in the school program, that grade was somewhat more likely to reflect the number of years they had spent in school. This difference probably stems from the fact that there were two teachers in the majority of four-year schools, one for each two grades, whereas most three-year schools had only one teacher. The amount of contact time between pupil and teacher was correspondingly greater in the four-year schools, which in turn made it easier to keep pace with the official schedule of instruction.

Finally, a number of zemstvos also studied the *age* at which pupils left the schools, whether as dropouts or as graduates. This information offers important clues to the relationship between economy and schooling, particularly regarding the impact of child labor on length of stay in the schools (the subject of the next chapter).

Vladimir statisticians discovered that the average age of male dropouts in the zemstvo schools was 10.7 years; female dropouts averaged 10.1 years of age. Four out of five male dropouts were between nine and twelve years old; only 12 percent were older than twelve. Among girls, three out of four dropouts were between nine and eleven years old, and only 12 percent were older than eleven. Boys dropped out in almost equal numbers each year over a four-year interval; the same total percentage of girls dropped out but over a *three-year* period.[46]

Studies of Vladimir and Iaroslavl' also pinpointed the ages at which students completed their schooling. In both provinces, the average age was eleven or twelve for between 75 and 80 percent of both boys and girls. Age at completion was thirteen for a respectable minority of boys (16 percent) and for half that percentage of girls. Only 3 percent of boys who graduated did so at age ten, but between 12 and 14 percent of female graduates received their certificate at that age.[47]

If we step back from the close detail, it is tantalizing to speculate that *pupils seemed to be striving to reach a point somewhere in the middle of the official program and that they would stay in school as long as it took to reach that point, but no longer.* To be sure, had this been so for *all* pupils, the dropout level would have approached 100 percent at that point (providing all schools followed the program precisely), though the length of stay would have differed. That this was not the strategy of all pupils (or their parents) is evident from the one in every three to four dropouts who left school during their first year of study (or, at least, who left the school in which they were registered at the time the survey was conducted). Yet the difference between three- and four-year schools in the relationship of years of stay to point of departure hints that for most pupils this point *did* exist and did represent the aim of schooling. (Had the contact time between teachers and pupils increased to a point where it would have been possible to keep pace with the official program everywhere, this trend might have been much more salient.) Thus, the goal for most pupils seemed to be mastering a certain level of skills, not receiving a certificate.

REPEATERS

To observers of Russian education, one of the most persistent and troubling features of the school system at the turn of the century was the high incidence of pupils repeating a grade. When a pupil had to repeat a year, he or she had obviously been unable to keep pace with the instructional schedule determined by the Model Program or, before 1897, by the requirements of the Military Benefits Examination. (Because the latter applied to boys, we would expect to find a higher incidence of repeating among boys than among girls, who could be whisked through the system more easily.) When many students in each class were forced to repeat, sometimes more than once, it could be argued that the very pace of instruction, or perhaps the methods, were unsuitable for village conditions.

How pervasive was repetition, and how frequently did it occur? Who were the repeaters? At what point in their studies did pupils run into snags? Did the introduction of the Model Program (1897) or the repeal of the Military Benefits Act (1906) change the frequency of repeating? Did repeating reflect economic conditions in the countryside, which, by impinging on attendance, health, and the pupil's ability to concentrate on learning, disrupt the smooth flow from one grade to another? Did repetition more accurately reflect the lack of fit between program demands and peasant needs, or was it simply a case of inadequate contact time between pupil and teacher, caused by the teaching of three grades simultaneously? Were the rural schools in Russia any worse than elsewhere in this regard?

Beginning in the 1890s, scattered reports from the countryside suggested that each year one or two of every ten pupils was forced to repeat a grade. In Khar'kov, the local zemstvo reported in 1899 that of every four boys in the first grade, roughly three proceeded to the next level and one remained behind. In the second grade, of every two boys, one went on and one stayed behind. In the Church parish schools, the percentage remaining behind in the first grade was somewhat higher, although it was somewhat lower in the second grade. In both the zemstvo and Church schools, a slightly higher percentage of girls than boys remained behind in the first grade, but fewer remained behind in the second. This study failed to explain, however, how the 20.7 percent of male students and 28.8 percent of female students who dropped out each year fit into the picture; the most one could conclude was that repeating was widespread in Khar'kov among both sexes and in both major types of schools.[48]

Table 30

Percentage of Pupils by Grade Who Had
Repeated a Grade at Any Point

	BOYS	GIRLS
Iaroslavl' (1896)		
First grade	13.0%	8.5%
Second grade	22.0	13.0
Third grade	32.0	18.0
Vladimir (1900)		
First grade	20.0%	17.0%
Second grade	32.0	24.0
Third grade	40.0	24.5

SOURCES: Iaroslavskoe gubernskoe zemstvo (Iaroslavl'), *Nachal'noe obrazovanie,* 88–92; Vladimirskaia gubernskaia zemskaia uprava (Vladimir), *Sbornik statisticheskikh* 3:98–101, 104.

NOTE: The Iaroslavl' study included 36,109 boys and 17,670 girls; the Vladimir study included 38,960 boys and 12,754 girls from all but eleven schools in the province.

To learn the dimensions of repeating at the turn of the century, investigators in Iaroslavl' and Vladimir compared the grade distribution of all pupils who had repeated (Table 30) with the length of stay in the schools. Proceeding on a number of complicated assumptions, Vladimir statisticians made the following inferences: 19.3 percent of boys stayed back in the first grade; in the second grade, 11.7 percent stayed a second year, and 3.7 percent a third. In the third grade, 3.8 percent stayed a second and only 1.3 percent a third year. That is, whereas one boy of every five was held back in the first grade, only one in eight or nine fell behind in the second grade. Fewer than four percent of those who made it to the third grade were forced to repeat. By that time, 25 percent had already repeated at least one grade.[49]

The 1911 Zemstvo Survey investigated repetition in zemstvo

Table 31
Grade Repetition in Three-Year Zemstvo Schools,
1910–1911

	GRADE DISTRIBUTION OF ALL ENROLLED PUPILS	GRADE DISTRIBUTION OF ALL REPEATERS	PERCENTAGE OF PUPILS REPEATING
First grade	47%	45%	17.4%
Second grade	35	43	23.0
Third grade	18	12	11.7
Three grades combined	100	100	18.0

SOURCE: *Svodka svedenii*, sec. 1, 30–31.

NOTE: Information was received for three-year schools from 122 districts in nineteen provinces, including 5,973 schools and 70,710 repeaters.

schools in most of European Russia. Information provided by the provincial boards for three-year schools shows the concentration of repeaters compared with all enrolled pupils (Table 31). For every three-year school, which averaged sixty-six pupils, twelve (18 percent) stayed back in any given year. Of thirty-one pupils in first grade, five to six (17.4 percent) were forced to repeat the first grade; of twenty-three in the second grade, five (23 percent) stayed back; and of twelve in the third grade, one to two (11.7 percent) were held back.[50]

The information collected for the 1911 Zemstvo Survey matches that drawn together earlier in Iaroslavl' and Vladimir. Not only did the annual incidence of repeating fall within the range of one to two of every ten pupils, but the tendency was also, as it had been earlier, for the vast majority of repeaters to find themselves trapped in the first or second grade. Among graduates who had repeated one year, the third grade presented the greatest hurdle, but the second grade did not offer easy passage, either. One interesting conclusion we can draw from comparing the earlier local studies and the 1911 Zemstvo Survey is that the imposition of the Model Program in 1897 had no perceptible impact on the performance of the schools—at least not when such performance was measured in terms of successful promotion.

Was staying back a grade the first step toward dropping out? Were only the "failures" held back? A separate study of *graduates* of primary schools was conducted in Iaroslavl' in 1901. That year, among rural school graduates, fully 31 percent of boys, but only 11 percent of girls, had been forced at some time in their school career to repeat at least one year—altogether, one out of four graduates. Of every one hundred male graduates who had stayed back in zemstvo schools, fourteen had done so in the first grade, thirty-nine in the second, forty in the third. Among girls, of every one hundred delayed graduates, eighteen had repeated the first grade, forty-nine the second, and twenty-seven the third (although, overall, girls were much less likely to have stayed back). In the Church parish schools, one in seven late graduates of both sexes (13 percent of boys and 15 percent of girls) had stayed behind in the first grade, one-third in the second (31 percent of boys and 35 percent of girls), and one-half in the third (51 percent of boys and 48 percent of girls).[51]

Were these figures another sign that two distinct groups of children were passing through the schools? According to this interpretation, the large majority consisted of the 75 to 80 percent of students whose studies were confined to two grades (and often three years) and who frequently repeated the first year in order to leave the schools with rudimentary skills in reading, writing, and counting. But there was a much smaller group, composed especially of boys, whose members were determined to learn the basics of *proper* writing and spelling and who were willing to spend one or even two years cramming to pass the examinations.

Who were the repeaters, and why did they stay back? A study of school records in Dmitrov district (Moscow) in 1911 concluded that of 431 pupils who stayed behind, 45 percent did so because of poor performance; 24 percent because of basic inability; 12 percent because of illness; 8 percent for frequent absenteeism, commonly related to distance of residence from the school; 6 percent because of interruptions caused by frequent transfers of teachers or because of overcrowding (insufficient individual attention); and 5 percent because of pupil laziness. In addition, the author of this study provided a list of repeaters compiled by one woman teacher in Dmitrov district, a list that offers a fascinating glimpse into the world of the schoolchild:

Repeated first grade:

Child #1.   Ten years old. Studied poorly because of lack of ability.

Child #2.   Nine years old. Spoiled by parents; missed twenty-eight school days with no good reason, and her parents did not want to give her an extra work load to help her catch up, because they feel the school demands too much.

Child #3.   Eight years old. Suffers from anemia and chronic headaches; missed thirty-three school days.

Child #4.   Eight years old. Fell from a horse, fractured his collarbone and damaged his reproductive organs. Placed in a hospital and missed forty-nine days.

Child #5.   Nine years old. Came down with scarlet fever. Placed in a hospital and missed forty-five days.

Repeated second grade:

Child #6.   Ten years old. Poor achievement because of laziness, carelessness, and mischievousness. Parents notified but paid no attention.

Child #7.   Nine years old. Taken out of school by the doctor because other members of family had scarlet fever and had not been removed from home because there were no beds in the hospital.

Child #8.   Ten years old. Missed thirty-eight class days because he had no shoes or warm clothes.[52]

A more systematic survey of the reasons underlying the high incidence of repeating was carried out by the zemstvos for the 1911 Congress. In the questionnaire sent to all zemstvo schools, teachers with three or more years of experience were asked to list the reasons contributing to the pattern of repeating and also to give the primary reason each individual had been forced to stay back. (The sample included 13,819 answers and covered 33,434 repeaters.) The compilers then grouped the responses into three general categories: *individual* causes stemming from "underdevelopment" (intellectual inability), indifference to school work, or illness; *school conditions,* including length and scope of the program and the difficulties stemming from one teacher coping with three different sections; and *domestic conditions,* causes stemming from the local way of life, whether economic or cultural (in Russian, *byt*—a term corresponding closely to Robert Redfield's use of "style of life," which includes both values and ideas, on the one hand, and "means of subsistence," on the other).[53]

When asked what factors generally *contributed* to the incidence of repeating, 81 percent of the teachers pointed to defects in individual abilities; 68 percent also blamed *byt,* and only 25 percent blamed school conditions. When asked for the *single* most important reason individual pupils had repeated a year, teachers blamed individual causes in 63 percent of the cases, *byt* in 33 percent, and school conditions in only 5 percent (Table 32). In no province were school conditions reported as the leading factor; Kherson was the only province in which *byt* was considered most important. In the Central Industrial provinces, the proportion of cases blamed on *byt* (one in five, or 22 percent) was significantly lower than in the agricultural regions, where one in every three instances of repeating was attributed primarily to way of life.[54]

It would be futile to rely too heavily on these figures; after all, what was the dividing line between the influence of one's way of life and individual characteristics, which included physical development and illnesses? For example, under the category of individual characteristics, illness was listed as a contributing factor by only one out of every four teachers and as the primary cause of repetition in only one of nine instances (11 percent). But what were the underlying causes of the "intellectual and moral backwardness" pointed to by so many teachers? Were pupils slow of wit because they had been undernourished in infancy or even later suffered from a poor diet?[55]

Several overlapping explanations were indicated by "individual" causes. Of the 81 percent of teachers who felt that intellectual deficiencies *contributed* to the rate of repeating, slightly more than one-third blamed negligence and poor attitudes, another one-third blamed disease, and only one in twenty-eight referred to the age of the pupil as a problem. When asked to pinpoint the *major* reason each pupil stayed back, intellectual shortcomings accounted for

Table 32

Number and Percentage of Pupils Repeating a
Grade, by Primary Reason for Repetition,
1909–1910

PRIMARY REASON FOR REPETITION	NUMBER OF PUPILS REPEATING	PERCENTAGE OF ALL PUPILS REPEATING	DISTRIBUTION OF PUPILS WITHIN EACH CATEGORY OF REASONS
Individual			
Intellectual inability	13,818	41.3%	65.4%
Poor attitude	3,106	9.3	14.7
Illness	3,852	11.5	18.2
Other	350	1.1	1.7
Total	21,126	63.2%	100.0%
Byt (Way of life)			
Irregular attendance	6,998	20.9%	66.4%
Late arrival/early departure	2,482	7.4	23.5
Farm work	526	1.6	6.5
Parental indifference	404	1.2	4.3
Lack of clothing	337	1.0	3.6
School closings (epidemics)	116	0.3	1.2
Distance (poor roads)	99	0.3	1.0
Ethnic differences (poor knowledge of Russian)	161	0.5	1.7
Total	10,587[a]	33.2%	108.2%[a]
School organization	1,731	5.1%	100.0%

SOURCES: *Anketa,* 80–91, tables 24, 24A, 25, 25A, 26A, and 27.

[a] In the original table, as here, the total number of pupils repeating in this category is given as 10,587, although the total of the separate entries is 11,123. The discrepancy is explained by a number of multiple entries (instances in which more than one cause of grade repetition was listed). For the same reason, the distribution of pupils in this category totals 108.2 percent, rather than 100 percent. Similarly, in the original, the grand total of entries is listed as 33,434, but a tally based on the subtotals above comes to 33,444.

two-thirds of all twenty-one thousand instances on which information concerning individual causes was forthcoming. Teachers blamed the child's attitude in only one in eleven cases.

Only 31.7 percent of all instances of repetition were blamed mainly on *byt*, though more than two-thirds of the teachers (68.4 percent) felt that it *contributed* to the problem. Of the roughly 30 percent of students who stayed back because their way of life had placed obstacles in their path, two-thirds had been hindered by erratic attendance. But among all repeaters, only one in five instances of staying back could be traced directly to poor attendance, a statistic that lends credence to records demonstrating a remarkably high attendance rate for children in Russia's schools. Only 7.4 percent of the repeaters had been thrown off course by late fall entry or early spring departure. This figure did not mean that children overwhelmingly arrived in school on time or remained until the official closing day but rather that the rural school had successfully adapted itself to the work rhythm of the countryside. It is true that the adjustment was not perfect: according to the 1911 Zemstvo Survey, which also presented the above information separately for each individual province, the industrial provinces as a group were less afflicted by *byt*-related problems than agricultural provinces such as Voronezh, Perm', Orel, Poltava, Tambov, Kherson, and Khar'kov, which had (relatively) striking rates of late enrollment and early departure from the schools. This pattern confirms what common sense suggests: where agriculture held sway, the school year was sometimes disrupted by the harvest and planting cycle, despite the best efforts of school authorities to adjust.[56]

Two other aspects of this 1911 study bear emphasis. One is the remarkable infrequency of references to parental attitudes as the major cause of pupils' poor performance (only four hundred references in over thirty-three thousand instances, or 1.2 percent of the total). Equally striking was the low incidence of problems related to school organization. Although the periodical press was full of complaints about the overload imposed by the Model Program, by overcrowding and understaffing, teachers themselves blamed only one in twenty cases of repetition on school organization. Problems with school organization were listed in only 25 percent of teachers' reports, even as a contributing factor. By far the most common specific complaint, listed by 20 percent of teachers as contributing to pupils' poor performance, was the need to teach three sections simultaneously; far less frequent were references to the school curriculum per se—that is, to overloading the pupils with work.

Surprisingly, only 1 percent of teachers listed lack of warm clothing as the major condition affecting performance, and only 0.3 percent listed distance or poor roads. Even as a contributing factor, lack of clothing was mentioned by only 3 to 4 percent of teachers, and distance by only about 1 percent. To be sure, this picture must be tempered by recalling the pupils who simply never enrolled because schools were located too far away, those who dropped out because distance or lack of warm clothing prevented them from coming to school, and those who were kept indoors by poor health and physical disabilities. Yet the number of such students was surely dwindling. The impact of the Russian winter, distance, and poverty, although evident, has clearly been overdrawn.

SUMMARY

The studies of enrollment patterns, distribution of pupils by grade, numbers of graduating pupils, dropout levels, and repeating leave little doubt that by the standards of most educators the Russian school system was malfunctioning. There was good reason to be proud that the investment of money and energy in school construction had succeeded in increasing the enrollment level to a point at which, in the European provinces at least, universally accessible education was just over the horizon. Yet if the goal was to provide the type of education embodied in the curriculum guides and handbooks for three- and four-year schools, something was clearly amiss.

How much education—whether instruction or character molding—could be imparted when the school system seemed to be a revolving door with children completing only a small portion of an already minimal program? A system that enrolled half the school-age population at any given time and held only 5 to 10 percent of all children in school long enough to complete the program could not produce the child envisioned by educators—whether their aim was to produce a citizen who was obedient, patriotic, and religious; one who was innovative, creative, versatile, and imaginative; or a productive, disciplined, and responsible worker. The goals set forth for the school as an institution that could convert the coarse, ignorant, surly, undisciplined, and often violent peasant into a modern citizen—and a Russified one, at that—had perhaps never been feasible in the first place, and such goals were certainly not feasible for the majority of pupils in the short time allotted the Russian schoolteacher.

The combination of a high level of attrition, regular attendance by students, rapidly increasing enrollments, and pressure for expansion to meet unsatisfied demand should make us pause. Were the schools a failure? The answer depends on the definition of success and failure. Peasants and educators did not necessarily share a common definition; what educators saw as failure may have served peasant purposes well. Once enrolled, children attended school with remarkable regularity. Although most children dropped out before completing three grades, a very large number spent two and even three years in the schools. Attrition and repetition were pervasive; but was this "wastage," or did it reflect a process of adjustment to the "natural cycle" of the village? Why were peasant parents taking their children out of the school system at such an early point, and at such a consistent rate throughout the country, with little consideration for type of school, local economy, or external conditions? These questions require an investigation of opportunity costs.

12

Child Labor and the Schools

From at least the 1880s, educators had been concerned with the seemingly obvious link between poverty and low attendance rates in the village schools. Attempts were made to connect literacy and enrollment rates with landholding and land usage, with family or village occupations, and with industrial cycles. These investigations were the photographic negative of the widespread belief that literacy and schooling were connected to productivity, discipline, and innovation, whether in the factory or on the farm. Studies produced a plethora of evidence, often in depressing detail, about the impact of stark, extreme poverty on the well-being of the population, about the powerful influence of opportunity-cost considerations on school enrollment, and about the vicious cycle of poverty and ignorance. Even as the school system grew and enrollments rose, poverty continued to leave a measurable imprint on initial enrollments.

Yet only in the early twentieth century did investigators, reconsidering the question of the economy and literacy, begin to make finer distinctions among types of occupation and to look separately at the impact of the economy and family wealth on initial enrollments and dropout rates. When studies began to differentiate between employment in factories and in *kustar'* (cottage) in-

352

dustries and to differentiate among the many occupations included within these general categories, it soon became clear that the relationship between literacy and industry was highly complex and subtle, extending far beyond simplistic gradations of the complexity of skills required.[1]

Far more important, when initial failure to enroll and dropout rates were considered separately, educators made the surprising discovery that occupation, extent of landholding, and type of land usage had remarkably little impact on the latter rate. No matter how wealthy the parents and no matter what their occupation, children dropped out at roughly the same rate. The implications of these discoveries merit consideration in some detail; they are relevant to contemporary studies of the history of schooling in the West as well as to the social history of Imperial Russia.

DISCOVERY OF PROBLEMS

The first studies of the relationship between the economy and education made little distinction between initial failure to enroll and dropping out before completion. One investigation that did look specifically at the latter was the famous survey of Moscow province by V. I. Orlov. When zemstvo statisticians discovered that between 10 and 20 percent of all pupils were dropping out each year, that up to 49 percent left before completing the second year, and that between 25 and 50 percent of all those pupils who actually made it to the third year withdrew before completion, "on the eve of receiving their diplomas," the statistical board sent out a questionnaire to the schools and to other village correspondents to ascertain the reasons. Orlov examined 3,061 answers from teachers; the reasons given for students' withdrawal are summarized in Table 33.

The prominent zemstvo activist V. Iu. Skalon concluded in reviewing this study that pupils who had left to work might in fact be grouped with those who had left because of "domestic and family" circumstances (as might those who withdrew because of illness, death, or poverty—this last reason having been included in the "other" category). In his words,

Table 33
Reasons Cited by Teachers for Students'
Withdrawal from School, Moscow Province,
1882–1883

	BOYS	GIRLS	ALL STUDENTS
Family, or domestic circumstances	53.7%	67.6%	57.7%
Work in factory, shop, or on farm	16.6	3.3	12.8
Transfer[a]	6.2	5.1	5.8
Sickness or death	7.2	8.1	7.1
Other	16.5[b]	15.9	16.3[b]

SOURCE: Orlov (Moscow), *Narodnoe obrazovanie*, 119–120.
[a] Only formally equivalent to dropping out.
[b] In the original table, as here, the figures for boys total slightly more than 100 percent and the figures for all students total slightly less.

What in fact are these domestic circumstances, consisting of "work at home" and "outside," as well as "exhaustion" and "sending off to the factory," if not proof of the precarious economic situation of the family, depriving it of the opportunity of making ends meet without the aid of the ten- to twelve-year-old child's labor?[2]

Skalon's observation that poverty narrowed peasant opportunities and made schooling short-lived was undoubtedly correct. Yet employment outside the home accounted for only one in eight responses, and, together, illness and domestic circumstances constituted nearly two-thirds of the causes cited. The categories, though related, were not identical. Illness, lack of warm clothing, and inability to pay transportation, lodging, or tuition fees were tied up with the *direct costs* of schooling, with the provision of education. Employment outside the home stemmed from the *indirect,* or opportunity, costs—how much parents would sacrifice by sending their children to school (or whether they could defer income now in the expectation of returns later).

Family circumstances must be considered a third category, separate from illness or outside employment. This category often involved babysitting, tending livestock, doing chores, or helping in local cottage industry production. But "family circumstances" also involved parents' assertion of their own role in socializing their children—parents taking children out of school to teach them production tasks within the family division of labor and to ensure their integration into the family hierarchy of authority. In many cases, there was actually a surplus of laborpower, with idle adults at hand who could have done the same work. In such instances, applying a strict cost-benefit analysis would be projecting a narrowly economic mode of thought onto a household production and consumption unit in which profit maximization was often subordinate to security, and monetary gain (whether immediate or deferred) secondary to the integrity of the family. Even more striking, in such studies, "ignorance" was also explained by and classified under "poverty," or the economic costs of schooling. Thus, parental attitudes, opportunity costs, family strategies, and severe poverty—the indirect and direct costs of education—were all lumped together under the general concept of "poverty."

Orlov's study confirmed the obvious fact that poverty, compounded by poor health, disrupted family life to the point that school enrollment was affected, but it left many questions unanswered. Why was the withdrawal rate entirely unaffected by the diverse occupational structures of the districts in Moscow province? It seemed to matter little whether an area was dominated by agriculture, cottage industry, or factories. Why was the dropout rate so high in the third year? Surely, if parents could have deferred earnings until the middle of the third grade, they could have waited a few more months, assuming that a graduation certificate had some impact on prestige, social mobility, or economic opportunity. Why did work in factories, shops, or the fields (which, apparently, meant hiring out to work for other families) account for only 12 percent of all dropouts?

During the 1890s, studies in several other provinces confirmed that economic conditions prevented a segment of the population from taking advantage of the existing schools. These studies established a direct correlation between size of family landholdings and initial school enrollment *or* literacy. In a highly influential study of

Kherson province, N. Borisov presented data showing that as family landholdings increased, so did the percentage of households with literate members; in the category of families who owned more than twenty desiatinas of land, the incidence of literacy was nearly 90 percent. (Such studies ordinarily counted the number of families with at least one literate *or* enrolled person.) Peasant households without livestock (43.3 percent of all households in the region) accounted for only 18.3 percent of enrolled students. Families with livestock (56.7 percent) were responsible for 81.7 percent of the students. Borisov concluded that "the rural school serves primarily the interests of the middle and rich strata of the peasant world, while the poor make only extremely limited use of its services."[3]

In Moscow province in 1893, I. P. Bogolepov, a renowned educator, statistician, and zemstvo employee, as well as a co-author of the Orlov study, carried out a survey of eight hundred villages in the districts of Mozhaisk and Moscow, with the help of a team of trained field workers. These districts were as different as night and day in terms of population density, communications networks, local employment, and—perhaps most interesting—amount of money per capita spent by the local zemstvos on primary education. Bogolepov, after a detailed study of enrollment figures in the two districts, arrived at a number of conclusions. He found that the absence of schools within a reasonable distance from peasant homes was an important factor in Mozhaisk, but only secondarily so in Moscow. In neither district were "family attitudes" an obstacle to primary education for boys, but in both districts there was significant reluctance to send girls to school.[4]

Bogolepov conclusively demonstrated the combined impact of economic conditions and distance from school. Specifically, he showed that it was infeasible for most families to send their children to school more than three versts from their homes; even prosperous families were hard-pressed to pay for the room and board required in such cases. Again, girls were the first to suffer when parents had to decide whether or not to spend between 60 and 100 kopecks (1 ruble) each month, but for poor families there was no question of spending even this modest sum on children of either sex. Most important, as in 1883, the primary cause of the school network's failure to reach the entire school-age population was economic circumstances. The need for a "helping hand" at home affected girls more severely than boys.[5] Most striking was Bogolepov's observation that, despite the marked economic and demographic differences between Mozhaisk and Moscow districts, the two school systems had many negative features in common:

The most common and overriding cause for nonattendance is one and the same for the relatively fortunate Moscow district and the completely destitute Mozhaisk district. . . . There can be no doubt that the prevalent cause of illiteracy among children of school age is to be found in economic conditions—poverty in all its aspects.[6]

Bogolepov graphically depicted his conclusions in a table, which drew considerable attention at the time and which continues to be used by historians today to illustrate the deleterious effects of poverty on the Russian countryside (Table 34).

Zemstvo studies typically showed that distance from the nearest school exacerbated economic obstacles to enrollment. Thus, when villages were dominated by industries whose workers had low literacy rates, school attendance dipped even lower when schools were situated any distance from the villages. In the same way, when families owning little land and few livestock (conditions commonly accompanying low literacy rates) lived any distance from schools, literacy and enrollment levels plunged still lower. Because poorer families could not afford the clothing or overnight lodgings necessary for their children to attend school in the winter, it seemed to follow that as the school network spread, the retarding impact of distance from school would be reduced, in turn lessening the baneful influence of poverty on school attendance. A careful study of selected areas in Moscow province in 1906 even suggested that distance was the determining variable: as the school network spread and distance from school was reduced, the level of participation increased, regardless of size of landholding, land usage, or family employment.[7]

Yet two important studies conducted after the Bogolepov survey provided a rude jolt to those who hoped that simply reducing distance would solve the problem of nonenrollment. In Vladimir, the zemstvo board sent its correspondents a brief questionnaire asking, first, if all children in the village were enrolled and, second, that reasons be given for any nonenrollment. Four hundred thirty-

Table 34

Obstacles to School Attendance, 1893

	MOSCOW DISTRICT			MOZHAISK DISTRICT			BOTH DISTRICTS		
	Boys	Girls	All Children	Boys	Girls	All Children	Boys	Girls	All Children
External conditions (primarily distance from schools or lack of schools)	8.5%	8.6%	8.6%	21.5%	16.8%	18.0%	14.0%	11.8%	12.4%
School conditions (mainly overcrowding)	13.5	2.7	5.2	4.4	0.9	1.8	9.6	2.0	3.9
Popular attitudes (unwillingness on the part of parents or children)	2.9	13.7	11.3	2.7	18.2	14.3	2.8	0.5	12.2
Illness	32.5	10.0	14.9	20.7	5.1	9.1	27.5	7.9	12.6
Economic	27.3	38.0	35.6	41.9	33.8	35.9	33.5	36.5	35.7
Family (need for extra hands or babysitters at home)	7.9	22.5	19.3	5.9	23.5	18.9	7.1	22.9	19.1
Other	7.4	4.5	5.1	2.9	1.7	2.0	5.5	3.4	3.9

SOURCE: Bogolepov (Moscow), *Gramotnost' sredi detei*, 102, 110–112.

NOTE: This information is based on responses provided by parents and relatives directly to census workers. The total number of children not in school was 8,011; information was available for 71.7 percent of this number.

seven correspondents answered the second question. Of this number, 23 percent blamed distance; 18 percent cited poverty; 8 percent, lack of warm clothing or footwear; 15 percent, work at home; 15 percent, parental attitudes; 7 percent, dissatisfaction with the school (largely because of teacher turnover); and 11 percent blamed overcrowding. This study showed that even with the school network largely in place, distance was cited by more than one in four correspondents (more than one in four because reluctance to send girls to school was prominent in the category of parental attitudes; correspondents felt that parents believed girls were more "sensitive" to the elements and should not be exposed to long winter travel). But it was also clear from the survey that the economy, and poverty in general, continued to take a large toll on enrollment.[8]

A major survey of Nizhegorod district in 1910 produced even more disturbing results. Nizhegorod (in Nizhnii Novgorod province) had been one of the first districts in the country to develop a plan for universal education; by 1908, virtually the entire school network was in place. Yet in 1910, of the 15,190 school-age children in the district, only 11,120 were enrolled in elementary schools of all types. This figure seemed to mean that after completion of a school network making education universally accessible, 26.8 percent of all school-age children remained outside the doors of the school (13.6 percent of boys and 46 percent of girls).[9]

A close study of responses from parents and village elders in the 260 villages of the district led to the conclusion that once again the economy was to blame for failure to enroll; it seemed to be responsible for 53 percent of all nonenrollment. Poverty and need were directly cited in roughly 10 percent of these cases, and lack of shoes or warm clothing in another 9 percent. "Children run about virtually without outer clothing, so they are forced to [stay at home and] sew nets, which doesn't demand shoes or clothing," wrote one peasant. In the village of Kusakov, "there are seven children in one family with three sets of warm clothing and two pairs of warm boots, so they can't study." One village elder quipped that "whoever has the means, has the education" ("*kotorye sostoiatel'nye krest'iane, to i vse uchenye*"). (Interestingly, a number of correspondents noted that warmth was not the only issue; school attendance required more "respectable" [*poriadlivye*] dresses than girls ordinarily wore.) Babysitting—children staying at home to care

for younger children—accounted for another 8.3 percent of failures to enroll, and employment in local cottage industries (especially basket weaving) and "absence from the village" (ordinarily
to work elsewhere) took clusters of children out of school in various villages. "Parental ignorance" was blamed in 14 percent of all
cases (the vast majority of these regarding daughters); indifference
on the part of children was cited in 5 percent of the instances; disease in 4 percent. Distance was cited in 10 percent of the cases,
overcrowding in 4 percent, and dissatisfaction with existing
schools in only 1.3 percent.[10]

It seemed undeniable that opportunity-cost considerations,
and even direct poverty so extreme that warm clothing was beyond
the family's means, continued to prevent the enrollment of just
under one in four children, once schooling was universally accessible. Both the Vladimir and Nizhegorod studies offered harsh testimony that girls between the ages of five and ten were sometimes
kept home to work as many as twelve to sixteen hours a day, particularly when the mother took in laundry or worked at spooling.[11]

This problem existed on a large scale and reflected a level
of misery and suffering often eloquently described by doctors,
agronomists, and teachers working in the countryside. Curiously,
it led a number of prominent educators to once again reverse the
old saw about poverty and ignorance. In the 1870s and 1880s, universal education had been regarded as a pipe dream because Russia
was seen as too poor to afford schools; but, as the British school
inspector Darlington later noted, this sentiment changed, and in
the 1890s the educated public began to feel that *because* Russia was
poor, she had to have schools—as many and as soon as possible
(see Chapters 3 and 4). A decade later, Pavel Vikhliaev concluded
his study of the impact of the economy on education in Moscow
province with the comment that poverty might well prevent the
spread of schooling:

It would be fallacious to claim that instruction will be universally accessible when all links of the three-verst school network have been completed. Even under these conditions, it will be possible to say only that
relative universal accessibility of primary education has been attained in
those regions within reach of advanced urban industries, and then only
for boys and not for girls. . . . Legislation introducing compulsory edu-

cation, if introduced in Russia, and specifically in Moscow province (which occupies a leading position among the other provinces), would meet the most resistance not so much in the realm of mores (such as family authority) as in the economic conditions of life under which the bulk of the rural population lives. Even if enough schools were opened to accommodate all children of school age, universal education would not be achieved.[12]

Similarly, Chekhov, in a handbook on education compiled in 1914, admitted that all measures designed to reduce the impact of poverty, including hot dinners at schools and free lodgings, were but "palliatives." Arguing that a "good half" of all girls not enrolled in the schools were taking care of younger siblings while the parents worked and that a large proportion of child labor took place in cottage industries, Chekhov noted that neither of these forms of work was amenable to government restriction or legislation. He concluded that "without an improvement in economic conditions, universal education cannot be achieved."[13]

A SECOND LOOK

Thus, a battery of studies conducted by a number of sophisticated observers all pointed in one direction—to the negative impact of economic conditions on schooling. Bogolepov's study of the influence of poverty on enrollments had a major national impact. His specific recommendations were directly incorporated into the Moscow universal education plan in 1896, which in turn helped shape the 1908 School Bill. His data on the reasons for nonenrollment were reproduced again and again for the next two decades in studies of rural education and, with the publicity of the national literacy campaign, reached well beyond a specialized audience to the general educated public.

Yet the Bogolepov data have frequently been misunderstood. A careless reader could conclude from this study that half of all children were excluded from the school system by poverty or illness. In fact, as we have seen in an earlier chapter, as early as 1891–1892 in Moscow district only about 10 percent of boys and 50 to 60 percent of girls between the ages of eleven and fourteen had no schooling. Thus, at most 5 percent of boys and 25 to 30 percent of all girls had been barred from schooling by poverty. Moreover, as the school system expanded, the enrollment rate (as a percentage of eligible children) steadily increased, indicating not only that the impact of the economy on initial enrollments was declining but also that its significance may have been exaggerated from the beginning. At the very least, a distinction should be made between direct and indirect costs; the expanded provision of schooling might have reduced the direct costs (travel, clothing, overnight lodging, fees for tutors when no places were available in the public schools) by bringing schools closer, but it could not have altered the opportunity costs of schooling (except where, by bringing a school closer to home, a child could attend *and* help at home).

We must underscore that the Bogolepov study did *not* proclaim that because of poverty half of all children remained outside the schools, nor did the author present evidence about the reasons for withdrawal from school—his concern was for those who had never enrolled. Finally, whatever parents were telling the surveyors, and whatever the surveyors were writing down, we know that the provision of schooling and the level of enrollment were directly related. As schools became available, the size of the unschooled population dropped, and continued to drop. In 1911, there were no empty places in the schools; in fact, nearly one million children had applied for but been denied admission. These facts must be kept in mind when evaluating the relationship between the size of the village labor force and the demand for child labor, as well as the relationship between work at home, the division of labor, and the hierarchy of family authority.

Let us reconsider the Vladimir study. The same failure to distinguish between extreme and representative examples we earlier observed in comments on daily attendance levels can be seen here. The Vladimir zemstvo correspondents were asked two questions; in response to the first (whether *all* children attended school), 49 percent replied affirmatively, and another 8 percent replied that all boys, but not girls, attended. Moreover, the specific responses to the second question on the reasons for nonattendance reflected only the number of respondents listing that reason, not the number of children who actually remained outside the school throughout childhood.[14]

In contrast, the Nizhegorod study sought, through the school network and village elders, to learn just how many children remained untouched by schooling and why; yet it, too, made a major miscalculation. The slip was the same made by Bogolepov (or his readers): the study considered only those *currently* enrolled as belonging to the schooled population. To begin with, 490 children among the 4,188 "unenrolled" were twelve years old; thus, 11.7 percent of all "unenrolled" were not even nominally of school age. Moreover, from the comments of parents and village elders, it is obvious that many respondents understood nonenrollment to mean "not currently enrolled." Under the section on parental attitudes, we frequently encounter the comment, "He [or she] went a year or so, and that's that!" (*"pokhodil[a] godok i ladno"*). One teacher commented, "Many parents, having sent their children to school for a year-and-a-half or two, then leave them at home." (The same imprecision marked the Vladimir study as well.)[15] Thus, if the number of children currently enrolled was much lower than the number of children who had *ever* attended school, it must follow that far fewer than one in four of the children in Nizhegorod remained outside the school doors throughout childhood— even though they were not in school at the time the survey was conducted.

These observations are noteworthy, because the Nizhegorod study was conducted *after* the school campaign was launched (and well after the Bogolepov study), allowing us to test the results of that campaign. But if it were only for this, the study would deserve a mere footnote elsewhere in this volume. Perhaps the most interesting aspect of the Nizhegorod study was how it magnified the impact of the economy on school enrollments beyond its true dimensions. This overstatement is most graphically illustrated by comparing the Nizhegorod data as originally presented in the journal *Russian School* with a tabulation of the percentage of the entire school-age population affected by each contributing factor (even assuming that all nonenrolled children were also unschooled, which we know is not true), as shown in Table 35.

Of all school-age children in Nizhegorod, slightly more than one in four were not enrolled at the time of the survey. Of this contingent, approximately half were not in school because the economy in some way interfered with attendance; in short, about one in

Table 35
Reasons for Nonenrollment,
Nizhegorod District, 1909

	NUMBER OF CHILDREN AFFECTED[a]	PERCENTAGE OF ALL SCHOOL-AGE CHILDREN AFFECTED
Economic conditions	2,205	12.9%
Poverty	447	2.9
Lack of warm clothing	380	2.5
Babysitting responsibilities	346	2.3
Domestic work	211	1.4
Basket weaving	617	4.1
Absent from village	67	0.4
Parental attitudes	574	3.8
Children's attitudes	207	1.4
Distance	436	2.9

SOURCE: Iordanskii, "Teoriia i deistvitel'nost'," 86.

[a] The total number of school-age children included in this survey was 15,190; 4,071 were affected by these reasons for nonenrollment. This column adds up to 5,490, however, because of multiple entries.

every eight children found the economy an obstacle to enrollment. But, as we have been studying nonenrolled rather than unschooled children, we can say with relative certainty only that one in eight children found the economy an obstruction to enrollment *or* continued attendance.

Consider, too, the lack of warm clothing. Although almost one in ten who did not attend school were prevented from doing so because they could not dress properly for the winter weather, in Nizhegorod district this figure meant that 380 of 15,190 children, or 2.5 percent of *all school-age children,* were too poor to dress for the Russian winter. Certainly this was a painful problem—indeed, one calling for immediate measures—yet the question of *dimension,* of scale, is most relevant here—and at most, one in thirty to one in forty children found lack of warm clothing an obstacle. (Compare the data on repeating, Chapter 11, Table 32.)

A study supervised by Vikhliaev, a statistician and economist responsible for the massive 1898–1900 household survey of Moscow province, systematically addressed the relationship between family wealth or occupation and *length of stay* in school. Vikhliaev compared local school statistics with employment and landholding patterns at the village and household levels, hoping to clarify the impact of the economy on duration of stay in the schools.[16]

The results were disappointing, yet very significant. The message of page after page of tables measuring the relationship between individual occupations, size and usage of landholdings, and broad categories of labor was that, in most cases, no link could be found. Dropouts came from all strata of the village in roughly equal numbers, meaning either that *everyone* in the village was too poor to defer an adolescent's meager income for three years (patently untrue) or that factors other than economic ones were at work.

Consider Tables 36 and 37, which illustrate the relationship— or lack of one—between industry and landholding, on the one hand, and *length of stay* (rather than initial enrollment) in school, on the other. (Note, however, the qualifications expressed in Chapter 11 about using grade distribution as a proxy for length of stay.)

It is striking how little difference can be observed in the amount of time different strata of the peasantry spent in the schools. It mattered little how much land a family owned, to what use the land was put (other tables demonstrated the irrelevance of land usage for determining literacy levels), or what percentage of the villagers were primarily engaged in local industry—the type of work that had the most detrimental effect on initial enrollment patterns. If a boy's family owned the smallest measure of land (fewer than seven desiatinas), his chances, once enrolled, of reaching the third grade were about one in two (44.7 percent), not much different from those of a boy from the most prosperous family (landholdings of more than ten desiatinas), who had a 48.4 percent chance.

A slight difference in length of stay could be perceived among girls in relation to the size of the family landholdings. Still, this difference meant only that a girl from the poorest family, once en-

Table 36
Grade Distribution of Students, by Size of Family
Landholdings, Moscow Province, 1900

SIZE OF FAMILY LANDHOLDING	FIRST GRADE	SECOND GRADE	THIRD GRADE
	Boys		
Less than 7 desiatinas	44.5%	35.6%	19.9%
7–10 desiatinas	43.4	36.7	19.9
More than 10 desiatinas	42.7	36.6	20.7
Grade distribution for all boys enrolled	43.6	36.3	20.1
	Girls		
Less than 7 desiatinas	52.6%	34.7%	12.7%
7–10 desiatinas	50.8	36.0	13.2
More than 10 desiatinas	49.4	35.9	14.7
Grade distribution for all girls enrolled	51.0	35.5	13.5

SOURCE: Vikhliaev (Moscow), *Ekonomicheskie usloviia*, 57.
NOTE: This study included 57,283 students (36,179 boys and 21,104 girls).

rolled, had about one chance in four (24.1 percent) to reach third
grade, whereas a girl from the wealthiest family had almost three
chances in ten (29.8 percent). It can be argued that the wealthier
girl's greater chances reflected a slight disparity traceable to economic conditions. (But whether relatively wealthy or poor, school-
age girls had less than one chance in seven or eight of enrolling and
reaching—not completing—the third grade. Although economic
status and family occupation generally had little impact on length
of stay, there was a clear and constant pattern of attrition for girls
as a group. At the same time as the overall proportion of girls in the
school system was steadily increasing, girls were the first to drop
out.) Yet the overriding pattern, common to both sexes and super-

seding measurable economic differences, was one of students dropping out before the third grade.

Moreover, reducing the *distance* from home to school made little difference in the distribution pattern. This finding is particularly intriguing, because study after study had shown a direct and strong relationship between *initial* enrollment levels and distance from school. Put simply, the closer a school, the greater the chance

Table 37

Grade Distribution of Students, by Village
Industrial Employment, Moscow Province, 1900

ADULT VILLAGERS EMPLOYED IN LOCAL INDUSTRY	FIRST GRADE	SECOND GRADE	THIRD GRADE
	Boys		
Males			
Less than 5 percent	42.3%	36.8%	20.9%
5–10 percent	43.5	36.7	19.3
10–30 percent	44.0	35.8	20.2
More than 30 percent	46.4	35.2	18.4
Grade distribution for all boys enrolled	43.6	36.3	20.1
	Girls		
Females			
Less than 10 percent	50.2%	36.0%	13.8%
10–30 percent	50.9	35.1	13.7
More than 30 percent	54.3	34.2	11.5
Grade distribution for all girls enrolled	51.0	35.5	13.5

SOURCE: Vikhliaev (Moscow), *Ekonomicheskie usloviia*, 59–61.

NOTE: This survey included 57,283 students (36,179 boys and 21,104 girls). Vikhliaev also produced tables showing the effect of female adult employment on enrollment patterns of boys and the effect of male adult employment on enrollment patterns of girls, with similar results.

Table 38
Percentage of Students Enrolled in Third Grade, by Size
of Family Landholdings and Distance from School,
Moscow, 1900

SIZE OF FAMILY LANDHOLDING	HOME LESS THAN ONE VERST FROM SCHOOL	HOME ONE TO THREE VERSTS FROM SCHOOL	HOME THREE OR MORE VERSTS FROM SCHOOL
	Boys		
Less than 7 desiatinas	20.1%	18.9%	19.9%
7–10 desiatinas	19.9	19.2	19.9
More than 10 desiatinas	22.1	20.2	20.7
All boys	20.6	19.4	20.1
	Girls		
Less than 7 desiatinas	13.0%	12.1%	12.2%
7–10 desiatinas	14.9	11.1	13.7
More than 10 desiatinas	16.1	14.0	14.7
All girls	14.6	12.2	13.5

SOURCE: Vikhliaev (Moscow), *Ekonomicheskie usloviia*, 56.
NOTE: This study included 7,274 boys and 2,839 girls in the third grade.

a child would attend. When combined with poverty (measured by landholding), distance from school seemed to be a powerful disincentive to attend. No such pattern could be discerned when it came to *length* of stay, however. (See Table 38.)

All things being equal, the percentage of students who reached the third grade depended only very slightly on the distance of home from school. Only when the family's landholdings were largest and when the school was in the same village was there a measurable difference, but even in these extreme cases the slight differences in length of stay were overwhelmed by the pattern of steady attrition from first through third grade.

Vikhliaev also discovered that level of parental industrial engagement had little impact on the distribution pattern. Even when broad categories of occupations were disaggregated, the pattern varied only slightly. For example, the smallest percentage of boys (16 percent of enrolled male students) were in the third grade in villages where either cobbling and leather work or silk weaving at home was the dominant industry; the highest percentage of boys in third grade (23.6 percent) was found where the male population worked in ceramic and machine-building factories. For girls in villages where silk weaving at home was the primary occupation, the percentage of female students in the third grade sank to 8 percent (although in the first two grades the figures were virtually identical to those for other occupations). The other industries cited all had female third-grade enrollments within a narrow range of 12 to 14 percent.[17]

After considering each of the major professions in Moscow province individually, Vikhliaev noted:

Looking over the individual industrial occupations, nowhere is it possible to find a distribution of pupils by grade that might be considered normal. Among all our categories of [parental] occupation, the junior section [of the school] is two to three times more populous than the senior, which is an irrefutable indication of the brevity of stay in the school. In addition, with the exception of the extremes such as cottage weaving, on the one hand, and workers in the machine-building factories, on the other, no major difference in [children's grade] distribution can be observed among the various occupations. *The distribution of pupils by section is of a much more constant magnitude, changing little over time or space, little affected by distance of school from village, and much more weakly reflecting differences in economic circumstances, than is the case with general attendance patterns* [emphasis added].[18]

It followed, though Vikhliaev did not emphasize the point nor did contemporary readers of his dense volume focus on the observation, that "it is far easier to make education universally accessible, or even to increase the relative proportion of girls in the student body, than to lengthen the stay of children in the school system."[19]

A question on the 1911 Zemstvo Survey sent to twenty-three thousand teachers seemed to demonstrate conclusively that opportunity costs did cut a wide swath into schooling (measured in length of stay). But a closer look at the responses will demonstrate the porousness of the boundary between "the economy" and "parental attitudes." The question asked teachers to indicate the causes of early departure from the schools: economic reasons, dissatisfaction with school curriculum or organization, staying back, insufficient awareness on the part of parents or children of the importance of education, and so forth.[20]

Of the 14,426 teachers who replied, 10,352 (slightly less than 72 percent) blamed "economic reasons." (Only in Ufa and Kazan' did fewer than 60 percent cite economic reasons.) There was little difference between the agricultural and industrial provinces in frequency of references to economic causes. However, 10,094 (nearly 70 percent of all teachers) also blamed "family conditions," and virtually all who did (9,983, or almost 99 percent) specifically complained of a lack of "parental awareness." In all thirty-four provinces (except St. Petersburg), between 60 and 80 percent of teachers felt that parental indifference to a complete education was a major cause of the high dropout rate.[21]

Thus, seven out of ten teachers blamed the economy, and seven out of ten blamed parental attitudes. I believe that this study hit upon an essential aspect of peasant mentality often ignored by those who believed the school system was malfunctioning because it was not acting according to (elite) design and who blamed poverty for this malfunctioning. Peasants often *were* desperately poor and certainly could have used their children at home; on occasion, children's help was even necessary. But "work at home," which accounted for more than two-thirds of all references to "economic causes," also fulfilled a socializing (that is, educative) function that parents were not willing to relinquish to the schools. Such work reinforced the patriarchal authority of the head of the household, it introduced children into the family division of labor, and it also placed them into the family hierarchy of authority.

DIMENSIONS OF CHILD LABOR

Studies of initial enrollment levels, attendance patterns, and the dropout rate reveal, on careful consideration, that the connection between length of stay and frequency of attendance on the one hand, and economic circumstances, on the other, was surprisingly weak. One could infer, however, that virtually no children completed the full three-year program because everyone in the countryside was so poor that the small observable differentials in wealth and income made no difference—that the opportunity cost of a full elementary education was simply too great even for those peasant families who were slightly less miserable than their fellow villagers.

This volume is not the place either to enter the fray concerning the scale of economic differentiation in village society or to discuss the absolute degree of impoverishment of the Russian countryside. These issues trace their origins to the debates between populists and Marxists and between industrial and agricultural interests in the last quarter of the nineteenth century, and they continue to provoke a lively discussion. We should, however, pause briefly to look at the absolute level of child employment, both on farms and in factories. It can easily be shown, at least for Moscow province, that *employment in factory and cottage industries for the overwhelming majority of children of both sexes began well after the standard age for completing elementary education; the same was true for work involving heavy agricultural chores.* The only time opportunity costs might have been a major consideration was when both parents worked outside the home, and the functioning of the household economy required an older child to babysit for younger siblings.

Studies of other countries have shown that parents often conspired with factory management to circumvent child labor laws, and it is possible to find similar reports in Russia. Nevertheless, the most authoritative study of literacy, wages, and the industrial work force conducted in Russia before the 1917 Revolution concluded that the factory presented no obstacle to primary education for the overwhelming majority of school-age children. The study, compiled by the factory inspector I. M. Koz'minykh-Lanin and based on cards collected from more than sixty thousand factory workers in Moscow province, showed that by 1908 the most common age of entry into the factory was between fifteen and seventeen years for both boys and girls. Data collected for boys only indicated that, at an earlier date, the factories had indeed drawn some children out of school, but that since 1900 this had only seldom been the case.[22]

Table 39 demonstrates that after 1888 only about 3 percent of entering factory workers were twelve years old or younger and

Table 39
Age at Entry into Factory Work Force,
Moscow Province, 1908

			AGE				
ENTRY DATE	*6–8*	*8–10*	*10–12*	*12–15*	*15–17*	*Over 17*	N
1898–1908	0%	0%	0.5%	18.4%	48.0%	33.1%	41,415
1888–1898	0	0.5	2.6	28.6	34.7	33.5	14,579
1878–1888	0	5.1	14.0	36.6	18.3	25.7	8,483
1868–1878	0.7	15.5	18.4	38.7	13.0	13.8	3,940
Before 1868	2.1	30.8	20.5	31.2	9.3	6.1	951

SOURCE: Compiled from Koz'minykh-Lanin (Moscow), *Gramotnost' i zarabotki*, ix–x.
NOTE: Total N for this survey was 69,368 and included both male and female workers. The numbers are rounded to the nearest one tenth of one percent.

that between two-thirds and four-fifths of the workers had remained free until the age of fifteen. Not only were children free of factory employment long enough to complete their primary education, but they sometimes also had another two or three idle years beyond that. We have to return to the 1880s before finding any real conflict between school and factory, and even then only one in five entering workers was age twelve or younger.[23]

The data studied by Koz'minykh-Lanin came only from those manufacturing units under the supervision of the factory inspectorate; the cottage workshop was not included. Is there any way to determine directly how many children were engaged in cottage industries? We can look at the composition of the work force in these industries to see what percentage of these workers were school-age children.

The 1898–1900 household census of Moscow province shed light on this question. In three districts studied, children were a significant part of the work force in only a very few occupations in both factory and cottage industries.[24] A glance at Table 40 shows that a few crafts (or stages in the production process) heavily employed child labor. The most prominent among these were spooling, threading, and cigarette rolling, as well as domestic service (for girls). These percentages, of course, assume significance for school enrollments only if the absolute size of the work force engaged in these occupations comprised a significant number of workers. In fact, only 30,000 out of a total work force of 526,000 in Moscow province were spoolers and threaders. Another 17,900 were employed as cigarette rollers, 13,000 worked as embroiderers, and there were almost 29,000 domestics. Thus, as many as 10,000 children in Moscow province may have been prevented from remaining in school because of alternative employment as spoolers or threaders, and another few thousand may have left to work as cigarette rollers or domestics.[25] In a school-age population of 219,240,[26] perhaps 5 to 7 percent of the children found school in conflict with gainful employment outside the home.

Two qualifications should be considered, however. First, the two largest employers of child labor—spooling and cigarette rolling—were in rapid decline after 1896 in the face of mechanization. Second, many children categorized as being "under thirteen" were, of course, twelve years old and with any luck could have finished three years of schooling by the time employment was available. However we approach the data, the number of children employed in the economy, though measurable, can account for only a fraction of the school dropout rate. It is particularly intriguing that employment in spooling and cigarette rolling declined precipitously after 1895, for my own study of Moscow school records shows little change in the grade distribution pattern in the subsequent fifteen years.[27]

Whereas the 1898 household survey looked in detail at two districts heavily engaged in the textile industry, another survey conducted a decade later investigated three western districts dominated by flax cultivation, the farming of root crops, and migratory work. This study defined more precisely the age cohort in question in order to analyze what percentage of all peasant children were employed in some form of industry or trade (*promysl*).[28]

As Table 41 presents, only an inconsequential percentage of children under the age of twelve might have found employment. At the ages of twelve and thirteen, 14.3 percent of boys and 6.7 percent of girls were working in 1910. The differences between the western districts and the textile-dominated districts of Bronitsy and Moscow in the eastern half of the province are intriguing; they

Table 40

Employed Children Under the Age of Thirteen as a
Percentage of the Work Force in Each Occupation,
Moscow Province, 1898–1900

	BRONITSY DISTRICT	MOSCOW DISTRICT	VOLOKOLAMSK DISTRICT
		Boys	
Spooling	31.0%	—	30.0%
Threading (*razmotka nitei*)	25.0	14.5%	33.5
Cigarette rolling	12.0	19.0	—
Cobbling	6.0	—	2.0
Silver working	3.0	—	—
Hat making	2.0	—	—
Box making	—	7.0	—
Carpentry	—	2.0	—
Catering (*polovye*)	—	3.0	—
Percentage of total work force under age thirteen	1.8	1.1	1.2
		Girls	
Spooling	30.0%	—	24.0%
Threading	11.5	6.0%	18.0
Cigarette rolling	12.0	8.0	—
Weaving	3.0	1.0	2.0
Embroidering	—	6.0	—
Basket making	3.0	—	—
Domestic service	—	10.0	3.5
Percentage of total work force under age thirteen	7.2	5.1	4.2

SOURCE: Kablukov (Moscow), *Moskovskaia guberniia po mestnomu obsledovaniiu* 4:641–643.

Table 41

Employed Children as a Percentage of Total Age
Groups, Ruzs, Mozhaisk, and Volokolamsk
Districts, 1898 and 1910

	1898	1910
	Boys	
Younger than 11 years old	0.2%	0.2%
11 years old	3.5	4.0
12–13 years old	12.1	14.3
14–15 years old	48.8	50.9
16–17 years old	77.5	78.3
(Employed adults, 18–45)	(85.2)	(82.0)
	Girls	
Younger than 11 years old	0.3%	0.1%
11 years old	2.8	2.9
12–13 years old	5.6	6.7
14–15 years old	10.1	13.8
16–17 years old	16.4	21.6
(Employed adults, 18–45)	(13.1)	(13.6)

SOURCE: P. A. Vikhliaev, *Vliianie travoseianiia na otdel'nye storony krest'ianskogo khoziaistva* (Moscow, 1915), 9:10–17.

NOTE: This study was based on information collected from 27,179 males and 30,224 females in 1898, and 29,336 males and 32,711 females in 1910.

are partly explained by the prominent place of migratory labor in the former. Parents were understandably unwilling to let children leave the village for employment, and when they did, they let boys go first.

Yet these differences should not obscure the basic fact that in both eastern and western districts employment outside the home or in local cottage industries only rarely penetrated the basic school-age contingent. Undeniably, there was an overlap between school and child employment in specific localities such as Bronitsy district. But this overlap (as I will argue below) was a local, restricted phenomenon.

WORK ON THE FARM

Thus far, we have ignored what many would consider the chief culprit in the conflict between school and the economy—work on the farm. The conflict between agriculture and schooling has been observed by such leading authorities on the economics of education as E. G. West and Theodore Schultz. In a famous article on schooling in the West, Lawrence Stone points to widespread child employment in the countryside, with boys leaving school at about age ten, and girls at about ages fourteen to fifteen. M. J. Maynes, in an excellent article on schooling in the Midi, notes that between 1800 and 1850 the usual age of entry into the agricultural labor force was around ten to twelve years old, at which point parents permanently withdrew their children from school. Horn notes that in England the Agricultural Child Labor Act of 1873 was in fact a dead letter and that child farm labor remained widespread.[29] In Russia, the famous Kushner study of the village of Viriatino (Tambov province) observed:

Youngsters from earliest childhood were accustomed to the work of the peasant. Little girls were taught how to spin. From the age of seven or eight, the boys began to work along with their fathers, going out to the fields with them, fetching water or wood. By the age of eight or nine, the boys were sent out to tend the cattle, and by a boy's thirteenth year he would help his father in all his chores.[30]

A few historians, however, have questioned the dimensions of this conflict. Tyack points out that schools in many farm areas adjusted to the harvest schedule and that opportunity costs of schooling were minimal. Recent work by Karl Kaestle and Maris Vinovskis shows a "strong rural bias toward school going" and underscores the compatibility of schooling and agricultural labor.[31] Kaestle and Vinovskis argue that mass schooling preceded not only government intervention but also industrialization and urbanization in the United States, actually emerging first in *farming* communities. It was only *after* elementary education, they argue, "from the age of thirteen, that youth began experiencing choices, sometimes forced choices, between work and school."[32] The crèche function of schooling should not be overlooked: schools sometimes served as babysitters while parents labored in the fields. The demands of the farm and the school schedule undoubtedly overlapped, but the episodic nature of farm work allowed the school schedule to be adjusted—after all, such adjustment was the original function of school vacations. A conceptual imprecision in defining the boundaries between childhood and adolescence has led many historians to grossly overstate the conflict.

Consider data gathered by the Soviet historian A. G. Rashin to demonstrate a high incidence of child labor in agriculture—data that prove exactly the opposite, at least if we confine our notion of childhood to the school-age contingent (boys and girls less than twelve or thirteen years old). Rashin cites a number of sources. The first, a zemstvo doctor named Kudriavtsev, described agricultural laborers in the south: "The overwhelming majority of migrants are unmarried young men [*parubki*] and women. They make up 69.4 percent of farm workers. . . . These are young people from fifteen to twenty-two years old."[33]

One Dobrotovskii, writing about peasants hiring out to other peasant farms (*batraki*), noted:

The main contingent of *batraki* are adolescents (seventeen to eighteen years old) and children (twelve to thirteen). . . . The former help wherever needed—in the threshing, mowing, plowing, and so forth. The latter specifically tend the flocks; in the summer, they follow the horses to overnight pasture; in the winter, they carry hay to the barns for the stock, carry water, or join the owner in sawing or chopping wood. Of course, children are hired only when the household has none of its own. . . . Of all the *batraki* working on peasant farms, scarcely one-fifth to one-fourth are adults . . . the remainder are adolescents and children.[34]

These passages are revealing, suggesting that for the most part minors employed on farms were well over school age, as were the children employed (usually for room and board alone) to tend the livestock. These children, of course, were hired to work the land of other households; they were migrant laborers who were certainly from the poorer families in the countryside—those families who most needed extra income and were most likely to pull children out of school in search of a few extra family kopecks. The Dobrotovskii passage also indicates the age at which children or adolescents were considered strong or responsible enough for the work of plowing and threshing and when they were old enough to tend livestock. There is little reason to assume that children would have been entrusted with the same tasks at an earlier age on their own family's farm.

It has often been noted that in Russia, as in the West, tending sheep was primarily an occupation for children (especially boys). To the extent that tending the flocks conflicted with schooling, students left school early and enrolled late each year. We have previously demonstrated that the school year in Russia successfully adjusted to the demands of the agricultural cycle; and although the school year was short, once begun, it was not often disrupted, and attendance was the more regular for this adjustment. It thus seems unreasonable to argue that the need for shepherds to tend the flocks (especially in a climate where livestock had to be brought indoors quite early in the year) offers a meaningful explanation for the school dropout rate.[35]

To analyze participation in farm labor as a whole, we again turn to Vikhliaev's study of the western districts of Moscow. One might object that Moscow was an industrial province where agriculture was only subsidiary, but in fact the acreage cultivated in Moscow remained stable in the last decades before 1914. Most families were engaged in both subsidiary farming and industrial or cottage labor, and the crops grown (including flax and potatoes) were far more labor-intensive than were grain crops. One might expect child labor to have been higher in this area, with the heavy demand for labor power in both agriculture and industry.[36]

But it can be seen in Table 42 that in these three districts of Moscow province—including the center of the flax industry and an area of intensive truck gardening and dairy farming—children (even adolescents under eighteen) were only rarely called on to participate in the heavy labor of farming. Between one in four and one in five children eleven to thirteen years old regularly helped around the house. Very few children of that age had employment elsewhere; thus, we can only assume that the labor of school-age children could not have been in great demand.[37]

Perhaps most important, child labor on the farm, when it

Table 42

Participation in Farm Labor by Age Group, Ruzs,
Mozhaisk, and Volokolamsk Districts, 1910

	MALE	FEMALE
Farm Chores		
11–13 years old	21.4%	23.5%
14–15 years old	23.6	35.9
16–17 years old	3.1	9.1
18–45 years old	0.4	0.5
Plowing		
12–15 years old	2.5%	4.9%
16–17 years old	12.3	61.6
18–45 years old	22.5	69.8
Mowing		
12–15 years old	5.8%	9.6%
16–17 years old	31.3	72.8
18–45 years old	49.5	72.6

SOURCE: P. A. Vikhliaev, *Vliianie travoseianiia na otdel'nye storony krest'ianskogo khoziaistva* (Moscow, 1915), 9:26–34, esp. 33.

existed, was often socially rather than economically dictated. The Soviet historian A. M. Anfimov has estimated that at the turn of the century surplus labor in the countryside amounted to 23 million farmhands.[38] Detailed time-budget studies of the individual peasant household showed that peasant labor was heavily underutilized, with a maximum use rate of 50 percent in most areas of the country, even after crafts and trades had been taken into account.[39]

Of course, labor hours were distributed differently between the sexes and among various age groups (see the figure on p. 380). Unfortunately, budget studies did not distinguish between adoles-

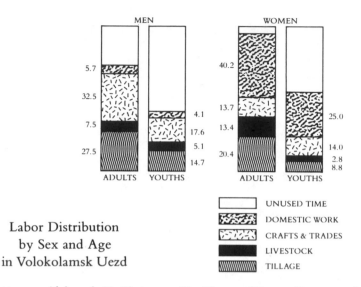

Labor Distribution
by Sex and Age
in Volokolamsk Uezd

UNUSED TIME
DOMESTIC WORK
CRAFTS & TRADES
LIVESTOCK
TILLAGE

SOURCE: Aleksandr V. Chaianov, *The Theory of Peasant Economy,* ed. and trans. Daniel Thorner, R. E. F. Smith, and Basil Kerblay (Homewood, Ill., 1966), 180.

cents and children nor did they set a precise age at which a young family member began to make a productive contribution to the farm. This lack of precision was understandable, for the transition from consumer to producer, from child to adult, involved a long apprenticeship. Nevertheless, it considerably weakens the usefulness of such studies.

Not surprisingly, adolescents worked fewer days than adults. Both adolescent and adult males had more unused time than their peers of the opposite sex. Boys and girls spent roughly the same amount of time on crafts; boys spent nearly twice as much time as girls tending livestock (though this activity took only a small portion of their day). Girls committed a substantial chunk of time to domestic work.[40]

Thus, if we keep in mind that the labor intensity curve of agriculture in Russia (as elsewhere) was very uneven, that the period of peak demand coincided with the school vacation, and that an absolute surplus of labor made child participation economically unnecessary in most cases, we can conclude that child labor on the farm was both episodic and socially determined.

PROVINCIAL COMPARISONS

A final and most direct way to investigate the impact of child labor and the economy in general on the length of schooling is to compare the grade distribution pattern of children in different provinces and regions. Initial enrollment patterns alone are not very good indicators; the enormous pressure for expanded schooling was reflected in the high incidence of denied admissions, and low enrollments often reflected the state of provision of schooling (supply) more than peasant attitudes (demand). If one million children were denied admission in 1910, if another six to seven million were enrolled, and if perhaps 25 to 50 percent of those not enrolled at the time had already had some schooling or were waiting for a place, the number of children outside the school gates cannot be used as a proxy for the number of school-age children needed in the local economy. Even when unemployed, these children may not have had the option of being in school—places may not have been available.

The distribution by grade of those enrolled, however, does offer a purified situation. Once enrolled, children could not be denied admission; the point of departure could only reflect parental attitudes or opportunity costs (assuming the school exerted no pressure on them to leave). If employment opportunities were the major explanation for the dropout rate, we would expect significant differences in the grade distribution pattern from province to province. We might also expect significant annual fluctuations in individual provinces, as the economy contracted and expanded.

In fact, we find extraordinary continuity. Moscow school records reveal that between 1901 and 1915 the number of boys in the third grade as a percentage of all enrolled boys remained at 19 to 20 percent; boys in the second grade made up between 37 and 38 percent. The grade distribution of girls was only slightly more uneven, ranging from 11 to 15 percent in the third grade, but only from 34 to 36 percent in the second grade. The fluctuation observed among girls in the third grade was largely a progression, from 11 percent of all enrolled girls in 1900 to 15 percent in 1915. In short, any significance that the annual perturbations of the local economy may have had for schooling was not reflected in the an-

Table 43
Length of Stay in School and the Regional Economy, 1910

	LENGTH OF STAY (PUPILS IN THIRD GRADE AS A PERCENTAGE OF TOTAL FIRST GRADE ENROLLMENT)	
	Boys	Girls
Provinces dominated by cottage industry Average employment per 10,000 population:		
High: 721 (five provinces)	46.00%	25.10%
Low: 76 (five provinces)	47.80	25.90
Provinces dominated by agriculture Average percentage of land cultivated:		
High: 74.2% (five provinces)	46.40	26.40
Low: 10.1% (six provinces)	48.45	26.85
Provinces dominated by factory production Average factory output per capita, in rubles:		
High: 105.0 (three provinces)	48.70	27.80
Low: 2.8 (eight provinces)	44.10	24.35

SOURCES: Rashin, *Formirovanie rabochego klassa Rossii,* 150, table 46; *Anketa,* i–iv; MNP, *Odnodnevnaia perepis'* 1:63, 65, 69, 71, 73; 2:138, 141, 143, 146, 149, 151, 154, 156, 159, 161, 163; 3:80, 85, 87, 90, 92; 4:61–66; 5:95–97; 6:67, 73, 77, 79, 107; 7:53–57.

nual grade distribution of children in Moscow province. In each year, the distribution of children was roughly the same: half in the first grade, slightly more than one-third in the second, and roughly one-sixth in the third.[41]

Comparisons at the provincial, national, and regional levels are also instructive because they allow us to draw tentative conclusions about the *scale* of the clash between school and local economy. In Table 43, provinces are grouped by occupational profile to determine if economic conditions had a significant impact on the distribution pattern or length of stay in school. In each category— cottage industry, agriculture, and factory labor—provinces with higher and lower engagement have been grouped together, and, for each group, the number of students in the third grade is shown as a percentage of enrollment in the first grade.

Despite enormous differences in the degree of involvement in factory production, cottage industries, and agriculture, the percentage of children of both sexes who, once enrolled, proceeded to the third grade was virtually the same in all these provinces. Only in those provinces characterized by factory production was there a variation in the length of stay of girls, but the range was not large. In the heavily industrialized provinces, a boy's chances, once enrolled, of staying into the third grade were 1 in 2.05; in the least industrialized provinces, the chances were 1 in 2.26—certainly not much of a difference.[42]

Thus, once children were enrolled in the school systems in these provinces, the rate of attrition from year to year was remarkably constant, and in all provinces girls tended to be weeded out more rapidly than boys. Roughly the same percentage dropped out each year, and the school systems in each area produced virtually the same proportion of graduates. For those who enrolled in school, the occupational profile of the area in which they lived had little effect on their length of stay in school or their chances of completing the program. Whether the area was predominantly concerned with farming, cottage industry, or factory labor, all children who went to school followed approximately the same pattern.

It is of course conceivable that a number of economic currents were at work, cancelling one another out when it came to school attendance, but one would expect some indication of this in the grade distribution pattern and dropout rate. As Bratchikov commented:

If the flight of pupils from the schools were a function exclusively of economic circumstances, then the dropout figures would fluctuate greatly from one region to another in Russia. But we see . . . that figures for those completing the program and for those dropping out, just like the pattern of distribution by section [grade], are very similar from one province to the next. There are enormous differences in the economic life of Moscow and Viatka, of Iaroslavl' and Khar'kov, of Perm' and Kherson, just to name a few. Yet even if we were to presume that the poverty of the population was more or less comparable in these provinces and throughout European Russia as a whole, this still would not explain the consistency of the dropout rate. When reference is made to the poverty [*neobespechennost'*] of the population to explain the flight from the schools, what is clearly meant is not a lack of food or clothing, but the economic order, which forces children out to work . . . and in this sense one can observe enormous differences from province to province. . . . If we keep in mind the [dynamics of school enrollments] and the wide variety of economic conditions, we must recognize that factors other than economic ones are impinging on the pupil's stay in school.[43]

CONCLUSIONS

The traditional depiction of conflict between school, on the one hand, and farm, factory, and cottage industry, on the other, is an overstated view, at least in Russia where the primary schools called for attendance only between the ages of eight and eleven. The authors of the works considered in this volume—Bogolepov, Iordanskii, Zviagintsev, Chekhov—were all exemplary men who devoted their entire working lives to the education of the common people, and their despairing comments on the continuing grip of poverty on the school system should not be lightly dismissed. Yet a careful reading of the material they themselves gathered and published suggests that by failing to maintain a clear distinction between statistics on initial enrollments and those indicating the length of stay in the school system, they missed an essential aspect of the situation. Their very closeness to the terrible poverty and misery of the countryside increased their impatience for improvement, and they seemed to overlook, or at least understate, the remarkable progress made in the half century following the Emancipation in enrolling the eligible school-age population of both sexes.

In fact, schools were proliferating, children were crowding at the doors, and literacy rates were climbing. What remained, as far as initial enrollments were concerned, was a final drive to clear up the pockets of educational backwardness in the European heartland and to spread schooling to the recently incorporated territories of Central Asia. In clearing up these pockets of backwardness, a major problem that faced school promoters was poverty. A small but significant minority of children were kept out of the schools by illness, retardation, or economic misery so profound warm clothing could not be found for the winter months. But this residual problem was just that; its dimensions were not identical with those of the "dropout" phenomenon, which was pervasive, ubiquitous, and unchanging in the twenty years after the 1891 famine, the period of massive elite intervention and support of schooling and rapid progress in initial enrollments.

Yet the confusion of the two phenomena—failure to enroll and dropping out once enrolled—and the unwarranted exaggeration of the former have created the impression that poverty and the economy wreaked havoc with the Russian school system and have convinced observers that the dropout rate reflected the impact of poverty and economic demands rather than a peasant strategy of reasserting control over a curriculum determined by the elite.

Reports from the countryside, though often referring to poverty as the chief cause of a high dropout rate, simultaneously observed that parents both wanted their children to read and write coherently *and* feared the effects of prolonged exposure to formal schooling. Moreover, what was labeled poverty often lumped together the effects of poor health, parental "backwardness," rural attitudes, and opportunity costs. Distance and lack of warm clothing prevented students from enrolling in only a small number of cases. We have been unable to discover any significant correlation between the grade distribution pattern and size of family landholdings or occupation of parents. Few adolescents began work at factories before the age of fifteen or sixteen. Only a handful of cottage industries in isolated districts employed child labor.

Children found work to do on the farm not only because they were needed but also because their parents did not want them to stay in school. When poverty was blamed for early departure, the parents' argument was "We need 'em on the farm, and besides, they've had enough schooling"—*not* "We can't get by without their help." On the peasant farm, work involved the child in a division of labor that also reflected the hierarchy of rank within the family. The acquisition of skills and experience and the performance of allotted tasks were means not only of increasing income but also of socialization, maintaining the authority of the household, defending the role of the family in the character development of the child. Forcing a child to carry out chores was a reassertion of the place of informal family education in the inculcation of values. In strict economic terms, given the enormous amount of slack labor available in rural areas most of the year, this work might have been carried out by adults or by older siblings who, it was often reported, hung around "chasing dogs" in the countryside after completing two years of schooling.

In short, we are often talking about family priorities and values as much as—or more than—strict economic necessity. Labor was socially allocated; it is misdirected to apply uncritically the notion of opportunity costs. A certain percentage of children did leave school after only one year (as discussed in Chapter 11), and child labor, poverty, and disease did cut a swath into the pattern of enrollments. But it is very difficult to disentangle the motives at work, to separate out local economy, opportunity costs, peasant demands and fears. When they are untangled, however, it can be seen that the reluctance to leave children in school, exposed to the agent of another culture, and the recognition that the graduation certificate often meant a net loss to the family farm (a topic elaborated in Chapters 14 and 15) were often enough to convince parents that they should find work for their children at home.

PART IV

The Results of Schooling

13

Mere Learning:

The Cognitive Results of Schooling

What were peasants learning in the primary schools? How well was knowledge retained? To what extent were parental expectations met, or fears justified? If we are to believe the numerous alarms sounded in the periodical press, regressive illiteracy was a widespread phenomenon, and it was not uncommon to meet recent graduates of primary schools who could barely spell their own names and who could not read at all. The shortcomings of the system were sometimes blamed on government interference and rigid control over curriculum.

Nearly a century later, however, we are more accustomed to functional illiteracy among adults with some schooling and less optimistic in general about the capabilities of schools. Perhaps most important, few today speak with confidence of a "proper way" to teach reading and writing. Surely anyone who has considered the successive waves of enthusiasm for phonics, the whole-word method, and "teaching the code" will treat with skepticism the progressive Russian educators' claim to possession of the true methods of teaching reading.[1] Ironically, government resistance to the whole-word method, which came into vogue in the early twentieth century, as well as official insistence on basic grammar lessons—to the dismay of progressive educators—may in fact explain the considerable success achieved by the school system in teaching the basics to peasant children.

The evidence collected in this chapter strongly suggests that if we ignore the shrill note of despair and frustration in contemporary commentaries and recognize that parental expectations often differed from educators' goals, we discover that the schools were indeed "delivering the goods." Peasant children were learning how to read, write, and count, often with surprising success. Russian pedagogy from the time of Korf until the 1917 Revolution was deeply concerned, because of the brevity of the school program, with promoting initiative and the urge to continue learning after the school stay had ended. Educators were sensitive to the problem of developing skills that today would be described as context-free: encouraging the transfer of conceptual rules to other areas of knowledge and facilitating an openness to new experience, to science, and to progress—a trait Inkeles considers characteristic of "modern man."[2] In particular, Russian teachers believed such skills could be developed through the practice of explanatory readings, open discussions, and encouragement of critical analysis.[3] Yet because the stay in school was brief and because both Military Statute and Model Program made rigorous demands for achievement in basic skills, teachers necessarily focused on lessons designed to help pupils master the ABCs, rather than spending much time on the less tangible goals of promoting curiosity, initiative, or receptivity to new experiences.

To analyze the results of schooling, it will be useful to keep in mind the distinction between *learning to read* and *learning from reading*. Jeanne Chall has broken the acquisition of reading skills into at least five stages. The first two—initial reading and decoding, and confirmation and fluency—are part of learning to read. Only with the third stage—"reading for learning the new," as the reader moves from familiar to unfamiliar text—does mastering the ideas conveyed become the dominant goal. Thus, if we wish to assess the ability to understand an unfamiliar text, the degree of transferable learning, generalized understanding, or reasoning skills, we must consider third-stage reading skills among Russian peasants.[4]

POST–EMANCIPATION SCHOOLS

What results were produced by the schools of the early post–Emancipation countryside? In a book written as a manual for new inspectors of public schools, Miropol'skii, a mainstream educator with little use for radicals but with considerable knowledge of German pedagogy and the Russian school system, complained of dismal results:

[Consider] the *gramotnik* [literate] of the old school [*starogo zakala*]; what does he know upon leaving school? The psalter, mechanically memorized; selections from the breviary learned the same way (moreover, he mixes up the answers and questions in one incoherent jumble); two or three rules of arithmetic and the ability to draw lines, write figures, and so forth; the lowly art of transcribing into a copy-book; the inability to sign his own name clearly and correctly; complete indifference and often even hostility to learning; the inability to develop further or to reason correctly. Listen to his reading—no understanding, no sense, no meaning. Pay attention to his arithmetic—he can't solve a simple problem. We have had occasion to note how former pupils who spent three or four years in school could not figure out how many kopecks were in one-eighth of a ruble or how much to pay a blacksmith for shoeing a horse, if each shoe cost 12 kopecks. And so, that's it from beginning to end—no useful information, no disposition to intellectual tasks. . . . Why should the peasant like the school?[5]

The pioneer of zemstvo education was Baron Korf, whose work in Ekaterinoslav prepared the groundwork for establishment of the three-year, three-grade primary school with one teacher and whose handbook on education was the most important reference and sourcebook for teachers in following decades. Korf's first-hand experience convinced him that Miropol'skii was wrong, that significant results *could* be achieved. According to Korf, after three years in the average zemstvo school children acquired the ability to read freely and correctly and with a clear understanding of the reading material. To demonstrate his point, he carried out a number of tests, organizing exams of former graduates in six villages in Ekaterinoslav province in 1881 and, at his initiative and according to his program, similar tests in Moscow, Vladimir, Smolensk, and

Tavrida.[6] In Ekaterinoslav, 555 former pupils showed up for the tests, which were the first attempts to measure the results of the school system. These former students were an average of 15.5 years old; they had attended school an average of 3.2 years (winters); and most had finished roughly four years earlier. Reading retention tests scored 8 percent of the pupils as "mechanical," or weak; 11 percent as fair; 21 percent satisfactory; and 60 percent excellent.[7]

Concerning these categories, Korf noted that for those who read "mechanically" (*mashinal'no*), "reading had ceased being a means for further education." He described as "satisfactory" any pupil who could read at the second grade level—that is, at the level of someone who had completed two years of schooling. "Fair" meant anyone who read "less fluently and rapidly," and "excellent" meant those who read better than the average graduate, "though only a minority read well enough that it was a pleasure to listen." Korf stressed that pupils in all three categories "read with full understanding" (*vpolne soznatel'no*). Thus, he concluded that at least four out of five graduates retained the skills of a second grade reader.[8]

Yet despite Korf's substantial reputation as an educator, his conclusions were by no means universally accepted. During the 1870s and 1880s, the question of how much pupils regressed after leaving public schools was hotly debated, not only in the press but also at zemstvo assembly meetings and teachers' congresses and within administrative circles. The question assumed tremendous significance, and many drew the extremely pessimistic conclusion that former public school pupils soon forgot everything and became newly illiterate. As early as 1870, an MNP report concluded that "children who, upon finishing school, are unable to find books for further reading often forget what they have learned in school and consequently have some right to consider [outlays for the] maintenance of schools as a waste of money, and studies as a waste of time."[9]

Scattered archival reports from the directors and inspectors of MNP schools also provide a glimpse of results. For example, the director of schools in Kazan' education circuit reported in 1872 that in village schools of Astrakhan' province the old method of teaching—*po skladam* (pronouncing each syllable)—predominated.

Lesson material was taught mechanically, without any comprehension of the subject. Pupils were forced to memorize, without any understanding, the central events of Bible history. Local inspectors could find only two or three pupils in each school (pupils who had already been there "several winters") who could read freely from a paragraph selected from a book, knew their prayers, and could recount a few events from the Bible. Such pupils could add and subtract, knew the multiplication tables, and could write satisfactorily. Again, however, these children were a small minority. "The rest of them chant the names of the letters, from the ABC book, or recite their lessons in unison from the same ABC book or from the Horologium." [10]

The same director reported that in Simbirsk, in the few schools where Bible instruction was taught with explanatory readings, pupils could read the prayers, New Testament, and Credo with comprehension, recite from Bible history, and explain the significance of the liturgy of the twelve Orthodox High Holidays and local holidays. In the majority of schools, however, the explanations by Bible teachers were far over the heads of the children. [11]

Nearly a decade later, a report of an inspection in Saratov province noted (in what was deemed a devastating criticism of teaching performance):

That success which is achieved in schools and described as satisfactory is limited to the mechanical reading of Russian and Church Slavonic, the use of math functions with whole numbers, the recitation from memory of the most common prayers, . . . a brief recitation of the main events from the Old and New Testament, Gospel history, and the ability to take dictation (if the teacher's pronunciation is good). In the very best schools, children learn to retell and to answer questions with understanding and thoroughness from material they have read, both in Russian and Church Slavonic, *as long as the content does not stray beyond the limited horizons of their impoverished daily life.* The best pupils can apply their basic arithmetic skills to simple everyday problems. *Within the limits of their general development and field of knowledge,* they can explain the content and meaning of the prayers and Credo and of Bible history, since teachers pay particular attention to this. The skill of independent exposition of thoughts and narrative retelling of even a very limited number of thoroughly mastered stories is possessed by a tiny number of pupils, most of *whom have regularly attended school for four or five winters* where the teacher was particularly dedicated [emphasis added].[12]

This summary made it clear that pupils were learning to read and count, that they were mastering at least the first two or three stages of literacy, and that they were able to utilize their skills in a familiar context. Transfer skills, or third- to fifth-stage literacy, seemed to come only after four or five years in school, but rudimentary reading—*learning to read*—was clearly within the capability of the school system.

RETENTION STUDIES, 1880–1911

The studies just described were fragmentary and impressionistic. But beginning in the 1880s and continuing until 1914, educators launched far more systematic attempts to measure the results of primary school education. On the following pages, we will examine these studies in chronological sequence rather than by subject tested. This method involves some overlap, but it offers the advantage of observing what was learned at different points over a third of a century, both before and after the imposition of the 1897 Model Program, and across an interval during which the quality of teaching personnel changed markedly.[13]

In 1885, the local zemstvo in Korsunov district, Simbirsk province, organized a test of those who had graduated from the local primary school during the previous decade. The test was announced through the local village elders; of 3,946 graduates, 2,842 showed up to participate. These tests were administered by commissions of independent observers, rather than by the pupils' teachers, and the results were classified according to the standard Russian five-point grading system.[14] Nearly a decade later, in January 1894, the local school board in Nizhedevitskii district, Voronezh province, instructed three of its members (one each from the Ministry of Education, the Ministry of the Interior, and the zemstvo) to test former graduates to verify the level of retention of school-acquired knowledge. These tests, carried out during Lent, included 1,038 of 1,914 graduates from the previous eighteen years.[15]

Between 1887 and 1896, other tests of former pupils were carried out in scattered areas of Russia, including Simbirsk, Stavropol, Riazan', Kherson, Tavrida, Ufa, Olonets, Moscow, Voronezh, and Kursk, most often in the schools of one district. The tests were not coordinated, and various approaches were tried: a few tests were conducted by mail, others by special teams of examiners (usually from the zemstvo or school board), and still others by individual educators.[16] In general, these tests attempted to measure the graduates' knowledge in all subjects taught by the primary schools and at the level required by the final examinations. The greatest variety in testing methods was found in tests of reading and writing. In some areas, former pupils were asked to read passages from old textbooks; in others, they were required to read from unfamiliar but simple works. In most, some attempt was made to measure speed, expressiveness, and comprehension. In some places, tests of "writing" were largely verification of penmanship and spelling (from dictation); in others, pupils had to put together a composition of their own or restate in their own words a passage read to them.

Particularly during the 1880s, the organization initiating the tests often clearly intended to defend outlays on the school system by proving that the efforts to teach literacy were not in vain. As one specialist on these surveys admitted, these "defensive aims may well have affected the results."[17] Furthermore, it was quite likely that only those who had best retained their school skills would voluntarily show up for such tests. In Simbirsk, for example, the rumor circulated that anyone who did poorly on the tests would lose the special military benefits granted by Article 56. Often, "the former pupil who has more or less slipped from literacy would not show up for the examinations out of an understandable confusion or fear of doing himself some harm [*nazhit' sebe kakuiu libo bedu*]."[18]

Nevertheless, the test results gain credence from the fact that everywhere the examiners were aware of these difficulties, made a good-faith attempt to control for self-selection, and in many cases took the trouble to learn why 40 to 50 percent of those summoned did not show up, discovering that generally the excuses offered were legitimate. In the words of a long-time observer of the schools, one with a notably critical eye for their deficiencies:

We consider, on balance, the fears of bias to be unwarranted. Not only were many of the tests [particularly in the 1890s, as the writer makes clear in another passage] carried out by people who cannot be called defenders of the public schools, but the reliability of the tests is further suggested by the fact that the results of the testing, regardless of locality, carried out completely independently each time, and under greatly differing circumstances, were remarkably similar, not only in outline but also in detail. Despite the different ways of surveying, registering, and evaluating the answers, as well as of compiling and evaluating the material, it is very easy to observe the similarity [in result].[19]

Table 44 summarizes the results of tests conducted in Simbirsk and Voronezh, two heartland provinces. In these two sets of tests conducted nearly a decade apart, the overwhelming majority of former pupils retained at least the rudiments of the skills acquired in the school system. Reading and math skills had slipped the least, whereas writing had suffered the most deterioration. Former pupils performed best when tested on basic math skills. The survey compilers listed a number of explanations: the demands of the school math programs were very limited and attainable (the four arithmetic functions, simple and compound numbers); teachers knew and taught this subject best; tests used examples from daily life rather than from textbooks; and, finally, basic math skills received constant reinforcement in the peasant's world.

Truly, the peasant practices his addition, subtraction, multiplication, and division throughout his life, no matter how modest—indeed, impoverished—his family circumstances, and no matter how simple and uncomplicated his social relations. He counts the strips in the field, the wood in his forest, his money in his pocket.

Most reports stated that pupils calculated rapidly and answered eagerly, often "more rapidly than well, for many had forgotten the formulas for carrying out math operations."[20]

Reading skills also held up well. Among the interesting discoveries of the Voronezh commission was that graduates read an average of eight to thirteen lines a minute of modern Russian, and six to twelve lines of Church Slavonic. (The examiners compared their own reading speed of twenty lines a minute for the same material.) Also, it appeared that the greater the time interval since graduation, the higher the reading score: the average reading score for those who had graduated ten or more years earlier was 3.7; for pupils graduating the year of the test, the average score was 3.5. Most startling, in the words of this commission's report: "*We didn't find a single individual who had entirely forgotten how to read or write.*"[21]

It was clear from individual reports that the measurement of reading skills largely focused on the "technique" of reading, for most of the commission members made a generous allowance for the backward conditions of the countryside and specifically noted that no major "cultural advances" could be observed among graduates. They pointed out that reading skills were maintained primarily by frequent reference to religious books and by the voracious consumption of the "low entertainment" offered by the *skazki* and the works of Nikolskii Rynok found at the local bazaars. Oral reading skills were particularly high, as literate readers were in high demand during long winter nights. Reading skills were seldom employed for learning *through* reading, as evidenced by the comment that the books least in demand among graduates in the Simbirsk countryside were those concerned with self-improvement, health, and agricultural methods, as well as by the compiler's statement that "in general among these people, there are very, very few books meriting serious attention. Virtually all the reports coming in from correspondents 'living close to the people' are full of statements noting the near absence of books, *but particularly of edificational and instructional books*" [emphasis added].[22]

Surveys conducted in the decade between the Simbirsk and Voronezh studies all concluded that many former pupils not only remembered how to read but had also markedly improved their speed and comprehension since graduation. Even reading in Church Slavonic yielded reasonably good results, "both in technique and in translation, as well as comprehension of Church Slavonic words and phrases." Participation in choir and Church services, along with the cheapness and availability of the Gospels and psalter, played a major role in reinforcing what had been learned in school. Indeed, throughout the country, the level of retention from Bible studies was probably best of all: "it was almost the universal impression that children who completed the school program knew best of all their Bible lessons; everywhere this subject stood in either first or second place."[23]

Table 44

Retention Test Scores, Simbirsk and Voronezh Provinces

	EXCELLENT 5	GOOD 4	SATISFACTORY 3	COMBINED 4 AND 3	FAILURE 2 AND 1
			Simbirsk, 1885 [a]		
Bible	20%	34%	37%	71%	9%
Church Slavonic	20	36	36	72	8
Reading	25	38	33	71	4
Writing	14	29	43	72	14
Math	21	38	36	74	5
Overall	19.8	35.1	36.8	71.9	8.1
			Voronezh, 1894 [b]		
Bible	15%	—	—	70%	15%
Church Slavonic	15	—	—	69	16
Reading	18	—	—	70	12
Writing	10	—	—	66	24
Math	17	—	—	73	10

	Voronezh, 1894, Graduating Pupils[c]			
Bible	62.5%	27.5%	10.0%	—
Reading	50.0	37.5	12.5	—
Writing	30.0	47.5	22.5	—
Math	42.5	37.5	20.0	—

SOURCE: Data for Simbirsk from Krasev, "Chto daët," 67–70; data for Voronezh from Bunakov, *Sel'skaia shkola*, 175–176, 184–185.

[a] For unexplained reasons, the total number of former pupils tested differed by subject, ranging from 2,833 in Bible to 2,878 in reading. Seven percent of the total had graduated fifteen years earlier, 20 percent no fewer than ten years earlier, 40 percent no fewer than five, and 33 percent had graduated within the previous three years. The examiners noted in their report that they had occasion to check the reading and writing of many graduates who did not show up and found their scores as high or higher than those tested.

[b] Total of 1,038 tested.

[c] Forty graduating pupils from five schools. These figures are the results of the official certifying exams.

All studies produced evidence that writing skills regressed rapidly after pupils left school. In Simbirsk district, of 2,305 former pupils, 1,314 continued to write regularly after leaving school, 649 only infrequently, and 342 not at all.[24]

Although the five-point system of evaluation did not establish firm criteria for writing skills, the general standards were indicated in one comment:

The majority of pupils received a two or three in writing. . . . The weak, smudgy strokes of the pen and gross spelling mistakes observed in the pupils in increasing numbers as the time away from school lengthens give me reason to believe that former pupils of village schools have little practice in writing. Others [whose scores were better] write elegantly and firmly. Many practice by copying out of books or by keeping record books of revenues and expenditures, and some keep in practice by writing letters. . . . Boys practice writing much less frequently than reading . . . and for that reason penmanship suffers. However, I learned through inquiry that they all carry out various brief forms of correspondence and keep a variety of records at home.[25]

In other studies during this period, former pupils tested in composition produced lamentable results in spelling and grammar but showed a clear mastery of basic technique. A report from Simbirsk province was representative:

Those examined who were asked to write down a well-known tale from the Bible did a very good job. But the same cannot be said for those who were required to write, not using familiar material but thinking up material or composing by themselves—for example, the composition of letters, or discussion of uncomplicated themes, or the description of some frequently observed natural phenomenon. Written work of this type was very unimaginative and impoverished in content; the letters were made up almost entirely of greetings, while judgments and descriptions were a jumble of phrases without any internal unity, incorrectly put together.[26]

Clearly, many examiners were looking for logical sequence of thought and flawless style. As to the *mechanics* of writing, virtually without exception the tests showed much more satisfying results: almost none of the pupils showing up for the tests had completely forgotten how to write. In the one study where true regressive illiteracy—in terms of the ability to write—was measured, only 21 of 1,028 former pupils had completely regressed.[27]

A study of Kursk province listed the most commonly encountered mistakes:

First of all, in the whole pile of papers what strikes the eye is the uncertain handwriting, sloppiness, abundance of corrections, and huge number of mistakes. You can find just about everything: capital-case letters in the wrong places, hard signs after vowels [e.g., *portnoi'*] and absent where they are needed, . . . words run together and others improperly separated.[28]

Such mistakes suggest that pupils were simply transcribing on paper what they heard in daily life, resulting in the phonetically correct reproduction of local dialects rather than exposition in "proper Russian." Lamentably, 35 percent of 720 former pupils could not spell their own names correctly. In six to seven lines of test dictation, improper word boundaries were observed in 50 percent of the pupils' samples, word distortion in 29 percent, omission of hard or soft signs in 34 percent. By far the most mistakes were found with the redundant Church Slavonic elements in the orthographical system, such as the letter *jat'*, which 64 percent of the pupils used incorrectly. (This letter and the hard *jers*, which also caused much trouble, were eliminated with the orthographic reforms of 1917. The hard *jers* was dropped in word-final position but retained medially.)[29]

But these troublemakers were of little or no semantic importance. Word distortion may often be a sign of the persistence of significant dialects in popular speech, and the high level of improper word separation suggests a low degree of familiarity with the written word. To be sure, 20 to 25 percent of the written compositions were given failing grades and judged fundamentally incoherent. But for the remaining 75 to 80 percent the difficulties observed were essentially reading, grammar, or spelling problems—not fundamental regression to illiteracy.[30]

In sum, a compiler of the surveys conducted between 1880 and 1905 noted that in all areas the rudimentary information provided by the school system remained firmly implanted in the pupils' minds long after graduation. He cautioned, however, that the yardstick being used was a very short one:

It is necessary to emphasize that the examinations touched on the retention of the most basic skills—reading, writing, and arithmetic. Concerning specific areas of knowledge and information in fields such as geography, natural science, and history, there was no inquiry. Obviously there was no point in even asking if the school provides its wards real knowledge in these areas.[31]

Yet both the numerical results of the retention studies and individual observations of competency levels indicate that in all subjects former pupils had retained the basic functional skills needed in the countryside—reading for pleasure or religious purposes, carrying out basic calculations, and maintaining simple correspondence and household accounts. Perhaps this school-acquired knowledge was not often used to ameliorate peasants' lives or to help them move out of the countryside, but neither were these skills allowed to deteriorate to the stage of regressive illiteracy or innumeracy.

THE 1911 ZEMSTVO SURVEY

The most thorough study of skill retention was carried out shortly before World War I for the 1911 All-Zemstvo Congress. Data from this study are useful both because the information came from all thirty-four zemstvo provinces and because more than a decade had passed since the imposition of the 1897 Model Program and almost five years since the repeal of the benefits conferred by the Military Benefits Exam. Over eleven thousand teachers in rural zemstvo schools responded in writing to this question:

How well have your former pupils retained, three to five years after completion of the final examinations, their knowledge and skills acquired in the following areas: reading speed; comprehension and the ability to reformulate orally what they have read; handwriting and spelling; the four functions of arithmetic; knowledge and understanding of the prayers; knowledge and understanding of the central events from the Old and New Testaments?[32]

Zemstvo surveyors tabulated the results (which many teachers obtained by special tests, others simply by personal observation). Teachers' responses for general subject categories are shown in

Table 45
Teachers' Perceptions of Primary School
Graduates' Knowledge and Skills Retention, 1911

	PERCENTAGE OF TEACHERS' RESPONSES			
	Skills Forgotten	*Skills Declined*	*Skills Retained*	*Skills Improved*
Russian	—	16.9%	76.9%	6.2%
Arithmetic	—	23.9	74.5	1.6
Bible	0.1%	43.1	56.1	0.7
Penmanship	0.3	69.4	29.7	0.6
Spelling	2.2	84.5	13.3	—
Reading skills				
Speed	0.1	17.9	76.7	5.3
Comprehension	0.1	15.0	77.3	7.6
Retelling (*pereskaz*)	0.0	17.4	76.8	5.8

SOURCE: *Anketa,* 63, 64.

NOTE: The figures in this table are based on 9,362 tabulated survey responses. When there was room for doubt, entries were listed under one of the two middle columns rather than under the extremes. Numbers indicate the general responses of teachers, not the number of students observed.

Table 45. But some of the more specific responses in the various categories can also be informative. Retention of language skills— whether reading speed, comprehension, or oral recitation—was uniformly high, with less than 20 percent of teachers observing a decline in any of these skills after graduation. Retention of basic math skills was also high, but not as uniformly so. Three to five years after leaving school, pupils were considerably more adept at solving simple problems orally than at carrying out written operations; compound numbers and basic division seemed to give the most trouble. It was commonly observed that "adults can count out loud with much greater facility than can schoolchildren, but when it comes to solving the simplest bookish problem in writing, for the most part they are completely lost!" [33]

A higher degree of slippage was found in Bible studies, particularly in the comprehension of prayer and of episodes from the

Scriptures. Knowledge of basic Biblical events and rote recitation of prayers from the Old and New Testaments were stronger:

Graduates of the public schools are able to recite by heart the most commonly used prayers, but knowledge of the text is seldom accompanied by the ability to retell the content in everyday language. They are able to give a brief exposition of the main events from the Old and New Testaments and have mastered the core of the Orthodox service and the basic concepts of the Orthodox catechism. This amounts to the assimilation, as far as this is possible for children aged eleven to thirteen, of the basic dogma of Orthodox teaching and only rarely to a conscious grasp and understanding of the foundations of Christian morality.[34]

Teachers explained the backsliding observed in this particular subject by the indifference and erratic attendance of Bible teachers, but at the same time they complained that rote memorization was the core of Bible classes and that the use of Church Slavonic prevented comprehension. Ironically, the Holy Synod archives contain inspectors' reports complaining that the level of Bible instruction was lowest in Church schools. This situation, as we now know, had a very mundane explanation: the priest received no remuneration for his efforts at the parish school and often neglected lessons there to teach Bible in the zemstvo schools, where he was paid.[35]

In 1911, as earlier, the worst regression had taken place in spelling and in penmanship. As for spelling, the familiar complaints about *jers* and *jat'* abound: "After two or three months, the students can only spell phonetically," wrote a teacher from Orel. Another from Perm' noted, "Three to four months after completing the program, pupils show up for the certificate and can hardly sign their own names without violating some grammar rule." From Viatka: "When I handed out the certificates, not one of the pupils could write his first name, patronymic, and surname correctly!"[36]

Local dialects still crept into writing and overran proper spelling. But, despite the evident frustration of teachers, the regression they observed did not generally affect the fundamental ability to read or write, albeit with frequent lapses from educated, proper Russian. In some cases, peasants clearly didn't care about proper

Russian: "Upon leaving school, the students pay no attention to spelling rules. They explain to me that spelling rules have no force once they are outside the school, as long as the meaning of the word and the thought are clear. They say, 'Who cares how to write it, as long as it makes sense!'"[37]

In other cases, however, a deterioration in penmanship and spelling stemmed from a simple lack of application of these skills:

Proper penmanship is completely lacking, because the callused hands lose the feel for such a tiny instrument as the pen. Still, these hands, used to work, manage painfully to scratch out what is asked of them.

After the axe and the saw, it's hard to hold a pen in the hand; that's what all the pupils themselves say.

The majority never pick up a pen after finishing school. They say that there's no reason to write. After they put down the "official" pen, they don't buy their own.[38]

There were obviously still pockets of isolation from the written word, still peasants whose daily activities seldom brought them into contact with documents. But these were indeed little more than pockets, for when the surveyors tried to compare the responses by region, they found little difference between industrialized and agricultural provinces in retention of the ability to handle numbers or letters.

Nevertheless, it would be incorrect to ignore the existence of some regressive illiteracy or what may have been the failure of the schools to teach *all* registered pupils how to read and write. Individual observers of the countryside frequently made comments such as this: "It often happened that a peasant would approach me with a request to write a letter, and when I asked him, 'Wait a minute, isn't your son literate?' he would answer with a wave of his hand, 'Not at all; he's of no use' ['*nikak ne mozhet, nikuda ne godit'sia*']."[39]

A few individual comments culled from contemporary writings, representative of the lot, show that most observers were finding results similar to those of the Zemstvo Congress study. One report was based on a special examination of 1,143 former students in 1910. (Of the sample, 300 had graduated before 1907, and 523 between 1907 and 1910; information on graduation dates was not available for the remainder.) Note how the observer's expectations subtly alter the tone:

Concerning knowledge of modern Russian, many can read with ease, know the rules of spelling, and write from dictation without gross mistakes; but they are unable to state the meaning in their own words. They know the parts of speech, conjugation, and declension. There are those who can take a sentence apart. They have memorized poems and fables. In some schools [however], explanatory reading is conducted this way: they read out loud, "The children sat at the table and ate *kasha* with a spoon." Then the questions begin: "Who sat? Where did they sit? What did they do? What did they eat?" . . . In the end, the children, distracted from the meaning by the questions, answer that the *kasha* ate the spoon, or that the children sat at the *kasha* and ate the table. The little articles included in the readers serve only as exercises in reading and grammar, while the contents do not serve to morally uplift or to develop aesthetic qualities; they are not linked with the moral principles provided by religion.[40]

In a speech to the 1911 Zemstvo Congress, the progressive educator Zviagintsev complained:

When one attends graduation examinations, one is amazed not so much by how little pupils know, as by how many words they know but do not understand and how easily they rush to pronounce them with no effort at understanding. During their years in school, children develop a fine art of being satisfied with a limited [*skudnoe*] comprehension of those words which they read in books or which the teacher forces them to memorize in preparation for the examinations. The semi-knowledge with which the pupil grows content is not only useless but also positively harmful. The German pedagogue Lai is fully correct in comparing such words with hollow nutshells: of no real use, they only create the illusion of nutrition [*tsennost'*]. This fine art of learning how to be satisfied with "empty shells" is even nurtured in the pupil the longer he stays in school; with time, the healthy striving for awareness that he brought to school and that search for precise conceptions fostered in children before school . . . become attenuated and die out.[41]

The tone of these comments must be separated from the facts being reported. If the job of the school was to teach the basics, it was clearly successful. Certainly, a degree of regression followed graduation, and this slippage was exacerbated by a shortage of books, libraries, and "culture" in the countryside. But such regression only rarely involved a return to full illiteracy; much of the perceived loss was not in the ability to communicate but rather in spelling and proper speech—perhaps reflecting the dominance of dialect and local idiom over a unified national language. Reports explicitly stated that former pupils could spell "phonetically," that they could communicate their needs in writing, and that they could certainly still read simple prose. What teachers and others were observing was the failure of pupils to meet the standards of communication necessary for participation in *privileged* society. Proper writing remained a "socially privileged form of expression," but the pupils took home with them—and kept—the ability to communicate meaning in prose.[42]

In 1894, the Voronezh district school board requested Nikolai Bunakov to take part in the annual certifying examinations for primary school graduates. His comments on the reading abilities of new graduates speak directly to the issues of learning to read and learning from reading:

Reading, both in modern Russian and Church Slavonic, of print and of manuscript, was generally unhesitating, confident, and intelligent [*tolkovyi*]. In almost all schools, the weak side of reading was the [frequency of] gross local pronunciation and the lack of even the most primitive expressiveness. The same can be said for the manner of reading poetry aloud. The pupils of all five schools knew and had memorized poems, but by no means did all show any understanding. . . . Still, when all is said and done, the results in reading, in the sense of being able to take apart and read out loud a printed text, were good in all five schools.[43]

Then Bunakov addressed the question of transfer, or learning from reading:

But in my mind the question of reading is inseparably linked with that of what is acquired by the student by means of reading, which must not be simply art for art's sake, reading for the sake of reading alone, as with Gogol's Petrushka [a character in *Revizor* who read everything indiscriminately and in whatever sequence found], but reading as a tool for expanding one's knowledge and conceptions [*poniatiia*]. Frankly speaking, during the exams it was discovered that the pupils of only one school used reading as a source for expanding their understanding, for the acquisition of knowledge. . . . In the other schools, apparently, no attention was given to the goal of teaching and familiarizing the pupils with the use of books for the acquisition of knowledge.[44]

These comments suggest striking parallels to Eugen Weber's observations about rural schools in nineteenth-century France. Weber notes that schools began their work by propagating an artificial language—"the literary or written language children learned in schools was as alien to the spoken tongue as spoken French itself was to their native dialect"—and that "the French of the schools was an alienating as well as an integrative force." But a key to participation in the national culture, to becoming a *citoyen*, a Frenchman and not a peasant, was the ability to use the language created at school, to be at ease with the "symbolism of images" and the "common points of reference." Weber found a striking example of this transition in France in the files of gendarmerie reports, where the language reflected the painful attempts of the newly literate to relate events in proper French, resulting in a stilted administrative style with awkward and convoluted phrases. It is possible that Russian peasants, in a similar situation, were simply drawing out *what was useful in their own familiar world,* in which no one "cares how you write it, as long as it makes sense," and that they had little interest in "participating in the national culture."[45]

The subject of numeracy—the ability to count and do basic calculations—deserves more attention and is probably as important as literacy. Yet it has generally been ignored (not only in Russia) by those investigating the spread of literacy to the countryside. According to zemstvo studies carried out between 1895 and 1900, the primary schools spent five hours a week (21 percent of class time) working on arithmetic. It is not difficult to discover what was expected of the teacher, for the Military Benefits Exam conferring reduced terms of service was very specific in its demands. The examinees had to know "the first four functions" (addition, subtraction, multiplication, division) and be able to apply this knowledge to simple practical tasks "encountered in everyday life." They were also required to "have a clear notion" of Russian measures of length, weight, time, liquid and dry substances, and monetary units. Model lesson plans to teach these particular skills have been preserved.[46]

From the first surveys conducted in the 1880s to those of the immediate prewar period, retention studies did consider the issue of numeracy, but the comments coming from the countryside were not entirely uniform: in some places, math scores were better than those in other subjects; in other places, they were worse. Although this discrepancy may have reflected the occupational needs of the population, it may also have been simply a statement of the obvious—that some teachers taught math better than others.

As with grammar, there were frequent complaints that "book learning" of mathematics was unrelated to real life. We should be somewhat skeptical of such comments, however, for in the first decade of the twentieth century progressive pedagogy was swept up in a movement to relate learning to life and to entirely remove the teaching of grammar from the schools. Similar criticisms were leveled against math books for their sterility and abstractness, as well as for the remoteness from everyday life of the problems used in such textbooks.[47] These complaints may have been far more accurate than those brought up in the war against grammar; still, the studies and individual comments make it clear that most graduates of the primary schools were able to work with basic numbers.

Interesting as these results are, it would be rash to draw conclusions about the level of numeracy in the villages until further material has been unearthed. This seemingly innocuous subject promises to tell us much about the degree of peasant participation in the modern world. Although mathematics did not directly threaten peasant values, as the stories included in a basic reader might have, teachers were being asked to carry out a minor revolution in peasant perceptions, for traditionally the Russian peasant had little use for official weights and measures, relying instead on complicated local systems of calculation.[48] One wonders how successful the schools were in imparting numeracy to the vast majority of students who never made it to the final examinations. If the reports that in most areas pupils could solve problems at the daily level are correct, then a new skill with broad ramifications had indeed been introduced. As Daniel and Lauren Resnick have observed, mathematics was introduced into elite curricula in eighteenth-century

Europe because it was regarded as the key to effective reasoning.[49] What ripple effects on the cognitive make-up of the peasant did basic math have? It is a question that bears further investigation. Certainly, if the peasants' strategy of schooling was defensive— to avoid being cheated—basic numeracy must have been a high priority.

INSTRUCTION IN
THE CHURCH PARISH SCHOOLS

Church school inspectors' reports to the Holy Synod in the years just prior to World War I deserve special attention precisely because they mirror the information collected on the zemstvo schools. In contrast to the annual reports filed immediately after 1887, which were largely repetitive, formulaic, and uncritical of the Church schools, reports from a later period were sometimes quite sophisticated, refreshingly candid, and reflected the same concerns bothering progressive educators: children were learning the mechanics of reading and writing, but they were not learning how to learn from reading; Bible instruction concentrated on rote learning and memorization to the detriment of the message of Christianity; and so forth. These reports, not intended for public consumption, indicate that at least some inspectors shared the same views about child upbringing and instruction as those educators who used the Church schools as whipping boys and treated inspectors as universally ignorant, harsh, and indifferent to children's welfare. Indeed, these reports completed by the Church provided much of the ammunition for the liberal assault on the parish school.

Consider first Samara province. There, Church inspectors reported that pupils mastered Bible history and their prayers best and knew least about their catechism and liturgy, subjects that were seldom covered in full. They noted that in many schools teachers neglected the lower and intermediate classes in order to prepare the upper-level pupils for the examinations and that often the "prayers [were] learned mechanically, without even an elementary explanation of individual words or phrases or discussion of content."

Teaching Bible history, some instructors spent little time "encouraging the coherent, free, and comprehending" retelling of what was read (*pereskaz*). Inspectors found little effort to "uncover the meaning of the prophecies and prophets of the Old Testament."[50]

In general, the teaching of Church Slavonic was rated as satisfactory, but inspectors complained of parish schools where the teachers had only a secular education: "Pursuing, as a rule, the development in the pupil of external mechanical qualities of reading, the teachers pay little attention to the development of the skill of fluent translation with comprehension into [modern] Russian."[51]

Almost everywhere, the phonics method was employed to teach modern Russian, and "success was quite marked."[52] The program requirements were met in almost all schools; those who completed the full course

learn to read fluently and are able to retell with some understanding what they have read; they know a sufficient number of poems and fables, [have some knowledge of] the most important events from Russian history, and can locate major historic sites on the map. In most schools, children quite adequately perform grammatical and syntactical exercises [*razbor*], are competent at dictation, and can carry out expository exercises.[53]

Nevertheless, the inspectors complained, insufficient attention was given to exposition in many schools, partly because of the shortage of workbooks and teachers' handbooks and partly "because of the ingrained habit of spending time on mechanical dictation." In general, much more time was given to "mechanical rather than explanatory reading," and little effort was made to "reason out the general plan of the article being read, to grasp the main argument, or to give a coherent summary in one's own words." In math, all of the program requirements were fulfilled, except that in the third grade many schools did not learn how to work with square and cubic dimensions or master the multiplication or division of fractions. Little attention was paid to problem solving (*zadachi po tipam*).[54]

The annual report of the Church school director of Saratov province for 1913–1914 contained an unusually detailed statement of school performance. In the report, one inspector was quoted thus:

The children [in the schools in his district] learned their prayers, Credo, and so forth. . . . They could recite events from Bible history and had some understanding of the Church services. They could read Church Slavonic texts fluently, correctly, and with understanding. Reading [out loud] in Russian was clear and comparatively expressive; moreover, the more capable could retell passages from a book they read, without prompting from the teacher. . . . In arithmetic, the children could carry out all four functions on paper, had some understanding of compound numbers, and were reasonably facile at counting in their heads with numbers of up to one hundred. . . . The main shortcoming was the mechanical application of the acquired skills and learning.[55]

Other inspectors were less sanguine. Although the majority of Church schools in Saratov province completed the official Church school program, the level of thoroughness varied considerably from school to school and by subject. In the larger villages with a church nearby, Bible lessons were generally, though not always, adequately mastered; in the hamlets, the majority of pupils had little knowledge of the catechism or Church services. Pupils stumbled over unfamiliar words in the prayerbooks, showed little understanding of the texts or the Commandments, "couldn't draw moral lessons from the Parables, had difficulty with the historical events of the Old and New Testaments, didn't know the last Testament, . . . couldn't understand the Church miracles, had no notion of even the basics of Orthodox iconology." Judging by the results of the examinations, "children had great difficulty coherently retelling this or that event from Bible history, though they were clearly familiar with the event and could satisfactorily answer individual questions about it." Children generally learned only the "commonly used school prayers and a few Church service canticles." Schools only rarely completed the requirements for choir instruction; there were numerous parish schools where choir was simply not taught.[56]

In Saratov, instruction in Church Slavonic was generally satisfactory, though there were numerous comments about "mechanical reading," "distortion of text," misplaced stress, "hastiness," "lack of rhythm," and an inability to read "psalmodically." In many schools, however, the older children could read quite well and took part in Church services. The teaching of modern Russian was quite successful—in the overwhelming majority of Church schools in Saratov, pupils could read from a Russian text freely while observing proper breaks. They could retell the text, the older students independently and those at the intermediate level with the coaching of the teacher. "During explanatory readings, the teachers tried to develop the intellectual capacities of the pupil not only in a 'formal' way, but also by enriching their knowledge of their native history and geography, of natural science and other topics." The only complaints noted were that in many schools the pupils lacked expressiveness and comprehension in their recitation and that only a few pupils used flawless grammar and spelling in their written composition. Moreover, teachers seldom paid sufficient attention to the neatness of pupils' workbooks, and penmanship was sadly deficient.[57]

In math, pupils learned to work with tens and hundreds during the first year, with hundreds and thousands during the second, and with numbers of any magnitude during the third. The Saratov Church school inspector concluded his annual report: "Within these limits, the students in the majority of schools could carry out the four functions, both written and orally." In some schools, he lamented, the pupils did not learn square and cubic dimensions, fractions, or counting time. Although the level of achievement was generally satisfactory, little attention was paid in some schools to oral calculations; in many schools, students did have a firm grasp of basic rules and formulas and were able to figure out the tricky problems in the textbook, but they were often unable to develop approaches to simple everyday math problems.[58] (Most retention studies pointed in exactly the opposite direction, however; graduates became adept at problem solving from direct experience but were unable to handle trick problems from math books.)

Finally, we turn to a report on Church schools in Vladimir province. In 1911–1912, teachers managed to go beyond the requirements of the Church school program and to add supplementary material in Bible study, fractions in mathematics, and Russian history and geography in 183 out of 515 full three-year schools. In 193 schools, the program requirements were met satisfactorily, and in only 39 did the teachers fail to complete the official program.[59]

In all schools included in the report, the full Bible study program was covered, though examinations conducted on the spot showed a considerable variety of thoroughness and success. In the best schools, the pupils were outstanding in retention, as well as in comprehension. According to the archival reports, these pupils could explain "how the teachings of the Church [were] interrelated, and how applied in everyday life." In other schools, although the knowledge "was firm, one noticed a certain mechanical quality." (We should note that this Church school inspector was measuring success not only by rote memorization but also by level of comprehension.) "It was obvious that the teacher was primarily working on the memory of the children; the children in their answers often simply reproduced the textbook and ran into difficulty when asked to interpret. . . . Of course, such knowledge is not solid."[60]

The director of Vladimir Church schools complained that the fault lay with many Bible teachers who "look on Bible instruction simply as a classroom subject and strive mainly to bring about a firm mastery of the material from the Program, as if they have forgotten that Scripture is studied not in order to master a certain volume of dogmatic and moral prescriptions but mainly to learn how to think, feel, and live in accordance with these teachings." As to Church Slavonic, however, the director reported that instruction was satisfactory in all schools and that children learned how to read "correctly, fluently, and psalmodically. . . . [But] as far as reading with understanding is concerned, especially when it comes to the Psalms, . . . this is only achieved with the greatest difficulty and by no means in all schools."[61]

Perhaps the most interesting comments in this extraordinarily detailed and candid report concern the success of teaching reading. (The phonics method was followed in all Vladimir Church schools.)

Modern Russian is taught on a high level of complexity in the primary schools; here the child must learn correct and expressive reading and must become familiar with the elements of Russian grammar and the major rules of spelling. He must learn how to express his thoughts both orally and in writing. At the same time, the child is being introduced to various information about Russian history and geography and so forth.

As far as fluent and correct reading is concerned, an adequate level is achieved in virtually all schools; children are capable of reading reasonably freely in any book, not only those used during class time [emphasis added].

In the majority of schools, children are also adequately taught conscious reading; they can retell and explain the meaning of something they have read without undue difficulty. But not everywhere have children sufficiently mastered the logical analysis of what they have read, the exposition of the basic idea and organization of the articles they have read.[62]

Finally, the director reported that it was extremely difficult for the three-year schools to meet all the math requirements but that everywhere children were learning to add, subtract, multiply, and divide with simple numbers and even to work with basic fractions.

In sum, everything we have said about the results of education in the zemstvo schools can reasonably be applied to the results of learning in the Church schools in these provinces. Anyone who has read the criticism of Church schools by secular educators at the turn of the century will realize that such a conclusion would have been anathema at that time. Yet, according to Church archives, the vast majority of teachers in the parish schools had secular backgrounds and had been trained in secular schools, and by 1900 the textbooks used in Church and zemstvo schools were often identical, and almost always comparable, in content and treatment. The Holy Synod waged a bitter and often underhanded campaign against the secular schools, but a bureaucratic struggle between two large organizations within the Russian government—the MNP and the Holy Synod—should not obscure the basic fact that, at least after the turn of the century, the schools were achieving basically the same instructional results.

GRADUATES AND DROPOUTS

This chapter has investigated the retention levels of school-based knowledge primarily among those who actually graduated from school. But graduates represented only a minority of enrolled pupils, and one would expect to find a higher degree of regressive illiteracy among dropouts. Kulomzin, the specialist in the Ministry of Finance who drew up influential plans for implementing universal education, argued heatedly against proposals that would have reduced the length of the school program from three to two years as a temporary expedient until enough funds could be found and teachers trained to offer more; he declared that "experience shows that even a stay of three years does not provide for full mastery of the *kurs* [program requirements]; most who finish take four years to do so."[63]

S. A. An'skii (Rappoport) directly addressed this question in a book on village literates published in 1914. Noting that the primary school graduate was a rare figure in the countryside, he described instead the "average village reader," one who had spent about two winters in the village schools: "[He] reads slowly and haltingly and without a clear understanding of the significance of punctuation marks. Even in the case of simple books, understanding comes with great difficulty. His understanding of literary forms is limited to that which he encounters in the *lubok* [chapbook] literature."[64]

An'skii, like other contemporary observers, seemed to be concerned about advanced, or "comprehensive," literacy and to regard basic reading skills, or learning to read, as inadequate. Yet the similarity between his observations on the average village literate and reports on the reading skills of school graduates is striking.

Both direct and indirect evidence support the notion that retention levels of graduates and dropouts were comparable. A very detailed Vladimir study, which treated graduates and dropouts without distinction, arrived at results closely corresponding to those derived from studies of graduates alone.[65] The school commission in Nizhedevitskii district, Voronezh province, concluded its 1894 study of retention levels of graduates with this comment on dropouts:

As far as schoolchildren who left the program before completion are concerned, the examining commission happened by chance to gather some information pertaining to twenty such pupils from two larger villages who also took the tests. It turned out that they all could read and write satisfactorily, although many of them had left school long ago, and some were in their thirties.[66]

This statement carries particular force, for the level of reading and writing skills demanded by this commission was clearly above the level of simple decoding or initial reading and in fact implied comprehension and fluency.

Moreover, Bunakov and other teachers testified that it was indeed possible to teach village youth the mechanics of reading and writing in two winters, or perhaps even one.[67] During the 1890s, F. Ol'denburg, a highly respected statistician and educator, produced an analysis of contemporary statistical sources on education in which he also addressed the question of what the schools were teaching. He argued that pupils in MNP schools who completed at least the first two years generally came away with basic literacy skills. In his estimation, between two-thirds and three-fourths of those with some schooling were able to "read with comprehension the most basic and accessible works and had the rudiments of writing and arithmetic." He claimed that although pupils enrolled in Church literacy schools learned virtually nothing, peasant-sponsored literacy schools had much better results. Ol'denburg admitted that the statistical sources for measuring results were scattered at best, but his unmatched familiarity with the original sources lends weight to even crude inferences.[68] We may conclude that the retention studies of graduates present a picture of learning skills acquired and retained that applies just as well to the vast majority of peasant children who spent two to three winters learning their ABCs but dropped out before qualifying for the graduation certificate.

This inference is also supported by a conclusion drawn indirectly from the enrollment and dropout patterns and the nature of the school curriculum. By all testimony, the third year of school was spent in intensive study of the basics in preparation for the spring examinations. Thus, the main difference between those who finished the third year and those who did not was that the former had the opportunity to memorize obscure grammar and spelling rules (which were the "first to fly away"), rather than covering new content of any substance. Certainly, this stay in the third grade must have helped imprint the basics through endless repetition. Yet many who did not graduate chose instead the path of remaining an extra year in the lower grades, where the rudiments were covered without any need to memorize the rules of proper grammar or spelling, rules that it made no sense to acquire if a peasant had no intention or opportunity of advancing socially. Therefore, the difference between a third year spent in the second grade and a third, or even perhaps fourth, year in the third and final grade would have been marginal in the long-term retention of basic skills.[69]

❖

The comments of individual educators with a lifetime of experience, the results of detailed teacher surveys, the retention tests carried out among former pupils of the school systems, and reports by inspectors in zemstvo and Church parish schools—all recount essentially the same tale: pupils were learning to read. To be sure, they read haltingly, they made mistakes in spelling, and their grammar left much to be desired. But they could read, they could write, and they could count within the limits prescribed by the needs of the family and village. This was true for graduates as well as dropouts, and for pupils of Church as well as zemstvo schools. The curriculum was humble, and the results were modest, but the achievements of these pupils should not be ignored or dismissed simply because they did not live up to the expectations of educators. In fact, they may have conformed instead to the wishes of the peasantry, who had a pedagogy of its own—one oriented toward survival rather than liberation.

14

Hidden Curriculum:

Moral Education and
the Impact of Schools

Formal lessons were but one component of schooling; character development was equally important to all educators. The state, the gentry, and liberal educators shared a paternalistic view of the peasantry, though they often differed over how peasant children should be taught. As in France during the Second Empire, education for the masses had "a regulatory notion, a sense of directing them along the proper road as much as freeing their minds." Whether the mission of the school was to "civilize the masses," diminish pauperism and criminality, foster patriotism, promote social stability and moral unity, or "modify the habits of bodily cleanliness and hygiene, social and domestic manners, and the way of looking at things and judging them," everyone agreed that the school was to play a major role in forming citizens.[1]

It was the organization of space and time, the routines and discipline, rather than the actual content of instruction, that made the school, with the army, an important agent of modernization, easing the transition from traditional village culture to modernity. Scholars have recently concluded that in Western Europe, where as late as 1914 the overwhelming majority of children completed their formal schooling by age eleven, schools failed to facilitate mobility or select talent. But despite this failure,

Europe's elementary schools had influenced their pupils in a number of ways. They had learned how to handle their national language and been exposed to new attitudes. . . . Rural pupils had become aware of a broader society beyond their native villages. This awareness was combined with feelings of patriotism. . . . they had at least been shown how to become acceptable employees and citizens in the eyes of the middle and upper classes.

The social mobilization of young men . . . was completed during their term of military service. . . . Basic training in military camps was simpler than it is today, but it did try to instill hygiene, discipline, and obedience to authority. . . . drilling for hours, like sitting still in the classroom when they were children, conditioned these men to the requirements of modern work discipline. And penalties for breaches of discipline in school and in the army prepared them for similar penalties on the job.[2]

In Russia at the turn of the century, there was widespread agreement that the civilizing mission of the schools was a failure. As in Europe, the hopes of educators had been pinned on emancipating people from supersition and ignorance, promoting general progress, remedying specific moral weaknesses such as criminality and pauperism, and regulating and indoctrinating.[3] But in Russia virtually all agreed that schooling was not working. To be sure, despite educators' laments and widespread despair at the meager results of instruction, children *were* learning how to read, write, and count. But values and habits, more than skills, were what educators hoped the schools would shape.

In this chapter, we will try to sort out the available evidence concerning the impact of schools on children's lives. Admittedly, measuring the larger impact of schooling is no easy task, even when investigators can design and supervise their own tests. In contrast, the studies reviewed here were primitive and incomplete; the very questions asked were sometimes ambiguous. Yet for the historian they do offer insights, however murky, into the changes wrought by the school in the villages. We begin with a brief summary of observations by individual educators, reading specialists, and others who measured the pulse of schooling. We then turn to the

1911 Zemstvo Survey, which carried out a systematic, though flawed, investigation of the school's impact on the lives of village youth.

✤

Writing in the early 1870s, the prominent educator Miropol'skii commented bitterly:

[Perhaps we can] pick out the literate ones [in the village]. . . . Perhaps they have learned to improve their work habits and labor productivity? Perhaps they reveal advanced consciousness? Perhaps they serve as models for society? Perhaps they can be distinguished by the cleanliness and refinement of their daily habits, as well as by their truthfulness and the honesty of their convictions? Perhaps, as defenders of public property, spokesmen for local interests, and representatives of a local intelligentsia, they are exerting a beneficial influence on society? . . . Whoever takes such hopes seriously or who turns to our countryside with such expectations has never in his life seen our villages or hamlets.[4]

Miropol'skii lamented that when one encountered literate peasants and asked them why it was necessary to study, the most forceful answer they would provide was that literacy was a good way to pick up some extra cash.

Miropol'skii was writing when the zemstvo school was in its infancy and the majority of literates had received their "schooling" outside the schools. But, although the classroom routines and teacher behavior prescribed in handbooks written by Korf, Bunakov, A. I. Anastas'ev, and others were designed to wrap literacy instruction in a code of proper conduct, few observers picked up successful results during the following decades, either.

Writing in the 1880s, S. Krasev, a friend and junior colleague of Ul'ianov (Lenin's father) and an author of the Simbirsk retention studies, complained:

How powerful and irresistible is man's milieu! The ritualistic observance of religion, the vulgarity of mores, all the blemishes of society, the abnormal relations to elders and relatives and, conversely, to the young and to one's offspring, as well as to women, . . . are soon picked up by the pupils who, upon leaving school, cast away everything that is necessary for further self-education. Thus our pupils sink in the end, with rare exceptions, almost to the level of their parents and relatives who never attended school.[5]

The comments of educators on the eve of World War I were, if anything, more despairing still. Even after schools had been in the villages for a generation or more, the volumes of reports to the 1911 Zemstvo Congress were full of complaints that the schools' influence was virtually negligible, that even the graduate of the primary school soon sank back into the morass of peasant village life. In one of the first reports to the congress, N. F. Ezerskii spoke disparagingly of the school's place in the village:

If we take a glimpse at the position of the school in the village, what strikes our eyes is that it stands in isolation, on the fringes of village life. The villagers send their children to school, because nowadays everyone sees that it is necessary; but what the school does, what it is trying to accomplish and why, neither the pupils nor the parents understand. . . . When the child leaves school, the thread of learning is cut and nothing in the life around him is likely to restore it. . . . This is why even in those places where a school has been in operation for twenty or thirty years it has had no cultural impact whatsoever . . . and the teacher, living in the middle of the village, feels himself an outsider in his village, feels that his school is an oasis, a cultural hermitage . . . but not an organic part of village life.[6]

The inspectors' reports in the archives of the Holy Synod echoed the views frequently expressed in the secular press. The inspector of Church schools in Vladimir diocese, whose reports were unusually informed and candid, noted in 1911:

Unfortunately, the beneficial influence of the schools ends early; by the age of eleven or twelve, children have already left school and their further development and upbringing no longer depend on the school. Thus, the good habits acquired in school are sometimes attenuated or even disappear under the pressure of another type of formative influence—life. This attenuation . . . is noticeable not only in the towns and factory centers, where after completing their education children cut all ties with the school, but, in recent times, has also been observed in hamlets and villages. It is well known that in the last few years debauchery and hooliganism have grown rapidly among village youth. . . . This debauchery [*zapushchennost'*] also affects adolescents who have recently left school and seems to undercut the positive impact of the school.[7]

Did the school have a significant impact on peasants' lives? Were careers altered, respect for science and medicine imparted, changes in the local economy effected, or hygiene, health, and relations with authority, with fellow villagers, and with family members improved? One report from the countryside declared that "in terms of moral fiber our literate peasants are no better than the illiterate," and it continued on a note of despair:

The question arises: Has the graduate of the school made any improvements in his household economy or methods of working the soil? Is he acquainted with improved agricultural implements, does he know how to combat unfavorable conditions, does he take better care of the vegetable plot and the livestock? Did the school give him, if not the ability, at least the wish and will for something better? The answer is no, nor did it think to give him this. . . . Does the former schoolchild show any striving to improve his daily life? Is he tidier, does he have any notion of hygiene? If no, there are no signs of it.[8]

Iakubovich, the author of this report, included a diatribe against the baneful impact of schooling, a diatribe that hints at some growing generational tensions in the countryside:

The only thing observed [as a result of schooling] is a heightened interest in tasteless and useless dandyism. In many areas, the normal peasant dress is being replaced by urban styles, which cut deeply into the peasants' skimpy budget, hindering major improvements to other, far more important sides of peasant life.

What has the school given the village, through the villagers' offspring, by way of family life? Family ties, the very foundation of the well-being of state and society, have been deeply shaken. Complaints about insubordination to parents and elders are ubiquitous. Young men and adolescents often verbally abuse their elders and even beat them; they file complaints in the courts and remove from the home whatever [possessions] they can. It seems that parents have lost all authority over their children and do not have the strength to call a halt to the outrages. Animosity and large-scale fights between siblings can be seen everywhere.[9]

Abundant evidence in contemporary sources indicates that rural customs, dress, games, diet, and general way of life were being undercut by the spread of urban culture. Today, historians note that generational conflict and crime were also on the rise in the Russian countryside before World War I. (However, at least two recent accounts also stress the retention of peasant dress, speech, and village residential patterns in the city, emphasizing that factories emerged in Russia in "symbiosis" with the countryside and that cities as large as Moscow continued to be dominated by peasant culture.)[10]

The degree of survival of peasant culture in the face of rapid economic and social change cannot be determined by teachers' and educators' reports alone. Nevertheless, even a passing acquaintance with the pedagogical press after 1905 is enough to show that teachers *felt* that the countryside was being swamped by the degenerate aspects of urban culture: violence, drunkenness, the break-up of family ties, brawling, and venereal disease. But is there any evidence that the school could be blamed for this deterioration or heightened conflict? Teachers seemed to be saying that schools were powerless to exert any moral influence or to provide the personal examples, positive guidance, or code of behavior needed to replace the "moral economy"—traditional views of social norms and obligations—which was being swept away.

Certainly, the school had *some* impact. Just one example, entirely overlooked by the press of the day, might be mentioned: schools sometimes brought together the youth of several villages and kept them together for several years. This mixing was often the first such contact for children. To what extent did this sustained contact strengthen the influence of peer relations over those of the family? How important was it in breaking down village autarky? In the north in particular, where settlements were scattered, pupils often remained at school overnight, or even the entire week, returning home only on Saturday after classes. Moreover, in many areas, the schools enrolled a mixed population of Russians and indigenous minorities—Chuvashi, Bashkiry, Mordva, or any of a hundred or so nationalities—and sometimes merged Old Believers with Orthodox, or even Muslim, children. It is odd that no one at the time seems to have paid attention to this development; but the historian should certainly not overlook it.

The 1911 Zemstvo Survey investigated whether the school had any effect on peasant *byt*, posing the question in positive terms: "Have you noticed any significant influence of the school on those who have *completed* the program? If so, in what way?" The survey recorded replies from 11,822 teachers; of this number, fewer than 1 percent observed a harmful impact, roughly 15 percent noticed no impact at all, and 9,912, or almost 84 percent, observed changes for the better.[11] A breakdown of the positive changes observed is presented in Table 46.

More than half the teachers (58.5 percent) cited beneficial educational (cognitive) changes in their pupils. Of this group, 47 percent (or 27 percent of *all* teachers) noticed intellectual development measured by verbal communication, vocabulary, and scope of knowledge; one-half (nearly 30 percent of all teachers) noticed a heightened curiosity about the world, seen in a quest for knowledge, respect for science, and continued reading; 20 percent (almost 12 percent overall) recorded a greater sympathy for educational efforts, whether by the family or the community; and 14 percent (8 percent of all teachers) observed a reduction in "superstitious attitudes" among school graduates.[12]

The teachers did not make a consistent distinction between academic instruction and character molding; the category represented by the first column in Table 46 included features such as intellectual curiosity and a search for broadened horizons, as well as cognitive gains. The 30 percent of all respondents who observed heightened intellectual curiosity and the 12 percent who noticed greater sympathy for efforts to spread education could equally well be included in the second column of the table, which indicates moral and cultural influence.

Nearly 40 percent of all teachers stated that a complete primary education influenced the moral and cultural levels of the graduates. Notably, the percentage who observed such an impact was somewhat higher in the Central Agricultural region than in the Central Industrial region where, it was argued, the influence of *otkhozhie* (work away from the village) counteracted whatever positive influence the school may have had. Also, whereas two-

Table 46
Percentage of Teachers Citing Various Positive Changes in
Primary School Graduates, by Region, 1911

REGION	EDUCATIONAL (COGNITIVE)	MORAL AND CULTURAL	RELIGIOUS ADHERENCE	FAMILY TIES	CIVIC INVOLVEMENT	ECONOMIC STATUS	HEALTH
Central Industrial	62.0%	36.0%	4.0%	13.0%	13.0%	22.0%	5.0%
Central Agricultural	55.0	42.0	6.0	15.0	16.5	28.0	7.0
Ukraine	54.0	42.0	7.0	13.5	14.5	43.0	7.0
Volga	60.0	39.0	16.0	16.0	18.0	28.0	9.0
Northern Forest	59.0	37.5	7.0	12.0	14.5	28.0	5.0
All respondents	58.5	39.2	6.7	15.4	16.5	27.5	7.6

SOURCE: *Anketa*, 138.

NOTE: The figures in the table are percentages of *all* respondents (11,822). In many cases, teachers listed more than one change.

fifths of all respondents observed some positive impact in the moral–cultural sphere, many others noted specifically that they had not observed any positive change and, further, that they *knew* there had been none.[13]

Zemstvo statisticians found a strong negative correlation between the crime rate in specific areas and the percentage of teachers who felt that the schools were exerting a positive moral–cultural influence on graduates. Thus, in the Central Agricultural region, where the rate of convictions was lowest, the incidence of perceived influence was considerably higher than in the Central Industrial region, where crime was much more widespread. The ethnic composition of the population seemed to be of little importance: in regions where non–Russians were more densely clustered (such as the Ukraine and Volga), the perceived moral–cultural impact of the school seemed to be less marked than in the Central Agricultural region, but significantly greater than in the Central Industrial area.[14]

Among teachers observing some moral–cultural influence, approximately half (or 20 percent of all teachers surveyed) specified improvements in external behavior—tidiness, politeness, deference to elders, less profanity. Five hundred seven teachers (or more than 4 percent of the total) distinctly noted that graduates were deferential to elders and to civil and religious authorities. This percentage is not particularly impressive, but as a spontaneously volunteered indication of influence, it does suggest that the schools helped instill respect for authority among some graduates.[15]

Nine hundred fifty-two, or about 8 percent of all teachers, saw "internal changes" among their pupils, primarily described as honesty, respect for law, continued striving for self-improvement, and greater consideration for other people, as well as for animals. Lamentably, only 399 (slightly more than 3 percent of the total number of teachers responding) believed that education helped reduce the level of drunkenness in the countryside.[16]

In slightly more than a quarter of all responses (27.5 percent), teachers observed that the school had an economic influence on graduates. For 5.7 percent, such influence meant the development of "businesslike attitudes"; for 10.5 percent, it meant concrete improvements in agricultural practices; and for 9.7 percent, a search for better work. In only 157 cases (1.3 percent) did teachers discern a "higher level of economic knowledge" on the part of graduates.

Even fewer teachers (132, or 1.1 percent) noted a practical application of acquired economic information, and 150 (1.2 percent) perceived an improvement in material conditions. In some regions, a few respondents felt that peasants who had completed primary school were more likely to take advantage of the Stolypin reforms, to separate their household and farmland from the commune and set out on their own.[17]

A zemstvo survey carried out in Perm' a decade earlier contained far more specific information on the socializing impact of the school and was reasonably positive about the influence of a full primary education on agricultural practice. Of 678 zemstvo correspondents, 343, or slightly more than half, claimed to observe a distinct difference in the way graduates managed their farms. Among Perm' correspondents who observed some change as a result of schooling, only a few referred to the use of books for gaining information on improving production. A greater number noted that graduates were more receptive than others to the advice proffered by the zemstvo agronomist, that they consciously tried to reduce labor expenditure and increase output, that they were more "enterprising," more resourceful and willing to take risks, prompter and more conscientious in their work, and more receptive to innovations such as new rotation systems and new equipment.[18]

Of those who noted no differences between primary school graduates and others, many commented that graduates were often still in subordinate positions in the household and had not yet had the opportunity to make their own decisions about how to run the farms. But it was also pointed out that former schoolchildren were not likely to become heads of households until the age of forty or more and, by that time, they would "have sunk into the morass of village ways." Many others complained that former pupils "became soft" or "unstable" and lost any desire for farming, or that they left in search of factory work or domestic service. Interestingly, one correspondent reported that peasants often equated soldiers and school graduates because both looked for ways out of the villages.[19]

The 1911 Zemstvo Survey also collected information on the relationship between education and the search for more lucrative or socially prestigious work. There was a puzzling but significant fluctuation from province to province in the percentage of teachers

Table 47

Percentage of Teachers Citing Education as
Influence on Search for Better Work
Opportunities, by Region, 1911

REGION	PERCENTAGE OF LAND CULTIVATED	TEACHERS CITING EDUCATION AS INFLUENCE
Central Agricultural	66.5%	13.2%
Ukraine	65.4	12.0
Volga	48.5	10.0
Northern Forest	10.7	9.6
Central Industrial	30.4	8.8
(Total respondents)		(9.7)

SOURCE: Compiled from *Anketa,* 150–153 (tables).

who noted that education led to a search for better work opportunities, with apparently dissimilar provinces such as Tula, Orel, Kaluga, Tambov, Moscow, and Iaroslavl' all reporting a considerably higher than average number of such observations. Grouped into regions, however, using the survey's criteria of occupations, land usage, ethnicity, and crime rate, the provincial rates do reveal a certain pattern, shown in Table 47.

Fewer teachers felt that graduates were striving to leave the farm in the Central Industrial provinces than in the three areas with the highest proportion of land under the plow and the highest percentage of the population engaged in either agriculture, hunting, or fishing. The contrast between the Central Agricultural and the Ukrainian provinces, on the one hand, and the industrialized heartland provinces, on the other, is particularly striking. Again, although the statistical difference is not large, the fact that these responses were unsolicited, spontaneous descriptions of how schooling affected pupils allows us to speculate that even a 5 percent difference in responses may be important.

The influence of schooling on the civic behavior of graduates was observed by 16.5 percent of all teachers involved in the zemstvo

Table 48
Teachers' Observations of Changes in Graduates'
Civic Behavior, 1911

	NUMBER OF TEACHERS CITING CHANGE	TEACHERS CITING CHANGE AS A PERCENTAGE OF ALL TEACHERS SURVEYED
Greater participation in local self-government	1,084	9%
Higher incidence of election to communal posts	216	2
Closer relations with local intelligentsia	828	7
Greater efforts to promote local education	797	7
Greater participation in various groups	77	1

SOURCE: *Anketa,* 153.

survey. Specific changes in such behavior are outlined in Table 48. The earlier Perm' survey also contained pertinent detail. When asked whether literacy (by which most zemstvo correspondents understood complete schooling) had a measurable impact on the conduct of volost' affairs and village gatherings, a full 77 percent of the correspondents answered affirmatively. Many reported that educated peasants enjoyed respect from fellow villagers and that the word of a literate peasant carried more authority than that of others. The Perm' study also noted that former schoolchildren were more likely to be elected to positions of authority in the village. The compiler of this survey summarized the reports:

The literate is better able to grasp matters under discussion; he conducts himself in exemplary fashion, does not shout without reason, "understands procedures better," "can make better sense of written material," is "more articulate" and "reasonable."

As one correspondent concluded, "Wherever you find a village gathering where many former pupils are in attendance, you will see much more civilized behavior and the disappearance of former practices such as *kashtanstvo* [gross acquisitiveness] and bribery with liquor."[20]

The 1911 Zemstvo Survey found that only 15 percent of all teachers responding to the survey believed a complete primary education had some impact on families of the pupils. In nearly three-quarters of these instances, this impact translated into a heightened interest in and tolerance of education by the entire family. In roughly one-third (that is, among approximately 5 percent of all teachers), an unspecified "moral" improvement in family relations was noted.[21]

The last two categories in which the influence of education was observed were religion (6.7 percent) and health (7.6 percent). Five hundred twenty-seven teachers (more than 4 percent) discerned a greater concern for cleanliness among graduates, and 122 (1 percent) argued that former pupils were more likely to turn to a doctor when confronted with health problems. The perceived influence of education on religion, slight as it was, was greatest in those areas with a large proportion of non-Orthodox adherents and only half as great in the Central Industrial and Central Agricultural regions. (What was apparently being measured was the rate of conversion to Orthodoxy.)[22]

Stepping back from these deceptively precise numbers, what can we learn from the responses of the eleven thousand rural teachers? Perhaps we should initially consider what should *not* be inferred from the study. First, the survey posed only one question— did the schools have an impact on the graduate?—and left it up to the teacher to specify the particular changes observed. Thus, silence on any topic was much less meaningful than a negative reply to a precise query about the influence of education on, say, career patterns or agriculture might have been. In only one area of the country did a sizable proportion of teachers spontaneously venture that the school had *no* moral or cultural impact on graduates. In addition, because teachers were not responsible for Bible study, they may have considered religion outside their purview and simply neglected to discuss changes or improvements in this subject.

Perhaps most important, the 1911 Zemstvo Survey (though not the Perm' study) investigated the influence of the school on the *graduate,* the child who had completed the full three- or four-year program. We now know that this included somewhere between one in six and one in ten village youth. The study recorded not the absolute number of former pupils influenced in one way or another, but the numbers of teachers who assigned particular importance to one or another type of impact. Thus, the conclusions represent only a relative weighting and can in no way be combined with the actual number of graduates to determine, for example, the true number of peasant children who were pursuing new careers, improving their speech patterns, or participating in civic affairs.

But even with all these reservations, the 1911 Zemstvo Survey remains extremely interesting, strongly suggesting that, among the small minority of children who made their way through the entire three-year program (not necessarily all those who stayed in the school three years), teachers perceived specific changes in behavior and values. The most commonly observed changes were alterations of speech patterns, richer vocabulary, heightened curiosity about the outside world, increased respect for science, and an attempt to "clean up" behavior, to become more respectable. Much less frequently, teachers noted changes in the economic attitudes or well-being of former pupils, and, more rarely, improvements in family relations or civic behavior. The lower incidence of these last two changes might well have signified resistance in the community to the graduates' new attitudes, as well as family resistance to the new way of life urged by the educated offspring. It is also intimated, but by no means convincingly demonstrated, by the study that graduates were often being given new ambitions in life without the opportunity to fulfill them.

THE KEY THAT OPENED NO DOORS

Among the changes observed in some graduates of the primary schools was a striving for economic betterment, which often meant a desire to leave the village. This striving had long been noted by those close to the countryside and the village school. Soon after the establishment of zemstvo schools, Baron Korf pointed out:

"Our public school, . . . in the majority of cases, leads to the following result: those who come out of its doors either soon forget what they have learned or they strive to leave their own milieu."[23] Similarly, in the 1880s, responding to a query concerning the local needs of public education, a representative from the Urzhumsk district zemstvo in Viatka province commented: "Our public school provides no knowledge applicable to daily life; its graduates soon forget what they have learned or search for ways to leave the countryside."[24] Kulomzin, one of the architects of the 1908 School Bill, also commented in his proposal for universal schooling that literates, and especially school graduates, fled the villages precisely because literacy was a rarity and provided opportunities for social mobility. He added hopefully that with the implementation of universal education, literacy would no longer be in short supply and the drain from the villages would cease as outside opportunities dried up.[25]

Throughout the last quarter of the nineteenth century, conservatives often expressed anxiety that the schools were in fact promoting social and geographic mobility, which they predicted would have dire consequences for the society as a whole. On the one hand, they expressed the age-old concern that education would encourage a striving for social advancement that would either tear down the old class barriers or, when frustrated, increase dissatisfaction with one's lot in life and lead to popular disturbances. On the other hand, they argued that education could only worsen the deepening agrarian crisis by siphoning off the most talented and enterprising peasants from the villages, placing them in nonmanual jobs in the towns and cities.

These issues bring us to the question of what happened to those few pupils who managed to complete the primary school program. With the rapid expansion of industry and the growth of the bureaucracy in late nineteenth-century Russia, one would expect a good deal of accompanying mobility. For the newly literate, particularly the young man who could read and write correctly, express himself properly, and count with ease, the opportunities could have been legion.

But the evidence concerning such opportunities is enigmatic; in fact, it points in two different directions, both of which spelled a net loss for peasant households, if not necessarily for the children themselves. When educated young people successfully found employment outside the village, they often cut all ties with home. The family thus lost the direct investment in the child's education and a labor unit for the farm, as well as the parents' main guarantee of social and economic security in their old age. The "backwash effect," observed in many developing countries, in which investment in rural education simply increases the outflow of labor skills from the countryside, can cause not only severe imbalance in national economies but also major problems for family farms. This backwash effect was—and is—present in Russia as well.[26]

Unfortunately, I have found no data concerning the relationship between a complete primary education, family economic status, and the occupation of the graduate. Yet widespread parental indifference to the school certificate, particularly after the law granting military deferments and reduced terms to those passing exams was rescinded, suggests that one teacher was correct when he declared that "a complete education is a key that opens no doors" (*"budet davat' v ruki kliuchi kotorym nechego otpirat"*).[27]

Why did so many pupils drop out during their third year of schooling, without bothering to take the one last step of acquiring the certificate? One school inspector from Saratov pointed out:

While not denying the usefulness of literacy and eagerly sending their children to school, especially their boys, the peasants make only modest demands: to teach their children the prayers, the Bible, and how to read, write, and count. The peasants don't like to keep their children in school long. They let them come for two, often for three, winters, and that is all. . . . The examinations conflict with the beginning of field work or spring chores. What is more, [the peasants] don't show a special interest in examinations because [these tests] no longer offer any particular benefits.[28]

A Church school inspector wrote that children would show up for their examinations only when the teacher hired them as day laborers. "'Little Father,' a peasant who was bringing his child to the final examination once told me, 'it's not our children but rather the teachers who need the examinations. After all, you know, they receive 10 rubles for every [child] who passes the test.'"[29] There was a measure of truth to this statement, the inspector concluded. Since the pupils received no real benefits, and since inspectors often measured a school's success by a count of those completing the program, it was indeed in the teacher's interest to produce as many pupils as possible for the final examination. These observations are supported by others who worked in the countryside.[30]

Although finding testimony that parents were often indifferent to the examination process and school certificates is no problem, it is much more difficult to find evidence supporting parental fears that a complete basic education would enable the child to find a "soft berth," as a Perm' study of peasant attitudes labeled the problem. In fact, in this study, when respondents were asked if graduates of the schools left agricultural work, only 38 replied that a "significant number" did; 269 claimed that only a few left; and 324 reported none at all left. In Perm', efforts to leave the village were greatest among former military recruits and individuals from large families. This same study noted that the degree of knowledge provided by the primary school was insufficient to gain access to official service (*sluzhba*), even as a lowly volost' clerk.[31]

Studies of primary school graduates also suggested that the vast majority remained in agricultural work. Orlov's famous 1882 study of education in Moscow included a survey of the fate of the 318 male recipients of the military benefits certificate in Moscow. Information was found on 246 of these graduates. Two had died; of the remaining 244, 11 (4.5 percent) were continuing full-time education elsewhere; 33 (13.5 percent) continued to attend the same school; 11 (4.5 percent) attended Sunday or refresher courses; and 7 (2.9 percent) took special courses in choir or drafting. One hundred ninety-one graduates did not continue their schooling; 112 of these (45.9 percent of the total group) were employed at home, 16 (6.5 percent) in cottage industry, 13 (5.3 percent) at liquor establishments; 14 (5.7 percent) worked in factories; 8 (3.3 percent) were engaged in commerce; 5 (2 percent) worked as draymen; 9 (3.7 percent) had clerical jobs at the volost' office; and 3 (1.3 percent) had other employment.[32]

A study in Simbirsk during the 1880s determined the occupations of 2,873 former pupils. Of this group, 77.4 percent were engaged in agriculture, 6.6 percent in "trades," 2 percent in factories, 3.5 percent "at home," 2.1 percent as clerks, and 6.3 percent in other employment (including commerce, continued education, shepherding, and so on). No specific employment was listed by

Table 49

Occupations of Male Primary School Graduates,
Kursk Province, 1890

	PERCENTAGE OF GRADUATES SURVEYED
Agriculture	80.7%
Trades	8.1
Commerce	3.9
Military	1.8
Continuing education	1.4
Pisar' (clerk in office, or village scribe)	1.2
Prikazchik (steward, or merchandise clerk)	0.9
Teacher	0.5
Priest or other clergy	0.3
Official	0.2
Service (*sluzhashchii*)	0.2
Painter	0.1
Other[a]	0.7

SOURCE: Belokonskii (Kursk), *Narodnoe nachal'noe obrazovanie*, 303.

NOTE: In Kursk in 1890, 39,974 male students received certificates. Data are presented here for 32,695 graduates.

[a] Includes medical (50), police (24), and others.

2.1 percent.[33] A far more inclusive study of over thirty thousand graduates in Kursk province in the 1890s yielded the results shown in Table 49. If these studies are representative of the entire country, we can conclude that only one in five graduates "left" agriculture—and certainly many of these children came from families already primarily engaged in trade, handicrafts, and factory labor.

We must also consider the findings of the 1911 Zemstvo Survey that a complete education did lead—among some former pupils—to a striving for economic betterment. To the degree that this effort meant a search for work opportunities outside of agriculture, rather than an attempt to rationalize production, a conflict between the striving and the results can be detected. Is it plausible that this search itself, rather than actual movement, caused parents' unhappiness, resulting in generational friction and attempts by parents to restrict the length of schooling to the necessary minimum? Certainly, the reports from the countryside cited at some length in our discussion of parental attitudes hint that this was the case. The key that opened no doors may well have opened a Pandora's box of strife. The Perm' study explicitly noted that education produced friction between the generations over the graduate's place in the family hierarchy and the choice of occupation to be pursued. When measuring peasant attitudes, it would be impossible to draw a line between hostility and indifference toward a complete primary education—the two attitudes must have overlapped. But it may not be unfounded to suggest that there was hostility, and that this hostility was grounded not in peasant slothfulness but in realistic observations of the consequences of a full primary education.

15

Beyond Primary School

Wh'''hat use did the peasant have for a primary school certificate?
Until 1906, one immediate benefit was a reduced term of military
service. Another possible road opened by the certificate allowed
some graduates a chance to continue their education. The importance of measuring what Lawrence Stone has called the "regulated
trickle," the progress of students through the successive stages
of the educational system, can hardly be exaggerated. As Stone
points out, "It is precisely because education is so powerful a force
in preserving existing social distinctions that change [in educational systems] is always a highly explosive political issue, and is
always so bitterly resented and resisted."[1]

The gateway between primary and secondary schooling, as
well as that between secondary and higher education, provided a
measure of sponsored mobility when opened; when closed, it
helped maintain stratification in society. Stone argues that the educational level at which status barriers are erected differs from society to society and that the determination of that level is crucial
in understanding social formations, the configuration of social
classes, and tensions between groups.[2]

Although a substantial body of literature exists on secondary
and higher education in Western Europe, the workings of the Rus-

sian secondary school system and its links with the primary schools remain largely unelucidated. This subject—encompassing frequent policy changes, a bewildering variety of secondary and higher elementary schools, and an even greater variety of entrance requirements and programs—is too complex to be analyzed here, though its exploration promises to yield important insights into the social history of late Imperial Russia.[3] Instead, the task of this chapter is more limited: to determine how many children proceeded on from the primary schools to further education, where they went, and what they did with their education, with the emphasis, once more, on peasant motivation and peasant choice.

NEITHER BEAUTY NOR BEAST

A persistent and central issue in Russian education circles was the debate over access to secondary education. At the turn of the century, pressure increased to support "advanced" elementary schools that facilitated direct access to secondary education—a vital rung in the ladder for peasants willing and able to continue their schooling. Pressure for an expanded school program led, on the one hand, to a movement, which rapidly gained momentum after 1905, to convert the basic primary schools into four-year institutions and also led, on the other hand, to the establishment of a growing number of five-year schools (called "two-class" because one teacher supervised grades one through three in one classroom, while a second teacher instructed the fourth and fifth grades in another) in the villages, as well as an assortment of advanced elementary schools in the towns. The drive culminated in the establishment of a unified higher elementary school by a decree issued on 25 July 1912. But even before 1912, an amorphous, somewhat ramshackle structure of advanced primary education had been established by a process of accretion, providing a bewildering variety of schools that offered vocational training or intermediate education for those determined to gain entrance to a secondary school.

The government had given itself a black eye in 1887 when Minister of Education Delianov released his famous "Cooks' Children" circular in an attempt to restrict the lower classes from continuing their education. Like all measures since the time of Nicholas I that were designed to restrain commoner access to advanced education, the circular was entirely ineffective. It would be fascinating to trace the debate over access to advanced education, linking it to larger social issues as well as to the ongoing discussion of school curriculum, but this would lead us far astray. Suffice it to note that not all progressives were united in the effort to create a unified ladder providing unhindered access to higher education, nor was the bureaucracy united in opposing such access.

Ironically, the "Cook's Children" circular seemed to fit the mood of much of the rural population. This mood is most evident in the results of a questionnaire concerning popular attitudes toward higher education that was sent out through the zemstvo correspondent network in Moscow province at the turn of the century and tabulated by V. V Petrov. Petrov complained that zemstvo interest in continued education had actually declined since the late 1870s, when at least there had been widespread recognition of the inadequacies of the three-year program. But the data he collected also seemed to indicate that the population was neither willing nor able to take advantage of courses beyond the third year of instruction. In the few existing five-year, two-class schools established by the Ministry of Education and supported by the provincial zemstvo, only 55 percent of those enrolled in the third year continued to the fourth.[4]

These five-year schools were concentrated in the more central, populous, and commercially oriented settlements in Moscow, as they were in other provinces. The majority of pupils who entered the final two years were children of factory personnel, local merchants, and wealthy peasant traders. Those who pursued the fourth year of study were primarily interested in low-level service careers, whereas the bulk of the population had no interest in the advanced primary education certificate.[5]

A significant proportion of the children in our two-class schools are the offspring of the petty bourgeoisie, the clergy, bureaucrats, impoverished nobility, and prosperous peasants . . . sometimes living as far as twenty to thirty versts from the schools. . . . The knowledge and skills these children carry away from the schools are more readily and fully applied in their lives . . . than in the peasant milieu; thus, they value the school more and look for more than simple literacy from it. Moreover, for many of these parents, their children's education is often linked with the hope— sometimes the only hope—of opening a way for them in life, since this . . . is achieved mainly through the knowledge, skills, rights, and privileges provided by the school. Consequently, the more taken from the school, the greater the chances of achieving a position for oneself. This explains the insistence with which individuals from these groups often work to gain greater advantages for their children through the school.[6]

Among the peasantry, only those with substantial resources could consider taking advantage of such schools:

For the peasant with land, the possession and tilling of the land provide him [a living] and fully decide the future of his children; thus he does not base his hopes on what the school system will give. He doesn't need rights from the school, but rather needs the literacy, which he values as a practical tool to meet the demands imposed by life. Only a surplus of means, such as the ownership of a subsidiary cottage industry, involvement in trade, or—and this is much rarer—the ambitious dream of bringing his child into society, encourages the peasant to take the maximum offered by the school. For this, the family must deny itself the income earned by the adolescent; as is known, this is not always possible, despite the practical benefits offered by assimilating the complete school curriculum.[7]

Referring to two-class schools, one teacher wrote that "these schools are not even known to everyone; they have clearly not taken root among the population and willy-nilly lead an invisible existence, unnoticed by the masses for whom they were created."[8] Petrov's survey contained a wealth of evidence from both Moscow and other provinces suggesting that the two–class school was used primarily by the more prosperous elements of the peasantry as a springboard for entry into the municipal or secondary schools. Complaints were frequent that the successful termination of the two–class school "wrenches the peasant child away from the occupation of his father and prods him to seek out easier jobs." Petrov argued that the advanced elementary school, rather than adding to the "intellectual forces" of the countryside, would only facilitate the further drain of talent and skills from the villages.[9] Here, of course, he was touching on the "backwash effect" that

so bothers developmental economists today. Petrov was also observing what Furet and Ozouf note in their history of literacy in
France: paradoxically, by recruiting talent and ambition away from
the village, advanced schools tended to reinforce rather than break
down the isolation and cultural autarky of the village community
as a whole.[10]

Despite this discouraging evidence, a number of other zemstvos that carried out statistical studies of popular attitudes toward
advanced elementary education between 1899 and 1910 discovered
a growing interest in such schools.[11] (See Table 50.) Comparing the
results of several surveys conducted during these years, one statistician concluded that the evident growth of interest in advanced
elementary education could be explained only by the cultural and
political impact of the 1905 Revolution and by "the new socioeconomic relations unfolding in the country as a whole, penetrating the countryside as well, and forcing the population to reach for
greater knowledge than that provided by the elementary school."[12]

In a study conducted in Moscow in 1910 (repeating Petrov's

Table 50
Perception of Popular Demand for
Advanced Education

PROVINCE	YEAR OF SURVEY	TEACHERS OR ZEMSTVO CORRESPONDENTS NOTING POPULAR INTEREST IN ADVANCED EDUCATION
Perm'	1899	46.5%
Kursk	1905	52.5
Kherson	1906	96.8
Moscow	1910	72.8

SOURCE: N. Kazimirov, "Otnoshenie naseleniia k shkolam povyshennogo tipa,"
in *Statisticheskii ezhegodnik Moskovskoi gubernii za 1911 god* (Moscow, 1912), 77.
NOTE: These figures reflect teachers' or zemstvo correspondents' perceptions, not
an actual measurement of demand.

earlier survey), 72 percent of the zemstvo correspondents questioned noted an interest in advanced elementary education among the rural population. Of the 323 correspondents surveyed, 68.4 percent were peasants engaged in agriculture, and more than four-fifths of these peasants replied affirmatively. But of the rural intelligentsia surveyed, only 50 percent perceived an interest in further elementary schools among the peasants—a rather striking difference in perceptions.[13]

The Moscow survey seemed to indicate a fairly substantial demand for such schools by a significant minority of the population in the countryside. Most important, in many localities peasants were themselves now taking the initiative by passing resolutions at both volost' and village-level gatherings. From Ploskovsk volost' in Volokolamsk, we read that "the peasants in our village wanted a town school and built a two-story building for the purpose." From Ramensk volost' in Bronitsy district, one peasant wrote that he had inquired widely and that his peers "talked about a two-class school as if it were their only dream in life." From Klin, Vereia, and Kolomna, peasants reported that village gatherings had either discussed or actually drawn up resolutions calling for advanced elementary schools and proposing measures to prod the zemstvo into action.[14] A report to the Moscow district zemstvo stated: "The demand for schools of an advanced type is registered in the frequent petitions we receive to open such schools, in the large number of candidates for zemstvo stipends, . . . and in the overcrowding of existing ministerial schools."[15]

Where cottage industries were not widespread, the demand for continued education was pronounced, for there was no local employment to draw in children immediately after their completion of the three-year primary school. From Kulpinsk volost' in Volokolamsk district, one correspondent complained, "After [the children] finish school, they often loiter about [*b'iut baklushi*] all winter long, for they can't find work, nor can they study without the help of a teacher." Another peasant correspondent wrote from Tashirovsk volost' in Vereia: "When the children finish school, they are only twelve years old, and until they are fifteen neither the factory nor the local workshop will take them." A peasant in Boiarkinsk volost', Kolomna district, noted: "The peasants finish school at thirteen and have to 'chase dogs' for two years until the factory will take them."[16] Such problems were also described in provinces other than Moscow:

Young people are often left without work after finishing school. Although a few of them love to read, in the company of others they become delinquents [*razgul'nymi*] and begin to commit various anti-social acts: they fight, write obscene words, smoke, and drink wine.[17]

According to observers, another major stimulus to advanced education was the mushrooming cooperative movement. Peasant participation in agricultural societies, as well as credit, dairy, and other cooperatives made clear the advantages of having a solid basic education.[18] In such organizations, literacy and numeracy were essential, for records, correspondence, and calculations were extremely important.

By far the most thorough study of popular demand for and utilization of advanced education was contained in the 1911 Zemstvo Survey. Teachers were asked, for example, to rate public satisfaction with existing primary schools. Although the responses fluctuated widely from province to province, overall only 38.7 percent of the 13,558 teachers responding believed peasants were content with the schools, and only 4.1 percent reported indifference. Of the 57.2 percent reporting dissatisfaction, the overwhelming majority (72.5 percent) called for a more extended program of study, whereas a sizable minority (30.6 percent) urged that the school curriculum be given a more vocational or "professional" character. (Of those urging a more specialized curriculum, 2,373 called for "professional," 2,015 for "trade," and 800 for "agricultural" training.) "First in one place, and then another, the demand from the peasants to have advanced schools and to open trade schools in the vicinity frequently pops up in reports and resolutions of the zemstvos."[19]

Yet, as we discovered when considering surveys on dropouts, repeating, opportunity costs, and absenteeism, reports that at first seem to be discussing a large-scale phenomenon often turn out to be deceptive. The magnitude of demand for advanced education was in fact rather small. Of the 7,755 teachers who reported popular dissatisfaction with the existing schools, 72.5 percent called for lengthening the program; of this group, 49 percent called for a four- or five-year *basic* program, and 27 percent for two-class schools. (A few favored both.) In short, of 13,558 teachers queried, only about 11 percent (1,536) specifically called for advanced general education, and only 20 percent thought it necessary to expand the program to four or five years.[20]

Given that we are dealing with teachers' perceptions of the need for advanced schools, and not with absolute numbers of pupils who would have utilized such schools, it seems likely that the zemstvo survey was recording the existence of a small fraction of the population in the countryside who were anxious and financially able to continue their children's studies beyond the three- or four-year point. The existence of this small group, an upwardly mobile peasant minority in the village, is a significant question for the political history of twentieth-century Russia. Yet for the majority of peasants, advanced schools were still of little importance.

A regional grouping of teachers' perceptions showed little difference between agricultural and industrial areas in popular aspirations for continued education, whether in the Ukraine, Volga, Central Agricultural, or Central Industrial regions. The only slight differences may have been in the Volga and Ukrainian regions, where minorities constituted a significant proportion of the population; mandatory instruction in Russian often impeded educational progress, and the peasants seemed to recognize that they had to keep their children in school longer in order to master the basics.[21]

Other studies confirmed the suspicion that interest in advanced education was limited to a small segment of the population. Even the fourth year tacked onto the basic program enjoyed limited popularity, though by 1911 nearly one out of every four zemstvo schools (23.6 percent) offered the additional year.[22]

The Church schools, which in some areas had begun even earlier to convert to a four-year program, met the same problem. In Saratov, just before World War I, the director of Church schools noted that where two-class (four-year) schools had been established, the population showed little interest in the final year, with attendance reflecting this lack of interest. Trying to explain this, he observed, "Children don't find a position after graduating, and, even worse, having completed advanced education [*bol'shaia nauka*], they are unfit for their native agriculture." The director of Church schools in Vladimir also found little support among the population for four-year schools, and he commented that half or fewer of those who had completed the third year returned for the fourth. There were even schools where *no* children enrolled in the fourth year.[23]

Among Old Believers, there was strong pressure for universal education but also no interest in extending the program. A questionnaire sent out in preparation for the Ninth Congress of Old Believers discovered that only 5 percent of the respondents felt any need for advanced schools in the countryside.[24]

Still another question included in the 1911 Zemstvo Survey concerned the obstacles that prevented pupils from continuing their education in advanced schools. Teachers were asked: "What is most important in preventing primary school graduates from continuing their education in secondary or other advanced schools: insufficient means; lack of appropriate schools; lack of fit between primary school and advanced school programs; the absence of desire on the part of the pupil or the parents; or other reasons?" The answers received from 14,350 teachers of three-year schools were quite revealing.

Throughout the country, teachers were virtually unanimous (94.2 percent, ranging from 87 percent in Ufa to 97 percent in Smolensk) in the sentiment that economic considerations kept graduates from continuing their education. Under this rubric were the familiar references to the indirect, or opportunity, costs of education. Correspondents noted that children eleven to twelve years old were expected to begin contributing to the welfare of the household. According to many reports, this expectation was particularly true in *razdel* households, where the father and the sons had separated their holdings, the number of adults in each home had been reduced, and labor needs increased correspondingly. By far the largest number of correspondents did not elaborate on the situation, however, but simply limited their answers to a terse "insufficient means."[25]

In an earlier discussion of child labor and the school dropout rate, we saw that most children did not become full-fledged working members of the household until the age of fourteen or fifteen, thus discounting child labor, forced by poverty, as a major explanation of the high dropout rate. But the teachers' argument that cited "insufficient means" may be much more credible when used to explain why many primary school graduates were unable to continue their education.

First, we should keep in mind that a fairly substantial proportion of graduating pupils had been in school longer than three years and were thus over the age of eleven. The 1911 Zemstvo Survey found that as many as 35 percent of graduates from three-year schools had spent four or more years completing the program. In the third grade, 30 percent of pupils were twelve years old, and 18 percent were thirteen or older. According to the 1911 School Census, only 72 percent of all rural elementary pupils in the Empire were ages eight through eleven.[26] Thus, children who had actually graduated from primary schools were closer to the ages at which they *would* be subject to economic pressure to join the work force.

Second, and perhaps most important, the teacher surveys referred to here made no distinction between direct and indirect (opportunity) costs. Although almost all zemstvo and Church schools provided instruction, textbooks, and materials free of charge to the individual family (the peasant commune often contributed a sizable amount), making basic education virtually free, enrollment in advanced schools involved substantial outlays for tuition, textbooks, clothing, and housing—costs that could easily exceed the total earnings of a peasant family. Even the two-class schools could be prohibitive. In Moscow in 1900, although tuition was only 3 rubles a year, it cost those who lived at a distance another 2 to 4 rubles a month for a child's room and board in town.[27] The small number of advanced schools in the Empire only increased the direct costs of sending children to school outside the village, because they generally had to travel long distances to find a school. One report in the 1910 Moscow questionnaire estimated: "For every pupil, it is necessary to find an apartment costing no less than 2 rubles a winter, as well as no less than three-eighths of a pound of tea; there is also the cost of transportation, no fewer than fifty times a winter (two to three times a week), and not everyone has that kind of money."[28] Thus, teachers who pointed to insufficient means as the overriding obstacle to continued education sounded a note of truth, for peasants were indeed confronted with both direct and indirect economic outlays if they wished to keep their children in school.

Teachers perceived parental attitudes—a lack of conviction that advanced education was useful—as the second most important obstacle to continued education, with 36.3 percent of the teachers citing this factor. The fluctuation of responses from province to province was fairly wide, ranging from 24 percent in Poltava to 52 percent in Ufa, but it is difficult to discern any pattern of regional or urban-rural differences.[29] In fact, a look at some of the particular responses indicates that the distinction between family attitudes and economic causes was somewhat tenuous; many parents were simply not convinced that further education would yield major economic benefits. One correspondent from Saratov wrote, "Many local residents look at advanced education from the business point of view. They are prepared to make outlays on education for their children, but only with the guarantee that the money doesn't simply go for nothing [*ne propali zria*] . . . that it yields dividends."[30]

There were instances when pupils, failing to find work commensurate with their education, ended up the odd-man-out in their own milieu. A correspondent from Perm' warned, "If you send your children to study in the advanced schools, you're likely to end up with neither peasant nor lord [*ne muzhik, ne barin*]. They become ill-adapted for agricultural work but fail to gain a better position in life." Another correspondent wrote:

A fellow, during his stay at the municipal school, becomes unaccustomed to farm work, but with this education alone it is almost impossible to find work that challenges his mind. The result? As the saying goes, Matrëna became neither a beauty nor a crow! [*i sdelalas' Matrëna ni pava ni vorona!*][31]

Because all advanced elementary schools were located in towns or cities and charged fees, the outlays on tuition, as well as room and board, were considerable—even prohibitive—for all but the wealthiest peasant families. The prospect of an investment being lost to the family often discouraged peasants from sending their children to these schools. To be sure, children who made their way into the world of service occupations and who retained a degree of family loyalty might have sent money home. In areas where land was limited and hands plentiful—such as the Central Agricultural region—the investment might have seemed justified. But the risk was also high. As one Perm' correspondent wrote in a different survey, the peasant child was likely "to shove off from one shore but not make it to the other" ("*ot odnogo berega otstanet a k drugomu ne pristanet*").[32]

Often, however, peasants looked unfavorably on the prospect of their children becoming "beauties"—on the prospect of the success that education might bring. From Ekaterinoslav, we read that parents "fear advanced education as a means of alienating a member of the family from the patriarchal conditions of domestic life. . . . They look at the educated son as some kind of *barin*, incapable of hard work, and they expect no support for themselves in their old age."[33] Many such responses could be cited.

At least one delegate to the Zemstvo Congress considered the problem important enough to bring to the attention of the assembled representatives:

We must strive to make the school useful to the population. Peasants want the school to provide literacy that will not tear their children away from the land and the family. . . . Today we often see peasant children who, having graduated from the urban schools, don't return to their families, but who remain in the town in search of easy work and who are ashamed, when at home, to harness a horse or clean up the yard [*dvor*], not to speak of participating in actual field work. Peasant girls, torn away from their families, after completing the pro–gymnasium avoid physical labor, don't as a rule know how to cut, sew, bake bread, or fix a dinner.[34]

The distinction between "economic conditions" and "parental attitudes" as obstacles to continued education indeed blurs on closer investigation. But a comparison of the reasons given by teachers for pupils not continuing on to advanced education with the reasons given for premature withdrawal from the elementary schools reveals a significant difference, shown in Table 51. It may be that economic considerations prevailed when parents decided not to send their children to more advanced schools, whereas family attitudes were more important in causing withdrawal from the elementary school program. At first glance, this explanation might seem to contradict one of this book's basic arguments, that by 1911

Table 51

Obstacles to Education Cited by Teachers, 1911

	PERCENTAGE OF TEACHERS' RESPONSES		
	Economic Considerations	*Parental Attitudes*	*School Organization or Conditions*
Cited as obstacle to continued (advanced) education	94.2%	36.3%	33.0%
Cited as cause of elementary school attrition	71.7	70.0	21.0

SOURCE: *Anketa*, 122.

there was widespread recognition among peasants of the usefulness of literacy and primary education. But the apparent contradiction disappears when we sort out the various strands involved.

Because the potential income of children between the ages of twelve and fifteen was much greater than the marginal labor contributions of younger boys or girls, opportunity-cost considerations obviously carried more weight with the parents of older children. Since the economic justification for the younger set dropping out of school was less substantial, the relative importance of cultural factors (parental attitudes) was magnified. Similarly, reluctance on the part of the children themselves was more frequently cited as a reason for early departure (19.9 percent) than for failure to continue education (6.3 percent)—possibly, as zemstvo statisticians suggested, because ignorance of the value of education was often transmitted from parents to children.[35]

The school system was listed more frequently as an obstruction to continued education than to completing elementary school precisely because the establishment of advanced elementary schools lagged far behind the building of three-year schools, with access to the former accordingly much more restricted. This difference reflected both the substantial gains made in the zemstvo provinces in bringing basic primary education to the rural population and the distance still to be covered before the ladder system could be introduced on a wide scale.[36]

Although the school system itself was more frequently an obstacle to continued education than to successful completion of the basic program, it is surprising how infrequently teachers referred to the system (school organization) as a problem. After all, complaints were common in the press about the shortage of advanced schools, overcrowding, and severe competition for places. Criticism of the lack of fit between the primary school program and entrance requirements for advanced higher and secondary schools was even more vociferous. Yet in all, only one out of three teachers in the countryside felt that the school system could be even partially blamed for the failure of peasants to continue their education. Among this number, 78 percent specifically noted the shortage of schools and the distance from the nearest advanced schools, and 29 percent referred to the incompatibility of school curricula.[37] Thus, only one out of four of all zemstvo teachers considered distance or shortage of schools a problem, and only one in ten believed that the missing rungs in the ladder (incompatibility of curriculum) actually created obstacles.

It is remarkable that teachers' opinions diverged so sharply from the views that dominated the educational world. If "fit" was not a major problem, what, after all, was the significance of the large-scale struggle waged by progressive circles for a "unified" school system and direct access to all levels of the educational ladder? Once again, the problem of "fit" may in reality have been a matter of poor integration of the peasants' perceived needs and wishes and those of progressive educators.

MEASURING THE REGULATED TRICKLE

For most of the peasantry, continued education was not a major issue. Yet for the historian interested in measuring social mobility and in the question of an upwardly mobile peasant minority emerging at the end of the nineteenth century, it is important to measure the size of the stream, or trickle, of peasants who continued on from the primary schools. We can determine precisely what proportion of zemstvo primary school graduates were continuing their education, for the question was carefully investigated in preparation for the 1911 Zemstvo Congress. Questionnaires sent directly to schools asked how many graduates were preparing to continue their education, and how many actually succeeded in enrolling.[38]

The survey demonstrated that a relationship existed between teachers' observations of the level of popular satisfaction with the school system and the incidence of continued education, for the latter was limited indeed.[39] Throughout the zemstvo provinces, almost exactly half of all zemstvo schools (50.7 percent) had *no* graduates continuing, or planning to continue, their education. Overall, 11.9 percent of graduates intended to or actually enrolled in advanced schools. In 1910, the zemstvo schools produced 15,098 pupils preparing to continue their education. Of this group, almost four out of five, or 9.5 percent of all graduates, actually enrolled—12,280 pupils who moved to the next rung of the educational ladder. The percentages of graduates continuing their education fluctuated wildly from province to province (from 3 percent in Samara and Tavrida to 15 percent in Novgorod, Smolensk, and Vologda), but the fluctuation suggests no obvious correlation with economic conditions.[40]

Using the above figures, we can make a rough estimate of the number of peasants from *all* rural schools who continued their education. The figure is approximate, for it assumes the same distribution and dropout rate, as well as the same percentage of graduates continuing, for all types of schools. The first two assumptions might be fairly safe, however, for we have seen that distribution and dropout rates did not vary significantly between the two major types of schools, zemstvo and Church.

According to the 1911 School Census, 624,392 pupils (9.42 percent of all enrolled) graduated from one- and two-class schools in the Empire in 1910. Ninety-two percent of schools included in the census offered courses of four years or less (a basic, rather than an advanced, elementary program). Assuming that the distribution of pupils roughly corresponded to the number of schools in each category, we can calculate a total graduating class size of 574,441. If the percentage of graduates continuing their education was the same in all types of schools, 68,358 pupils were preparing a move on to a higher rung on the educational ladder, and 54,572 pupils actually made it to that next rung.

By 1911, a child in the Russian Empire had roughly a 50 percent chance of enrolling in a primary school. (See Chapter 10.) The child who did enroll in primary school had about one chance in three or four of completing the program. If he completed the program and graduated, he then had one chance in twelve of continuing his education. If "he" were a she, the chances of passing each stage were much slimmer. Children who were born in the countryside also faced somewhat lower chances. Children born in Central Asia of non-Russian parents had virtually no chance of even reaching primary school, not to mention continuing from there.

What were the individual peasant's chances of receiving an advanced education? What were the odds that a peasant child born in 1900 would have the opportunity to move beyond the lowest rung of the school ladder? Estimating the number of school-age children in 1910 at 13,852,167, we can assume that one out of three or one out of four (between 4,571,215 and 3,463,041) should have graduated each year. This number would have approximated the "flow" into higher schools annually if all children had been enrolling, graduating, and continuing on. Instead, with 54,572 graduates continuing their education annually, a child's chances of moving beyond lower elementary school were between one and one-and-a-half in one hundred.

Table 52 indicates that even among the zemstvo provinces there was great variation in the life chances of an individual proceeding to advanced schools. In Moscow, roughly three in every one hundred peasants could hope to do so, but in Orel the chances were only one in two hundred.

The 1911 Zemstvo Survey noted that the average village school graduated eleven or twelve pupils each year; of these students, one or two were likely to continue their education. Interestingly, among schools where at least one student continued, the tendency was actually for two or three to go on; in a few areas, as many as one-quarter of all graduating students remained in school.[41] We have no way of knowing the reason for this clustering, but it suggests that the availability of advanced schools in the area may have been very important.

What choice of schools did primary school graduates have?

Table 52
Continued Education, Selected Provinces, 1911

	PERCENTAGE OF CHILDREN AGED 8-II ENROLLED IN PRIMARY SCHOOLS	PERCENTAGE OF PRIMARY SCHOOL STUDENTS GRADUATING	PERCENTAGE OF PRIMARY SCHOOL GRADUATES CONTINUING THEIR EDUCATION	INDIVIDUAL LIFE CHANCE OF RECEIVING ADVANCED EDUCATION
Kazan'	38.1%	38.4%	10.0%	1.5%
Moscow	84.2	36.9	9.8	3.0
Olonets	59.7	42.0	10.2	2.6
Orel	48.3	25.2	4.2	0.5
Tula	62.9	23.1	9.8	1.4
Kherson	50.5	23.7	10.5	1.3

SOURCES: Compiled from *Anketa,* 104–107, tables 29, 30; *Svodka svedenii,* sec. 1, 23; Malinovskii, "Nekotorye vyvody," 75–76.

They were eligible to enroll in the fourth year of the five-year, two-class elementary school without taking a qualifying exam, and they could then move (also without examination) into the fifth year of the municipal (1872) school, which offered an advanced primary education. The two-class schools also prepared graduates for the entrance examinations to teachers' seminaries and *fel'dsher* and agricultural schools. According to the 1911 School Census, 466 zemstvo-sponsored two-class schools (all but eight in villages) enrolled 67,000 pupils in all grades. In addition, another 2,368 five- and six-year schools with 334,767 pupils were directly under the MNP. Chekhov states that in 1915 there were thirteen different types of five- and six-year schools under the MNP, a total of 6,812 schools, of which 5,694 were located in the countryside. If these figures are comparable, it means that a substantial expansion of these advanced schools took place in the last three years before World War I.[42]

Primary school graduates could also go directly to the municipal school, enrolling in the first class (first or second year) or sometimes in the first year of the second class (third year)—but only after passing entrance exams certifying they had the equivalent of a basic primary education. From the municipal schools, students gained access to the preparatory class of the secondary technical schools without examination; they could also enroll in a two- or three-year pedagogical program ancillary to a large number of the municipal schools. After 1912, when municipal schools were converted to Higher Elementary Schools (VNUs), pupils who completed the first or second class (fifth and sixth years) had the right to enroll in the second or third class of a general secondary school after passing examinations in both a foreign and a classical language.[43] As of 1911, there were 1,136 municipal schools, with 154,387 pupils, as well as 115 district schools with 18,000 pupils—although the latter type of school was to have been phased out in 1872. Primary school graduates could also enroll directly in trade schools or in the two-year preparatory class attached to three-year agricultural schools and to commercial schools (whose basic program corresponded to that offered in the 1872 municipal schools).

Even these possibilities did not exhaust the options open to ambitious peasant graduates. In theory, they qualified for entrance into virtually any secondary or higher elementary school, provided they could pass the entrance examinations. These examinations, of course, could pose major problems. As a handbook for teachers and parents noted:

What entrance examinations in which schools can the recent graduate of the primary school expect to pass? . . . We can only say that the graduate might take the examinations for the boys' and girls' gymnasiums, for the pro-gymnasiums, for the *realschulen,* for the clerical schools, the municipal schools, and so forth, but it is impossible to be certain of a favorable outcome in any of these instances. . . . Almost every institution . . . has requirements peculiar to it alone, which it tests during the entrance examinations. In addition, the flood of those wanting to enroll and the shortage of places is forcing the examiners to raise the standards on the entrance examinations.[44]

Among the schools allowing direct entrance to primary school graduates, the best-attended was the two-class school, followed by lower trade schools, municipal schools, lower commerce and agricultural schools, teachers' seminaries, and clerical schools. Yet choice was affected not only by difficulty of entrance and location of school but also by the direct costs involved. In the clerical seminaries, tuition cost from 20 to 40 rubles a year; in the municipal schools, tuition was only 3 to 6 rubles, but the estimated cost of housing, feeding, and clothing a child in the large towns ranged from 60 to 200 rubles—well beyond the means of most peasants.[45]

Graduates of the primary school could also enroll in teachers' seminaries. These seminaries were designed primarily for peasants, but they admitted only candidates who were sixteen years old or older, and the entrance examinations tested for knowledge at the level of the fifth year of two-class schools. Still, the seminaries offered scholarships, which must have been tantalizing. A comment from a handbook suggests that many peasants did apply directly, noting that "the aspirant who has only completed the primary school program must prepare very thoroughly for these entrance examinations."[46]

If we could determine the ratio of applicants to entering pupils for each of these schools, we could learn to what degree the pressure for social advancement through continued education was being released or dammed at the exit gates of primary education. Scattered reports strongly suggest that the competition for places was keen indeed. One educator, writing shortly after the 1917 Revolution, minced no words: "The number of upper primary and former municipal schools was so insignificant that, according to official statistics, only one such school existed per 135,000 population. As a result, the needs of the population for that particular type of school remained largely unsatisfied." Moreover, "the number of newly established two-class schools remained far below the rapidly growing demands of the population."[47]

We do not have the data to quarrel with this point. Nevertheless, a rough comparison of the size of the 1910 graduating class and the scattered enrollment figures for the various types of advanced primary and lower secondary schools casts doubt on the notion that a large volume of repressed demand existed; such a comparison suggests that places could have been found for most graduates who were ready to continue their education. If we add to this the relatively low incidence of teachers' complaints that advanced schools were not available and the chorus of voices claiming that peasants were just not interested in anything beyond the basics, we might argue that the burden of proof rests with those who contend that upward mobility was thwarted by the school system. We can in fact posit that mobility through the system was both extremely limited *and* adequate—if by adequacy we refer to articulated peasant needs and the capacity of the system to meet them. Again, however, this question will be answered only through further detailed study.

With only one child in every ninety to one hundred advancing beyond the basic primary school, it seems obvious that peasant society as a whole was little affected by the school system. Yet it is of intrinsic interest to learn what happened to these ambitious and fortunate children once they left the village. The 1911 Zemstvo Survey offers a unique glimpse into the fate of these exceptional youths (see Table 53).

The largest percentage of graduates who continued their education, 41.6 percent, did so by enrolling in advanced elementary schools.[48] The survey was carried out just before the establishment of Higher Elementary Schools (VNUs), so teachers who referred to "advanced" schools meant the two-class, five-year Ministry of education and zemstvo schools, generally located in the villages. Unfortunately, the survey muddied the waters by including in this category four-year schools, which were rapidly becoming the standard primary school in the countryside. This figure, then, does tell us that an undetermined number of graduates felt it worthwhile to proceed to a four-year school, either to conclude their education or to prepare for entrance examinations to more advanced schools. The fact that some children chose this route, rather than simply repeating the last year of a three-year school, implies, contrary to much contemporary testimony, that the fourth year did offer new material or skills, rather than a rehash of the hastily presented content of the 1897 Model Program.

The second most common destination was the municipal school, in which 24.9 percent of graduates continuing their studies enrolled. Third in preference was the secondary school, in which roughly one out of five (19.7 percent) enrolled. Next came the pedagogical institutions, which enlisted 6.1 percent of the graduates, and the vocational schools were last, with 4.7 percent.

From Table 53 and other information gathered for the Zemstvo Congress, we see that the overwhelming majority (86 percent) of

Table 53

Schools Attended by Primary School Graduates
Who Continued Their Education, 1911

TYPE OF SCHOOL	PERCENTAGE OF PRIMARY SCHOOL GRADUATES WHO ATTENDED	RANGE OF PERCENTAGES THROUGHOUT PROVINCES
Secondary (includes gymnasiums, pro-gymnasiums, *realschulen,* commercial and diocesan schools)	19.7%	7–34%
Pedagogical (includes teachers' institutes, seminaries, and Church "second class" [*vtoroklassnye*] teachers' schools)	6.1	2–15
Municipal (1872)	24.9	5–46
Advanced primary (includes both four-year and five-year [two-class] schools)	41.6	13–79
Vocational and trade (includes agricultural schools)	4.7	0–18
Unknown	2.9	1–11

SOURCES: *Svodka svedenii,* sec. 7, 111, table 33; *Anketa,* 111.
NOTE: This survey covered 12,280 pupils in thirty-four zemstvo provinces.

those who continued their education enrolled in general education schools, of which the advanced elementary—both two-class and municipal—were the most heavily utilized, enrolling more than six out of ten who continued their education.[49] As we might expect, enrollment figures are inversely related to the level of the school: most graduates entered the two-class schools, fewer proceeded directly to the municipal schools, and still fewer to the secondary level.

Yet two figures should give us pause. Given the rigors of the entrance requirements and the meager fare offered in the primary schools, how did one out of five of these graduates move directly to secondary school? Why too, given their numbers, did the vocational (including agricultural) schools receive such a small share of enrollments? The first question concerns a tiny number of village youth—roughly one in five hundred from the villages. Nevertheless, the imbalance is intriguing. Could teachers have underestimated the degree to which a shortage of advanced elementary schools affected the flow of peasants into higher schools? Were some peasant families choosing more advanced schools because they saw an advantage in moving directly into an institution offering far more privileges to the graduate? We can only speculate, for the documents at hand do not answer these questions.

WASTAGE

Entrance into an advanced school was one step beyond primary education, but successful completion of an advanced program involved several more steps. Just how many children managed to complete the full program once enrolled? Fortunately, records exist for 130,000 pupils in two-class (five- and six-year) schools and for nearly 8,000 municipal school pupils. Information from these records is presented in Table 54.

In the lower primary schools, between one out of three and one out of four enrolled eventually graduated. In the two-class schools, attrition was nearly as bad. In the five-year schools, for example, the size of the graduating class would ideally have been 20,528; in fact, it was only 7,690, with only one in three pupils finishing. In the six-year schools, only 2,259—two out of five—walked out the right door.[50]

At first glance, it would seem that the attrition rate in advanced elementary schools was as severe as that in the lower schools. This pattern would make little sense, however, given that children entering upper elementary schools were from that small minority who saw some benefit in continued education and had the resources both to cover direct expenses and to accept the sacrifice of income involved.

In fact, the situation was not nearly so dismal. The five- and

Table 54

Distribution of Pupils by Grade,

Advanced Elementary Schools, 1911

	FIRST GRADE	SECOND GRADE	THIRD GRADE	FOURTH GRADE	FIFTH GRADE	SIXTH GRADE
Two-class schools[a]						
Five-year	33.9%	27.3%	18.6%	12.6%	7.4%	—
Six-year	28.4	24.4	18.0	11.0	11.3	6.6
Municipal schools[b]	—	—	35.1	29.3	20.5	14.8

SOURCE: *Svodka svedenii,* sec. 2, 4–6.

[a] N = approximately 130,000 pupils.

[b] N = approximately 8,000 pupils.

six-year (two-class) schools included a basic primary program during the first three years and an advanced division for the fourth and fifth years. If we consider these as separate schools, which, in a way, they were, we see that six out of ten who entered the second class in the five-year school completed the program. In the six-year school, the percentage was nearly identical. Although these were rural schools supposedly enrolling a greater proportion of peasants, I have found no systematic information analyzing the composition of these classes—whether the pupils came from distant villages, how wealthy their families were, and so forth. But one may plausibly argue that these students were the "cream," that they represented wealthier peasant families who were moving their children into positions that allowed social and economic advancement and who were therefore willing, indeed determined, to keep them in school until completion. One characteristic distinguishing the two-class from the three-year schools was the simple fact that many of those "continuing" in the fourth year were actually transfers from other schools. This fact strengthens the argument that the two classes of these schools should be treated here as separate institutions.

Petrov noted in his Moscow study:

Only the children of more prosperous parents make it to the end of the two-class program. If—and we encounter this very infrequently—the parents are not particularly prosperous, then they have set themselves the task of advancing their children into "society," particularly the most capable children among them. But the two-class schools are eagerly used by people of other estates and all those who are striving and have the means to provide their child with a diploma, which serves as one of the conditions making it easier to find less arduous and better-paid work.[51]

From Smolensk province, another report at the turn of the century commented that "of all those completing the program of the two-class schools, only a fraction continued to engage in agriculture."[52]

In the municipal schools, six out of ten of those enrolling (59.6 percent) also graduated. Again, at first glance one might have expected a better rate. As Petrov noted,

If we recall that the municipal schools are overwhelmingly located in cities [a few were located in villages] and that enrollment is linked with significant outlays on tuition, textbooks, and uniforms, then it becomes entirely clear that the enrolling contingent is drawn from the more or less prosperous, attracted by the specific privileges [the school provides] when entering government service or enrolling in other educational institutions.[53]

The compilers of the 1911 Zemstvo Survey neglected to note that such schools also enrolled a large number of urban children who were not nearly as prosperous but for whom the direct cost of initial enrollment (housing, travel) was not nearly as prohibitive. Given this mixture, the graduation rate was very high. Most important, compared to the lower primary schools with their high attrition rates, these advanced elementary schools, whether two-class village or municipal schools, were clearly far more successful in keeping their pupils in class until graduation. *In these schools, graduation was the criterion of success; in the lower primary schools, mastery of the basics was the goal, and graduation was often a matter of no import, or even a step to be avoided.* In the case of the lower primary schools, we are talking about the overwhelming majority of the population, for whom too much education would have made a child "neither beauty nor beast," since the family did not have the resources to bring extended education to a successful conclusion—that is, to establish a "career." In the case of the advanced schools, a tiny village elite of individual families could carefully plot the careers of selected children and allocate household resources correspondingly. Notably, scattered references indicate that children in the two-class schools often came from larger families, hinting that some families adopted the strategy of sponsoring one particular child through the educational network.

CAREERS

Zemstvo statisticians also followed the careers of 5,591 pupils who graduated from the higher elementary schools. Of these graduates, 30.3 percent (1,696) returned home to work on the farm or in local industry, 31.8 percent (1,780) enrolled in other institutions, and 25.5 percent (1,424) took up service careers, while the fate of 12.4 percent (691) remained unknown. Of those who continued their education, 57.7 percent (1,027) enrolled in secondary-level general education schools, and 42.3 percent (753) entered specialized institutions. Of the 1,424 graduates entering service careers, 7.8 percent (111) began work with the zemstvos, 35 percent (498) went into the professions and government service, 32.5 percent (463) took jobs with commercial enterprises, and 24.7 percent (352) worked with private individuals.[54]

Paradoxically, it was easier to enter the secondary schools from two-class schools than to do so from municipal schools, although two-class schools were theoretically on a lower level— graduates of the two-class schools applied to the second- or third-year levels of secondary schools, whereas municipal school graduates had to apply to enroll in the fourth- or fifth-year classes. Graduates of the two-class schools were also more likely than their peers from the municipal schools to find work in commercial or industrial enterprises (particularly given that the bulk of Russian industry at the turn of the century was located in the countryside). In contrast, however, graduation from the municipal schools eased entry into government service and facilitated enrollment in specialized secondary schools; not only were government offices and spe-

Table 55
Destination of Recent Graduates of Advanced
Primary Schools, 1911

	GRADUATES OF TWO–CLASS SCHOOLS	GRADUATES OF MUNICIPAL SCHOOLS
Remained at home	40.0%	27.7%
Enrolled in general secondary schools	16.0	7.0
Enrolled in specialized secondary schools	14.0	21.0
Employed by zemstvo, other public or government service	6.0	22.0
Employed by trade, industrial, or credit institution	17.0	12.5
Employed by private individual	6.0	9.0
Other	1.0	1.5

SOURCE: *Zakliuchitel'nyi tom,* vol. 12 of *Trudy pervogo obshchezemskogo s"ezda po narodnomu obrazovaniiu* (Moscow, 1912), 110.
NOTE: Data for 4,164 graduates.

cialized schools located in towns, but the average age and educational background of municipal school graduates also qualified them. Table 55 illustrates the fate of graduates of these two types of schools most commonly utilized by peasants.

A strikingly higher percentage of those graduating from rural, two-class schools remained in their villages after graduation, compared to the municipal school graduates.[55] This pattern confirms the observations of contemporaries that the very shortage of schools and the tendency to locate them in large towns accelerated the "backwash effect": children streamed out of the countryside into the town to gain a better education and, once there, seldom returned to the villages. Locating two–class schools in the villages helped reduce this outflow.

But two–class schools also had a contingent of poor peasants who were trying to pull themselves out of the *mir* into a better existence, whether at home or as far away as possible. The following description of families with children in these schools illustrates this well:

Here are the Golubevs, a family with ten members, living only off the tiny income provided by a small shop. Here are the Rogozhnikovs, a family of eight deeply sunk in debt. Here are the Zhukovs—the father is a barrel-maker who earns from 60 to 70 kopecks a day and has no land; on this, he must support six people. Here are the Studenovs, a family of eight with no allotment land and no working hands (the pupil is the oldest)—the father is an agricultural day worker, the mother earns 4 rubles and 50 kopecks (the father provides nothing); she has enrolled two sons, feeds and dresses the whole family. Here are the Mukhins—a family of six people, again without allotment land, whose main source of income is begging.[56]

Individual reports also made it clear that some poor peasants saw the lower trade·schools as a gateway out of the village. F. I. Ierusalimskii, an inspector of trade schools in Sapozhnikov district, noted:

The majority of graduates [of trade schools] are from poor families and have no liquid assets with which to open up their own shops—the initial cost of which might be as high as 2,000 rubles. Instead, these families eke out a miserable existence, earning from 30 to 40 kopecks a day in a local cottage workshop, under an employer much less educated and civilized than they; seeing no future in Sapozhnikov district, the graduates don't look for work, but instead try to enroll [in a higher school], gain more skills, and later find work in factories.[57]

Perhaps these students were the unfortunate ones who struggled into the upper reaches of the primary school system, found their resources exhausted, could not continue, and yet were unwilling to work behind the plow.

The career patterns of graduates from lower agricultural and trade schools suggest that whatever impact these schools had on the lives of individuals, they did little to improve the level of production expertise in the villages. Information on 131 students who graduated from eleven agricultural schools in 1908–1909 showed that in 1911, 56.5 percent were employed "in their specialty," whereas 20.6 percent were self-employed "at home." A closer look at the reports, however, showed that although nearly 80 percent were nominally pursuing careers in agriculture, many who remained home were only waiting to gain a more "fitting" position either in the zemstvo offices or as a teacher.[58] Similarly, a large proportion of those "engaged in their own specialty" were living in the district towns, employed by the zemstvo in the executive board offices as paper-pushers. For this reason, many zemstvo educators doubted that the agricultural schools were fulfilling their mission of spreading improved agricultural techniques, or even education and culture, to the villages. Instead, many peasants seemed to be using these schools as the most accessible passage to careers away from the village or to secondary schools.

The tendency of some, even many, pupils to use the lower agricultural school as a stepping-stone out of the villages was very evident in a survey carried out by the Okhansk district zemstvo (Perm' province), tracing the destinations of graduates from a zemstvo-supported agricultural trade school. Of the seventeen graduates who responded, three were working in the agricultural sphere (but not at manual labor) in the same district, eight had given up their agricultural specialty and taken jobs as clerks and office workers, two were in the military, and only three remained on the land. Of these three, one had lost a leg, another had taken up beekeeping, and a third was farming, by his own admission, only until he could find a teaching post. Another nineteen graduates did not reply to the survey, and it was discovered that all had left the district.[59]

The same phenomenon was noted in the numerous trade schools founded or supported by the zemstvos, where, similarly, many former pupils never applied the skills they learned in these schools. To be sure, of 318 pupils who graduated in 1908–1909 from fourteen trade schools, 67 percent were engaged in the agricultural specialty they had studied, another 13 percent remained at home, and only 5 percent were continuing their education in 1911. But a similar study in Riazan' province, surveying all those who had graduated from one school over a fourteen-year period, revealed that, although 169 of 204 former pupils were nominally working "in their specialty," 53 of these 169 were in fact working on the railroads, 38 were in factories, 7 were with the government, and 71 were working in their trade, either within or outside the district.[60]

To contemporaries, these studies were an ominous sign that lower trade and agricultural schools had failed to advance the productive forces of the countryside by raising the level of technological sophistication of farming and cottage industries. What seemed to be happening was precisely what is happening in the Soviet countryside today: as large sums are poured into improving the educational and professional qualifications of the rural labor force, the vast majority of those benefiting from such training use it as a ticket to leave the villages and move into the skilled blue-collar work force in the cities, with capital investment thus resulting in a large net loss. In fact, the retention ratio, the proportion of those who did stay in the villages, was, at over one in three, higher in the pre-Soviet countryside than it is today.

What must be considered a loss to the economy as a whole, and to the villages in particular, could well be considered successful mapping of career strategies for those who left the villages for white-collar or skilled jobs in the towns. But our conclusions concerning the advanced elementary and vocational schools as gateways of social mobility must remain tentative at this point. How many of the large proportion of graduates who "remained at home" found lucrative employment and used their skills to improve the local economy? How justified was the peasant complaint that the pupil with "too much science" became unfit for the farm, without finding lucrative outside employment? Scattered evidence suggests that those who made it to the higher schools were from more prosperous families and tended to drop out less frequently than those enrolled in the lower primary schools. It also suggests that these schools, whatever their profile, could be used as stepping-stones out of the villages and into the skilled work force. Although the absolute number of pupils making this advance was so tiny that village society overall could hardly have been affected, these pupils may have constituted a small peasant elite deserving closer study.

SECONDARY SCHOOLS AND UNIVERSITIES

Historians have often pointed to the great increase in the number of commoners enrolled in secondary and higher institutions in the Russian Empire during the second half of the nineteenth century and the first decade of the twentieth. Some have even drawn ponderous conclusions about the democratization of Imperial Russia from the rising percentage of commoners.[61] Such conclusions are, of course, unfounded; they rest on a simple confusion of access percentage—the percentage of all members of a specified social group who were enrolled at a specific level—with distribution percentage—the percentage of all students at that level who were from a given social group. (See, for example, Tables 56 and 57.)

Enrollments in secondary schools tripled in relation to popu-

Table 56

Access to Advanced Education, Russian Empire,
1897 (Access Percentage)

	SECONDARY EDUCATION	POST- SECONDARY EDUCATION	COMBINED (EITHER SECONDARY OR POST–SECONDARY EDUCATION)
Nobility and bureaucracy	26.7%	5.3%	32.0%
Clergy	34.5	1.0	35.5
Urban estates	2.8	0.2	3.0
Rural estates [a]	0.1	0.003	0.1

SOURCE: Piskunov, *Ocherki istorii shkoly,* 559.

NOTE: These figures include those enrolled in 1897, as well as those who had already received a complete or partial education of the type indicated.

[a] In the original chart, this category included a numerically insignificant listing of other social estates. In general, these percentages must be regarded as crude approximations, since one's legal estate and one's social class could differ widely in Russia, particularly in the case of urban workers who continued to be registered in their villages and listed as peasants.

Table 57
Percentage of Students from Peasantry,
by Type of Advanced School, Russian Empire
(Distribution Percentage)

	1876	—	1895	1904	1911
Normal schools	7.6%	—	11.8%	19.3%	32.1%

	1874	1880	—	1904	1911
Men's gymnasiums	6.4%	6.9%	—	10.6% }	20.0%
Men's pro-gymnasiums	9.4%	10.3%	— }		

	—	1880	1898	1904	1911
Women's gymnasiums	—	4.4%	5.3%	14.2% }	25.5%
Women's pro-gymnasiums	—	12.8%	16.1% }		

	1863	1880	1895	1907	1913
Universities	1.6%	3.3%	6.8%	6.9%	13.3%

SOURCE: Rashin, "Gramotnost'," 71–78.

lation in the last two decades of tsarist rule, rising from 13.3 enrollees per ten thousand population in 1895 to 36 per ten thousand
in 1914.[62] Moreover, Rashin and others have correctly pointed out
that the distribution percentage of peasants in gymnasiums and
pro-gymnasiums for men doubled in the last decade before World
War I (from 10.6 percent to 20 percent) and rose from 7.6 percent
to 32.1 percent in the *realschulen* between 1876 and 1914. These
were impressive gains, but they hardly affected the individual
peasant's actual life chances of pursuing an education; after all, only
thirty thousand peasants were enrolled in all general secondary
schools in 1914.[63]

Records from 1897 show that twenty in ten thousand rural
males and ten in ten thousand rural females (aged ten to twenty-

nine) had a secondary or university education—for a total of thirty per twenty thousand, or fifteen per ten thousand in that year.[64] Estimates made above by extrapolating from the total number of children in zemstvo schools and the average in any school suggest that by 1911 one village youth in a hundred continued beyond the lower primary school. Using the same data, we can estimate that in 1911 twenty-nine youths in ten thousand could expect to reach the secondary school level (that is, beyond the advanced primary school). These figures would suggest an improvement of 100 percent or more in the individual access of rural youth to advanced schools between 1897 and 1911. Nevertheless, despite the rapid expansion of overall enrollments, even despite the doubling of the *distribution* percentage (an extremely important democratization of the universities and secondary schools), the degree of educational mobility remained very slight indeed in the countryside, for the actual number of peasant youth in secondary schools remained but an insignificant fraction of the rural population.

SUMMARY

For the overwhelming majority of rural youth, the hope of continuing their education beyond the lower primary level was very slim. For most, even the expectation of completing the three-year program was illusory. A key distinction existed, however, between dropping out during the first three years and failing to continue one's education. In the first case, economic considerations were marginal; the direct and indirect costs of keeping a child in school were ordinarily not prohibitive, but the positive benefits of the school diploma were very limited. Peasant parents often believed that too prolonged a stay in school could have a harmful impact on children's attitudes toward work and toward their place in the family.

The case of advanced education was very different. For those who had graduated from a village school, the obstacles to continuing their study were quite formidable. At the same time, the benefits of an advanced elementary or even a secondary education were sometimes enough to justify the substantial expenditure involved. Both the direct costs—tuition, room and board, and other outlays—as well as the indirect, opportunity costs of advanced elementary education proved an insurmountable barrier for most village families. But a small minority of students overcame these barriers and, once in the schools, generally remained to complete the program. This chapter has measured that "trickle" and traced its path.

Yet the most important fact to be gleaned from this investigation, if we are concerned primarily with the relationship of school and community, is that these schools provided an exit from the village for that small minority of peasant students. As Furet and Ozouf observe in their study of France, one reason that literacy remained restricted, in impact as well as in content and distribution, for three centuries was that the more advanced schools offered upward social mobility *coupled* with emigration to a small fraction of the population; in so doing, the effect, at least for the first few generations, was to reinforce village isolation by removing "potential modernizers." By offering a chance of escape, "the school raised a barrier between the community and its potential modernizers; it helped to entrap the community in its tradition."[65]

The question left unanswered in the case of Russia is to what degree aspirations created among gifted children in basic primary school were frustrated by the gap preventing all but the wealthiest from moving to the next rung. It is plausible to argue that village autarky was actually reinforced by the existence of the trickle. At the same time, a hint of growing intergenerational tension, of frustrated ambitions, is contained in the references to peasants altered by their complete primary education but provided no outlet for these new strivings.

Conclusion

In Russia after the Emancipation, literacy made steady progress among the peasantry. The level of schooling trailed the level of literacy until the 1890s, after which the government and the zemstvos launched a major, and successful, universal education campaign, removing the direct cost of schooling from the peasant communities, building thousands of schools, and improving teachers' salaries and benefits. By 1914, more than half the children of school age (eight to eleven years old) in the Empire were enrolled in primary schools, and in many provinces in European Russia the proportion was much greater. Applying an argument first made by West in discussing schooling in England—that census enrollments markedly understated the number of children who at one time or another had contact with the schools—we have seen that by World War I Russia had proceeded far down the road toward universal education. Although many minority regions were still deprived of schooling, what remained elsewhere was largely a "mopping-up" operation. The Soviet authorities in fact inherited a large-scale school network.

Central to this study have been the questions of initiative and periodization—who was responsible for the organization and expansion of education, and what the stages of this process were.

471

Consider first the state and the educated public. Occasionally before 1890 a local zemstvo actively promoted public schooling, but, as a whole, the Russian elite, both official and public, gave low priority to peasant education. As long as the primary purpose of schooling was seen as benefiting the individual and providing personal fulfillment, the sentiment was widespread that "because we are poor, we cannot afford schooling." The remarkable expansion of literacy and schooling that occurred in the quarter century following the Emancipation took place largely through the efforts of the peasant community, not the elite. Peasants appreciated the utility of basic education and were aided only infrequently by the local zemstvo, more often by the priest. Zemstvo activity in this period was largely confined to reorganizing, asserting control over, and improving the existing, unregistered peasant schools.

Only in the 1890s, when Russia underwent a series of economic and social upheavals and fell behind other nations in military capacity, was the school treated as an important source of military strength, national integration, economic productivity, labor discipline, and political stability. Whether the school was to promote proper work habits and attitudes toward authority, create the future citizens of democratic Russia, or contribute to the diffusion of technological innovation and labor skills, the educated public and officialdom now joined hands to bring about universal basic education. Now it was said, "Because we are poor, we *must* have schools." Whether the goal was subordination or liberation, the common ethos was paternalistic intervention between peasants and their children.

Many historians have blamed apparent zemstvo lethargy before the turn of the century on the overgrown, reactionary Russian bureaucracy, which stifled all independent local activity. Yet an important conclusion drawn in this study is that the conflict between educational bureaucrats and zemstvos has been significantly overstated. The local school inspector has been unjustly vilified, the bureaucracy did not generally restrain progress in local education, the zemstvo had de facto control over local school boards and the day-to-day affairs of the school, and, contrary to most descriptions, relations between local zemstvo and school authorities were generally amicable and businesslike. When there was tension, it often arose over efforts by the local inspector to prod the zemstvo into activity, not from efforts to prevent the spread of schooling. The study of local school boards reveals, parenthetically, just how tenuous central control at the district level was, well into the twentieth century. The British inspector Darlington noted:

The amount of control which the state is able to exercise over teaching in primary schools is limited. . . . It is one of the paradoxes of Russian life that in spite of the elaborate bureaucratic machinery created by the state . . . the schools are, in fact, less strictly supervised from the educational point of view by the officials of the central government than in England.[1]

The implementation of the 1908 School Bill marked a third stage in the history of mass schooling in Russia; in the first, peasants built schools; in the second, zemstvos took them over; and in the third, on the eve of World War I, the Ministry of Education began to wrench the schools away from the zemstvos. Paradoxically, conflicts among school boards, inspectors, and zemstvos tended to increase as the goal of universal education came within reach, that is, during the period of greatest progress.

The school inspector was not the sole victim of a lopsided press which declared that only "local control" could provide quality education; claims that schooling had to be secular as well as locally controlled meant that the Church parish school often became another victim (although the Synod itself was also a notorious mudslinger). The sharp contrast often drawn between secular and Church schools had little basis in reality for the period under study. Though the Church schools were supposedly deficient in quality and the zemstvo schools much preferred by the peasantry, the peasants themselves saw little difference between the two types of schools. When they did prefer one over the other, it was often for simple, practical considerations: one was "free" (i.e., supported by the entire community) and the other charged fees for each pupil; or some parents preferred the talk-and-chalk pedagogy of Church schools and officialdom to the child–centered progressivism of zemstvo activists. Even more striking, teachers in the two types of schools took similar approaches to curriculum, discipline, learning methods, and testing. Ironically, the priest or seminary graduate was more likely to be found in the zemstvo school, whereas Church schools often employed lay teachers. Evidence demonstrates that zemstvo and Church parish schools were siblings of common parentage—the free peasant school. The Church school was the undernourished sibling, but their common origins and environment are evident in the similar paths pursued by both types of school.

It is one matter to demonstrate a significant increase in the availability of schooling or to show that most children were going to school, and quite another to discuss the significance of this expansion. One obvious yardstick is the spread of literacy, which is commonly treated as an indicator of "psychological modernization." Yet in Russia literacy often preceded schooling. Scholars in the West have recently uncoupled learning to read from going to school; one is not an epiphenomenon, or even a necessary result, of the other. Recent work also justifiably questions the significance of statistics registering crude or signature literacy. Literacy may be a skill that can be integrated into village life with minimal disruption. The achievement of comprehensive literacy, or learning *from* reading rather than learning *to* read, may instead be the crucial stage. Many of the cognitive and attitudinal changes associated with "becoming modern" take place not through literacy as such but rather through time spent in a formal school, where learning is context-free and the opportunities for "transfer" are maximized. Thus, schooling rather than literacy must be used to measure the impact of formal education, and the place to start is with the questions of *length of stay* in school and *regularity of attendance* while enrolled.

Very few children remained in Russian village schools more than two or three years. The grade distribution and intensity of schooling remained virtually unchanged during the last thirty years of the Empire, despite the increased availability of schooling and soaring enrollments. No more than one in six of all school-age children completed the full three grades and received the certificate of completion (though many others stayed three years).

In short, by most standards, education was a failure in rural Russia. Although schooling was more widespread than is commonly believed, it was also very shallow, or short-winded. The peasant child barely had time to learn the ABCs before returning to the world. The high incidence of what is now called "wastage" was the most convincing proof that the schools were not accomplishing their mission.

But views differed on the nature of this mission. Social history and recent work in the history of education tell us that the peasantry must be given its rightful place as policy maker alongside the educated public and the state, as one of several forces vying for control over the education of peasant children. What were the peasants' views? Why were the schools operating as revolving doors? Why did children leave before they could complete even the modest three-year cycle set forth in the 1897 Model Program? At the time, educators blamed poverty, either directly in that parents could not afford the warm clothing needed by their children, or indirectly in the form of opportunity costs (lost work in the home, field, or factory). Poverty *did* exact a toll, keeping some children from enrolling. Zemstvo yearbooks, educational journals, and numerous questionnaires addressed to teachers provide poignant illustrations of this fact.

Yet poverty does not fully explain the patterns of enrollment, withdrawal, and grade repetition. Studies of early departure showed almost no correlation between time of departure and wealth (measured in landholding and use) or parental employment in the village. Children from both poor and wealthy families left the schools well before graduation. Furthermore, investigators produced convincing evidence that children who left school by the age of eleven or twelve were seldom employed for plowing or other heavy agricultural tasks, nor did they find work in factory or cottage industry until the ages of fifteen or sixteen. Local conditions varied considerably, and areas dominated by cottage industries had markedly different literacy levels than other areas; but these differences in economy and employment did not seem to affect the intensity or duration of schooling.

I do not question the prevalence of poverty in the Russian countryside. *I do suggest that poverty, particularly in the guise of opportunity costs, was not the only—and perhaps not the major—cause of attrition from the schools.* The disillusionment and despair expressed by many zemstvo educators must be placed in context; their laments were particularly shrill because of high expectations for literacy, schooling, and the written word in advancing social and cultural progress. We do not always share those expectations today.

Let us use as our model of the rational actor in peasant society not the individual profit-maximizer, but rather the cautious peasant who approached economic transactions as part of a zero–sum game. His view of the "bad life" and his precarious, marginal existence taught him to value survival and security over profit and risk-taking. For him, literacy was a means of protection against, rather than advancement in, a hostile world. For the peasant, estimates of the opportunity costs of schooling, which measure only deferred income and immediate costs, would have missed the mark. A simple calculation of the relative pull of schooling against the push of the factory, cottage industry, or farm tells us only how *we* might have acted as "optimizing" peasants, heads of families investing resources at our disposal, not how the peasant family actually utilized its resources, set its priorities, allocated its energies, protected its foundations, and maintained its equilibrium under the stress of economic change. To understand peasant strategies, we must keep in mind the distinction between the optimizing peasant and the rational-actor peasant. What was best for the individual child (maximizing opportunity) often threatened the overall interests of the family farm and security in old age for the parents. The child might use that education to leave for good. At the least, too much education threatened the authority of elders, and hence the equilibrium of village life.

Perhaps the pattern of "escalation" of schooling without "intensification" reflected the imposition of popular will on a system nominally controlled from above. This pattern stemmed from a life strategy, imperfectly implemented but relentlessly pursued. Peasants recognized that their children had to learn how to read, write, and count in order to survive in a world increasingly crowded with written documents, but they had no use for the cultural baggage that accompanied basic instruction. Educators wanted to civilize the peasant; villagers wanted to produce children in their own image. Thousands of reports from teachers confirmed this attitude, while also castigating peasant sloth and cultural backwardness.

Because peasants sought both to sponsor and to limit, the interaction between community and outside world in the sphere of education was complex. Peasant goals remained substantially the same throughout the entire half century following the Emancipation, but the tactics peasants adopted to pursue their goals changed as they struggled with the outside world, adapted to changing circumstances, and responded to initiatives from above. Until the large-scale intervention of the 1890s, the peasant approach consisted mainly of direct action to provide education in a virtual vacuum—this action is the elusive history of *vol'nye* schools.

Activity by the peasants forced the state to respond to their persistent demands, but after the state and zemstvo stepped in on a large scale, the peasants ceased to be the dominant sponsors of education. No longer was it a question of whether or not the peasants should learn their ABCs; rather, the issues became who should teach them, how they should be taught, and what they should learn. Elite intervention led peasants to adopt subtler tactics to control their children's education as the official school system spread to European Russia—that is, as peasant schools were registered, "organized," and brought under first zemstvo, and then state, supervision. As the state began to assume most of the direct costs of schooling, peasants limited their children's participation in the system. They used the schools for their own purposes, sifting out those aspects of schooling meant to intrude into, interfere with, or alter their lives and traditions. This tactic was a variant of a traditional peasant approach to the city the world over, what Redfield calls the "institutionalized provision for strangers," allowing resident strangers to live in the village but not to be *of* it, to "serve it in a specialized and instrumental capacity."[2] Does it matter that the stranger was an institution rather than an individual?

By the second half of the nineteenth century, life was making demands that threatened the hierarchy of peasant family authority. Much evidence suggests that peasants recognized the tremendous importance of literacy and numeracy. But the schools, where these skills were most easily obtained, bypassed the system of "brokers" by which communal autarky was maintained and contact with the outside world mediated to filter out disruptive elements. Schools "introduced into the [child's] mind patterns which were not in agreement with that system"; by separating education from the division of labor, they "wrested a child away from the harmonious system of labor," mounting an assault on an entire rhythm and way of life, the smallest disruption of which threatened the whole system.[3]

In his outstanding work on Russian agriculture, Confino describes how the three-field system, communal repartition, technology, tools, and division of labor of the peasant household were all tightly interconnected—an ecology and a *mentalité* in which piecemeal change destroyed the integrity of the whole.[4] The fierce and stubborn peasant resistance often met by outsiders when they tried to introduce new methods or tools stemmed from the same considerations that prompted peasant resistance to self-help literature and the hidden curriculum of the schoolroom. Peasants knew the tremendous risks of tinkering with the system. They also knew that outsiders were determined to "improve" the peasant way of life. Most of all, they knew that with guidance came control from the outside. It is striking that peasants themselves made the same distinction between literacy and the *process* of schooling emphasized by specialists.

Only if we take into account the opposing pulls of an environment in which the ability to read, write, and count was essential, but where the solidarity of the community and family farm required sifting these skills from the matrix in which they were embedded, is it possible to understand the contradictory reports on popular attitudes toward education and to place the cycle of schooling in Russia into perspective. It would be incorrect to argue that *all* peasant children got the schooling they or their parents wanted and incorrect to treat peasants as a homogeneous mass. But it *is* useful to think in terms of broad strategy, of a natural cycle of schooling, rather than of "wastage." The latter term implies that if schools did not function in ways envisioned by legislators and educators, they did not function at all.

Peasant pedagogy was a survival philosophy, an adaptive strategy in a harsh, hostile, and changing world. Peasants supported literacy, but they were not "becoming modern"—optimistic, receptive to risk, open to science and to the outside world. Anthropologists, responding to a romantic tendency to idealize peasant culture and the holistic view of the "good life," have recently argued that peasants see the world as generally threatening, and they talk of the peasant view of the "bad life." As Kenneth Lockridge notes, the onset of literacy in America did not bring "attitudinal liberation" there, either:

Nor . . . did the new man emerging seem to be as socially optimistic, emphatic, outgoing or constructive as some have suggested. In this perspective, higher literacy appears as an epiphenomenon of a broader movement toward a mentality which involved the careful husbanding of every resource in a . . . society ever more crowded, commercial and complex. . . . While this had revolutionary implications for man's fate, it did not necessarily revolutionize or still less broaden human consciousness. . . .

Millions of men and women [in the course of three centuries], then, were led to pick up the potentially radical tool of literacy, often for reasons deeper than its ever greater availability. But it would be wrong always to associate the social forces moving them with progress or with upward mobility. There is evidence for a more skeptical and pessimistic account of the social forces behind this new instrument.[5]

Peasant pedagogy should also be evident in the results of schooling. According to the press at the time, regressive illiteracy was a widespread phenomenon; it was not uncommon to meet graduates of the primary schools who, ten years later, could not read a word and could barely sign their own names. But detailed and systematic retention studies carried out over three decades by zemstvo commissions, as well as a systematic survey of teachers' opinions conducted for the 1911 Zemstvo Congress, showed that graduates, and even students who did not finish, had in fact learned to read. Former pupils could read simple texts out loud and restate them in their own words. Basic computation had been mastered and retained in most provinces. Everywhere, the lowest scores were given for composition; here, however, logical sequence of thought and style were being tested, not rudimentary writing. The most commonly observed writing problems (improper word boundaries, word distortion) suggest that pupils learned to write phonetically, in their local dialect, but had not assimilated the national language of civilized discourse, which Eugen Weber has eloquently shown was a crucial stage in the modernization of the French peasantry. Nevertheless, and most important, peasants *were* learning how to read, write, and count—and they were retaining these skills. The zemstvo studies were confirmed by the annual reports of inspectors and directors from both the MNP and the Holy Synod.

Contemporary educators saw little purpose in teaching the ABCs if peasants were not also freed from superstitions and prejudices. The state favored a heavy dose of patriotism and proper (Orthodox) religion. Progressives and conservatives differed over goals, but neither valued instruction without character education. Yet it is evident that for the bulk of the population, who spent only two winters in the school, the civilizing, integrating mission of schooling was largely a failure. Peasant families were extracting the necessary information and skills from the village school, but the school remained on the fringes of village society and had little impact on mores.

The rural teacher has been an important figure in this narrative. The state and the educated public drew up curricula, provided funds, and selected and purchased textbooks, but the teacher delivered the goods. It has been argued that Russian rural teachers were so ill prepared they could not possibly have succeeded in their mission. Using standards of adequacy developed by UNESCO, looking at the teachers' level of education, and considering their own perceptions of their readiness for teaching, this study has shown that most were, in fact, moderately well prepared for their limited tasks. Indeed, given the widespread tendency for teachers in developing countries to flee the countryside for more lucrative employment elsewhere, the tsarist strategy of maintaining a low intellectual profile for rural teachers was, in developmental terms, an optimal approach for using scarce human resources.

Were teachers role models for children? Were they carriers of new beliefs, habits, and attitudes? Did teachers radicalize the countryside by disseminating revolutionary ideas? Using the concepts of "brokers," "outsiders," and "resident strangers" from anthropology, I have produced a demographic profile of teachers and studied the incidence of turnover in the villages (that is, length of contact with peasants) to show that teachers did not play an influential role in village culture. Efforts to introduce "civilization" through the teacher were analogous to efforts to introduce "rational medicine" through the zemstvo medical orderly, who found himself in competition with traditional healers and deliverers and had to adapt their methods of treatment.

Reports from the countryside showed that teachers were materially dependent on the village, commanded little respect, were vulnerable to harassment from local authorities and the village elite, received very little support from the zemstvo, and often looked to the inspector for protection against the village. A core of pedagogical activists and radicals were influential at the national level, but this core never comprised more than 5,000 to 7,000 teachers. At the local level, the vast majority of the 140,000 teachers in the villages were "rabbits," terrified of peasant violence and hopeful that the state would provide them protection and material security. Thus, teachers, though reasonably effective in communicating the rudiments of knowledge, were probably not effective carriers of radical political values or modern culture. Teachers were, in a sense, "contaminated," as the government feared, but not by radical ideas. The "contamination" came from contact with children and peasants, which lowered the status of teachers in the eyes of the elite, and from contact with the elite, which polluted teachers in the eyes of the peasants.

Peasants, then, were learning to read, but not yet learning from reading. Peasant reading habits were simply an extension of traditional oral readings, with a marked preference for entertainment, popular narrative, and hagiography, and little use for self-help literature or tracts on science, hygiene, or agriculture. School, book, and teacher had come to the village, but they had been incorporated only as "resident strangers," accepted only when they donned village garb and adapted to the natural cycle.

In the West, Harvey Graff and others have argued that "as education became a dominant tool for social stability and hegemony, morality formed the basis for tutelage in literacy." The processes were mutually reinforcing, "literacy speeding and easing moral instruction, and morality guiding and restraining the potentially dangerous uses of literacy."[6] Yet what happens when literacy and morality are separated, when the old "moral economy" begins to disintegrate, but instruction does not "inculcate the rules for social and economic behavior in a changing and modernizing society"? In the case of Russia, is it not feasible that those agents of socialization commonly identified as easing the transition to the modern industrial order—armies, trade unions, and schools—were all dysfunctioning (if their function was to discipline and integrate) and that the failure of these integrating mechanisms helps explain the *buntarstvo,* the elemental, anarchic hostility to all educated and privileged elites so characteristic of the late Imperial period and the wave of disorder that swept away the Old Regime?

Rimlinger argues that trade unions, tardily legalized and to the end hamstrung by government restrictions, provided little experience in the orderly articulation of demands and had little overall impact on the Russian workforce.[7] John Bushnell has recently shown that the army, which essentially reconstructed the social relations of the old serf estate, did little to modernize the peasant.[8] Now we see that the peasant commune, preserved and reinforced by the Emancipation legislation, was capable of at least temporarily absorbing the village school and turning it to its own ends. How long this strategy could have worked, given the rapid industrialization of Russia, is another question. We might argue that the longstanding "symbiosis" of village and city observed by Robert Johnson in his recent study of the Moscow work force was finally breaking down by 1914, that rising generational tensions (noted by Shanin) were threatening the peasant household, and that intravillage conflict was eroding the legendary solidarity of the commune.[9] William Rosenburg notes, in a discussion of the countryside in 1917, that "one gets a sense . . . of the growing problem of rural-urban relations generally and of the . . . process of introversion . . . which involved a closing off of the village and the development of a virulent hostility on the peasant's part" to all outsiders.[10]

I have argued that peasants did have an adaptive strategy of education and that it did produce results. Such an argument does not exclude the possibility of mounting tensions, culminating in a rupture, and the anomic violence of despair. The study of peasant education reinforces the conclusion that to the very end of the Old Regime there remained a significant "psychological gulf" between the folk and the educated public (*narod* and *obshchestvennost'*) and that the arrival of literacy, the school, and the teacher did little to bridge that gulf.

Appendix A: Instruction in Russian Primary Schools

1. 1897 Model Program
(Abridged Program of Primary Schools)

RELIGION

In the first year, the most common daily prayers are taught, and the children learn by heart the Creed and the Ten Commandments. In the second year, the main events of the history of the Old and New Testaments are studied. In the third year, the children are taught the Short Catechism and receive lessons on the liturgy, the significance of the chief acts of worship connected with the service of the Orthodox Church, and so forth.

CHURCH SLAVONIC

Instruction in Slavonic reading begins as soon as the children have mastered the mechanical difficulties of Russian reading, that is, about the middle of the first year of schooling. The first year of Church Slavonic includes study of the Slavonic alphabet and its peculiarities, as compared with the Russian; reading of the most commonly used prayers; practical acquaintance with diacritical signs and abbreviations; and reading exercises from the primer. In the second year, children read the gospels and the Chasoslov (Horologium) and study Slavonic numerals. The third year includes reading the Gospels and the psalter.

RUSSIAN

First Year

Analysis of words by syllables and syllables by sounds. Letters and their combinations. Reading separate words and short phrases composed of the letters learned. Reading short and easy connected passages, with special attention to marks of punctuation and with the pupil asked to reproduce the subject in response to the teacher's questions. Learning short fables and other poems by heart.

Division of words into syllables, and rules for carrying over part of a word to the next line. Capital and small letters; use of capital letters. Vowels and consonants; the hard vowels and the corresponding soft sounds. Use of the hard and soft signs after consonants. Use of certain alternative vowel symbols. Vowels that may not follow certain consonants. Hard and soft pronunciation of consonants. Accents; changes in meaning of words according to position of accent. Writing individual words and shorts sentences from dictation, to allow the scholars to practice the rules of orthography they have learned; the dictation exercise preceded by an explanation of the correct method of writing certain words with which the scholars might make mistakes. Copying from book passages.

Second Year

Practice in fluent and (so far as possible) expressive reading with oral reproduction of subject matter in response to teacher's questions. Written reproduction of short passages, assisted by teacher's questions. Learning poems and fables by heart.

Words signifying a thing (object), the quality of a thing, the action or state of a thing. The substantive; its gender, number, and case-endings in response to questions. Personal pronouns replacing the substantive. Verbs: tenses and persons, imperative and infinitive moods. The preposition standing by itself and in the form of a prefix.

Proper letter to be used in cases where the pronunciation of a vowel or consonant in a word is obscure. Use of the full stop, colon (in certain specified cases), quotation marks, hyphen, and comma before vocative case. Dictation preceded by a warning against errors and a review of rules of orthography already learned. Copying from book. Writing previously learned matter from memory.

Third Year

Intelligent and expressive reading with oral and written reproduction of subject matter. Reading of ordinarily legible manuscript. Learning poems, fables, and elegant prose extracts by heart.

The adjective: agreement with the substantive in gender, number, and case; case-endings; degrees of comparison; full and short endings. Cardinal and ordinal numbers. The subject and predicate of a sentence; exercises in the proper use of punctuation between sentences and parts of a sentence (not including comma and semicolon). Exercises on the use of the letter in the middle or at the end of words. Dictation for purposes of recapitulation and testing pupil's knowledge. Copying from book. Writing letters and simple descriptions according to a given model.

WRITING

In the first year, the pupils first learn the proper way to sit and hold their pens; they are then taught how to form the elements of letters, the letters themselves and complete words. By the end of the year, they should be able to write sentences in large hand between lines. The second year's work consists chiefly in helping the children become accustomed to a smaller handwriting, the copy exercises being from either headlines or the blackboard. The pupils continue to write between lines until the third year, when they begin to write on one line. Greater attention is, of course, paid to legibility than to speed of writing, but by the end of the third year a fair amount of speed is expected.

ARITHMETIC

First Year

Counting, directly and otherwise, up to one hundred.

The four primary functions with numbers not exceeding twenty.

Knowledge of figures and the signs of arithmetical operations.

Examples of fundamental arithmetical concepts (for example, add, subtract, multiply, divide, how many times one number is contained in another, how much more or less or how many times more or less one number is than another).

Roman numeration to XX.

Note: The requirements may be exceeded only if a thorough knowledge of the rules within the limits indicated has been attained.

Second Year

Numeration and application of the four functions from one hundred to one thousand.

Explanation of arithmetical expressions: addition, subtraction, multiplication, division. Comparison of numbers.

Multiplication and division by ten and one hundred.

Acquaintance with the most commonly used Russian measures.

Solution of problems, orally and in writing, based on the arithmetical rules learned.

Elementary knowledge of fractions that are commonly used in practical life (for example, ½, ¼, ⅛, ¹⁄₁₀, ⅓, ⅙, ⅑).

Third Year

Numeration and the four primary operations with numbers of any magnitude; proofs of these operations.

Operations with compound concrete numbers.

Very simple calculations with fractions.

Solution of problems, oral and written.

SINGING

The chief aim of instruction in this subject is to familiarize the pupils with the chants and hymns most frequently used in the Church, though in all three divisions the singing of national and patriotic songs is, as far as possible, made part of the instruction. The chants chosen are of progressive difficulty; singing by note is introduced in the second year.

Source: This is a modified version of the abridged translation found in Thomas Darlington, *Education in Russia,* Board of Education, Special Reports on Education, vol. 23 (London, 1909), 296–299. The full text in Russian can be found in N. Verigin, *V pomoshch uchashchim v nachal'nykh narodnykh uchilishchakh,* 5th ed. (Moscow, 1915), 50–73.

2. Time Allocation by Subject in Russian Primary Schools at the Turn of the Century

	HOURS PER WEEK	HOURS PER SCHOOL YEAR	PERCENTAGE OF CLASS HOURS
Bible	6	156	25.0
Church Slavonic	3	78	12.5
Russian	8	208	33.4
Penmanship	2	52	8.3
Arithmetic	5	130	20.8
Total	24	624	100.00

SOURCE: Adapted from F. F. Korolëv, *Ocherki po istorii sovetskoi shkoly i pedagogiki, 1917–1920* (Moscow, 1958), 14 (originally compiled by A. I. Afanas'ev in *Narodnaia shkola: Rukovodstvo dlia uchitelei,* 10th ed. [Moscow (?), 1915]).

NOTE: Data assume twenty-six school weeks per year, twenty-four class hours per week. Time allocation by subject was virtually the same for the first, second, and third grades.

Appendix B: Structure of the Russian School System

1. Varieties of Primary Education

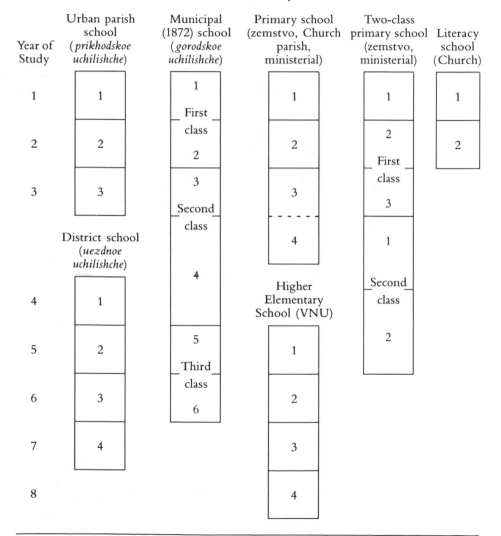

SOURCE: Modified from N. V. Chekhov's original graph, found in *Tipy russkoi shkoly v ikh istoricheskom razvitii* (Moscow, 1923), 42.

2. The Russian School System in 1914

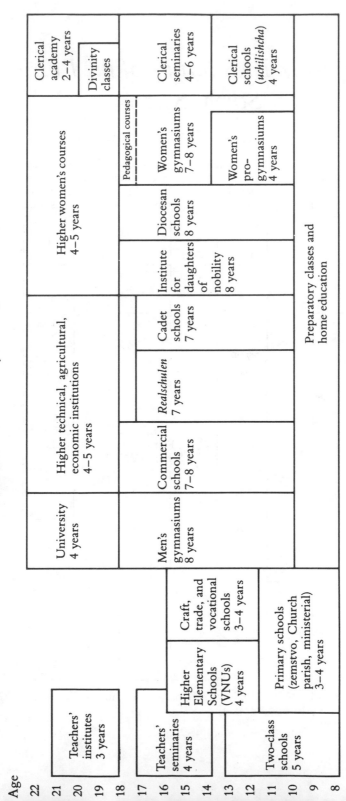

Age								
22								Clerical academy 2–4 years
21	Teachers' institutes 3 years	University 4 years	Higher technical, agricultural, economic institutions 4–5 years	Higher women's courses 4–5 years				Divinity classes
20								
19						Pedagogical courses	Women's gymnasiums 7–8 years	Clerical seminaries 4–6 years
18								
17	Teachers' seminaries 4 years	Men's gymnasiums 8 years	Commercial schools 7–8 years	*Realschulen* 7 years	Cadet schools 7 years	Institute for daughters of nobility 8 years	Diocesan schools 8 years	Women's pro-gymnasiums 4 years	Clerical schools (*uchilishcha*) 4 years
16								
15	Higher Elementary Schools (VNUs) 4 years	Craft, trade, and vocational schools 3–4 years						
14								
13								
12	Primary schools (zemstvo, Church parish, ministerial) 3–4 years					Preparatory classes and home education		
11								
10	Two-class schools 5 years							
9								
8								

SOURCE: F. F. Korolëv, *Ocherki po istorii sovetskoi shkoly i pedagogiki, 1917–1920* (Moscow, 1958), 14.

Notes

INTRODUCTION

1. Marc Raeff, *The Birth of the Russian Intelligentsia* (New York, 1966), 123–126. Roberta J. Manning comments: "All too often many gentry liberals, like their conservative counterparts, tended to treat the worker and peasant masses as little more than childlike creatures, moved mainly by irrational passions and desires" ("Zemstvo and Revolution: The Onset of the Gentry Reaction, 1905–1907," in *The Politics of Rural Russia,* ed. Leopold Haimson [Bloomington, Ind., 1979], 54).

2. Daniel Field, *Rebels in the Name of the Tsar* (Boston, 1976), 213.

3. Jack Goody, *The Domestication of the Savage Mind* (Cambridge, England, 1977); see also Philip Rieff, *Freud: The Mind of the Moralist* (New York, 1959), esp. 208. But compare the treatment in Robert A. Nisbet, *Social Change and History* (New York, 1969).

4. The classic statement of this view is found in Robert Redfield, *The Primitive World* (Ithaca, N.Y., 1953), 26–54, 84–110. For more recent works, see Teodor Shanin, ed., *Peasants and Peasant Society* (Baltimore, Md., 1971); and Jack M. Potter et al., eds., *Peasant Society: A Reader* (Boston, 1967).

5. See the "Introduction" by Peter Burke to *The New Cambridge Modern History,* ed. Peter Burke (Cambridge, England, 1979), 13:1–14, esp. 4; and Emmanuel LeRoy Ladurie, "Peasants," in the same work, 115–163. See also Peter Stearns, *European Society in Upheaval* (New York, 1975), 34.

491

6. Marx's phrase is from *The Holy Family* and is cited in François Furet and Jacques Ozouf, "Three Centuries of Cultural Cross-Fertilization in France," in *Literacy and Social Development in the West: A Reader,* ed. Harvey J. Graff (Cambridge, England, 1981), 214.

7. See Charles Tilly, "Did the Cake of Custom Break?" in *Consciousness and Class Experience in Nineteenth-Century Europe,* ed. John M. Merriman (New York, 1979), 17–44, esp. 21—a critique of modernization theory and, specifically, of the work of Eugen Weber.

8. LeRoy Ladurie, "Peasants," 148; C. Arnold Anderson, "Literacy and Schooling on the Threshold," in *Education and Economic Development,* ed. C. Arnold Anderson and Mary Jean Bowman (Chicago, 1965), 347. For a recent bibliography of the history of literacy, see Harvey J. Graff, ed., *Literacy in History: An Interdisciplinary Research Bibliography* (New York, 1981).

9. This summary is drawn from the work of Sylvia Scribner and Michael Cole. See especially: "Cognitive Consequences of Formal and Informal Education," *Science,* no. 182, 9 November 1973, 552–558; and "Literacy Without Schooling: Testing for Intellectual Effects," *Harvard Educational Review* 48 (November 1978): 448–461. Scribner and Cole have recently published a more extensive discussion of their conclusions in *The Psychology of Literacy* (Cambridge, Mass., 1981). For an additional discussion, see the essay by Tela Zasloff, "Readings on Literacy," in *Literacy in Historical Development,* ed. Daniel Resnick (Washington, D.C., 1983), 155–170.

10. On "becoming modern," see Alex Inkeles, "The School as a Context for Modernization," in *Education and Individual Modernity in Developing Countries,* ed. Alex Inkeles and Donald Holsinger (Leiden, 1974), 8–23. On "psychic mobility," see Daniel Lerner, *The Passing of Traditional Society* (Glencoe, Ill., 1958), 55–61. For an interesting application of modernization theory to literacy in Russia, see Barbara Anderson, *Internal Migration During Modernization in Late Nineteenth Century Russia* (Princeton, N.J., 1980); and Marc Blaug, "Literacy and Economic Development," *School Review* 74 (1966): 393–417. For a critique, see Charles Tilly, "Talking Modern," *Journal of Peasant Studies* 6 (1977): 66–68.

11. M. D. Shipman, *Education and Modernization* (London, 1971), 40.

12. Ibid., 46–47. On American schools, see especially David Tyack and Elizabeth Hansot, *Managers of Virtue: Public School Leadership in America, 1820–1980* (New York, 1982). A good recent example of the glorification of the American school is Wayne E. Fuller, *The Old Country School: The Story of Rural Education in the Middle West* (Chi-

cago, 1982). Recent debates on American school history are summarized in Marvin Lazerson, "Revisionism and American Educational History," *History of Education Review* 43, no. 2 (1973): 269–283.

13. See Patrick L. Alston, "Recent Voices and Persistent Problems in Tsarist Education," *Paedagogica Historica* 16, no. 2 (1976): 203–215; also Allen Sinel, "Problems in the Periodization of Russian Education: A Tentative Solution," *Slavic and European Education Review,* no. 2 (1977): 54–61. On the centralist, standardizing bias of American reformers and the negative view of rural education stemming from this bias, see Karl E. Kaestle and Maris A. Vinovskis, *Education and Social Change in Nineteenth-Century Massachusetts* (Cambridge, England, 1980), esp. 100–101. For recent works on Russian institutional history of education, see the Bibliography.

14. David Pace, *Claude Lévi-Strauss: The Bearer of Ashes* (London, 1983), 129, also 130–133 and chapters 5–7. See also Goody, *Domestication,* 1–19.

15. As Jack Goody has observed, we cannot "neglect the fact that cognitive activities of individuals do differ from society to society in many ways." The observer must avoid "extreme relativism" but at the same time stay away from a "we/they division which is both binary and ethnocentric," which treats differences "almost as if human minds themselves differed in their structure like machines of an earlier and later design" (Goody, *Domestication,* 2).

16. For a discussion and summary of the literature, see Harvey J. Graff, *The Literacy Myth: Literacy and Social Structure in the Nineteenth-Century City* (New York, 1979); and his "Introduction" to *Literacy and Social Development,* 1–13. See also Jack Goody and Ian Watts, "The Consequences of Literacy," in *Literacy in Traditional Societies,* ed. Jack Goody (Cambridge, England, 1969), 27–68.

17. Elizabeth Eisenstein, "Some Conjectures About the Impact of Printing on Western Society and Thought: A Preliminary Report," *Journal of Modern History* 40, no. 1 (1968): 1–56.

18. Natalie Zemon Davis, *Society and Culture in Early Modern France* (Stanford, Calif., 1975), esp. 189–226.

19. Graff, *The Literacy Myth,* 5, also 303–304, 322–324.

20. Daniel P. Resnick and Lauren B. Resnick, "The Nature of Literacy: An Historical Exploration," *Harvard Educational Review* 47 (August 1977): 370–371.

21. Evelyn S. Rawski, *Education and Popular Literacy in Ch'ing China* (Ann Arbor, Mich., 1979), 5–6.

22. Goody, *Domestication,* 10.

23. Furet and Ozouf, "Three Centuries," in Graff, *Literacy and Social Development,* 222–231. See also Zasloff, "Readings on Literacy," 156–158, in the same work; and David Olson, "From Utterance to Text," *Harvard Educational Review* 48 (August 1978): 341–377.

24. Patrick J. Harrigan, "Historians and Compilers Joined: The Historiography of the 1970s and the French Enquêtes of the Nineteenth Century," in *The Making of Frenchmen: Current Directions in the History of Education in France,* ed. Donald N. Baker and Patrick J. Harrigan (Waterloo, Ontario, 1980), 10.

25. See the discussion in Zasloff, "Readings on Literacy," esp. 157–158; and Scribner and Cole, note 9, above.

26. Scribner and Cole, "Cognitive Consequences," 552–558.

27. Thomas Laqueur, "Towards a Cultural Ecology of Literacy in England," in Resnick, *Literacy in Historical Development,* 45, also 43–57. See also Laqueur's "The Cultural Origins of Popular Literacy in England, 1500–1850," *Oxford Review of Education* 2, no. 3 (1976): 255–275.

28. See especially John E. Craig, "The Expansion of Education," *Review of Research in Education* 9 (1981): 151–213.

29. See Lawrence Stone's seminal article, "Literacy and Education in England, 1640–1900," *Past and Present* 42 (1969): 69–137.

30. Tyack and Hansot, *Managers of Virtue,* 21.

31. Furet and Ozouf, "Three Centuries," 215, 231. But see LeRoy Ladurie, "Peasants," 138–139, for a different view; also see the brilliant work by Eugen Weber, *Peasants into Frenchmen: The Modernization of Rural France, 1870–1914* (Stanford, Calif., 1976).

32. Egil Johansson, "The History of Literacy in Sweden," in Graff, *Literacy and Social Development,* 155–182.

33. Shipman, *Education and Modernization,* 44, 52.

34. Lazerson, "Revisionism," 271. For an important statement of this view, see Michael Katz, "The Origins of Public Education: A Reassessment," *History of Education Quarterly* 16 (Winter 1976): 381–407.

35. Katz has observed that we must "study the relationship between the way schools are organized and what they are supposed to do," but the logic of the revisionist argument that schools "replicate" society has not been backed up by solid historical research demonstrating *how* the classroom experience does this (Katz cited in Lazerson, "Revisionism," 277).

36. For example, Harvey Graff has argued recently that the primary

function of schooling was not formal learning, but rather disciplining for the new factory order: "To 'educate' the workers was necessary. But it was not an education in reading and writing; rather it was the need to educate the first generation of factory workers to a new factory discipline. . . . One of the consequences was the preoccupation with the character and morals of the working class which [is] so marked a feature of the early stages of industrialization" (*The Literacy Myth,* 228–229). Dan and Lauren Resnick, however, stress the element of continuity, arguing that, despite the secularization of schools in Europe and America in the nineteenth century, educational theory retained a strong moral component, whether in the inculcation of individual codes of behavior or the fostering of patriotism and "citizenship": "Despite the new curriculum in France, many of the criteria for literacy embedded in seventeenth- and eighteenth-century religious instruction were allowed to persist" ("Nature of Literacy," 379).

37. Michael Confino, *Systèmes agraires et progrès agricole: L'assolement triennal en Russie aux XVIIIᵉ–XIXᵉ siècles. Étude d'économies et des sociologies rurale* (The Hague, 1969); Moshe Lewin, *Russian Peasants and Soviet Power,* trans. Irene Nove (London, 1968); Field, *Rebels.* See also Teodor Shanin, *The Awkward Class: Political Sociology of Peasantry in a Developing Society, Russia, 1910–1925* (Oxford, 1972); David Ransel, ed., *The Family in Imperial Russia* (Urbana, Ill., 1978); and Dorothy Atkinson, *The End of the Russian Land Commune, 1905–1930* (Stanford, Calif., 1983).

38. Daniel Orlovsky, *The Limits of Reform: The Ministry of Internal Affairs in Imperial Russia, 1802–1881* (Cambridge, Mass., 1981); Neil Weissman, *Reform in Tsarist Russia: The State Bureaucracy and Local Government, 1900–1914* (New Brunswick, N.J., 1981); Roberta J. Manning, *The Crisis of the Old Order in Russia: Gentry and Government* (Princeton, N.J., 1982); Klaus Fröhlich, *The Emergence of Russian Constitutionalism* (Boston, 1981); Geoffrey Hosking, *The Russian Constitutional Experiment: Government and Duma, 1907–1914* (Cambridge, England, 1973); and Terence Emmons and Wayne S. Vucinich, eds., *The Zemstvo in Russia: An Experiment in Local Self-Government* (Cambridge, England, 1982).

39. John Brewer, "Rowlandsonian," *London Review of Books,* no. 14 (1982): 4. See also, for example, Hugh Seton-Watson, *The Russian Empire, 1801–1917* (Oxford, 1967), 477–480.

40. Jacob Walkin, *The Rise of Democracy in Pre-Revolutionary Russia: Political and Social Institutions Under the Last Three Czars* (New York, 1962), 120; N. Timashev, *The Great Retreat* (New York, 1946).

41. One need only compare *The Making of Frenchmen,* the recent collectively authored work edited by Baker and Harrigan, to see how little has been done in Russian studies.

42. See Henry A. Giroux, *Ideology, Culture and the Process of Schooling* (Philadelphia, Pa., 1981), esp. 97.

43. Kaestle and Vinovskis, *Education and Social Change in Massachusetts,* 11.

44. On education statistics in Russia, see especially I. M. Bogdanov, *Obzor izdanii gubernskikh zemstv po statistike narodnogo obrazovaniia* (Khar'kov, 1913); I. M. Bogdanov, ed., *Trudy pervogo vserossiiskogo s"ezda po statistike narodnogo obrazovaniia* (Khar'kov, 1912); B. P. Vologdin, "Zemskaia statistika narodnogo obrazovaniia," in *Iubileinyi zemskii sbornik,* ed. B. B. Veselovskii and Z. G. Frenkel' (St. Petersburg, 1914), 399–411; I. Z. Kaganovich, *Ocherk istorii razvitiia statistiki shkol'nogo obrazovaniia v SSSR* (Moscow, 1957); P. A. Vikhliaev, *Kratkoe rukovodstvo po statistike narodnogo obrazovaniia* (Moscow, 1919).

45. See the brief comments by Kaestle and Vinovskis in *Education and Social Change in Massachusetts,* 9; also M. J. Maynes, "Work or School? Youth and the Family in the Midi in the Early Nineteenth Century," in Baker and Harrigan, *The Making of Frenchmen,* 123. On deducing strategies from aggregate behavior, see the general comments by Craig in his "Expansion of Education."

46. Thomas Darlington, *Education in Russia,* Board of Education, Special Reports on Education, vol. 23 (London, 1909), 303.

47. See three articles by Eric R. Wolf: "Aspects of Group Relations in a Complex Society: Mexico," *American Anthropologist* 58, no. 6 (1956): 1065–1078; "Types of Latin American Peasantry," in *Tribal and Peasant Economies,* ed. George Dalton (Garden City, N.J., 1967), 501–524; and "Closed Corporate Peasant Communities in Mesoamerica and Central Java," in Potter, *Peasant Society,* 230–246.

48. See Shanin, *The Awkward Class,* 177–179. For another excellent discussion, see Hamza Alavi, "Peasant Classes and Primordial Loyalties," *Journal of Peasant Studies* 1, no. 1 (October 1972): 43–49.

49. In this context, anthropologists speak of "hinge men" or "brokers" who watch over the crucial "junctures" or "synapses" of relationships linking the local system to the larger whole. Traditionally, these "brokers," who often serve as elders or headmen and are responsible for tax collection and the maintenance of law and order, are not the true moral leaders of the community. Instead, they are agents of both

government and village, and their authority in the community is severely compromised by the posture of humility they must adopt toward officialdom and by the contamination of sustained contact with outsiders. In Russia, the role of mediator was often adopted by the elder (both volost' *starshina* and village *starosta*). See George Foster, "Peasant Society and the Image of Limited Good," in Potter, *Peasant Society,* 300–324; and Joseph Lopreato, "How Would You Like To Be a Peasant?" in the same work, 419–438.

See also F. G. Bailey, "The Peasant View of the Bad Life," in Shanin, *Peasants and Peasant Society,* 299–321, esp. 303. In the same volume, see Kazimierz Dobrowolski, "Peasant Traditional Culture," 277–298; and Sutti Ortiz, "Reflections on the Concept of Peasant Culture and Peasant Cognitive Systems," 322–336.

Recent Soviet work by Zyrianov, Alexandrov, and Prokof'eva has helped illuminate the workings of the peasant local community. In particular, Zyrianov points to the existence of an "official elder" and a "field elder" and notes that it was the latter who enjoyed genuine authority in the village; see P. N. Zyrianov, "Nekotorye cherty evoliutsii krest'ianskogo 'mira' v poreformennuiu epokhu," in *Ezhegodnik po agrarnoi istorii vostochnoi Evropy, 1971* (Vilnius, 1974), 380–387; V. A. Alexandrov, *Sel'skaia obshchina v Rossii* (Moscow, 1976); L. S. Prokof'eva, *Krest'ianskaia obshchina v Rossii* (Leningrad, 1981).

50. From yet another perspective, the unique role of rural teachers places them in a strategic position in the modernization process. François Furet and Jacques Ozouf have linked the spread of general literacy (especially the ability to write) with the end of the "control of the small group," of tradition; with a "modification of the social fabric itself" by breaking up the group in favor of the individual; with the establishment of direct communication between the individual and the state; and with the establishment of a modern, national political unit to replace the bonds of the community. To them, "it is through the written word, which short-circuits the barriers erected by the oral community . . . that political individualization takes place." In France, however, the process of transition from restricted to general literacy took fully three centuries, and the authors eloquently describe how "restricted" literacy had little impact on traditional structures ("Three Centuries," esp. 222–224).

In Russia, just as economic modernization was compressed into the brief period between 1880 and 1914, so the political and cultural transformation from restrictive to general literacy described by Furet and Ozouf had to proceed at a forced pace in order to keep up—it had to be induced by outside agents. Yet the very mission of the teacher posed a direct threat to the position of hinge men or mediators such as the elder, the village priest, or even the entire older generation, and the teacher's work threatened to "short-circuit" the barriers erected by the community, threatened to dissolve the culture. The place occupied by the village teacher in the community serves as an excellent marker of the stage of disintegration of the oral community or, alternatively, of its continuing vitality and capacity to maintain equilibrium and integrity under strain.

CHAPTER 1

1. Joseph L. Black, *Citizens for the Fatherland* (Boulder, Colo., 1979), 3. See also M. F. Shabaeva, ed., *Ocherki istorii shkoly i pedagogicheskoi mysli narodov SSSR: XVIII v.–pervaia polovina XIX v.* (Moscow, 1973), 19–23. On this period, see V. V. Grigor'ev, *Istoricheskii ocherk russkoi shkoly* (Moscow, 1900), 59–182; S. A. Kniaz'kov and N. I. Serbov, *Ocherki istorii narodnogo obrazovaniia v Rossii do epokhi reform Aleksandra II* (Moscow, 1910); M. I. Demkov, *Istoriia russkoi pedagogiki,* vol. 2 (St. Petersburg, 1897); O. N. Smirnov, "Narodnoe prosveshchenie i narodnyi uchitel' dorevoliutsionnoi Rossii," Arkhiv akademii pedagogicheskikh nauk SSSR (hereafter APN) (1946), f. 50, op. 1, d. 33; V. I. Charnoluskii, "Narodnoe prosveshchenie v dorevoliutsionnoi Rossii," (1929?), APN f. 19, op. 1, d. 8.
2. On enrollments, see *Narodnaia entsiklopediia nauchnykh i prikladnykh znanii* (Moscow, 1912), 10:8.
3. Black, *Citizens,* 28.
4. E. N. Medynskii, *Istoriia russkoi pedagogiki,* 2d ed. (Moscow, 1938), 64–66; Black, *Citizens,* 30; Shabaeva, *Ocherki istorii shkoly,* 35–44; G. E. Zhurakovskii, *Iz istorii prosveshcheniia v dorevoliutsionnoi Rossii,* ed. E. D. Dneprov (Moscow, 1978), 18–31.
5. Darlington, *Education in Russia,* 93; Isabel de Madariaga, *Russia in the Age of Catherine the Great* (New Haven, Conn., 1981), 494; *Narodnaia entsiklopediia* 10:11–12; Shabaeva, *Ocherki istorii shkoly,* 67–194. On the Boards of Social Welfare and their overall place in local government, see the article by S. Frederick Starr, "Local Initiative in Russia Before the Zemstvo," in Emmons and Vucinich, *The Zemstvo in Russia,* 5–31.
6. Cited in Paul Dukes, *Catherine the Great and the Russian Nobility* (Cambridge, England, 1967), 191. See also M. D. Kurmacheva, "Problemy obrazovaniia v ulozhenoi komissii 1767 g.," in *Dvorianstvo*

i krepostnoi stroi Rossii XVI–XVIII vv., *Sbornik statei posveshchënnyi pamiati A. A. Novosel'skogo* (Moscow, 1975), 240–264.

7. Dukes, *Catherine the Great*, 191; but see de Madariaga, *Russia in the Age of Catherine*, 491.

8. N. I. Novikov, cited in Black, *Citizens*, 108. The same issue has provoked a debate about the overall goals of Catherinian education legislation. Okenfuss has traced the transformation of Enlightenment views into a Germanic regimen of discipline and has argued that Catherine's reforms "were part of the conservative reaction against the contagion of progressive education, that is, the ideal of educating the whole man" (Max J. Okenfuss, "Education and Empire: School Reform in Enlightened Russia," *Jahrbücher für Geschichte Osteuropas* 27 [1979]: 68).

De Madariaga, in her recent work on Catherine, counters: "Where, one might ask, was there a school, let alone an educational system, run on Rousseauian lines?" She argues that Catherine saw no contradiction between good citizenship and the acceptance of hierarchy, on the one hand, and self-development and fulfillment, on the other (*Russia in the Age of Catherine*, 501, 496–499). Indeed, Chisick has recently demonstrated that in France—and it was with the French Enlightenment that Catherine flirted—the question of educating *le menu peuple* (in the sense of the lower classes, not the nation or the collectivity) was complicated by the incompatibility of different strands in Enlightenment thought: the synthesis of classicism and Christianity that constituted the Enlightenment yielded not only naturalism, rationalism, and humanism but also a distrust of the lower classes. Even Voltaire once asserted that the children of peasants should remain illiterate.

According to Chisick, there was a basic problem in the Enlightenment approach to education: on the one hand was the belief that education dissipated ignorance and superstition; on the other was fear and distrust of the common people and opposition to the spread of education. A resolution was finally found in Jansenist views that education could be used as a form of social control and in the emergence of the belief in "an education fitting to one's place in society, and an education designed to induce the lower classes to accept their place in the constituted social order" (Harvey Chisick, *The Limits of Reform in the Enlightenment: Attitudes Toward the Education of the Lower Classes in Eighteenth-Century France* [Princeton, N.J., 1981], 116–119).

Approached from this perspective, the question of Catherinian views is less problematic. The debate among historians is whether

Catherine was most influenced by Betskoi, Felbiger, or Basedow, and whether there was a contradiction between self-development and education useful to the state—but the debate concerned citizens and subjects, not serfs. Until Radishchev and the spread of sentimentalism in Russia, serfs were regarded as little more than cattle. On those rare times when their education (let alone well-being) was considered and the question of their proper schooling emerged, the Russian state was squarely within the Enlightenment tradition when it sought a "fitting education" for serfs.

Although de Madariaga has recently noted that early drafts of the 1786 Statute did mention rural schools, the final version overlooked them; and the provision that free subjects could be admitted to schools left out the lowly serf. On this question, see also Black, *Citizens,* 89, 142; *Narodnaia entsiklopediia* 10:11–12; Darlington, *Education in Russia,* 27; Shabaeva, *Ocherki istorii shkoly,* 146n. Interesting material on elite attitudes toward popular education in seventeenth-century Russia, especially on Catherine's commission, can be found in Zhurakovskii, *Iz istorii prosveshcheniia,* 35–78. M. D. Kurmacheva has recently published a book on the "peasant intelligentsia," including three chapters on schools: *Krepostnaia intelligentsiia Rossii* (Moscow, 1983), esp. 58–112.

9. S. V. Rozhdestvenskii, *Ocherki po istorii sistem narodnogo prosveshcheniia v Rossii v XIII–XIX vv.* (St. Petersburg, 1912), 1:611–613.

10. Black, *Citizens,* 145, 148–149. See also Rozhdestvenskii, *Ocherki po istorii,* 604–611; and Shabaeva, *Ocherki istorii shkoly,* 143–154.

11. Nicholas Hans, *History of Russian Educational Policy, 1701–1917* (New York, 1964), 27. See also Patrick L. Alston, *Education and the State in Tsarist Russia* (Stanford, Calif., 1969), 3–42; P. Miliukov, *Ocherki po istorii russkoi kul'tury,* 3d ed. (St. Petersburg, 1902), 2:295–330; N. A. Konstantinov and V. Ia. Struminskii, *Ocherki po istorii nachal'nogo obrazovaniia v Rossii,* 2d ed. (Moscow, 1953), 37–84.

12. Darlington, *Education in Russia,* 24. See also P. F. Kapterev, *Istoriia russkoi pedagogiki* (St. Petersburg, 1909), 126n.

13. For a discussion of the emphasis on secondary and higher education in the Russian tradition, see Michael Kaser, "Education in Tsarist and Soviet Development," in *Essays in Honor of E. H. Carr,* ed. C. Abramsky (London, 1974), 229–254; and, more recently, James C. McClelland, *Autocrats and Academics: Education, Culture, and Society in Tsarist Russia* (Chicago, 1979), 9. See also McClelland's "Diversification in Russian-Soviet Education," in *The Transformation of Higher Education,* ed. Komad H. Jarausch (Stuttgart, 1983), 180–196;

K. Bendriakov, "Shkol'naia sistema v Rossii pered fevral'skoi revo-liutsiei," *Narodnoe obrazovanie,* no. 3 (1947): 47; and Medynskii, *Istoriia russkoi pedagogiki,* 79—83.

14. M. I. Demkov, *Nachal'naia narodnaia shkola: Eia istoriia, didaktika i metodika,* 2d ed. (Moscow, 1916), 48—49. On the history of educational districts, see Grigor'ev, *Istoricheskii ocherk russkoi shkoly,* 294—295, 330—331, 399—400.

15. Hans, *History of Russian Educational Policy,* 44—45; but see Shabaeva, *Ocherki istorii shkoly,* 195—223, on the foreign origins of Alexander's system (the author denies any French inspiration). See also Alston, *Education and the State,* 22; Konstantinov and Struminskii, *Ocherki po istorii,* 84—117; Grigor'ev, *Istoricheskii ocherk russkoi shkoly,* 294—326; S. V. Rozhdestvenskii, ed., *Istoricheskii obzor deiatel'nosti ministerstva narodnogo prosveshcheniia, 1802—1902* (St Petersburg, 1902); and Demkov, *Istoriia russkoi pedagogiki* (Moscow, 1909), 3:1—210.

16. Cited in *Narodnaia entsiklopediia* 10:18—20. See also Demkov, *Nachal'naia narodnaia shkola,* 49. Here the term *parish* was a geographic referent and had no relation to the type of school. Later in the century, parish schools sprang up under the Holy Synod, while Alexander's parish schools, modified and actively promoted under Nicholas I, continued to exist under the Ministry of Education as 1828 Parish Schools. Historians have sometimes confused the two types of schools, which by the end of the century fulfilled entirely different missions and were subordinated to different authorities. The overwhelming majority of Church parish schools were located in the countryside in the second half of the century; the Parish Schools targeted for the countryside by Alexander came to life only when Nicholas began to establish them in the *towns,* where they remained.

17. Cited in Demkov, *Nachal'naia narodnaia shkola,* 49—50.

18. On the district schools, see *Narodnaia entsiklopediia* 10:21; S. I. Miropol'skii, *Shkola i gosudarstvo: Obiazatel'nost' obucheniia v Rossii (Istoricheskii etiud),* 3d ed. (St. Petersburg, 1910), 3—49; and especially two articles by M. Sukhomlinov, "Zametki ob uchilishchakh i narodnom obrazovanii v Iaroslavskoi gubernii," *Zhurnal ministerstva narodnogo prosveshcheniia* (hereafter *ZhMNP*) 117, sec. 3 (January 1863): 103—189; and "Uchilishcha i narodnoe obrazovanie v Chernigovskoi gubernii," *ZhMNP* 121, sec. 3 (January 1864): 1—94. This last work is very rich in first-hand observation.

19. M. N. Pokrovskii, ed., *Istoriia Rossii v XIX veke* (St. Petersburg, 1906), 4:78.

20. Hans, *History of Russian Educational Policy,* 59. See also Konstantinov and Struminskii, *Ocherki po istorii,* 92–93; and the judgments of Grigor'ev, *Istoricheskii ocherk russkoi shkoly,* 325–327.

21. On the Lancaster schools in Russia, see Grigor'ev, *Istoricheskii ocherk russkoi shkoly,* 306–307; and Judith Cohan Zacek, "The Lancaster School Movement in Russia," *Slavonic and East European Review* 45 (1967): 343–367. Other scholars note that few other countries in Western Europe at the time had followed the Prussian policy of active government intervention in support of primary education: Carlo M. Cipolla, *Literacy and Development in the West* (Baltimore, Md., 1969), 62–100; Hugh M. Pollard, *Pioneers of Popular Education, 1760–1850* (Cambridge, Mass., 1957), 3–12, 125–133, 135–146, 281–295; Alston, *Education and the State,* 19; Black, *Citizens,* 159.

22. Miropol'skii, *Shkola i gosudarstvo,* 64; Grigor'ev, *Istoricheskii ocherk russkoi shkoly,* 380–387.

23. *Narodnaia entsiklopediia* 10:21, 22. Also cited in Pokrovskii, *Istoriia Rossii v XIX veke* 4:96–97.

24. Hans, *History of Russian Educational Policy,* 32–33. Pokrovskii, *Istoriia Rossii v XIX veke* 4:102; Shabaeva, *Ocherki istorii shkoly,* 207–210.

25. Hans, *History of Russian Educational Policy,* 67–68; Konstantinov and Struminskii, *Ocherki po istorii,* 94–96; Pokrovskii, *Istoriia Rossii v XIX veke* 4:97; Darlington, *Education in Russia,* 67–68; and T. V. Kolchina, "Narodnye uchilishcha v Rossii v 30–50–kh godakh XIX veka" (Candidate diss., Moskovskii oblastnoi institut pedagogiki imeni N. K. Krupskoi, Moscow, 1973), esp. 14–36. On this period, see also Cynthia Whittaker, *The Origins of Modern Russian Education: An Intellectual Biography of Count Sergei Uvarov, 1786–1855* (Dekalb, Ill., 1984).

26. William Mathes, "The Process of Institutionalization of Education in Russia, 1800–1917," in *Russian and Slavic History: Papers from the Banff 1974 Conference,* ed. Don K. Rowney and G. Edward Orchard (Columbus, Ohio, 1977), 35.

27. Miropol'skii, *Shkola i gosudarstvo,* 141. See also Miliukov, *Ocherki po istorii russkoi kul'tury* 2:373–376; Hans, *History of Russian Educational Policy,* 233.

28. On volost' schools, see Struminskii and Konstantinov, *Ocherki po istorii,* 97–101; G. A. Fal'bork and V. I. Charnoluskii, *Narodnoe obrazovanie v Rossii* (St. Petersburg, 1899), 28–30, 40, 166–168; William H. Johnson, *Russia's Educational Heritage* (Pittsburgh, Pa., 1950), 101; N. V. Chekhov, *Narodnoe obrazovanie v Rossii s 60-kh*

godov XIX veka (Moscow, 1912), ch. 1; and Charnoluskii, "Narodnoe prosveshchenie," 10–15, 26–56.

29. Pokrovskii, *Istoriia Rossii v XIX veke* 4:86.

30. Konstantinov and Struminskii, *Ocherki po istorii,* 97–98.

31. Pokrovskii, *Istoriia Rossii v XIX veke* 4:116.

32. Chekhov, *Narodnoe obrazovanie,* 92–94. Also Pokrovskii, *Istoriia Rossii v XIX veke* 4:127; *Narodnaia entsiklopediia* 10:24.

33. Both Mosolov and Kulomzin are cited in Miliukov, *Ocherki po istorii russkoi kul'tury* 2:376. See also Pokrovskii, *Istoriia Rossii v XIX veke* 4:110.

34. N. M. Druzhinin, *Gosudarstvennye krest'iane i reforma, P. D. Kiselëva* (Moscow, 1958), 2:251. There is abundant evidence that the Church was not the only promoter of "paper schools." See, for example, Miropol'skii, *Shkola i gosudarstvo,* 141; and Fal'bork and Charnoluskii, *Narodnoe obrazovanie,* 4, 28–30, 166–168. See also V. I. Kaganovich, "Ocherk istorii shkol'noi statistiki v Rossii" APN (1957), op. 20, d. 3, esp. 13–14; and N. N. Iordanskii, "Istoriia narodnoi shkoly," APN (n.d.), f. 20, op. 1, d. 3, 82. This school inspector showed that neither the Ministry of Appanages, the state peasant bureaucracy, nor the MNP had any idea how many schools they had.

35. Chekhov, *Narodnoe obrazovanie,* 92–94.

36. Laqueur, "Cultural Origins of Popular Literacy," 257.

37. See *Illiustrirovannye avtobiografii neskol'kikh nezamechatel'nykh russkikh liudei,* 2d ed. (Moscow, 1896), 78–102, for an excellent example of the devoted efforts of a village priest to spread literacy.

38. Druzhinin, *Gosudarstvennye krest'iane* 2:255; Pokrovskii, *Istoriia Rossii v XIX veke* 2:109.

39. Pokrovskii, *Istoriia Rossii v XIX veke* 4:111.

40. Konstantinov and Struminskii, *Ocherki po istorii,* 99.

41. On Kiselëv, see especially Olga Crisp, "The State Peasants Under Nicholas II," in her *Studies in the Russian Economy before 1914* (London, 1976), 73–96; and Druzhinin, *Gosudarstvennye krest'iane* 2:248–262.

42. Pokrovskii, *Istoriia Rossii v XIX veke* 4:106–107; also Druzhinin, *Gosudarstvennye krest'iane* 2:248–251; and *Narodnaia entsiklopediia* 10:24.

43. Pokrovskii, *Istoriia Rossii v XIX veke* 4:106–107.

44. Druzhinin, *Gosudarstvennye krest'iane* 2:248.

45. Pokrovskii, *Istoriia Rossii v XIX veke* 4:107.

46. Druzhinin, *Gosudarstvennye krest'iane* 2:251.

47. *Narodnaia entsiklopediia* 10:24.

48. Pokrovskii, *Istoriia Rossii v XIX veke* 4:109; Druzhinin, *Gosudarstvennye krest'iane* 2:248. Peasants sometimes showed up with eggs, poultry, or pigs, asking that their children be "released" (Iordanskii, "Istoriia narodnoi shkoly," 9–10).

49. A. G. Rashin, "Gramotnost' i narodnoe obrazovanie v Rossii v XIX i na .hale XX veka," *Istoricheskie zapiski* 37 (1951): 54; Pokrovskii, *Istoriia Rossii v XIX veke* 4:120–123; Fal'bork and Charnoluskii, *Narodnoe obrazovanie,* 32.

50. These sixteen provinces were Petersburg, Saratov, Moscow, Kherson, Ekaterinoslav, Smolensk, Lifland, Vil'no, Orel, Voronezh, Orenburg, Tavrida, Iaroslavl', Khar'kov, Novgorod, and Vladimir (Rashin, "Gramotnost'," 52–53).

51. Darlington, *Education in Russia,* 86, 103; Fal'bork and Charnoluskii, *Narodnoe obrazovanie,* 32–33. But see Rashin, "Gramotnost'," 56; he estimates a ratio of 1:143 for all the schools in the entire Empire.

52. Rashin, "Gramotnost'," 57, 65–67; Fal'bork and Charnoluskii, *Narodnoe obrazovanie,* 33; Ia. E. Vodarskii, *Naselenie Rossii za 400 let (XVI–XX vv.)* (Moscow, 1973), 55.

53. Pokrovskii, *Istoriia Rossii v XIX veke* 4:104–105; see esp. the citation on page 105.

54. McClelland, *Autocrats and Academics,* 5; Mathes, "Process of Institutionalization," 41.

55. Darlington, *Education in Russia,* 103. K. P. Tsebrovskii, in "Nachal'noe obrazovanie v Iaroslavskoi gubernii v poreformennyi period" (Candidate diss., Moskovskii gosudarstvennyi pedagogicheskii institut, Moscow, 1955), 382–383, discusses these schools and claims that in the 1860s there were at least as many unofficial peasant schools as there were official schools.

56. Demkov, *Nachal'naia narodnaia shkola,* 47.

57. Ibid., 49; D. Uspenskii, "Pomeshchiki o gramotnosti krest'ian," *Russkaia mysl'* 25, no. 3 (1904): 19–30. See also Kurmacheva, *Krepostnaia intelligentsiia,* 84–113; and Tsebrovskii, "Nachal'noe obrazovanie," 81–95, 380–385.

58. Pokrovskii, *Istoriia Rossii v XIX veke* 4:124. Also see *Narodnaia entsiklopediia* 10:17. For descriptions of pre-reform schools, see Iordanskii, "Istoriia narodnoi shkoly," 90–120; Kolchina, "Narodnye uchilishcha," 37–95; A. S. Gatsiskii, *Shkol'noe delo v Nizhegorodskom povolzh'e* (Kazan', 1873), esp. 1–16; V. Kolpenskii, "Sel'skaia shkola nakanune krest'ianskoi reformy," *Arkhiv istorii truda v Rossii,* vol. 4

(1922); I. Paul'son, *Metodiki grammatiki po istoricheskim i teoreticheskim dannym,* vol. 1 (St. Petersburg, 1887–1892). Also see the remarkable autobiography of the rural teacher E. Strel'tsov (*Iz dvadtsatipiatiletnei praktiki sel'skogo uchitelia,* vol. 1: *Sel'skaia shkola, 1848–1864* [St. Petersburg, 1875]). A concise summary of zemstvo investigations of pre-1864 conditions is found in E. A. Zviagintsev, *Polveka zemskoi deiatel'nosti po narodnomu obrazovaniiu* (Moscow, 1915), 1–15; see also V. A. Petrov, "Zemskaia nachal'naia shkola Viatskoi gubernii" (Candidate diss., Moskovskii oblastnoi pedagogicheskii institut, Kirov, 1955), 8–42.

59. Miropol'skii, *Shkola i gosudarstvo,* 66–70.

60. N. A. Rubakin, *Sredi knig* (Moscow, 1913), 2:419.

61. Black, *Citizens,* 74.

62. Marc Raeff's description of seminary education is found in *Michael Speransky: Statesman of Imperial Russia* (The Hague, 1957), 3–7.

63. Zviagintsev, *Polveka,* 9.

64. V. I. Orlov, *Narodnoe obrazovanie v Moskovskoi gubernii,* vol. 9 of *Sbornik statisticheskikh svedenii po Moskovskoi gubernii,* Moskovskaia gubernskaia zemskaia uprava, Otdel khoziaistvennoi statistiki (Moscow, 1884), 5; Volokolamsk district zemstvo board cited in Moskovskaia gubernskaia zemskaia uprava, Otdel khoziaistvennoi statistiki, *Izvestiia Moskovskoi gubernskoi zemskoi upravy* (January-February 1912), Appendix, 12. See also V. V. Petrov, *Obzor dvadtsatipiatiletnei deiatel'nosti Moskovskogo zemstva po narodnomu obrazovaniiu* (Moscow, 1892), 13.

65. *Doklad Kolomenskoi uezdnoi zemskoi upravy zemskomu sobraniiu* (Ocherednaia sessiia, December 1869) (Kolomna, 1870). Also see Petrov, *Obzor,* 13, 14–16; V. V. Petrov, ed., *Voprosy narodnogo obrazovaniia v Moskovskoi gubernii* (Moscow, 1897), 1:34–37.

66. Considerable detail on the schools of the immediate pre-zemstvo period exists in the numerous surveys of zemstvo educational activity published at the end of the century and before World War I. All of the following examples are from Tula: P. S. Sheremet'ev, ed., *Narodnye uchitelia i uchitel'nitsy v Tul'skoi gubernii: Istoriko-statisticheskii ocherk* (Tula, 1898), 12–16. See also note 58, above.

67. Druzhinin, *Gosudarstvennye krest'iane* 2:250.

68. Ibid., 251.

69. Ibid.

70. Ibid.

71. Zviagintsev, *Polveka,* 9–11.

72. Ibid., 7.

73. Druzhinin, *Gosudarstvennye krest'iane* 2:252. See also Konstantinov and Struminskii, *Ocherki po istorii*, 99.

74. Weber, *Peasants into Frenchmen*, 305–307. Also see Pamela Horn, *Education in Rural England, 1800–1914* (New York, 1978), 18–23; P. H. J. H. Gosden, *How They Were Taught* (Oxford, 1969), 11–12.

75. Richard Gawthrup and Gerald Strauss, "Protestantism and Literacy in Early Modern Germany," *Past and Present*, no. 104 (1984): 31–55. But see also Pollard, *Pioneers of Popular Education*, 94–95.

76. Geroid T. Robinson, *Rural Russia Under the Old Regime: A History of the Landlord-Peasant World and a Prologue to the Peasant Revolution of 1917* (Berkeley and Los Angeles, Calif., 1967), 54; Miropol'skii, *Shkola i gosudarstvo*, 126–127.

77. Mathes, "Process of Institutionalization," 41.

78. Okenfuss, "Education and Empire," 68.

79. Mathes, "Process of Institutionalization," 34ff.

CHAPTER 2

1. S. S. Tatishchev, *Imperator Aleksandr II, Ego zhizn' i tsarstvovanie* (St. Petersburg, 1903), 2:232.

2. Nicholas Hans, *The Russian Tradition in Education* (London, 1963), 54–56; V. Z. Smirnov, *Ocherki po istorii progressivnoi russkoi pedagogiki XIX veka* (Moscow, 1963), 163–184. For a general discussion of the issues and personalities, see Kapterev, *Istoriia russkoi pedagogiki*, 228–286; and Chekhov, *Narodnoe obrazovanie*, 5–21. The text of Pirogov's article is found in M. I. Demkov, *Russkaia pedagogika v glavneishikh eia predstaviteliakh*, 2d ed. (Moscow, 1916), 136–152. For a more recent discussion, see William Mathes, "N. I. Pirogov," *Slavic Review* 31 (March 1972): 44–50. In the Soviet Union, Pirogov has received considerable attention, as have the educational debates of the sixties in general: see E. D. Dneprov, *Sovetskaia literatura po istorii shkoly i pedagogiki dorevoliutsionnoi Rossii: Bibliograficheskii ukazatel'* (Moscow, 1979), for lists of dissertations, articles, and monographs.

3. V. Z. Smirnov, *Reforma nachal'noi i srednei shkoly v 60-kh godakh XIX veka* (Moscow, 1954), 26–166. This is a very solid work, based on extensive archival research.

4. Ibid., 25, 30; Darlington, *Education in Russia*, 102–104; Hans, *Russian Tradition*, 55; Hans, *History of Russian Educational Policy*, 100–102.

5. Smirnov, *Reforma,* 132–134. See also Fal'bork and Charnoluskii, *Narodnoe obrazovanie,* 38.

6. S. Frederick Starr, *Decentralization and Self-Government in Russia, 1830–1870* (Princeton, N.J., 1972), 244.

7. Rozhdestvenskii, *Istoricheskii,* 454; Fal'bork and Charnoluskii, *Narodnoe obrazovanie,* 39.

8. Smirnov, *Reforma,* 159. See Chekhov, *Narodnoe obrazovanie,* 209–210, for a summary of the evolution of officially proclaimed goals of primary education from 1828 to 1911; for the 1864 Statute, see *ZhMNP* 123, sec. 4 (July 1864): 39–47. For the earlier drafts concerning program, length of hours, and course of study, see Smirnov, *Reforma,* 28–40, 64–66, 87–94, 99–108.

   For summaries of the 1864 and 1874 statutes, see Rozhdestvenskii, *Istoricheskii,* 444–456, 543, 556; V. I. Charnoluskii, *Zemstvo i narodnoe obrazovanie* (St. Petersburg, 1910), 1 : 4–17; F. Ol'denburg, "Zakonodatel'stvo i spravochnye izdaniia po nachal'nomu narodnomu obrazovaniiu," in *Vseobshchee obrazovanie v Rossii,* ed. D. M. Shakhovskii (Moscow, 1902), 1–21. Smirnov, *Reforma,* 143–151, 161–165, is also an excellent summary. The full text of the 1874 Statute is in *ZhMNP* 174, sec. 4 (August 1874): 227–237; and *Svod zakonov Rossiiskoi Imperii* (St. Petersburg, 1893), 11 : 294–310, part 1.

9. See Smirnov, *Reforma,* 148, for a different interpretation of the boards; also Alston, *Education and the State,* 75; Charnoluskii, *Zemstvo i narodnoe obrazovanie* 1 : 4–6; Allen Sinel, "Educating the Russian Peasantry: The Elementary School Reforms of Count Dmitry Tolstoi," *American Slavic and East European Review* 27, no. 1 (1968): 53; E. A. Zviagintsev, "Zemstvo i uchebnoe vedomstvo," in Veselovskii and Frenkel', *Iubileinyi zemskii sbornik,* 360.

10. Charnoluskii, *Zemstvo i narodnoe obrazovanie,* 1 : 10–11.

11. Darlington, *Education in Russia,* 103–104; Chekhov, *Narodnoe obrazovanie,* 37–42.

12. In the West, the generally enthusiastic assessment of zemstvo activities derives at least partially from the tendency of an earlier generation of émigré historians, themselves often connected with zemstvo politics, to overstate the importance of the zemstvos and to ignore their elitist, blatantly pro-gentry economic politics. Roberta Manning's work on the role of the zemstvos in the 1905 Revolution (*The Crisis of the Old Order in Russia: Gentry and Government*) does much to rectify this. In addition, Emmons and Vucinich's *The Zemstvo in Russia* has also gone far toward correcting the longstanding imbalance. Ironically, in the Soviet Union, where the zemstvos

have been almost entirely ignored or contemptuously dismissed, younger historians have been promoting a more positive reassessment of the local economic, educational, and welfare measures of the zemstvos. In particular, a projected study of zemstvo education petitions promises to break new ground.

13. The word *zemstvo* has been translated as "territorial assembly" and compared with the Prussian *Landtag*. But most historians prefer not to translate *zemstvo*. "The very word conjured up romanticized memories of the seventeenth-century *zemskii sobor*. . . . Despite strenuous official counteraction, the aura of popular sovereignty and indigenous Muscovite constitutionalism clung to the local assemblies from the moment of their conception" (Gr. Dzhanshiev, *Iz epokhi velikikh reform* [Moscow, 1894], 310). As Hosking has commented: "Russians talked of local self-government [*mestnoe samoupravlenie*] to distinguish it from the soulless machinery of the central bureaucracy, which also had its local agencies. The word *zemstvo*, and its adjective *zemskii* [and, we should add, the word for zemstvo activist, *zemets*], came to carry attributes of humanity, cooperative effort, closeness to the soil, love of the people" (Hosking, *Russian Constitutional Experiment*, 152–154). But see also Starr, *Decentralization*, 294; as well as the article by Kermit McKenzie, "Zemstvo Organization and Role Within the Administrative Structure," in Emmons and Vucinich, *The Zemstvo in Russia*, 33–34.

14. See especially Alexander Vucinich, "The State and the Local Community," in *The Transformation of Russia*, ed. C. Black (Cambridge, Mass., 1960), 195; Walkin, *Rise of Democracy*, 154; Alfred Rieber, "Alexander II: A Revisionist View," *Journal of Modern History* 43, no. 1 (1971): 48; Terence Emmons, "Conclusion," in Emmons and Vucinich, *The Zemstvo in Russia*, 432; and N. M. Pirumova, *Zemskoe liberal'noe dvizhenie: Sotsial'nye korni i evoliutsiia do nachala XX veka* (Moscow, 1977), 27. See also V. V. Garmiza, "Zemskaia reforma i zemstvo v istoricheskoi literature," *Istoriia SSSR*, no. 5 (1960): 85–89. For bibliographies of works on the zemstvo, see V. V. Garmiza, *Podgotovka zemskoi reformy 1864 goda* (Moscow, 1957); B. B. Veselovskii, *Istoriia zemstva za sorok let* (St. Petersburg, 1909), 1:595–628; and P. P. Gronskii, "Teoriia samoupravleniia v Russkoi nauke," in Veselovskii and Frenkel', *Iubileinyi zemskii sbornik*, 76–86. See also S. Ia. Tseitlin, "Zemskaia reforma," in Pokrovskii, *Istoriia Rossii v XIX veke* 3:215–230 and 5:79–139.

15. Walkin, *Rise of Democracy*, 179:

In the contest between state and society, which became so sharp toward the close of the nineteenth century, the zemstvo became the natural center for political activity and political leadership. . . . Had there been no war, there are good grounds for believing that Russian society's growing maturity and its new ways of action at the lowest levels would have forced the central government to adjust its ways of action. . . . There can be no question that Russia was following the major European powers in moving from absolute monarchy to constitutional democracy.

16. Cited in Garmiza, "Zemskaia reforma," 82; I. V. Orzhekhovskii, *Iz istorii vnutrennei politiki samoderzhaviia v 60–70–kh godakh XIX veka* (Gorkii, 1974), 83–107.

17. Vucinich, "The State and Local Community," 195–197.

18. George Yaney, *The Systematization of Russian Government* (Urbana, Ill., 1973), 231.

19. Starr, *Decentralization,* 298, 313–315.

20. McKenzie, "Zemstvo Organization," 32–36.

21. Thomas Fallows, "The Zemstvo and the Bureaucracy," in Emmons and Vucinich, *The Zemstvo in Russia,* 178.

22. See McKenzie, "Zemstvo Organization," 49, 53, for detail; for subsequent modifications, organization, and the "roof and foundation" notion, see Garmiza, "Zemskaia reforma," 94; Walkin, *Rise of Democracy,* 158; K. K. Arsen'ev et al., *Melkaia zemskaia edinitsa: Sbornik statei* (St. Petersburg, 1903), particularly the "Introduction"; N. N. Avinov, "Glavnye cherty v istorii zakonodatel'stva o zemskikh uchrezhdeniiakh," in Veselovskii and Frenkel', *Iubileinyi zemskii sbornik,* 1–35; and Veselovskii, *Istoriia zemstva* 3:551–575. The figures are drawn from V. V. Alekhin and K. V. Sivkov, *Moskovskii krai* (Moscow, 1925), 7–9; and Tsentral'nyi statisticheskii komitet, *Moskovskaia guberniia,* vol. 24 of *Pervaia vseobshchaia perepis' naseleniia Rossiiskoi imperii* (St. Petersburg, 1905), 7–9.

23. For a detailed description, see L. G. Zakharova, *Zemskaia kontrreforma 1890 g.* (Moscow, 1968); B. B. Veselovskii, *K voprosu o klassovykh interesakh v zemstve* (St. Petersburg, 1905), 1–92, esp. 33–55; Vladimir Trutovskii, *Sovremennoe zemstvo* (Petrograd, 1914), 13–38; Roberta Manning, "The Zemstvo and Politics," in Emmons and Vucinich, *The Zemstvo in Russia,* 142; Pirumova, *Zemskoe liberal'noe dvizhenie,* 77–82; and the article by N. I. Lazarevskii, "Zemskoe izbiratel'noe pravo," in Veselovskii and Frenkel', *Iubileinyi zemskii sbornik,* 50–76.

The revised 1890 Statute significantly increased the property requirement. The system was further complicated by the superimposition of class qualifications through a complicated method of indirect voting in the various curias and by arbitrary quotas set by the government. After 1890, the gentry gained 55.2 percent of the seats in the district zemstvos and between 80 and 90 percent of the seats at the provincial level. According to Manning, after 1907, outside the four peasant provinces, the gentry "accounted for at least two-thirds of all zemstvo deputies at the district level and virtually all the provincial deputies." Indeed, in the period from 1890 to 1893, 87 percent of provincial delegates were hereditary nobility and 60 percent were large landowners (holding over 500 desiatinas).

24. McKenzie, "Zemstvo Organization," 43. In 1906, Article 52, allowing the governor to *select* peasant delegates, was repealed.

25. N. A. Zinov'ev, ed., *Otchet po revizii zemskikh uchrezhdenii Moskovskoi gubernii* (St. Petersburg, 1904), 1:10–17. See also "Iz istorii Moskovskogo zemstva," in Moscow, *Izvestiia* (January–February 1914), 3:9–12; and Veselovskii, *K voprosu,* 53–54.

26. Veselovskii, *K voprosu,* 42–43; George Fischer, *Russian Liberalism: From Gentry to Intelligentsia* (Cambridge, Mass., 1958), 9. See also S. N. Prokopovich, *Mestnye liudi o nuzhdakh Rossii* (St. Petersburg, 1904), 139–149.

27. Dorothy Atkinson, "The Peasant and the Zemstvo," in Emmons and Vucinich, *The Zemstvo in Russia,* 113; Donald McKenzie-Wallace, *Russia on the Eve of War and Revolution* (New York, 1964), 216; Starr, *Decentralization,* 295; Robinson, *Rural Russia Under the Old Regime,* 132. But see Sergei Pushkarev, *The Emergence of Modern Russia* (New York, 1963), 149–150, for a much more positive assessment of gentry-peasant relations in the zemstvo.

28. V. D. Kuzmin-Karavaev, "Krest'ianstvo i zemstvo," in *Velikaia reforma,* ed. A. K. Dzhivelegov, S. P. Mel'gunov, and V. I. Pichet (Moscow, 1911), 6:277–287; the translation is from Emmons, "Conclusion," 426. See also Ben Eklof, "Spreading the Word: Primary Education and the Zemstvo in Moscow Province, 1864–1910" (Ph.D. diss., Princeton University, 1977). Further comments are in Veselovskii, *K voprosu,* 36–39; M. Surin, *Chto govoriat krest'iane o nuzhdakh derevni* (Moscow, 1906), 106; A. Levitskii, "O vyborakh zemskikh glasnykh ot krest'ian," in Moscow, *Izvestiia* (January–February 1915), 4:10–12.

29. Veselovskii, *Istoriia zemstva* 3:305; Trutovskii, *Sovremennoe zemstvo,* 149; McKenzie, "Zemstvo Organization," 54.

30. Veselovskii, *Istoriia zemstva* 4:439–442; Trutovskii, *Sovremennoe zemstvo,* 38–54; L. D. Briukhatov, "Znachenie tret'ego elementa v zhizni zemstva," in Veselovskii and Frenkel', *Iubileinyi zemskii sbornik,* 186–206. See also several articles on Third Element personnel in Emmons

and Vucinich, *The Zemstvo in Russia:* Robert Johnson, "Liberal Professionals and Professional Liberals: The Zemstvo Statisticians and Their Work," 343–364; Nancy M. Frieden, "The Politics of Zemstvo Medicine," 315–342; and Samuel C. Ramer, "The Zemstvo and Public Health," 279–314.

31. Zinov'ev, *Otchet po revizii zemskikh* 1:131–137; Trutovskii, *Sovremennoe zemstvo,* 47. On the "righting" of the zemstvos, see Manning, "Zemstvo and Revolution," 184–218. See also L. K. Erman, *Intelligentsiia v pervoi russkoi revoliutsii* (Moscow, 1966), 183–190, 313–321; and Veselovskii, *Istoriia zemstva* 4:42–49, 64–75, 417, 422.

32. Trutovskii, *Sovremennoe zemstvo,* 49–50, 226–227.

33. Veselovskii, *K voprosu,* 38, 162. See also Chapters 7 and 8.

34. For a more thorough discussion, see Avinov, "Glavnye cherty," 1–35; and V. F. Karavaev, "Zemskie smety i rasklady," 155–180 (both in Veselovskii and Frenkel', *Iubileinyi zemskii sbornik*). McKenzie, "Zemstvo Organization," 45, contains detail on zemstvo functions. According to McKenzie, the deletion of the term "economic" (*khoziaistvennye*) from the phrase "management of local economic welfare and needs" in the 1890 Statute substantially broadened zemstvo powers. A long debate ensued over whether the framers of the legislation meant "management," "participation," or "looking after."

35. Starr, *Decentralization,* 312–313. On arrears, see also Veselovskii, *K voprosu,* 118; and Atkinson, "The Peasant and the Zemstvo," 105–109. The entire history of zemstvo finances is inadequately understood and merits closer study. See N. Kazimirov, *Krest'ianskie platezhi i zemskaia deiatel'nost' v Moskovskoi gubernii* (Moscow, 1906); and Trutovskii, *Sovremennoe zemstvo,* 58–59, 69, 70, where the author argues that peasant land was assessed at a much higher rate than was the land of the nobility. Also see A. I. Shingarev, "Vopros ob uluchshenii zemskikh finansov," in Veselovskii and Frenkel', *Iubileinyi zemskii sbornik,* 107, 134.

36. See Charnoluskii, *Zemstvo i narodnoe obrazovanie* 1:4; Starr, *Decentralization,* 286; Smirnov, *Reforma,* 142. The relevant section of the statute is VII, Article 2.

37. The precise wording of the clause was also the result of an intense bureaucratic struggle, the ramifications and significance of which extend well beyond the subject of this book, and which have been the subject of much interesting recent work in both the West and the Soviet Union. The entire problem of local government, of which the Zemstvo Statute was but one chapter, remained unsolved until the revolution; some historians have suggested that the problems surfac-

ing between 1861 and 1881 had considerable impact on the course of 1917.

38. On this view of the Great Reforms, see especially Rieber, "Alexander II."

39. Chekhov, *Narodnoe obrazovanie,* 37–42.

40. On the rescript, see ibid., 43. On the textbook section, see Allen Sinel, *The Classroom and the Chancellery: State Educational Reform in Russia Under Count Dmitry Tolstoi* (Cambridge, Mass., 1973), 60–61. In addition, a decree of 17 November 1879 ordered inspectors or school boards to directly supervise the distribution of *all* primary school textbooks. On the Temporary Regulations of 1865, see Daniel Balmuth, *Censorship in Russia, 1865–1905* (Washington, D.C., 1979), 13–42. A history of the textbook committee is found in A. I. Georgievskii, *K istorii uchenogo komiteta ministerstva narodnogo prosveshcheniia* (St. Petersburg, 1902).

41. Chekhov, *Narodnoe obrazovanie,* 43; A. I. Anastas'ev, *Narodnaia shkola: Rukovodstvo dlia uchitelei i uchitel'nits narodnykh shkol. Nastol'-naia spravochnaia kniga,* 7th ed. (Moscow, 1910), 1:126–127. On peasants concealing schools, see Tsebrovskii, "Nachal'noe obrazovanie."

42. In fact, the 1869 legislation for the central European provinces was preceded in 1863 by the establishment of inspectors in a number of provinces in the troubled southwest region, where the central government was acting firmly to undercut the position of the Polish nobility and the Catholic Church.

43. On zemstvo teacher training, see Charnoluskii, *Zemstvo i narodnoe obrazovanie* 1:34–38; Medynskii, *Istoriia russkoi pedagogiki,* 252; N. N. Kuz'min, *Uchitel'skie seminary Rossii i ikh mesto v podgotovke uchitelei nachal'noi shkoly* (Kurgan, 1970); F. G. Panachin, *Pedagogicheskoe obrazovanie v Rossii: Istoriko-pedagogicheskie ocherki* (Moscow, 1979).

44. Chekhov, *Narodnoe obrazovanie,* 46; Pokrovskii, *Istoriia Rossii v XIX veke* 7:127–131; A. I. Piskunov, ed., *Ocherki istorii shkoly i pedagogicheskoi mysli narodov SSSR. Vtoraia polovina XIX v.* (Moscow, 1976), 198.

45. *Narodnaia entsiklopediia* 10:33. This rescript has been cited by virtually every history of Russian education. See also the discussion and citations following in Chapter 5. On the bureaucracy, see especially Alfred J. Rieber, "Bureaucratic Politics in Imperial Russia," *Social Science History* 2, no. 4 (Summer 1978): 399–413.

46. See Anastas'ev, *Narodnaia shkola* 1:29–53. See also the comments by Smirnov, *Reforma,* 161–165.

47. Sinel, "Educating the Russian Peasantry," 57. On the marshalls of the nobility, see references following in Chapter 5.
48. Fal'bork and Charnoluskii, *Narodnoe obrazovanie*, 85–120, esp. 93, for the important Senate decision.

CHAPTER 3

1. Chekhov, *Narodnoe obrazovanie*, 37–40; Kapterev, *Istoriia russkoi pedagogiki*, 228–240; Miropol'skii, *Shkola i gosudarstvo*, 73–110. Studies consulted for this chapter but not directly cited may be found in the list of provincial studies in the Bibliography. See also bibliographical guides to zemstvo statistical studies, particularly Bogdanov, *Obzor izdanii gubernskikh zemstv;* and *Spisok izdanii zemskikh i gorodskikh samoupravlenii po narodnomu obrazovaniiu: K 1 ianv. 1912* (St. Petersburg, 1914). Also helpful is the list of Soviet dissertations, mainly provincial studies, included in Dneprov, *Sovetskaia literatura*.
2. Vakhterov cited in Demkov, *Nachal'naia narodnaia shkola*, 4; Starr, *Decentralization*, 35.
3. Darlington, *Education in Russia*, 104 (see also Chekhov, *Narodnoe obrazovanie*, 68); Piskunov, *Ocherki istorii shkoly*, 68.
4. Cited in Piskunov, *Ocherki istorii shkoly*, 69.
5. The Lancaster (or, properly speaking, the Bell-Lancaster) system was a method of instruction by monitors (older children). In 1814, it spread from England to the Continent and within a few years enjoyed considerable success in France, Spain, Italy, Greece, Denmark, Sweden, and Norway. The system was designed to maximize the teacher's effectiveness by soliciting the cooperation of the most advanced pupils in instructing their peers. The economies achieved through such a method proved more important than the arguments advanced by other zemstvo delegates in favor of the prestigious Prussian system based on the methods of Pestalozzi. See Petrov, *Obzor*, 25–29; Pollard, *Pioneers of Popular Education*, 85–99; and Zacek, "Lancaster School Movement."
6. *Doklady Moskovskomu gubernskomu zemskomu sobraniiu*, report no. 58 (Moscow, 1866), 67–83.
7. Petrov, *Obzor*, 28.
8. See Moskovskaia gubernskaia zemskaia uprava, Otdel khoziaistvennoi statistiki, *Sbornik postanovlenii Moskovskogo gubernskogo zemskogo sobraniia s 1865 po 1897* (Moscow, 1902), 5:10, 11–16, where the debate is presented.

9. For a summary of the two positions, see Charnoluskii, *Zemstvo i narodnoe obrazovanie* 1:17–21.

10. P. F. Kapterev, *Novye dvizheniia v oblasti narodnogo obrazovaniia i srednei shkoly* (Moscow, 1913), 17, 21–22. For a different view, see Charnoluskii, *Zemstvo i narodnoe obrazovanie* 1:13.

11. Kapterev, *Novye dvizheniia*, 18.

12. Veselovskii, *Istoriia zemstva* 4:476; N. N. Iordanskii, "Narodnaia shkola i zemstvo Nizhegorodskoi gubernii v 60–70 gody XIX veka," *Sovetskaia pedagogika*, no. 4 (1941): 81–82.

13. Veselovskii, *Istoriia zemstva* 1:1–99, 105–107; Yaney, *Systematization*, 348; Moscow, *Sbornik postanovlenii* 5:18.

14. This argument, of course, did not prevent the Moscow zemstvo from offering subsidies to the Fifth Gymnasium in Moscow, where peasants were not admitted.

15. Moscow, *Sbornik postanovlenii* 5:3. See also V. V. Akimov, "Zemskaia deiatel'nost' po narodnomu obrazovaniiu v Moskovskoi gubernii," *ZhMNP*, n.s. 7, sec. 3 (March 1907): 174–191; n.s. 8, sec. 3 (May 1907): 1–43; and Zinov'ev, *Otchet po revizii zemskikh* 1:195.

16. Veselovskii, *Istoriia zemstva* 1:461–467.

17. On Korf, see Piskunov, *Ocherki istorii shkoly*, 313–320; Kapterev, *Istoriia russkoi pedagogiki*, 256–267; and Smirnov, *Ocherki*, 233–253. For a full biography, see M. L. Peskovskii, *Nikolai Aleksandrovich Korf: Ego zhizn' i deiatel'nost'* (St. Petersburg, 1913).

18. Veselovskii, *Istoriia zemstva*, 2:415.

19. See Miropol'skii, *Shkola i gosudarstvo*, 46–109. For further detail, see O. Kaidanova, *Ocherki po istorii narodnogo obrazovaniia v Rossii i SSSR* (Berlin, 1938), 1:73–75; Veselovskii, *Istoriia zemstva* 3:165; Piskunov, *Ocherki istorii shkoly*, 91–92; A. V. Ososkov, *Voprosy istorii nachal'nogo obrazovaniia v Rossii* (Moscow, 1975), 2:9–11; E. O. Vakhterova, *V. P. Vakhterov: Ego zhizn' i rabota* (Moscow, 1961), 258–259. For a good discussion of sources, see Kapterev, *Novye dvizheniia*, 86–89.

20. Chekhov, *Narodnoe obrazovanie*, 9; Kapterev, *Novye dvizheniia*, 9 (the debate in St. Petersburg); Vakhterova, *Vakhterov*, 258–259. A study of zemstvo resolutions showed that in many cases where individual zemstvos favored compulsory education, peasants had sponsored the resolutions (N. Belokonskii, "Zemstvo i vseobshchee obuchenie k 30-letnemu iubileiu zemskikh uchrezhdenii, 1864–1894," *Russkaia shkola* 4, no. 12 [1894]: 108–127). In other instances, zemstvos called

for universal education but failed to allocate any money (Kapterev, *Novye dvizheniia,* 10–17; Veselovskii, *Istoriia zemstva* 3:165–166.

21. Veselovskii, *Istoriia zemstva* 3:166.

22. Vakhterova, *Vakhterov,* 261, 277.

23. Piskunov, *Ocherki istorii shkoly,* 92; Ososkov, *Voprosy istorii* 2:10, 60–61.

24. Miliukov, *Ocherki po istorii russkoi kul'tury* 3:384–386.

25. On gentry land, reassessments, and taxation, see Veselovskii, *Istoriia zemstva* 1:69, 85–87; V. Skalon, "Zemskie finansy," in *Entsiklopedicheskii slovar' Brokgauza-Efrona* (St. Petersburg, 1890–1906), 24:528; and Eklof, "Spreading the Word," ch. 2. On Moscow in particular, see Zinov'ev, *Otchet po revizii zemskikh* 1:187–190; and Kazimirov, *Krest'ianskie platezhi.* See also Johnson, "Liberal Professionals." For a caustic discussion of zemstvo finances, taxes, and reluctance to invest in welfare and education, see the comment by E. M. Stratanov, *Tekushchie voprosy nachal'nogo obrazovaniia i nizshei shkoly* (Moscow, 1910), 17–25.

26. A. P. Pogrebinskii, *Gosudarstvennye finansy tsarskoi Rossii v epokhu imperializma* (Moscow, 1968), 29; Veselovskii, *Istoriia zemstva* 1:32.

27. Kapterev, *Novye dvizheniia,* 19–21. See also Veselovskii, *Istoriia zemstva* 4:663, 674, 676, for a description of how the Perm' zemstvo as late as the 1890s resisted all efforts by the local governor and educational curator to have the zemstvo contribute to peasant education. In a speech delivered in 1881, delegate E. Kushtinov lashed out at the zemstvo for lavishing money on secondary schools. In contrast, some districts such as Orlovsk, where peasants had a sizable representation, actively resisted the movement to "economize" on schooling. Tsebrovskii presents telling detail on zemstvo inactivity throughout his enormous work "Nachal'noe obrazovanie." (See also Iordanskii, "Narodnaia shkola," 79–81.) Zviagintsev lamented that, as late as 1914, some district zemstvos were still inactive (*Polveka,* 49).

28. UNESCO has adopted a similar concept of "nuclear" or "godfather" schools offering extended cycles around which short-cycle (the Russian "filial") schools could be clustered. But the zemstvo version of the filial school did not provide for the "godfather" (Herbert Moore Phillips, *Basic Education: A World Challenge* [London, 1975], 136).

29. For a detailed discussion of Moscow activities and of the gradual drift away from the incentive program to direct sponsorship and more energetic measures, see Eklof, "Spreading the Word." See also G. I. Chernov, *Stranitsy proshlogo: Iz istorii dorevoliutsionnoi shkoly Vladimirskoi gubernii* (Vladimir, 1970), on schools in Vladimir province.

30. Ben Eklof, "Peasant Sloth Reconsidered: Strategies of Education and Learning in Rural Russia Before the Revolution," *Journal of Social History* 14, no. 3 (Spring 1981): 362–366.

31. Ibid., note 29. On *vol'nye shkoly,* see especially N. Bunakov, *O domashnikh shkolakh gramotnosti v narode (Po materialam, sobrannym St. Peterburgskim komitetom gramotnosti)* (St. Petersburg, 1885); A. S. Prugavin, *Zaprosy naroda i obiazannosti intelligentsii v oblasti prosveshcheniia i vospitaniia,* 2d ed. (St. Petersburg, 1895), 31–52; Chekhov, *Narodnoe obrazovanie,* 28–34; V. Devel', "Krest'ianskie vol'nye shkoly gramotnosti v Tverskoi gubernii," *Russkaia shkola* 1, nos. 4, 5, 6 (1890): 99–111, 131–147, 121–134. A detailed survey can be found in Iordanskii, "Istoriia narodnoi shkoly."

32. Chekhov, *Tipy russkoi shkoly v ikh istoricheskom razvitii* (Moscow, 1923), 35.

33. Sheremet'ev, *Narodnye uchitelia,* 23; Vladimirskaia gubernskaia zemskaia uprava, *Sbornik statisticheskikh i spravochnykh svedenii po narodnomu obrazovaniiu v Vladimirskoi gubernii* (Vladimir, 1900), 3:40; I. Voronov, *Materialy po narodnomu obrazovaniiu v Voronezhskoi gubernii* (Voronezh, 1899), 26–27. The Tavrida study can be found in Statisticheskoe biuro Tavricheskogo gubernskogo zemstva, *Sbornik po shkol'noi statistike* (Simferopol', 1903), 1:30.

34. Prugavin, *Zaprosy naroda,* 31–52; Bunakov, *O domashnikh shkolakh gramotnosti,* 1–23. See also (Novgorod) *Ocherk narodnogo obrazovaniia v Novgorodskoi gubernii za 1884–1885 uchebnyi god* (Novgorod, 1887), 77–80, and the descriptions of individual schools in part 3; and Tsentral'nyi gosudarstvennyi istoricheskii arkhiv Leningrada (hereafter TsGIAL) (1911), f. 803, op. 83, d. 130 (Vladimir province). A particularly valuable table, showing the main sponsor of each school in the province and testifying to the role of both clergy and peasantry in founding zemstvo schools, is found in Vladimir, *Sbornik statisticheskikh* 3:43–45.

35. Veselovskii, *Istoriia zemstva* 1:509–510. For a different view more favorable to the zemstvo effort, see the argument by I. P. Belokonskii, "Narodnoe obrazovanie v Moskovskoi gubernii," *Russkaia shkola* 2, no. 2 (1891): 135.

36. Charnoluskii, *Zemstvo i narodnoe obrazovanie* 1:68. For local examples, see (Vologda) *Nachal'noe obrazovanie v Vologodskoi gubernii po svedeniiu 1898–1899* (Vologda, 1901), 1:237–266; (Novgorod) *Soderzhanie nachal'nykh sel'skikh shkol i otnoshenie naseleniia k shkolam,* no. 4 of *Polozhenie narodnogo obrazovaniia v Novgorodskoi gubernii*

(Novgorod, 1904), 32; A. K. Reingardt, *Istoriia nachal'noi shkoly v Orlovskoi gubernii: Ocherki deiatel'nosti uezdnykh zemstv po narodnomu obrazovaniiu* (Orel, 1897), ch. 3; (Simbirsk) *Nachal'noe narodnoe obrazovanie v Simbirskoi gubernii po dannym 1902–1903 goda* (Simbirsk, 1905), 47–53.

37. A. N. Kulomzin, *Dostupnost' nachal'noi shkoly v Rossii* (St. Petersburg, 1904), 44; Veselovskii, *Istoriia zemstva* 1:655–657; Yaney, *Systematization,* 348. For a recent discussion of zemstvo revenues and peasant taxation, see Fallows, "The Zemstvo and the Bureaucracy," 177–243; and Atkinson, "The Peasant and the Zemstvo," 79–133. A local study of Iaroslavl' district in 1903–1907 placed the annual value of labor obligations provided by the peasants for each school at 125 rubles (B. V. N. Nadezhdin, *Ocherk deiatel'nosti Iaroslavskogo uezdnogo zemstva za 1903–1907* [Iaroslavl', 1907], 13). According to another study of 207 districts in Russia at the turn of the century, 75.4 percent of zemstvos were paying teachers' salaries; 78 percent were defraying the costs of textbooks and paraphernalia; 21 percent assumed responsibility for school building repairs; and only 14.5 percent paid for maintenance (*Doklad gubernskoi zemskoi upravy po narodnomu obrazovaniiu Iaroslavskomu gubernskomu sobraniiu* [Iaroslavl', 1904], 267).

38. Veselovskii, *Istoriia zemstva* 1:508–510. See also Shkol'naia komissiia Iaroslavskogo gubernskogo zemstva, *Kratkii obzor zemsko-shkol'nogo dela v Rossii (Po dannym Iaroslavskoi vystavki severnago kraia, 1903)* (Iaroslavl', 1906), 13–14, 22–23, for more systematic data on the zemstvo contribution to secondary education. See especially Voronov, *Materialy po narodnomu obrazovaniiu,* 164–165, in which a detailed study showed that the peasant contribution in 1897 constituted 30.7 percent of the total funding but ranged from 12 percent to 79 percent. Also see Iaroslavskoe gubernskoe zemstvo, *Nachal'noe obrazovanie v Iaroslavskoi gubernii po svedeniiam za 1896–1897 uchebnyi god,* part 1 (Moscow, 1902), 377–385, 392–397.

39. Ministerstvo narodnogo prosveshcheniia (hereafter MNP), *Odnodnevnaia perepis' nachal'nykh shkol Rossiiskoi imperii proizvedënnaia 18 ianvaria 1911,* ed. V. I. Pokrovskii (Petrograd, 1916), 16:194. This argument—that the best way to promote primary education is to invest in secondary schooling—has its supporters today (Cipolla, *Literacy and Development,* 70–71).

40. See MNP, *Odnodnevnaia perepis'* 16:124.

41. For tables and details of zemstvo outlays, see Veselovskii, *Istoriia zemstva* 1:569, 576. Also see *Svodka svedenii,* vol. 6 of *Trudy pervogo*

obshchezemskogo s"ezda po narodnomu obrazovaniiu (Moscow, 1912), "Raskhody zemstva," 3–4, 11; Trutovskii, *Sovremennoe zemstvo*, 76.

42. Fal'bork and Charnoluskii, *Narodnoe obrazovanie*, 192–193; Pogrebinskii, *Gosudarstvennye finansy*, 15–30. The estimates of government allocations were reached by combining tables 1 and 2 in Hans, *History of Russian Educational Policy*, 229–230. Hans's budget totals include extraordinary state expenditures as well as the regular state budget, but his estimates of MNP outlays do not include money allocated to teacher training institutions, which by 1914 was a considerable sum.

43. Hans, *History of Russian Educational Policy*, 229–230.

44. *Svodka svedenii*, "Raskhody zemstv," 1–11; B. B. Veselovskii, "Zemskie finansy," in Veselovskii and Frenkel', *Iubileinyi zemskii sbornik*, 170.

45. See the discussion in Veselovskii, *Istoriia zemstva* 1 : 1–226, esp. 43–89; for comparisons of outlays and results by province and per capita, see MNP, *Odnodnevnaia perepis'* 16 : 60–125.

46. Trutovskii, *Sovremennoe zemstvo*, 76.

47. Charnoluskii, however, observed from data collected for the 1911 Zemstvo Congress that in some areas the peasant contribution remained substantial even at that late date ("Voprosy narodnogo obrazovaniia na pervom obshchezemskom s"ezde," *Russkaia shkola* 22, no. 9 [1911]: 68).

CHAPTER 4

1. Fischer, *Russian Liberalism*, 72. See also Veselovskii, *Istoriia zemstva* 3 : 433–434; I. P. Belokonskii, *Zemskoe dvizhenie* (Moscow, 1910), 31–37; N. Cherevanin, "Dvizhenie intelligentsii," in *Obshchestvennoe dvizhenie v Rossii v nachale XX-ogo veka*, ed. P. Maslov et al. (St. Petersburg, 1909), 1 : 259–291.

2. Cited in *Narodnaia entsiklopediia* 10 : 62.

3. Darlington, *Education in Russia*, 150. See also V. I. Malinin, "Progressivnaia russkaia obshchestvennost' v bor'be za vseobshchuiu gramotnost'," *Sovetskaia pedagogika*, no. 10 (1976): 103.

4. The unfortunate tendency to treat the Russian bureaucracy as a monolithic entity has been challenged in recent years. The reader can find a sophisticated discussion of the bureaucracy in *Social Science History* 2, no. 4 (Summer 1978), especially articles by Alfred J. Rieber ("Bureau-

cratic Politics in Imperial Russia," 399–413) and Cyril E. Black ("Japan and Russia: Bureaucratic Politics in a Comparative Context," 414–426).

5. Chekhov, *Narodnoe obrazovanie,* 77–78; Darlington, *Education in Russia,* 109. Oddly enough, some recent Soviet works subscribe wholeheartedly to this view; see in particular Piskunov, *Ocherki istorii shkoly,* 68; P. A. Zhil'tsov and V. M. Velichkina, *Uchitel' sel'skoi shkoly* (Moscow, 1973), 13, 55, where the authors cite N. Krupskaia, Lenin's wife, to buttress their argument that the zemstvos made a "positive contribution." But there also seems to be a new hard line, similar to the diatribes characteristic of the Stalinist era. See, for example, Ososkov, *Voprosy istorii* 1:8–9, 30–33. Korolëv's attack on Struminskii (both prominent educational historians)—which was leveled in 1951, not the best time for dispute—for the latter's favorable treatment of zemstvo schools suggests that the assessment of the zemstvo contribution has long been a bone of contention among Soviet historians and represents an ideological divide. See F. F. Korolëv, "Narodnoe obrazovanie v Rossii nakanune fevral'skoi revoliutsii 1917 goda," *Sovetskaia pedagogika,* no. 12 (1951): 48–49.

6. Veselovskii, *Istoriia zemstva* 3:386; Pokrovskii, *Istoriia Rossii v XIX veke* 7:158; V. R. Leikina-Svirskaia, *Intelligentsiia v Rossii vo vtoroi polovine XIX-ogo veka* (Moscow, 1971), 261; Pirumova, *Zemskoe liberal'noe dvizhenie,* 118–119. An adequate discussion of the conventions of the Society for the Dissemination of Technical Knowledge is found in Konstantinov and Struminskii, *Ocherki po istorii,* 208–209, 248–258; and a more comprehensive analysis in S. Ia. Batyshev, ed., *Ocherki istorii professional'no-tekhnicheskogo obrazovaniia v SSSR* (Moscow, 1981), 59–62.

7. Membership in the Moscow Literacy Committee rose from 316 in 1890 to 866 in 1895, then dropped to 133 in 1900, rising again to 400 by 1905; see Vakhterova, *Vakhterov,* 99–103, 121–124, 142; P. Shestakov, "Stolichnye komitety gramotnosti," *Russkaia mysl'* 17, nos. 5 and 9 (1896): 107–124, 107–124. In St. Petersburg, the Literacy Committee (later Society) had the following membership: 289 in 1891, 1,025 in 1895, 134 in 1900, 408 in 1906, and 189 in 1910 ("Pedagogicheskaia khronika," *Russkaia shkola* 22, no. 4 [1911]: 111). For a list of other societies promoting education in Russia, see A. I. Kairov et al., eds., *Pedagogicheskaia entsiklopediia* (Moscow, 1964–1968), 2:457; Piskunov, *Ocherki istorii shkoly,* 353–359; *Narodnaia entsiklopediia* 10:175–191; and Pokrovskii, *Istoriia Rossii v XIX veke* 7:157–159.

8. Kairov et al., *Pedagogicheskaia entsiklopediia* 2:627; Piskunov, *Ocherki istorii shkoly*, 357. The history of the League of Education is still unwritten.

9. On periodicals, see A. G. Kalashnikov et al., eds., *Pedagogicheskaia entsiklopediia* (Moscow, 1927–1930), 1:395–415; M. V. Mashkova, *Istoriia russkoi bibliografii nachala XX veka* (Moscow, 1969), 251; V. A. Zelenko, "Voprosy prosveshcheniia v otrazhenii pedagogicheskikh zhurnalov," *Russkaia shkola* 26, no. 3 (1915): 43–75; N. N. Ablov, *Pedagogicheskaia periodicheskaia pechat', 1803–1916* (Moscow, 1937). See also T. D. Krylova, "Bibliografiia v pedagogicheskoi zhurnalistike v period novogo revoliutsionnogo pod'ema, 1910–1914" (Candidate diss., Leningradskii institut kul'tury, Leningrad, 1975); L. N. Litvin, "*Russkaia shkola* (1890–1917), O narodnom obrazovanii, obuchenii, i vospitanii" (Candidate diss., APN, Moscow, 1975); and Z. G. Poluiaktova, "Zhurnal *Vestnik vospitaniia* i ego obshchestvenno-pedagogicheskoe napravlenie" (Candidate diss., Leningradskii gosudarstvennyi pedagogicheskii institut imeni A. I. Gertsena, Leningrad, 1967).

10. Pokrovskii, *Istoriia Rossii v XIX veke* 7:162.

11. Vakhterova, *Vakhterov*, 108, 122.

12. F. G. Panachin, "Uchitel'stvo Rossii na zare XX stoletiia," *Narodnoe obrazovanie*, no. 9 (1973): 86; V. A-v, "Dve vystavki po narodnomu obrazovaniiu v Moske," *Russkaia mysl'* 17, no. 2 (1896): 115–127; Belokonskii, *Zemskoe dvizhenie*, 98; *Narodnaia entsiklopediia* 10:82.

13. N. V. Chekhov, "Narodnoe obrazovanie," in *Nuzhdy derevni, po rabotam komitetov o nuzhdakh sel'sko-khoziaistvennoi promyshlennosti*, ed. K. K. Arsen'ev (St. Petersburg, 1904), 1:364; Pokrovskii, *Istoriia Rossii v XIX veke* 7:162.

14. Veselovskii, *Istoriia zemstva* 1:16, 3:389, 4:6; *Narodnaia entsiklopediia* 10:64.

15. Veselovskii, *Istoriia zemstva* 3:398–412, 4:103; N. F. Bunakov, "O zhelatel'nykh zadatkakh v sovremennoi russkoi shkole," in Shakhovskii, *Vseobshchee obrazovanie*, 22–29.

16. Robert H. Dodge, "Peasant Education and Zemstvo Schools in the Moscow Province, 1865–1905," *Topic: 27*, 14 (1974): 60.

17. V. A. Kumanëv, *Revoliutsiia i prosveshchenie mass* (Moscow, 1973), 68. See also Konstantinov and Struminskii, *Ocherki po istorii*, 201. Asserting a relationship between literacy and economic change does little to elucidate precisely what that relationship is. Soviet historians seem to be woefully oblivious of recent Western writing that skill-

fully casts doubt on the existence of a direct causal relationship between the "needs" of industry and the spread of literacy. On this question, see Laqueur, "Cultural Origins of Popular Literacy"; C. Arnold Anderson and Mary Jean Bowman, "Education and Economic Modernization in Historical Perspective," in *Schooling and Society,* ed. Lawrence Stone (Baltimore, Md., 1976), 3–20; Stone, "Literacy and Education in England"; and, especially, Graff, *The Literacy Myth.*

But what is important for our discussion here is not so much the actual relationship between industry and literacy as the widespread perception that "a reasonable bit of schooling made better workers," a belief as widespread in Russia as in England at an earlier date. See Richard Daniel Altick, *The English Common Reader: A Social History of the Mass Reading Public, 1800–1900* (Chicago, 1957), 142–172, for an excellent discussion of these beliefs; also Shipman, *Education and Modernization,* 136.

18. I. I. Ianzhul et al., eds., *Ekonomicheskaia otsenka narodnogo obrazovaniia,* 2d ed. (St. Petersburg, 1899); in that volume, see especially E. N. Ianzhula, "Vliianie gramotnosti na proizvoditelnost' truda," 75–83; A. I. Chuprov, "Ob ekonomicheskom znachenii obrazovatel'nykh i vospitatel'nykh uchrezhdenii dlia rabochego klassa," 68–74; V. N. Stanchinskii, "Gramotnost' rabochikh v nekotorykh zavedeniiakh Tverskoi gubernii," 143–150. This work provided most of the material for Arcadius Kahan's well-known study of Russian factory workers' literacy ("Russian Statesmen and Scholars on Education as an Investment," in Anderson and Bowman, *Education and Economic Development,* 3–10).

19. Ianzhul et al., *Ekonomicheskaia otsenka,* 5.

20. Quoted in K., "Voprosy narodnoi shkoly na II s"ezde deiatelei po tekhnicheskomu i professional'nomu obrazovaniiu," *Russkaia mysl'* 17, no. 4 (1896): 88. It is noteworthy that the work by A. Gorbunov ("O vliianii obshchago nachal'nogo obrazovaniia na proizvoditel'nost' truda"), which was not reprinted in *Ekonomicheskaia otsenka* but appeared in *Russkaia mysl'* 17, no. 3 (1896): 67–80, begins with a quotation from an 1874 translation of John Stuart Mill's *Foundations of Political Economy,* stating that the mind of the worker is the most important component of labor productivity.

21. *Narodnaia entsiklopediia* 10:278–279. For studies of education and industry presented to the Nizhnii Novgorod fair of 1896, see Ososkov, *Voprosy istorii* 2:66.

22. Ianzhula, "Vliianie gramotnosti," 77, 82.

23. Ianzhul et al., *Ekonomicheskaia otsenka*, 50. See also Chekhov, "Narodnoe obrazovanie," 364, 379. Current wisdom supports this argument; Erich Jacoby, the former head of the United Nations Food and Agricultural Organization (FAO), writes that "the correlation is obvious between literacy and the adoption of improved praxis [in agriculture]" (*Man and Land* [London, 1971], 310).

24. I. G. Mizhuev, "Elementarnoe obrazovanie," in *Entsiklopedicheskii slovar' Brokgausa-Efrona* (St. Petersburg, 1890–1906), 80:624.

25. Nancy Frieden, "Child Care: Medical Reform in a Traditionalist Culture," in Ransel, *The Family in Imperial Russia*, 257.

26. Mizhuev, "Elementarnoe obrazovanie," 623.

27. *Narodnaia entsiklopediia* 10:13.

28. Shipman, *Education and Modernization*, 54–55.

29. A. N. Strannoliubskii, "Sostoianie narodnogo obrazovaniia v sëlakh evropeiskoi Rossii," *Russkaia shkola* 4, no. 3–4 (1893): 164–165.

30. Shipman, *Education and Modernization*, 41–42.

31. Graff, *The Literacy Myth*, 26.

32. Cited in Shestakov, "Stolichnye komitety gramotnosti," no. 9, 107.

33. Cited in Pirumova, *Zemskoe liberal'noe dvizhenie*, 152.

34. V. P. Vakhterov, "Usloviia dostizheniia vseobshchego obrazovaniia," in Ianzhul et al., *Ekonomicheskaia otsenka*, 113–114.

35. V. V. Akimov, "Kniga v derevne," *ZhMNP*, n.s. 2, sec. 3 (September 1906): 24–26.

36. Kulomzin cited in Ososkov, *Voprosy istorii* 2:9.

37. A published version of Vakhterov's speech, from which the comments that follow are taken, appears in his "Vseobshchee nachal'noe obuchenie," *Russkaia mysl'* 15, no. 7 (1894): 1–18. See also Vakhterova, *Vakhterov*, 266–280; Kaidanova, *Ocherki po istorii narodnogo obrazovaniia* 1:76; and N. T-va, "V Moskovskom komitete gramotnosti," *Russkaia shkola* 4, no. 7 (1894): 185–190.

38. See Vakhterova, *Vakhterov*, 269, for a summary of responses to the speech.

39. Ibid., 274. See also Ianzhul et al., *Ekonomicheskaia otsenka*, 281; and Darlington, *Education in Russia*, 330–331.

40. After a heated discussion, the General Section of the 1896 Congress on Technical and Professional Education voted in favor of three general propositions: one expressed support for universal education; a second called for retaining control of education in local hands but also for financial assistance from the state; and a third, passed by a

narrow margin, favored imposing compulsory minimum contributions on local bodies (intended to end zemstvo foot-dragging).

On the more technical questions of how to quantify the need for schools, a special committee proposed that the number of school-age children be estimated at sixty-seven per one thousand population, that the number of children per school be set between forty and sixty, that the "school radius" be set at three versts, and, finally, that teachers' salaries be set at 240 to 400 rubles, "depending on local circumstances." (See Darlington, *Education in Russia*, 330–331; and Vakhterova, *Vakhterov*, 281.)

41. Miliukov, *Ocherki po istorii russkoi kul'tury* 2:389; Chuprov cited in Vakhterova, *Vakhterov*, 279.

42. Darlington, *Education in Russia*, 151. Kulomzin collected Nicholas's every utterance on education; records are in Kulomzin's personal archive (TsGIAL, f. 1642, d. 668).

43. In Russian, *prosveshchenie* (enlightenment) and *zatmenie* (eclipse). Soviet historians sometimes credit this statement to Lenin.

44. Akimov, "Kniga v derevne," 18.

45. Cited in Ososkov, *Voprosy istorii* 2:38–39.

46. The proposal may be found in V. I. Farmakovskii, "K voprosu o vseobshchem obuchenii," *ZhMNP* 345, sec. 4 (January–February 1903): 124–144.

47. Ososkov, *Voprosy istorii* 2:5. See also A. Chekini, "Nachal'noe narodnoe obrazovanie," in *Novyi entsiklopedicheskii slovar' Brokgauza-Efrona* (Petrograd, 1916), 28:142.

48. For a discussion of this legislation, see Ososkov, *Voprosy istorii* 2:32–108; V. G. Savel'eva, "Politika tsarizma v voprosakh obrazovaniia, 1907–1911" (Candidate diss., Leningradskii gosudarstvennyi universitet, Leningrad, 1975).

49. Hans, *History of Russian Educational Policy*, 213–214; Hoskings, *Russian Constitutional Experiment*, 178–179 (which is, despite this minor flaw, an excellent work).

50. A law establishing Higher (advanced) Elementary Schools was passed in 1912, however.

51. Ososkov, *Voprosy istorii* 2:108–155.

52. Hans, *History of Russian Educational Policy*, 213–214; Chekini, "Nachal'noe narodnoe obrazovanie," 143–146; Kapterev, *Novye dvizheniia*, 45–47. Chekhov, *Narodnoe obrazovanie*, 219, includes a much-cited table describing how close each education district was to achieving universally accessible education in 1911. The best sum-

mary of the terms and long-range legal implications of the late Imperial legislation is N. N. Iordanskii, "Usloviia osushchestvleniia vseobshchago obucheniia v Rossii," *Russkaia shkola* 25, no. 1 (1914): 1–23.

53. Chekini, "Nachal'noe narodnoe obrazovanie," 143–146.

54. Hans, *History of Russian Educational Policy,* 229; Chekini, "Nachal'noe narodnoe obrazovanie," 145. See also Kapterev, *Novye dvizheniia,* 43–45.

55. Iordanskii, "Usloviia osushchestvleniia," no. 2, 27–29; Zviagintsev, "Zemstvo i uchebnoe vedomstvo," 359–370.

CHAPTER 5

1. Sinel, *The Classroom and the Chancellery,* 237–238.

2. Orlovsky, *Limits of Reform,* 139–151.

3. Sinel, *The Classroom and the Chancellery,* 237. See also Pirumova, *Zemskoe liberal'noe dvizhenie,* 44–52.

4. Especially important in this network were the Department of Public Instruction, the Council of the Ministry, and the Academic Council, all under the MNP.

5. Darlington, *Education in Russia,* 184, also 206. Darlington, who conducted his research at the turn of the century, overlooked the fact that such bartering of money for control was taking place between the district and provincial zemstvos and would be the tool used by the MNP after 1908 to gain control over zemstvo schools.

6. Sinel, *The Classroom and the Chancellery,* 78; V. I. Farmakovskii, "Nachal'naia shkola MNP," *Russkaia shkola* 10, no. 4 (1899): 112. For a survey of the politics of education in the Baltic and western provinces, see Darlington, *Education in Russia,* 161–182; Fal'bork and Charnoluskii, *Narodnoe obrazovanie,* 95–102; and the excellent collection of articles edited by Edward C. Thaden, *Russification in the Baltic Provinces* (Princeton, N.J., 1981). In the Soviet Union, Eduard Dneprov is currently completing a major work on the subject.

7. Sinel, *The Classroom and the Chancellery,* 83–84.

8. Darlington, *Education in Russia,* 223–224. For information on the commercial schools, see the Soviet study by Batyshev, *Ocherki istorii.*

9. Alston, *Education and the State,* 94; John Bushnell, "Peasants in Uniform: The Tsarist Army as a Peasant Society," *Journal of Social History* 13, no. 4 (1981): 565–566; Darlington, *Education in Russia,* 192. See also V. Ivanovich, "Novyi zakon ob obuchenii voisk," *Vestnik*

vospitaniia 13, no. 8 (1902): 152–162; and Dzhanshiev, *Iz epokhi velikikh reform,* 501, note 20.

10. This information on the army and literacy was supplied by John Bushnell, whose data are based on the *Ezhegodnyi voennyi sbornik* (St. Petersburg, 1910), 286; and Rashin, "Gramotnost'," 45. See also Eklof, "Peasant Sloth Reconsidered," 363–364.

11. Starr, *Decentralization,* 9.

12. E. A. Zviagintsev, *Inspektsiia narodnykh uchilishch* (Moscow, 1914), 8–10. In the Soviet Union, Dneprov has recently completed a massive project involving the compilation from personnel files (*formuliarnye spiski*) of data on the origins, education, and service records of over four hundred inspectors in 1863, 1874, and 1896. Analysis and publication of this effort should greatly enhance our knowledge of the inspectorate.

13. The duties of the inspector as set forth in the law books included exclusive supervision over all one- and two-class schools maintained by the MNP, as well as joint supervision with the local school boards over all other schools (until the 1884 Regulations for Church schools established the Synod's jurisdiction over parish schools). Inspectors were required to visit schools "as frequently as possible" and to provide annual reports on *all* schools, both to their immediate superiors and to the local school boards. More specifically, the inspectors' functions included a voice in the hiring of teachers (the zemstvo hired, the inspector certified, and the school board confirmed); observation of teachers' moral and professional qualities, as well as their relations with local residents; temporary suspension of unfit teachers and referral of such cases to the local school board for final action; pedagogical guidance and encouragement of teachers; and supervision of the school curriculum, specifically "supervision of the scope and content and . . . the method and overall nature [*kharakter*]" of each subject, as well as encouragement of gymnastics, choir, and vocational courses wherever appropriate.

The inspector kept watch over the length of the school day and school year and the allocation of class time. He was to make sure that only those textbooks and readers approved by the MNP were used in the classroom and made available in school libraries, encouraging the purchase of those books "recommended" and "approved," rather than merely "allowed," by the textbook commission. The inspector oversaw the maintenance of school facilities and equipment, as well as health conditions in the classroom. In addition, he was mandated to promote the spread of schools by encouraging the activities of local organizations. He was charged with keeping an eye on teachers' seminaries, schools, and courses, and with participating in the school board meetings. Finally, the inspectors and directors were responsible for annual reports; for ensuring that accurate and detailed class journals, library records, and inventories were maintained in all schools; and for the proper flow of paperwork moving through or originating in the local school board.

These responsibilities, delineated in the 1871 Instructions and elaborated in the 1874 School Statute, remained in force until 1917, though the MNP and the Senate had to issue numerous circulars and decisions clarifying—or sometimes further obfuscating—the controversial questions of who really hired and fired teachers; just what relations should exist among school board, zemstvo, and inspector; and just how academic, organizational, and economic functions were to be divided among the various parties. At a later date, the inspectors were further burdened with supervising all extramural functions of the schools and administering the complicated teacher pension plan enacted by the state in 1900.

For the full text of the 1871 Instructions, see Anastas'ev, *Narodnaia shkola* 1:10–29.

14. Zviagintsev, *Inspektsiia narodnykh uchilishch*, 13–15, 63. See N. Verigin, *V pomoshch uchashchim v nachal'nykh narodnykh uchilishchakh*, 5th ed. (Moscow, 1915), 104–105; and P. Salomatin, *Kak zhivët i rabotaet narodnyi uchitel'* (St. Petersburg, 1913), 98–181, for many graphic examples. Zviagintsev noted that with the increase in inspectors' budgets after 1908, many were released from routine paperwork to spend more time in the field. While complaining that inspectors were mere paper-pushers, he now lamented that this new development boded ill for the schools because the inspectors could now spend more time inspecting. Thus if they stayed in their offices, they were bureaucrats; if they went on the road, they were intrusive officials—by definition, they could do no good.

15. Charnoluskii, *Zemstvo i narodnoe obrazovanie* 2:247; Medynskii, *Istoriia russkoi pedagogiki*, 319; Panachin, *Pedagogicheskoe obrazovanie*, 71; Sinel, *The Classroom and the Chancellery*, 238; Scott J. Seregny, "Professionalism and Political Activism: The Russian Teachers' Movement, 1864–1908" (Ph.D. diss., University of Michigan, 1982), 58. See also Stratanov, *Tekushchie voprosy*, 114; the memoirs of the educator N. I. Bratchikov, "Vospominaniia o rabote uchitelei v nachal'noi zemskoi shkole," APN (1946), f. 18, op. 1, d. 209, 75–76; and two Soviet dissertations: Petrov, "Zemskaia nachal'naia shkola," 234,

323–326; and A. K. Rymakov, "Krupnyi deiatel' zemskoi shkoly N. N. Iordanskii" (Candidate diss., Nauchnyi institut teorii i istorii pedagogiki, APN, RSFSR, Moscow, 1964), 96.

16. For works on Ul'ianov, see Dneprov, *Sovetskaia literatura,* 199–225; almost two hundred entries are listed. For an example of atrocious biography as hagiography, see Zh. Trofimov and Zh. Mindubaev, *Ilia Nikolaevich Ul'ianov* (Moscow, 1981). For descriptions of active, supportive inspectors, see S. Losev, "Ob inspektorakh i direktorakh narodnykh uchilishch," *Russkii nachal'nyi uchitel',* no. 3 (1911): 134–146.

17. See, for example, Zviagintsev, *Inspektsiia narodnykh uchilishch,* 24, 30–32; Pokrovskii, *Istoriia Rossii v XIX veke* 7:151; Kapterev, *Novye dvizheniia,* 29; Medynskii, *Istoriia russkoi pedagogiki,* 319. The original work itself is M. T. Iablochkov, *Russkaia shkola: Nastavleniia direktora narodnykh uchilishch* (Tula, 1895).

18. Zviagintsev, *Inspektsiia narodnykh uchilishch,* 30–31, 49–53.

The "Berdiansk episode" was one of the most celebrated instances of an inspector abusing his powers. Berdiansk district, in Tavrida, was a peasant zemstvo that early became renowned for its energetic efforts to spread schooling. In 1872, it petitioned for the right to provide for and select a "zemstvo inspector," but the petition was turned down. In 1877, the district petitioned the government to send its own inspector, and one arrived that year. As soon as he arrived, Inspector Iankovskii began to fire and transfer many teachers, leaving schools empty in the middle of the year. He declared the existing zemstvo role in school affairs illegal and prohibited the zemstvo from collecting information on the schools. He forbade the school board chairman to permit the zemstvo board to read the inspector's reports, declaring that it was an unjustified intrusion into the pedagogical side of school affairs. This charming gentleman then forced the zemstvo to purchase textbooks only through the school board (his legal right)—and only with his signature. In fact, he required that his personal signature or emblem be on every textbook in use. As a result, books piled up in the school board offices, the schools experienced shortages, and an ambitious textbook procuring effort dried up. Finally, Iankovskii sent out a circular to teachers requiring them to prepare a written outline of each lesson beforehand and to keep all outlines on file; when visiting schools, he prohibited all oral questions, requiring that all communication be in writing. On Berdiansk, see N. A. Korf, *Nashi pedagogicheskie voprosy* (Moscow, 1882), 67–90; Zviagintsev, *Inspektsiia narodnykh uchilishch,* 49–53; Kapterev, *Novye dvizheniia,* 38–39.

19. "Institut direktorov i inspektorov narodnykh uchilishch," *ZhMNP,* n.s. 19, sec. 3 (January 1909): 49–59.

20. Ibid. See also Bratchikov, "Vospominaniia o rabote uchitelei," 71, on education.

21. Circular No. 34121, cited in Zviagintsev, *Inspektsiia narodnykh uchilishch,* 37–38. See also A. Ropp, *Chto sdelala tret'ia gosudarstvennaia duma dlia narodnogo obrazovaniia* (St. Petersburg, 1912), 66–81. But E. M. Stratanov states that inspectors received 900 rubles per year, not 2,000 (*Tekushchie voprosy,* 120), and a quick look at Dneprov's records seems to indicate that the salary was ordinarily around 1,000 rubles, with another 1,000 to 2,000 rubles as an allowance for expenses, in the 1890s. Rymakov observes that an article written by Baron Korf in 1882 drew an idealized portrait of the inspectors and helped justify government service for many who might have been reluctant to enter the field ("Iordanskii," 99–101). For the article itself, see Korf, *Nashi pedagogicheskie voprosy,* 221–242.

22. Zviagintsev, *Inspektsiia narodnykh uchilishch,* 34. See also his final chapter, listing numerous incidents cited in the press in 1912–1913.

23. Sinel, *The Classroom and the Chancellery,* 69–70. To be sure, the Minister of Education often appealed for more inspectors, but his requests were not met because of financial stringency. According to Stratanov, there were six hundred schools for each inspector in the zemstvo provinces in 1872. In 1874, the MNP proposed to the State Council that the maximum number of schools for each inspector should be one hundred, but in fact the average remained approximately two hundred. Thus, if there were 150 school days, each school would have been allotted three-quarters of a day—if we ignore travel time and the substantial office work required of each inspector. By the MNP estimates, each inspector in 1875 covered an area of 37,986 square versts, with an average distance between schools of 23 versts. By 1904, each inspector was responsible for 10,000 square versts in the zemstvo provinces, but for 50,000 versts in the Empire as a whole; the number of schools under each inspector was 110 and 162, respectively. Each inspector generally covered two districts (Stratanov, *Tekushchie voprosy,* 120).

24. M. V. Sedel'nikova, *N. V. Chekhov: Vidnyi deiatel' narodnogo prosveshcheniia* (Moscow, 1960), 30–31.

25. Hans, *History of Russian Educational Policy,* 233.

26. Zviagintsev, *Polveka,* 52; Fal'bork and Charnoluskii, *Narodnoe obrazovanie,* 169–170.

27. See also the information and debates over adequacy in TsGIAL, f. 733, op. 171, d. 2148, 357–413.

28. TsGIAL, f. 703, op. 203, d. 1190 (Simbirsk educational circuit); TsGIAL, f. 703, op. 203, d. 1658 (Khar'kov circuit); Zviagintsev, *Inspektsiia narodnykh uchilishch,* 40, 45. On the Trans-Baikal region, see F. Zharov, "Sposoby proizvodstva ekzamenov v nachal'noi shkole," *Russkaia shkola* 25, no. 1 (1914): 80. See also Bratchikov, "Vospominaniia a rabote uchitelei," 76; Petrov, "Zemskaia nachal'naia shkola," 516–518; Ia. V. Panfilov, "Shkola Kurskoi gubernii nakanune i v pervye gody posle velikoi sotsialisticheskoi revoliutsii" (Candidate diss., Nauchnyi istoricheskii institut teorii i istorii pedagogiki, APN, RSFSR, Moscow, 1955), 72–76.

29. Trofimov and Mindubaev, *Ul'ianov,* 74–78. See also TsGIAL, f. 733, op. 172, d. 1869, 80–90, a lengthy report by a director, discussing the impossibility of visiting schools and the burden of paperwork.

30. The questionnaire and the teachers' comments that follow are cited in Zviagintsev, *Inspektsiia narodnykh uchilishch,* 114–132.

31. Chekhov, *Narodnoe obrazovanie,* 64.

32. Ibid., 65.

33. Zviagintsev, "Zemstvo i uchebnoe vedomstvo," 362–363.

34. Charnoluskii, *Zemstvo i narodnoe obrazovanie* 2:245; TsGIAL, f. 733, op. 228, d. 41, 45 (Poltava).

35. Zviagintsev, "Zemstvo i uchebnoe vedomstvo," 363; see also Chekhov, *Narodnoe obrazovanie,* 66; Charnoluskii, *Zemstvo i narodnoe obrazovanie* 2:245.

36. Zviagintsev, "Zemstvo i uchebnoe vedomstvo," 363. For instances (in Viatka) in which zemstvos vetoed candidates for inspector, see Bratchikov, "Vospominaniia o rabote uchitelei," 69, 72–73; Rymakov, "Iordanskii," 101; and Petrov, "Zemskaia nachal'naia shkola," 429–437.

37. Veselovskii found eight instances at the provincial level and two hundred at the district level in which the marshall served as chairman of the executive board as well as presiding over the zemstvo assembly and local school board. Recent research confirms the suggestion that the inspectors were the social inferiors of the local marshalls. Gary Hamburg's work demonstrates that the marshalls were generally quite wealthy, often well educated, and frequently had both titles and high standing at court. They were politically diverse and included several participants in the liberal opposition (Hamburg, "Portrait of

an Elite: Russian Marshalls of the Nobility, 1861–1917," *Slavic Review* 40, no. 4 [1981]: 585–602).

As the Soviet historian N. M. Pirumova discovered in her analysis of over eleven hundred zemstvo delegates between 1890 and 1893, one-third held high positions (III–VIII) in the Table of Ranks, half held lower official ranks (IX–XIV), and two-thirds held elective (other than zemstvo) or administrative posts in the provinces—as justices of the peace, land captains, marshalls of the nobility, and so forth. The number of zemstvo activists who were invited to serve in influential positions in the administration, especially as governors and vice-governors, steadily increased at the end of the century (Pirumova, *Zemskoe liberal'noe dvizhenie,* 82–83).

See also Manning, "The Zemstvo and Politics," 138–140, 156–157; and Chekhov, *Narodnoe obrazovanie,* 66. E. M. Stratanov argues that the marshalls of the nobility were virtually unaccountable to higher authority (*Tekushchie voprosy,* 110). One director filed a report complaining of pressure exerted by local marshalls (TsGIAL [1869], f. 733, op. 172, 80–90). Senate inspection (*reviziia*) of Saratov and Samara in 1880 also noted the power of the marshalls and their ability to transfer inspectors who offended them (TsGIAL, f. 733, op. 171, d. 440, 11).

38. Zviagintsev, *Inspektsiia narodnykh uchilishch,* 75–82, 84–85. But see the comments by Zinov'ev, *Otchet po revizii zemskikh* 1:226–227; and a discussion of education administration in St. Petersburg circuit, published in *Svodka svedenii,* sec. 11, 13 for evidence of a lack of friction.

39. On the "righting of the zemstvos" after 1905, see Roberta Manning's excellent study "The Zemstvo and Politics," 133–176; and her article "Zemstvo and Revolution," 30–66; as well as the massive documentation in Veselovskii, *Istoriia zemstva* 4:54–79. William Gleason also observed that the turn to the right had almost no impact on social programs ("The All-Russian Union of Zemstvos and World War I," in Emmons and Vucinich, *Zemstvo in Russia,* 365–382).

40. Zviagintsev, *Inspektsiia narodnykh uchilishch,* 89–90.

41. Sinel, *The Classroom and the Chancellery,* 229. But see Medynskii, *Istoriia russkoi pedagogiki,* 254.

42. Chekhov, *Narodnoe obrazovanie,* 63–64.

43. Verigin, *V pomoshch,* 85–86. See also *Svodka svedenii,* sec. 11, 4; and Charnoluskii, *Zemstvo i narodnoe obrazovanie* 2:251, for comment on this controversial article.

44. *Svodka svedenii,* sec. 11, 6–7.

45. Zinov'ev, *Otchet po revizii zemskikh* 1:203–207. For other examples and comment, see A. I. Shingarev, "Osnovania zemskogo sanitar-nago nadzora za nachal'nymi shkolami," in Shakhovskii, *Vseobshchee obrazovanie*, 101; Charnoluskii, *Zemstvo i narodnoe obrazovanie* 2:250. See Anastas'ev, *Narodnaia shkola* 1:50 for the pertinent laws.

46. On the 1901 conference, see Zviagintsev, *Inspektsiia narodnykh uchilishch*, 83–84. For information on Moscow province, see Zinov'ev, *Otchet po revizii zemskikh* 1:200. For Kursk and Viatka, see Charnoluskii, *Zemstvo i narodnoe obrazovanie* 2:267–268. Stratanov also noted: "Gathering together now and then, the members of the school board hastened to wrap up business, rushing off who knows where and what for" (*Tekushchie voprosy*, 110).

47. Sources include Zinov'ev, *Otchet po revizii zemskikh* 1:200–203; and TsGIAL (1869–1871), f. 733, op. 203, d. 561, 73. Several districts— most likely those not throbbing with activity—filed no reports at all. The frequency of meetings ranged from four to fourteen meetings in Viatka, from two to fourteen in Samara, two to ten in Saratov, four to thirteen in Simbirsk, two to twelve in Petersburg, three to nine in Pskov, five to ten in Novgorod, four to thirteen in Vologda, and four to eight in Olonets.

48. Zinov'ev, *Otchet po revizii zemskikh* 1:201–202. See also Paul Vinogradoff, *Self-Government in Russia* (New York, 1915), 59–60; in this work, the author significantly omits any mention of school boards.

49. Veselovskii, *Istoriia zemstva* 1:544–545, 3:148–154. Also see the discussion in Charnoluskii, *Zemstvo i narodnoe obrazovanie* 2:249–250.

50. Veselovskii, *Istoriia zemstva* 1:544–555; Pirumova, *Zemskoe liberal'noe dvizhenie*, 49.

51. Charnoluskii, "Voprosy narodnogo obrazovaniia," no. 11, 92–93.

52. Ososkov, *Voprosy istorii* 2:117.

53. Seregny, "Professional and Political Activism," 77–86, esp. 82.

54. Charnoluskii, *Zemstvo i narodnoe obrazovanie* 2:253–271; Zviagintsev, *Inspektsiia narodnykh uchilishch*, 25; Veselovskii, *Istoriia zemstva* 1:518.

55. Charnoluskii, *Zemstvo i narodnoe obrazovanie* 2:258–259; Veselovskii, *Istoriia zemstva* 1:518.

56. According to a 1906 study of twenty-one provincial education commissions, eleven commissions included the entire zemstvo executive board; four included only the chairman or selected members of the board. Zemstvo delegates were included on fourteen commissions (between three and twelve delegates on each). On various other pro-

vincial commissions, one could find the local zemstvo doctors, representatives of the school board (including inspectors), representatives from the district zemstvos, zemstvo directors of education, and marshalls of the nobility. At the district level, the members of the commission were a comparable mix of local authorities, zemstvo representatives, and hired professionals; in particular, the local school inspector was a voting member on ten of twenty-six district boards on which information was collected. Charnoluskii points to the frequent litigation that arose concerning zemstvo school commissions, centering on the interpretation of Article 105 of the Zemstvo Statute (*Zemstvo i narodnoe obrazovanie* 2:260). In 1899, a legal clarification (*raz"iasnenie*) was published, specifically granting the right to hire personnel and establish commissions, but in subsequent years a number of Senate rulings progressively chipped away at this right (ibid., 260–264).

For a detailed description of zemstvo teachers' conferences at the zemstvo board and of zemstvo freedom of activity, see N. N. Potapova, "Istoriia zemskoi shkoly Moskovskoi gubernii v nachale XX-ogo veka" (Candidate diss., Moskovskii oblastnoi pedagogicheskii institut, Moscow, 1945), 109–110, 124–126.

57. Charnoluskii, *Zemstvo i narodnoe obrazovanie* 2:261–263.

58. In Moscow the practice of "collective guardianship" was initiated in 1902 (Zinov'ev, *Otchet po revizii zemskikh*, 226). For the text of the decree on guardians, see A. Lebedev, *Shkol'noe delo* (Moscow, 1909–1911), 2:76–80; and Anastas'ev, *Narodnaia shkola* 1:36 (for Article 124 of the Statute of Emancipation).

For descriptions of guardians, see Vladimir, *Sbornik statisticheskikh* 3:166–167; I. P. Belokonskii, ed., *Narodnoe nachal'noe obrazovanie v Kurskoi gubernii* (Kursk, 1897), 264–268; Novgorod, *Ocherk narodnogo obrazovaniia*, 28–31; (Tula) *Nachal'noe narodnoe obrazovanie v Tul'skoi gubernii v 1896–1897 uchebnom godu* (Tula, 1898), 64–70.

In Anton Chekhov's story "The Schoolmistress," the school guardian was an "almost illiterate peasant, the head of a tanning business, unintelligent, rude," yet someone in whose presence the schoolmistress would not venture to sit down and with whom she felt compelled to use the deferential mode of speech (Avrahm Yarmolinsky, ed., *A Treasury of Great Russian Short Stories* [New York, 1944], 814).

59. Charnoluskii, *Zemstvo i narodnoe obrazovanie* 2:269–270.

60. Anastas'ev, *Narodnaia shkola* 1:37–38.

61. Charnoluskii, "Voprosy narodnogo obrazovaniia," no. 9, 72; and *Svodka svedenii*, sec. 11, 9.

62. *Svodka svedenii,* sec. 11, 9.

63. Cited in Sedel'nikova, *Chekhov,* 30–31. Iordanskii, who worked for the Moscow zemstvo after 1912, points out the same thing (Rymakov, "Iordan,skii," 328).

64. Sedel'nikova, *Chekhov,* 39.

65. Charnoluskii, *Zemstvo i narodnoe obrazovanie* 2:260, 267–269.

66. Zviagintsev, *Inspektsiia narodnykh uchilishch,* 84.

67. Charnoluskii, "Voprosy narodnogo obrazovaniia," no. 9, 73.

68. *Svodka svedenii,* sec. 9, 3–4. I am currently developing a study of primary school textbooks and have compiled an extensive list of studies of textbooks. For a brief discussion of the variety found in Moscow province, see Eklof, "Spreading the Word," 355–366; and *Svodka svedenii,* sec. 9, 4–5.

CHAPTER 6

1. Piskunov, *Ocherki istorii shkoly,* 82; Paul N. Ignatiev, Dmitry Odinetz, and Paul Novgorodtsev, *Russian Schools and Universities in the World War,* Carnegie Endowment for International Peace, Economic and Social History of the World War: Russian series (New Haven, Conn., 1929), 7; Fal'bork and Charnoluskii, *Narodnoe obrazovanie,* 60; Darlington, *Education in Russia,* 331–338. But also see N. I. Bratchikov, "Uchebno-vospitatel'naia chast' v nachal'noi shkole," *Russkaia shkola* 20, no. 1 (1909): 96.

   In addition to the sources cited in the notes below, see the following works on Church schools: Grigor'ev, *Istoricheskii ocherk russkoi shkoly,* 517–538; A. M. Vanchakov, *Tserkovnye shkoly pri zakonakh o vseobshchem obuchenii* (Petrograd, 1917); A. M. Vanchakov, *Kratkii istoriko-statisticheskii obzor razvitiia tserkovnoi shkoly s 1884 i do nastoiashchego vremeni (1884–1909)* (St. Petersburg, 1909); O. Krzhizhanovskii, "Znachenie dukhovenstva v istorii narodnogo obrazovaniia v Rossii (Istoricheskii ocherk)," *Obrazovanie* 4, nos. 3, 5–6, 7–8, 9 (1895): 231–249, 470–498, 21–58, 30–52; and A. K. Rozhdestvenskii, *Slovo pravdy o tserkovnoi shkole* (Rybinsk, 1906). Many local zemstvo studies and Soviet dissertations on education in various provinces include chapters on Church schools. See, for example, T. N. Vostrukhina, "Istoriia narodnogo obrazovaniia vo Vladimirskoi gubernii s 60-kh godov XIX veka do oktiabr'skoi revoliutsii" (Candidate diss., Moskovskii gorodskoi pedagogicheskii institut imeni V. P. Potemkina, Moscow, 1955), 40–44, 279–299; *Istoricheskii ocherk tserkovnoi shkoly Moskovskogo uezda, 1884–1909* (n.p., 1909).

2. Robert F. Byrnes, *Pobedonostsev: His Life and Thought* (Bloomington, Ind., 1968), 274; Pokrovskii, *Istoriia Rossii v XIX veke* 7:127; Chekhov, *Narodnoe obrazovanie*, 92–94. See S. I. Miropol'skii, *Ocherki istorii tserkovno-prikhodskoi shkoly ot pervago eia vozniknoveniia do nastoiashchago vremeni*, nos. 1–3 (St. Petersburg, 1895), for the period preceding the Great Reforms.

3. See Chapter 1; and Pokrovskii, *Istoriia Rossii v XIX veke* 7:127.

4. Tatishchev, *Imperator Aleksandr II* 2:232–233; Piskunov, *Ocherki istorii shkoly*, 77–78; Farmakovskii, "Nachal'naia shkola MNP," no. 4, 113–114, 116.

5. See Farmakovskii, "Nachal'naia shkola MNP," no. 4, 113. See also Article 2 of the 1874 School Statute and its subsequent modification in the 1893 edition of the *Svod Zakonov;* and N. P. Malinovskii, "Istoricheskii ocherk po reforme dukhovnoi shkoly," *Russkaia shkola* 23, no. 11 (1912): 117–137.

6. Alston, *Education and the State*, 79; *Narodnaia entsiklopediia* 10:33. The need to improve the material status of priests in order to enhance their contribution to education was recognized in the Committee of Ministers and State Council deliberations over a Church school statute (TsGIAL, f. 1152, op. 9, d. 465, 666; and TsGIAL [1879–1886], f. 703, op. 171, d. 1654 [MNP]).

7. Blagovidov cited in Pokrovskii, *Istoriia Rossii v XIX veke* 7:129. Sinel argues that Tolstoy hoped to use priests simply to reduce the costs of teacher training to the state (*The Classroom and the Chancellery*, 227).

8. Chekhov, *Narodnoe obrazovanie*, 94; Fal'bork and Charnoluskii, *Narodnoe obrazovanie*, 189–190; Piskunov, *Ocherki istorii shkoly*, 79; Hans, *History of Russian Educational Policy*, 157. According to one account in the house journal of the Holy Synod, this decline stemmed partially from local priests turning over their schools to the zemstvos (*Narodnoe obrazovanie*, no. 9 [1909]: 203–212). Massive studies of zemstvo schools in Novgorod and Moscow in the 1880s show that many zemstvo schools were in fact founded by priests. Count Tolstoy admitted in 1872, however, that of 1,948 Church schools listed on the books in seven provinces, only 263 really existed (Orzhekhovskii, *Iz istorii*, 144).

9. Piskunov, *Ocherki istorii shkoly*, 80. According to Kapterev, of forty schools on the books, Korf found only two even nominally functioning (*Novye dvizheniia*, 9).

10. Pokrovskii, *Istoriia Rossii v XIX veke* 7:129. (Also see note 8 above.) There are many examples of priests organizing schools and then

turning them over to the zemstvo. Rozhdestvenskii compiled a list based on district zemstvo studies in Iaroslavl' province (*Slovo pravdy o tserkovnoi shkole,* 14–16). See also Iordanskii, "Istoriia narodnoi shkoly," 11–12; I. Meshcherskii, "Ocherki shkol'nogo dela v Rossii," *Russkii nachal'nyi uchitel',* nos. 10 and 12 (1886): 492–501, 596–604.

11. For discussion and documentation of the role played by priests in rural disturbances earlier in the century, see Ia. I. Lincoln, *Ocherki istorii krest'ianskogo dvizheniia v Rossii v 1825–1861* (Moscow, 1952), 102–103. For the later period, and a standard Soviet interpretation, see E. F. Grekulov, *Tserkov', samoderzhavie i narod* (Moscow, 1969), esp. 44–64 and 145–151; and L. I. Emil'iakh, *Krest'iane i tserkov' nakanune oktiabria* (Leningrad, 1976).

12. Sinel, *The Classroom and the Chancellery,* 227. It is noteworthy that Rachinskii, the lion of Church school education among the peasants, in his correspondence opposed turning over MNP schools to the Church because he believed priests in the main not up to the task (Smirnov, "Narodnoe prosveshchenie," 112–113).

13. E. G. West, *Education and the Industrial Revolution* (New York, 1975), 99.

14. See P. Zaionchkovskii, *The Russian Autocracy in Crisis,* trans. Gary Hamburg (Gulf Breeze, Fla., 1979), 62. See also Darlington, *Education in Russia,* 143–144; *Istoricheskii ocherk razvitiia tserkovnykh shkol za istekshee dvadtsatipiatiletie, 1884–1909* (St. Petersburg, 1909), 7.

15. See *Pobedonostsev,* the biography by Robert Byrnes.

16. On the commission to draw up a statute for Church parish schools, see the discussion in *Istoricheskii ocherk razvitiia,* 7–23; Malinovskii, "Istoricheskii ocherk," 117–137; and Piskunov, *Ocherki istorii shkoly,* 81–82.

17. On the 1884 and 1902 legislation, see Anastas'ev, *Narodnaia shkola* 1 : 395–421; Darlington, *Education in Russia,* 144–145; Hans, *History of Russian Educational Policy,* 158–160; *Narodnaia entsiklopediia* 10 : 49; and V. Dobronravov, *Tserkovnaia shkola vo Vladimirskoi eparkhii s 1884 po 1909* (Vladimir, 1909), 84–85. The texts of the statutes are in the *Polnoe sobranie zakonov Rossiiskoi imperii,* third series, vol. 4, no. 2318. For the modified program, see *Programmy dlia tserkovnoprikhodskikh shkol* (St. Petersburg, 1905); G. A. Fal'bork and V. I. Charnoluskii, *Nastol'naia kniga po narodnomu obrazovaniiu* (St. Petersburg, 1899–1911), 3 : 255; A. S. Prugavin, *Zakony i spravochnye svedeniia po nachal'nomu narodnomu obrazovaniiu,* 2d ed. (St. Petersburg, 1904), 365–426.

18. Pokrovskii, *Istoriia Rossii v XIX veke* 7:150. Piskunov points to the sanctions imposed by the Church on malingerers as evidence that it was not always easy to persuade the clergy to teach peasants (*Ocherki istorii shkoly*, 86–87). In 1885, only one year after the regulations establishing parish schools, instruction was made obligatory for deacons (*d'iakony*); in 1892, the Synod imposed fines of one-third of a priest's salary for those who neglected their teaching obligations, and in the same year graduates of clerical seminaries were required to teach for two to three years in a Church parish school before they could be eligible for a post with the Church. On poor relatives of clergy serving as teachers, see N. L. Peterson, *Prosveshchenie. Svod trudov mestnykh komitetov po 49 guberniiam evropeiskoi Rossii dlia vysochaishe uchrezhdennogo osobogo soveshchaniia o nuzhdakh sel'skokhoziastvennoi promyshlennosti* (St. Petersburg, 1904), 32–36.

19. The military exemption was particularly important in that it exerted a tremendous influence on the school curriculum and brought instruction in the Church parish schools in line with that in the zemstvo schools, in large measure overriding the differences in the formal programs.

20. Both V. Dobronravov and P. I. Sokolov, defenders of the Church schools, recognized that the diocesan schools were stillborn. See especially the description in *Istoricheskii ocherk razvitiia*, 28.

21. Hans, *History of Russian Educational Policy*, 159. However, according to Article 39 of the 1896 Church School Administrative Statute, Church parish schools remained open to supervision by the MNP inspectors, and an MNP official was a permanent member of district as well as diocesan boards and also sat on the School Council that ran school affairs under the Holy Synod (Farmakovskii, "Nachal'naia shkola MNP," no. 4, 117).

22. *Istoricheskii ocherk razvitiia*, 63. See TsGIAL, f. 803, op. 10, d. 1065, for material on the *ukaz* (decree) of 3 June 1887. There is a discussion of Church school board annual reports and statistics, with a high estimation of their quality, in Kaganovich, "Ocherk istorii shkol'noi," 19–22.

23. See A. Petrishchev, *Zametki uchitelia* (St. Petersburg, 1905), 335–337; Kapterev, *Istoriia russkoi pedagogiki*, 383; Pokrovskii, *Istoriia Rossii v XIX veke* 7:149; Chekhov, *Narodnoe obrazovanie*, 103. All these sources offer roughly the same description of this episode.

24. Chekhov, *Narodnoe obrazovanie*, 102. Also see Byrnes, *Pobedonostsev*, 276; and Piskunov, *Ocherki istorii shkoly*, 83.

25. Chekhov, *Narodnoe obrazovanie*, 103; Rashin, "Gramotnost'," 65. For the increase in the number of Church schools by province between 1890 and 1911, see N. P. Malinovskii, "Nekotorye vyvody po dannym shkol'noi perepisi 1911-ogo goda," *Russkaia shkola* 22, no. 5–6 (1911): 81–82. See Dobronravov, *Tserkovnaia shkola*, 77–81, for a listing of the sources of funding for Church schools in Vladimir on a year-to-year basis. Many local zemstvo studies also analyzed Church school financing: see Novgorod, *Polozhenie narodnogo obrazovaniia*, 17; Iaroslavl', *Nachal'noe obrazovanie*, 430–452. Piskunov briefly discusses the school tax issue (*Ocherki istorii shkoly*, 85).

26. Darlington, *Education in Russia*, 146; Piskunov, *Ocherki istorii shkoly*, 83; Miliukov, *Ocherki po istorii russkoi kul'tury* 2:388.

27. But see A. A. Shteven, *Iz zapisok sel'skoi uchitel'nitsy* (St. Petersburg, 1895), for a description of the experiences of one teacher who eagerly worked to help increase the number of Church parish schools and was rebuffed by Church authorities. The "Shteven incident" became a cause célèbre in education circles.

28. On proposals during the period 1887–1897 to merge Church and zemstvo schools, see Piskunov, *Ocherki istorii shkoly*, 84. The records of the Joint Committee from 1889 to 1901 are found in TsGIAL, f. 733, op. 171, d. 2148; and TsGIAL, f. 803, op. 1, d. 1094. See also Rozhdestvenskii, *Istoricheskii*, 565, 649–652, 672; Kapterev, *Istoriia russkoi pedagogiki*, 381.

29. See *Istoricheskii ocherk razvitiia*, 645–688, for a very partisan discussion of the attacks in the periodical press. For examples of the attacks, see N. V. K-vich, "Tserkovno-shkol'noe delo v Rossii," *Vestnik evropy* 36, no. 5 (September 1901): 218–247; and Medynskii, *Istoriia russkoi pedagogiki*, 322.

30. K-vich, "Tserkovno-shkol'noe delo," 235–240. For examples of the reports made by these Church school inspectors, see Chapter 13.

31. Seregny, in "Professionalism and Political Activism," discusses the systematic attack launched by Church authorities on secular teachers during 1905. Also see Grekulov, *Tserkov'*, 65–102.

32. *St. Peterburgskie vedomosti*, 13 April 1899, no. 100, cited in *Istoricheskii ocherk razvitiia*, 665.

33. See TsGIAL, f. 992, op. 1, d. 180, for the journal of a conference of school curators in August 1904, with references to clashes between Church and Ministry of Education authorities over opening new schools. Numerous references can also be found in the chronicle sections of such periodicals as *Vestnik vospitaniia*, *Russkaia shkola*, and *Narodnoe obrazovanie*.

34. The most thorough discussion of the debate in the Duma over Church schools is in A. V. Ososkov, *Ocherki istorii narodnogo obrazovaniia v dorevoliutsionnoi Rossii* (Moscow, 1975), 2:143–151. See also Charnoluskii, "Voprosy narodnogo obrazovaniia," no. 11, 91–101; Ropp, *Chto sdelala,* 100–110; Savel'eva, "Politika tsarizma," 114–116, 124, 140, 154–170. The Church position is stated in *Tserkovnye vedomosti,* no. 12 (1910): 59–70.

35. The decline of conditions in the Church schools after 1906 is amply documented in the inspectors' reports; see TsGIAL (1912–1913), f. 803, op. 10, d. 1038, 5–9 (Samara); and TsGIAL (1913–1914), f. 803, op. 10, d. 1063, 4–11 (Saratov). See the description in Dobronravov, *Tserkovnaia shkola,* 103, 142–144; and Ososkov, *Ocherki* 2: 57–59.

36. Progressives never seemed to recognize the inconsistency of their position. See V. I. Charnoluskii, *Osnovnye voprosy organizatsii shkoly v Rossii* (St. Petersburg, 1909), 53–66.

37. K-vich, "Tserkovno-shkol'noe delo," 248.

38. See the chapter on school libraries in my forthcoming manuscript (tentatively entitled *The Archaeology of Education*).

39. Bratchikov, "Uchebno-vospitatel'naia," no. 1, 96, 90–95.

40. Kapterev, *Istoriia russkoi pedagogiki,* 380; Darlington, *Education in Russia,* 337. On the 1884 Church school program, see numerous zemstvo studies which also showed that the time allotted each subject in zemstvo and Church schools was roughly comparable. See especially Vladimir, *Sbornik statisticheskikh* 3:203–234. Rozhdestvenskii offers a word-for-word comparison of official programs and a discussion of textbooks in use (*Slovo pravdy o tserkovnoi shkole,* 5–7).

41. Samarin cited in *Istoricheskii ocherk razvitiia,* 650. See also Iaroslavl', *Nachal'noe obrazovanie,* 219; and Kulomzin, *Dostupnost' nachal'noi shkoly,* 28. In an interesting discussion, Kapterev cites Church authorities who concede that Church school instruction was overly formalistic (*Istoriia russkoi pedagogiki,* 372–373, 378); see also K-vich, "Tserkovno-shkol'noe delo," 235–240. Chekhov correctly notes that between 1884 and the early 1900s the Church school program was gradually expanded and the general education content increased (*Narodnoe obrazovanie,* 105).

42. Peterson, *Prosveshchenie,* 66. See also TsGIAL (1914), f. 803, op. 1063, d. 154 (Samara); TsGIAL (1911), f. 803, op. 10, d. 130 (Vladimir); Chekhov, *Narodnoe obrazovanie,* 100–101; and K-vich, "Tserkovnoshkol'noe delo," 233–234; as well as the personal experiences of one teacher related in Salomatin, *Kak zhivët,* 107–116. In an account of

Poltava schools, we learn that a priest opened a school in 1881 and in the next year turned it over to the zemstvo so he could receive some money for his efforts at Bible instruction; see TsGIAL, f. 733, op. 228, d. 41, 19–22. Also see TsGIAL, f. 733, op. 171, d. 440, which describes an inspection of Saratov province noting that children often could not take the certifying exam because the priest had never taught them Bible and noting other instances in which children passed the exam only because the priests who never showed up to teach were the same ones who "tested" them. In Ufa, secular teachers taught Bible because priests were not available (TsGIAL, f. 733, op. 175, d. 365, 42–46).

43. Peterson, *Prosveshchenie,* 64–65.

44. Chekhov, *Narodnoe obrazovanie,* 104; the Perm' study is cited in Kapterev, *Istoriia russkoi pedagogiki,* 383. See also (Viatka) *Issledovaniie polozheniia nachal'nogo obrazovaniia v Viatskoi gubernii* (Viatka, 1900–1902), 1:80–81; and Voronov, *Materialy po narodnomu obrazovaniiu,* 14–45 (Voronezh).

45. See TsGIAL, f. 803, op. 10, d. 63, 141 (Saratov); TsGIAL (1913), f. 803, op. 10, d. 1038 (Samara); and TsGIAL (1911), f. 803, op. 10, d. 130 (Vladimir), for testimony. Also see Dobronravov, *Tserkovnaia shkola,* 115, 121–123; and K-vich, "Tserkovno-shkol'noe delo," 248. Piskunov presents a different view (*Ocherki istorii shkoly,* 84). In 1893, the Church school inspector in Moscow complained that peasants were closing down Church schools, turning them into zemstvo schools to avoid paying twice for schools (TsGIAL, f. 803, op. 10, d. 695, 57–58).

46. See Chapter 10 for more on this issue. A Synod circular of 12 June 1884 forbade the local clergy to open schools in villages where a zemstvo school was already functioning (although this restriction was rescinded in 1906) (TsGIAL, f. 733, op. 175, d. 139, 208–209). Darlington pointed out the speciousness of arguing popularity based on size of enrollment (*Education in Russia,* 331). On MNP-Church rivalry and the practice of placing rival schools in the same village, leaving other villages bereft, see Iaroslavl', *Nachal'noe obrazovanie,* 12.

47. See Piskunov, *Ocherki istorii shkoly,* 86; and Kapterev, *Istoriia russkoi pedagogiki,* 380.

CHAPTER 7

1. Ignatiev, Odinetz, and Novgorodtsev, *Russian Schools and Universities,* 15–16.

2. Erman, *Intelligentsiia*, 314; A. V. Ushakov, *Revoliutsionnoe dvizhenie demokraticheskoi intelligentsii v Rossii, 1895–1904* (Moscow, 1976), 17–40; A. A. Korestelov et al., eds., *Uchitel' i revoliutsiia* (Moscow, 1925), 161–163. The one exception to this general view is Leikina-Svirskaia, *Intelligentsiia v Rossii*, 147–173. For an anthology of fictional portraits of teachers, see D. Blagoi, ed., *Uchitel' v russkoi khudozhestvennoi literature* (Moscow, 1927). See also Ben Eklof, "The Village and the Outsider: The Rural Teacher in Russia," *Slavic and European Education Review*, no. 2 (1979): 1–29.

3. Moscow, *Sbornik postanovlenii* 5:27.

4. Petrov, *Obzor*, 12; Sheremet'ev, *Narodnye uchitelia*, i–xxiv, esp. xxiii, for the Kashirsk incident. See also Miropol'skii, *Shkola i gosudarstvo*, 5; Petrov, *Obzor*, 6–12; Miliukov, *Ocherki po istorii russkoi kul'tury*, 2:376; Zviagintsev, *Polveka*, 11–20; Chekhov, *Narodnoe obrazovanie*, 108; Viatka, *Issledovaniie* 1:129; *Narodnaia entsiklopediia* 10:150–152; Pokrovskii, *Istoriia Rossii v XIX veke* 4:78–80. A summary of the zemstvo studies is found in Iordanskii, "Istoriia narodnoi shkoly," 100.

5. Surveys of teachers' salaries never distinguished between teachers working full-time and those for whom teaching was a supplementary occupation; thus, comparisons between early and later periods overstate improvements.

6. Fal'bork and Charnoluskii, *Narodnoe obrazovanie*, 171–175, 201; MNP, *Odnodnevnaia perepis'* 16:2–4, 49. Figures for the 1890s differ considerably. One estimate actually put the number of elementary school teachers in 1899 at 200,000 (L. Blinov, "Narodnyi uchitel' v Rossii," in Shakhovskii, *Vseobshchee obrazovanie*, 63). But most estimate the number of teachers in MNP schools at approximately 60,000; see Farmakovskii, "Nachal'naia shkola MNP," no. 10, 147; Leikina-Svirskaia, *Intelligentsiia v Rossii*, 167. This figure did not include either the 21,299 Bible teachers working in MNP schools in the European provinces (Fal'bork and Charnoluskii, *Narodnoe obrazovanie*, 182, 200) or perhaps as many as 67,000 religious teachers in the Russian Empire as a whole. Blinov estimates as many as 70,000 teachers in Church parish schools and literacy schools, another 15,000 in Jewish schools, 12,000 in Moslem "confessional" schools, and yet another 12,454 in schools for soldiers, but these figures are undoubtedly exaggerated.

7. L. K. Erman, "Sostav intelligentsii v Rossii v kontse XIX i nachale XX v.," *Istoriia SSSR*, no. 1 (1963): 163; V. R. Leikina-Svirskaia, *Russkaia intelligentsiia v 1900–1917 godakh* (Moscow, 1981), 47–49,

50–51, 63. Another 52,000 officers and bureaucrats were in the armed services.

8. For estimates of need, see Kulomzin, *Dostupnost' nachal'noi shkoly,* 34; Leikina-Svirskaia, *Russkaia intelligentsiia,* 63; Kapterev, *Novye dvizheniia,* 93. Kapterev argued that Russia needed another 100,000 teachers before universal literacy could be achieved. See also Eklof, "Spreading the Word," 390, note 4.

9. The number of teachers' seminaries (colleges) rose from only 49 in 1872 to 72 in 1904, but then increased to 92 in 1910 and to 183 in 1915. By 1915, these seminaries were producing 3,610 teachers annually. However, the total number graduated between 1900 and 1913 (20,300) only equaled the number experts estimated the country would need *each year;* Veselovskii estimated that the country needed another 600 seminaries. Another 150 permanent pedagogical courses were attached to general secondary or incomplete secondary schools (district schools, for example), offering a program lasting one to three years and graduating between 1000 and 1,700 teachers annually. These graduates were not regular students of the host institutions but enrolled specifically in pedagogical courses (*Istoricheskii ocherk razvitiia,* 426).

   The Holy Synod also maintained a number of specialized teacher training institutions. There were a very limited number of teachers' schools (20 in 1910, graduating 293 teachers), as well as many more "second class" schools (*vtoroklassnye shkoly*) offering two years of teacher training beyond the basic primary program. In 1908, 328 of these schools graduated 4,687 teachers. The "second class" schools, however, only prepared teachers to work in literacy schools and in fact declined rapidly after 1911; their graduates should not be included in any general estimate of the annual output of qualified teachers.

10. Panachin, *Pedagogicheskoe obrazovanie,* 93; Johnson, *Russia's Educational Heritage,* 250; Alston, *Education and the State,* 239, 242; Leikina-Svirskaia, *Russkaia intelligentsiia,* 63.

11. Kulomzin, *Dostupnost' nachal'noi shkoly,* 34; B. B. Veselovskii, "Vseobshchee obuchenie i zemstvo," in Veselovskii and Frenkel', *Iubileinyi zemskii sbornik,* 391–399; Rashin, "Gramotnost'," 74–76; Farmakovskii, "Nachal'naia shkola MNP," no. 8, 176. These estimates of the pool of secondary school graduates are based on the average number of graduates from each institution in 1910 and on the corresponding number of institutions in 1915–1916; we assume that the average size of each graduating class was constant.

12. For the rules on certification, see Kalashnikov et al., *Pedagogicheskaia entsiklopediia* 1:1021.

13. University or secondary school graduates without pedagogical training could be certified by proving competence through giving a few trial lessons conducted under the supervision of the local inspector or school board or by serving an apprenticeship under a certified teacher (Farmakovskii, "Nachal'naia shkola MNP," no. 8, 175; Darlington, *Education in Russia,* 259).

14. Horn, *Education in Rural England,* 113–114.

15. Chekhov, *Narodnoe obrazovanie,* 111; MNP, *Odnodnevnaia perepis'* 16:89. See also Farmakovskii, "Nachal'naia shkola MNP," no. 8, 155–157, 160–161.

16. Samuel Bowles and Herbert Gintis, *Schooling in Capitalist America: Educational Reform and the Contradictions of Economic Life* (New York, 1976), 171; Stone, "Literacy and Education in England," 95. See also Farmakovskii, "Nachal'naia shkola MNP," no. 8, 161; TsGIAL, f. 992, op. 1, d. 1980, 145 (conference of education administrators); Kulomzin, *Dostupnost' nachal'noi shkoly,* 32; Zhil'tsov and Velichkina, *Uchitel' sel'skoi shkoly,* 30–42. Richard Stites argues that lack of alternative opportunities put women in this field (*The Women's Liberation Movement in Russia* [Princeton, N.J., 1978], 173).

17. S. T. Semënov, *Dvadtsat' piat' let v derevne* (Petrograd, 1915), 47. See also Salomatin, *Kak zhivët,* 58–60, for graphic examples of peasant disdain for and abuse of women teachers.

18. Chekhov, *Narodnoe obrazovanie,* 111; Salomatin, *Kak zhivët,* 59–60. See also Iaroslavl', *Nachal'noe obrazovanie,* 371.

19. Salomatin, *Kak zhivët,* 66–77.

20. MNP, *Odnodnevnaia perepis'* 16:95, table 40 (a-b).

21. Ibid. See Eklof, "Spreading the Word," 397, for information on provincial differences in social origins of rural teachers, both male and female. See also Leikina-Svirskaia, *Intelligentsiia v Rossii,* 163.

22. Orlov, *Narodnoe obrazovanie,* 63, 76; Novgorod, *Ocherk narodnogo obrazovaniia,* 25; Iaroslavl', *Nachal'noe obrazovanie,* 249. (The figures in the Iaroslavl' table do not add up properly; also, the male-female columns for Church schools were improperly reversed in the original.)

23. In 1911, 96 percent of rural teachers were provided with housing, which was sometimes attached to the school, sometimes a separate unit. Teachers' level of satisfaction with this housing, however, was quite low; see Ben Eklof, "*Kindertempel* or Shack? Russian School

Buildings at the Turn of This Century" (Indiana University, 1983, photocopy).

24. *Uchitelia i uchitel'nitsy zemskikh shkol,* vol. 2 of *Polozhenie narodnogo obrazovaniia vo Vladimirskoi gubernii po issledovaniiu 1910 goda,* Vladimirskaia gubernskaia zemskaia uprava (Vladimir, 1910–1911), 32. See also Salomatin, *Kak zhivët,* 184.

25. Farmakovskii, "Nachal'naia shkola MNP," no. 8, 162–163; V. Evteev, ed., *Trudy pervogo vserossiiskogo s"ezda predstavitelei obshchestv vspomoshchestvovaniia litsam uchitel'skogo zvaniia* (Moscow, 1907), 2: 105, 844–857, 945–946. The Evteev volumes contain the reports to the tumultuous 1902 Teachers' Mutual Aid Congress in Moscow, described in detail in Seregny, "Professionalism and Political Activism." See also A. Koridalin, "Material'noe polozhenie uchashchikh," in *Doklady,* vol. 3 of *Trudy pervogo obshchezemskogo s"ezda po narodnomu obrazovaniiu* (Moscow, 1912), no. 18, 193. For an attempt to correlate marital status by gender and salary, see Moskovskaia gubernskaia zemskaia uprava, Otdel khoziaistvennoi statistiki, "Svedeniia ob uchashchikh v zemskikh shkolakh Moskovskoi gubernii," in *Statisticheskii ezhegodnik Moskovskoi gubernii za 1891* (Moscow, 1892), 19.

26. Chekhov, *Narodnoe obrazovanie,* 110–113. See also Vladimir, *Sbornik statisticheskikh* 3:133, for the percentage of teachers, by type of school, for whom teaching was a full-time occupation. According to this study, teaching was a supplementary occupation for 50 percent of those employed in Church schools.

On vacations, see Moscow, "Svedeniia ob uchashchikh," 21; and V. A. Gol'tsev, "K voprosu o polozhenii uchashchikh narodnykh shkol," *Russkaia mysl'* 18, no. 12 (1897): 68, which uses material from the 1894 Literacy Committee survey on how teachers spent their vacations. According to this survey, 51 percent of teachers in Kazan' school district traveled to the nearest town "only rarely." Also in Kazan', despite difficult material circumstances, observers claimed that the number of teachers who did not express a desire to change work was four times greater than those who did indicate such a desire (although in Kazan' most teachers were peasants). The same study noted that the number of teachers living with family far exceeded the number married (Gol'tsev, "K voprosu o polozhenii uchashchikh," 62).

27. MNP, *Odnodnevnaia perepis'* 16:4–6. In the zemstvo schools, 11,740 of 44,368 teachers were married.

28. For data on teachers' ages, see ibid., 86, table 29.

29. Ibid., 4, 89, and, for provincial figures, 93.

30. Ibid., 86. The Zemstvo Congress Survey and the 1911 School Census showed enormous regional variations in the professional qualifications of rural teachers, variations caused by the locations of different types of teacher training institutions, by the living conditions and school salaries offered in different areas, and by the draw of great economic and cultural centers such as St. Petersburg and Moscow or of the sunny coast of the Crimea (V. V. Akimov, "Zemskaia rabota po podgotovke narodnykh uchitelei," *ZhMNP,* n.s. 56, sec. 3 [March 1915]: 179–183; n.s. 57, sec. 3 [May 1915]: 6; n.s. 58, sec. 3 [July 1915]: 151). The difficulty of attracting and keeping trained teachers in the rural hinterlands is a chronic complaint of educators in the Soviet Union today; as the 1911 School Census shows, the roots of this problem extend back before the 1917 Revolution. On the flight from the countryside today, see David E. Powell, "Soviet Society in Flux: The Rural Exodus," *Problems of Communism* 22, no. 6 (November–December 1974): 5–7.

31. *Anketa uchashchim zemskikh shkol* (hereafter *Anketa*), vol. 5 of *Trudy pervogo obshchezemskogo s"ezda po narodnomu obrazovaniiu* (Moscow, 1911), 15–16. See Eklof, "Spreading the Word," 403, table 10–4, for a more detailed listing.

32. For the curriculum of the teacher training schools, see Farmakovskii, "Nachal'naia shkola MNP," no. 8, 170–172; Panachin, *Pedagogicheskoe obrazovanie,* 85. For an overview, see Kuz'min, *Uchitel'skie seminary Rossii.*

33. On government pressure to locate teachers' seminaries in rural areas, see Pokrovskii, *Istoriia Rossii v XIX veke* 7:130; Alston, *Education and the State,* 239; Sinel, *The Classroom and the Chancellery,* 242; Darlington, *Education in Russia,* 247.

34. Farmakovskii, "Nachal'naia shkola MNP," no. 8, 172.

35. Korolëv, "Narodnoe obrazovanie," 49. The harsh critic of the seminaries was one Gubkin, cited in Evteev, *Trudy pervogo vserossiiskogo s"ezda* 2:1113–1116, 1127.

   Revealingly, when the Novgorod zemstvo petitioned to give its teachers' seminaries the status of secondary schools, the local school director agreed that the seminaries' graduates were receiving the equivalent of a secondary education. But the MNP, in a report to the Council of Ministers, refused to go along with the request, not because it disagreed but because it felt this move would increase the outflow of graduates from primary school teaching to more attractive professions (TsGIAL, f. 733, op. 175, d. 365, 107–108, 205).

36. Farmakovskii, "Nachal'naia shkola MNP," no. 8, 172; Piskunov, *Ocherki istorii shkoly*, 198–200.

37. Panachin, *Pedagogicheskoe obrazovanie*, 96.

38. Sinel, *The Classroom and the Chancellery*, 241.

39. According to Darlington, the only difference between the religious seminary and the gymnasium was a greater concentration on religion, theology, and philosophy in the fifth and sixth classes of the seminary. Religious schools (*uchilishcha*) accepted children from the ages of ten to twelve, and the seminaries (the second four years of a combined eight-year program) fixed the age of admission at fourteen to eighteen (Darlington, *Education in Russia*, 234). For information on the curriculum, see ibid., 286–288; Hans, *History of Russian Educational Policy*, 124.

40. Darlington, *Education in Russia*, 237, 292; Zhil'tsov and Velichkina, *Uchitel' sel'skoi shkoly*, 37.

41. Darlington, *Education in Russia*, 236, 288–289. Beginning in 1864 in the Fourth Section gymnasiums, many schools also offered separate two- or three-year programs (*kursy*) in pedagogy. After 1897, a uniform three-year course was established. Graduates of the seven-year gymnasium program, however, like graduates of the diocesan schools, automatically received teaching certificates without participation in these specialized affiliated pedagogical *kursy*, and few graduates of the *kursy* seem to have trickled into the rural public schools.

42. Bratchikov, "Uchebno-vospitatel'naia," no. 2, 119–120.

43. See Verigin, *V pomoshch*, 129–133, for the regulations governing qualifying examinations and certification. For certification of Church parish school teachers, see Anastas'ev, *Narodnaia shkola* 1:413–414.

44. Zhil'tsov and Velichkina, *Uchitel' sel'skoi shkoly*, 38–39.

45. Farmakovskii, "Nachal'naia shkola MNP," no. 8, 178; Salomatin, *Kak zhivët*, 156.

46. Farmakovsii, "Nachal'naia shkola MNP," no. 8, 177.
    The question of teacher training was the focus of a number of thorough and excellent reports to the 1911 Zemstvo Congress, and, according to Charnoluskii, the discussion at the second session (charged with teachers' affairs) was valuable and comprehensive. At the general session of the congress, a number of resolutions calling for a comprehensive plan of teacher training—rather than the existing fragmentary, casual approach—were adopted virtually without objection. The resolutions declared that teachers should have no less than a general secondary education, as well as both theoretical and

practical pedagogical training, and that they should be encouraged to develop an "active independent personality, with an advanced striving for development and growth, for improving methods of *vospitanie* and instruction, with high sensitivity [*zhivaia otzyvchivost'*] to the surrounding population, with respect not only for mental but also for physical work, [with] love of nature. . . . Teachers should also master the skills of drawing, singing, and handicrafts." More concretely, it was resolved that the zemstvo should not hire individuals with significantly less than a secondary education, because the gap in general education could not be filled by training provided by the pedagogical *kursy*. The basic contingent of teachers should be from among graduates of the teachers' seminaries (reformed) or graduates of general secondary schools with supplementary instruction from pedagogical *kursy* (Charnoluskii, "Voprosy narodnogo obrazovaniia," no. 11, 111–116).

47. Horn, *Education in Rural England*, 111–112; Tyack and Hansot, *Managers of Virtue*, 19.

48. *Anketa*, 21–42.

49. Alston, *Education and the State*, 239.

50. *Anketa*, 21–42. This discussion is continued in Chapter 8.

51. Iaroslavl', *Nachal'noe obrazovanie*, 265.

52. It is not possible to learn precisely how long teachers remained at their posts. To do this, we would have to learn how long those who were leaving their posts had served prior to resignation, death, or dismissal. Instead, surveys generally inquired how long those currently on the job had been working *to that date*. This information provides a cross section; it gives us some idea of the strength of the bond between teacher and village community, but it does not really answer the original question. For length of stay at any given point to accurately reflect teachers' tenure, the school system would have to be intact and stable. But because the system grew rapidly after 1890, the numbers of new recruits required to fill new openings would, in our cross section, tend to reduce the average tenure of the village teacher. See Iaroslavl', *Nachal'noe obrazovanie*, 265–268, for a discussion of these statistical problems.

53. MNP, *Odnodnevnaia perepis'* 16:86. The data on length of stay are muddied by the 1905 Revolution. Historians have frequently stated, based on the testimony of one Duma representative with links to the police, that some 23,000 teachers were dismissed in the aftermath of the revolution. No other source has verified this extraordinary claim, however. Using the data from the 1911 School Census and working

with a *normal* annual attrition level of 10 percent (Ignatiev, Odinetz, and Novgorodtsev, *Russian Schools and Universities*, 16), it is possible to make some indirect estimates. Without political reprisals, there should have been between 53,200 and 61,200 new teachers in the system; in fact, there were 68,173. Thus, given the normal attrition rate and the number of school openings between 1906 and 18 January 1911, there were between 7,000 and 15,000 more new teachers than we would expect; this figure may well represent the number of teachers who suffered reprisals after 1905. Though substantially fewer than the 23,000 often cited, these dismissals were certainly a severe blow to the system—a great loss of experience and human capital, as well as a personal loss for those who suffered. (These calculations are based on data from MNP, *Odnodnevnaia perepis'* 16:4, 65, 86.)

54. Vladimir, *Uchitelia i uchitel'nitsy zemskikh shkol,* 15. But see also Tavrida, *Sbornik po shkol'noi statistike* 1:40; (Pskov) *Materialy k voprosu ob uchastii Pskovskogo gubernskogo zemstva v raione nachal'nogo narodnogo obrazovaniia* (Pskov, 1898–1899), 1:3; Iaroslavl', *Nachal'noe obrazovanie,* 268; Sheremet'ev, *Narodnye uchitelia,* 31.

55. Moscow, "Svedeniia ob uchashchikh," 14; and Moscow, *Statisticheskii ezhegodnik,* 210.

56. Summary statement from Moscow, "Svedeniia ob uchashchikh," 6; studies are found in Iaroslavl', *Nachal'noe obrazovanie,* 270–271; Moscow, "Svedeniia ob uchashchikh," 4–8; Sheremet'ev, *Narodnye uchitelia,* 35 (Tula); and Vladimir, *Sbornik statisticheskikh* 3:138–139. For qualifications by province, see *Anketa,* 17 (reproduced in Eklof, "Spreading the Word," 403, table 10–4).

57. Iaroslavl', *Nachal'noe obrazovanie,* 274.

58. Ibid., 276.

59. Vladimir, *Sbornik statisticheskikh* 3:141; Tavrida, *Sbornik po shkol'noi statistike* 2:41; Iaroslavl', *Nachal'noe obrazovanie,* 276; Sheremet'ev, *Narodnye uchitelia,* 31 (Tula); Moscow, "Svedeniia ob uchashchikh," 8. See also Evteev, *Trudy pervogo vserossiiskogo s"ezda* 1:257.

60. Vladimir, *Uchitelia i uchitel'nitsy zemskikh shkol,* 15, 21.

61. Cited in Evteev, *Trudy pervogo vserossiiskogo s"ezda* 2:1040.

62. Vladimir, *Uchitelia i uchitel'nitsy zemskikh shkol,* 18; Moscow, *Statisticheskii ezhegodnik,* 218.

63. Phillips, *Basic Education,* 50–53. Using the example of the new math, Susan Jacoby notes that clinging to routine, along with resistance to the additional labor and the adjustment involved in introducing new curriculum, was the biggest obstacle to successful implementation of

the so-called Zankov reforms of the early seventies (*Inside Soviet Schools* [New York, 1974], 91–94).

64. Phillips, *Basic Education*, 60. Because of the difficulty of gaining access to higher schools, teachers' seminaries were virtually the only places where peasants could receive a free education, and even a stipend and housing, as well as schooling beyond the two-class schools. Many thus enrolled in school not to pursue teaching careers but in search of a higher rung on the education ladder and social and economic mobility (Zhil'tsov and Velichkina, *Uchitel' sel'skoi shkoly*, 34–35).

CHAPTER 8

1. *Anketa*, 224.

2. Chekhov, *Narodnoe obrazovanie*, 112–113; Orlov, *Narodnoe obrazovanie*, 52. In 1902, the death by starvation of a teacher in Novgorod caused a national furor; see Seregny, "Professionalism and Political Activism," 278.

3. Petrov, *Voprosy narodnogo obrazovaniia* 4:175–176.

4. Moscow Literacy Committee data cited in Blinov, "Narodnyi uchitel'," 75–76; Iaroslavl', *Nachal'noe obrazovanie*, 308. In the Crimea, where the zemstvo teacher earned an average of 400 rubles, the Church school teacher earned 133 rubles. In Tver', however, the Church school teacher's miserable salary of 142 rubles was not much lower than the 154 rubles earned by a zemstvo teacher. See also Tavrida, *Sbornik po shkol'noi statistike* 1:43; Sheremet'ev, *Narodnye uchitelia*, 37.

   A survey conducted by the Synod in 1899 showed that of thirty-three thousand teachers, nineteen thousand earned less than 100 rubles annually, whereas only three thousand earned over 200 rubles; these figures included sextons and literacy school teachers, however (A. Nikolaev, *Sel'skii uchitel'* [St. Petersburg, 1906], 6).

5. Moscow, "Svedeniia ob uchashchikh," 6. See S. I. Miropol'skii, *Inspektsiia narodnykh shkol i eia zadachi* (St. Petersburg, 1877), 82, for descriptions of teachers leaving the villages for better jobs.

6. On zemstvo teacher pension programs, see Farmakovskii, "Nachal'naia shkola MNP," no. 10, 163–167.

7. See Seregny, "Professionalism and Political Activism," 258, for a graphic MNP circular from 1903. For the pension regulations, see Verigin, *V pomoshch*, 32–49 (statute of 12 June 1900, and modifica-

tions of 3 March 1903 and 19 April 1904; laws of 15 January and 1 June 1910).

8. The 1914–1915 Teachers' Congress endorsed a beginning salary of 600 rubles, with supplements that could bring it to 960 rubles (Nikolai Sokolov, "Voprosy shkol'noi politiki v postanovleniiakh s"ezda po narodnomu obrazovaniiu," *Russkaia shkola* 25, no. 3 [1914]: 99–100).

9. Johnson, *Russia's Educational Heritage,* 210; Charnoluskii, "Voprosy narodnogo obrazovaniia," no. 11, 109. In fact, from a developmental perspective, the restraints on teacher salaries were certainly not cost-effective because they encouraged flight from the schools.

The 1908 law was unquestionably a mixed blessing for liberal zemstvo educators. Although welcoming the release of substantial funds in the zemstvo budget that could now be diverted to other purposes and the stimulus to the universal education campaign provided by the Treasury salary supplements, they feared losing the leverage provincial zemstvos had formerly enjoyed by providing grants with strings attached. In particular, zemstvo educators were apprehensive that teachers would come to regard themselves as employees of the government rather than of the zemstvo. In retrospect, it can be seen that such a change was precisely what the government intended; the pension plan of 1900 was only the first step, and the 1908 law the second, for in 1913 and 1914 the Ministry of Education issued regulations forbidding teachers from taking part in zemstvo-sponsored activities and even from communicating directly with the zemstvo assembly or executive board (Zviagintsev, "Zemstvo i uchebnoe vedomstvo," 368; Ignatiev, Odinetz, and Novgorodtsev, *Russian Schools and Universities,* 19–20). Yet, to teachers, just who employed them may have been less significant than how much they were paid, and, for them, the 1908 law and government intervention unquestionably improved their lot.

10. Vladimir, *Uchitelia i uchitel'nitsy zemskikh shkol,* 23. Twenty-five percent continued to receive less than 300 rubles a year, however.

11. MNP, *Odnodnevnaia perepis'* 16:95, table 41.

12. Although 64 percent of the 279 districts surveyed paid their teachers no less than 360 rubles a year, 56 districts (20 percent) still paid zemstvo teachers between 240 and 360 rubles yearly, and 35 districts (11 percent) paid even lower average salaries.

13. MNP, *Odnodnevnaia perepis'* 16:67. For international comparisons, see G. Genkel', *Narodnoe obrazovanie na zapade i u nas* (St. Petersburg, 1911), 37, 51, 55, 64, 76, 90, 100.

14. Trutovskii, *Sovremennoe zemstvo*, 226–227; S. I. Dubrovskii, *Sel'skoe khoziaistvo Rossii v period imperializma* (Moscow, 1973), 334. See Leikina-Svirskaia, *Russkaia intelligentsiia*, 59, for information on the *fel'dshery*; also, Koridalin, "Material'noe polozhenie uchashchikh," 195.

15. The question of the adequacy of teachers' salaries is particularly difficult to answer. Regional variations in salaries were still marked (ranging, for example, from 195 rubles in Tula to 430 in Ekaterinoslav zemstvo schools). Moreover, costs differed considerably from province to province and region to region. Most important, the needs of the individual teacher varied, in both objective and subjective terms. A married teacher with children had far greater basic needs than a bachelor or a single woman; subjectively, urban-raised gymnasium graduates may have included in a "living wage" many items that peasant graduates of a teachers' seminary, who may also have kept their own gardens, may well have regarded as frills (Johnson, *Russia's Educational Heritage*, 209; Alston, *Education and the State*, 239; Kulomzin, *Dostupnost' nachal'noi shkoly*, 33–34; Ushakov, *Revoliutsionnoe*, 18; Eklof, "Spreading the Word," 423, esp. note 27).

    For these reasons, it is not surprising that even those estimates based on careful budget studies produced a variety of responses concerning a tolerable salary for the rural teacher. These estimates ranged from as low as 338 rubles in Kaluga and 480 rubles in Novgorod for a married teacher to 600 rubles for a single teacher and 1,200 for a married teacher—the estimate presented by Koridalin to the 1911 Zemstvo Congress. Teachers themselves volunteered in the congress questionnaire that a salary of 480–600 rubles was adequate, if supplements for rent, fuel, and other expenses were also provided (Koridalin, "Material'noe polozhenie uchashchikh," 183–196; Charnoluskii, *Zemstvo i narodnoe obrazovanie* 2:273; *Anketa*, 223). Budget studies revealed not only the teachers' material needs but also their status anxieties. Koridalin's minimum budget of 600 to 1,200 rubles, for instance, allowed a number of discretionary expenditures, including domestic help, travel, theater, books, and periodicals. It was, in other words, not a survival norm but an income allowing a life fitting the intellectual and cultural needs of the *intelligent*, or professional. But very few teachers made 600 rubles or more, and many of those living on 300–350 rubles were married with children.

16. Koridalin, "Material'noe polozhenie uchashchikh," 191; Darlington, *Education in Russia*, 350. See also Eklof, "Spreading the Word," 412, for a table listing individual complaints made by teachers to the 1911 Zemstvo Congress.

17. Some teachers took over Bible lessons and received a portion of the Bible teacher's salary (the priest usually took the rest); other teachers gave private lessons (apparently not in high demand) or taught supplementary courses. In the summer, when teachers had some free time, it was virtually impossible to find work except as an agricultural laborer (Iaroslavl', *Nachal'noe obrazovanie,* 315; Salomatin, *Kak zhivët,* 184–188).

According to studies a decade later (after the turn of the century), the practice of moonlighting continued, despite salary increases. In Moscow, for example, of 1,712 zemstvo teachers, 293 earned an average of 12–34 rubles by running local libraries; 149 earned an average of 33 rubles teaching crafts or singing; another 96 earned 12 rubles each conducting public readings; 7 worked as insurance agents earning 307 rubles each; and 3 ran pedagogical museums, earning an average of 60 rubles. Thus, although one of every three teachers had supplementary earnings during the school year, for most the amounts were small (*Svodka svedenii,* sec. 7, 15).

In Vladimir in 1910, 8 percent of teachers received an average of 55 rubles a year teaching Bible, and 10 percent (24 percent of men, but only 5 percent of women) had other sources of income averaging 85 rubles overall—102 for men and 49 for women. As in Moscow, most of this income came from running the local library, teaching handicrafts or singing, or coaching for entrance examinations. Such supplementary work came during the school year, when teachers often already had more than fifty hours a week of contact time with pupils without this added effort (Vladimir, *Uchitelia i uchitel'nitsy zemskikh shkol,* 26–27). Thus, time constraints imposed harsh limits on such supplements. Moreover, work befitting one's station could not always be found, and the newspapers noted a few extreme cases where, for want of money, a local teacher hired out as a *batrak* (farm laborer), a shepherd, or a painter. In more extreme cases, teachers left the profession entirely to become clerks in the state-run liquor stores, police constables, tax officials, full-time insurance agents, or even pest exterminators for the zemstvo (Salomatin, *Kak zhivët,* 188–190).

18. V. V. Akimov, "Zemskaia deiatel'nost' po narodnomu obrazovaniiu v Moskovskoi gubernii," *ZhMNP,* n.s. 8, sec. 3 (May 1907): 15–17. See also A. Nikolaev, "Neskol'ko slov o biudzhete narodnogo uchitelia," *Russkaia shkola* 23, no. 5–6 (1912): 89–95, for detail on the impact of salaries on diet and the distribution of expenditures by single and married teachers.

19. *Anketa,* 223.

20. Petrov, *Voprosy narodnogo obrazovaniia* 1:185. For a general discussion of salaries, see Charnoluskii, *Zemstvo i narodnoe obrazovanie* 2:272–297. See Phillips, *Basic Education,* 53, for comparisons with the developing world today.

21. Petrov, *Voprosy narodnogo obrazovaniia* 1:185.

22. Ibid.

23. This semi-professional position was not unique to Russia; Seregny notes that "teaching is the most profoundly contaminated (secularized) profession. . . . With the rise of mass education its mystique is compromised [since] the tasks it performs are within the competency of all who have been taught themselves, and since those on whom it practices are children. Many of these functions [are] substitutes for parental roles in any case" (Scott Seregny, "Professional Activism and Association Among Russian Teachers" [Paper presented to the Conference on Professions and Professionalization in Imperial Russia, University of Illinois, Champaign-Urbana, 24–26 June 1982], 2–3).

24. I. A. Bunin, "Uchitel'," in *Polnoe sobranie sochinenii* (Petrograd, 1915), 2:48–80.

25. Evteev, *Trudy pervogo vserossiiskogo s"ezda* 2:1020; also cited in Seregny, "Professionalism and Political Activism," 237.

26. Richard Pipes, *Russia Under the Old Regime* (New York, 1974), 152–154. Also compare Horn, *Education in Rural England,* 158.

27. According to Senate interpretation, the sponsor of the school "nominated" the teacher, and the inspector "admitted" the teacher to school duties. A year later, on receipt of a certificate of competence and political reliability, the school board confirmed the teacher in office. The teacher could be temporarily suspended by the inspector of schools, but dismissal had to be confirmed by the school board. The teacher had the right of appeal, first to the provincial school board and then to the Senate. However, the teacher had neither the right of self-defense before the school board nor the right to request copies of the papers pertaining to the dismissal, nor even the right to an explanation from the school board for the dismissal. In addition, although regulations stipulated that reasons for dismissal were not to be stamped on a teacher's certificate, a notation was added specifying the length and location of the job and inviting direct correspondence from a new place of work. It was not uncommon for a teacher to be shadowed by the past and to be dismissed from one post after another once the incriminating documents caught up. Finally, in two separate ordinances in 1914 (2 February and 11 October), the inspector was

given exclusive power first to appoint and then to dismiss teachers. This was another major step in the appropriation of direct control over the schools from the zemstvo.

An excellent source on this topic is the report to the 1902 Teachers' Congress: "Doklad komissii po vyiasneniiu pravogo polozheniia uchashchikh," in Evteev, *Trudy pervogo vserossiiskogo s"ezda* 1:351. On the legislation itself, see Verigin, *V pomoshch*, 95–101. A good summary of the hiring procedures is in *Narodnaia entsiklopediia* 10:162. See also Chekhov, *Narodnoe obrazovanie*, 62; Darlington, *Education in Russia*, 143; and Ia. K., "Pravovoe polozhenie narodnogo uchitelia," *Russkaia shkola* 19, no. 5–6 (1908): 128–145. Salomatin's description of the "Berednik episode" is of particular interest (*Kak zhivët*, 145–148); for later legislation, see the brief note in Ignatiev, Odinetz, and Novgorodtsev, *Russian Schools and Universities*, 20.

Until 1914, however, appointment and dismissal procedures were somewhat cumbersome, and it was far more common for a teacher to resign "voluntarily" (under pressure) or for teachers to be transferred to other schools in the same district. Transfers were a means of introducing finer gradations of punishment short of dismissal and were widely employed in the Russian countryside. Transfers refined the available measures of control and simplified the procedures involved, for teachers had no defense against arbitrary decisions by the inspector to move them to other schools. Indeed, Salomatin produced some truly amazing records of inspectors arbitrarily transferring virtually all the teachers in one district (*Kak zhivët*, 138–141, 141–145, 150).

Perevod (transfer) was often confused with *perekhod* (voluntary moves), however; as noted earlier, teachers themselves often left their schools in the spring in the hope that conditions would be better elsewhere. Moreover, some of the transfers reported in the press were obvious attempts by the inspector to end a troublesome conflict between villagers and an unwelcome teacher or to *protect* a teacher from the accusations or harassment of the village priest or local peasant officials. When a conflict arose, it was easier for the inspector to move t.1e teacher to another school than to sort out the rights and wrongs or, much more difficult, to appease the various parties. Thus, the high incidence of transfer, endemic to the school system, was a sign of conflict and strain. It typified the powerlessness of the teacher, but it was not merely a measure of the abuse of power by the inspector or of tensions between inspector and teacher; just as often, it seems to have been an attempt by the inspector to maintain peace in the village or even to protect the teacher.

28. Cited in Evteev, *Trudy pervogo vserossiiskogo s"ezda* 1:259.

29. Iablochkov cited in Kapterev, *Novye dvizheniia*, 29.
30. See Salomatin, *Kak zhivët*, 157, for the Chistopol'sk case. See also K., "Pravovoe polozhenie narodnogo uchitelia," 141–143; and Evteev, *Trudy pervogo vserossiiskogo s"ezda* 1:252, 257.

    Zhil'tsov and Velichkina cite an example of a teacher being forced to get on his knees in front of his class for the inspector (*Uchitel' sel'skoi shkoly*, 26–27). In his memoirs, Bratchikov recalls watching a young teacher in conversation with the inspector. As the inspector mounted some stairs, the teacher was forced to walk sideways up the same stairs, facing the inspector all the while ("Vospominaniia o rabote uchitelei," 79–80). Also see the instructions to teachers contained in a handbook for students at teachers' seminaries: A. Tarnovskii, *Ob obiazannostiakh uchitelia nachal'nogo narodnogo uchilishcha* (Moscow, 1896), 3, 35–37.
31. Cited in Evteev, *Trudy pervogo vserossiiskogo s"ezda* 1:389–390.
32. Salomatin, *Kak zhivët*, 104–105, 107, 176–181. See also K., "Pravovoe polozhenie narodnogo uchitelia," 140.
33. Salomatin himself was ultimately dismissed for failure to use the proper form of deferential address when writing to a priest (he used *ego vysokoblagorodiiu* instead of *ego vysokoblagosloveniiu*) and for refusing to teach Bible lessons in the priest's stead.

    Scott Seregny has argued that as Russia suffered military defeat and experienced social dislocation and disorders among minorities at the turn of the century, priests often became local crusaders for a militant Orthodox patriotism, with secular teachers often the targets of this crusade. Seregny has produced documentary evidence to support this claim, but the argument must be balanced with evidence from other areas that sometimes priests were in fact the most enthusiastic sponsors of popular education and even leaders of peasant revolts ("Professionalism and Political Activism," 545–547).
34. K., "Pravovoe polozhenie narodnogo uchitelia," 138–139; Evteev, *Trudy pervogo vserossiiskogo s"ezda* 1:251; Belokonskii, *Narodnoe nachal'noe obrazovanie*, 138; Salomatin, *Kak zhivët*, 99–100.
35. Bratchikov, "Uchebno-vospitatel'naia," no. 2, 116.
36. Chekhov, *Narodnoe obrazovanie*, 113–114.
37. Cited in Nikolaev, *Sel'skii uchitel'*, 12.
38. Evteev, *Trudy pervogo vserossiiskogo s"ezda* 1:248.
39. Miropol'skii, *Inspektsiia narodnykh shkol*, 84–88; Sheremet'ev, *Narodnye uchitelia*, xviii. See Zyrianov, "Nekotorye cherty," 380–387, for a discussion of the term *miroedy* ("commune-eaters").

40. Furet and Ozouf, "Three Centuries," 222–226. On "restricted" literacy, see Goody and Watts, "The Consequences of Literacy," 58.
41. Orlov, *Narodnoe obrazovanie,* 203–204.
42. Petrov, *Voprosy narodnogo obrazovaniia* 1 : 185.
43. Shigin cited in Evteev, *Trudy pervogo vserossiiskogo s"ezda* 1 : 266.
44. *Anketa,* 27, also 30, 34.
45. Evteev, *Trudy pervogo vserossiiskogo s"ezda* 2 : 1033.
46. Ibid.
47. Ibid., 1037. See also Sheremet'ev, *Narodnye uchitelia,* 43–46; and Iaroslavl', *Nachal'noe obrazovanie,* 303–309.
48. Ignatiev, Odinetz, and Novgorodtsev, *Russian Schools and Universities,* 15–16.
49. Evteev, *Trudy pervogo vserossiiskogo s"ezda* 1 : 473.
50. Sheremet'ev, *Narodnye uchitelia,* xviii–xix, xxi.
51. Petrov, *Voprosy narodnogo obrazovaniia,* 1 : 187. See also Blinov, "Narodnyi uchitel'," 79.
52. Petrov, *Voprosy narodnogo obrazovaniia* 1 : 186; Chekhov, *Narodnoe obrazovanie,* 112–113; and Evteev, *Trudy pervogo vserossiiskogo s"ezda* 1 : 477, 487.
53. Sheremet'ev, *Narodnye uchitelia,* 45–46.
54. "Na podvode" (literally, "On the Cart"), translated as "The Schoolmistress," in Yarmolinsky, *A Treasury of Great Russian Short Stories,* 814.
55. Iaroslavl', *Nachal'noe obrazovanie,* 302–308; Sheremet'ev, *Narodnye uchitelia,* 43–46.
56. *Svodka svedenii,* sec. 7, 12; Salomatin, *Kak zhivët,* 117–118; Evteev, *Trudy pervogo vserossiiskogo s"ezda* 1 : 248, 257, 527. See also Gol'tsev, "K voprosu o polozhenii uchashchikh," 65.
57. Iaroslavl', *Nachal'noe obrazovanie,* 308–309.
58. Evteev, *Trudy pervogo vserossiiskogo s"ezda* 1 : 477. A handbook written for use in teachers' seminaries recommended that teachers take up manual crafts both to improve their lot and to demonstrate that teachers were not averse to manual labor. From the suggestion, it is clear that the author believed teachers did in fact look down on manual labor (Tarnovskii, *Ob obiazannostiakh uchitelia,* 8).
59. By 1902 there were 171 mutual aid societies in operation, representing about 22,000 teachers. By 1917 there were also some 106 savings and loan funds for teachers. See Konstantinov and Struminskii,

Ocherki po istorii, 238; Seregny, "Professionalism and Political Activism," 209–246, 850–854. Also see Chekhov, *Narodnoe obrazovanie,* 122; Panachin, *Pedagogicheskoe obrazovanie,* 116–117; and Salomatin, *Kak zhivët,* 171, for analyses of the decline of membership in mutual aid societies after 1900. See also Ronald Hayashida and Hideo Hayashida, "The Unionization of Russian Teachers, 1905–1908: An Interest Group Under the Autocracy," *Slavic and European Education Review,* no. 2 (1981): 1–16.

60. See, for example, Piskunov, *Ocherki istorii shkoly,* 188–190.

61. Seregny, "Professionalism and Political Activism," 137–208; Panachin, *Pedagogicheskoe obrazovanie,* 112–113; Piskunov, *Ocherki istorii shkoly,* 190; E. P. Ol'khovskii, "Narodnyi uchitel' v revoliutsionnom dvizhenii 60–70–kh godov XIX veka," *Sovetskaia pedagogika,* no. 7 (1967): 121–129; A. M. Vezhlev, "Uchitel'skie s"ezdy i kursy v Rossii (Vtoraia polovina XIX veka)," *Sovetskaia pedagogika,* no. 7 (1958): 79–88 (the Orzhevskii citation is found on page 84). According to Ol'khovskii (121), 433 teachers were brought to trial in the 1860s and 1870s, constituting 8 percent of all revolutionaries arrested. Sergei Nechaev's revolutionary activities as a teacher are described in the biography *Nechaev,* by Philip Pomper (New Brunswick, N.J., 1979).

62. Kapterev, *Novye dvizheniia,* 40–41; Seregny, "Professional Activism and Association," 15–16.

63. Seregny, "Professional Activism and Association," 30–31.

64. Chekhov, *Narodnoe obrazovanie,* 125.

65. Vladimir, *Uchitelia i uchitel'nitsy zemskikh shkol,* 35–36.

66. Seregny, "Professionalism and Political Activism," 657; Seregny, "Professional Activism and Association," 12.

67. Blinov, "Narodnyi uchitel'," 72.

68. Petrov, *Voprosy narodnogo obrazovaniia* 2:36–37.

69. Bratchikov, "Uchebno-vospitatel'naia," no. 2, 127.

70. Iaroslavl', *Nachal'noe obrazovanie,* 280–291; Bratchikov, "Uchebno-vospitatel'naia," no. 2, 129; Evteev, *Trudy pervogo vserossiiskogo s"ezda* 1:666–667. See also Vladimir, *Uchitelia i uchitel'nitsy zemskikh shkol,* 33–36.

71. Cited in Evteev, *Trudy pervogo vserossiiskogo s"ezda* 1:688.

72. Petrov, *Voprosy narodnogo obrazovaniia* 2:4–7.

73. Seregny, "Professionalism and Political Activism," 726–727. On teachers' allegiance to the Socialist Revolutionaries, see Eklof,

"Spreading the Word," 239–248; also Erman, *Intelligentsiia,* 314; Stites, *Women's Liberation Movement,* 271; and Richard H. Eiter, "Organizational Growth and Revolutionary Tactics: Unity and Discord in the Socialist Revolutionary Party, 1901–1907" (Ph.D. diss., University of Pittsburgh, 1978). (I am grateful to John Bushnell for this last reference.)

74. Seregny, "Professionalism and Political Activism," 192.

75. Evteev, *Trudy pervogo vserossiiskogo s"ezda* 1:266. In the same work (1:385–390 and 2:1127), the author complains that the activist teacher was being replaced by the drillmaster. Petrov, in his study of Moscow (*Voprosy narodnogo obrazovaniia*), came to the same conclusion, as did many activist teachers from the seventies and eighties, writing of the late eighties and nineties. See also Seregny, "Professionalism and Political Activism," 247.

76. Seregny, "Professionalism and Political Activism," 680–690.

CHAPTER 9

1. Craig, "Expansion of Education," 168.

2. Bratchikov, "Uchebno-vospitatel'naia," no. 1, 115.

3. Maynes, "Work or School?" 115–134.

4. Field, *Rebels,* 4.

5. Works by N. A. Korf include *Nashe shkol'noe delo* (Moscow, 1873); *Russkaia nachal'naia shkola. Rukovodstvo dlia zemskikh glasnykh i uchitelei sel'skoi shkoly* (St. Petersburg, 1870), a volume that went through twenty-four editions; and *Nashi pedagogicheskie voprosy* (Moscow, 1882). M. Sukhomlinov's observations are found in "Zametki ob uchilishchakh i narodnom obrazovanii v Iaroslavskoi gubernii," *ZhMNP* 117, sec. 3 (January 1863): 103–189; and "Uchilishcha i narodnoe obrazovanie v Chernigovskoi gubernii," *ZhMNP* 121, sec. 3 (January 1864): 1–94. V. Zolotov's comments are recorded in "Izsledovanie krest'ianskoi gramotnosti po derevniam preimushchestvenno Tverskoi gubernii i chastiiu Moskovskoi," *ZhMNP* 118, sec. 3 (April 1863): 400–444; 120, sec. 3 (October 1863): 156–197. Many of the local zemstvo histories of education published at the end of the century included chapters on the 1860s and 1870s, providing accounts drawn from district-level reports and investigations.

6. Sukhomlinov, "Uchilishcha i narodnoe obrazovanie," 74.

7. N. F. Bunakov, "Ocherk narodnogo obrazovaniia v Vologodskoi gubernii," *ZhMNP* 122, sec. 3 (April 1864): 127.

8. Sukhomlinov, "Zametki ob uchilishchakh," 172.

9. Sukhomlinov, "Uchilishcha i narodnoe obrazovanie," 74.

10. N. P. Malinovskii, "Rol' krest'ian v rasprostranenii narodnogo obra- zovaniia v sviazi s osvobozhdeniem ikh ot krepostnoi zavisimosti," *Russkaia shkola* 22, no. 2 (1911): 65.

11. Ibid., 66–67.

12. Chernigov study cited in Sukhomlinov, "Uchilishcha i narodnoe obrazovanie," 75; Zolotov, "Izsledovanie krest'ianskoi gramotnosti," 409–410; Sukhomlinov, "Uchilishcha i narodnoe obrazovanie," 77.

13. Herbert Moore Phillips, *Literacy and Development* (New York, 1970), 15.

14. Zolotov, "Izsledovanie krest'ianskoi gramotnosti," 410; Sukhomli- nov, "Uchilishcha i narodnoe obrazovanie," 75.

15. Korf, *Russkaia nachal'naia shkola,* 37.

16. Sukhomlinov, "Uchilishcha i narodnoe obrazovanie," 76.

17. Zolotov, "Izsledovanie krest'ianskoi gramotnosti," 408; Sukhomli- nov, "Uchilishcha i narodnoe obrazovanie," 61, 76; Sukhomlinov, "Zametki ob uchilishchakh," 175.

18. Malinovskii, "Rol' krest'ian," 67.

19. Many accounts related that peasants continued to equate school at- tendance with *barshchina* or with conscription; schooling was seen as a substitute. See, for example, Vologda, *Nachal'noe obrazovanie* 2:9.

20. Malinovskii, "Rol' krest'ian," 67.

21. Bunakov, "Ocherk narodnogo obrazovaniia," 109; Malinovskii, "Rol' krest'ian," 67, 73; Sukhomlinov, "Zametki ob uchilishchakh," 174.

22. TsGIAL, f. 733, op. 202, d. 255, 133; Miropol'skii, *Inspektsiia narod- nykh shkol,* 157.

23. Cited in Miropol'skii, *Inspektsiia narodnykh shkol,* 170.

24. Korf, *Russkaia nachal'naia shkola,* 4–5.

25. Malinovskii, "Rol' krest'ian," 67. The zemstvo surveys of provincial education are full of descriptions of incidents following the hiring of an incompetent teacher. See also Chapter 8.

26. Malinovskii, "Rol' krest'ian," 69.

27. Korf, *Russkaia nachal'naia shkola,* 4–5.

28. Malinovskii, "Rol' krest'ian," 67.

29. Sukhomlinov, "Uchilishcha i narodnoe obrazovanie," 74.

30. Zolotov, "Izsledovanie krest'ianskoi gramotnosti," 404–409.

31. Sukhomlinov, "Zametki ob uchilishchakh," 150.

32. Patrick J. Harrigan, *Mobility, Elites, and Education in French Society of the Second Empire* (Waterloo, Ontario, 1980), 87–88. See also Graff, *The Literacy Myth*, 1–21, 225–233.

33. Teodor Shanin, in *The Awkward Class,* argues that the generational struggle must be considered as significant a source of tension in the countryside as intervillage conflicts, the rural-urban split, and class differences in the village (157, 168–169, 175–177). For evidence of the generational struggle, see Semënov, *Dvadtsat' piat let v derevne;* and P. I. Kushner, *The Village of Viriatino,* trans. Sula Benet (New York, 1970). Reginald Zelnick summarizes the fascinating biographies of two peasants-turned-workers in his article "Russian Rebels: An Introduction to the Memoirs of Semen Kanatchikov and Matvei Fischer," *Russian Review* 35, no. 3 (July 1976): 249–289; no. 4 (October 1976): 417–447.

34. Andrei Gartvig, "Soznana-li naseleniem potrebnost' vo vseobshchem obuchenii?" *Russkaia shkola* 6, no. 4 (1895): 135.

35. Ibid., 134.

36. Weber, *Peasants into Frenchmen,* 325–326.

37. Gartvig, "Soznana-li naseleniem," 136.

38. D. M. Bobylev, *Kakaia shkola nuzhna derevne* (Perm', 1908), 40. Similar studies were repeated, with identical results, in many other provinces. See, for example, Petrov, *Voprosy narodnogo obrazovaniia,* vol. 3.

39. S. A. Rachinskii, *Sel'skaia shkola,* 6th ed. (St. Petersburg, 1910), 56–57; cited in Demkov, *Nachal'naia narodnaia shkola,* 120–131.

40. N. F. Bunakov, *Sel'skaia shkola i narodnaia zhizn'* (St. Petersburg, 1901), 12.

41. Korf, *Russkaia nachal'naia shkola,* 56.

42. Rachinskii, *Sel'skaia shkola,* 57.

43. Gartvig, "Soznana-li naseleniem," 145–147.

44. Ibid.

45. Petrov, *Voprosy narodnogo obrazovaniia* 3:2–15.

46. I. K. Ozerov, *Na bor'bu s narodnoi t'moi* (Berlin, n.d.), contains a large number of Russian proverbs expressing the fear that illiteracy placed the individual in danger of being cheated and outwitted by outsiders as well as by fellow villagers. Bunakov's observation is found in *Sel'skaia shkola,* 12. See Bobylev, *Kakaia shkola nuzhna derevne,* 40, for a summary and a table arguing that peasant motivations were diverse. This table is also reproduced in Ben Eklof, "Schooling and

Literacy in Imperial Russia," in Resnick, *Literacy in Historical Development,* 116.

47. See Eklof, "Spreading the Word," 209–211, 335–336; as well as Petrov, *Voprosy narodnogo obrazovaniia* 3:3–15, from which these statements are culled.

48. *Anketa,* 98–102.

49. Ibid.

50. E. A. Zviagintsev, *Narodnaia zhizn' i sel'skaia shkola* (Moscow, 1912), 2:20.

51. Bunakov, *Sel'skaia shkola,* 33–34. This emphasis on composing letters is fully understandable, Bunakov continued, for "the demand for written communications in peasant life is growing and growing with every passing year." Bunakov mentions in particular universal military service, seasonal farm labor, and *otkhod* (migratory labor) in general—all of which separated individuals from their native villages. "He who leaves does not want to cut ties with his native fields and home folk, nor do those who remain behind want him to disappear without a trace. This is where the growing demand for correspondence originates. Just a few years ago, the only person able to carry out such correspondence . . . was the local sexton; for him, such correspondence was an item of profit—but for the peasants, it was a burdensome expenditure."

52. Samarin cited in Belokonskii, "Narodnoe obrazovanie," no. 2, 132. The practice of levying separate fees for reading and for writing was noticed by many observers.

53. N. N. Iordanskii, "Teoriia i deistvitel'nost' v oblasti vseobshchago obucheniia," *Russkaia shkola* 22, no. 1 (1911): 86–87.

54. Sukhomlinov, "Zametki ob uchilishchakh," 159.

55. V. P. Vakhterov, "Zaprosy naroda i nasha nachal'naia shkola," in *Obshchee delo: Sbornik statei po voprosam rasprostraneniia obrazovaniia sredi vzroslogo naseleniia,* ed. V. Kostramina (Moscow, 1900–1912), 2:14–16.

56. Ibid.

57. Bobylev, *Kakaia shkola nuzhna derevne,* 82–87. I am currently working on a manuscript that will include a lengthy discussion of Baranov's basal reader and other textbooks in use in the Church and zemstvo schools. For the 1897 Model Program, see Appendix A.

58. Iordanskii, "Teoriia i deistvitel'nost'," no. 1, 91.

59. A. A. Krasev, "Chto daët krest'ianam nachal'naia narodnaia shkola?" *Russkaia mysl'* 8, no. 2 (1887): 116–117. To be sure, Krasev con-

tinued, with time "the relatively rapid rate of progress in their studies, the entertaining books with pictures used by children, . . . the almost unfailing kindness of teachers in dealing with children, . . . and, finally, the warm feelings held for the school by the children themselves have already produced quite a strong impression on the peasants and have significantly shaken their former, not entirely benevolent, view of the school."

60. TsGIAL (1870), f. 733, op. 203, d. 200, 145 (St. Petersburg school district).

61. Orlov, *Narodnoe obrazovanie,* 202.

62. Jeffrey Brooks, "Readers and Reading at the End of the Tsarist Era," in *Literature and Society in Imperial Russia, 1800–1914,* ed. William M. Todd III (Stanford, Calif., 1978), 132. See also Zolotov, "Izsledovanie krest'ianskoi gramotnosti," 404–407.

63. Orlov, *Narodnoe obrazovanie,* 143, 144–147.

64. Ibid., 202.

65. Ibid., 176.

66. TsGIAL, f. 803, op. 10, d. 695 (Moscow province).

67. TsGIAL, f. 803, op. 10, d. 470 (Kazan').

68. Bunakov, *Sel'skaia shkola, 7.* On the persistence of *dvoeverie,* see Orlov's comments in his work *Narodnoe obrazovanie,* 205–206. For a cautionary note on the prevailing belief that peasant societies are everywhere dominated by such dual faith, see Emmanuel LeRoy Ladurie, *Montaillou,* trans. B. Bray (New York, 1978), 288–305.

69. Bunakov, *Sel'skaia shkola,* 70.

70. Devel', "Krest'ianskie vol'nye shkoly."

71. Shakhovskii quoted in ibid., no. 4, 108.

72. Devel', "Krest'ianskie vol'nye shkoly," no. 4, 100; no. 5, 135–138, 143–147.

73. Gartvig, "Soznana-li naseleniem," 147.

74. Dm. G., "Devochka v narodnoi shkole," *Russkaia shkola* 22, no. 1 (1911): 63. Also see Eklof, "Spreading the Word," 211.

75. Petrov, *Voprosy narodnogo obrazovaniia* 1:147; I. P. Bogolepov, *Gramotnost' sredi detei shkol'nogo vozrasta v Moskovskom i Mozhaiskom uezdakh* (Moscow, 1894), 100–103.

76. Gartvig, "Soznana-li naseleniem," 147. See also the discussion in Chapters 10–12.

77. Petrov, *Voprosy narodnogo obrazovaniia* 3:10–11.

78. Bogolepov, *Gramotnost' sredi detei,* 67–68.

79. Petrov, *Voprosy narodnogo obrazovaniia* 3:9.

80. Bogolepov, *Gramotnost' sredi detei,* 69; Gartvig, "Soznana-li naseleniem," 162.

81. Vladimir, *Sbornik statisticheskikh* 3:82.

82. Ibid., 88.

83. Weber, *Peasants into Frenchmen,* 325–326.

84. Gartvig, "Soznana-li naseleniem," 147.

85. Stone, "Literacy and Education in England," 120. Also see West, *Education and the Industrial Revolution,* 32.

86. The most influential statement of the viewpoint that schools should prepare pupils for "life in general" was found in N. F. Bunakov, *Shkol'noe delo,* 3d ed. (St. Petersburg, 1906), 6–14. See also Hans, *History of Russian Educational Policy,* 97–101.

CHAPTER 10

1. Cipolla, *Literacy and Development,* 32.

2. The terms are from Kaestle and Vinovskis, *Education and Social Change in Massachusetts,* 4, 11. The authors write: "If we wish to assess the 'impact' or 'influence' of schooling, we need to know more about daily attendance rates, the length of the school year, the average number of years attended per child, the distribution of schooling patterns by social groups, . . . but the first task is to determine how many people were going to school."

3. *Svodka svedenii,* sec. 8, 11–12. See also Hans, *History of Russian Educational Policy,* 213–214; Chekhov, *Narodnoe obrazovanie,* 219; Iordanskii, "Usloviia osushchestvleniia"; and Kapterev, *Novye dvizheniia,* 45–57.

4. Charnoluskii, "Voprosy narodnogo obrazovaniia," no. 9, 71.

5. Kapterev, *Novye dvizheniia,* 45–57. The 1911 School Census estimated the number of school-age children to be 14.8 million (MNP, *Odnodnevnaia perepis'* 16:104). According to Chekhov (*Narodnoe obrazovanie,* 146), most statisticians used an annual population increase figure of .0149 for their calculations.

6. See Ososkov, *Voprosy istorii* 1:48; Frank Lorimer, *The Population of the Soviet Union: History and Prospects* (Geneva, 1946), 37; *Narodnaia entsiklopediia* 10:87.

7. Kulomzin, *Dostupnost' nachal'noi shkoly,* 25. The figure of 5,619 villages is from V. I. Kovalevskii, ed., *Proizvoditel'nye sily Rossii* (St.

Petersburg, 1896), 49. See *Svodka svedenii,* sec. 8, 14–18, for other technical difficulties in drawing up network plans. Also see Stratanov, *Tekushchie voprosy,* 56; the excellent article by E. P. Kovalevskii, "Usloviia dostizheniia vseobshchago obrazovaniia," in *Doklady,* vol. 3 of *Trudy pervogo obshchezemskogo s''ezda po narodnomu obrazovaniiu* (Moscow, 1912), 604–623; N. V. Chekhov, "Mery i uchrezhdeniia, oblegchaiushchie naseleniiu pol'zovanie shkolami," in *Narodnoe obrazovanie v zemstvakh: Osnovy organizatsii i praktiki dela. Sbornik statei,* ed. E. A. Zviagintsev et al. (Moscow, 1914), 372–375; N. Kazimirov, "Peresmotr shkol'nykh setei," in Zviagintsev et al., *Narodnoe obrazovanie v zemstvakh,* 360–372; Chekhov, *Narodnoe obrazovanie,* 199–200; and Charnoluskii, "Voprosy narodnogo obrazovaniia," no. 11, 103.

8. Kulomzin, *Dostupnost' nachal'noi shkoly,* 47. The Soviet claim that it would have taken two hundred years to achieve universal literacy is based on calculations made *before* 1908 (the year of the School Bill's passage) and offered in a 1906 article in *Vestnik vospitaniia,* cited in L. M. Zak et al., *Stroitel'stvo sotsializma v SSSR: Istoriograficheskii ocherk* (Moscow, 1971), 171. See also Chekhov, *Narodnoe obrazovanie,* 146.

9. According to the compilers of the 1856 study, however, rural schools made up only one-fourth of all primary schools. After 1856, the number of rural schools as a percentage of the total rapidly increased, and by 1878 they made up no fewer than twenty thousand of the twenty-five thousand primary schools on the books.

10. West, *Education and the Industrial Revolution,* 8–30.

11. MNP, *Odnodnevnaia perepis'* 16:2–12, 68–70; U.S. Education Office, *Annual Report of the Commissioner* (Washington, D.C., 1910), 2:1333–1341. For a complete table of enrollment figures, see Eklof, "Schooling and Literacy," 126.

12. MNP, *Odnodnevnaia perepis'* 16:60. Information on enrollment and ages when children left school in the West can be found in Paul Monroe, ed., *A Cyclopedia of Education,* vols. 1–5 (New York, 1911–1913); see entries for individual countries. For length of school stay in England in 1870, see Nigel Middleton and Sophia Weitzman, *A Place for Everyone: A History of State Education from the End of the Eighteenth Century to the 1970's* (London, 1976), 76. According to Edward R. Tannenbaum, "the overwhelming majority of pupils in Europe's public elementary schools finished their formal education by age eleven" (*1900: The Generation Before the Great War* [New York, 1976], 32).

13. MNP, *Odnodnevnaia perepis'* 16:110. The 24 percent figure is used by Rashin in his often-cited work on literacy and education in tsarist Russia, yet the Soviet historian does not use the eight-to-eleven age group nor does he point out the discrepancy between the school-age base and the actual length of the school program ("Gramotnost'," 28–40).

14. West, *Education and the Industrial Revolution,* 19.

15. Kulomzin, *Dostupnost' nachal'noi shkoly,* 19. See also the discussion in Bogolepov, *Gramotnost' sredi detei,* 30–43.

16. For enrollment figures by province, see MNP, *Odnodnevnaia perepis'* 16:2, 22–23, 104–107, 140. For 1915 figures, see Chekhini, "Nachal'noe narodnoe obrazovanie," 123–149, and i–vi (appendix). Lenin wrote that "the rural population has virtually no access to learning"; see Kumanëv, *Revoliutsiia i prosveshchenie mass,* 55. Richard Altick is cited in West, *Education and the Industrial Revolution,* 42.

17. A flow chart describing precise enrollments would have to include (separately for each sex) an allowance for the imbalance caused by the annual expansion of the system, which swelled the first grade in comparison to the others; a precise reckoning of length of stay in the schools; the incidence of repeating; the proportion of children over and under the proper school age who were enrolled in the schools; and some estimate of multiple entries (through repeated dropping out and transfer).

18. See Bogolepov, *Gramotnost' sredi detei,* 22–42.

19. Darlington, *Education in Russia,* 310.

20. MNP, *Odnodnevnaia perepis'* 16:115, table 57. The famous Church educator Rachinskii saw precisely the connection between overnight stays and socialization; he is cited in Chekhov, *Narodnoe obrazovanie,* 98. In a forthcoming manuscript I discuss the practice of providing overnight lodging and its impact on schooling. (Official figures, based on space available rather than actual usage, understated the frequency of overnight stays by pupils.)

21. It is also possible to argue that the commonly established correlation between density of population or urbanization, on the one hand, and receptivity to schooling (or level of literacy), on the other, confuses cause and effect—or rather, that it *phrases as an issue of demand what is really a matter of supply.* This is what Iaroslavl' statisticians had to say:

> The denser the population, the more pupils a given locality can yield, and, therefore, the cheaper the cost of schooling (i.e., the unit cost); the denser the population, the less the distance to a school; the more convenient, all other considerations being equal, to use the school.

When a significant population density is achieved, schools will be so crowded that it will be necessary to invite another teacher and this in its turn . . . will favorably affect the course of instruction. On the other hand, with sparse population, and particularly with small settlement size, the ordinary school radius will be incapable of yielding a sufficient school-age contingent. In such cases the provision of a sufficient number of schools is linked with formidable outlays, for the unit costs of educating each pupil will be that much greater. Moreover, in the case of schools opened in sparsely settled areas, the distance from home to school will be that much greater and, all other considerations being equal, the same quantity of population will be less eager to make use of the school (further reducing the school-age contingent enrolling)(Iaroslavl', *Nachal'noe obrazovanie*, 74).

For Russian settlement patterns, see Y. Taniuchi, "Note on the Territorial Relationship Between Rural Societies, Settlements, and Communes," Center for Russian and East European Studies, Discussion Papers Series RC/D, no. 3 (Birmingham, England, 1966); and Basil Kerblay, *L'Isba d'hier et d'aujourd 'hui* (Lausanne, 1973).

22. Phillips, *Basic Education*, 30.

23. For information on staggered enrollments, see *Svodka svedenii*, sec. 1, 65–69; Kapterev, *Novye dvizheniia*, 90; and Belokonskii, *Narodnoe nachal'noe obrazovanie*, 139.

24. Compare the information presented in this chapter with the following observation on popular demand in the less developed world today: "The popular demand of the mass of parents for primary education for their children is urgent and unabated. It is quite common to see parents waiting in numbers in front of schools and educational offices with their children, hoping to obtain enrollment, even when there are no places; and they are often prepared to make considerable sacrifices" (Phillips, *Basic Education*, 73).

25. Vladimir, *Sbornik statisticheskikh* 3:39; Farmakovskii, "Nachal'naia shkola MNP," no. 7, 195; Fal'bork cited in Viatka, *Issledovaniie* 1:52–53; I. P. Bogolepov, "K voprosu o sostavlenii proektov normal'noi seti uchilishch," in Shakhovskii, *Vseobshchee obrazovanie*, 33.

26. Vladimir, *Sbornik statisticheskikh* 3:121–122; Belokonskii, "Narodnoe obrazovanie v Moskovskoi gubernii," no. 2, 139, and no. 3, 164.

27. (Moscow), "Obzor narodnogo obrazovaniia," in *Statisticheskii ezhegodnik Moskovskoi gubernii za 1914* (Moscow, 1915), 207; Tavrida, *Sbornik po shkol'noi statistike* 1:34.

28. MNP, *Odnodnevnaia perepis'* 16:59, 69, table 20.

29. The extremely high level of denied admissions in Poland was probably the result of 1906 language liberalization measures. After that

date, a flood of repressed demand, which had been languishing since the 1880s, was released into the school system.

30. Almost exactly two-thirds of all children rejected were boys, but it is impossible to determine whether this figure reflected a preferential admission policy or the differentiated nature of demand among the population.

31. MNP, *Odnodnevnaia perepis'* 16:2–3.

32. F. Ol'denburg, *Narodnye shkoly evropeiskoi Rossii v 1892–1893: Statisticheskii ocherk* (St. Petersburg, 1896), 28; Iaroslavl', *Nachal'noe obrazovanie*, 46; Tavrida, *Sbornik po shkol'noi statistike* 1:46.

33. Iaroslavl', *Nachal'noe obrazovanie*, 8–9. In each of the categories described here, the total adds up to less than 100 percent because of unexplained cases in which two teachers taught two groups each in a three-year school or three sections each in a four-year school, and so forth.

34. MNP, *Odnodnevnaia perepis'* 16:48–49, 53, 58–59; *Svodka svedenii*, sec. 1, 14.

35. Iaroslavl', *Nachal'noe obrazovanie*, 9; Tavrida, *Sbornik po shkol'noi statistike* 1:46.

36. West, *Education and the Industrial Revolution*, 34; Middleton and Weitzman, *A Place for Everyone*, 75. For Ontario, see Graff, *The Literacy Myth*, 274, 275–277. See also Monroe, *Cyclopedia of Education* 3:75.

37. Cipolla, *Literacy and Development*, 32. But see Phillips, *Basic Education*, 40, for ratios in the developing world.

38. In contrast, see Phillips's discussion of the UNESCO experience in literacy campaigns. He argues that ages six to ten are the vital period for the development of logical abilities, attitudes toward new knowledge, and curiosity about the outside world, and he declares that intake *must* begin by age six (*Basic Education*, 40ff.).

39. For studies of individual provinces, see Iaroslavl', *Nachal'noe obrazovanie*, 114–115; Viatka, *Issledovaniie* 1:50, 53–55 (in Viatka at the turn of the century, a *majority* of schoolgirls aged fourteen and fifteen were in the first grade); Vladimir, *Sbornik statisticheskikh* 3:97–98; MNP, *Odnodnevnaia perepis'* 16:104, table 45.

   See also Kaestle and Vinovskis, *Education and Social Change in Massachusetts*, 28, 63–64, 69–70; West, *Education and the Industrial Revolution*, 19, 28; Phillips, *Basic Education*, 5, 156.

   On Russian views, and particularly on Ushinskii, see K. El'nitskii, *Shkol'noe obuchenie*, 2d ed. (Petrograd, 1914), 87–90; Chekhov, *Tipy russkoi shkoly*, 96–111; Korf, *Russkaia nachal'naia shkola*, 10.

40. Darlington, *Education in Russia,* 322–333; Miropol'skii, *Inspektsiia narodnykh shkol,* 144.

41. Korf, *Russkaia nachal'naia shkola,* 36–37.

42. See Verigin, *V pomoshch,* 141; *Zakliuchitel'nyi tom,* vol. 12 of *Trudy pervogo obshchezemskogo s"ezda po narodnomu obrazovaniiu* (Moscow, 1912), 223–226.

43. P. A. Vikhliaev, *Ekonomicheskie usloviia narodnogo obrazovaniia v Moskovskoi gubernii* (Moscow, 1910), 14.

44. Pokrovskii, *Istoriia Rossii v XIX veke* 4:122–123.

45. Chekhov, *Narodnoe obrazovanie,* 145; MNP, *Odnodnevnaia perepis'* 16:22–23, 60, table 14, 104; *Svodka svedenii,* sec. 1, 17, table 7; Iaroslavl', *Kratkii obzor zemsko-shkol'nogo,* 6–7.

Curiously, in some areas the proportional enrollment of girls was higher in Church schools, whereas in other areas it was higher in zemstvo schools. For example, in Kursk in 1904–1905, 21 percent of the students in zemstvo schools and 33 percent in Church parish schools were girls. In Poltava (1906), the proportion was 17 percent in zemstvo schools and 41 percent in Church parish schools; in Tavrida (1904), the figures were 25 percent and 45 percent, respectively; and in Kherson (1904), 22 percent and 33 percent. Yet studies of all Church schools (1898) and all zemstvo schools (1903), conducted separately, showed little difference overall—22.9 percent of the students in Church schools and 23.5 percent in zemstvo schools were girls. It is interesting to speculate whether in some areas more deeply religious peasants preferred to send their girls to the Church (i.e., state) schools. This may have been true here and there, but a number of other forces were also tugging at gender enrollment statistics.

In Vladimir, for example, it was discovered that regardless of type of school, the size of the building seemed to determine the proportion of girls enrolled; the bigger the school, the higher percentage of girls were enrolled. Such a trivial observation led to a startling conclusion: low female enrollments simply reflected the deficient provision of schooling. When local districts were divided into five groups according to the availability of schools, those areas with greater access to schools also had a higher proportion of girls enrolled. This finding led to the conclusion that girls were indeed being turned away from the schools until there was adequate space for boys.

But in other provinces, as Bratchikov discovered, the higher proportion of girls in Church schools was a result of the strategy of Church authorities; in many large villages that already boasted a zemstvo school, the Church opened a second primary school exclusively for girls. This practice seemed to be especially widespread in the Crimea. Elsewhere, notably in Voronezh, correspondents reported that the peasants believed the zemstvo schools provided a better education and, apparently by community agreement, sent their boys to these schools while relying on the less solid Church schools for the overflow of girls. These local observations do not mesh well with data collected in the 1911 School Census for all schools, in which the number of rejections was just as high for Church as for zemstvo schools, and the proportion of girls among all rejected was approximately the same as the proportion of girls in the school population as a whole. The only observation that seems to hold is that as the provision of education increased, so did the proportional representation of girls. (See Bratchikov, "Uchebno-vospitatel'naia," no. 1, 99, for a compilation of local studies. See also Vladimir, *Sbornik statisticheskikh* 3:82.)

46. Rashin, "Gramotnost'," 69.
47. See MNP, *Odnodnevnaia perepis'* 16:66, table 18, 105–108, table 48.
48. Ibid., 103–105.

CHAPTER 11

1. E. P. Thompson, "Time, Work-Discipline, and Industrial Capitalism," *Past and Present,* no. 38 (1967): 56–97.
2. Theodore W. Schultz, *The Economic Value of Education* (New York, 1963), 30.
3. West, *Education and the Industrial Revolution,* 31, 32–34. See also Maynes, "Work or School?" 119–120; Stone, "Literacy and Education in England," 115.
4. David Tyack, "Ways of Seeing: An Essay on the History of Compulsory Schooling," *Harvard Educational Review* 46 (August 1976): 381.
5. Chekhov, *Tipy russkoi shkoly,* 81–83.
6. Petrov, *Voprosy narodnogo obrazovaniia* 1:139–141; Iaroslavl', *Nachal'noe obrazovanie,* 196–199; Vladimir, *Sbornik statisticheskikh* 3: 205–207; Viatka, *Issledovaniie* 1:120–123.

   In all three provinces, the majority of schools opened their doors in September or early October (in Iaroslavl', for example, of the 42 percent of schools opening in October, 40 percent did so in the first ten days of the month) and closed their doors in very late April or in May. (In Iaroslavl', of the 35 percent closing in April, five out of seven closed in the last ten days of the month.) There were exceptions, most notably in Vladimir where 7 percent of Church schools closed in March. Based on this information, local statisticians calculated the length of the school year. In Iaroslavl', the school year lasted 147 days for rural zemstvo schools and 134 for Church parish schools; in Vladimir, it lasted 163 days (the average for all schools); and in Moscow, it ran to over 150 days. To be sure, the average concealed a remarkable variety, ranging from 51 to 201 days in Viatka, from "under 115" to 190 in Iaroslavl', and from "under 100" to 201 and more in Vladimir. But it is readily apparent from the tables in the statistical yearbooks that the largest cluster of schools fell within the range of 126 to 160 days.

7. Iaroslavl', *Nachal'noe obrazovanie*, 197–200.

8. MNP, *Odnodnevnaia perepis'* 16:69, table 20.

9. Both citations are from V. V. Akimov, "Postanovka uchebnogo dela v zemskikh shkolakh," *ZhMNP*, n.s. 63, sec. 3 (May 1916): 55. See also *Svodka svedenii*, sec. 1A, 34–41.

10. Chekhov, *Tipy russkoi shkoly*, 83. Zemstvo studies commonly noted that children arrived in shifts.

11. *Svodka svedenii*, sec. 1A, 34–41.

12. Moscow, "Obzor narodnogo obrazovaniia" (1913), 233–235. See also Iaroslavl', *Nachal'noe obrazovanie*, 197–199.

13. Petrov, *Voprosy narodnogo obrazovaniia* 1:142.

14. Moscow, "Obzor narodnogo obrazovaniia" (1913), 232–236.

15. In the Moscow study, 915 schools were closed for village holidays, each for an average of three days. It should be noted that although only 3 percent of schools had closings for village holidays in 1893, 16 percent had them in 1914. A partial explanation of this significant discrepancy is that the earlier study counted only closings of more than three days, and the latter counted all closings. In Iaroslavl', a study of school holidays showed that in addition to the week given at Easter, 82 percent of all zemstvo and Church schools closed for local holidays, although for an average of only four days a year (Iaroslavl', *Nachal'noe obrazovanie*, 201).

16. But see (Vladimir) *Tekushchaia zemskaia shkol'naia statistika po Vladimirskoi gubernii za 1910–1911 uchebnyi god* (Vladimir, 1912), 104–107. In Vladimir, schools missed, on the average, seven days. On teacher mortality levels, see P. M. Shestakov, "Narodnye uchitelia i uchitel'nitsy," in *Zhurnal komiteta gramotnosti* (Moskovskogo) (Moscow, 1894), 87–89; Tula, *Nachal'noe narodnoe obrazovanie*, 53; and Salomatin, *Kak zhivët*, 51–57. An especially vivid description of contagious diseases among teachers is given by S. V. Anikin in Evteev,

Trudy pervogo vserossiiskogo s"ezda 1:258—Anikin notes that "no doctor ever risks his family's life as the teacher does daily!" A gripping description of health conditions in Russian schools can be found in Andrei Shingarev's article, "Osnovania," esp. 100–102. Compare this with the descriptions of school sanitary conditions in the West found in Weber, *Peasants into Frenchmen,* 303–304; Cipolla, *Literacy and Development,* 36–37; and, especially, Middleton and Weitzman, *A Place for Everyone,* 75–76.

17. Tyack, "Ways of Seeing," 360; Chekhov, *Tipy russkoi shkoly,* 82; Kaestle and Vinovskis, *Education and Social Change in Massachusetts,* 24, 81. Chekhov notes that although the official U.S. school year lasted 153 days, average yearly attendance amounted to only 112 days for enrolled children.

18. Bowles and Gintis, *Schooling in Capitalist America,* 152–153. Bowles and Gintis, basing their estimates on U.S. census returns, speak of the school year in terms of actual attendance rather than calendar dates for opening and closing; nevertheless, the comparison still holds—although the Russian school year was generally shorter, attendance was far more regular, perhaps for that very reason.

Also compare a school year of 210 days in England in the mid-nineteenth century (West, *Education and the Industrial Revolution,* 87) and years of 275 to 300 days in Germany and England by the end of the same century (Chekhov, *Tipy russkoi shkoly,* 76–91).

19. Craig, "Expansion of Education," 171–173. Iaroslavl' statisticians concluded that the economy could be blamed for 83 percent of all abbreviated years, the weather for 5 percent, and internal school conditions for 12 percent. Yet they noted:

> One naturally concludes, if we correlate [references to economic reasons with type of school as well as district of origin], that in addition to economic causes the routine [*praktika*] of a given school has an enormous impact on the length of the school year and that to a significant extent the economy is unjustly blamed.
>
> In the first place, if the economy primarily determined the length of the school year, one would expect to find fewer references to economic problems in those districts where the school year was the longest. In fact, we find just the opposite to be true. For example, in Rostov district, where the school year is longest, economic reasons were blamed for 93 percent of all school closings. . . . In Poshekhonsk district, where the school year is most abbreviated, the economy was blamed in only 69 percent of all incidents. [The proportion of schools reporting in each district was approximately the same.] Thus, in Rostov [district], despite references to poverty, work at home and in the fields, and so forth, the school year lasted 163 days!

The absence of a strict correlation between length of school year and economic *byt* stands out in even sharper relief if we keep in mind that although economic conditions are rather homogeneous within the boundaries of each district, the length of the school year is different in zemstvo and Church schools . . . and longer in two-class than in one-class schools under the same authority (by as much as twenty-five days). . . . So, although conditions of *byt* impose limits on the length of the school year, . . . these limits are very elastic in response to internal school conditions. . . . *References to the economy, always brought up to justify the brevity of the school year, are most often mere conventions and very often conceal the truth that by no means has the primary school everywhere taught the population to observe and respect school routines or to look on schooling as important,* in deference to which it is sometimes necessary to make minor sacrifices at home [*radi kotoroi nuzhno prenebrech' inogda melochnymi khoziaistvennymi udobstvami*]" [emphasis added] (Iaroslavl', *Nachal'noe obrazovanie*, 198–199).

20. Petrov, *Voprosy narodnogo obrazovaniia* 1:144. See also Iaroslavl', *Nachal'noe obrazovanie*, 213; and Obshchezemskii s"ezd po statistike narodnogo obrazovaniia, *Polozhenie statistiki nachal'nogo narodnogo obrazovaniia v gubernskikh zemstvakh* (Khar'kov, 1913), 1–105, for information on how attendance statistics were compiled. (The latter work was edited by I. M. Bogdanov and republished in Khar'kov in 1913 as a separate volume entitled *Obzor izdanii gubernskikh zemstv po statistike narodnogo obrazovaniia.*) For a cautionary note, see Malinovskii, "Nekotorye vyvody," 72.

21. Tyack, "Ways of Seeing," 360; Horn, *Education in Rural England,* 123–124, 139–140, 266–267; Graff, *The Literacy Myth,* 266–267, 273–277. See also West, *Education and the Industrial Revolution,* 87; Middleton and Weitzman, *A Place for Everyone,* 76; P. W. Musgrave, *Society and Education in England Since 1800* (London, 1968), 40.

22. Korf, *Russkaia nachal'naia shkola,* 30.

23. Orlov, *Narodnoe obrazovanie,* 116–132.

24. For lower attendance figures, see the study by Devel' of zemstvo and free peasant literacy schools in Tver' ("Krest'ianskie vol'nye shkoly," no. 5, 139–141); the author adds, however, that in general peasant children attended *vol'nye* schools with great regularity. See also Vladimir, *Sbornik statisticheskikh* 3:294–295, tables 10 and 11, for figures comparable to those of Moscow. An excellent study of Kherson province shows much higher levels of absenteeism (N. Borisov, *K voprosu o vliianii zaniatiia na narodnoe obrazovanie* [Aleksandriia, 1899], esp. ix–xvi).

25. Petrov, *Voprosy narodnogo obrazovaniia* 2:145.

26. MNP, *Odnodnevnaia perepis'* 16:65, table 18.

27. Also see Kapterev, *Novye dvizheniia,* 145–146; Vladimir, *Sbornik statisticheskikh* 3:123–125, 339–340, tables 29 and 30.

28. Bogolepov, *Gramotnost' sredi detei,* 1–174; Strannoliubskii, "Sostoianie narodnogo obrazovaniia," 161–196. Bogolepov's study is examined here in Chapter 12.

29. N. N. Iordanskii observed that many parents sent their children to school to relieve overcrowding at home ("Uchitel' i naselenie derevni," APN [ca. 1914], f. 20, op. 1, d. 30, 2–3).

30. On the idea that there is a "natural cycle" to schooling, see Phillips, *Basic Education,* 55–56, 165–166.

31. Bratchikov, "Uchebno-vospitatel'naia," no. 1, 103–104.

32. Iaroslavl', *Nachal'noe obrazovanie,* 18–19. This pattern seems to confirm what many educators observed: teachers did not allow a pupil to take examinations until they were confident the student would be successful. A high incidence of failure on examinations, rather than a high dropout rate, jeopardized a teacher's reputation with the school authorities. See also *Svodka svedenii,* sec. 1, 21–22, 27; Tavrida, *Sbornik po shkol'noi statistike* 1:29.

33. Figures for the seventies and eighties are culled from Fal'bork and Charnoluskii, *Narodnoe obrazovanie,* 182–183; Kaganovich, "Ocherk istorii shkol'noi," 19–25; Ol'denburg, *Narodnye shkoly,* 1–15. For Moscow data, see Belokonskii, "Narodnoe obrazovanie v Moskovskoi gubernii," no. 2, 138–141.

34. Fal'bork and Charnoluskii, *Narodnoe obrazovanie,* 206; Bratchikov, "Uchebno-vospitatel'naia," no. 1, 103–104; Iaroslavl', *Nachal'noe obrazovanie,* 21.

35. I call attention to the word *effectiveness* because, like *wastage,* it assumes that the success of the school system could best be measured by determining the proportion of enrolled students who graduated.

36. For a comparison of the success rates of boys and girls, see *Svodka svedenii,* sec. 1, 17, 19, 24; Iaroslavl', *Kratkii obzor zemsko-shkol'nogo,* 7–9.

37. Vladimir, *Sbornik statisticheskikh* 3:110–112; Iaroslavl', *Nachal'noe obrazovanie,* 96. Kulomzin estimated that it took most graduates an average of four years to complete the program (*Dostupnost' nachal'noi shkoly,* 16). See also Tavrida, *Sbornik po shkol'noi statistike* 1:29; Orlov, *Narodnoe obrazovanie,* 112–117.

38. *Svodka svedenii,* sec. 1A, 26–27. A number of other provinces produced studies of how long graduates remained in school in the

countryside; taken together, these studies suggest that organizational or pedagogical aspects of schooling in some areas forced many children who were determined to complete the entire program to remain longer than ordinarily required. It is hard to conceive of economic or ethnic factors that would have affected Kherson, Poltava, Saratov, and St. Petersburg provinces alike to produce lengthier stays in village schools for graduates than were found in other provinces. One might suspect that some provinces included only zemstvo schools, and others both zemstvo and Church. Yet in this case the zemstvo schools would have had the lengthiest average stay; the data for zemstvo schools only in St. Petersburg seem to confirm this suspicion. It is puzzling that in provinces where the flow of pupils through the system seemed to be proceeding in otherwise similar ways, a sharp difference existed in the length of time it took graduates to make it through the schools. (See Bratchikov, "Uchebno-vospitatel'naia," no. 1, 106; and Inkeles, "The School as a Context for Modernization," 21–22.)

39. Iaroslavl', *Nachal'noe obrazovanie,* 94–96. See also Viatka, *Issledovaniie* 1:90; and Bratchikov, "Uchebno-vospitatel'naia," no. 1, 107–109, for a study of Murom district (Vladimir). In this study, the average stay for all pupils, both graduates and dropouts, was given as follows: 13 percent of boys and 36 percent of girls stayed one year; 14 percent of boys and 34 percent of girls stayed two years; 31 percent of boys and 19 percent of girls for three years, and 39 percent of boys and only 1 percent of girls stayed four or more years. (Length of stay for the remainder of the students was listed as unknown.)

40. Vladimir, *Sbornik statisticheskikh* 3:110–112.

41. Ibid., 112.

42. Bratchikov, "Uchebno-vospitatel'naia," no. 1, 109; but see also Viatka, *Issledovaniie* 1:89–90, 107–109. Based on returns from fifteen thousand village schools under the MNP in the thirty-four zemstvo provinces, Kovalevskii, editor of an article on education for a volume put together for the 1896 Nizhnii Novgorod Fair, arrived at the following estimates: Almost four-fifths of all enrolled pupils were in the first and second years, 11.7 percent were in the second and third years, and 2.1 percent were in their fourth year (the rest were not accounted for). Almost the same relationship prevailed in the town schools. Thus, three-fourths of enrolled children in elementary schools in Russia studied no longer than two years, and only one-tenth extended their education to or through a third year (Kovalevskii, *Proizvoditel'nye sily Rossii,* 49). (From these data, one might infer that 25 percent entered the third year but only 10 percent completed it.)

43. *Svodka svedenii*, sec. 1A, 28.

44. Ibid., 29. The survey does not explain why only 34 pupils dropped out from the first grade with four years of study, while 1,241 dropped out of the same grade with five or more years. Surprisingly, the same anomaly existed in four-year schools, where 17 pupils dropped out of the first grade with four years of study, and 404 dropped out with five years.

45. Ibid., 29–31.

46. Vladimir, *Sbornik statisticheskikh* 3 : 113.

47. Ibid., 117; Iaroslavskoe gubernskoe zemstvo, *Svedeniia o nachal'nykh uchilishchakh Iaroslavskoi gubernii i ob okonchivshikh v nikh kurs za 1899–1900 uchebnyi god* (Moscow, 1901), 29. See also Tavrida, *Sbornik po shkol'noi statistike* 1 : 29; Viatka, *Issledovaniie* 1 : 113–114.

48. Bratchikov, "Uchebno-vospitatel'naia," no. 1, 109; P. Kazantsev, "Dvizhenie uchashchikhsia nachal'noi shkoly po otdeleniiam," *Russkaia shkola* 23, no. 1 (1912): 150 (for Dmitrov district, Moscow province).

49. Vladimir, *Sbornik statisticheskikh* 3 : 98–101, 104 (data collected on thirty-nine thousand boys and thirteen thousand girls in all but seventy-seven schools in the district); Iaroslavl', *Nachal'noe obrazovanie*, 88–92.

     From these studies, investigators learned that the Vladimir zemstvo schools were much more rigorous in their demands than the Iaroslavl' schools, that Church schools in both provinces tended to promote children more rapidly than zemstvo schools did, and that girls in both provinces (but particularly in Iaroslavl') were more likely than boys to proceed on schedule. However, while suggesting that organizational differences from province to province could affect the flow of pupils through the system and pointing to more lenient treatment of girls (who did not have to take the certifying examinations), the figures were muddied by other complications. For example, an accurate measurement of the difficulties encountered in moving from grade to grade would have to account for attrition—the proportion of discouraged pupils who dropped out when not promoted. In other words, the higher proportion of boys who stayed back in the third grade could have been as much a measure of persistence and determination as of "wastage" (i.e., interrupted passage). See also MNP, *Odnodnevnaia perepis'* 16 : 114–115, tables 55 and 56.

50. *Svodka svedenii*, sec. 1, 30–31. By 1911, four-year schools accounted for one-quarter of all zemstvo schools and commonly employed at

least two teachers, thus increasing teachers' *contact* time with individual grade groups from one-third to one-half or more of all classroom hours. In such schools, the distribution of repeaters more closely matched the distribution of pupils by grade. Again, a bulge of repeaters was found in the second grade, but it was slightly less prominent. Overall, the incidence of repeating in four-year schools was lower—by 3 percent—than in three-year schools. The proportion of those reaching the fourth grade who had to repeat that year before leaving school was slightly lower than in the three-year schools.

Why was the gap so slight? As the share of *three-year* schools with two teachers increased, the amount of contact time each pupil had in such schools would have been greater than in four-year schools with two teachers, and the difference in contact time for each student in the two types of schools would have been gradually lessened. But, although the growing trend was to employ two teachers in three-year schools, this was not yet prevailing practice, and the narrow gap in the frequence of repeating cannot be explained solely by such developments. Either contact time in both types of schools was inadequate to keep up with the demands of the school program, or other causes were at work somewhat equally in both three- and four-year schools. The question remains: if the three-year program was too rushed, as teachers complained, why didn't a fourth year significantly reduce the rate of repeating?

51. Iaroslavl', *Svedeniia*, 36.

52. Kazantsev, "Dvizhenie uchashchikhsia," 153–158.

53. *Anketa*, 80–91; Redfield, *The Primitive World*, 50–51.

54. *Anketa*, 81–82.

55. The comment on health is not flippant; it is quite possible that malnutrition severely impaired the learning abilities of many village youth. For recent research on the impact of nutrition on the brain, see Richard W. Restak, *The Brain: The Last Frontier* (New York, 1979), esp. 128. Zemstvo studies demonstrated that between 10 and 40 percent of all schoolchildren were poorly fed, even in years with successful harvests, and that between 15 and 35 percent of all schoolchildren were ill. See the unsigned article "Shkol'nye zavtraki," in *Prakticheskaia shkol'naia entsiklopediia: Nastol'naia kniga dlia narodnykh uchitelei i drugikh blizhaishikh deiatelei v oblasti narodnogo obrazovaniia,* ed. N. V. Tulupov and P. M. Shestakov (Moscow, 1912), 346–363.

56. See *Anketa*, 80–94, for data on individual provinces and regions.

CHAPTER 12

1. This chapter makes no claim to exhausting a very complex topic. For a recent study of the relationship between literacy and the work force in factories, see Olga Crisp, "Labor and Industrialization in Russia," in *The Cambridge Economic History of Europe* (Cambridge, England, 1978), 7: part 2, 308–415.

2. V. Iu. Skalon, "Narodnaia shkola pod Moskvoi," *Vestnik evropy* 2, no. 3 (1883): 122.

3. Borisov is cited in Kumanëv, *Revoliutsiia i prosveshchenie mass*, 44–48. See also Charnoluskii, *Zemstvo i narodnoe obrazovanie* 2:337; N. Bychkov, "Gramotnost' sel'skogo naseleniia," *Iuridicheskii vestnik* 1 (July-August 1890): 309–332; Voronov, *Materialy po narodnomu obrazovaniiu*, 21–25, 112–146.

4. Bogolepov, *Gramotnost' sredi detei*, 4–20.

5. Ibid., 100–102, 111. For estimates of the cost of food, clothes, and lodging, see also Chekhov, "Mery i uchrezhdeniia," 387.

6. Bogolepov, *Gramotnost' sredi detei*, 21, 67–69.

7. Vikhliaev, *Ekonomicheskie usloviia*, 92–93.

8. Vladimir, *Sbornik statisticheskikh* 4:27–30 (appendix).

9. Iordanskii, "Teoriia i deistvitel'nost'," no. 1, 76–92; no. 2, 25–37.

10. Ibid., no. 1, 77–78.

11. Ibid., 79–84; G., "Devochka v narodnoi shkole," 64–65.

12. Vikhliaev, *Ekonomicheskie usloviia*, 68–69.

13. Chekhov, "Mery i uchrezhdeniia," 388.

14. Vladimir, *Sbornik statisticheskikh* 4:27–30.

15. Iordanskii, "Teoriia i deistvitel'nost'," no. 1, 86; Vladimir, *Sbornik statisticheskikh* 4:29.

16. Vikhliaev, *Ekonomicheskie usloviia*, 56–64.

17. Ibid., 59, 62–64.

18. Ibid., 63.

19. Ibid., 64.

20. *Anketa*, 96.

21. "School organization" was noted as an obstacle by 21.6 percent of the teachers; in four out of five such instances, this response meant frequent repetition of grades. One in five teachers complained of a lack of striving among children, or "other specificities" pertaining to the child (ibid., 96–103).

22. I. M. Koz'minykh-Lanin, *Gramotnost' i zarabotki fabrichno-zavodskikh rabochikh Moskovskoi gubernii. Materialy po statistike Moskovskoi gubernii,* no. 4 (Moscow, 1912), ix (introduction by P. A. Vikhliaev).

23. It is true that when workers were separated by type of employment and by sex a slightly different picture emerged. In the machine-building factories at the turn of the century, the most common age of entry had shifted from the eleven-to-fifteen age range to the range between fifteen and seventeen; by the decade of 1898 to 1908, only 6 percent of new workers entered the factories before the age of fifteen. But in the textile industry, between 20 and 25 percent of new entries during the same interval were between twelve and fifteen years old. Moreover, it was quite clear that at an earlier date textile factories *had* cut into school enrollments. In the 1880s, 16 percent of female and 24 percent of male workers entering the work force had been under twelve years old, and during the 1870s the figure had been even higher: 32 percent of female workers and 42 percent of males (ibid., xi).

    See also S. N. Antonova, *Vliianie stolypinskoi reformy na izmenenie v sostave rabochego klassa* (Moscow, 1951).

24. N. Kablukov, ed., *Moskovskaia guberniia po mestnomu obsledovaniiu, 1898–1900* (Moscow, 1905–1908), 4: part 2, 641–643.

25. Ibid., 65–70, 344, 346, 449–490.

26. The school-age population is estimated by calculating 9 percent of a population of 2,436,000 (A. G. Rashin, *Naselenie Rossii za 100 let [1811–1913]* [Moscow, 1956], 44, table 19).

27. To be sure, the 1898 Moscow household survey also looked at the numbers of all children of both sexes who were engaged in industry (whether cottage industry or factories), and the results seemed to indicate a high incidence of female child labor in the textile districts (Kablukov, *Moskovskaia guberniia* 4: part 2, 49–50).

    In Bronitsy and Moscow, 24 percent and 18 percent of girls under thirteen years of age, or virtually one in four, were employed. Nevertheless, the same study, which made a careful distinction between work in the same village and work away (*otkhozhie*), showed that only one in every twenty-four employed girls was working outside her native village (that is, one in ninety-six children). Most important, of the 22.7 percent of all girls under thirteen listed as employed in their own villages, only a small fraction were engaged year-round. For boys, the percentage was insignificant: only one of every one hundred school-age boys was employed full-time in a province (or districts) dominated by the textile industry or other handicrafts. Similarly, among girls, between one and three of every one hundred faced full-time employment. Of course, by "part-time" the survey may have meant "seasonal." Thus interpreted, cottage industries could have presented serious obstacles to schooling for as many as one in five girls. When these studies are juxtaposed with the data on the age structure of the active work force, however, the two sets of information strongly indicate that school and *kustar'* (cottage) industry and school and factory were seldom in conflict.

28. P. A. Vikhliaev, *Vliianie travoseianiia na otdel'nye storony krest'ianskogo khoziaistva* (Moscow, 1915), 9:10–17.

29. West, *Education and the Industrial Revolution*, 35; Schultz, *Economic Value of Education*, 30; Stone, "Literacy and Education in England," 116; Maynes, "Work or School?" 115–134; Horn, *Education in Rural England*, 136.

    See also Anita Baker, "Deterioration or Development? The Peasant Economy of Moscow Province Prior to 1914," *Russian History* 5, no. 1 (1978): 1–23; and Cipolla, *Literacy and Development*, 70.

30. Kushner, *The Village of Viriatino*, 122. See also Ososkov, *Ocherki* 2:117–131.

31. Tyack, "Ways of Seeing," 381; Kaestle and Vinovskis, *Education and Social Change in Massachusetts*, 86.

32. Kaestle and Vinovskis, *Education and Social Change in Massachusetts*, 98.

33. A. G. Rashin, *Formirovanie rabochego klassa Rossii* (Moscow, 1958), 290.

34. Ibid., 292.

35. See, for example, Vladimir, *Sbornik statisticheskikh* 3:203; in that province, tending stock outdoors began in May and ended in the fall.

36. Baker, "Deterioration or Development?" 12. See Robert Eugene Johnson, *Peasant and Proletarian: The Working Class of Moscow in the Late Nineteenth Century* (New Brunswick, N.J., 1979), for a detailed study of the Moscow labor force.

37. Vikhliaev, *Vliianie travosenianiia* 9:26–34, esp. 33.

38. A. M. Anfimov, *Krest'ianskoe khoziaistvo evropeiskoi Rossii, 1881–1904* (Moscow, 1980), 24. Hans Rogger notes that the surplus of rural laborers may have risen to 32 million by 1913 (*Russia in the Age of Modernization and Revolution* [New York, 1983], 127).

39. Aleksandr V. Chaianov, *The Theory of Peasant Economy*, ed. and trans. Daniel Thorner, R. E. F. Smith, and Basil Kerblay (Homewood, Ill., 1966), 74, 79.

40. Ibid., 59.
41. Eklof, "Spreading the Word," 205–206, 328; Vikhliaev, *Ekono-micheskie usloviia,* 22–23.
42. Several of the least industrialized provinces were also the most backward in outlays for education. If these provinces—Pskov, Chernigov, and Penza—are eliminated from the averages shown in Table 43, there is virtually no difference between the most and least industrialized provinces in length of stay. Indeed, the one item that did seem to affect length of stay was provincial allocation of money for education. The average outlay per capita for the five highest provinces was 130.8 kopecks; the average for the five lowest provinces was 43.4 kopecks. In provinces with the highest outlays, the number of male students in the third grade equaled 54 percent of first grade enrollment, and female students equaled 32 percent. Corresponding figures for provinces with lower outlays were 40 percent for boys and 21 percent for girls.
43. Bratchikov, "Uchebno-vospitatel'naia," no. 1, 109.

CHAPTER 13

1. Jeanne S. Chall, *Learning to Read: The Great Debate* (New York, 1967); Thomas Wolf, "Reading Reconsidered," *Harvard Educational Review* 47 (August 1977): 411–429.
2. Alex Inkeles and David Smith, *Becoming Modern* (Cambridge, Mass., 1974). See also Lerner, *The Passing of Traditional Society,* 43–75; and Peter Stearns, *The Face of Europe* (St. Louis, 1977), 198.
3. It can be argued that explanatory reading was important not only in the direct development of abstract skills but also because of the new and potentially disruptive content provided.

> When comparing school learning to informal learning, anthropologists and psychologists most commonly emphasize differences in content. . . . In some subject matter the information dispensed by the school contradicts commonly accepted knowledge and beliefs. The history curriculum obliterates the oral tradition and replaces it with "world history" whose people and events were previously undreamed of in the child's culture. The subject called geography transforms the child's known physical universe into an unfamiliar one whose properties are not derived from the senses. These changes in overlapping content areas have been epitomized in the saying that in school "science lays common sense to rest." In addition, school introduces new subjects, such as grammar, mathematics, and the sciences, which may have no cultural counterparts at all. Not only the

content, but the basic organizing concepts of these fields of knowledge may conflict with the traditional culture's way of understanding and interpreting the world (Scribner and Cole, "Cognitive Consequences," 556).

4. See Chall, *Learning to Read,* 307, where the author distinguishes between "code emphasis" and "meaning emphasis."

5. Miropol'skii, *Inspektsiia narodnykh shkol,* 159.

6. Korf, *Nashi pedagogicheskie voprosy,* 144–209, esp. 167. This work summarizes a large number of early investigations.

7. Cited in S. A. An'skii [S. A. Rappoport], *Narod i kniga: Opyt kharakteristiki narodnogo chitatelia.* Appendix to *Narod i voina* (Moscow, 1913), 34–35.

8. Ibid.

9. Ibid.

10. TsGIAL (1872), f. 733, op. 202, d. 255, 171 (Kazan' education district).

11. Ibid.

12. TsGIAL (1880–1881), f. 1291, op. 1, d. 139, 1234 (*reviziia* of Saratov province). See also TsGIAL (1875), f. 733, op. 202, d. 166, 154 (Moscow education district).

13. See Zviagintsev, *Narodnaia zhizn',* vol. 1, for a summary of some of these tests. Soviet dissertations also commonly include rather detailed analyses of test results; for example, Tsebrovskii, "Nachal'noe obrazovanie," 307–340; and Petrov, "Zemskaia nachal'naia shkola," 186–206, 286–319, 395–422, 452–472, 499–515. See also the school board reports of Iordanskii for Makar'evsk district, Nizhegorod province, in Rymakov, "Iordanskii," 100–101, 115. See *Vestnik Pskovskogo zemstva,* no. 7, 1896, for test results for those who had graduated between 1871 and 1889; and the *reviziia* of Saratov and Samara provinces conducted by Senator Shamsin, for similar reports (TsGIAL [1882], f. 733, op. 171, d. 440). For a comparable study of the school instruction of French peasants, see Maynes, "Work or School?" 125.

14. Krasev, "Chto daët." (Krasev later reconsidered this study in *Chto mogut i dolzhny davat' narodu nashi nachal'nye narodnye shkoly* [St. Petersburg, 1906], esp. 4–14.)
   Of the 1,104 graduates who did not appear for the Simbirsk test, all but 176 had convincing reasons for not coming (death, military service, work away from the village), and in most cases, the occupa-

tions of former students suggest high retention. Thus, at most, 176 might have been too "ashamed" of regression to have shown up.

15. Bunakov, *Sel'skaia shkola*, 175–176, 184–185.

16. Zviagintsev, *Narodnaia zhizn'* 1:3–29.

17. Ibid., 4.

18. Ibid., 8.

19. Ibid., 14.

20. Krasev, "Chto daët," 67–70.

21. Bunakov, *Sel'skaia shkola*, 176.

22. Krasev, "Chto daët," 60.

23. Zviagintsev, *Narodnaia zhizn'* 1:18.

24. Krasev, "Chto daët," 60, 63–64, 68.

25. Bunakov, *Sel'skaia shkola*, 182.

26. Zviagintsev, *Narodnaia zhizn'* 1:17.

27. Ibid.

28. Ibid., 23.

29. Ibid., 24–25.

30. Ibid., 24. For a comparison, see the results of a 1911 study in *Anketa*, 73–75.

31. Zviagintsev, *Narodnaia zhizn'* 1:25.

32. *Anketa*, 61. See also comments by teachers and a lengthy discussion of retention of individual subjects in Vladimir, *Sbornik statisticheskikh* 3:223–231, 386–387 (table).

33. *Anketa*, 76.

34. *Doklady*, vol. 3 of *Trudy pervogo obshchezemskogo s"ezda po narodnomu obrazovaniiu*, 169–170.

35. Stratanov, *Tekushchie voprosy*, 110. See also the earlier discussion in Chapter 6, as well as the comments in Krasev, *Chto mogut*, 21–38.

36. *Anketa*, 73.

37. Ibid., 74.

38. Ibid.

39. *Doklady*, vol.3 of *Trudy pervogo obshchezemskogo s"ezda*, 171.

40. *Doklady*, vol. 4 of *Trudy pervogo obshchezemskogo s"ezda po narodnomu obrazovaniiu* (Moscow, 1912), 515–517.

41. Doklady, vol. 3 of *Trudy pervogo obshchezemskogo s"ezda*, 236–237. See also *Anketa*, 77–78; and A. Bulatov, "K voprosu o retsedive bezgramotnosti," *Russkaia shkola* 18, no. 6 (December 1907): 41, 45.

42. Weber, *Peasants into Frenchmen*, 337. But see Bunakov, *Sel'skaia shkola*, 195–197, for a more disillusioned view.

43. Bunakov, *Sel'skaia shkola*, 187.

44. Ibid.

45. Weber, *Peasants into Frenchmen*, 336.

46. On the Military Benefits Exam, see Chapter 5. For time spent on various subjects, see F. F. Korolëv, *Ocherki po istorii sovetskoi shkoly i pedagogiki, 1917–1920* (Moscow, 1958), 18.

47. For discussions of basic math books in use, see E. A. Zviagintsev, ed., *Voprosy i nuzhdy uchitel'stva* (Moscow, 1909–1911), 6:10–34, 9:61–80; also Demkov, *Nachal'naia narodnaia shkola*, 304–315.

48. Moskovskaia gubernskaia zemskaia uprava, Otdel khoziaistvennoi statistiki, *Formy krest'ianskogo zemlevladeniia*, vol. 4 of *Sbornik statisticheskikh svedenii* (Moscow, 1879), 25–29. See also the recent Soviet monograph by Prokof'eva, *Krest'ianskaia obshchina v Rossii*, on peasant life in the villages of the vast Sheremet'ev estates.

49. Resnick and Resnick, "Nature of Literacy," 374.

50. TsGIAL (1912), f. 803, op. 10, d. 1038, 10 (Samara).

51. Ibid., 14.

52. Given that the whole-word method (borrowed from the United States by zemstvo educators but now largely rejected as inappropriate for the phonetic Russian language) was used in zemstvo schools, it is conceivable that better results were achieved in parish than in zemstvo schools.

53. TsGIAL, f. 803, op. 10, d. 1038, 15.

54. TsGIAL (1911), f. 803, op. 10, d. 1037, 18.

55. TsGIAL (1913), f. 803, op. 10, d. 1038, 6ff. (Saratov).

56. Ibid.

57. Ibid.

58. Ibid.

59. TsGIAL (1911), f. 803, op. 10, d. 130, 2 (Vladimir).

60. Ibid.

61. Ibid.

62. Ibid.

63. Kulomzin, *Dostupnost' nachal'noi shkoly*, 16.

64. An'skii, *Narod i kniga*, 38.

65. Vladimir, *Sbornik statisticheskikh* 3:221–230, 386–387.

66. Bunakov, *Sel'skaia shkola*, 182.

67. Ibid., 33–34, 37, 183–190, 207. See also Phillips, *Basic Education,*
166, 208–220. In Kairov et al., *Pedagogicheskaia entsiklopediia* 3:166,
the unnamed author of an article on "literacy instruction" notes that
the time needed to "master reading" with phonics is between ten
weeks and four months.

    Parents often contracted with tutors to teach their children how to
read in one or two months (*Ocherk deiatel'nosti Rybinskogo zemstva
po narodnomu obrazovaniiu, 1865–1900* [supplement to the district
zemstvo school commission report] [Rybinsk, 1902], 6–8). In the archives, I often encountered inspectors' reports on mid-winter visits,
noting that first-year pupils were already reading "tolerably." See
also Iordanskii, "Istoriia narodnoi shkoly," 98.

    I have recently discovered a report from vol. 21 of *Sbornik Permskago
zemstva,* 1885 (cited in K. Verakso, "Razvitie nachal'nogo obrazovaniia na Urale" [Candidate diss., Nauchnyi issledovatel'skii institut
teorii i istorii pedagogiki, APN, RSFSR, Sverdlovsk, 1949], 247), of
a teacher who divided former pupils in her district into groups. One
group, pupils who had studied for only one year, could read "a bit"
several years later. Another group, former pupils who had studied
for two years, could "read well, but wrote poorly"—they tended to
retain reading skills but rapidly lose the ability to write. The third
group included graduates, all of whom knew some Russian history
and geography and could read, write, and count well.

68. Ol'denburg, *Narodnye shkoly,* 87–89. Ol'denburg also attempted to
measure regressive illiteracy by comparing school enrollment figures
with the number of literates recruited into the army several years
later. But the results fluctuated wildly from province to province—in
many areas, recruit literacy was much higher than school enrollment,
though in others it was far lower. Because it was impossible to control for "wild," or unschooled, literacy, on the one hand, or for
schools that existed only on paper, on the other, the results were not
significant.

    Ol'denburg also observed that it was impossible to generalize
about the quality of instruction in Church parish schools overall.
Much depended on the enthusiasm of the local priest, on the availability of state funding (which varied considerably from area to area),
and on the ethnic and religious composition of the local population.

69. Kulomzin, *Dostupnost' nachal'noi shkoly,* 15–16; TsGIAL, f. 733, op.
172, d. 430, 114. But Verakso, "Razvitie," 247, shows that in the
Urals, because few pupils graduated, teachers concentrated on the
middle grade to consolidate skills and left the third grade to independent study.

CHAPTER 14

1. Harrigan, *Mobility, Elites, and Education,* 120; Weber, *Peasants into Frenchmen,* 330. See also Stone, "Literacy and Education in England," 94–95: "The conversion of childhood, which is normally and naturally a time of play and random physical activity, into [a time] of sedentary book-learning must have important effects on the adult character, producing the self-discipline and punctuality needed for a modern society."

2. Tannenbaum, *1900,* 32–33.

3. Harrigan, *Mobility, Elites, and Education,* 118–121.

4. Miropol'skii, *Inspektsiia narodnykh shkol,* 157–158.

5. Krasev, "Chto daët," 56. See also the confessions of disillusionment by both Bunakov in *Sel'skaia shkola,* 203–208; and An'skii in *Narod i kniga,* 18.

6. *Doklady,* vol. 3 of *Trudy pervogo obshchezemskogo s"ezda,* 2. For further discussions of socialization and schooling, see other reports to the same 1911 Zemstvo Congress (*Trudy pervogo obshchezemskogo s"ezda*): vol. 1, *Postanovleniia* (Moscow, 1911), 16, 41–42, 163–177, 197–202, 215–235, 542–547; vol. 2, *Doklady* (Moscow, 1912), 74–79, 98–99, 206–217, 516, 524, 654–659, 747–751, 758–759.

7. TsGIAL, f. 803, op. 130, d. 10, 18 (Vladimir). See also TsGIAL, f. 803, op. 10, d. 1063, 125 (Saratov).

8. *Doklady,* vol. 3 of *Trudy pervogo obshchezemskogo s"ezda,* 165.

9. Ibid.

10. Johnson, *Peasant and Proletarian,* 193; Joseph Bradley, *Muzhik and Muscovite: Urbanization in Late Imperial Russia* (Berkeley and Los Angeles, 1985). See also the autobiographical account by S. T. Semënov, *Dvadtsat' piat' let v derevne.*

11. *Anketa,* 125.

12. Ibid., 138.

13. Ibid., 139, 144.

14. Ibid., 7, 144.

15. Ibid., 146.

16. Ibid., 147.

17. Ibid., 148–149.

18. Bobylev, *Kakaia shkola nuzhna derevne,* 48–53.

19. Ibid.

20. Ibid., 60–62.

21. *Anketa,* 155–156.
22. Ibid., 157–158.
23. Korf, *Nashi pedagogicheskie voprosy,* 139–140.
24. V. P. Vakhterov, "Obshcheobrazovatel'nye zadachi narodnoi shkoly," *Russkaia mysl'* 18, no. 11 (1897): 88.
25. Kulomzin, *Dostupnost' nachal'noi shkoly,* 6–10.
26. T. Balogh and P. P. Steeten, "The Planning of Education in Backward Countries," in *The Economics of Education: Selected Readings,* ed. Mark Blaug (Baltimore, Md., 1968), 2:389; Seymour M. Lipset and Reinhard Bendix, *Social Mobility in Industrial Society: A Study of Political Sociology* (Berkeley and Los Angeles, 1959), 11. For other sources, see Harrigan, *Mobility, Elites, and Education,* 4, note 8. The enormous flow of educated laborpower from the villages in the Soviet Union today has been repeatedly observed in the specialized literature.
27. Petrov, *Voprosy narodnogo obrazovaniia* 4:120.
28. TsGIAL, f. 823, op. 10, d. 1063, 20–23 (Saratov).
29. Ibid.
30. See, for example, Bunakov, *Sel'skaia shkola,* 35; *Svodka svedenii,* sec. 8, 15.
31. Bobylev, *Kakaia shkola nuzhna derevne,* 116.
32. Orlov, *Narodnoe obrazovanie,* 53–54.
33. Krasev, "Chto daët," 55.

CHAPTER 15

1. Stone, "Literacy and Education in England," 73.
2. Ibid.
3. On the Russian secondary school system during the period prior to 1900, see Darlington, *Education in Russia,* 346–428, 508–528; Ignatiev, Odinetz, and Novgorodtsev, *Russian Schools and Universities,* 28–56; Batyshev, *Ocherki istorii,* 12–140; and McClelland, *Autocrats and Academics,* 12–17, 40–49.
4. Petrov, *Voprosy narodnogo obrazovaniia* 4:108; *Svodka svedenii,* sec. 2, 5–6. Thus, if 30 percent of the enrolled school-age population in 1897 actually reached the third year, half of them (15 percent) actually entered the fourth year—and 5 percent graduated.
5. Petrov, *Voprosy narodnogo obrazovaniia* 4:115–121.
6. Ibid., 115.

7. Ibid.

8. Ibid., 118–119.

9. Ibid., 121.

10. Furet and Ozouf, "Three Centuries," 231. See also Balogh and Streeten, "Planning of Education," 389.

11. N. Kazimirov, "Otnoshenie naseleniia k shkolam povyshennogo tipa," in *Statisticheskii ezhegodnik Moskovskoi gubernii za 1911 god,* Moskovskaia gubernskaia zemskaia uprava, Otdel khoziaistvennoi statistiki (Moscow, 1912), 77–78.

12. Ibid. See also Charnoluskii, *Zemstvo i narodnoe obrazovanie* 1:117; as well as his *Voprosy narodnogo obrazovaniia na pervom obshchezemskom s"ezde* (St. Petersburg, 1911), 20 (Charnoluskii's *Russkaia shkola* article republished as a book).

Nevertheless, in Nizhnii Novgorod the compilers of a 1910 survey could find only three teachers who thought an extended program would draw more pupils. But the same survey noted that the provincial zemstvo executive board sometimes received petitions directly from the peasants requesting that advanced elementary schools be opened. Pupils who often remained four or five years in schools with three-year programs might also have represented a suppressed desire for more education; yet even these children generally returned to the home and farm after overextending their stay in the basic school (Iordanskii, "Teoriia i deistvitel'nost'," no. 2, 33–34).

13. Kazimirov, "Otnoshenie naseleniia," 77–84.

14. Ibid., 81.

15. Ibid., 77.

16. Ibid., 84.

17. *Anketa,* 220.

18. Kazimirov, "Otnoshenie naseleniia," 77.

19. *Anketa,* 169–183, esp. 170–174, tables 51–53. The percentage of teachers reporting popular satisfaction with schools fluctuated from 17 to 51 percent among the thirty-four provinces; the percentage reporting dissatisfaction ranged from 37 to 81 percent; and the proportion of those reporting indifference varied from 2 to 10 percent. Among those reporting dissatisfaction, a range of 54 to 93 percent called for expanded education, whereas 12 to 42 percent called for a more vocational curriculum.

See also Eklof, "Spreading the Word," 381; and *Svodka svedenii, Zakliuchitel'nyi tom,* "Narodnye shkoly povyshennogo tipa," 11.

20. *Anketa,* 172–174.

21. Ibid., 180.

22. *Svodka svedenii,* sec. 1, 10, 30, table 3.

23. TsGIAL (1913–1914), f. 803, op. 10, d. 63, 120 (Saratov); TsGIAL (1911), f. 803, op. 10, d. 130, 19 (Vladimir).

24. Sovet vserossiiskikh s"ezdov staroobriadtsev, *Voprosy narodnogo obrazovaniia sredi staroobriadtsev* (Moscow, 1909), 107–113.

25. *Anketa,* 115–120, esp. table 26.

26. *Svodka svedenii,* sec. 1, 26, 33, tables 12 and 16; MNP, *Odnodnevnaia perepis'* 16:104, table 46b.

27. Petrov, *Voprosy narodnogo obrazovaniia* 4:115. For other estimates of the costs of advanced schooling, see especially Bogolepov, *Gramotnost' sredi detei,* 69–70.

28. Kazimirov, "Otnoshenie naseleniia," 88.

29. *Anketa,* 116.

30. Ibid., 118.

31. Ibid., 119.

32. Bobylev, *Kakaia shkola nuzhna derevne,* 100.

33. *Anketa,* 119.

34. *Doklady,* vol. 3 of *Trudy pervogo obshchezemskogo s"ezda,* 44–45.

35. *Anketa,* 122.

36. Ibid., 123–124.

37. Ibid., 116, 121.

38. Ibid., 103–114.

39. Ibid., 182. The study compared *reports* of dissatisfaction and the *actual incidence* of continued education.

40. Ibid., 104–107, 114, tables 29 and 30.

41. Ibid., 114.

42. Malinovskii, "Nekotorye vyvody," 75–76. For the number of two-class schools, see MNP, *Odnodnevnaia perepis'* 16:9, table 6; and Chekhov, *Tipy russkoi shkoly,* 49.

43. For the most succinct description of enrollment requirements, see Tulupov and Shestakov, *Prakticheskaia shkol'naia entsiklopediia,* 424–428.
    For the curriculum of advanced primary and secondary schools, see S. A. Cherepanov, "Uchebnye plany obshcheobrazovatel'noi shkoly v dorevoliutsionnoi Rossii," *Izvestiia akademii pedogogicheskikh nauk RSFSR* 33 (1951): 190–209. The teacher Salomatin complained that it was easier for a "camel to pass through the eye of a needle" than for peasants to make their way into an advanced school (*Kak zhivët,* 80).

44. Tulupov and Shestakov, *Prakticheskaia shkol'naia entsiklopediia,* 426.
45. Ibid.
46. Ibid.
47. Ignatiev, Odinetz, and Novgorodtsev, *Russian Schools and Universities,* 6–7.
48. Interestingly, as many as one-fourth (26.5 percent) of the pupils enrolled in five-year schools were girls. Even more intriguing, of 235,138 pupils enrolled in the second class (fourth and fifth years) of two-class schools in 1915, 73,191, or 31 percent, were girls (MNP, *Odnodnevnaia perepis'* 16:9; Chekhov, *Tipy russkoi shkoly,* 49).
49. *Svodka svedenii,* sec. 2b, sec. 3, 3–31; *Anketa,* 111–121.
50. *Svodka svedenii,* sec. 2, 4–6.
51. Petrov, *Voprosy narodnogo obrazovaniia* 4:121.
52. Cited in ibid., 121.
53. *Svodka svedenii,* sec. 2, 4–6; Petrov, *Voprosy narodnogo obrazovaniia* 4:121.
54. *Svodka svedenii,* sec. 2, 9–10.
55. The contrast in successful completion rates between urban and rural schools may be somewhat overstated. Peasants and urban children mixed in the municipal schools; naturally, more peasants would "return home" to work after completing school. After all, how many urban children could return home to find work?
56. *Svodka svedenii,* sec. 2, 11.
57. Ibid.
58. *Svodka svedenii,* sec. 3, 12–14.
59. Ibid., 11.
60. Ibid., 13.
61. See, for example, Timasheff, *The Great Retreat;* and Walkin, *Rise of Democracy.*
62. Johnson, *Russia's Educational Heritage,* 196–197.
63. Rashin, "Gramotnost'," 75–78; Piskunov, *Ocherki istorii shkoly,* 550–551. For a discussion of access and distribution percentages, see Fritz K. Ringer, *Education and Society in Modern Europe* (Bloomington, Ind., 1979), 26.

    On this same issue, see also Arcadius Kahan, "Social Structure, Public Policy and the Development of Education and the Economy in Tsarist Russia," in Anderson and Bowman, *Education and Economic Development,* 363–375. The debate in Russian society over educational opportunity for the lower classes is discussed in Smirnov, "Narodnoe prosveshchenie," 291–298.

64. Johnson, *Russia's Educational Heritage,* 286, table 31. For an interesting comparison to my results, see Maynes, "Work or School?" 115–134, which traces the careers of successful peasants in the Midi. See also the brief discussion of the developing world in Phillips, *Basic Education,* 74.

65. François Furet and Jacques Ozouf, *Reading and Writing: Literacy in France from Calvin to Jules Ferry* (Cambridge, England, 1982), 322.

CONCLUSION

1. Darlington, *Education in Russia,* 303.

2. Redfield, *The Primitive World,* 34.

3. Boguslaw Galeski, *Basic Concepts of Rural Sociology,* trans. H. C. Stevens (Manchester, England, 1972), 44–45.

4. Confino, *Systèmes agraires et progrès agricole.*

5. Kenneth Lockridge, "Literacy in Early America, 1650–1800," in Graff, *Literacy and Social Development,* 200.

6. Graff, *The Literacy Myth,* 26.

7. G. V. Rimlinger, "Autocracy and the Factory Order in Early Russian Industrialization," *Journal of Economic History* 20, no. 1 (1960): 67–92.

8. Bushnell, "Peasants in Uniform," 565–576.

9. Johnson, *Peasant and Proletarian;* Shanin, *the Awkward Class.*

10. William Rosenburg, "The Zemstvo in 1917 and Its Fate under Bolshevik Rule," in Emmons and Vucinich, *The Zemstvo in Russia,* 383–422.

Bibliography

EXPLANATORY NOTE

Before writing on Russian peasant schools, I spent years investigating zemstvo history, as well as Russian rural society in general. When I turned to peasant schools as a sourcebook of peasant culture, I originally intended to include in this volume studies of textbooks, readers, school schedules, school buildings, peasant reading habits, Russian school science, and other topics. These have now been removed to a second, future volume concerning the process, rather than the dynamics, of schooling. In addition, I glibly hoped to include in this present work a description of schooling in the minority regions, from the Baltic to the Caucasus. I collected much data on that topic, only to realize that the subject was far too complex, demanded several languages not in my possession, and could not be subsumed under a general chapter on minority policy without a simultaneous "history from below," or study of popular pedagogy for each of the minority peoples.

In the bibliography that follows, I have excluded references to works in all of the fields mentioned above, except for a few classic studies or bibliographies that provide excellent summaries or handy references to basic sources. In particular, the reader is referred to the works by Veselovskii (*Istoriia zemstva*) and Zakharova for information on the zemstvo, to the work on minorities edited by Ul'ianov, and to the volumes by Lebedev, Anastas'ev (vol. 1), and Tulupov and Shestakov on the process of schooling in Russia. For concise descriptions of prerevolutionary school curricula and schedules, see the writings by Veselov, Cherepanov, and Eliseev; for laws, rulings, and other codifications, see Fal'bork and Charnoluskii (*Nastol'naia kniga*), Rubakin, Antsiferov, and Anastas'ev (vol. 1).

Studies of Russian education statistics are sprinkled throughout the bibliography; readers should especially note the 1957 Soviet work by Kaganovich, a handy—and surprisingly positive—assessment and description. For biographies of Russian educators, as well as editions of their collected works, see Dneprov's important and thorough bibliography and the recent Soviet multi-authored period histories of Russian education, which are listed here separately under the names of the various editors: Kuzin, Piskunov, and Shabaeva. For a bibliography of literacy studies in the West, see Graff's *Literacy in History*.

I have excluded most recent Western histories of the Russian bureaucracy and the zemstvo, but the reader will find numerous references to these topics in the text and notes, as well as in the works, listed here, by Pintner and Rowney, Whelan, Orlovsky, and Emmons and Vucinich.

The bibliography is organized into several sections. The first lists archival material, largely from the Central State Historical Archives in Leningrad, the holdings of the Ministry of Education (MNP) and the Holy Synod, and the holdings of the Archives of the Academy of Pedagogical Sciences in Moscow. Of great value were the yearly inspectors' reports contained in the archives of the Synod and the MNP, as well as the unpublished manuscripts written during the Soviet period by leading educators who had spent most of their working lives in the tsarist school systems or zemstvo bureaus.

In the second section of this bibliography, I have listed useful bibliographies of Russian education; I know of no other such compilation. The third section includes studies that focus on one province, or a district within a province. These are largely, but not exclusively, zemstvo studies. Works on individual provinces that were generated by zemstvo statistical boards but were edited or written by a single individual are listed alphabetically by author under the name of the province.

In the fourth section, I list other studies, in Russian, of Russian education. Particularly noteworthy is the multi-volume one-day census of schools in the Russian Empire, a census that was carried out on 18 January 1911 and published over the next five years. This survey (*Odnodnevnaia perepis'*, listed here under "Ministerstvo narodnogo prosveshcheniia" [MNP]) is a rich and still underutilized source. My research is indebted above all to the survey carried out by zemstvo statisticians in preparation for the 1911 All-Zemstvo Congress on Education and to the papers presented to that congress. This material is collected in twelve volumes in the

Trudy of the congress, listed below as *Trudy pervogo obshchezemskogo s"ezda po narodnomu obrazovaniiu*.

The final section of the bibliography lists works in Western languages on Russian education and on education and peasant society in areas other than the Russian Empire. Entries on Western education, literacy, and peasant society include only those works that have shaped the ideas underlying this volume.

A few abbreviations used frequently in the endnotes or text can be listed here. TsGIAL refers to the Central State Historical Archives in Leningrad; MNP stands for the Ministry of Education, and *ZhMNP* for the Journal of the Ministry of Education. APN is the Academy of Pedagogical Sciences and may refer to material found in the Academy Archives, to books published under its auspices, or to dissertations written under the Academy.

I. ARCHIVAL SOURCES

Arkhiv akademii pedagogicheskikh nauk SSSR (APN)
    fond 7, V. P. Vakhterov
    fond 18, Materialy gosudarstvennykh uchrezhdenii, obshchestvennykh organizatsii, i chastnykh lits—arkhivnaia kollektsiia
    fond 19, V. I. Charnoluskii
    fond 21, N. V. Chekhov
    fond 50, O. N. Smirnov
    Note especially the following works:
        Bratchikov, N. I. "Vospominaniia o rabote uchitelei v nachal'noi zemskoi shkole" (f. 18, op. 1, d. 209, 1946)
        Charnoluskii, V. I. "Narodnoe prosveshchenie v dorevoliutsionnoi Rossii" (f. 19, op. 1, d. 8, 1929?)
        Iordanskii, N. N. "Istoriia narodnoi shkoly" (f. 20, op. 1, d. 3, n.d.)
        Smirnov, O. N. "Narodnoe prosveshchenie i narodnyi uchitel' dorevoliutsionnoi Rossii" (f. 50, op. 1, d. 33, 1946)
Tsentral'nyi gosudarstvennyi istoricheskii arkhiv Leningrada (TsGIAL)
    fond 91, Sankt Peterburgskii kometit gramotnosti
    fond 231, Materialy dokladov 2-ogo s"ezda po tekhnicheskomu i professional'nomu obrazovaniiu (1895)
    fond 733, Department narodnogo prosveshcheniia
        opis 117, Otchet MNP (1870–1916)
        opis 120–123, Inspektorskii razriad
        opis 170–184, 227, Uchitel'skie seminarii i nachal'nye uchilishcha (1863–1917)

opis 185, Dela o nachal'nykh uchilishchakh, peredannykh iz Ministerstva gosudarstvennykh imushchestv

opis 186, Razriad po vseobshchemu obucheniiu

opis 187, Razriad po vseobshchemu obucheniiu (shkol'naia set')

opis 188, Materialy perepisi nachal'nykh shkol

opis 193–197, Razriad obshchikh del

opis 201, Sekretnoe deloproizvodstvo (1906–1917)

opis 233, Proekty shkol'nykh zdanii i smety na nikh

fond 803, Sviateishii sinod

opis 1, Uchilishchnyi sovet sinoda

opis 10, Otchety nabliudatelei i inspektorov (1893–1914)

fond 846, O vyrabotke programm dlia narodnykh shkol

fond 1152, Gosudarstvennyi sovet

opis 9–12, various

fond 1263, Materialy komiteta ministrov po narodnomu obrazovaniiu

opis 1, Zhurnal komiteta ministrov (1865–1891)

opis 2, Zhurnal komiteta ministrov (1891–1899)

Gosudarstvennyi arkhiv Iaroslavskoi oblasti

fond 33, Istoricheskaia spravochnaia biblioteka

fond 156, Direktsiia narodnykh uchilishch

fond 459, Popechitel' uchebnogo okruga

fond 485, Zemskaia uprava i zemskoe sobranie

fond 549, Direktsiia narodnykh uchilishch Iaroslavskoi gubernii

fond 553, Iaroslavskii gubernskii uchilishchnyi sovet

fond 1123, Iaroslavskii eparkhial'nyi uchilishchnyi sovet

Gosudarstvennyi arkhiv Vologodskoi oblasti

fond 438, Vedomosti o shkolakh poseshchennykh inspektorami narodnykh uchilishch Vologodskoi gubernii

fond 465, Vologodskii eparkhial'nyi uchilishchnyi sovet

Tsentral'nyi istoricheskii arkhiv goroda Moskva

fond 156, Moskovskii gubernskii uchilishchnyi sovet

fond 459, Otchety direktora i inspektorov i otchetnye zapiski

II. BIBLIOGRAPHIES OF RUSSIAN EDUCATION

Ablov, N. N. *Pedagogicheskaia periodicheskaia pechat', 1803–1916.* Moscow, 1937.

Alchevskaia, Kh. D. *Chto chitat' narodu: Kriticheskii ukazatel' knig dlia narodnogo i detskogo chteniia.* 3 vols. St. Petersburg and Moscow, 1884–1906.

Berkov, P. N. "Materialy dlia bibliografii literatury o russkikh narodnykh (lubochnykh) kartinkakh." In *Russkii fol'klor: Materialy i issledovaniia,* vol. 2, 353–362. Moscow and Leningrad, 1956.

Bogdanov, I. M. *Obzor izdanii gubernskikh zemstv po statistike narodnogo obrazovaniia.* Khar'kov, 1913.

Brickman, William W. "Selected Bibliography on the History of Education in Russia to 1917." *Paedagogica Historia* 14 (1974): 164–169.

Charnoluskii, V. I. "Bibliografiia narodnogo prosveshcheniia." In *Pedagogicheskaia entsiklopediia,* edited by A. G. Kalashnikov et al., vol. 2, 601–606. 2d ed. Moscow, 1928.

Dneprov, E. D. *Sovetskaia literatura po istorii shkoly i pedagogiki dorevoliutsionnoi Rossii: Bibliograficheskii ukazatel'.* Moscow, 1979.

Flerov, A. E. *Ukazatel' knig po voprosam vospitaniia i obucheniia: Kriticheskii obzor pedagogicheskoi literatury.* Vypusk 2. Moscow, 1906.

Imperatorskoe vol'noe ekonomicheskoe obshchestvo. *Sistematicheskii obzor russkoi narodno-uchebnoi literatury,* vol. 1. St. Petersburg, 1878.

————— —————. Supplement 1. St. Petersburg, 1882.

————— —————. 2d ed. St. Petersburg, 1895.

Kaganovich, I. Z. *Ocherk istorii razvitiia statistiki shkol'nogo obrazovaniia v SSSR.* Moscow, 1957.

Karavaev, V. F. *Bibliograficheskii obzor zemskoi statisticheskoi i otsenochnoi literatury, 1864–1903,* nos. 1 and 2. St. Petersburg, 1906, 1913.

Katalog pedagogicheskoi biblioteki po nachal'nomu obrazovaniiu. Prilozhenie: Ukazatel' statei pomeshchennykh v imeiushchikhsia v biblioteke pedagogicheskikh zhurnalov s 1900 po 1 sent. 1910. St. Petersburg, 1910.

—————. *Pervoe dopolnenie.* St. Petersburg, 1912.

Katalog-ukazatel' zemskoi literatury po narodnomu obrazovaniiu, sobrannyi k s"ezdu: Prilozhenie k zakliuchitel'nomu tomu. In *Trudy pervogo obshchezemskogo s"ezda po narodnomu obrazovaniiu.* Moscow, 1912.

Khrustaleva, V. A. "Obzor osnovnykh ukazatelei pedagogicheskoi literatury za period ot 1856–1917." *Sovetskaia pedagogika,* no. 2 (1939): 139–147.

Kufaev, M. N. "Bibliografiia russkikh pedagogicheskikh zhurnalov." In *Pedagogicheskaia entsiklopediia,* edited by A. G. Kalashnikov et al., vol. 1, 395–416. 2d ed. Moscow, 1927.

Kuzin, N. P., M. N. Kolmakova, and Z. I. Ravkin, eds. Bibliography in *Ocherki istorii shkoly i pedagogicheskoi mysli narodov SSSR, 1917–1941.* Moscow, 1981.

Mel'nikova, V. E., ed. *Narodnoe obrazovanie. Pedagogicheskie nauki: Annotirovannyi ukazatel' k otechestvennym bibliograficheskim posobiiam na russkom iazyke, opublikovannykh s serediny XIX po 1978 god.* Moscow, 1981.

Ol'denburg, F. F. Chap. 1 in *Narodnye shkoly evropeiskoi Rossii v 1892–1893 gody: Statisticheskii ocherk.* St. Petersburg, 1896.

Ostrogorskii, A. N. "Bibliograficheskii ukazatel' materialov po istorii russkoi shkoly." *Pedagogicheskii sbornik,* nos. 3, 7, 10 (1899); nos. 1, 3, 7, 9, 11 (1900); and nos. 1, 4, 6, 9 (1901).

Pedagogicheskaia bibliografiia. 3 vols. Moscow, 1967–1973.

Piskunov, A. I. *Sovetskaia istoriko-pedagogicheskaia literatura (1918–1957): Sistematicheskii ukazatel'.* Moscow, 1960.

————, ed. Bibliography in *Ocherki istorii shkoly i pedagogicheskoi mysli narodov SSSR: Vtoraia polovina XIX veka,* 563–584. Moscow, 1976.

Prugavin, A. S. *Zakony i spravochnye svedeniia po nachal'nomu narodnomu obrazovaniiu.* 2d ed. 4 vols. St. Petersburg, 1904.

Rubakin, N. A. *Sredi knig.* 3 vols. Moscow, 1913.

Samokhvalov, I. S. *Kratkii ukazatel' literatury po statistike narodnogo obrazovaniia v Rossii.* Moscow, 1920.

Seriia ukazatelei po otdel'nym voprosam. No. 1, *Narodnoe obrazovanie.* Moscow, 1916.

Shabaeva, M. F., ed. Bibliography in *Ocherki istorii shkoly i pedagogicheskoi mysli narodov SSSR: XVIII–pervaia polovina XIX vv.,* 565–586. Moscow, 1973.

Sologub, B., and V. Simonovskii. *Ukazatel' luchshikh, po otzyvam pechati, uchebnikov, nachal'nykh uchebnykh posobii i rukovodstv na russkom i ukrainskom iazykakh.* St. Petersburg, 1909.

Spisok izdanii zemskikh i gorodskikh samoupravlenii po narodnomu obrazovaniiu: k 1 ianv. 1912. St. Petersburg, 1914.

Ul'ianov, G. K. *Obzor literatury po voprosam kul'tury i prosveshcheniia narodov SSSR.* Moscow and Leningrad, 1930.

Veselovskii, B. B. "Sistematicheskii ukazatel' literatury po zemskim voprosam." In *Istoriia zemstva za sorok let,* vol. 1, 608–612; vol 4., 44–60. St. Petersburg, 1909, 1911.

Vikhliaev, P. A. *Kratkoe rukovodstvo po statistike narodnogo obrazovaniia.* Moscow, 1919.

Vologdin, V. P. "Zemskaia statistika narodnogo obrazovaniia." In *Iubileinyi zemskii sbornik,* edited by B. B. Veselovskii and Z. G. Frenkel', 399–411. St. Petersburg, 1914.

Zelenin, D. K. *Bibliograficheskii ukazatel' russkoi etnograficheskoi literatury, 1700–1910.* St. Petersburg, 1913.

Zinevich, N. A. "Bibliografiia pedagogicheskaia." In *Pedagogicheskaia entsiklopediia,* edited by I. A. Kairov et al., vol. 1, 211–221. Moscow, 1964.

III. PROVINCIAL STUDIES

Chernigov

Sukhomlinov, M. "Uchilishcha i narodnoe obrazovanie v Chernigovskoi gubernii." *ZhMNP* 121, sec. 3 (January 1864): 1–94.

Eniseisk

Zholudev, G. D. "Iz istorii narodnogo obrazovaniia v Krasnoiarskom krae (Eniseiskoi gubernii), 1861–1917." Candidate dissertation, Krasnoiarskii pedagogicheskii institut, Krasnoiarsk, 1959.

Iaroslavl'

Iaroslavskoe gubernskoe zemstvo. *Nachal'noe obrazovanie v Iaroslavskoi gubernii po svedeniiam za 1896–1897 uchebnyi god,* part 1. Moscow, 1902.

―――. *Svedeniia o nachal'nykh uchilishchakh Iaroslavskoi gubernii i ob okonchivshikh v nikh kurs za 1899–1900 uchebnyi god.* Moscow, 1901.

Shkol'naia komissiia Iaroslavskogo gubernskogo zemstva. *Kratkii obzor zemsko-skhol'nogo dela v Rossii (Po dannym Iaroslavskoi vystavki severnago kraia, 1903).* Iaroslavl', 1906.

Sukhomlinov, M. "Zametki ob uchilishchakh i narodnom obrazovanii v Iaroslavskoi gubernii." *ZhMNP* 117, sec. 3 (January 1863): 103–189.

Tsebrovskii, K. P. "Nachal'noe obrazovanie v Iaroslavskoi gubernii v poreformennyi period." Candidate dissertation, Moskovskii gosudarstvennyi pedagogicheskii institut, Moscow, 1955.

Uspenskii, K. P. *Tserkovnye shkoly Iaroslavskoi eparkhii za 25 let (1884–1909).* Iaroslavl', 1909.

Zhurnal Iaroslavskogo gubernskogo zemskogo sobraniia. Iaroslavl', 1868–1869.

Kaluga

Peshekhonov, A. *Kratkii obzor deiatel'nosti Kaluzhskogo gubernskogo zemstva po narodnomu obrazovaniiu.* Kaluga, 1898.

Kazan'

Narodnoe obrazovanie v Kazanskoi gubernii. Vol. 1, Voprosy vneshkol'nogo obrazovaniia. Kazan', 1905.

Kherson

Bulgakov, I. V. Narodnaia shkola po otzyvam naseleniia Aleksandriiskogo uezda Khersonskoi gubernii. Aleksandriia, 1910.

Istoricheskii ocherk deiatel'nosti Khersonskogo gubernskogo zemstva za 1866–1899. Vol. 3, Nachal'noe obrazovaniie. Kherson, 1906.

Kursk

Akimov, V. V. "Deiatel'nost' Kurskogo zemstva po narodnomu obrazovaniiu, 1865–1906." ZhMNP, n.s. 28, sec. 3 (July 1910): 1–36; n.s. 29, sec. 3 (October 1910): 113–154; n.s. 30, sec. 3 (November 1910): 1–44.

Belokonskii, I. P., ed. Narodnoe nachal'noe obrazovanie v Kurskoi gubernii. Kursk, 1897.

Blagoveshchenskii, N. D. Sbornik statisticheskikh svedenii po Kurskoi gubernii. Vol. 1, Krest'ianskaia gramotnost' i obrazovanie tsentral'nogo raiona Kurskoi gubernii. Kursk, 1885.

Panfilov, Ia. V. "Shkola Kurskoi gubernii nakanune i v pervye gody posle velikoi sotsialisticheskoi revoliutsii." Candidate dissertation, Nauchnyi istoricheskii institut teorii i istorii pedagogiki, APN, RSFSR, Moscow, 1955.

Tekushchaia shkol'naia statistika, za 1906–1907. Kursk, 1908.

Moscow

Akimov, V. V. "Zemskaia deiatel'nost' po narodnomu obrazovaniiu v Moskovskoi gubernii." ZhMNP, n.s. 7, sec. 3 (March 1907): 174–191; n.s. 8, sec. 3 (May 1907): 1–43.

Belokonskii, I. P. "Narodnoe obrazovanie v Moskovskoi gubernii." Russkaia shkola 2, nos. 2 and 3 (1891): 131–142, 151–165.

Bogolepov, I. P. Gramotnost' sredi detei shkol'nogo vozrasta v Moskovskom i Mozhaiskom uezdakh. Moscow, 1894.

———. "Statisticheskoe svedenie o gramotnosti krest'ianskogo naseleniia Moskovskoi gubernii, po podvornoi perepisi 1869 i 1883." In Statisticheskii ezhegodnik Moskovskoi gubernii za 1895, 1–27. Moscow, 1896.

Bogoslovskii, S. *Zemskii meditsinskii biudzhet Moskovskogo gubernskogo zemstva, 1883–1905.* Moscow, 1905.

Doklady Moskovkomu gubernskomu zemskomu sobraniiu. Moscow, 1864–1914.

Kablukov, N., ed. *Moskovskaia guberniia po mestnomu obsledovaniiu, 1898–1900.* 4 vols. Moscow, 1905–1908.

Kazimirov, N. *Krest'ianskie platezhi i zemskaia deiatel'nost' v Moskovskoi gubernii.* Moscow, 1906.

——————, ed. *Statisticheskii ohzor narodnogo obrazovaniia v Moskovskoi gubernii za 1911–1915.* 4 vols. Moscow, 1912–1916.

Klevezal, V. P. "K voprosu o vliianii shkol na fizicheskoe razvitie detei." In *Trudy desiatogo gubernskogo s''ezda vrachei Moskovskoi gubernii,* part 3, 18–27. Moscow, 1889.

Koz'minykh-Lanin, I. M. *Gramotnost' i zarabotki fabrichno-zavodskikh rabochikh Moskovskoi gubernii. Materialy po statistike Moskovskoi gubernii,* no. 4. Moscow, 1912.

Krandievskii, V. "O vvedenii obshchedostupnago nachal'nago obucheniia v Moskovskoi gubernii." *Russkaia mysl'* 17, no. 6 (1896): 92–103.

Moskovskaia gubernskaia zemskaia uprava, Otdel khoziaistvennoi statistiki. *Doklady Moskovskoi gubernskoi zemskoi komissii po narodnomu obrazovaniiu, 1867–1916.* 19 vols. Moscow, 1867–1916.

——————. *Doklady Moskovskoi gubernskoi zemskoi revizionnoi komissii, 1878–1915.* 47 vols. Moscow, 1878–1915.

——————. *Doklady Moskovskoi gubernskoi zemskoi upravy zemskomu sobraniiu, 1867–1916.* 76(?) vols. Moscow, 1867–1916. [Yearly reports on education normally designated no. 2; reports on agriculture listed as no. 4.]

——————. *Istoricheskii ocherk ekonomicheskikh meropriiatii Moskovskogo gubernskogo zemstva.* Moscow, 1895.

——————. *Izvestiia Moskovskoi gubernskoi zemskoi upravy, 1911–1917.* 7 vols. Moscow, 1911–1917.

——————. *Sbornik postanovlenii Moskovskogo gubernskogo zemskogo sobraniia s 1865 po 1897.* 5 vols. Moscow, 1899–1902.

——————. *Sbornik statisticheskikh svedenii po Moskovskoi gubernii.* Vols 4, 5, 7, and 9. Moscow, 1879–1899. *Also see* Orlov, *Narodnoe obrazovanie v Moskovskoi gubernii.*

——————. "Svedeniia ob uchashchikh v zemskikh shkolakh Moskovskoi gubernii." In *Statisticheskii ezhegodnik Moskovskoi gubernii za 1891,* 1–25. Moscow, 1892.

Orlov, V. I. *Narodnoe obrazovanie v Moskovskoi gubernii.* Vol. 9 of *Sbornik statisticheskikh svedenii po Moskovskoi gubernii,* Moskovskaia gubernskaia zemskaia uprava, Otdel khoziaistvennoi statistiki. Moscow, 1884.

Petrov, V. V. *Obzor dvadtsatipiatiletnei deiatel'nosti Moskovskogo zemstva po narodnomu obrazovaniiu.* Moscow, 1892.

————. "Tserkovno-prikhodskie shkoly Moskovskoi gubernii." *Vestnik vospitaniia* 10, no. 7 (1899): 122–163.

————, ed. *Voprosy narodnogo obrazovaniia v Moskovskoi gubernii.* 5 vols. Moscow, 1897–1907.

Potapova, N. N. "Istoriia zemskoi shkoly Moskovskoi gubernii v nachale XX-ogo veka." Candidate dissertation, Moskovskii oblastnoi pedagogicheskii institut, Moscow, 1945.

"Pravila po postroike shkol'nykh domov v seleniiakh Moskovskoi gubernii." In *Trudy II-ogo s"ezda zemskikh vrachei Moskovskoi gubernii,* 44–49. Moscow, 1889.

Serpukhovskaia uezdnaia zemskaia uprava. *Obzor tridtsatiletnei deiatel'nosti po narodnomu obrazovaniiu.* Serpukhov, 1895.

Vikhliaev, P. A. *Ekonomicheskie usloviia narodnogo obrazovaniia v Moskovskoi gubernii.* Moscow, 1910.

Nizhnii Novgorod

Gatsiskii, A. S. *Shkol'noe delo v Nizhegorodskom povolzh'e.* Kazan', 1873.

Iordanskii, N. N. *Bytovye i semeinye usloviia zhizni shkol'nikov v Nizhnem-Novgorode.* Nizhnii Novgorod, 1907.

————. *Istoricheskii ocherk razvitiia vseobshchego obucheniia v Nizhegorodskom uezde v sviazi s rabotoi zemstva po narodnomu obrazovaniiu.* Nizhnii Novgorod, 1911.

————. "Narodnaia shkola i zemstvo Nizhegorodskoi gubernii v 60–70 gody XIX veka." *Sovetskaia pedagogika,* no. 4 (1941): 76–89.

————. *Otchet o sostoianii nachal'nykh uchilishch v Nizhnem Novgorode za 1900–1907.* 7 vols. Nizhnii Novgorod, 1901–1908.

Novgorod

Ocherk narodnogo obrazovaniia v Novgorodskoi gubernii za 1884–1885 uchebnyi god. Novgorod, 1887.

Samsonov, V. *Byt uchashchikh v Novgorodskoi gubernii.* Novgorod, 1907.

Soderzhanie nachal'nykh sel'skikh shkol i otnoshenie naseleniia k shkolam.

Polozhenie narodnogo obrazovaniia v Novgorodskoi gubernii, no. 4. Novgorod, 1904.

Orel

Reingardt, A. K. *Istoriia nachal'noi shkoly v Orlovskoi gubernii: Ocherki deiatel'nosti uezdnykh zemstv po narodnomu obrazovaniiu.* Orel, 1897.

―――. *Sbornik statisticheskikh svedenii po nachal'nomu narodnomu obrazovaniiu v Orlovskoi gubernii za 1895–1896 uchebnyi god.* Orel, 1898.

Perm'

Osorin, N. A. *Narodnoe nachal'noe obrazovaniie v Permskoi gubernii so vvedeniia zemskikh uchrezhdenii po 1900.* Kazan', 1900.

Sbornik svedenii o polozhenii nachal'nogo narodnogo obrazovaniia v Permskoi gubernii. Perm', 1903.

Udintsev, S. A. *Ocherk razvitiia narodnogo obrazovaniia v Irbitskom uezde Permskoi gubernii.* Irbit, 1892.

Verakso, K. L. "Razvitie nachal'nogo obrazovaniia na Urale." Candidate dissertation, Nauchnyi issledovatel'skii institut teorii i istorii pedagogiki, APN, RSFSR, Sverdlovsk, 1949.

Poltava

Iatsevich, N. Y., ed. *Nachal'noe narodnoe obrazovanie v Poltavskoi gubernii.* Poltava, 1894.

Statisticheskii ezhegodnik Poltavskogo gubernskogo zemstva na 1903. Poltava, 1903.

Statisticheskii ezhegodnik Poltavskogo gubernskogo zemstva na 1904. Poltava, 1904.

Pskov

Materialy k voprosu ob uchastii Pskovskogo gubernskogo zemstva v raione nachal'nogo narodnogo obrazovaniia. 2 vols. Pskov, 1898–1899.

Po voprosu ob ekonomicheskom znachenii narodnogo obrazovaniia i o polozhenii ego v Pskovskoi gubernii. Pskov, 1900.

Riazan'

Materialy po istorii Riazanskogo gubernskogo zemstva. Riazan', 1903.

Sbornik statisticheskikh svedenii po Riazanskoi gubernii. Vol. 13, *Nachal'nye shkoly.* Riazan', 1889.

Subbotin, P. A. *Obzor deiatel'nosti Riazanskogo uezdnogo zemstva po narod-nomu obrazovaniiu za vremiia, 1865–1900.* Moscow, 1902.

Saratov

Polozhenie narodnogo obrazovaniia v Saratovskoi gubernii za vremia sushche-stvovaniia v nei zemskikh uchrezhdenii. Saratov, 1894.

Simbirsk

Akimov, V. V. "Deiatel'nost' Simbirskogo zemstva po narodnomu obra-zovaniiu." *ZhMNP,* n.s. 17, sec. 3 (September 1908): 43–85; n.s. 17, sec. 3 (October 1908): 121–144; n.s. 18, sec. 3 (November 1908): 1–33.

Nachal'noe narodnoe obrazovanie v Simbirskoi gubernii po dannym 1902–1903 goda. Simbirsk, 1905.

Superanskii, M. *Nachal'naia narodnaia shkola v Simbirskoi gubernii: Istoricheskii-statisticheskii ocherk.* Simbirsk, 1906.

Tambov

Sbornik materialov i statisticheskikh svedenii po narodnomu obrazovaniiu v Tambovskoi gubernii. Tambov, 1899.

Tavrida

Statisticheskoe biuro Tavricheskogo gubernskogo zemstva. *Sbornik po shkol'noi statistike.* 2 vols. Simferopol, 1903–1905.

Tula

Akimov, V. V. "Deiatel'nost' Tul'skogo zemstva po narodnomu obrazo-vaniiu." *ZhMNP* 343, sec. 3 (October 1901): 149–182; 344, sec. 3 (December 1901): 121–161.

Nachal'noe narodnoe obrazovanie v Tul'skoi gubernii v 1896–1897 uchebnom godu. Tula, 1898.

Seropolko, S. O. *Kratkii obzor tridtsatiletnei deiatel'nosti Tul'skogo gubern-skogo zemstva v oblasti narodnogo obrazovaniia.* Tula, 1902.

Sheremet'ev, P. S., ed. *Narodnye uchitelia i uchitel'nitsy v Tul'skoi gubernii: Istoriko-statisticheskii ocherk.* Tula, 1898.

Tver'

Narodnoe obrazovanie. Vol. 8, *Materialy po istorii Tverskogo gubernskogo zemstva, 1866–1908.* Tver', 1910.

Ufa

Grigor'ev, P. N. *Ocherk deiatel'nosti Ufimskogo gubernskogo zemstva po narodnomu obrazovaniiu za vremia, 1875–1910.* Ufa, 1911.

Viatka

Akimov, V. V. "Deiatel'nost' Viatskogo zemstva po narodnomu obrazovaniiu." *ZhMNP,* n.s. 11, sec. 3 (October 1907): 1–46; n.s. 12, sec. 3 (December 1907): 117–172.

Blinov, N. *Narodnoe obrazovanie v Viatskoi gubernii za poslednie desiat' let (1864–1874).* Viatka, 1875.

Issledovaniie polozheniia nachal'nogo obrazovaniia v Viatskoi gubernii. 2 vols. Viatka, 1900–1902.

Nachal'nye narodnye uchilishcha Viatskoi gubernii; Ocherki o vozniknovenii uchilishch s 1786 po 1898. Viatka, 1900.

Petrov, V. A. "Zemskaia nachal'naia shkola Viatskoi gubernii." Candidate dissertation, Moskovskii oblastnoi pedagogicheskii institut, Kirov, 1955.

Sel'skie obshchestvennye biblioteki v Viatskoi gubernii. Statisticheskii ezhegodnik Viatskoi gubernii za 1899, sec. 2, part 1. Viatka, 1901.

Tanaevskaia, V. V., and M. M. Sherstennikov. *Kratkii obzor deiatel'nosti Viatskogo gubernskogo zemstva za 35 let (1867–1902),* vol. 1. Viatka, 1906.

Vladimir

Chernov, G. I. *Stranitsy proshlogo: Iz istorii dorevoliutsionnoi shkoly Vladimirskoi gubernii.* Vladimir, 1970.

Dobronravov, V. *Tserkovnaia shkola vo Vladimirskoi eparkhii s 1884 po 1909.* Vladimir, 1909.

Vladimirskaia gubernskaia zemskaia uprava. *Polozhenie narodnogo obrazovaniia vo Vladimirskoi gubernii po issledovaniiu 1910 goda.* 2 vols. Vladimir, 1910–1911.

———. *Sbornik statisticheskikh i spravochnykh svedenii po narodnomu obrazovaniiu v Vladimirskoi gubernii.* 6 vols. Vladimir, 1899–1902.

Vostrukhina, T. N. "Istoriia narodnogo obrazovaniia vo Vladimirskoi gubernii s 60-kh godov XIX veka do oktiabr'skoi revoliutsii." Candidate dissertation, Moskovskii gorodskoi pedagogicheskii institut imeni V. P. Potemkina, Moscow, 1955.

Vologda

Bunakov, N. F. "Ocherk narodnogo obrazovaniia v Vologodskoi gubernii." *ZhMNP* 122, sec. 3 (April 1864): 117–132.

Griazovetskaia uezdnaia zemskaia uprava Vologodskoi gubernii. "O polozhenii uchashchikh nachal'nykh narodnykh uchilishch." In *Doklady*, vol. 2 of *Trudy pervogo obshchezemskogo s"ezda po narodnomu obrazovaniiu*, no. 23a, 247–268. Moscow, 1912.

Nachal'noe obrazovanie v Vologodskoi gubernii po svedeniiu 1898–1899. 2 vols. Vologda, 1901.

Voronezh

Ocherk o sostoianii nachal'nogo narodnogo obrazovaniia v Voronezhskoi gubernii v 1911. Voronezh, 1912.

Shchebin, F. A. *Voronezhskoe zemstvo, 1865–1899: Istoricheskii-statisticheskii obzor*. Vol. 18, *Narodnoe obrazovanie*. Voronezh, 1891.

Voronov, I. *Materialy po narodnomu obrazovaniiu v Voronezhskoi gubernii*. Voronezh, 1899.

IV. GENERAL WORKS IN RUSSIAN

A-v, A. "Institut direktorov i inspektorov narodnykh uchilishch." *ZhMNP*, n.s. 19, sec. 3 (January 1909): 48–59.

A-v, I. "Iz zhizni russkogo narodnogo uchitelia." *Russkaia shkola* 22, nos. 10 and 11 (1911): 66–86, 51–75.

A-v, V. "Dve vystavki po narodnomu obrazovaniiu v Moskve." *Russkaia mysl'* 17, no. 2 (1896): 115–127.

Akimov, V. V. "Pervyi vserossiiskii s"ezd po voprosam narodnogo obrazovaniia." *ZhMNP*, n.s. 49, sec. 3 (November 1913): 107–145.

———. "Postanovka uchebnogo dela v zemskikh shkolakh." *ZhMNP*, n.s. 62, sec. 3 (March 1916): 33–90; n.s. 63, sec 3 (May 1916): 1–61.

———. "Zemskaia rabota po podgotovke narodnykh uchitelei." *ZhMNP*, n.s. 56, sec. 3 (March 1915): 145–183; n.s. 57, sec. 3 (May 1915): 1–26; n.s. 58, sec. 3 (July 1915): 129–168.

Anastas'ev, A. I. *Narodnaia shkola: Rukovodstvo dlia uchitelei i uchitel'nits narodnykh shkol. Nastol'naia spravochnaia kniga*. 7th ed. 2 vols. Moscow, 1910.

Anketa uchashchim zemskikh shkol. Vol. 5 of *Trudy pervogo obshchezemskogo s"ezda po narodnomu obrazovaniiu.* Moscow, 1911.

Ansimov, V. I. *Sviaz' gramotnosti krest'ianskogo naseleniia s ego khoziaist-vennym blagosostoianiem.* Moscow, 1898.

An'skii, S. A. [S. A. Rappoport]. *Narod i kniga: Opyt kharakteristiki narod-nogo chitatelia.* Appendix to *Narod i voina.* Moscow, 1913.

Antsyferov, S. I. *Spravochnaia kniga po nizshemu obrazovaniiu.* 8 vols. St. Petersburg, 1905.

Arsen'cv, K. K., et al. *Melkaia zemskaia edinitsa: Sbornik statei.* St. Petersburg, 1903.

Arsen'ev, K. K., ed. *Nuzhdy derevni, po rabotam komitetov o nuzhdakh sel'sko-khoziaistvennoi promyshlennosti.* St. Petersburg, 1904.

Batyshev, S. Ia., ed. *Ocherki istorii professional'no-tekhnicheskogo obrazo-vaniia v SSSR.* Moscow, 1981.

Beliavskii, A. *Istoricheskii ocherk razvitiia elementarnoi shkoly v biografiiakh zamechatel'nykh pedagogov i po ustavam pravitel'stva.* 2d ed. St. Petersburg, 1905.

Belokonskii, I. P. *Derevenskie vpechatleniia (Iz zapisok zemskogo statistika).* St. Petersburg, 1900.

————. *Zemskoe dvizhenie.* Moscow, 1910.

Bendriakov, K. "Narodnoe obrazovanie v Rossii pri vremennom pra-vitel'stve." *Narodnoe obrazovanie,* no. 6 (1947): 50–60.

————. "Skhol'naia sistema v Rossii pered fevral'skoi revoliutsiei." *Narod-noe obrazovanie,* no. 3 (1947): 41–60.

Blagoi, D., ed. *Uchitel' v russkoi khudozhestvennoi literature.* Moscow, 1927.

Blagoveshchenskii, I. I. *Svodnyi statisticheskii sbornik po zemskim podvor-nym perepisiam.* Vol. 1, *Krest'ianskoe khoziaistvo.* Moscow, 1893.

Bobylev, D. M. *Kakaia shkola nuzhna derevne.* Perm', 1908.

Bogdanov, I. M. *Gramotnost' i obrazovanie v dorevoliutsionnoi Rossii i v SSSR.* Moscow, 1964.

Bratchikov, N. I. "Uchebno-vospitatel'naia chast' v nachal'noi shkole." *Russkaia shkola* 20, nos. 1, 2, 3 (1909): 89–118, 107–131, 78–93.

Bunakov, N. F. *Izbrannye pedagogicheskie sochineniia.* Moscow, 1953.

————. *O domashnikh shkolakh gramotnosti v narode (Po materialiam, so-brannym St. Peterburgskim komitetom gramotnosti).* St. Petersburg, 1885.

————. *Sel'skaia shkola i narodnaia zhizn'.* St. Petersburg, 1901.

Bychkov, N. "Gramotnost' sel'skogo naseleniia." *Iuridicheskii vestnik* 1 (July-August 1890): 309–332.

Charnoluskii, V. I. *Itogi obshchestvennoi mysli v oblasti obrazovaniia.* St. Petersburg, 1906.

————. *Osnovnye voprosy organizatsii shkoly v Rossii.* St. Petersburg, 1909.

————. *Sputnik narodnogo uchitelia i deiatelia narodnogo obrazovaniia.* St. Petersburg, 1908.

————. "Voprosy narodnogo obrazovaniia na pervom obshchezemskom s"ezde." *Russkaia shkola* 22, nos. 9, 10, 11, 12 (1911): 50–78, 87–109, 91–116, 87–116.

————. *Zemstvo i narodnoe obrazovanie.* 2 vols. St. Petersburg, 1910.

————, ed. *Svod zakonov, tsirkuliarov i spravochnykh svedenii po narodnomu obrazovaniiu.* Moscow, 1908.

Charushin, V. A. *O roli narodnykh uchitelei v ozdorovlenii russkoi derevni.* Perm', 1910.

Chekhov, N. V. *Narodnoe obrazovanie v Rossii s 60-kh godov XIX veka.* Moscow, 1912.

————. *Tipy russkoi skholy v ikh istoricheskom razvitii.* Moscow, 1923.

Chekini, A. "Nachal'noe narodnoe obrazovanie." In *Novyi entsiklopedicheskii slovar' Brokgauza-Efrona,* vol. 28, 123–149. Petrograd, 1916.

Cherepanov, S. A. "Uchebnye plany obshcheobrazovatel'noi shkoly v dorevoliutsionnoi Rossii." *Izvestiia akademii pedagogicheskikh nauk RSFSR* 33 (1951): 158–209.

Demkov, M. I. *Istoriia russkoi pedagogiki.* 3 vols. St. Petersburg, 1897–1909.

————. *Nachal'naia narodnaia shkola: Eia istoriia, didaktika i metodika.* 2d ed. Moscow, 1916.

————. *Ocherki po istorii russkoi pedagogiki.* 2d ed. Moscow, 1916.

————. *Russkaia pedagogika v glavneishikh eia predstaviteliakh.* 2d ed. Moscow, 1916.

Devel', V. "Krest'ianskie vol'nye shkoly gramotnosti v Tverskoi gubernii." *Russkaia shkola* 1, nos. 4, 5, 6 (1890): 99–111, 131–147, 121–134.

Dido. *Zametki i nabliudeniia (Iz zametok byvshego sel'skogo uchitelia).* St. Petersburg, 1902.

Dneprov, E. D. "Sotsial'nyi sostav uchashchikhsia russkoi shkoly vo vtoroi polovine XIX v." *Sovetskaia pedagogika,* no. 10 (1976): 101–112.

Druzhinin, N. M. *Gosudarstvennye krest'iane i reforma, P. D. Kiseleva.* 2 vols. Moscow, 1946, 1958.

Dubrovskii, A. V. "Statisticheskiie svedeniia o sel'skikh uchilishchakh v evropeiskoi Rossii i privislianskikh guberniiakh, po obsledovaniiu 20 marta 1880." In *Statisticheskii vremennik Rossiiskoi imperii,* series 3, no. 1. St. Petersburg, 1884.

―――. "Svedeniia po statistike narodnogo obrazovaniia 1872–1874 v evropeiskoi Rossii." In *Statisticheskii vremennik Rossiiskoi imperii,* series 2, no. 16. St. Petersburg, 1879.

Dzhivelegov, A. K., S. P. Mel'gunov, and V. I. Pichet, eds. *Velikaia reforma.* 6 vols. Moscow, 1911.

Eliseev, V. *Programmy i pravila vysshikh nachal'nykh uchilishch.* Odessa, 1915.

El'nitskii, K. *Russkie pedagogi vtoroi poloviny XIX stoletiia.* Petrograd, 1915.

―――. *Shkol'noe obuchenie.* 2d ed. Petrograd, 1914.

Evteev, V., ed. *Trudy pervogo vserossiiskogo s"ezda predstavitelei obshchestv vspomoshchestvovaniia litsam uchitel'skogo zvaniia.* 2 vols. Moscow, 1907.

Fal'bork, G. A. *Vseobshchee obrazovaniie v Rossii.* Moscow, 1908.

Fal'bork, G. A., and V. I. Charnoluskii. *Narodnoe obrazovanie v Rossii.* St. Petersburg, 1899.

―――. *Nastol'naia kniga po narodnomu obrazovaniiu.* 4 vols. St. Petersburg, 1899–1911.

―――. "Otchet o polozhenii statistiki narodnogo obrazovaniia v Rossii, proizvodimago Imperatorskim vol'nym ekonomicheskim obshchestvom." St. Petersburg, 1895.

―――, eds. *Nachal'noe narodnoe obrazovanie v Rossii.* 4 vols. St. Petersburg, 1900–1905.

Farmakovskii, V. I. "K voprosu o vseobshchem obuchenii." *ZhMNP* 345, sec. 4 (January–February 1903): 124–144.

―――. "Nachal'naia shkola MNP." *Russkaia shkola* 10, nos. 4, 5, 6, 7, 8, 10, 12 (1899): 105–127, 149–178, 157–186, 189–231, 146–181, 147–168, 127–142. [Also published as a book under the same title. Moscow, 1902.]

Filatova, A. V. "Sredi krest'ianskikh detei." *Russkaia shkola* 23, no. 5–6 (1912): 153–163.

―――. *Vospominaniia uchitel'nitsy, 1874–1907.* Moscow, 1929.

Flerov, Vs. "Chem my sil'ny." *Russkaia shkola* 23, no. 2 (1912): 27–43.

G., Dm. "Devochka v narodnoi shkole." *Russkaia shkola* 22, no. 1 (1911): 60–69.

Ganelin, Sh. I. *Ocherki po istorii srednei shkoly v Rossii vtoroi poloviny XIX veka.* 2d ed. Moscow, 1954.

Garmiza, V. V. *Podgotovka zemskoi reformy 1864 goda.* Moscow, 1957.

———. "Zemskaia reforma i zemstvo v istoricheskoi literature." *Istoriia SSSR,* no. 5 (1960): 81–107.

Gartvig, Andrei. "Soznana-li naseleniem potrebnost' vo vseobshchem obuchenii?" *Russkaia shkola* 6, no. 4 (1895): 130–153.

Genkel', G. *Narodnoe obrazovanie na zapade i u nas.* St. Petersburg, 1911.

Gol'tsev, V. A. "K voprosu o polozhenii uchashchikh narodnykh shkol." *Russkaia mysl'* 18, no. 12 (1897): 61–78.

Gorbunov, A. "O vliianii obshchago nachal'nogo obrazovaniia na proizvoditel'nost' truda." *Russkaia mysl'* 17, no. 3 (1896): 67–80.

Grigor'ev, V. V. *Istoricheskii ocherk russkoi shkoly.* Moscow, 1900.

Iablochkov, M. T. *Russkaia shkola: Nastavleniia direktora narodnykh uchilishch.* Tula, 1895.

Ianson, A. K. "O podgotovke uchitelei." In *Doklady,* vol. 2 of *Trudy pervogo obshchezemskogo s"ezda po narodnomu obrazovaniiu,* 218–232. Moscow, 1912.

Ianzhul, I. I., A. I. Chuprov, E. N. Ianzhula, V. P. Vakhterov et al. *Ekonomicheskaia otsenka narodnogo obrazovaniia.* 2d ed. St. Petersburg, 1899.

Imperskoe russkoe tekhnicheskoe obshchestvo. *S"ezd russkikh deiatelei po tekhnicheskomu i professional'nomu obrazovaniiu v Rossii.* Vol. 1. St. Petersburg, 1891.

———. *Trudy IX sektsii II s"ezda russkikh deiatelei po tekhnicheskomu i professional'nomu obrazovaniiu.* St. Petersburg, 1896.

Iordanskii, N. N. "Teoriia i deistvitel'nost' v oblasti vseobshchago obucheniia." *Russkaia shkola* 22, nos. 1 and 2 (1911): 70–92, 25–39.

———. "Usloviia osushchestvleniia vseobshchago obucheniia v Rossii." *Russkaia shkola* 25, nos. 1 and 2 (1914): 1–23, 13–32.

Istoricheskii ocherk razvitiia tserkovnykh shkol za istekshee dvadtsatipiatiletie, 1884–1909. St. Petersburg, 1909.

Ivanov, N. "Zemstvo." In *Novyi entsiklopedicheskii slovar' Brokgauza-Efrona,* vol. 18, 652–680. Petrograd, 1916.

Ivanovich, V. "Zemstvo i tserkovnaia shkola." *Russkoe bogatstvo* 7 (July 1903): 159–168.

K. "Voprosy narodnoi shkoly na II s"ezde deiatelei po tekhnicheskomu i professional'nomu obrazovaniiu." *Russkaia mysl'* 17, no. 4 (1896): 79–94.

K., Ia. "Pravovoe polozhenie narodnogo uchitelia." *Russkaia shkola* 19, no. 5–6 (1908): 128–145.

K-vich, N. V. "Tserkovno-shkol'noe delo v Rossii." *Vestnik evropy* 36, no. 5 (September 1901): 218–247.

Kabardin, N. P. "Odnodnevnaia perepis' nachal'nykh shkol Rossiiskoi imperii." *ZhMNP,* n.s. 69, sec. 3 (May 1917): 22–38.

Kaidanova, O. *Ocherki po istorii narodnogo obrazovaniia v Rossii i SSSR.* 2 vols. Berlin, 1938.

Kairov, A. I., et al., eds. See *Pedagogicheskaia entsiklopediia* (1964–1968).

Kalashnikov, A. G., et al., eds. See *Pedagogicheskaia entsiklopediia* (1927–1930).

Kantor, I. M. *Pedagogicheskaia leksikografiia i leksikologiia.* Moscow, 1968.

Kapterev, P. F. *Istoriia russkoi pedagogiki.* St. Petersburg, 1909.

———. *Novaia russkaia pedagogika.* St. Petersburg, 1914.

———. *Novye dvizheniia v oblasti narodnogo obrazovaniia i srednei shkoly.* Moscow, 1913.

Kapterev, P. F., and A. F. Myzychenko, eds. *Sovremennye pedagogicheskie techeniia.* Moscow, 1913.

Karyshev, N. A. *Zemskie khodataistva, 1865–1884.* Moscow, 1900.

Kaufman, A. A. "Zemskaia statistika." In *Novyi entsiklopedicheskii slovar' Brokgauza-Efrona,* vol. 18, 618–632. Petrograd, 1916.

Kazantsev, P. "Dvizhenie uchashchikhsia nachal'noi shkoly po otdeleniiam." *Russkaia shkola* 23, no. 1 (1912): 150–158.

Kivshenko, N. *Dnevnik sel'skoi uchitel'nitsy.* St. Petersburg, 1887.

Kniaz'kov, S. A., and N. I. Serbov. *Ocherk istorii narodnogo obrazovaniia v Rossii do epokhi reform Aleksandra II.* Moscow, 1910.

Kolosov, S. *V pogone za sel'sko-khoziaistvennymi znaniiami v vospitanii narodnogo uchitelia 70–80–kh godov.* Gzhansk, 1909.

Konstantinov, N. A., M. F. Medynskii, and M. F. Shabaeva. *Istoriia pedagogiki.* Moscow, 1974.

Konstantinov, N. A., and V. Ia. Struminskii. *Ocherki po istorii nachal'nogo obrazovaniia v Rossii.* 2d ed. Moscow, 1953.

Korestelov, A. A., et al., eds. *Uchitel' i revoliutsiia.* Moscow, 1925.

Korf, N. A. *Nashe shkol'noe delo.* Moscow, 1873.

———. *Nashi pedagogicheskie voprosy.* Moscow, 1882.

———. *Russkaia nachal'naia shkola. Rukovodstvo dlia zemskikh glasnykh i uchitelei sel'skoi shkoly.* St. Petersburg, 1870.

———. *Zemskii vopros o narodnom obrazovanii.* St. Petersburg, 1867.

Koridalin, A. *K voprosu o material'noi neobespechennosti narodnogo uchitelia.* Sergiev-Posad, 1911.

Kornilov, I. P., ed. *Zadachi russkogo prosveshcheniia v ego proshlom i nastoiashchem: Sbornik statei.* St. Petersburg, 1902.

Korolëv, F. F. "Fevral'skaia revoliutsiia i narodnoe obrazovanie." *Sovetskaia pedagogika,* no. 2 (1953): 47–71.

―――. "Narodnoe obrazovanie v Rossii nakanune fevral'skoi revoliutsii 1917 goda." *Sovetskaia pedagogika,* no. 12 (1951): 41–67.

―――. *Ocherki po istorii sovetskoi shkoly i pedagogiki, 1917–1920.* Moscow, 1958.

―――, ed. *Ocherki po istorii sovetskoi shkoly i pedagogiki, 1921–1931.* Moscow, 1961.

Kovalevskii, E. P. "Usloviia dostizheniia vseobshchago obrazovaniia." In *Doklady,* vol. 3 of *Trudy pervogo obshchezemskogo s"ezda po narodnomu obrazovaniiu,* 604–623. Moscow, 1911.

Kovalevskii, V. I., ed. *Proizvoditel'nye sily Rossii.* St. Petersburg, 1896.

Krasev, A. A. "Chto daët krest'ianam nachal'naia narodnaia shkola?" *Russkaia mysl'* 8, nos. 1 and 2 (1887): 49–72, 100–130.

―――. *Chto mogut i dolzhny davat' narodu nashi nachal'nye narodnye shkoly.* St. Petersburg, 1906.

Krasnoperov, I. M. "Rezul'taty odnodnevnoi perepisi narodnykh shkol v Rossii 18 ianvaria 1911 g." *ZhMNP,* n.s. 55, sec. 3 (July 1914): 1–32.

Kratkii obzor zemsko-shkol'nogo dela v Rossii. Iaroslavl', 1906.

Krzhizhanovskii, O. "Znachenie dukhovenstva v istorii narodnogo obrazovaniia v Rossii (Istoricheskii ocherk)." *Obrazovanie* 4, nos. 3, 5–6, 7–8, 9 (1895): 231–249, 470–498, 21–58, 30–52.

Kulomzin, A. N. *Dostupnost' nachal'noi shkoly v Rossii.* St. Petersburg, 1904.

Kumanëv, V. A. *Revoliutsiia i prosveshchenie mass.* Moscow, 1973.

―――. *Sotsializm i vsenarodnaia gramotnost'.* Moscow, 1967.

Kurmacheva, M. D. *Krepostnaia intelligentsiia Rossii.* Moscow, 1983.

―――. "Problemy obrazovaniia v ulozhenoi komissii 1767 g." In *Dvorianstvo i krepostnoi stroi Rossii XVI–XVIII vv. Sbornik statei posveshchënnyi pamiati A. A. Novosel'skogo,* 240–264. Moscow, 1975.

Kuzin, N. P., M. N. Kolmakova, and Z. I. Ravkin, eds. *Ocherki istorii shkoly i pedagogicheskoi mysli narodov SSSR, 1917–1941.* Moscow, 1981.

Kuz'min, N. N. *Uchitel'skie seminary Rossii i ikh mesto v podgotovke uchitelei nachal'noi shkoly.* Kurgan, 1970.

Lapshin, N. P. "Iz istorii russkoi dorevoliutsionnoi inspektsii narodnykh uchilishch, 1869–1917." *Uchenye zapiski Elabuzhskogo gosudarstvennogo pedagogicheskogo instituta* 11, no. 4 (1962): 1–29.

Lebedev, A. *Shkol'noe delo.* 2 vols. Moscow, 1909–1911.

Leikina-Svirskaia, V. R. *Intelligentsiia v Rossii vo vtoroi polovine XIX-ogo veka.* Moscow, 1971.

———. *Russkaia intelligentsiia v 1900–1917 godakh.* Moscow, 1981.

Leont'ev, A. A. *Krest'ianskoe pravo. Sistematicheskoe izlozhenie osobennostei zakonadatel'stva o krest'ianstve.* 2d ed. St. Petersburg, 1914.

Lositskii, A. E. *K voprosu ob izuchenii gramotnosti naseleniia Rossii.* Chernigov, 1900.

Lubenets, T. G. "Kakie trebovaniia pred'iavliaet narod k shkole." *ZhMNP,* n.s. 39, sec. 3 (March 1912): 195–205.

Luppov, P. "O statistike tserkovnykh shkol." In *Trudy podsektsii statistiki XI s"ezda estestvoispytatelei i vrachei,* 213–230. St. Petersburg, 1902.

Malinovskii, N. P. "Istoricheskii ocherk po reforme dukhovnoi shkoly." *Russkaia shkola* 23, nos. 11 and 12 (1912): 117–137, 58–86.

———. "Korennye nuzhdy sovremennoi nachal'noi narodnoi shkoly." In *Doklady,* vol. 2 of *Trudy pervogo obshchezemskogo s"ezda po narodnomu obrazovaniiu,* 708–760. Moscow, 1912.

———. "Nekotorye vyvody po dannym shkol'noi perepisi 1911-ogo goda." *Russkaia shkola* 22, no. 5–6 (1911): 71–92.

———. "Rol' krest'ian v rasprostranenii narodnogo obrazovaniia v sviazi s osvobozhdeniem ikh ot krepostnoi zavisimosti." *Russkaia shkola* 22, no. 2 (1911): 61–74.

Medynskii, E. N. *Istoriia russkoi pedagogiki.* 2d ed. Moscow, 1938.

Miliukov, P. *Ocherki po istorii russkoi kul'tury.* 3d ed. St. Petersburg, 1902.

Ministerstvo narodnogo prosveshcheniia (MNP). *Odnodnevaia perepis' nachal'nykh shkol Rossiiskoi imperii proizvedёnnaia 18 ianvaria 1911.* Edited by V. I. Pokrovskii. 16 vols. Petrograd, 1916.

Mironositskii, P. *Dnevnik uchitelia tserkovno-prikhodskoi shkoly.* 2d ed. St. Petersburg, 1901.

Miropol'skii, S. I. *Inspektsiia narodnykh shkol i eia zadachi.* St. Petersburg, 1877.

———. *Ocherk istorii tserkovno-prikhodskoi shkoly ot pervago eia vozniknoveniia do nastoiashchago vremeni,* nos. 1–3. St. Petersburg, 1895.

————. *Shkola i gosudarstvo: Obiazatel'nost' obucheniia v Rossii (Istoricheskii etiud)*. 3d ed. St. Petersburg, 1910.

————. *Uchitel' narodnoi shkoly. Ego prizvanie i kachestva, znachenie, tseli.* St. Petersburg, 1890.

Mizhuev, I. G. "Elementarnoe obrazovanie." In *Entsiklopedicheskii slovar' Brokgauza-Efrona*, vol. 80, 619–630. St. Petersburg, 1890–1906.

Mizhuev, P. G. *Vliianie narodnogo obrazovaniia na narodnoe bogatstvo, zdorov'e, nravstvennost' i drugie storony obshchestvennoi zhizni.* St. Petersburg, 1901.

MNP. *See* Ministerstvo narodnogo prosveshcheniia.

Narodnaia entsiklopediia nauchnykh i prikladnykh znanii. Vols. 9 and 10. Moscow, 1911, 1912.

Nikolaev, A. "Neskol'ko slov o biudzhete narodnogo uchitelia." *Russkaia shkola* 23, no. 5–6 (1912): 89–95.

————. *Sel'skii uchitel'.* St. Petersburg, 1906.

Odnodnevnaia perepis'. *See* Ministerstvo narodnogo prosveshcheniia.

Ol'denburg, F. *Narodnye shkoly evropeiskoi Rossii v 1892–1893: Statisticheskii ocherk.* St. Petersburg, 1896.

————. "Zapiski po statistike nachal'nago obrazovaniia v Rossii." *ZhMNP* 340, sec. 3 (March 1901): 103–140.

Ol'khovskii, E. P. "Narodnyi uchitel' v revoliutsionnom dvizhenii 60–70–kh godov XIX veka." *Sovetskaia pedagogika,* no. 7 (1967): 121–129.

Orzhekhovskii, I. V. *Iz istorii vnutrennei politiki samoderzhaviia v 60–70–kh godakh XIX veka.* Gorkii, 1974.

Ososkov, A. V. "Nachal'noe narodnoe obrazovanie i IV gosudarstvennaia duma." *Sovetskaia pedagogika,* no. 7 (1947): 80–91.

————. *Nachal'noe obrazovanie v dorevoliutsionnoi Rossii (1861–1917).* Moscow, 1982.

————. *Voprosy istorii nachal'nogo obrazovaniia v Rossii.* Vols. 1 and 2. Moscow, 1974, 1975.

Ozerov, I. Kh. *Na bor'bu s narodnoi t'moi.* Berlin, n.d.

Panachin, F. G. "Narodnoe uchitel'stvo v revoliutsii 1905–1907." *Narodnoe obrazovanie,* no. 5 (1975): 89–93.

————. *Pedagogicheskoe obrazovanie v Rossii: Istoriko-pedagogicheskie ocherki.* Moscow, 1979.

————. *Pedagogicheskoe obrazovanie v SSSR.* Moscow, 1975.

————. "Uchitel'stvo Rossii na zare XX stoletiia." *Narodnoe obrazovanie,* no. 9 (1973): 83–89.

Pedagogicheskaia entsiklopediia. 2d ed. 3 vols. Edited by A. G. Kalashnikov et al. Moscow, 1927–1930.

Pedagogicheskaia entsiklopediia. 4 vols. Edited by I. A. Kairov et al. Moscow, 1964–1968.

Pedagogicheskii slovar'. 2 vols. Moscow, 1960.

Peterson, N. L. *Prosveshchenie. Svod trudov mestnykh komitetov po 49 guberniiam evropeiskoi Rossii dlia vysochaishe uchrezhdennogo osobogo soveshchaniia o nuzhdakh sel'sko-khoziastvennoi promyshlennosti*. St. Petersburg, 1904.

Petrova, I. B. *Iz dnevnika narodnoi uchitel'nitsy*. Moscow, 1915.

Pirogov, N. I. *Izbrannye pedagogicheskie sochineniia*. Moscow, 1952.

Pirumova, N. M. *Zemskoe liberal'noe dvizhenie: Sotsial'nye korni i evoliutsiia do nachala XX veka*. Moscow, 1977.

Piskunov, A. I., ed. *Ocherki istorii shkoly i pedagogicheskoi mysli narodov SSSR. Vtoraia polovina XIX v*. Moscow, 1976.

Pokrovskii, M. N., ed. *Istoriia Rossii v XIX veke*. 9 vols. St. Petersburg, 1906.

Pokrovskii, V. I. *O shkol'noi perepisi 18 ianvaria 1911*. St. Petersburg, 1911.

"Polozhenie o nachal'nykh narodnykh uchilishchakh." *ZhMNP* 123, sec. 1 (July 1864): 39–47.

"Polozhenie o nachal'nykh narodnykh uchilishchakh." *ZhMNP* 174, sec. 1 (August 1874): 127–137.

Propp, V. Ia. *Russkie agrarnye prazdniki*. Leningrad, 1963.

Protopopov, D. D. *Istoriia St. Petersburgskogo komiteta gramotnosti (1861–1895)*. St. Petersburg, 1898.

Prugavin, A. S. *Zakony i spravochnye svedeniia po nachal'nomu narodnomu obrazovaniiu*. 2d ed. St. Petersburg, 1904.

———. *Zaprosy naroda i obiazannosti intelligentsii v oblasti prosveshcheniia i vospitaniia*. 2d ed. St. Petersburg, 1895.

Rachinskii, S. A. *Sel'skaia shkola*. 6th ed. St. Petersburg, 1910.

Raevskii, V. *Iz zhizni narodnykh uchilishch. Ocherk i kharakteristiki uchilishch, popechitelei ikh, zakonouchitelei, uchitelei, uchitel'nits i detei*. Nizhnii Novgorod, 1896.

Rappoport, S. A. *See* An'skii, S. A.

Rashin, A. G. *Formirovanie rabochego klassa Rossii*. Moscow, 1958.

———. "Gramotnost' i narodnoe obrazovanie v Rossii v XIX i nachale XX veka." *Istoricheskie zapiski* 37 (1951): 28–80.

———. *Naselenie Rossii za 100 let (1811–1913)*. Moscow, 1956.

Ropp, A. *Chto sdelala tret'ia gosudarstvennaia duma dlia narodnogo obra-zovaniia.* St. Petersburg, 1912.

Rozhdestvenskii, A. K. *Slovo pravdy o tserkovnoi shkole.* Rybinsk, 1906.

Rozhdestvenskii, S. V., ed. *Istoricheskii obzor deiatel'nosti ministerstva narod-nogo prosveshcheniia, 1802–1902.* St. Petersburg, 1902.

————. *Ocherki po istorii sistem narodnogo prosveshcheniia v Rossii v XVIII–XIX vv.* Vol. 1. St. Petersburg, 1912.

Rubakin, N. A. *Etiudy o russkoi chitaiushchei publike.* St. Petersburg, 1895.

————. "Gramotnost'." In *Entsiklopedicheskii slovar' Brokgauza-Efrona,* vol. 18, 537–549. St. Petersburg, 1890–1906.

Ruttsen, V. "Prodolzhitel'nost' kursa v russkoi nachal'noi shkole." *Russ-kaia shkola* 25, no. 3 (1914): 34–41.

Rymakov, A. K. "Krupnyi deiatel' zemskoi shkoly N. N. Iordanskii." Candidate dissertation, Nauchnyi institut teorii i istorii pedagogiki, APN, RSFSR, Moscow, 1964.

S-, K. "Sorokaletie Khar'kovskago obshchestva gramotnosti." *Russkaia shkola* 22, no. 5–6 (1911): 99–108.

Salomatin, P. *Kak zhivët i rabotaet narodnyi uchitel'.* St. Petersburg, 1913.

Samsonov, V., and G. Rumanov, eds. *Trudy pervago vserossiiskogo s"ezda uchitelei.* 2 vols. St. Petersburg, 1910.

Savel'eva, V. G. "Politika tsarizma v voprosakh obrazovaniia, 1907–1911." Candidate dissertation, Leningradskii gosudarstvennyi universitet, Leningrad, 1975.

Savenkov, I. *Uchitel' russkoi narodnoi shkoly i ego obiazannosti.* Warsaw, 1900.

Semënov, S. T. *Dvadtsat' piat' let v derevne.* Petrograd, 1915.

Shabaeva, M. F., ed. *Ocherki istorii shkoly i pedagogicheskoi mysli narodov SSSR: XVIII v.-pervaia polovina XIX v.* Moscow, 1973.

Shakhovskii, D. M., ed. *Vseobshchee obrazovanie v Rossii.* Moscow, 1902.

Shestakov, P. "Stolichnye komitety gramotnosti." *Russkaia mysl'* 17, nos. 5 and 9 (1896): 107–124, 107–124.

Shteven, A. A. *Iz zapisok sel'skoi uchitel'nitsy.* St. Petersburg, 1895.

Skalon, V. "Zemskie finansy." In *Entsiklopedicheskii slovar' Brokgauza-Efrona,* vol. 24, 515–531. St. Petersburg, 1890–1906.

————. "Zemskie uchrezhdeniia." In *Entsiklopedicheskii slovar' Brok-gauza-Efrona,* vol. 24, 532–542. St. Petersburg, 1890–1906.

Smirnov, V. Z. *Ocherki po istorii progressivnoi russkoi pedagogiki XIX veka.* Moscow, 1963.

————. *Reforma nachal'noi i srednei shkoly v 60-kh godakh XIX veka.* Moscow, 1954.

Sokolov, Nikolai. "Voprosy shkol'noi politiki v postanovleniiakh s"ezda po narodnomu obrazovaniiu." *Russkaia shkola* 25, no. 3 (1914): 80–100.

Sovet vserossiiskikh s"ezdov staroobriadtsev. *Voprosy narodnogo obrazovaniia sredi staroobriadtsev.* Moscow, 1909.

Strannoliubskii, A. N. "Sostoianie narodnogo obrazovaniia v sëlakh evropeiskoi Rossii." *Russkaia shkola* 4, no. 3–4 (1893): 161–196.

Stratanov, E. M. *Tekushchie voprosy nachal'nogo obrazovaniia i nizshei shkoly.* Moscow, 1910.

Strel'tsov, E. *Iz dvadtsatipiatiletnei praktiki sel'skogo uchitelia.* Vol. 1, *Sel'skaia shkola, 1848–1864.* St. Petersburg, 1875.

Surin, M. *Chto govoriat krest'iane o nuzhdakh derevni.* Moscow, 1906.

Svavitskii, Z. M., and N. A. Svavitskii. *Zemskie podvornye perepisi: Pouezdnye itogi, 1880–1913.* Moscow, 1926.

Svodka svedenii. Vol. 6 of *Trudy pervogo obshchezemskogo s"ezda po narodnomu obrazovaniiu.* Moscow, 1912.

Svodka svedenii o sostoianii zemskoi statistiki narodnogo obrazovaniia. Khar'kov, 1913.

"Svod ustavov uchebnykh uchrezhdenii i uchebnykh zavedenii vedomstva Ministerstva narodnogo prosveshcheniia." In *Svod zakonov Rossiiskoi imperii,* vol. 11, part 1, 214–310. St. Petersburg, 1893.

Titlinov, V. *Dukhovnaia shkola v Rossii XIX stoletiia.* 2 vols. Vil'no, 1908–1909.

Trudy pervogo obshchezemskogo s"ezda po narodnomu obrazovaniiu. 12 vols. Moscow, 1911–1912.
    Vol. 1, *Postanovleniia.* Moscow, 1911.
    Vol. 2, *Doklady.* Moscow, 1912.
    Vol. 3, *Doklady.* Moscow, 1912.
    Vol. 4, *Doklady.* Moscow, 1912.
    Vol. 5, *Anketa uchashchim zemskikh shkol.* Moscow, 1911.
    Vol. 6, *Svodka svedenii.* Moscow, 1912.
    Vol. 7, *Zhurnal s"ezda.* Moscow, n.d.
    Vol. 8, *Zhurnal s"ezda.* Moscow, n.d.
    Vol. 9, *Zakliucheniia.* Moscow, 1912.
    Vol. 12, *Zakliuchitel'nyi tom.* Moscow, 1912.
    Katalog-ukazatel' zemskoi literatury po narodnomu obrazovaniiu, sobrannyi k s"ezdu: Prilozhenie k zakliuchitel'nomu tomu. Moscow, 1912.

Trutovskii, Vladimir. *Sovremennoe zemstvo.* Petrograd, 1914.

Tulupov, N. V., and P. M. Shestakov, eds. *Prakticheskaia shkol'naia entsiklopediia: Nastol'naia kniga dlia narodnykh uchitelei i drugikh blizhaishikh deiatelei v oblasti narodnogo obrazovaniia.* Moscow, 1912.

Ushinskii, K. D. *Sobranie sochinenii.* 7 vols. Moscow and Leningrad, 1948–1952.

Uspenskii, D. "Pomeshchiki o gramotnosti krest'ian." *Russkaia mysl'* 25, no. 3 (1904): 19–30.

Vakhterov, V. P. "Knizhnye sklady v provintsii." *Russkaia mysl'* 15, no. 1 (1894): 1–13.

———. "Obshcheobrazovatel'nye zadachi narodnoi shkoly." *Russkaia mysl'* 18, no. 11 (1897): 79–96.

———. *Spornye voprosy obrazovaniia.* Moscow, 1907.

———. "Vseobshchee nachal'noe obuchenie." *Russkaia mysl'* 15, no. 7 (1894): 1–18.

———. *Vseobshchee obrazovanie.* Moscow, 1897.

Vakhterova, E. O. *V. P. Vakhterov: Ego zhizn' i rabota.* Moscow, 1961.

Vanchakov, A. M. *Kratkii istoriko-statisticheskii obzor razvitiia tserkovnoi shkoly s 1884 i do nastoiashchego vremeni (1884–1909).* St. Petersburg, 1909.

Vasil'evich, V. [V. Kir'iakov]. *Shag za shagom. K istorii ob"edineniia narodnykh uchitelei.* Helsinki, 1913[?].

Veletskii, S. N. *Zemskaia statistika.* Part 1, *Istoriia i metodologiia.* Moscow, 1899.

Venkulev, P. "15-letie deiatel'nosti S. Peterburgskogo obshchestva gramotnosti, 1896–1911." *Russkaia shkola* 22, no. 5–6 (1911): 108–120.

———. "Sorokoletie Khar'kovskago obshchestva gramotnosti." *Russkaia shkola* 22, no. 5–6 (1911): 99–121.

Verigin, N. *V pomoshch uchashchim v nachal'nykh narodnykh uchilishchakh.* 5th ed. Moscow, 1915.

Veselov, M. O. *Uchebnye plany nachal'noi i srednei shkoly.* Moscow, 1937.

Veselovskii, B. B. *Istoriia zemstva za sorok let.* 4 vols. St. Petersburg, 1909–1911.

———. *K voprosu o klassovykh interesakh v zemstve.* St. Petersburg, 1905.

Veselovskii, B. B., and Z. G. Frenkel'. *Iubileinyi zemskii sbornik.* St. Petersburg, 1914.

Vezhlev, A. M. "Uchitel'skie s"ezdy i kursy v Rossii (Vtoraia polovina XIX veka)." *Sovetskaia pedagogika,* no. 7 (1958): 79–88.

Vladimirov, I. "Material'noe i dukhovnoe obespechenie narodnogo uchiteliia." *Russkaia shkola* 25, nos. 9–10, 11, 12 (1914): 97–124, 122–136, 16–29.

Vodarskii, Ia. E. *Naselenie Rossii za 400 let (XVI–XX vv.)*. Moscow, 1973.

Vospominaniia narodnogo uchitelia. St. Petersburg, 1911.

Vserossiiskii s"ezd po voprosam narodnogo obrazovaniia. *Trudy pervogo vserossiiskogo s"ezda po voprosam narodnogo obrazovaniia, 23 dekabria – 3 ianvaria, 1914*. 2 vols. Petrograd, 1915.

Zakharova, L. G. *Zemskaia kontrreforma 1890 g*. Moscow, 1968.

"Zakon o nachal'nom obrazovanii v Imperii." In *Voprosy i nuzhdy uchitel'stva*, edited by E. A. Zviagintsev, vol. 3, 73–92. Moscow, 1909.

Zapankov, N. A. *Uchitel' narodnoi shkoly*. St. Petersburg, 1906.

Zharov, F. "Sposoby proizvodstva ekzamenov v nachal'noi shkole." *Russkaia shkola* 25, no. 1 (1914): 73–98.

Zhelbakov, N. A., ed. *Istoriia russkoi pedagogiki s drevneishikh vremen do velikoi proletarskoi revoliutsii*. Vol. 4, part 2 of *Khrestomatiia po istorii pedagogiki*, edited by S. A. Kamenev. Moscow, 1936.

Zhil'tsov, P. A., and V. M. Velichkina. *Uchitel' sel'skoi shkoly*. Moscow, 1973.

Zhurakovskii, G. E. *Iz istorii prosveshcheniia v dorevoliutsionnoi Rossii*. Edited by E. D. Dneprov. Moscow, 1978.

Zinov'ev, N. A., ed. *Otchet po revizii zemskikh uchrezhdenii Moskovskoi gubernii*. 3 vols. St. Petersburg, 1904.

Zolotov, V. "Izsledovanie krest'ianskoi gramotnosti po derevniam preimushchestvenno Tverskoi gubernii i chastiiu Moskovskoi." *ZhMNP* 118, sec. 3 (April 1863): 400–444; 120, sec. 3 (October 1863): 156–197.

Zviagintsev, E. A. *Inspektsiia narodnykh uchilishch*. Moscow, 1914.

———. *Narodnaia zhizn' i sel'skaia shkola*. 2 vols. Moscow, 1912.

———. *Polveka zemskoi deiatel'nosti po narodnomu obrazovaniiu*. Moscow, 1915.

———. *Shkola, zemstvo i uchitel'*. Moscow, 1911.

———, ed. *Voprosy i nuzhdy uchitel'stva*. 10 vols. Moscow, 1909–1911.

Zviagintsev, E. A., S. O. Seropolko, N. V. Chekhov et al., eds. *Narodnoe obrazovanie v zemstvakh: Osnovy organizatsii i praktiki dela. Sbornik statei*. Moscow, 1914.

Zyrianov, P. N. "Krakh vnutrennei politiki tret'eiiun'skoi monarkhii v oblasti mestnogo upravleniia (1907–1914)." Candidate dissertation, Akademiia nauk SSSR, Moscow, 1972.

———. "Nekotorye cherty evoliutsii krest'ianskogo 'mira' v poreformennuiu epokhu." In *Ezhegodnik po agrarnoi istorii vostochnoi Evropy, 1971*, 380–387. Vilnius, 1974.

V. WORKS IN WESTERN LANGUAGES

Abercrombie, Nicholas. *Class, Structure, and Knowledge: Problems in the Sociology of Knowing*. New York, 1980.

Alavi, Hamza. "Peasant Classes and Primordial Loyalties." *Journal of Peasant Studies* 1, no. 1 (October 1972): 23–61.

———. "Peasants and Revolution." *Socialist Register* 1, no. 1 (1965): 241–277.

Alston, Patrick L. *Education and the State in Tsarist Russia*. Stanford, Calif., 1969.

———. "Recent Voices and Persistent Problems in Tsarist Education." *Paedagogica Historica* 16, no. 2 (1976): 203–215.

Altick, Richard Daniel. *The English Common Reader: A Social History of the Mass Reading Public, 1800–1900*. Chicago, 1957.

Anderson, C. Arnold. "A Footnote to the Social History of Modern Russia: The Literacy and Education Census of 1897." *Genus* 12, no. 1 (1956): 166–181.

Anderson, C. Arnold, and Mary Jean Bowman, eds. *Education and Economic Development*. Chicago, 1965.

Anweiller, Oskar. "Russian Schools." In *Russia Enters the Twentieth Century*, edited by George Katkov et al., 287–314. London, 1971.

Apostol, Paul N., and Alexandr Michelson. *Russian Public Finance During the War*. Carnegie Endowment for International Peace, Economic and Social History of the World War: Russian series. New Haven, Conn., 1928.

Archer, Margaret. *Social Origins of Educational Systems*. Beverly Hills, Calif., 1979.

Atkinson, Dorothy. *The End of the Russian Land Commune, 1905–1930*. Stanford, Calif., 1983.

Bach, Theresa. *Educational Changes in Russia*. Washington, D.C., 1919.

Baker, Donald N., and Patrick J. Harrigan, eds. *The Making of Frenchmen: Current Directions in the History of Education in France*. Waterloo, Ontario, 1980.

Balmuth, Daniel. *Censorship in Russia, 1865–1905.* Washington, D.C., 1979.

Banton, Michael, ed. *The Social Anthropology of Complex Societies.* New York, 1966.

Berelowitch, Wladimir. "L'École russe en 1914." *Cahiers du monde russe et soviétique* 19, no. 3 (July-September 1978): 185–300.

Bissonnette, Rev. Georges. "Peter the Great and the Church as an Educational Institution." In *Essays in Honor of G. T. Robinson,* edited by John Shelton Curtiss, 3–19. Leiden, 1963.

Black, Cyril E., et al. *The Modernization of Japan and Russia.* New York, 1975.

Black, Joseph L. *Citizens for the Fatherland.* Boulder, Colo., 1979.

Blaug, Mark, ed. *The Economics of Education: Selected Readings,* vol. 2. Baltimore, Md., 1968.

———. "The Economics of Education in English Classical Political Economy, A Re-Examination." In *Essays on Adam Smith,* edited by Andrew S. Skinner and Thomas Wilson, 256–287. Glasgow, 1976.

Boucher, Leon. *Tradition and Change in Swedish Education.* New York, 1982.

Bourdieu, Pierre, and Jean-Claude Passeron. *Reproduction in Education, Society and Culture.* Translated by Richard Nice. London, 1977.

Bowles, Samuel, and Herbert Gintis. "The Problem with Human Capital Theory—A Marxist Critique." *American Economic Review* 65 (1975): 74–82.

———. *Schooling in Capitalist America: Educational Reform and the Contradictions of Economic Life.* New York, 1976.

Buisson, Ferdinand. *Nouveau Dictionnaire de pédagogie et d'instruction primaire.* Paris, 1911.

Bushnell, John. "Peasants in Uniform: The Tsarist Army as a Peasant Society." *Journal of Social History* 13, no. 4, (1981): 565–576.

Byrnes, Robert F. *Pobedonostsev: His Life and Thought.* Bloomington, Ind., 1968.

Calhoun, Daniel. *The Intelligence of a People.* Princeton, N.J., 1973.

Callahan, Raymond E. *Education and the Cult of Efficiency.* Chicago, 1962.

Chaianov, Aleksandr V. *The Theory of Peasant Economy.* Translated and edited by Daniel Thorner, R. E. F. Smith, and Basil Kerblay. Homewood, Ill., 1966.

Chall, Jeanne S. *Learning to Read: The Great Debate.* New York, 1967.

Chisick, Harvey. *The Limits of Reform in the Enlightenment: Attitudes Toward the Education of the Lower Classes in Eighteenth-Century France.* Princeton, N.J., 1981.

Cipolla, Carlo M. *Literacy and Development in the West.* Baltimore, Md., 1969.

Confino, Michael. *Systèmes agraires et progrès agricole: L'assolement triennal en Russie aux XVIIIe–XIXe siècles. Étude d'économies et de sociologies rurales.* The Hague, 1969.

Conroy, May Schaeffer. "School Hygiene in Late Tsarist Russia." *Slavic and European Education Review,* no. 2 (1981): 17–26.

Darlington, Thomas. *Education in Russia.* Board of Education, Special Reports on Education, vol. 23. London, 1909.

Davis, Natalie Zemon. *Society and Culture in Early Modern France.* Stanford, Calif., 1975.

de Madariaga, Isabel. "The Foundation of the Russian Educational System by Catherine II." *Slavic and East European Review* 57 (1979): 369–395.

———. *Russia in the Age of Catherine the Great.* New Haven, Conn., 1981.

Dodge, Robert H. "The Moscow Zemstvo and Elementary Education, 1868–1910." Ph.D. dissertation, Syracuse University, 1970.

Eisenstadt, S. N. "Studies of Modernization and Sociological Theory." *History and Theory* 13 (1974): 225–252.

Eisenstein, Elizabeth L. "Some Conjectures About the Impact of Printing on Western Society and Thought: A Preliminary Report." *Journal of Modern History* 40, no. 1 (1968): 1–56.

Eklof, Ben. "The Myth of the Zemstvo School: The Sources of the Expansion of Rural Education in Imperial Russia, 1864–1914." *History of Education Quarterly* 24 (Winter 1984): 561–584.

———. "Peasant Sloth Reconsidered: Strategies of Education and Learning in Rural Russia Before the Revolution." *Journal of Social History* 14, no. 3 (Spring 1981): 355–385.

———. "Spreading the Word: Primary Education and the Zemstvo in Moscow Province, 1864–1910." Ph.D. dissertation, Princeton University, 1977.

Emmons, Terence, and Wayne S. Vucinich, eds. *The Zemstvo in Russia: An Experiment in Local Self-Government.* Cambridge, England, 1982.

Febvre, Lucien, and Henri Jean Martin. *The Coming of the Book: The Impact of Printing, 1450–1800.* Translated by David Gerard. London, 1979.

French, Frances Graham. "Education in Russia." In *Report of the Commissioner of Education for 1890–1891,* vol. 1, part 1, 195–262. Washington, D.C., 1894.

Furet, François, and Jacques Ozouf. *Reading and Writing: Literacy in France from Calvin to Jules Ferry.* Cambridge, England, 1982.

Galeski, Boguslaw. *Basic Concepts of Rural Sociology.* Translated by H. C. Stevens. Manchester, England, 1972.

Galskoy, Constantin. "The Ministry of Education Under Nicholas I, 1826–1836." Ph.D. dissertation, Stanford University, 1977.

Giroux, Henry A. *Ideology, Culture and the Process of Schooling.* Philadelphia, Pa., 1981.

Goodman, David, and Michael Redclift. *From Peasant to Proletarian: Capitalist Development and Agrarian Transitions.* New York, 1982.

Goody, Jack. *The Domestication of the Savage Mind.* Cambridge, England, 1977.

Gosden, P. H. J. H. *How They Were Taught.* Oxford, 1969.

Graff, Harvey J. *The Literacy Myth: Literacy and Social Structure in the Nineteenth-Century City.* New York, 1979.

———, ed. *Literacy and Social Development in the West: A Reader.* Cambridge, England, 1981.

———, ed. *Literacy in History: An Interdisciplinary Research Bibliography.* New York, 1981.

Graham, Hugh. "Did Institutionalized Education Exist in Pre-Petrine Russia?" In *Russian and Slavic History: Papers from the Banff 1974 Conference,* edited by Don K. Rowney and G. Edward Orchard, 261–271. Columbus, Ohio, 1977.

Greer, Colin. *The Great School Legend: A Revisionist Interpretation of American Public Education.* New York, 1972.

Guroff, Gregory, and S. Frederick Starr. "A Note on Urban Literacy in Russia, 1890–1914." *Jahrbücher für Geschichte Osteuropas* 19 (1971): 520–531.

Hans, Nicholas. *History of Russian Educational Policy, 1701–1917.* New York, 1964.

———. *The Russian Tradition in Education.* London, 1963.

Harman, David. "Illiteracy: An Overview." *Harvard Educational Review* 40 (May 1970): 226–243.

Harrigan, Patrick J. *Mobility, Elites, and Education in French Society of the Second Empire.* Waterloo, Ontario, 1980.

Hayashida, Ronald, and Hideo Hayashida. "The Unionization of Russian

Teachers, 1905–1908: An Interest Group Under the Autocracy." *Slavic and European Education Review,* no. 2 (1981): 1–16.

Horn, Pamela. *Education in Rural England, 1800–1914.* New York, 1978.

Ignatiev, Paul N., Dmitry Odinetz, and Paul Novgorodtsev. *Russian Schools and Universities in the World War.* Carnegie Endowment for International Peace, Economic and Social History of the World War: Russian series. New Haven, Conn., 1929.

Inkeles, Howard, and David Smith. "Some Social and Psychological Effects and Non-Effects of Literacy in a New Nation." *Economic Development and Cultural Change* 16 (1967–1968): 1–14.

Johnson, Robert Eugene. *Peasant and Proletarian: The Working Class of Moscow in the Late Nineteenth Century.* New Brunswick, N.J., 1979.

Johnson, William H. *Russia's Educational Heritage.* Pittsburgh, Pa., 1950.

Kaestle, Karl E., and Maris A. Vinovskis. *Education and Social Change in Nineteenth-Century Massachusetts.* Cambridge, England, 1980.

Kahan, Arcadius. "Determinants of the Incidence of Literacy in Rural Nineteenth-Century Russia." In *Education and Economic Development,* edited by C. Arnold Anderson and Mary Jean Bowman, 298–302. Chicago, 1965.

————. "The 'Hereditary Workers' Hypothesis and the Development of a Factory Labor Force in Eighteenth- and Nineteenth-Century Russia." In *Education and Economic Development,* edited by C. Arnold Anderson and Mary Jean Bowman, 291–297. Chicago, 1965.

————. "Russian Statesmen and Scholars on Education as an Investment." In *Education and Economic Development,* edited by C. Arnold Anderson and Mary Jean Bowman, 3–10. Chicago, 1965.

————. "Social Structure, Public Policy and the Development of Education and the Economy in Tsarist Russia." In *Education and Economic Development,* edited by C. Arnold Anderson and Mary Jean Bowman, 363–375. Chicago, 1965.

Kaser, Michael. "Education in Tsarist and Soviet Development." In *Essays in Honor of E. H. Carr,* edited by C. Abramsky, 229–254. London, 1974.

Katz, Michael B. "The Origins of Public Education: A Reassessment." *History of Education Quarterly* 16 (Winter 1976): 381–407.

Kushner, P. I. *The Village of Viriatino.* Translated by Sula Benet. New York, 1970.

Landes, William, and Lewis Solman. "Compulsory Schooling Legislation: An Economic Analysis of Law and Social Change in the Nineteenth Century." *Journal of Economic History* 36 (March 1972): 54–97.

Laqueur, Thomas. "The Cultural Origins of Popular Literacy in England, 1500–1850." *Oxford Review of Education* 2, no. 3 (1976): 255–275.

Laurie, Arthur P., ed. *The Teachers' Encyclopedia of the Theory, Method, Practice, History, and Development of Education at Home and Abroad.* 7 vols. London, 1911–1912.

LaVopa, Anthony J. *Prussian Schoolteachers: Profession and Office, 1763–1848.* Chapel Hill, N.C., 1980.

Lazerson, Marvin. "Revisionism and American Educational History." *History of Education Review* 43, no. 2 (1973): 269–283.

McClelland, James C. *Autocrats and Academics: Education, Culture, and Society in Tsarist Russia.* Chicago, 1979.

McLelland, David. "Does Education Accelerate Economic Growth?" *Economic Development and Cultural Change* 14 (1965–1966): 257–278.

Mathes, William. "The Process of Institutionalization of Education in Russia, 1800–1917." In *Russian and Slavic History: Papers from the Banff 1974 Conference,* edited by Don K. Rowney and G. Edward Orchard, 27–48. Columbus, Ohio, 1977.

Mathews, Mitford M. *Teaching to Read: Historically Considered.* Chicago, 1966.

Mattingly, Paul. *The Classless Profession: American Schoolmen of the Nineteenth Century.* New York, 1975.

Middleton, Nigel, and Sophia Weitzman. *A Place for Everyone: A History of State Education from the End of the Eighteenth Century to the 1970's.* London, 1976.

Monroe, Paul, ed. *A Cyclopedia of Education.* 5 vols. New York, 1911–1913.

Moody, Joseph N. *French Education Since Napoleon.* Syracuse, N.Y., 1978.

Moore, Barrington, Jr. *Social Origins of Dictatorship and Democracy: Lord and Peasant in the Making of the Modern World.* Boston, 1966.

Musgrove, Frank. *School and the Social Order.* New York, 1979.

Neuburg, Victor E. *Popular Education in Eighteenth Century England.* London, 1971.

Okenfuss, Max J. "Education and Empire: School Reform in Enlightened Russia." *Jahrbücher für Geschichte Osteuropas* 27 (1979): 41–68.

Ong, Walter J. *Orality and Literacy: The Technologizing of the Word.* London and New York, 1982.

Orlovsky, Daniel T. "Recent Studies of the Russian Bureaucracy." *Russian Review* 35, no. 4 (October 1976): 448–467.

Paulsen, Friedrich. *German Education: Past and Present*. Translated by T. Lorenz. New York, 1908.

Pethybridge, Roger. "Spontaneity and Illiteracy in 1917." In *Reconsiderations on the Russian Revolution: Papers from the Banff '74 Conference*, edited by Richard C. Elwood, 80–91. Cambridge, Mass., 1976.

Phillips, Herbert Moore. *Basic Education: A World Challenge*. London, 1975.

———. *Literacy and Development*. New York, 1970.

Pintner, Walter M., and Don K. Rowney, eds. *Russian Officialdom: The Bureaucratization of Russian Society from the Seventeenth to the Twentieth Century*. Chapel Hill, N.C., 1980.

Pollard, Hugh M. *Pioneers of Popular Education, 1760–1850*. Cambridge, Mass., 1957.

Popkewitz, Thomas S., and B. Robert Tabachnick. *The Study of Schooling: Field-Based Methodologies in Educational Research and Evaluation*. New York, 1981.

Rawski, Evelyn S. *Education and Popular Literacy in Ch'ing China*. Ann Arbor, Mich., 1979.

Redfield, Robert. *The Little Community* and *Peasant Society and Culture*. Chicago, 1965.

Reiber, Alfred. "Alexander II: A Revisionist View." *Journal of Modern History* 43, no. 1 (1971): 42–58.

Resnick, Daniel, ed. *Literacy in Historical Development*. Washington, D.C., 1983.

Resnick, Daniel P., and Lauren B. Resnick. "The Nature of Literacy: An Historical Exploration." *Harvard Educational Review* 47 (August 1977): 370–385.

Ringer, Fritz K. *Education and Society in Modern Europe*. Bloomington, Ind., 1979.

Robinson, Geroid T. *Rural Russia Under the Old Regime: A History of the Landlord-Peasant World and a Prologue to the Peasant Revolution of 1917*. Berkeley and Los Angeles, Calif., 1967.

The Russian Ministry of Public Education at the World's Columbian Exposition. St. Petersburg, 1893.

Santa Maria, Phillip. "The Question of Elementary Education in the Third Russian State Duma, 1907–1912." Ph.D. dissertation, Kent State University, 1977.

Schofield, Roger S. "The Measurement of Literacy in Pre-Industrial England." In *Literacy in Traditional Societies*, edited by Jack Goody, 311–325. Cambridge, England, 1968.

Schultz, Theodore W. *The Economic Value of Education*. New York, 1963.

———. *Transforming Traditional Agriculture*. Chicago, 1964.

Scribner, Sylvia, and Michael Cole. "Cognitive Consequences of Formal and Informal Education." *Science,* no. 182 (9 November 1973): 552–558.

———. "Literacy Without Schooling: Testing for Intellectual Effects." *Harvard Educational Review* 48 (November 1978): 448–461.

———. *The Psychology of Literacy*. Cambridge, Mass., 1981.

Selleck, Richard J. W. *The New Education, 1870–1914*. London, 1968.

Seregny, Scott J. "Professional Activism and Association Among Russian Teachers." Paper presented to the Conference on Professions and Professionalization in Imperial Russia, University of Illinois, Champaign-Urbana, 24–26 June 1982.

———. "Professionalism and Political Activism: The Russian Teachers' Movement, 1864–1908." Ph.D. dissertation, University of Michigan, 1982.

Shanin, Teodor. *The Awkward Class: Political Sociology of Peasantry in a Developing Society, Russia, 1910–1925*. Oxford, 1972.

———, ed. *Peasants and Peasant Society*. Baltimore, Md., 1971.

Shipman, M. D. *Education and Modernization*. London, 1971.

———. *The Sociology of the School*. London, 1968.

Silver, Harold. *The Concept of Popular Education*. London, 1965.

Simkhovich, V. I. G. "History of the School in Russia." *Educational Review* 8 (May 1907): 486–522.

Sinel, Allen. "The Campaign for Primary Education in Russia, 1890–1904." *Jahrbücher für Geschichte Osteuropas* 30 (1982): 481–507.

———. *The Classroom and the Chancellery: State Educational Reform in Russia Under Count Dmitry Tolstoi*. Cambridge, Mass., 1973.

———. "Count Dmitry Tolstoi and the Preparation of Russian School Teachers." *Canadian Slavic Review* 3, no. 2 (Summer 1969): 246–262.

———. "Educating the Russian Peasantry: The Elementary School Reforms of Count Dmitry Tolstoi." *American Slavic and East European Review* 27, no. 1 (1968): 49–70.

———. "Problems in the Periodization of Russian Education: A Tentative Solution." *Slavic and European Education Review,* no. 2 (1977): 54–61.

Smith, Frank. *A History of English Elementary Education, 1760–1902*. London, 1931.

Soltow, Lee, and Edward Stevens. *The Rise of Literacy and the Common*

School in the United States: A Socioeconomic Analysis to 1870. Chicago, 1981.

Spring, Joel. *American Education: An Introduction to Social and Political Aspects.* New York, 1978.

Starr, S. Frederick. *Decentralization and Self-Government in Russia, 1830– 1870.* Princeton, N.J., 1972.

Stewart, W. A. C. *Progressives and Radicals in English Education, 1750–1970.* Clifton, N.J., 1972.

Stone, Lawrence. "Literacy and Education in England, 1640–1900." *Past and Present* 42 (1969): 69–137.

Sutherland, Gillian. *Elementary Education in the Nineteenth Century.* London, 1971.

————. *Policy Making in Elementary Education, 1870–1895.* Oxford, 1973.

Tibble, J. W., ed. *An Introduction to the Study of Education.* London, 1971.

Timberlake, Charles E. "The Leningrad Collection of Zemstvo Publications." *Slavic Review* 26, no. 3 (1967): 475–481.

Tönnies, Ferdinand. *Community and Society (Gemeinschaft und Gesellschaft).* Translated by C. P. Loomis. New York, 1957.

Tyack, David. *The One Best System: A History of American Urban Education.* Cambridge, Mass., 1974.

————. "Ways of Seeing: An Essay on the History of Compulsory Schooling." *Harvard Educational Review* 46 (August 1976): 355–389.

Tyack, David, and Elisabeth Hansot. *Managers of Virtue: Public School Leadership in America, 1820–1980.* New York, 1982.

UNESCO. *World Illiteracy at Mid-Century.* Monographs on Fundamental Education, no. 11. Paris, 1957.

Wardle, David. *The Rise of the Schooled Society: The History of Formal Schooling in England.* London, 1974.

Watson, Foster. *The Encyclopedia and Dictionary of Education.* London, 1921–1922.

Weber, Eugen. *Peasants into Frenchmen: The Modernization of Rural France, 1870–1914.* Stanford, Calif., 1976.

West, E. G. *Education and the Industrial Revolution.* New York, 1975.

Whelan, Heide. *Alexander III and the State Council: Bureaucracy and Counter-Reform in Late Imperial Russia.* New Brunswick, N.J., 1982.

Wiebe, Robert H. "The Social Functions of Education." *American Quarterly* 21 (Summer 1969): 148–164.

Williams, Raymond. *The Long Revolution.* London, 1961.

Wolf, Eric R. "Aspects of Group Relations in a Complex Society: Mexico." *American Anthropologist* 58, no. 6 (1956): 1065–1078.

———. *Peasants*. Englewood Cliffs, N.J., 1966.

Wolf, Thomas. "Reading Reconsidered." *Harvard Educational Review* 47 (August 1977): 411–429.

Woods, Ronald George, ed. *Education and Its Disciplines*. New York, 1972.

Zacek, Judith Cohan. "The Lancaster School Movement in Russia." *Slavonic and East European Review* 45 (1967): 343–367.

Zelnik, Reginald. "Passivity and Protest in Germany and Russia: Barrington Moore's Conception of Working-Class Responses to Injustice." *Journal of Social History* 15, no. 3 (Spring 1982): 485–499.

———. "Russian Rebels: An Introduction to the Memoirs of Semen Kanatchikov and Matvei Fischer." *Russian Review* 35, no. 3 (July 1976): 249–289; no. 4 (October 1976): 417–447.

———. "The Sunday-School Movement in Russia, 1859–1862." *Journal of Modern History* 37, no. 4 (1965): 151–170.

Index